PSYCHOPATHOLOGY

A Competency-Based Assessment Model for Social Workers

Susan W. Gray
Barry University
Ellen Whiteside McDonnell School of Social Work

Australia • Brazil • Mexico • Singapore • United Kingdom • United States

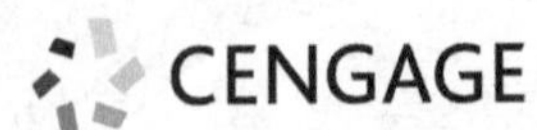

***Psychopathology: A Competency-Based Assessment Model for Social Workers,* Fourth Edition**
Susan W. Gray

Product Director: Jon-David Hague

Product Manager: Julie Martinez

Content Developer: Hahn Consulting

Product Assistant: Stephen Lagos

Content Project Manager: Tanya Nigh

IP Project Manager: Brittani Morgan

IP Analyst: Deanna Ettinger

Manufacturing Planner: Judy Inouye

Production Service and Compositor: Lumina Datamatics, Inc.

Photo and Text Researcher: Lumina Datamatics, Inc.

Cover Image: Reflection in glass ball of Caledon Badlands, © Patty Maher Photography/Getty Images

Library of Congress Control Number: 2015948210

ISBN: 978-1-305-10193-7

Cengage
20 Channel Street
Boston, MA 02210
USA

Cengage is a leading provider of customized learning solutions with employees residing in nearly 40 different countries and sales in more than 125 countries around the world. Find your local representative at: **www.cengage.com**.

Cengage products are represented in Canada by Nelson Education, Ltd.

To learn more about Cengage platforms and services, register or access your online learning solution, or purchase materials for your course, visit **www.cengage.com**.

Printed at CLDPC, USA, 09-21

To my beloved husband,
Kenneth E. Gray, JD
... you are my inspiration.

Contents

PREFACE

INTRODUCTION

All of us engage in behaviors that we usually do not think a lot about—from eating, to talking, feeling, thinking, remembering, playing, buying things, or even going to the bathroom, to list a few. However, these behaviors can potentially have a maladaptive component that can be diagnosed as a mental disorder. These dysfunctions are a source of substantial concern to many different mental health professions whose members hold differing opinions regarding the etiology, pathology, and treatment of these disorders. Professionals think in terms of their "language," and in order to be able to meaningfully communicate with one another, it is important to share a common vocabulary. The *Diagnostic and Statistical Manual of Mental Disorders* (DSM) published by the American Psychiatric Association (APA, 2013) offers an official diagnostic nomenclature, making it a powerful document. It plays a significant role in how practitioners, their agencies, funding sources, social programs, and the general public conceptualize and respond to problematic and maladaptive behaviors (Schwartz & Wiggins, 2002).

Among the 500,000 mental health professionals in the United States who use the DSM-5, the largest group is social workers (U.S. Department of Labor, Bureau of Labor Statistics, 2010) followed by mental health counselors (American Counseling Association, 2011), psychologists (American Psychological Association, 2012), and psychiatrists (APA, 2011). Moreover, social work practice specific to the field of mental health is the largest subspecialty within the profession (Whitaker, Weismiller, Clark, & Wilson, 2006). Historically, the use of the psychiatric nomenclature in social work practice has been controversial and has generated considerable discussion within the profession (Washburn, 2013). To some extent, mental disorders are the constructions of practitioners and researchers rather than proven diseases and illnesses (Maddux, Gosselin, & Weinstead, 2008). On the other hand, the diagnoses found in the DSM are not necessarily lacking credibility or empirical support.

THE *DIAGNOSTIC AND STATISTICAL MANUAL OF MENTAL DISORDERS* AND ITS FIFTH EDITION

The publication of the DSM-5 in 2013 is the fifth edition of the DSM, representing the first major revision to the manual in more than 30 years (APA, 2013). The DSM has a profound influence on all mental health professions. Certainly there have been numerous controversies surrounding the DSM-5 including the overall reliability of the system, poor research for field trials, its seeming slant toward a biological approach, the relative lack of participation of professional groups other than psychiatry, and the inclusion and definition of particular mental disorders—most notably the autism spectrum (First, 2010; Frances, 2012, 2013; Friedman, 2012; Jones, 2012; Pomeroy & Anderson, 2013). Admittedly, the DSM-5 may contain flaws, but for the most part it describes what is reasonably understood by most practitioners and researchers to be the predominant forms of psychopathology. The psychiatric diagnosis is primarily a way of communicating and the categories of the different disorders can be useful without necessarily being "the final word" about how people function. The DSM-5 may be imperfect and sometimes biased, but no one has questioned whether the manual should be used at all or suggested that there is an alternative way to move forward. Regardless of the criticisms, the reality is that the DSM remains as the primary classification system across the counseling professions for diagnosis and reimbursement purposes (Washburn, 2013). If we are to provide our clients with the best possible services, then the ability to make an accurate diagnosis is an important step in that direction. Regardless of where you stand, it is essential to become familiar with the changes in the DSM-5 and its potential impact on clients. In fact, using the DSM-5 is unavoidable for many clinical social workers. For instance, the Association of Social Work Boards (ASWB) includes questions specific to the DSM on its licensing exams, which are required by almost every state (Frazer, Westhuis, Daley, & Phillips, 2009). Beginning in July 2015, the licensure test questions shifted to testing knowledge of the DSM-5.

Revising the DSM has been an enormous undertaking and no diagnostic process is perfect. Keep in mind that a work of this magnitude will have some errors. The APA has made every effort to keep up with the listing of errata, and you are encouraged to check the association's website (http://www.dsm5.org), which posts corrections to the manual. It is anticipated that minor text edits will be corrected in later publications.

In the prior edition of this book I shared the experience of one of my students on a field trip we took to an agency that works with the severely and persistently mentally ill organized around the clubhouse model. Essentially this student had reservations around working with "those people" until she met a real client and had the chance to get to know him a little better as he proudly showed us around the agency. I still remember this client's greeting as we approached the front door of the agency. He had a big smile and proudly announced, "Hi, I'm Danny and I have schizophrenia. Welcome to our clubhouse. I can't wait to show you around." I remembered thinking, who knows more about mental illness than someone who lives with a disorder on a daily basis? Danny's symptoms may wax and wane, but ultimately they do not go away. The competency-based approach to the assessment process takes into account a client's lived experiences with a diagnosis. From this perspective, Danny's diagnosis becomes but a part of his identity and does not define him. The intent of the competency-based model is to advance the assessment process to one that recognizes each person's uniqueness rather than to focus solely on a diagnostic label.

Lacasse and Gomory (2003) analyzed a sample of psychopathology syllabi from top graduate schools of social work around the country and found that the most frequently required texts were authored by psychiatrists. No course had a stand-alone text authored by a social worker. As social workers, we are familiar with working from a strengths perspective with our clients, and this orientation somehow becomes lost in books from other disciplines. This book is written by a social worker for social workers. Learning about psychopathology and related diagnoses is like learning a new language. Best to learn this language with a social work accent!

THE BOOK'S ORGANIZATION

The changes in the DSM-5 will require practitioners to relearn how to classify and conceptualize some mental disorders. The aim of this book's fourth edition is to help readers understand the new features of the DSM-5 to the extent that you can take this information and, by incorporating the competency-based assessment model, apply diagnoses correctly. As with prior editions, case studies are provided to highlight diagnostic criteria and to differentiate among the different diagnoses.

Stigma and misunderstanding of mental illness is pervasive, and many still consider mental health problems to be the result of personal shortcomings. The book is organized around the competency-based model, which highlights the biological (including neurological), psychological, and social aspects of a person's life as a part of the diagnostic process. In this way, understanding psychopathology will not focus on character flaws or personal weakness but include a strengths-based orientation to the assessment, which looks to how someone like Danny copes with and rebounds from the challenges of living with a mental disorder. The diagnosis understands the individual's biopsychosocial makeup, cultural and political influences, coping methods, and factors that are a basis for strengths, resiliency, and resources. This orientation balances psychopathology with a parallel appreciation of factors related to strengths and resiliency. It goes without saying that using the DSM requires skill in order to be able to distinguish the client's symptom picture. The competency-based assessment extends this understanding and looks beyond a review of the client's symptoms to consider how a disorder is experienced, how it is expressed, and how symptoms are interpreted by the person and those close to him or her.

INTRODUCTION TO ENHANCED CONTENT

You will find a number of changes in each of the chapters. The DSM-5 definition of mental illness takes into account the neurological features of mental disorders. In order to familiarize the social work practitioner with the neurological contributions to psychopathology, Chapter 1 expands the review of the biopsychosocial framework supporting the competency-based assessment by including content on the role of the brain and related systems in psychopathology. Subsequent chapters include a discussion of these influences around particular disorders. A review of changes to the reorganization of the DSM are also included.

The DSM-5 classification system cuts across all developmental stages, thus eliminating the need for a separate chapter on the disorders of infancy, childhood, and adolescence as seen in the DSM-IV-TR. From a life-span perspective, disorders specific to early development are placed in the second chapter on neurodevelopmental disorders, and a later chapter on neurocognitive disorders addresses late life developments. This approach to DSM reorganization also attempts to better reflect the relative strength of relationships among disorder groups. For example, although there is an overlap of symptoms among the anxiety disorders, obsessive-compulsive disorder, posttraumatic stress disorder, and acute stress disorder, each has a different clinical presentation and are now included in separate chapters on the basis of overt symptoms in the DSM-5. However, clients with any one of these closely related disorders can show comorbid disorders from among this spectrum (Bienvenu et al., 2011).

Consistent with this approach to the DSM classification system, new chapters have been added; for example, obsessive-compulsive and related disorders, and trauma- and stressor-related disorders, to list a few. To remain consistent with prior editions, all of the chapters from 2 through 16 in the book have been ordered around how they appear in the DSM. You will find a review of the specific disorders followed by an updated discussion of prevailing patterns, and the differential diagnosis. Case vignettes are presented followed by a diagnosis and the competency-based assessment. An assessment summary reviews possible alternative diagnoses so that readers can become familiar with the process of distinguishing symptoms and client competencies in reality-based situations. In this way, readers may learn to take the client's "whole person" into account when making a diagnosis of mental illness. Not every disorder addressed in the DSM-5 appears in the book. The intent is to provide a more in-depth review of those syndromes social workers will more than likely encounter in their everyday practice. As before, each chapter is designed to stand alone. This feature was kept in order to facilitate individual instructor preference around sequencing the teaching of content about a particular disorder. In addition, it is easier for readers who might want to re-review a diagnosis.

New case stories have been added throughout the book to illustrate the new diagnoses included in the DSM-5. For example, you will notice the case of John Laughlin highlighting disruptive mood dysregulation disorder in the depressive disorders chapter, and Larry Dalton's experiences with gambling disorder in the substance-related and addictive disorders chapter. There are numerous familiar case studies from prior editions, but the diagnosis has been updated to reflect the DSM-5 diagnostic criteria. For example, Rudy Rosen still struggles with schizophrenia, but the way it has been diagnosed is different. To add context to the diagnostic shifts, each chapter ends with a summary of the changes from the DSM-IV-TR to the DSM-5. Sometimes a diagnosis that the practitioner will more than likely not see in the average practice situation was reviewed, and this was done to expand the overall understanding of the diagnostic categories in the DSM-5. For instance, you will find Patty Nemeth's story about separation anxiety in the chapter featuring the anxiety disorders, and Mary Ellen Creamer's struggles with pica in the feeding and eating disorders chapter. The DSM-5 has moved away from a categorical approach to the diagnosis—that is, either you meet criteria for a diagnosis or not—and more toward a dimensional perspective. Reflective of this shift, you will find more listings of diagnostic specifiers and severity ratings for each of the diagnoses.

The fourth edition of the book remains a part of the Cengage Learning Empowerment Series and continues to integrate the Council on Social Work Education (CSWE) Educational Policy and Accreditation Standards (EPAS). However, in March 2015, CSWE approved a new set of standards, referred to as practice competencies. This newly revised set of practice behaviors has been integrated into each chapter, thus further supporting the book's emphasis on a performance-based orientation to learning that links theory and action; that is, using real-life case examples to highlight the assessment process. Competency notes are provided at the end of each chapter that describe each competence and its relationship to chapter content. The Appendix contains test questions for each chapter, and they have been expanded to reflect the revisions to this edition.

While the book targets social workers, it can be used by all mental health professionals taking courses in psychopathology, human behavior, or direct practice. It is also a good reference for practitioners who want to review the basics of psychopathology or to prepare for a licensure exam. Supervisors will find it a useful reference for psychiatric diagnoses. The case studies are drawn from real-life practice experiences, and I hope readers will find the diversity reflective of contemporary practice. All case stories have been changed to protect anonymity, and some represent a compendium of different client experiences. Any resemblance to a real-life client is accidental and not intentional. The cases can be used by both instructors and supervisors as a part of a homework assignment, to supplement lectures, or adapted to provide evidence of students' understanding of the assessment process in practice.

INSTRUCTOR SUPPLEMENTS

For this edition of the textbook, the author has crafted a detailed Instructor's Manual to support your use of the new edition. The manual includes chapter summaries, practitioner reflections that can be used as student exercises, suggestions for further study, and additional online and print resources. There is also a detailed test bank and a set of classroom PowerPoint slides that accompany the text.

This material can be found at http://www.cengage.com.

ACKNOWLEDGEMENTS

The DSM-5 created the opportunity for making significant changes in the book. It did not take very long for me to realize that an undertaking like this could be accomplished only with a lot of help and support. I would especially like to acknowledge all of the helping hands behind the scenes who worked diligently to make this edition of the book a reality. Looking back, I find it hard to believe that 15 years have passed since the first edition was published. Back then I could not have predicted that the competency-based assessment would make such an enduring contribution to the mental health field. I am always collecting case stories—from my own practice, students, supervisees, and colleagues—and continue to be impressed by the strength and resilience of those who struggle with a mental disorder. Thank you to all who have shared their "stories" with me.

Diagnosing clients is not an easy task. The DSM-5 provided an exciting opportunity to look at this process through the lens of the values of our profession and then applying those values in contemporary practice. Over and over again, readers have shared that this textbook, with its real-life case stories, has helped them to learn psychopathology in a way that keeps in mind the uniqueness of each person who struggles with the challenges associated with living with a mental disorder.

Thank you for encouraging me to continue this work. When each client's diagnosis is individualized through the competency-based assessment, we move in the direction of a societal culture that encourages a change in the negative perceptions of mental illness and the stigma that surrounds those who seek help for these challenges.

I would like to thank Gordon Lee, Product Manager–Anthropology and Social Work, who was involved at the outset, and Julie Martinez, Product Manager–Counseling, Human Services, and Social Work, who saw this edition through to its successful completion. I would also like to acknowledge those who assisted with the production phase of the book, including Tanya Nigh, Senior Content Project Manager, Jeffrey Hahn, J. L. Hahn Consulting Group, and Valarmathy Munuswamy, Associate Program Manager, Lumina Datamatics, Inc. Cengage Learning wishes to recognize the many contributions made by Marilyn Zide to the first edition of this book. I know there are many others on the Cengage team and I do want to acknowledge their contributions.

As a last step, I wish to thank my husband, Kenneth, whose support has made all of this possible. As with his experiences with my work on prior editions, there were many times we would miss meals, eat take out, or have lunch at 3:00 or 4:00 p.m. because I was on the computer and, "just need another minute to finish this thought." He claims not to know anything about social work but somehow manages to provide the right words of encouragement at the right time. His faith in me is something special!

REFERENCES

American Counseling Association. (2011). *2011 statistics on mental health professions.* Alexandria, VA: Author.

American Psychiatric Association. (2011). *American Psychiatric Association.* Retrieved on May 1, 2015 from: http://www.psychiatry.org/

American Psychiatric Association (APA). (2013). *Diagnostic and Statistical Manual of Mental Disorders* (5th ed.). Arlington, VA: Author.

American Psychological Association. (2012). *Support Center: How many practicing psychologists are there in the United States?* Retrieved on May 1, 2015 from: http://www.apa.org/support/practice.aspx

Bienvenu, O. J., Samuels, F. J., Wuyek, A., Liang, K-Y., Wang, Y., Grados, M. A., ... Nestadt, G. (2011). Is obsessive-compulsive disorder an anxiety disorder and what, if any, are spectrum conditions? A family study perspective. *Psychological Medicine*, *41*(1), 33–40.

First, M. B. (2010). Clinical utility in the revision of the Diagnostic and Statistical Manual of Mental Disorders (DSM). *Professional Psychology: Research and Practice*, *41*, 465–473.

Frances, A. J. (2012). DSM-5 is guide not bible—ignore its ten worst changes. *Psychology Today.* Retrieved on May 1, 2015 from: http://www.psychologytoday.com/blog/dsm5-in-distress/201212/dsm-5-is-guide-not-bible-ignore-its-ten-worst-changes

Frances, A. J. (2013). Two fatal technical flaws in the DSM-5 definition of autism. *Huffington Post.* Retrieved on May 1, 2015 from: http://www.huffingtonpost.com/allen-frances/two-fatal-technical-flaws_b_3337009.html

Frazer, P., Westhuis, D., Daley, J., & Phillips, I. (2009). How clinical social workers are suing the DSM: A national study. *Social Work in Mental Health*, *7*, 325–339.

Friedman, R. A. (2012). Grief, depression, and the DSM-5. *New England Journal of Medicine.* Retrieved on May 2, 2015 from: http://www.nejm.org/doi/full/10.1056/NEJMp1201794?query=TOC

Jones, K. D. (2012). A critique of the DSM-5 field trials. *Journal of Nervous and Mental Disease*, *200*, 517–519.

Lacasse, J. R., & Gomory, T, (2003). Is graduate social work education promoting a critical approach to mental health? *Journal of Social Work Education*, *39*, 383–408.

Pomeroy, E. C., & Anderson, K. (2013). The DSM-5 has arrived. *Social Work*, *58*(3), 197–200.

Schwartz. M. A., & Wiggins, O. P. (2002). The hegemony of the DSMs. In J. Sadler (Ed.), *Descriptions and prescriptions: Values, mental disorders and the DSM* (pp. 199–209). Baltimore, MD: Johns Hopkins University Press.

Maddux, J. E., Gosselin, J. T., & Weinstead, B. A. (2008). Conceptions of psychopathology: A social constructionist perspective. In J. E. Maddux & B. A. Weinstead (Eds.), *Psychopathology: Foundations for a contemporary understanding* (2nd ed., pp. 3–18). New York: Routledge/Taylor & Francis Group.

U.S. Department of Labor, Bureau of Labor Statistics. (2010). *Occupational outlook handbook: Social workers*. Retrieved on May 1, 2015 from: http://www.bls.gov/ooh/Community-and-Social-Service/Social-Workers.htm

Washburn, M. (2013). Five things social workers should know about the DSM-5. *Social Work, 58*(5), 373–376.

Whitaker, T., Weismiller, T., Clark, E., & Wilson, M. (2006). *Assuring the sufficiency of a frontline workforce: A national study of licensed social workers. Special report: Social work services in behavioral health care settings.* Washington DC: National Association of Social Workers.

About the Author

Susan W. Gray is Professor Emerita at Barry University's Ellen Whiteside McDonnell School of Social Work in Miami Shores, Florida. She received her PhD in social work from Barry University with a specialization in licensure and professional regulation, her EdD concentrating on adult education from Nova Southeastern University, her MBA from Barry University, and her MSW in clinical practice from Rutgers–the State University. She is a member of the National Association of Social Workers, the Academy of Certified Social Workers, and the Council on Social Work Education. She has been a member of the faculty since 1980, teaching a variety of courses across the curriculum, including foundation and advanced clinical social work practice courses specializing in working with individuals, families and groups, an elective course in crisis intervention, and a doctoral course in social work education. Among her accomplishments, Dr. Gray directed the Doctoral Program and spearheaded an extensive revision of its curriculum.

Dr. Gray is a Licensed Clinical Social Worker and registered clinical supervisor in Florida, where she also serves as a member of the Probable Cause Panel for the state licensure board. Dr. Gray holds a wide range of experience in direct clinical practice with individuals, families, and groups, having worked in a variety of clinical and community settings, including a half-way house for pregnant adolescents, family and children outpatient counseling centers, acute care medical settings, inpatient psychiatric units, and private practice. She also served as a member of the Florida Board of Clinical Social Work, Mental Health Counseling, and Marriage and Family Therapy.

Her practice interests include her work in supervision, professional regulation and licensure, rural practice, bereavement groups, intergenerational family assessment tools, the brief solution-focused model of practice, methods of classroom teaching, and aspects of cultural diversity. Dr. Gray's current research interests are in mental health assessment and practice. She has authored numerous publications, given presentations at local, state, national, and international social work conferences, and is also the author of *Competency-based Assessments in Mental Health Practice: Cases and Practical Applications*. Dr. Gray is known to be an informative and engaging speaker and has received numerous awards; most notably, she was honored as a mentor by the Council on Social Work Education's Council on the Role and Status of Women in Social Work Education and received the prestigious lifetime achievement award from both the Florida Miami–Dade National Association of Social Workers and nationally from the National Association of Social Workers. Dr. Gray's decision to become a teacher was based on her wish to continue to serve and to pay forward all of the mentoring and support she received throughout her professional career. Looking to the new generation of graduating social workers and experienced practicing social workers, she hopes that this book will set the stage for readers to find their way to positively influence the profession beginning each client, and one case at a time.

CHAPTER 1

An Introduction to the Competency-Based Assessment Model

INTRODUCTION

The now century-old tradition of psychiatric social work was one of several specializations, including medical social work and child welfare, that emerged during the early part of the twentieth century. While the field of psychiatric social work grew during the 1900s, social workers struggled when seeking employment because of negative professional attitudes directed toward them. French (1940) identified some of the problems associated with early psychiatric social work positions such as large caseloads, low pay, and in some cases requirements to live on the institution's premises and perform nonprofessional duties within the institution.

The profession changed over time, and in the last part of the twentieth century, social workers could be found serving all areas of the public and private mental health sectors. During the past five decades, social workers have had considerable flexibility in assessing clients, with the choice of using diagnostic categories found in various editions of the *Diagnostic and Statistical Manual of Mental Disorders* (*DSM*) (5th ed., *APA*, 2013 [*DSM-5*]) or other psychosocial or behavioral criteria. Looking at practice in the twenty-first century, some of the ways social workers have historically assessed clients is in jeopardy, especially regarding specific diagnostic descriptions and interventions based on presenting symptoms. In an effort to make the profession a convincing competitor in the marketplace, accountability is one of the central themes for present-day contemporary social work practice. The DSM classification system is often used to meet these accountability requirements and for third-party payments. As a consequence, social workers are called upon to balance the profession's traditional focus on client strengths and resilience with the symptom-based orientation organizing the DSM.

Looking to the future, changes in the service delivery structure of agencies, significant cost containment efforts, and the federal health care reforms enacted in 2010 have moved the profession toward a further reevaluation of the assessment process in clinical social work practice. The push toward reform of the private health insurance market, and to provide better coverage for those with preexisting conditions has set the stage for questions about spiraling medical expenses emerging in the form of increased costs for employee insurance coverage, as well as care for the poor and uninsured who currently seek medical treatment at emergency rooms and public clinics. The full extent of the repercussions of the overhaul of the American health care system are yet to be determined. Nonetheless, the implications of these initiatives are the merging of public and private services; the shifting of financial risk to service providers; the development of community-based service alternatives; and an increased emphasis on client strengths and social supports. Organized around theoretical underpinnings familiar to our profession, this book is about a competency-based assessment model that keeps sight of the complexities of life in vulnerable populations such as the mentally ill while formulating a differential diagnosis using the classification system found in the DSM.

Mental disorders are common, and in any given year, about 26.2 percent of American adults over age 18 suffer from a mental disorder (National Institute of Mental Health [NIMH], 2010). Looking to the rates of mental illness in children, approximately 7 percent of a preschool pediatric sample were given a psychiatric diagnosis in one study and approximately 10 percent of 1- and 2-year-olds receiving developmental screening were assessed as having significant emotional/behavioral problems (Carter, Briggs-Gowan, & Davis, 2004). Despite one's career direction within the field of social work, practitioners in today's practice arena are more than likely to encounter clients with mental illness. Those who work with individuals considered mentally ill recognize the need to learn how to decipher the DSM format. Part of the problem in using the manual is that one might come away from it questioning how the diagnostic criteria presented translate to the real-life clients and their struggles seen in practice. Social workers must know not only how to assess individuals effectively but also how to develop an appropriate intervention plan that addresses clients' needs.

The DSM format is not for amateurs and should not be considered a substitute for professional training in assessment or the other skills needed to work with clients. For example, tasks such as performing mental status exams and monitoring of medication (historically the sole domain of psychiatrists) are now routinely handled by social workers. It is important to recognize that using a classification system can never replace an assessment that considers "the basic fact that people are quintessentially social beings, existing with each other in symbiotic as well as parasitic relationships" (Gitterman & Germain, 2008a, p. 41). That is, the person is much more than his or her diagnosis. There have been a number of long-standing criticisms of the DSM (see e.g., Dumont, 1987; Kirk & Kutchins, 1994; Kirk, Siporin, & Kutchins, 1989; Kutchins & Kirk, 1987). Being a social work practitioner as well as an educator, my primary reason for writing this book is to help make the DSM format more understandable and accessible to other social workers. This book does not take a linear or traditional psychiatric approach; rather, it incorporates a competency-based assessment as a vehicle to support the profession's historical orientation to practice.

Developing a working knowledge of psychopathology is similar to mastering a foreign language; at first everything seems confusing, but gradually the language becomes understandable. Similarly, beginning social work students are often anxious when asked to formulate an initial diagnosis, feeling they are somehow perpetuating the tendency to pigeonhole, stereotype, or label people. The process is complicated because most textbooks about mental disorders are written by psychiatrists or psychologists and tend to be biased toward their authors' own professional alliances. I recognize that using the DSM-5 format has been a controversial topic within social work practice (e.g., see Frances, 2012; Frances, 2013; Friedman, 2012). Since the first introduction of the manual in the early 1950s, it has been used to describe and classify mental disorders. Admittedly, the DSM is an imperfect system, and it has the potential to stigmatize clients through labeling. However, despite its drawbacks, the DSM continues to serve as the standard for evaluation and diagnosis. The aim in writing this book is not to reinvent the proverbial wheel by creating a "wannabe" mini-DSM. Rather, my concern for social work practitioners is the emphasis that the DSM places on "disease" and "illness" obscures our profession's orientation, which centers on client strengths. While practicing from a strengths perspective, the social work practitioner does not ignore the hardships people living with a particular diagnosis must face. Schizophrenia, for example, presents some very real challenges. However, the competency-based assessment model expands the focus of the evaluation to include looking at a person's abilities, talents, possibilities, hopes, and competencies. Saleebey (2012) points out that people learn something valuable about themselves when they struggle with difficulty as they move through life. Although this book is organized around the DSM, I hope to simplify the language of psychopathology in a way that will help to influence the kinds of information gathered, how it is organized, and how it is interpreted. This interpretation includes looking at those strengths that would be useful to the person who struggles with mental illness and helps the social worker focus on the resourcefulness of a person, which is a beginning step in restoring hope. In essence, the social worker looks at how people survive and cope with a diagnosis of mental illness (Gitterman, 2014). A person's resourcefulness, strengths, and coping become a part of the assessment process, ensuring that the diagnosis does not become the center of his or her identity. The "whole story" of a person must include the parts of his or her struggle that have been useful to them and the positive information they have yielded.

Competency 7 b

The competency-based assessment includes the ability to differentially apply knowledge of human behavior (specifically bio-psycho-social-spiritual theories) to better understand the client's current functioning. Familiarity with the DSM diagnostic classification system is considered to be a part of this comprehensive approach to the assessment process. Competency-based practice emphasizes the importance of identifying client competencies, and it focuses on assets instead of deficits. More precisely, it strives to build and enhance the client's own skills as they attempt to deal with life conditions.

The mental disorders found in the DSM will be presented here from a social work perspective. Sometimes interesting historical information will be included; at other times editorial asides about exploration and assessment will be offered. In most cases, a clinical case vignette is presented to help the reader keep in mind the major features of assessment. Above all, the intent is to provide what social workers need in a format that will prove clinically relevant, understandable, and practitioner-friendly.

This book is not intended to address all of the specific DSM classifications, nor does it include all specific disorders. It is anticipated that assessment criteria will be advanced from a social work perspective while balancing the tensions inherent in the medical model. The competency-based assessment encompasses an ecological approach, the strengths perspective, and systems theory to determine what biopsychosocial factors contribute to the client's problems, as well as factors that may be useful in intervention planning. The struggle is to shift the lens away from defining pathology and toward focusing on internal processes in which all of the social and environmental factors that influence functioning are considered. Many current textbooks are starting to move away from terminology describing those considered mentally ill as "patients." The DSM format has also moved away from such negative descriptions. The ultimate challenge is to know how and when the DSM is effective and useful—and how and when to keep its classification system in perspective.

Competency 7 b

We now turn to a review of the DSM-5. This discussion is intended to update, and in some cases reintroduce the reader to the core concepts of the diagnostic assessment using the DSM-5.

THE DSM-5: APPROACHES TO THE ASSESSMENT

In December 2012, the American Psychiatric Association (APA) Board of Trustees voted to approve the new DSM-5. This much-anticipated revision has been received with both excitement and uncertainty. The manual was introduced at the APA's national conference in May 2013, and copies were made available to the public shortly thereafter. This latest version of the DSM represents the first major revision in nearly 20 years since the initial publication of the fourth edition (DSM-IV) in 1994. Unlike earlier editions, there was an unprecedented openness and transparency never before seen in the manual's revision process. Specifically, the APA published three separate drafts of the manual during 2012 on their website asking for feedback. This resulted in approximately 13,000 comments and thousands of emails and letters. National Institute of Mental Health (NIMH) director Thomas R. Insel, MD, wrote in an April 29, 2013, blog post (Insel, 2013): "The goal of this new manual, as with all previous editions, is to provide a common language for describing pathology. While DSM has been described as a 'Bible' for the field, it is, at best, a dictionary, creating a set of labels and defining each. The strength of each of the editions of DSM has been 'reliability'—each edition has ensured that clinicians use the same terms in the same ways."

Why has the DSM taken on such a large role in mental health practice? It may be related to the reality that the prevalence of mental disorders touches most people's lives or someone we know. Mental disorders are common in the United States. The Centers for Disease Control and Prevention (CDC) report, "Mental Illness

Surveillance among Adults in the United States," released on September 2, 2011, indicates that nearly 50 percent of U.S. adults will develop at least one mental illness during their lifetime (CDC, 2011). Fortunately, only about 5.8 percent of the U.S. population, or 1 in 17 adults, struggles with a severe mental disorder (NIMH, 2010). Considered as the "gold standard," the DSM establishes the almost universal measure by which medical professionals diagnose and ultimately treat mental disorders, making it an essential part of the field of psychiatry. In addition, the DSM is used by clinicians in the field of mental health, and also by researchers and health insurance companies. As well, the DSM's criteria for specific disorders is used to determine insurance coverage, grant funding, and new mental health policies. Even so, the final published edition of the DSM-5 was welcomed with both praise and challenge from mental health professionals.

As a response to criticism of the DSM-5, the DSM-5 task force chair, David Kupfer, MD, identified the conceptual framework that guided the development of the manual (Kupfer, 2013):

- Chapters of the specific disorders have been revised to signal how disorders may relate to each other based on underlying vulnerabilities or symptom characteristics.
- The specific disorders are framed in the context of age, gender, and cultural explanations in addition to being organized along a developmental life span within each chapter.
- Key disorders were combined (or reorganized) because the relationships among the different categories placed them along a single continuum, such as (the newly introduced) substance use disorder and autism spectrum disorder.
- A new section of the manual introduces emerging measures, models, and cultural guidance to help clinicians in their evaluation of patients. For the first time, self-assessment tools are included in the manual with the intent to directly include patients in their diagnosis and care.

There is also a greater alignment with the ICD-11. The number 11 represents the most recent version of the International Classification of Diseases (ICD), which is a coding system used to classify morbidity data from inpatient and outpatient records, physician offices, and most National Center for Health Statistics (NCHS) surveys. The NCHS serves as the World Health Organization (WHO) Collaborating Center for the Family of International Classifications for North America. In this capacity, the center is responsible for coordination of all official disease classification activities in the United States relating to the ICD and its use. The manual attempts to harmonize with the ICD-11, which is expected to be released sometime in 2015. The DSM-5 also places a greater reliance on the genetic and neurobiological research that support a biologic etiology of many psychiatric disorders; for example, schizophrenia, autism spectrum, or depressive disorders. The biological aspects are a good fit with the competency-based assessment, which looks at the range of factors affecting a client, including biological influences.

Consistent with previous editions of the manual, using the revised DSM underscores the need for clinical training and practice experience in order to accurately distinguish between normal reactions to things that can happen in a person's life and those responses that can be diagnosed as a mental disorder. Many of the changes in the DSM-5 will now require even experienced practitioners to relearn how to classify and conceptualize a number of disorders. These revisions support the focus of this edition of the book, which is intended to demystify what can be a complex and intimidating process to diagnose clients. You will notice a number of additional cases, which are intended to feature the diagnoses that are new to the DSM-5. Cases in the earlier editions of our book have been slightly modified to highlight the revised diagnostic process.

We now turn to the DSM-5 definition of a mental illness to set the stage for a more detailed review of how to use the DSM-5.

THE DSM-5 DEFINITION OF MENTAL ILLNESS

A long-standing challenge in the field of mental health practice has been making the distinction between what is a mental disorder and what can be regarded as a normal behavior. The DSM-5 proposed some changes to the definition of mental illness in an attempt to provide a more scientifically valid and clinically useful definition (Stein et al., 2010). According to the *DSM-5* (*APA*, 2013, p. 20), the following elements are required in order to diagnose mental illness:

> A mental disorder is a syndrome characterized by clinically significant disturbance in an individual's cognition, emotion regulation, or behavior that reflects a dysfunction in the psychological, biological, or developmental processes underlying mental functioning. Mental disorders are usually associated with significant distress or disability in social, occupational, or other important activities. An expectable or culturally approved response to a common stressor or loss, such as the death of a loved one, is not a mental disorder. Socially deviant behavior (e.g., political, religious, or sexual) and conflicts that are primarily between the individual and society are not mental disorders unless the deviance or conflict results from a dysfunction in the individual, as described above.

Using this definition, the practitioner approaches the assessment by looking for a behavioral or psychological syndrome or pattern that reflects an underlying psychobiological dysfunction. Mental illness is considered when the consequences of these conditions cause the person clinically significant distress or disability that is not an expectable response to common stressors and losses, a culturally sanctioned response to a particular event, or a result of social deviance or conflicts with society. Disorders are seen as a spectrum that can be scored in terms of severity rather than discrete categories. The rationale for moving in this direction is based on research that suggests the underlying biology of mental disorders is more dimensional than categorical (Kupfer & Regier, 2011). The guiding principles organizing the DSM-5 take into account the neurological and dimensional features of mental disorders.

Earlier versions of the DSM were organized around a categorical approach. For instance, if someone had four of nine symptoms of major depression, they did not meet the threshold for a diagnosis. In contrast, if five of nine symptoms were evident, then the person met criteria for a diagnosis of major depression. For all intents and purposes, the categorical approach is seen as an all-or-nothing approach to making a diagnosis. While a person must still meet criteria for a particular diagnosis, the dimensional perspective on assessment takes into consideration the complexity of a particular condition through the use of specifiers, subtypes, severity ratings, and cross-cutting symptom measures when formulating a diagnosis that otherwise might be restricted by the categorical approach.

Although ultimately the diagnosis is still dependent on the practitioner's "yes or no" decision around meeting diagnostic criteria, the dimensional perspective is rooted in data-based observation. However, the DSM-5 cautions the practitioner to avoid over-quantifying a specific behavior in order to push it to a higher level of severity or to assign an additional diagnosis. The challenge for the practitioner is to determine what is central to supporting a particular diagnosis and which symptoms are situation dependent.

We now turn to a more detailed review of the manual.

How the DSM-5 Is Organized

The DSM-5 is organized into three sections (Table 1.1). Section I provides instructions on how to use the manual. This introductory section also describes the process of the manual's revision, including the field trials, the public and professional review process, and expert review. It clearly states its goal to "harmonize" with the ICD systems and shares the organizational structures—such as the dimensional approach to diagnosis, developmental and life-span considerations, the focus on culture and gender issues, and the use of other specified and unspecified diagnoses. These latter categories replace the DSM-IV diagnostic categories of "not otherwise specified" (or NOS) and allows the practitioner to specify the reason that criteria for a specific disorder are not met or the option to forgo specification.

Section II delineates the categorical diagnoses including other conditions that may be a focus of clinical attention with a new organizational structure that eliminates the former DSM-IV multiaxial system. The multiaxial system was removed in an attempt to remove artificial distinctions between medical and mental disorders. Instead, this section is organized around a life span and developmental progression intended to demonstrate how disorders relate to one another. Throughout, the disorders are framed according to age, gender, and developmental characteristics.

Section III provides assessment measures including self-assessment tools, a cultural formulation for understanding the cultural context of mental illness, a dimensional alternative for the personality disorders, and conditions suggested for further research.

Table 1.1 Summary of the Three Major Sections of the DSM-5

Section:	Focus:
Section I	Introduction and information on how to use to use the manual
Section II	Information around the categorical diagnoses
Section III	Assessment measures, cultural formulation, alternative model for the personality disorders, conditions for further study

A CLOSER LOOK AT SECTION II

There are 20 chapters in Section II of the DSM-5 that describe specific disorder categories. Each disorder consists of three major components: the diagnostic classification, the diagnostic criteria sets, and the descriptive text. When considering a particular diagnosis, it is helpful to review the descriptive text, which further elaborates diagnostic criteria. While the descriptive text that follows each disorder varies slightly, it is generally explained under the following headings:

- Specifiers—Provide the option to define subgroupings that share features within a particular disorder.
- Recording procedures—Addresses specific coding requirements for the diagnosis.
- Diagnostic features—Elaborates the specific diagnostic criteria.
- Associated features supporting diagnosis—Considers additional features that can be seen in a particular diagnosis.
- Prevalence—Describes the occurrence of the disorder.
- Development and course—Addresses signs to look for when considering a disorder and its duration.
- Risk and prognostic factors—Addresses the environment, genetic, physiological, and other factors associated with a particular disorder.
- Culture-related diagnostic issues—Elaborates cultural influences to better inform the practitioner how a client's symptoms can be influenced by culture, race, ethnicity, religion, or geographic origin.
- Gender-related diagnostic issues—Reviews potential gender differences in the expression of the symptoms of a disorder.
- Functional consequences (of a specific disorder)—Describes specific behaviors related to a person's level of functioning.
- Diagnostic markers—Explains key indicators to look for when making the assessment.
- Differential diagnosis—Differentiates the diagnosis from other syndromes.
- Comorbidity—Describes other potential co-occurring disorders.
- Relationship to other classifications—Discusses other classification systems; for example, the ICD-11.

The chapters are organized developmentally, or as they become apparent across the life span. The first chapter introduces those diagnoses thought to reveal themselves early in life, such as the neurodevelopmental disorders, followed by the schizophrenia spectrum and other psychotic disorders. Subsequent chapters list those syndromes more commonly seen in adolescence and early adulthood (i.e., the bipolar, depressive, and anxiety disorders) and ends with those diagnoses applicable to middle and late adulthood (Kupfer, Kuhl, & Regier, 2009). Paris (2013) observes that in some cases, a person may have several diagnoses (often referred to as comorbidity) in his or her lifetime; that is, another diagnosis might be added, changed, or even deleted. Organizing the Section II chapters around developmental considerations helps the practitioner to explain to his or her clients why multiple diagnoses have been assigned or other diagnoses may have been added or changed over time (APA, 2013).

The developmental or life span approach is also evident within specific chapters. For example, the disorders that were first diagnosed in childhood listed in the DSM-IV as a separate chapter are now incorporated into the discussion of the anxiety, depressive, bipolar, trauma-related, schizophrenia, and eating disorders. In addition, the DSM-5 provides a review of specific diagnostic criteria and specifiers that relate to onset in childhood.

The DSM-5 also considers disorders clustered around what is termed internalizing and externalizing factors. The internalizing disorders are characterized by high levels of negative activity and are represented by prominent symptoms of anxiety, depressive, and somatic symptoms. These disorders include the depressive disorders, anxiety disorders, obsessive-compulsive and related disorders, trauma and stressor-related disorders, and dissociative disorders.

The group of externalizing disorders are characterized by symptoms of prominent antisocial behaviors, disruptive conduct, substance use and impulsive behaviors. They include, for example, the disruptive, impulse-control, and conduct disorders, and the substance-related and addictive disorders. The bipolar and related disorders are considered an intermediary position and listed between schizophrenia (and other psychotic disorders) and the emotional or internalizing disorders.

Using the DSM-5

The DSM-5 has eliminated the multiaxial system found in earlier versions of the DSM. To sort through the diagnostic process, the practitioner first lists the person's reason for the visit or the principal diagnosis. For example, the book features the case of Janet Sellar to illustrate the substance-related disorders—and she has several diagnoses. However, alcohol intoxication brought Janet to the practitioner's attention, so that diagnosis is listed first. In most cases, the practitioner adds the qualifying phrase, "principal diagnosis" or "reason for visit." In situations where several conditions may have equally contributed to a client's need for care, the principal diagnosis is listed first and the remaining disorders recorded in the order of attention and treatment.

When there is not enough data to support a formal diagnosis, a provisional diagnosis may be assigned and designated by placing the term "provisional" after the apparent diagnosis. In this way, the practitioner can follow-up to determine if criteria are fully met. The provisional diagnosis is generally used for a syndrome that is typically time dependent, such as schizophrenia spectrum and other psychotic disorders. For example, the active phase symptoms for schizophrenia and other psychotic disorders must last for at least 1 month; but if the practitioner does not have specific information about the duration of a person's active phase symptoms, then the diagnosis of "schizophrenia, provisional" would be assigned.

In situations where full criteria are not met, the practitioner considers whether the symptom picture meets criteria for the "other specified" or "unspecified" classifications. The book describes the case of Chris Oghee, who was suspected of having an avoidant personality disorder in addition to alcohol use. However, at the time the diagnosis was made, the social worker had not been able to distinguish all of the symptoms, so "unspecified personality disorder" was assigned. Personality disorders were formerly considered as Axis II disorders, but the DSM-5 now makes no distinction between the personality disorders (formerly listed on Axis II) and other disorder classifications.

Looking to medical disorders, formerly an Axis III designation, the medical condition is listed first in DSM-5 if there is a mental disorder that can be attributed to this medical condition. In this way, the medical disorder is given appropriate attention, and the mental disorder, while noted, may or may not resolve once the medical disorder is addressed. For instance, the case of Sarah Jean Pfohl shows that she has Alzheimer's disease and is also diagnosed with a neurocognitive disorder.

The DSM-5 has replaced the DSM-IV Axis IV, significant psychosocial and contextual features, with the specific diagnostic categories of "Other Conditions That May Be a Focus of Clinical Attention." They are not seen as mental disorders per se but may be assigned if it is the reason for the person's current visit or helps to explain the need for a certain test, procedure, or treatment. They were informally referred to as "V codes" in the DSM-IV. For example, returning to the case of Janet Sellar, she was convicted of a DUI (driving under the influence) and referred for mandated counseling. These problems support the addition of "conviction in criminal proceedings without imprisonment" to her diagnostic picture. For the DSM-5, these conditions can be coded from ICD-9-CM (usually V codes) and from ICD-10-CM (or Z codes).

The Global Assessment of Functioning Scale (GAF), noted on Axis V in the DSM-IV, has also been eliminated. Instead, the DSM-5 looks to an assessment of the severity of a person's symptoms (and related diagnosis), dangerousness to self or others, and disability in social and self-care. Relevant assessment measures were included in the printed edition of the DSM-5, but for the first time, supplemental assessment measures are available online (and accessible online at: http://www.psychiatry.org/dsm5). Using these assessment tools, the practitioner can obtain a picture of a person's symptom presentation and, with repeated administration, can track these symptoms over time. Additional scales included in the manual can be taken by clients themselves and/or administered by the practitioner. It is hoped that using these measures will offer the practitioner a way to detail the full range of a person's symptoms and inform further research.

Refining the Diagnosis

Overall, the disorders listed in the DSM-5 remain in specific diagnostic categories, but a number of options provide the opportunity for the practitioner to further refine the diagnosis by considering subtypes and/or specifiers as appropriate. Measures of severity (ranging from relatively mild and nonclinical deficits to severe), descriptive features (such as with good to fair insight, or in a controlled environment) and course (e.g., in partial remission, in full remission, or recurrent) are stipulated. In this way, the practitioner can better account for variations from person to person (Borges et al., 2010).

Subtypes offer the opportunity to further distinguish differences within a particular disorder. For instance, returning to our example of Sara Jean Pfohl, she has symptoms of a neurocognitive disorder. Since Sara Jean's condition is in the advanced stage, her diagnosis is a "major neurocognitive disorder" as distinguished from "minor neurocognitive disorder." The practitioner is then asked to "specify whether" her neurocognitive disorder is due to Alzheimer's disease or another of the neurocognitive disorders, such as from vascular disease or a traumatic brain injury. This step requires making a distinction among the various subtypes of neurocognitive disorders. The practitioner also asked to "specify" the level of severity. Next, the practitioner is able to "specify" behavioral disturbance. Since Sara Jean's disorder is due to Alzheimer's disease and her symptom picture supports a moderate level of severity with behavioral disturbance, her diagnosis is listed as "moderate major neurocognitive disorder due to probable Alzheimer's disease with behavioral disturbance." As an aside, if Sara Jean had "possible" major neurocognitive disorder, meaning that there is no evidence supporting Alzheimer's as the cause, then Alzheimer's disease would not be listed as a separate and co-occurring medical disorder.

The DSM-5 joined together diagnoses that were previously listed separately in the DSM-IV. One example is autism spectrum disorder (ASD), which combines four different disorders found in the DSM-IV. They are organized along a single spectrum focused on a continuum of two major diagnostic criteria of dysfunctional social communication and restricted, repetitive behaviors or interests. The practitioner is instructed to "specify" current level of severity (seen as ranging from "requiring support" to "substantial support"). As well, the diagnosis is further refined by asking the practitioner to "specify if" there is a level of intellectual impairment and language impairment. The vignette of Bobby Owens, highlighted in the book's chapter on neurocognitive disorders, illustrates severity levels with a diagnosis of: autism spectrum disorder requiring support for deficits in communication, and requiring support for restricted, repetitive behaviors, without accompanying intellectual impairment, and without accompanying language impairment. This is in contrast to the diagnosis for Chris Wells, who also struggles with ASD. Since his symptoms are more severe, his diagnosis is listed as: autism spectrum disorder requiring very substantial support for deficits in communication, and requiring substantial support for restricted, repetitive behaviors, without accompanying intellectual impairment, and with accompanying language impairment—no intelligible speech (nonverbal).

In essence, subtypes are subgroupings within a particular diagnosis, and they are indicated by the instruction "specify whether." On the other hand, to "specify" or "specify if" extends the diagnosis to further clarify the course, severity, or special features of a disorder. In some instances, a specifier is not mutually exclusive; that is, you expect to see the instruction to "specify if" (followed by a list of relevant features) when more than one diagnostic characteristic applies to a particular diagnosis. Returning to our earlier example of ASD, the DSM provides instructions to "specify if" there is accompanying intellectual impairment and if there is accompanying language impairment. Looking to another element of ASD, the practitioner is also instructed to "specify if" there are any known medical or genetic conditions or environmental factors. When you read the case stories for Bobby Owens and for Chris Wells, you will find there is no mention of any medical or genetic conditions or environmental factors as a part of the diagnostic picture, so this specifier was not applied.

As you will see throughout the book, the number of subtypes and specifiers for the diagnostic categories has been expanded, which is consistent with the DSM-5 dimensional approach to assessment. Keep in mind that the DSM-5 offers specific instructions along the way for considering the diagnostic criteria for each diagnosis. By reviewing the case examples in this book that highlight those diagnoses social workers commonly encounter in practice, it is anticipated that you will carefully evaluate your client's symptom picture and become more comfortable formulating an assessment.

The changes to the DSM-5 are a good fit with the book, which is organized around the competency-based assessment. Here, the multiple interactions of the biological, psychological, social, and cultural aspects of a client's life are considered, which leads to more detailed information around the diagnosis and its effects on a client's life. This perspective provides an integrated framework for considering a diagnosis and individualizes a person's encounter with mental illness. The competency-based model guides the practitioner in carefully exploring the full range of a client's problems, in attempting to understand their worldview, and in how to make sense of that information when considering a specific diagnosis.

We now turn our attention to the competency-based assessment model.

THE COMPETENCY-BASED ASSESSMENT MODEL

A competency-based assessment provides a conceptual framework using bio-psycho-social-spiritual theories and the DSM classification system to guide the process of assessment. In this way, the practitioner systematically reviews and understands an individual's past in order to distinguish among and interpret presenting concerns. The social worker gains a greater insight into a person's current functioning by looking at his or her history. Attention is focused on examining biological, psychological (including cognitive), and social systems variables. In his classic work, Bronfenbrenner (1979) suggests that practitioners who do not consider all the various environmental influences lose the breadth and depth of the client's life experiences. The biopsychosocial framework, together with an ecological approach, the strengths perspective, and systems theory, explicates this competency-based assessment model. The biopsychosocial framework validates the potential importance of biogenetic, psychological, social, and environmental factors in understanding human behavior; the ecological perspective draws attention to the client's multiple interactions with his or her environment; the strengths perspective draws attention to the attributes, capacities, experiences, and resources in a person's life that contribute to a positive and satisfying life and effective social functioning; and systems theory integrates these principles. Individualizing how *this* individual person is affected by "illness" is at the heart of this conceptualization.

Here is a brief overview of the components comprising the competency-based assessment model.

THE BIOPSYCHOSOCIAL FRAMEWORK

George Engel (1977, 1980, 1997) is considered the leading proponent of the biopsychosocial framework. According to Engel, the biological component addresses relationships among factors that include normal biology, disease processes, genetic influences, and their relationship to the person's biological functioning. Historically, there have been two major models explaining behavior: one is the biomedical model and the other is the psychodynamic model. The biomedical model delineates diagnostic criteria, whereas the psychodynamic model focuses on symptoms, behaviors, and underlying psychological processes. These two models, when integrated, contribute to the foundation for a biopsychosocial framework. Extending biological considerations is the emerging research supporting neurological contributions. This framework for assessment considers (a) genetic and biological factors in the pathogenesis of certain disorders (such as schizophrenia and mood disorders); (b) developmental experiences and/or conflicted family and social relationships (some individuals may be more vulnerable to certain types of illness); (c) current life stresses (which may precipitate the onset of certain psychiatric disorders and symptoms or contribute to the relapse of preexisting conditions).

As we have seen, the DSM-5 definition of mental illness takes into account the neurological features of mental disorders. This orientation places a greater reliance on the genetic and neurobiological research that support a biologic etiology, making it a good fit with the biopsychosocial framework. Neurobiology, a subdiscipline of both biology and neuroscience, studies the physiological, genetic, and developmental aspects of behavior. Neurobiology typically investigates cells of the nervous system beginning with the level of neurons, neurotransmitters, and the organization of these cells into functional circuits that process information and mediate behavior. In order to familiarize the social work practitioner with the neurological contributions to psychopathology, we briefly look into the role of the brain and related systems in psychopathology.

To begin, the nervous system is a network of cells that carries information to and from all parts of the body. The primary functions of the nervous system are to gather and process information, produce responses to stimuli, and coordinate the workings of different cells. The central nervous system includes the brain and spinal cord, which receives, processes, interprets, and stores information and then sends messages to the muscles, glands, and organs. The neurons are the basic building blocks of the nervous system. These specialized cells are the information-processing units of the brain that are responsible for sending and receiving messages within that system. Figure 1.1 illustrates the structure of the neuron.

The parts of the neuron that receive messages from other cells are called the dendrites. Notice that they look like tree branches and are attached to the cell body, or soma. The soma is the part of the cell that contains the nucleus, which keeps the entire cell alive and functioning. The axon is attached to the soma, and its function is to carry messages out to other cells. Dendrites receive signals to the cell body, while axons carry signals away from the cell body. Notice that the axon is wrapped in what is called a myelin sheath. Think of it as wrapping several layers of paper around your finger for added protection. The myelin sheath increases the speed at which nerve impulses are transmitted from one nerve cell to another. At the end of the axon is the axon terminal.

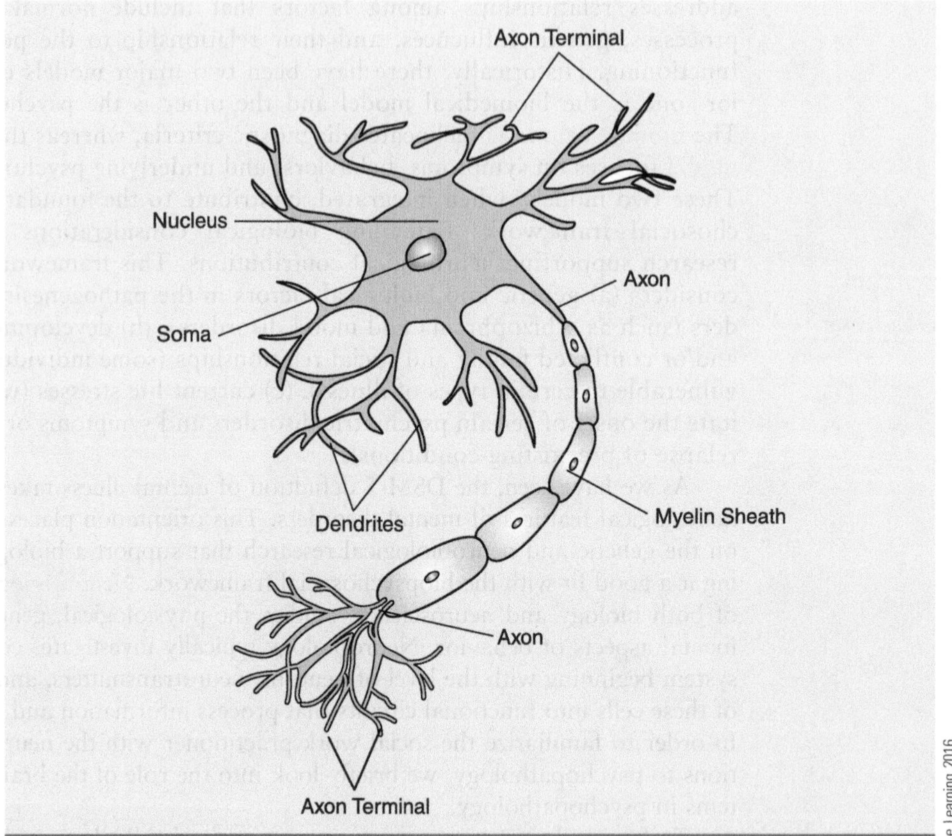

FIGURE 1.1 › THE STRUCTURE OF THE NEURON

The axon terminal contains synapses, or specialized structures, where neurotransmitter chemicals are released to communicate with target neurons (Figure 1.2). The neurotransmitters are released from this location and travel to an adjacent neuron. It is here that the nervous system comes to life with chemical couriers such as the neurotransmitters.

The neurons do not directly touch each other but are separated by a very small space called the synaptic cleft; that is, the place where the axon terminal of one neuron almost touches the dendrite or cell body of another neuron. The entire site is called a synapse—consisting of the axon terminal (or presynaptic neuron), the cleft, and the covering membrane of the receiving dendrite or cell (or postsynaptic neuron). At this point, synaptic vesicles (or tiny sacs in the axon terminal) open and release a few thousand molecules of a chemical substance called a neurotransmitter.

You may wonder at this point about how the neurotransmitters get across the gap. The synaptic vesicles release their neurotransmitters into the synaptic

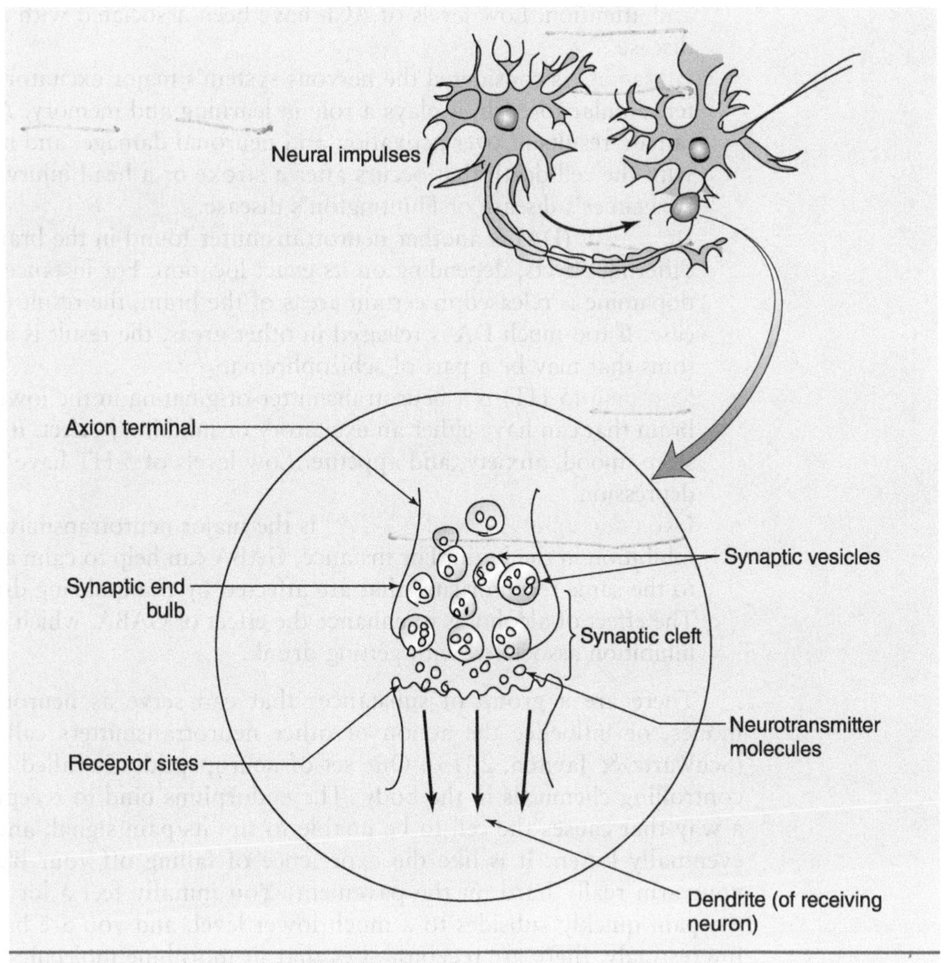

FIGURE 1.2 › TRANSMISSION OF MESSAGES ACROSS NEURONS IN THE BRAIN

gap. The molecules float across the synapse, and many of them fit themselves into the receptor sites and activate the next cell. Think of the receptor sites as tiny suction cups pulling in the neurotransmitters. The next cell can be a neuron, but it can also be a cell on a muscle or a gland. Figure 1.2 illustrates this process.

Through their effects on specific nerve circuits, the neurotransmitters can effect behavior that is revealed by mood, emotion, and/or psychomotor activity. The first neurotransmitter identified was named acetylcholine (ACh). Some of the better understood neurotransmitters and their effects are summarized as follows:

- Acetylcholine (ACh) is found in the hippocampus, an area of the brain responsible for forming new memories. It also plays a key role in memory, arousal, and attention. Low levels of ACh have been associated with Alzheimer's disease.

- Glutamate is considered the nervous system's major excitatory neurotransmitter. Similar to ACh, it plays a role in learning and memory. An excess of glutamate results in over activation and neuronal damage, and may be associated with the cell death that occurs after a stroke or a head injury, or with Alzheimer's disease or Huntington's disease.
- Dopamine (DA) is another neurotransmitter found in the brain and can have differing effects, depending on its exact location. For instance, if too little dopamine is released in certain areas of the brain, the result is Parkinson's disease. If too much DA is released in other areas, the result is a cluster of symptoms that may be a part of schizophrenia.
- Serotonin (5-HT) is a neurotransmitter originating in the lower part of the brain that can have either an excitatory or inhibitory effect. It is associated with sleep, mood, anxiety, and appetite. Low levels of 5-HT have been tied to depression.
- Gaba-aminobutyric acid (GABA) is the major neurotransmitter producing inhibition in the brain. For instance, GABA can help to calm anxiety by binding to the same receptor sites that are affected by tranquilizing drugs and alcohol. The effect of alcohol is to enhance the effect of GABA, which causes the general inhibition associated with getting drunk.

There are a group of substances that can serve as neurotransmitters, hormones, or influence the action of other neurotransmitters called neuropeptides (Schwartz & Javitch, 2013). One set of neuropeptides is called endorphins, pain-controlling chemicals in the body. The endorphins bind to receptors and work in a way that causes the cell to be unable to fire its pain signal, and pain sensations eventually lessen. It is like the experience of falling off your bike and smacking your arm really hard on the pavement. You initially feel a lot of pain, but then the pain quickly subsides to a much lower level, and you are back on your bike. Interestingly, there are receptor sites that fit morphine molecules perfectly, and so it is hypothesized that there must be some form of a natural substance in the body that has the same effect as morphine. The endorphins explain why heroin and other drugs derived from opium are so addictive; that is, when someone takes morphine or heroin, their body neglects to produce endorphins. However, when the drug wears off, they are left with no protection against pain; and everything hurts, so the person then wants more heroin—and the cycle of addiction begins.

The nervous system emerges from the assembly of neurons and is considered the most complex system in the body. It is split into the central nervous system, consisting of the brain and spinal cord, and the peripheral nervous system, which is made up of all the nerves and neurons that are not contained in the brain and spinal cord. The peripheral nervous system allows the brain and spinal cord to communicate with the sensory systems of the eyes, ears, skin, and mouth, and to control the muscles and glands of the body. It is estimated that the brain, the core of the nervous system, has about 100 billion neurons and 100 trillion synapses

(Williams & Herrup, 1998). Behavior normally involves thousands to millions of these neurons in several different areas of the brain. Many areas of the brain have multiple roles, and an in-depth review exceeds the focus of the book. However, we will briefly look into the section of the brain called the limbic system, which is the part of the brain that plays a role in a person's emotions, learning, memory, and motivation.

The limbic system, the part of the brain involved in emotions, motivation, memory, and learning, is found in the inner margin of the upper brain and includes the thalamus, hypothalamus, hippocampus, amygdala, and anterior cingulate cortex (see Figure 1.3). The thalamus is a somewhat round structure in the center of the brain that acts as a relay station for incoming information from the sensory organs. Much like the triage nurse in the emergency room, the thalamus relays information from the sensory organs (such as hearing, sight, touch, or taste) to the cerebral cortex. The hypothalamus, sitting just below and in front of the thalamus, regulates body temperature, thirst, hunger, sleeping and waking, sexual activity, and the aggression we feel. The hippocampus, located toward the middle temporal lobe on each side of the brain, is instrumental in forming long-term permanent memories that are then stored elsewhere in the brain. It plays a role in learning, memory, and the ability to compare sensory information to expectations. The amygdala is located near the hippocampus. It is involved in fear responses and memory of that fear. The amygdala plays a vital role in forming emotional memories (Squire & Kandel, 2009). The cingulate cortex resembles a collar surrounding the frontal part (or anterior section) of the corpus callosum and is actually found in the cortex. It plays an important role in emotional and cognitive processing and has

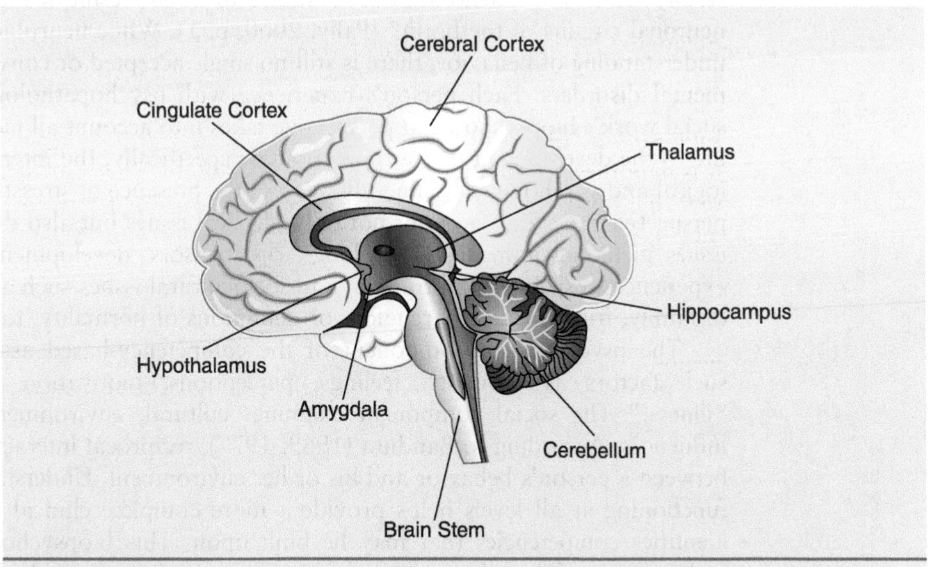

FIGURE 1.3 › THE LIMBIC SYSTEM

been shown to be implicated in a variety of disorders including attention-deficit/hyperactive disorder and bipolar disorder (Fornito, Yucel, & Pantelis, 2009; Maletic et al., 2007).

The limbic system can be seen in Figure 1.3. To orient you to its location in the brain, notice the cerebral cortex is illustrated. This is the largest part of the brain and can best be described as a cauliflower-like structure that is covered by several thin layers of densely packed cells collectively known as the cerebral cortex. Also notice the brain stem, which looks somewhat like a stalk. It is the part of the brain located at the top of the spinal cord. The cerebellum is also pictured. It is about the size of a small fist and is the part of the brain involved in cognitive and emotional learning along with contributing to a sense of balance and coordination of muscle movements (Timmann et al., 2010).

Environmental considerations, integral to the competency-based assessment, play a central role in neuronal development. During the sensitive period of a child's early care, connections in the infant's limbic system are proliferating at a high rate. Schore (2003) observes that changes in the social environment will activate genetic programs in the "microarchitecture of growing brain regions" and thus play a role in shaping each person's neuropsychological environment (p. 33). In sum, the brain's neural architecture reflects the environment that shapes it (Cozolino, 2002). For example, if the infant's social environment is either chronically stressful and overstimulating or lacking in sufficient stimulation and challenge, the neurotransmitter (and hormonal) changes in the brain can induce cell death in the affective areas of the limbic system. These changes lead to affect dysregulation and a compromised neural network.

Clearly, the brain and the mind work together in very dynamic ways, and, as a result, "all mental phenomena are assumed to be the result of biological activity of neuronal circuits of the brain" (Pally, 2000, p. 1). While neurobiology extends our understanding of behavior, there is still no single accepted or consistent cause of the mental disorders. Each person's experience with psychopathology is unique, and social work's biopsychosocial perspective takes into account all factors that contribute to the development of psychopathology; specifically, the interplay between biological and psychological vulnerability, and the presence of stressful life events. This perspective takes into account not only physical issues but also those psychological issues including immediate and long-term stressors, developmental problems, life experiences, psychological trauma, and sociocultural issues such as the expectations of family, friends, culture, religion, or definitions of normality, to list a few.

The psychological component of the competency-based assessment refers to such factors as thoughts, feelings, perceptions, motivation, and reaction to "illness." The social component examines cultural, environmental, and familial influences. According to Bandura (1969, 1977), reciprocal interactions are assumed between a person's behavior and his or her environment. Understanding the client's functioning at all levels helps provide a more complete clinical picture—one that identifies competencies that may be built upon. This biopsychosocial orientation makes it essential to discern the client's medical status, individual psychology, and sociocultural factors affecting behavior.

The biopsychosocial framework supports the competency-based assessment model in several ways. First, the significance of understanding the client's present functioning and its relationship to past events underscores the need for fully understanding each client's unique history. Second, this model relies on a thorough assessment and prioritizing of problems. Third, it pays attention to the multiple systems that affect the client, such as the biological, psychological, social, and cultural aspects of the client's life. A fourth characteristic is the focus on positive behaviors and events in the client's life rather than on deficits. Finally, a competency-based assessment focuses on the relationship between behavior and surrounding events—that is, those events that can either elicit or maintain problematic behaviors. This framework helps the client (and his or her family) maintain an identity apart from the "illness." Applying a competency-based assessment model underscores the importance of evaluating all aspects of the client's difficulties while looking for strengths.

The second element important to discussion of the competency-based assessment model incorporates an ecological perspective.

The Ecological Perspective

Competency 6 a

The competency-based assessment looks to therapeutic relationships with clients within the person-in-environment perspective. More than 40 years ago, Carel Germain (1973) introduced the "ecological metaphor" as a way to expand the focus of social work practice by emphasizing the interaction between people and their environment. This orientation draws attention to both the internal as well as external factors in a client's life. The ecological perspective primarily focuses on human ecology—the way human beings and their environments accommodate each other (Germain, 1991; Gitterman & Germain, 2008b). This interaction is considered dynamic; that is, the goodness of "fit" between individuals and their surroundings is achieved through mutual interaction, negotiation, and compromise. In essence, people are seen as being involved in dynamic and reciprocal interactions with their environment. Sheafor and Horejsi (2011) highlight the importance of understanding clients through an ecological point of view:

> It should be apparent that there is not always a good fit between concepts borrowed from another field, like ecology, and the values and purposes of the social work profession. Nevertheless, these ideas stretch our thinking and encourage us to view human behavior and problems and consider planned change in ways that are new and fresh. Above all else, ecology teaches us that people are shaped and influenced by their environment and, in turn, the environment is shaped and changed by humans. (p. 63)

The mental disorders in the DSM describe disease processes, not people; individuals with the same diagnosis often look very different from one another in terms of behaviors, personality, life experiences, or problems in living. Depending on the diagnostic criteria offered, clients may have remarkably different life experiences. While the DSM may be recognized as a useful diagnostic tool, it tells the practitioner little or nothing about the "why's" of mental illness—and it does not address client individuality.

One of the strengths of the ecological perspective is that it draws attention to each person's unique history and takes into account the complexities of the human experience. Some of the more salient concepts of the ecological perspective take into consideration are the following:

- **Person: environment fit**—This is viewed as the actual congruence or "fit" between an individual's or a group's needs and their surroundings. Considered a defining characteristic of social work practice, the person: environment fit requires an assessment that encompasses the person, their environment, and the interactions between them.
- **Adaptations**—Adaptations are regarded as the continuous, change-oriented, cognitive, sensory-perceptual, and behavioral processes people use to sustain or improve the fit between themselves and their environment.
- **Life stressors**—Life stressors include difficult social or developmental transitions, traumatic life events, or other issues that disturb the existing fit between people and their environments.
- **Stress**—Stress is considered the response to life stressors; stress is characterized by troubled emotional or physiological states (or both). It may be characterized by anxiety, guilt, anger, fear, depression, helplessness, or despair.
- **Coping measures**—Any efforts to regulate negative feelings about changes in the environment may be considered coping measures.

According to Antonovsky (1980), the most basic category of coping resources consists of beliefs and attitudes toward life. Other coping mechanisms relate to a person's knowledge of and successful experiences with life tasks; cognitive capacities and ability to reason; ability to control and use emotional affective responses to stress; and skills to carry out planned action, which usually come from past successful experiences.

The ecological perspective views individuals as moving through a series of life transitions that require environmental supports and coping skills. Stress may result if there is not a good fit between internal and external demands and available resources (Gitterman & Germain, 2008a). The practitioner looks at those transactions that either promote or inhibit growth and development. In addition, this perspective helps the practitioner to work collaboratively with clients to mobilize strengths and coping skills, locate resources, and explore opportunities within the client's environment that may pave the way for the client to achieve success rather than leave him or her feeling powerless or disenfranchised.

The third aspect integral to the competency-based assessment is the strengths perspective.

THE STRENGTHS PERSPECTIVE

Competency 7 c

As a part of the competency-based assessment, social workers are called upon to identify and articulate the client's strengths as well as vulnerabilities. The strengths perspective provides an avenue for the practitioner to identify and build upon client strengths. Strengths can be seen as any client resources, capabilities, knowledge, abilities, motivation, experience, intelligence, or other positive qualities that can play a role in solving problems and pursuing positive and satisfying life experiences (Blundo, 2008). This perspective serves to counterbalance the deficit-oriented approach so often associated with an assessment of pathology. Rather than solely focusing on what is wrong in a person's life, the strengths perspective looks to a consideration of the positive and functional aspects of behaviors and situations. The strengths perspective does not ignore the reality that a psychiatric diagnosis may impose limitations on a person's functioning but looks to those experiences as a potential source of strength and opportunity (Saleebey, 2012).

As a part of the competency-based assessment, the practitioner's focus shifts to an exploration of each person's unique experience with the challenges associated with mental illness. The strengths perspective presumes that every person has strengths, even when some of the behaviors associated with a particular diagnosis are considered seriously dysfunctional. The practitioner assumes that strengths can be found in all environments, no matter how difficult they might seem. As such, the practitioner looks for something positive and important that the client is doing, can do, or wants to do. Saleebey (2012) identifies the following principles that are the underpinnings of the strengths perspective:

- Every individual, group, family, and community has strengths.
- Trauma and abuse, illness and struggle may be injurious, but they may also be sources of challenge and opportunity.
- Assume that you do not know the upper limits of the capacity to grow and change and take individual, group, and community aspirations seriously.
- We best serve clients by collaborating with them.
- Every environment is full of resources.

In summary, the strengths perspective provides the structure to look for those capabilities and resources that differentiate each client's experience with mental illness.

The fourth and last element comprising the competency-based assessment model is systems theory.

Systems Theory

Systems theory was developed during the 1940s and 1950s by Ludwig von Bertalanffy (1968) as an approach to understanding the interconnectedness of the various relationships within a person's life. From its beginning, systems theory postulated that the behavior of any living system could be influenced by other conditions. Bertalanffy suggested that all social sciences can be integrated by using systems as the unit of analysis—that is, the biological system, the personality system, and the social system.

Systems theory organizes the practitioner's understanding of human development. The theory does not attempt to explain human behavior, but asserts that human behavior is viewed through three distinct frames of reference: biological, psychological, and social. Systems theory clarifies the person: situation gestalt by conceptualizing the client's world. It moves away from a linear explanation of cause and effect to appreciate the complex interactions between the individual and all aspects of their biopsychosocial system. In other words, the true role of systems theory is to help the social worker pay attention to those complex interactions between clients and their environment. The competency-based assessment complements using the DSM for assessing mental illness. This systems approach to assessment includes exploring how the client's current thoughts and feelings as well as environmental factors relate to functioning versus looking only at behavior as a sign of intrapersonal or personal concerns. Using the biopsychosocial framework fosters an evaluation based on "behaviors in situations" rather than on behaviors or situations alone. The competency-based assessment also considers capacities, motivation, and environmental qualities as components of ecological competence for the multiple transactions between people and their social environments. This approach changes the type of assessment questions asked—the social worker is more interested in finding out what is right about the client rather than focusing solely on what is wrong. This summary of the central ideas supporting the competency-based assessment model sets the stage for the constructs discussed in the following chapters.

Assessment is an ongoing process with a focus toward valuing client strengths. Sheafor and Horejsi (2011) distinguish the assessment from diagnosis in a number of ways:

> In direct practice with individuals, families, and small groups, the social worker's data gathering and assessment will be shaped and guided by the person-in-environment framework. In other words, attention is given to the client as a unique and whole person as well as the demands and constraints placed on the client by the context or environment in which he or she must function. (p. 172)

The competency-based assessment changes the emphasis in the questions a practitioner asks. The practitioner gives some attention to all dimensions of the whole person and considers any factors that may affect his or her social functioning. For example, when working with a client who is socially isolated and may be depressed, asking a question about how he or she manages to get through the day shifts the focus away from pathology and toward the client's own competency. This then provides the foundation for examining effective problem solving, self-change, viable alternatives, and solutions. From this example, using a wide-angle lens in formulating the assessment provides the opportunity to gather data that focuses on the client's experiences in coping with depression. The biological, psychological, and social elements found in the competency-based assessment, when merged with the DSM, provide an individualized way of looking at clients and their social contexts.

Competency 8 c

Systems theory supports the competency-based assessment and helps to inform interprofessional collaboration. Systems theory, for example, provides a perspective that helps practitioners better understand how assessment and related services are linked together. The social worker may consult with other professional disciplines to confirm a diagnosis or to monitor a client's medication. When professionals from different disciplines work together, they have the opportunity to formulate a diagnosis more accurately and deepen their understanding of a person's symptoms than when they conduct assessments independently. Seeking the advice and counsel of other professionals is integral to the competency-based assessment process and is supported by the National Association of Social Workers' (NASW) Code of Ethics (NASW, 2008). The Code specifically notes that social workers should put personal biases aside and act on behalf of clients based on professional social work knowledge, skills, and values to the best of their ability and in the client's best interest. This requires social workers to define what is unique about their professional perspective, have a solid professional identity, and know what falls outside their purview (Reamer, 2013). Interprofessional collaboration includes upholding the values and ethics of social work, respect for professional colleagues, an ecological holistic view of practice, and a perspective that is similar or complementary to the collaborators' perspectives (Bronstein, 2003).

In subsequent chapters, the connections among the biological, psychological, and social factors are presented. Figure 1.4 is a graphic representation of this approach. This pedagogical feature is repeated throughout the book, each time focusing on the specific disorder under discussion. The case illustrations are not to be considered as the final word, but seen as representations of assessment data.

By envisioning the convergence of these perspectives, it is anticipated that the practitioner will get a fuller picture of assessing for competence (or those skills that enable the client to function effectively) and the client's unique experience with mental disorders. The competency-based assessment is the process of clarifying competence within the client system, the unique features of the client's environment, the goodness of fit between the client and his or her environment, and the impact of mental illness. Gitterman and Germain (2008a) note,

> By immersing ourselves in clients' stories and environments, social workers are in a natural position to describe adaptive and dysfunctional patterns, as well as processes of change. Through detailed and rich descriptions, including direct quotes from clients and significant environmental figures, we capture the whole person within a life course and ecological perspective. (p. 129)

Our clients are seen as active, striving human beings who are capable of organizing their lives and realizing their potentialities, as long as they have appropriate

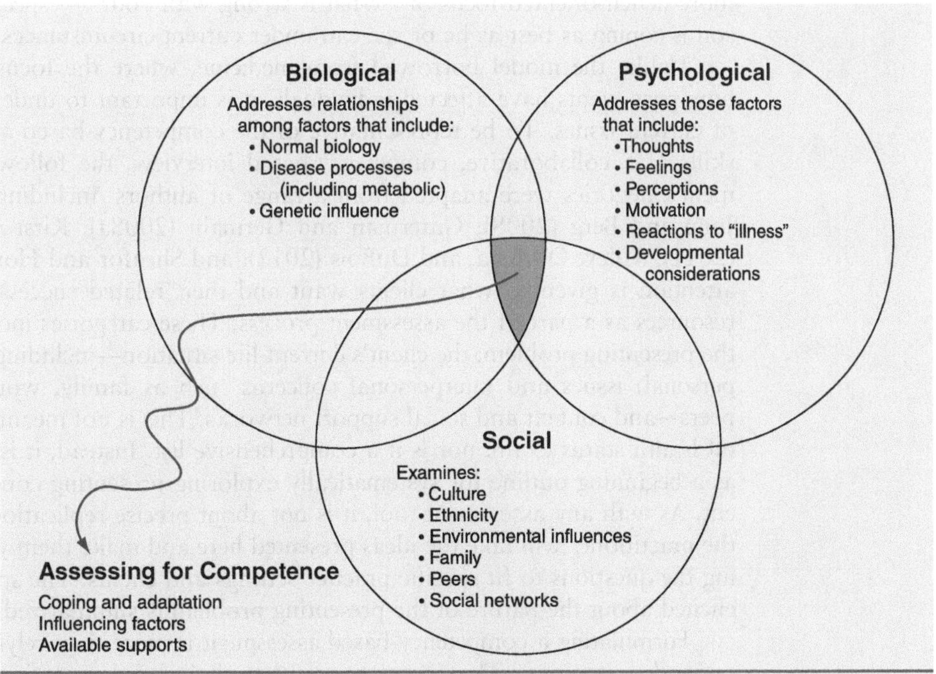

FIGURE 1.4 › The Competency-Based Assessment Model

resources that can be located in the family, their community, and/or the environment. The competency-based assessment is directed toward finding ways to support the client's strengths and coping strategies. The competency-based assessment model provides a framework for understanding persons with mental illness as unique and fosters the consideration of not only a person's illness but of his or her capacity to grow in relationships. The social worker, in collaboration with the client system, focuses on social adaptation, coping skills development, and empowerment. In addition, the practitioner identifies and amplifies the client's existing capacities in order to resolve problems and improve quality of life. The competency-based approach to the assessment can be seen as respectful toward and empowering of oppressed and vulnerable people such as those with mental illness.

UNDERSTANDING THE CLIENT

Competency 7 d

Competent social work practice includes the ability to critique and apply knowledge of human behavior in order to fully understand the client's presenting problems and the environmental interplay. Social work practice is distinguished from other professions by viewing the client as being in a reciprocal relationship with his or her social surroundings. The individual and his or her environment are mutually interdependent, but sometimes obstacles get in the way of the person's social functioning. The assessment should be guided by obtaining relevant information and understanding of the full range of the client's circumstances, which then informs the development of intervention strategies. Assessment should ask, "What's the matter?" instead of the more deficit-oriented focus of "What is wrong with you?"—especially since the person is coping as best as he or she can under current circumstances or events.

Unlike the model borrowed from medicine, where the focus is on examining how past events have affected individuals, it is important to understand the context of current issues. To be representative of the competency-based assessment and the skills of a collaborative, competency-based interview, the following major assessment categories were adapted from a range of authors, including, for example: de Jong and Berg (2008); Gitterman and Germain (2008a); Kirst-Ashman and Hull (2011); Miley, O'Melia, and DuBois (2012); and Sheafor and Horejsi (2011). More attention is given to what clients want and their related successes, strengths, and resources as a part of the assessment process. These categories include the nature of the presenting problem, the client's current life situation—including intrapersonal (or personal) issues and interpersonal concerns such as family, work or school, and peers—and context and social support networks. This is not meant to replace a mental health status exam, nor is it a comprehensive list. Instead, it is intended to serve as a beginning outline for systematically exploring presenting concerns with the client. As with any assessment tool, it is not about precise replication. It is hoped that the practitioner will take the ideas presented here and make them your own by revising the questions to fit specific practice settings and clients. The specific information elicited about the nature of the presenting problem is summarized in Table 1.2.

Formulating a competency-based assessment is more than relying on gut feelings or worker intuition. This is not to say that clinical judgment is unimportant, only that effective judgments concerning clients must instead be grounded in empirical

TABLE 1.2 THE NATURE OF THE PRESENTING PROBLEM

Identify the reason for referral:

What made the client seek help now and not before?

How has the client sought to solve the problem previously including other therapy (and with what results)?

What is the client's ability to identify and define problems, or to discuss probable causative factors?

Describe the events leading up to the referral or other factors precipitating the referral.

Identify the contributing conditions and components of the problem:

History

When did the problem first occur?

Is this a long-standing unresolved problem, or a recent one?

Duration

How long has the problem been going on?

Frequency

How often does the problem occur?

Magnitude

What is the intensity of the problem?

Antecedents

What happens immediately before the problem occurs?

Consequences

What happens immediately after the problem occurs?

Clarify the client's competence:

What are the unique capacities, skills, attitudes, motivations, strengths, and potentialities of the client?

What are the particular areas of coping strengths?

What are indicators of resilience in the person?

Which areas of competence need to be reinforced or supported?

Which life experiences can be mobilized to stimulate or support the process of change?

What client resources are available for solving the problem?

How does the client relate to the worker and demonstrate the ability to use help?

What is the social worker's perception of the problem?

How much agreement is there between the worker and the client concerning these problems?

Are there other difficulties associated with (or in addition to) the problem?

observations and documentation of client characteristics. In the author's experience, there is a temptation to diagnose first and then ask questions to support this clinical picture. Ordinarily, the social worker looks at the multiple influences in the client's life, for example, intrapersonal issues, patterns of interpersonal relationships, social context, and support networks. Table 1.3 provides suggestions for examining

Table 1.3 The Client's Current Life Situation

I. Intrapersonal (or personal) issues:

Cognitive functioning

What is the client's perception of the problem?
Is there evidence of the client's capacity to solve problems?
Is there evidence of rational (versus irrational) thoughts?

Emotional functioning

Describe the client's affect.
Is there evidence of appropriate (versus inappropriate) affect?
Has the client had difficulty managing any recent stresses or pressures?

Behavioral functioning

What is the client's physical appearance?
Does the client have any distinctive mannerisms?
Does the client have any disabilities?

Physiologic functioning

Has the client been seen medically during the past year?
If so, what are the results?
Has the client had any recent illnesses or surgery?
Is there evidence of drug and/or alcohol usage?
Is the client taking any medications?
Describe diet, caffeine use, nicotine use, etc.

Mental status

Note any of the following:
Disturbances in appearance, dress, or posture.
Disturbance in thoughts (such as hallucinations or delusions).
Disturbances in level of awareness (such as memory, attention).
Disturbances in emotional tone (deviations in affect or discrepancies between the client's verbal report of mood/affect and practitioner observation).
Degree of client awareness of the nature of the problem and need for treatment.

Client roles and role performance

What roles does the client perform (such as spouse or parent)?
Are the client's issues related to role performance?
Are the client's issues related to role satisfaction or dissatisfaction?
Are there any serious problems with children, marriage, and/or other close relationships?

Developmental considerations

Trace the birth, developmental history (including the mother's pregnancy), developmental milestones, or illnesses.
Explore sexual, marital, and family history (such as domestic violence, abuse).
Is there a legal history?
What has family life been like for the client?
Does the client recall any specific events while growing up (such as a parent's death or a divorce)?

TABLE 1.3 CONTINUED

II. Interpersonal family issues:

What is each family member's perception of the problem(s)?

Client's marital/partner status

What is the client's sexual, dating, partner, or marital history?

What is the quality of the client's intimate relationships?

At what age (or ages) did the client marry (or engage in a partner relationship)?

How many marriages (or partner relationships) has the client had?

Family structure

What is the quality of the client's family interactions?

Describe the family system, including composition, structure, boundaries, cohesion, flexibility, rules, family alliances, family power, negotiation, family decision making, problem solving, and communication patterns.

Has there been any recent serious illness or death in the client's family?

How does the client describe his or her parents and/or siblings (if any)?

III. Interpersonal work or school issues:

What is the client's occupation or grade in school?

How satisfied is the client with work/school?

Are there indicators of successful achievement in this setting?

Are there issues related to grades, performance, pay, or promotions?

Describe the client's relationships with colleagues/peers.

Does the presenting problem(s) occur in this setting?

If so, does it affect the client's ability to get along with peers, teachers, bosses, or other authority figures?

What is the client's academic/work history?

Is the client having any problems with money or with employment?

Is the client in debt?

IV. Interpersonal issues with peers:

Does the client have friends?

What is the quality of these relationships?

Is the client satisfied with his or her peer relationships?

biopsychosocial functioning and areas that delineate the fit between the person and his or her social networks.

Competency 1 b

As a part of the competency-based assessment, social work professionals recognize and manage their personal biases as they influence the relationship and assessment process. Practitioners are knowledgeable about the shifting societal mores and how they can potentially affect a client's well-being. This orientation to the assessment includes an exploration of the client's context and social support networks (see Table 1.4). This includes culture and ethnicity, which are an integral part of one's identity. It is important to explore the extent to which these factors can affect

TABLE 1.4 THE CLIENT'S CONTEXT AND SOCIAL SUPPORT NETWORKS

Clarify the environmental characteristics that influence coping and adaptive patterns of the client:

What environmental resources does the client have?

How adequate are the client's material circumstances—for example, housing, transportation, food?

What does the client know about community resources and how to use them?

What actual or potential supports are available in the environment?

Does the client have access to family or peer supports or support from agencies in the neighborhood that are not being used?

What are the risks and vulnerabilities in the client system?

What blocks, obstacles, and/or deficits interfere with the client's life processes and adaptive strivings?

What is the goodness of "fit" between the client system and his or her environment?

Are there any ethnic/cultural considerations for the client?

What is the client's ethnic or cultural group and is this a source of stress or support?

What is the degree of acculturation?

Is there evidence of prejudice or discrimination by others toward the client?

To what extent is there isolation from (or participation in) extra-familial groups and associations, such as ethnic or cultural groups?

What is the client's perception of the effect ethnic/cultural group identification has had?

How do sociocultural factors (such as racism, sexism, cultural values) affect the client's functioning?

Does the client experience any social and/or economic injustice?

Can the client draw from the resources of his or her culture or ethnic group?

a person with a mental illness. Along with respect for these considerations, the practitioner must remember to take into account his or her own attitudes and biases as they affect the assessment process and the therapeutic relationship (Lum, 2010; Thyer, Wodarski, Myers, & Harrison, 2010).

SUMMARY

The competency-based assessment model translates the process of summarizing, prioritizing, and classifying the information found in the DSM into a format that is more familiar to social work practitioners. However, the practitioner looks for strengths and resources in the individual and his or her related social systems that can be developed and supported. Additionally, individual, family, and socio-environmental systems in the client's life are reviewed. A thorough understanding of the client's problems often demystifies using a diagnostic label and provides clinical insight into what seems to be a complicated symptom picture (Gray, 2006, 2011). The worker must be knowledgeable about many factors related to presenting issues. Therefore, familiarity with the diagnostic conditions and the ability to apply them correctly is important to the competency-based assessment for social workers. While readers may regard this orientation as simply good old-fashioned social work practice, the competency-based perspective advances professional clinical social work practice by suggesting that an assessment grounded in strengths and possibilities increases opportunities to effectively serve those who seek help.

Recent legislative initiatives have transformed the landscape of mental health practice, and it is becoming increasingly necessary to conduct the kind of assessment that provides accurate information about a person's complex mental health symptoms. The need for interprofessional collaboration is becoming increasingly apparent. Social work practice in the twenty-first century has become more complicated and underscores the growing need for interprofessional collaboration, which draws upon the knowledge of other disciplines and professionals. There are a number of benefits to interprofessional collaboration. Merging the expertise and knowledge from different disciplines maximizes the creativity needed for fully understanding the symptoms experienced by those who are struggling with mental illness (Bronstein, 2003).

A crucial component of the competency-based assessment is its client-centered focus that values the unique strengths and perspectives of people who are struggling with mental illness. An important social work value relates to appreciating human worth and respecting dignity. We often see people who are not at their best. It goes without saying that the profession is committed to helping people who are oppressed and disempowered. The social worker focuses on the strengths of the person, thereby promoting both personal and societal competence despite the obstacles associated with mental illness. As a matter of fact, over 40 years ago, Siporin (1975) recognized that "a chief mandate of the social work profession is to work with people who are disenfranchised and oppressed" (p. 4). Social work values both the strengths and vulnerabilities of people. These values are integral to the competency-based assessment model, which incorporates both biopsychosocial factors and the relationship between the client's behavior and his or her context. This perspective provides a complete picture describing the individual's functioning at all levels.

Social workers have also traditionally been concerned with social justice, and this perspective has encouraged practitioners to look beyond a client's mental health diagnosis and consider the broader issues of a person's welfare, such as what it is like to live with a diagnosis. The competency-based assessment helps the practitioner to understand both a client's diagnosis and to consider the experience and impact of this diagnosis on his or her family, community, and social environment (Gray, 2011). This requires an understanding of the social and environmental contributors to mental illness, such as family welfare, housing, income security, and community or a sense of being a part of something or belonging somewhere.

In sum, the competency-based assessment focuses on relationships between behavior and surrounding events—those events that elicit or maintain problematic behaviors. The individual's present functioning is examined in relationship to past events, while considering biopsychosocial factors as well as environmental systems. The focus is on client strengths rather than deficits. Integral to the competency-based assessment is the assumption that clients have the capability to reorganize their lives as long as they have appropriate family, community, societal, and environmental resources and supports.

As the DSM transitions from the DSM-IV-TR (APA, 2000) to the current edition of the manual, Table 1.5 provides a brief summary of the changes made to the organization of the manual.

TABLE 1.5 SUMMARY COMPARISON BETWEEN THE DSM-IV-TR MULTIAXIAL SYSTEM AND THE DSM-5

DSM-IV-TR	DSM-5
Axis I—Clinical Disorders and Other Conditions That May Be a Focus of Clinical Attention Axis II—Mental Retardation and the Personality Disorders	Principal diagnosis is listed; there could be more than one that meets criteria (or comorbid disorders) If there is more than one diagnosis: • List reason for the client's visit first • And list the reason for the visit first • Include the phrase, "principal diagnosis" or "reason for visit" In some cases, add provisional diagnosis, if relevant • Applies when diagnostic criteria will be met but (at the time) the practitioner does not have enough information • Include the term "provisional" after the diagnosis
Axis III—General Medical Conditions	If there is a medical condition that appears to be the cause of the medical disorder, it is listed before the mental disorder
Axis IV—Psychosocial and Environmental Problems	Consider using the diagnostic categories of Other Conditions That May Be a Focus of Clinical Attention (detailed in the DSM-5, pages 715–727)
Axis V—Global Assessment of Functioning (GAF)	Replaced with a global measure of disability—the World Health Organization Disability Assessment Schedule (WHODAS), version 2 (refer to Section III, pages 745–748)

COMPETENCY NOTES

Competency 1 b—Social workers use reflection and self-regulation to manage personal values and maintain professionalism in practice situations (p. 27): Social workers recognize personal values and make the distinction between personal and professional values.

Competency 6 a—Social workers apply knowledge of human behavior and the social environment, person-in-environment, and other multidisciplinary theoretical frameworks to engage with clients (and constituencies) (p. 19): Social workers understand theories of human behavior and the social environment and critically apply this knowledge to facilitate engagement with clients (and constituencies) including families, groups, organizations, and communities.

Competency 7 b—Social workers are able to apply knowledge of human behavior and the social environment, person-in-environment, and other multidisciplinary theoretical frameworks in the analysis of assessment data (pp. 3, 4): Social workers understand theories of human behavior and the social environment and critically evaluate and apply this knowledge in the assessment process.

Competency 7 c—Social workers develop mutually agreed-on intervention goals and objectives based on the assessment of strengths, needs, and challenges within clients and constituencies (p. 20): Social workers recognize the implications of the larger practice context in the assessment process.

Competency 7 d—Social workers select appropriate intervention strategies based on the assessment, research knowledge, and values and preferences of clients and communities (p. 24): Social workers understand methods of assessment with diverse clients (and constituencies) to advance practice effectiveness.

Competency 8 c—Social workers use interprofessional collaboration, as appropriate, to achieve beneficial practice outcomes (p. 22): Social workers value interprofessional teamwork and recognize the beneficial outcomes that require interdisciplinary, interprofessional, and interorganizational collaboration.

References

American Psychiatric Association (APA). (2000). *Diagnostic and statistical manual of mental disorders* (4th ed., text revision). Washington, DC: Author.

American Psychiatric Association (APA). (2013). *Diagnostic and statistical manual of mental disorders* (5th ed.). Arlington, VA: Author.

Antonovsky, A. (1980). *Health, stress, and coping.* San Francisco: Jossey-Bass.

Bandura, A. (1969). *Principles of behavior modification.* New York: Holt, Rinehart & Winston.

Bandura, A. (1977). *Social learning theory.* Englewood Cliffs, NJ: Prentice Hall.

Bertalanffy, L. von (1968). General system theory: A critical review. In W. Buckley (Ed.), *Modern systems research for the behavioral scientist* (pp. 11–30). Chicago: Aldine.

Blundo, R. (2008). Strengths-based framework. In T. Mizrahi & L. E. Davis (Eds.), *Encyclopedia of social work* (20th ed., Vol. 4, pp. 173–177). Washington, DC: National Association of Social Workers and Oxford University Press.

Borges, G., Yu, Y., Cherpitel, C., Bond, J., Cremonte, M., Moskalewicz, J., . . . Rubio-Stipec, M. (2010). The dimensionality of alcohol use disorders and alcohol consumption in a cross-national perspective. *Addiction*, *195*(2), 240–254.

Bronfenbrenner, U. (1979). *The etiology of human development: Experiments by nature and design.* Cambridge, MA: Harvard University Press.

Bronstein, L. R. (2003). A model for interdisciplinary collaboration. *Social Work*, *48*(3), 297–306.

Carter, A. S., Briggs-Gowan, M. J., & Davis, N. O. (2004, January). Assessment of young children's social-emotional development and psychopathology: Recent advances and recommendations for practice. *Journal of Child Psychology and Psychiatry*, *45*(1), 109–134.

Centers for Disease Control and Prevention (CDC). (2011, September). Mental illness surveillance among adults in the United States. *Morbidity and Mortality Weekly Report*, *60*(3), 1–32. Retrieved on November 21, 2014 from: http://www.cdc.gov/Features/MentalHealthSurveillance/

Cozolino, L. (2002). *The neuroscience of psychotherapy: Building and rebuilding the human brain.* New York: Norton.

de Jong, P., & Berg, I. K. (2008). *Interviewing for solutions* (3rd ed.). Belmont, CA: Thompson.

Dumont, M. P. (1987). A diagnosis parable. *Readings*, *2*(4), 9–12.

Engel, G. L. (1977). The need for a new medical model: A challenge for biomedicine. *Science*, *196*, 120–136.

Engel, G. L. (1980). The clinical application of the biopsychosocial model. *American Journal of Psychiatry*, *137*, 535.

Engel, G. L. (1997). From biomedical to biopsychosocial: Being scientific in the human domain. *Psychosomatics*, *38*(6), 521–528.

Fornito, A., Yucel, M., & Pantelis, C. (2009). Reconciling neuroimaging and neuropathological findings in schizophrenia and bipolar disorder. *Current Opinion in Psychiatry*, *22*, 312–319.

Frances, A. J. (2012). DSM-5 is guide not bible—ignore its ten worst changes. *Psychology Today.* Retrieved on December 1, 2014 from: http://www.psychologytoday.com/blog/dsm5-in-distress/201212/dsm-5-is-guide-not-bible-ignore-its-ten-worst-changes

Frances, A. J. (2013). Two fatal technical flaws in the DSM-5 definition of autism. *Huffington Post.* Retrieved on December 1, 2014 from: http://www.huffingtonpost.com/allen-frances/two-fatal-flaws_b_3337009.html

French, L. M. (1940). *Psychiatric social work.* New York: The Commonwealth Fund.

Friedman, R. A. (2012). Grief, depression, and the DSM-5. *New England Journal of Medicine*, *366*, 1855–1857. Retrieved on December 1, 2014 from: http://www.nejm.org/doi/full/10.1056/NEJMp1201794?query=TOC

Germain, C. B. (1973). An ecological perspective in casework practice. *Social Casework*, *54*, 323–330.

Germain, C. B. (1991). *Human behavior in the social environment: An ecological view.* New York: Columbia University Press.

Gitterman, A. (2014). *Handbook of social work practice with vulnerable and resilient populations* (3rd ed.). New York: Columbia University Press.

Gitterman, A., &. Germain, C. B. (2008a). *The life model of social work practice* (3rd ed.). New York: Columbia University Press.

Gitterman, A., & Germain, C. B. (2008b). Ecological framework. In T. Mizrahi & L. E. Davis (Eds.), *Encyclopedia of Social Work* (e-reference edition). National Association of Social Workers and Oxford University Press. Retrieved on May 5,

2011 from: http://www.oxford-naswsocialwork.com/entry?entry=t203.e118

Gray, S. W. (2011). *Competency-based assessments in mental health practice: Cases and practical applications*. Hoboken, NJ: John Wiley & Sons.

Gray, S. W. (with Zide, M. R.) (2006). *Psychopathology: A competency-based treatment model for social workers*. Pacific Grove, CA: Brooks/Cole Thomson Learning.

Insel, T. R. (2013, April 29). Director's Blog: Transforming diagnosis. National Institute of Mental Health. Retrieved on November 20, 2014 from: http://www.nimh.nih.gov/about/director/2013/transforming-diagnosis.shtml

Kirk, S. A., & Kutchins, H. (1994, June 20). Is bad writing a mental disorder? *New York Times*, p. A17.

Kirk, S. A., Siporin, M., & Kutchins, H. (1989). The prognosis for social work diagnosis. *Social Casework*, *70*, 295–304.

Kirst-Ashman, K. K., & Hull, G. H. (2011). *Understanding generalist practice* (6th ed.). Belmont, CA: Thomson Brooks/Cole.

Kupfer, D. (2013, May 6). David Kupfer, MD, responds to criticism of DSM-5 by NIMH director. *Psychiatric News Alert*. Retrieved on November 30, 2014 from: http://www.psych.org/File%20Library/Advocacy%20and%20Newsroom/Press%20Releases/2013%20Releases/13-33-Statement-from-DSM-Chair-David-Kupfer–MD.pdf

Kupfer, D. J., Kuhl, E. A., & Regier, D. A. (2009). Progress in diagnostic classification: Consideration of factors related to later life development. *American Journal of Geriatric Psychiatry*, *17*, 355–358.

Kupfer, D. J., & Regier, D. A. (2011). Neuroscience, clinical evidence, and the future of psychiatric classification in DSM-5. *American Journal of Psychiatry*, *168*, 172–174.

Kutchins, H., & Kirk, S. A. (1987). DSM-III and social work malpractice. *Social Work*, *32*, 205–211.

Lum, D. (2010). *Culturally competent practice: A framework for understanding diverse groups and justice issues* (4th ed.). Belmont, CA: Brooks/Cole Cengage Learning.

Maletic, V., Robinson, M., Oakes, T., Lyengar, S., Ball, S. G., & Russell, J. (2007). Neurobiology of depression: An integrated view of key findings. *The International Journal of Clinical Practice*, *61*(12), 2030–2040.

Miley, K. K., O'Melia, M., & DuBois, B. (2012). *Generalist social work practice: Advances in theory and practice*. New York: Columbia University Press.

National Association of Social Workers (NASW). (2008). *Code of ethics*. Silver Springs, MD: Author.

National Institute of Mental Health (NIMH). (2010). Statistics. Retrieved on December 1, 2014 from: http://www.nimh.nih.gov/health/statistics/index.shtml

Pally, R. (2000). *The mind-brain relationship*. London: Karmac Books.

Paris, J. (2013). *The intelligent clinician's guide to the DSM-5*. New York: Oxford University Press.

Reamer, F. (2013). *Social work values and ethics* (4th ed.). New York: Columbia University Press.

Saleebey, D. (Ed.). (2012). *The strengths perspective in social work practice* (6th ed.). Boston: Pearson.

Schore, A. N. (2003). *Affect dysregulation and disorders of the self*. New York: Norton.

Schwartz, J. H., & Javitch, J. A. (2013). Neurotransmitters. In E. R. Kandel, J. H. Schwartz, T. M. Jessell, S. A. Siegelbaum, & A. J. Hudspeth (Eds.), *Principles of neural science* (5th ed., pp. 289–306). New York: McGraw-Hill.

Sheafor, B. W., & Horejsi, C. J. (2011). *Techniques and guidelines for social work practice* (9th ed.). Boston: Allyn and Bacon.

Siporin, M. (1975). *Introduction to social work practice*. New York: Macmillan.

Squire, L. R., & Kandel, E. R. (2009). *Memory: From mind to molecules*. Greenwood Village, CO: Roberts and Company Publishers.

Stein, D. J., Phillips, K. A., Bolton, D., Fulford, K. W., Sadler, J. Z., & Kendler, K. S. (2010). What is a mental/psychiatric disorder? From DSM-IV to DSM-V. *Psychological Medicine*, *40*(11), 1759–1765.

Thyer, B. A., Wodarski, J. S., Myers, L. L., & Harrison, D. F. (Eds.). (2010). *Cultural diversity and social work practice* (3rd ed.). Springfield, IL: Charles C. Thomas.

Timmann, D., Drepper, J., Frings, M., Maschke, M., Richter, S., Gerwig, M., & Kolb, F. P. (2010). The human cerebellum contributes to motor, emotional and cognitive associative learning: A review. *Cortex*, *46*(7), 845–857.

Williams, R. W., & Herrup, K. (1998). The control of neuron number. *Annual Review of Neuroscience*, *11*, 423–453.

CHAPTER 2

Neurodevelopmental Disorders

INTRODUCTION

The neurodevelopmental disorders are characterized by abnormalities in brain development affecting emotion, learning ability, self-control, and memory that unfold as a person grows (Ehninger, Li, Fox, Stryker, & Silva, 2008). Along with the early onset of symptoms, these disorders have traditionally been acknowledged when development of the nervous system is disturbed leading to a structurally compromised brain. Looking to the DSM's developmental focus and the related manifestation of disorders over the life span, the neurodevelopmental disorders are placed first in the manual. There are numerous causes contributing to the development of the neurodevelopmental disorders, ranging from childhood deprivation to genetic and metabolic diseases, immune disorders, infectious diseases, nutrition, physical trauma, and toxic and environmental factors. The specific DSM-5 disorders considered neurodevelopmental in origin or that have neurodevelopmental consequences when they occur in infancy and childhood are listed in Table 2.1.

Individuals with neurodevelopmental disorders, their families, and society in general experience significant mental, emotional, physical, and economic consequences. More than likely, special education, psychological, and medical services are needed that can drain resources and contribute further stress. This chapter provides a review of the specific disorders social workers will most often encounter beginning with intellectual disability (intellectual developmental disorder).

TABLE 2.1 THE DSM-5 NEURODEVELOPMENTAL DISORDERS

Intellectual Disabilities
Intellectual Disability (Intellectual Developmental Disorder) Global Developmental Delay Unspecified Intellectual Disability (Intellectual Developmental Disorder)
Communication Disorders
Language Disorder Speech Sound Disorder Childhood-Onset Fluency (Stuttering) Social (Pragmatic) Communication Disorder Unspecified Communication Disorder
Autism Spectrum Disorder *Attention-Deficit/Hyperactivity Disorder*
Attention-Deficit/Hyperactivity Disorder (ADHD) Other Specified Attention-Deficit/Hyperactivity Disorder Unspecified Attention-Deficit/Hyperactivity Disorder
Specific Learning Disorder *Motor Disorders*
Developmental Coordination Disorder Stereotypic Movement Disorder
Tic Disorders
Tourette's Disorder Persistent (Chronic) Motor or Vocal Tic Disorder Provisional Tic Disorder Other Specified Tic Disorder Unspecified Tic Disorder
Other Neurodevelopmental Disorders

INTELLECTUAL DISABILITY (INTELLECTUAL DEVELOPMENTAL DISORDER)

Intellectual disability (intellectual developmental disorder) is a disorder that appears before adulthood. It is characterized by an individual's significantly impaired cognitive functioning and deficits in adaptive behaviors, for example, self-help, communication, or interpersonal skills. Intellectual disability, or less frequently referred to by the older term of mental retardation, is the term used. These are the children who may take longer to learn to speak, walk, and take care of their personal needs such as dressing or eating. More than likely, they will have trouble learning in school. These individuals will learn, but it will take them longer and there may be some things they cannot learn. Intellectual disability has historically been defined by an intelligence quotient (IQ) score under 70 but the definition now includes both intellectual functions and the individual's functional skills within the environment.

As of 2003, the term "mental retardation" is still used by the World Health Organization's ICD codes, which have a section titled "Mental Retardation" (codes F70–F79). In the next revision, the ICD-10 CM replaces the term with "intellectual disability" (Carulla et al., 2011), and the DSM-5 has already moved toward this transition by replacing the diagnosis of mental retardation with "intellectual disability (intellectual developmental disorder)" (APA, 2013).

Prevailing Pattern

Approximately 4.6 million people in the United States have an intellectual disability (National Center on Birth Defects and Developmental Disabilities, 2005). Prevalence in the general population is approximately 1 percent, and specific rates vary by age (APA, 2013). As an example, more than 545,000 children ages 6 to 21 years have some level of intellectual disability and receive special education services in public schools under this category per the nation's special education law, the Individuals with Disabilities Education Act (IDEA) (U.S. Department of Education, 2010).

In 2003, the average lifetime cost of intellectual disability amounted to slightly over $1 million per person with an intellectual disability, or to be precise, $1,014,000 (CDC, 2004). This is slightly more than the costs associated with the diagnosis of cerebral palsy and double those associated with serious vision or hearing impairments. Of that $1,014,000, 14 percent was due to increased medical expenses (excluding what is normally incurred by the typical person), and 10 percent was attributed to nonmedical expenses such as the excess cost of special education compared to standard schooling. Some expenses, such as costs associated with living in a group home, were excluded from this calculation.

Differential Assessment

There are many signs of an intellectual disability (National Center on Birth Defects and Developmental Disabilities, 2005). For example, children with an intellectual disability may:

- Sit up, crawl, or walk later than other children;
- Learn to talk later, or have trouble speaking;
- Find it hard to remember things;
- Not understand how to pay for things;
- Have trouble understanding social rules;
- Have trouble seeing the consequences of their actions;
- Have trouble solving problems; and/or
- Have trouble thinking logically.

Competency 7 d

The child's stage of development offers another level of understanding the diagnostic picture. Some behaviors or emotions are expected at a certain age and are not necessarily symptoms of pathology, whereas at another age they would be considered age-inappropriate. Social workers use their knowledge about human behavior across the life course when making the distinction between "normal" versus "abnormal." To diagnose an intellectual disability, the social worker looks for the onset of symptoms during the child's developmental period and considers both mental abilities and adaptive skills (particularly in the conceptual, social, and practical domains). Both are highlighted in the U.S. special education law IDEA, which guides how early intervention and special education services are provided to infants, toddlers, children, and youth with disabilities. Accordingly, "intellectual disability" is defined per the Code of Federal Regulations, Title 34 Education, Part 300 Assistance to States for the Education of Children with Disabilities, Sub part A—General, Section 300.8(c)(6) Child with a Disability. The definition is a "significantly sub-average general intellectual functioning, existing concurrently with deficits in adaptive behavior and manifested during the developmental period, that adversely affects a child's educational performance" (34 CFR §300.8(c)(6)). Known as Rosa's Law and signed into law by President Barack Obama in October 2010, the term "mental retardation" was changed to "intellectual disability," the term now used in practice.

Congruent with the DSM-5 dimensional approach to diagnosis, intellectual disability takes into account the child's adaptive functioning along with IQ scores; that is, the diagnosis is not made rigidly. To determine the symptom picture, the practitioner considers the following criteria:

- Intellectual functions (such as reasoning, problem solving, planning, abstract thinking, judgment, academic learning, and learning from experience) confirmed by the practitioner's assessment and standardized intelligence testing.
- Adaptive functioning in multiple environments (such as home, school, work, and the community) provided by someone familiar with the person, and also the observations of the practitioner who is able to find out directly from the person what he or she can communicate, understand, and the like.
- Onset of symptoms during the developmental period.

In essence, the practitioner looks for two main things in the client's symptom picture:

- Ability to make sense of the world or the ability of the person's brain to learn, think, solve problems (or IQ/intellectual functioning).
- Whether the person has the skills needed to live independently (or adaptive functioning).

In order to assess severity, ranging from mild to profound, the DSM-5 details the conceptual, social, and practical domains of functioning. In other words, the person's adaptive functioning, and not IQ scores, characterize severity levels.

Intellectual functioning, or IQ, is usually measured by an IQ test, with the average score being 100. Those scoring in the range of 65 to 75 (or lower) are thought to have an intellectual disability. The DSM-5 cautions the practitioner that clinical training and judgment are essential to accurately interpret test results. When looking to adaptive functioning, the practitioner looks to what a child can do in comparison to other children of his or her age.

The case of Sam "Sammie" Blaylock illustrates intellectual disability (intellectual developmental disorder).

CASE The Case of Sam "Sammie" Blaylock

Sammie's younger sister, Cindy Blaylock Reynolds, was meeting the social worker for the first time at Winter Haven, the home where her 37-year-old brother, Sammie, has been living. Cindy lives out of state but after her parents died last year, she assumed the full responsibility for her brother. Cindy begins, "Sammie was already three years old when I was born. When he was real little everybody in the family called him Sammie and I guess the name stuck. For as long as I can remember ... you might say for my whole life, I've have had a big brother with severe intellectual disabilities. For me, the hard part was when I would hear the other kids in school call him a retard, moron, or even an idiot. Because I was so young, I wondered, 'How could people be so mean?' I guess they were uneducated about my big brother. For me, it was completely normal to have a brother like Sammie. You might think that sounds odd, but because I was born 3 years after Sammy I just accepted that he was the way he was. What did I know? He was just Sammy, my older brother. For the longest time, he couldn't talk or walk, or even eat or drink on his own. Truthfully, he could 'do' nothing on his own. It was really like having a baby brother instead of a big brother but I didn't know any different. Sometimes I wondered how Sammie felt. Back then he was so full of love and still is so he doesn't understand why everyone doesn't love his hugs."

Cindy continues, "Gosh! This sounds all about me. I'm sure you want to hear more about Sammie." The social worker reassured Cindy that her experiences with her brother were important and knowing more about the family is helpful. Cindy seemed reassured and continued, "I remember how hard it was on my parents. Both of them were working full-time and raising Sammie and me. They had us later in life plus they had all the challenges that come with having a child with a disability. I know Sammie has an IQ score of 35 but when we were little I remember Sammie didn't learn like other kids. Then he started having behavioral issues. From the very first, he didn't develop normally. I remember my parents were so worried because for the longest time Sammie couldn't speak. He would make sounds that were all his own. Then as he got older, he started to need more and more care. Now, with the help of the therapists at Winter Haven, you can understand him just fine. Sure Sammie uses simple phrases but you can pretty much get at what he's trying to say. I mean don't ask him to explain anything complicated but at least you can figure out what Sammie's trying to say. And, gosh! Sammie's always so happy to see me! At least at Winter Haven he's able to keep to a schedule which is important for people like him. I know Sammie needs to live where qualified staff can look after him 24/7 and Winter Haven provides the supervision he needs ... like helping him get dressed and even making sure he takes a shower. Daily care and stuff like that. Sammie needs a high fiber diet because of some internal issues he has and the dietician here makes it happen. I live out of state and just divorced. My plan is to move back here to be closer to Sammie. That way, I can be more accessible but I know I can't manage him on my own."

Cindy seemed lost in thought at this point, and looked out the window as if to catch her breath. After a few silent moments, she continued, "I remember how hard it was when Sammie was first brought to Winter Haven. Me? I was very sad. I lost my big brother and didn't understand. You know, back then there were no supports to help a family keep kids like Sammie at home. There weren't any of those specialized programs you see in the schools these days and you only went to see a social worker if you were a charity case."

Cindy looked embarrassed at this point and continued, "Oh, I'm sorry. I didn't mean to insult you. As a matter of fact, my parents always had good things to say about you. Like how helpful you have been ... especially when a problem would come up. Like the time Sammie decided he didn't like his roommate. Then there was helping him to participate in the social programs here at Winter Haven. Sure he needs a lot of help on those outings but Sammie always seems to have so much fun. It was like he felt like he was somebody special. We all need that, don't we?" The social worker noticed Cindy was talking a little faster at this point and seemed a little anxious, so she interjected, "Cindy, you didn't insult me, so no offense taken. A lot of people wonder what I do here. Since you are now Sammie's guardian, I hope I can be of help as you take on this responsibility and that we can work together on Sammie's behalf."

Cindy seemed relieved and added, "It's just that sometimes I feel so guilty that he is the way

CASE The Case of Sam "Sammie" Blaylock (Continued)

he is. Why did it happen to him and not me? You know, before my mother passed she told me something I will never forget. She said that Sammie is happy with who he is, he is happy with where he is, and we would never want to change him."

Sam "Sammie" Blaylock's DSM Diagnosis Is as Follows:

Intellectual Disability (Intellectual Developmental Disorder), Severe

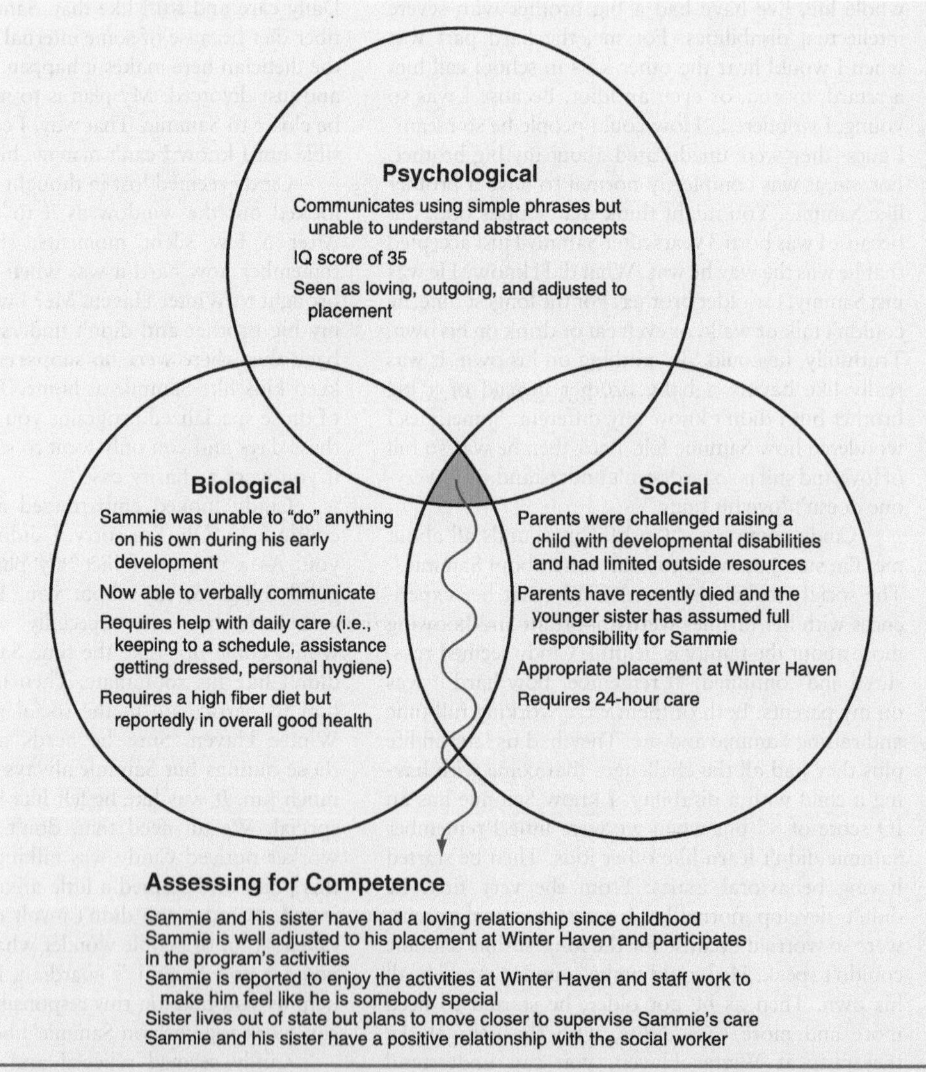

FIGURE 2.1 › Intellectual Disability (Intellectual Development Disorder.)
The interactions of the biological, psychological, and social variables in Sam "Sammie" Blaylock's life.

Competency 7 b

Assessment Summary In many ways, people with intellectual disabilities are not appreciated as full citizens in our society. As seen in Sammie's story, when he was growing up he was called derogatory names such as a retard, moron, or idiot. Sammie was placed at Winter Haven since his family was unable to provide the 24-hour care he needed. He has adjusted well, and it looks like the facility provides a person-centered approach that focuses on Sammie as someone with capacities and encourages his participation, which makes him feel like he is somebody special. This is congruent with the social work focus on advocacy and promoting the right of self-determination and self-direction by people with intellectual disabilities.

Competency 7 b

Intellectual disability commonly occurs with autism spectrum disorder; a disorder complicated by social communication and behavioral deficits. Though limited, Sammie does communicate and appears to relate well to his sister, the social worker, and others at Winter Haven. The communication and specific learning disorders are also comorbid with intellectual disability. In particular, the communication disorders include problems in language, speech, and communication. A specific learning disorder looks to a different way of learning. The syndrome is characterized by a disorder in one or more of the central nervous system processes involved in perceiving, understanding, and/or using concepts through verbal (spoken or written) language or nonverbal means. It becomes apparent when the person struggles in one or more of the following areas: attention, reasoning, processing, memory, communication, reading, writing, spelling, and calculation. That is, how a person takes in new information, how it is understood, and how it is linked to old information. However, since Sammie does not meet criteria, he is not considered to have these commonly co-occurring diagnoses.

Competency 7 c

Looking to the competencies in Sammie's life, despite being stigmatized by his intellectual limitations, his sister grew up seeing him as simply her big brother because she "didn't know any different." She is currently his guardian and is moving closer to where he is placed in order to better work with staff around his care and become more involved in his life. The setting seems appropriate for Sammie, and he has made a positive adjustment. He participates in the activities at Winter Haven and feels like he is somebody special and valued.

Other Related Disorders

Global Developmental Delay: Global developmental delay is the diagnosis used for individuals who are 5 years of age or younger and fail to meet expected developmental milestones in several areas of intellectual functioning. This diagnosis is reserved for the child who is not able to undergo a systematic assessment of intellectual functioning or is unable to participate in standardized testing.

Unspecified Intellectual Disability (Intellectual Developmental Disorder): This diagnosis applies to individuals who are 5 years of age or older but cannot participate in assessment procedures because of sensory or physical impairments; for example blindness, deafness, or severe problem behaviors.

We now turn to a review of autism spectrum disorder.

AUTISM SPECTRUM DISORDER

Autism spectrum disorder (ASD), sometimes just referred to as "autism," is a neurodevelopmental disorder where severity differs from person to person. ASD now encompasses the previous DSM-IV-TR diagnoses of autism, Asperger's syndrome, childhood disintegrative disorder, and pervasive developmental disorders not otherwise specified (PDD-NOS). These disorders are characterized by social deficits and communication difficulties, stereotyped or repetitive behaviors and interests, and in some instances, cognitive delays. Because of a very similar symptom picture, they now fall under the autism spectrum umbrella and are differentiated in the DSM-5 by clinical specifiers (e.g., dimensions of severity) and associated features (such as known genetic disorders, epilepsy, and intellectual disability/intellectual developmental disorder). This approach to the diagnosis of ASD uses a dimensional perspective.

Looking to severity measures, the DSM collapsed social and communication deficits into one domain. As such, the individual's diagnostic assessment is described in terms of severity of social communication symptoms, severity of fixated or restricted behaviors or interests, and associated features. Detailed descriptions of each domain are provided in the DSM to help the practitioner to consistently distinguish the features of these severity specifiers.

It should be noted that ASD frequently co-occurs with other disorders, particularly intellectual disability (intellectual developmental disorder) and language disorder. When that happens, both disorders are listed. The differential diagnosis is important as the key symptoms of communication impairments and restricted/repetitive behaviors can be elements of a number of other diagnoses; for example, Rett syndrome, selective mutism, the communication disorders (i.e., language disorder and social [pragmatic] communication disorder), stereotypic movement disorder, attention-deficit/hyperactivity disorder, and schizophrenia.

The cause of ASD has yet to be found, but it does seem likely that genetics (hereditary) and environmental factors (such as exposure to toxins) play a role (Tager-Flusberg, 2010). Researchers have identified a number of genes associated with the disorder, and the risks are greater if there is a family member with ASD. Other studies suggest that ASD could result from the disruption of normal brain development in the early development of the fetus caused by defects in genes that control brain growth and regulate how the brain cells communicate with each other possibly due to the influence of environmental factors (Rutter, 2000). While these findings hold promise, further study on the causes of ASD is needed.

Prevailing Pattern

Frequencies for ASD across the United States and in other countries have approached 1 percent of the general population (APA, 2013) with an estimated prevalence rate of 6 per 1,000 individuals (Newschaffer et al., 2007). The disorder is diagnosed 4 times more often in males than in females. Very little is known about the prevalence of ASD in older persons (APA, 2013). As autism is considered a universal disorder, these rates are consistent across cultures and ethnic groups (Mash & Barkley, 2002). It has become increasingly apparent that ASD is on the rise (Grandjean & Landrigan, 2006). However, it is unclear whether this is due to expanded diagnostic criteria that include subthreshold cases, increased awareness of the disorder, or simply a rise in the frequency of the disorder.

Differential Assessment

Competency 7 b

ASD is characterized by problems in communication and social interactions that vary on an individual basis. As we will see in the case of Chris Wells, symptoms must be present in the child's early developmental period. Each person's experience with ASD is different, and another of our case examples, Bobby Owens, provides an example of when a person's problems may not become fully apparent until social demands exceed limited capacities. Sometimes a person can develop strategies learned later in life that may mask symptoms, which underscores the importance of the social worker's knowledge of human behavior across the life course.

Looking to the domain of social communication, the diagnostic criteria include problems in social-emotional reciprocity such as the give-and-take in conversation or a reduced sharing of interests, emotions, or affect. This is the child who may not initiate or respond to social interactions.

A second domain that characterizes ASD is restricted, repetitive patterns of behavior that can be seen by stereotyped or repetitive motor movements, the use of objects (such as lining up toys in a "special" way), or speech. The individual insists on sameness, specific and inflexible routines, or ritualized patterns of (verbal or nonverbal) behavior. In other words, this is the youngster who becomes extremely distressed over the smallest change. Another criterion can be seen in the child's highly restricted, fixated interests that exceed the normal interest in something; for example, the child becomes exceptionally attached to or preoccupied with unusual objects such as only the wheels of a toy train. Hyper- or hyporeactivity to sensory input or an unusual interest in sensory aspects of the environment is also considered; for example, an adverse reaction to a sound or excessively smelling or touching something.

The practitioner, aided by a chart provided in the DSM explaining each of these domains, rates severity ranging from "requiring very substantial support" to "requiring support." The social communication difficulties domain is listed (and rated) separately from the domain of restricted, repetitive behaviors. Specifiers are included, as appropriate. They are:

- With or without accompanying intellectual impairment.
- With or without accompanying language impairment.
- Associated with a known medical or genetic condition or environmental factor (and the practitioner provides an additional code to identify the medical or genetic condition).
- Associated with another neurodevelopmental, mental, or behavioral disorder (and additional codes, as appropriate, are listed).
- With catatonia.

We now turn to the case of Chris Wells to illustrate the symptom picture of ASD.

CASE The Case of Chris Wells

Chris Wells, age 3½, was referred to the Children's Rehabilitation Center by his family pediatrician for a complete evaluation. The center uses a team to complete the evaluation, consisting of medical doctors, psychiatrists, social workers, nurses, and audiologists, as well as occupational, physical, and recreational therapists. The family had been concerned about their son for quite some time. The social worker on the team was assigned to conduct the social history. Following is the parents' story.

Mrs. Wells began, "Looking back, I didn't consider my pregnancy with Chris difficult. Well, there were some moments like when I didn't gain weight in the first trimester. Actually, I lost weight. Chris is my second child so I really didn't become too alarmed since I also lost a few pounds in my first pregnancy. I just figured it was part of 'morning sickness' and, like before, it would pass. By the fifth month I started to gain weight and continued to gain monthly so I figured all was fine. Let me tell you though. That last month was a bummer. Chris was really active when he was inside me. Seemed like my ribs and pelvic bone were getting a workout from all his hyperactivity. I couldn't wait to deliver! Then I went into premature labor. I went to the hospital and the labor was stopped by the use of some kind of IV medication to relax my muscles. I think they took the medication off the market since then. I'm sure you'll find the details in my medical records. Finally, I had Chris by a C-section, just like my first one. I was so relieved when he arrived very healthy and hearty. They could hear him cry from the delivery room all the way down to the other end of the hall."

Mrs. Wells continued, "Chris seemed to develop okay. Almost from the beginning he could hold up his head and by 10 months he was climbing out of his crib. On the other hand he did have some peculiarities. Right from the start, Chris did not especially like to be cuddled and he didn't like to be rocked to sleep. He never even held out his hands for me to pick him up. Even now, he doesn't look at you. It's like he's in his own little world. Chris slept through the night right away so when I couldn't get him to nap during the day I wasn't really too worried. Now traveling with him was another story. My oldest would fall asleep as soon as the car started but not Chris. He would cry and scream for the entire trip. It didn't matter if we were going around the block or if it was an hour drive. Nothing could console him. Chris was ready to walk by about 10 months but he couldn't. This was because he refused to put his whole foot on the floor. Instead, he could curl up his toes and walked on the tops of them. My husband reassured me that we probably had a budding basketball star but I still worried. Took him about 6 months to walk normally with his whole foot on the floor. But he still isn't talking. Don't get me wrong. I love my son but his behavior worries me." Mrs. Wells glanced in the direction of her husband, who nodded in agreement.

Mr. Wells then interjected, "At first we thought maybe he was deaf but all tests indicated normal physical functioning. While Chris didn't speak, he would make soft sounds. Seemed like they made sense only to him though. Odd, but Chris made no effort to communicate with us and often seemed oblivious to other people in the room. We sort of worked around it but now that he's in pre-kindergarten class, his behavior is more obvious. We thought it might be good for Chris to be with other children his age. Well, that's not really working out and I'm afraid maybe we made a mistake by pushing him too hard to socialize with other kids. The teacher tells us that he understands what's going on around him so he seems okay in the intelligence department but he has absolutely no friends and really looks as if he is always in his own world. His teacher tries to get him interested in the toys but Chris just doesn't appear to want to get involved. He loves his toy trains, though. That child will spend hours just spinning the wheels over and over and over. If you try to take his trains away he just screams until you give them back." Mrs. Wells nodded her head in agreement and Mr. Wells continued, "Seems Chris is more interested in his trains than people. When I was little I remember that I was interested in trains, too. But not like this. Seems he's more fascinated with the wheels rather than the whole train. Come to think of it, everybody told me stories about how I couldn't be separated from my special blanket. Chris? He loves those hard metal train wheels. He has to have all his train lined up just so, too. If not, he has a fit. Odd, don't you think? We're here to do whatever it takes to get him to be more like other kids. His older brother loves him, although I don't know why. They have so little in common. My older boy, though he's only 7, already wants to be on a baseball team. Can't start them too early, you know."

Mrs. Wells interjected, "Chris is still not talking and I hope you can find out why. At first our pediatrician reassured us that Chris would grow out of it but with no progress, he finally referred us here." She added, "Oh, and let me tell you about his motor skills. Like all babies he would reach for your glasses or jewelry. Well, Chris would go a step further. He would grab my husband's glasses and in 2 seconds flat would fling them across the room before you even realized it! I stopped wearing jewelry because he would do the same with me. Don't know where he inherited that aggressive streak. Not from us. Sometimes I'm afraid it will just get worse when he gets older. What do you think?"

CHRIS WELLS'S DSM DIAGNOSIS IS AS FOLLOWS:

Autism Spectrum Disorder requiring very substantial support for deficits in communication, and requiring substantial support for restricted, repetitive behaviors, without accompanying intellectual impairment, and with accompanying language impairment—no intelligible speech (nonverbal)

Competency 8 c

ASSESSMENT SUMMARY ASD can be detected as early as 18 months or even younger (Lord et al., 2006). Chris was seen by age 3½ at the rehabilitation center where a team approach is used to determine the final diagnosis. As such, Chris will be seen by the social worker along with other professionals at the agency. The clinical social work practitioner working in a setting like this one will be checking with other medical professionals, as needed, in order to confirm Chris's diagnosis; for instance, medical doctors, psychiatrists, nurses, audiologists, and occupational, physical, and recreational therapists.

Competency 7 b

The social worker listened carefully to Mr. and Mrs. Wells's account of their struggles in order to collect, organize, and interpret data around Chris's symptoms. As part of the diagnostic workup, this vignette highlights Chris Wells's developmental history, which supports a symptom picture of ASD. ASD is thought to follow two possible developmental courses. One course of development is characterized by normal or near-normal development followed by loss of skills or regression in the first 2 to 3 years of the child's life. A second course of development follows a gradual course of onset in which parents report concerns in development over the first 2 years of life and the diagnosis is made around 3 to 4 years of age. However, as seen in Chris's situation, most parents report the onset of symptoms within the first year of life (Zwaigenbaum et al., 2009). From the very beginning, Mrs. Wells described her son as somehow "different." He did not like to be cuddled, did not reach out for attention or affection, and did not even look at his parents. In fact, when Chris was held as an infant, he would aggressively grab his father's glasses and fling them across the room.

Adjusting to new circumstances also seemed difficult. For instance, Chris was described as being upset when taking car trips, no matter how long; that is, he would

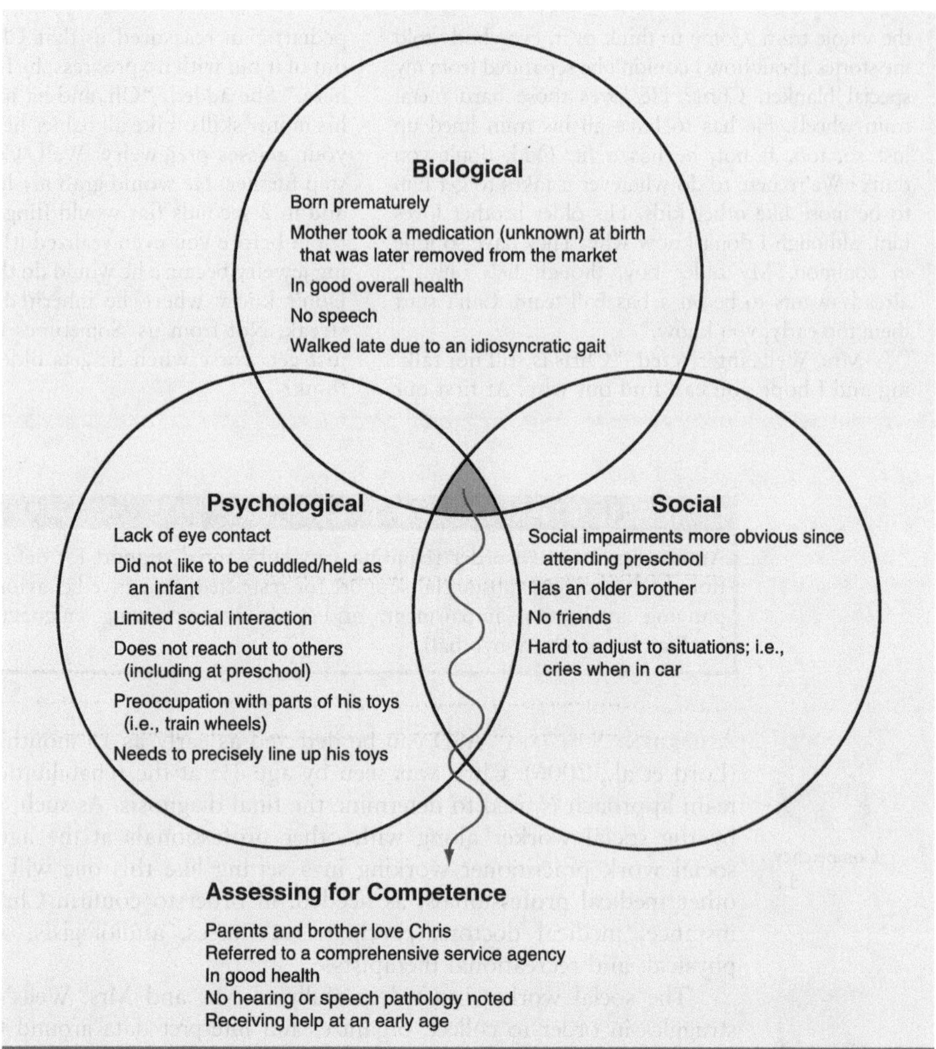

FIGURE 2.2 › AUTISM SPECTRUM DISORDER
The interactions of the biological, psychological, and social variables in Chris Wells's life.

cry the entire time. In addition to delays in talking, Chris did not walk right away although his parents saw him as "ready" at 10 months of age. This was because of his peculiar way of curling up his toes and walking on the tops of them.

Chris's play was described as odd. He would focus on his toy train wheels and was constantly spinning them. He would be upset if any of his trains were not lined up in precise order. Social interaction was further impaired. For example, Chris was described as unable to make friends in preschool. Further, Chris showed no enjoyment in the toys in the classroom. At the time he was referred to the rehabilitation center, Chris was still not talking, which further impaired his ability to socialize. He was characterized as being "in his own world."

Competency 7 a

A number of competencies are evident in Chris Wells's story. Mr. and Mrs. Wells are concerned about their son and willing to do "whatever it takes" to help him. Though they are worried and frightened by his behavior, they love their son and quickly followed up on the referral to the Children's Rehabilitation Center. The causes of ASD are unclear, and the clinic takes a comprehensive approach to the assessment in order to determine the final diagnosis. Chris has already had his hearing evaluated before coming to the center, and no abnormalities were found. In addition, the pediatrician found Chris to be in good health, thus ruling out any medically based explanation for his behavior. Therefore, the pediatrician referred the Wells family to the center for a more complete evaluation.

Keep in mind there are a number of disorders where the person's social interaction or communication skills may be problematic, such as Rett syndrome, selective mutism or the language disorders, and social (pragmatic) communication disorder, but not to the degree of impairment seen in autism spectrum disorder. For example, disruptions in social interaction can be seen in the regressive phase of Rett syndrome (usually between 1 and 4 years of age) but unlike Chris Wells, most of these individuals improve over time. Those with selective mutism typically do not show the disturbances in early development that we saw in Chris Wells's case story. The symptoms of impaired communication seen in selective mutism occur in specific contexts. Chris Wells's struggles can be seen across several contexts; for example, in school and at home. Someone with a language disorder does not exhibit the nonverbal communication problems associated with autism spectrum disorder, nor do they show the restricted repetitive patterns of behavior, interests, or activities evident in Chris Wells's vignette. Similarly, someone with social (pragmatic) communication disorder may have communication problems but do not show the repetitive patterns of behavior, interests, or activities found in the autism spectrum symptom picture. Difficulties with attention, such as being overly focused or easily distracted, can be seen in Chris Wells's story and can closely resemble the symptom picture of attention-deficit/hyperactivity disorder (ADHD). However, ADHD is considered when difficulties paying attention or hyperactivity go well beyond what is typically expected of someone of a comparable age.

To further illustrate the range of social and communication impairments along with the restricted/repetitive behaviors that define ASD, we turn to the case of Robert "Bobby" Owens.

CASE THE CASE OF ROBERT "BOBBY" OWENS

"Don't get me wrong," started Mrs. Owens. "I love my son but from the very first I thought something was 'off' with him. He was just so different from his brother, who is 20 months older." I asked Mrs. Owens to continue. "Bobby is 11 years old now but he has always been ...," she paused and continued, "Well, a little different. He doesn't seem to get the give-and-take of social interaction." Mrs. Owens stated that Bobby has a hard time understanding other people's perspectives and that he will speak impulsively. I asked her what she meant and Mrs. Owens indicated that Bobby just blurts out whatever he is thinking. "I remember once when we were in the grocery store and a rather heavyset woman was putting a huge box of cookies in her cart. Bobby just went up to her and announced that fat people should eat vegetables. He was so loud I know everybody around us could hear him. I was so embarrassed but Bobby just couldn't see what was wrong. It's like he has a hard time appreciating what other people might think."

CASE THE CASE OF ROBERT "BOBBY" OWENS (CONTINUED)

Mrs. Owens added that her son stands out in a group of children. "Bobby loves to read DC comic books. You know, Batman, Superman, and all those superheroes. He can tell you all about them in the minutest detail. All he wants to do is talk about those comic book stories and he can't seem to tell when you're bored. He just goes on and on and on. You might say Bobby has a narrow interest in things. Most of the boys in his class are involved in some kind of sport but Bobby just isn't interested. He would rather be reading those comic books of his, so it's tough for him to make friends."

I noticed that Mrs. Owens looked a little uncomfortable at this point, but she insisted that I needed to understand what was going on with her son. She continued, "Now that Bobby's in middle school he started showing some really serious behavior problems. It all began the past summer with his anger outbursts. He can't seem to have a conversation with you about his feelings. He doesn't seem to have the words to tell you how he feels and just explodes. I'm afraid that if we don't do something he'll be put in one of those special classes." Mrs. Owens looked directly at the social worker and continued, "We all know that's just a dumping ground for all the kids who don't fit in. That's why I came here. I'm hoping you can suggest some kind of program to help Bobby get along in school."

The social worker asked about Bobby's developmental history, and Mrs. Owens described it as unremarkable. However, she described her son as having a number of what she called "quirky" behaviors. Mrs. Owens stated, "For instance, things had to be a certain way for Bobby and you couldn't convince him otherwise. Like needing to eat from the same bowl, line up his toys in exact order, and travel the same way home. And then there were the issues with his clothes. All the tags had to be removed and for the longest time he wanted to wear his underwear inside out. If things were not the way he thought they should be then he would have a fit. You might say there were a lot of meltdowns in our house." The social worker reflected, "So that's what rigidly holding on to specific and nonfunctional routines looks like." Mrs. Owens continued, "It was like you were dealing with a two-year-old. You know, the 'terrible twos,' but only Bobby is much too old now for that kind of behavior. I thought maybe he had allergies or something so I took him to the doctor for a check-up. He told me that he didn't think Bobby was 'that bad.' All he said was Bobby was just immature for his age and then ran a bunch of tests. I don't think he had a clue about what could be wrong." The social worker noted that no medical problems were found that might better explain Bobby's behavior. She also planned to ask Mrs. Owens for consent to release information so she could obtain Bobby's medical history.

Mrs. Owens indicated that she had hoped her son would grow out of his behaviors, adding, "What with all his temper outbursts this past summer I finally came to the realization that my son is turning into a different person." About a month into summer vacation, she noticed that Bobby was getting more and more upset. Mrs. Owens added that unstructured time was generally hard for Bobby, and he needed everything to be planned, with no deviation in his schedule. As the summer progressed, Bobby became more and more agitated and withdrawn. Then he started yelling at everyone who tried to talk to him. Mrs. Owens added, "Things started going from bad to worse. He began to say that everyone hated him. My heart sank when he said that I hated him. I just didn't know what to do for him and he was so unhappy. You never knew what to expect next. All those days of yelling and worrying were taking a toll on everybody in the family. We couldn't go to the store, shopping, or even to the movies. Bobby just couldn't get along with anybody. I thought that things would get better when school started back up. Boy was I wrong on that one," said Mrs. Owens.

Bobby started the sixth grade, and for the first time he was going to middle school. It was a new school for him and much larger than his elementary school. He also had all new teachers. "Those teachers decided to treat Bobby as if he was 'choosing' his behaviors. Bobby always had bad handwriting but his teachers seemed to think he wasn't trying hard enough. No one seemed to care about him, and on most days he would be in tears in the vice principal's office. He started to go into his own world and block everyone completely out. He would not listen. He would just stare right through you as if you weren't there. Then there were the anger issues. It got so that Bobby had alienated all the kids he knew from elementary school. And if that wasn't bad enough, I just learned a couple of weeks ago about the bullies who were tormenting Bobby. He doesn't know how to stand up for himself. My husband and I complained to the school but nothing was done. To make matters worse, those bullies were smart enough to not get caught. Since Bobby was seen as so explosive by the teachers, if something did happen, it was seen as his fault. Right there and then my husband and I decided we needed help. That's why we're here." said Mrs. Owens.

ROBERT "BOBBY" OWENS'S DSM DIAGNOSIS IS AS FOLLOWS:

Autism Spectrum Disorder requiring support for deficits in communication, and requiring support for restricted, repetitive behaviors, without accompanying intellectual impairment, and without accompanying language impairment

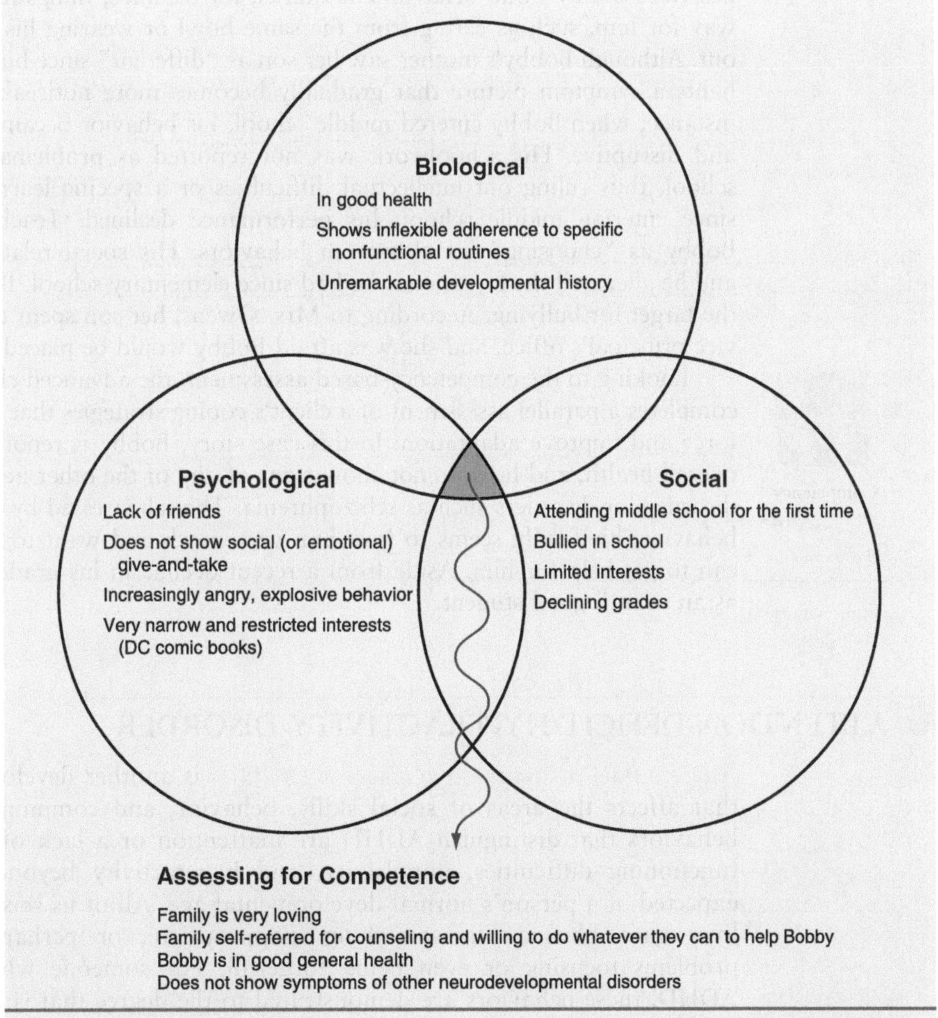

FIGURE 2.3 › AUTISM SPECTRUM DISORDER
The interactions of the biological, psychological, and social variables in Robert "Bobby" Owens's life.

Competency 7 b

ASSESSMENT SUMMARY The symptom picture for ASD differs for each individual, and this vignette illustrates how Bobby Owens's struggles are different and yet in some ways similar to those of Chris Wells. Like Chris, Bobby's mother also noticed that her son's behavior was not quite right almost since he was born. In contrast, a consistent theme for Bobby is his difficulty making friends, and he shows a lack in the give-and-take of social relationships or reciprocity. Mrs. Owens describes the time in the supermarket when Bobby told a heavyset stranger who was putting cookies into her cart that she needed to be eating vegetables instead. He was oblivious of the impact his remarks might have on the stranger. Bobby was described as showing a deep and narrow interest in DC comics and being unable to discern when others would get bored when he talked about the comic book heroes.

Unlike Chris Wells, Bobby's parents had hoped he would outgrow his peculiar behaviors, but that changed when he started sixth grade. At first, Mrs. Owens describes Bobby's odd behaviors as quirks; for instance, things had to be a certain way for him, such as eating from the same bowl or wearing his underwear inside out. Although Bobby's mother saw her son as "different" since birth, his story highlights a symptom picture that gradually becomes more noticeable over time. For instance, when Bobby entered middle school, his behavior became more aggressive and disruptive. His schoolwork was not reported as problematic in elementary school, thus ruling out intellectual difficulties or a specific learning disorder; but since entering middle school, his performance declined. Teachers characterized Bobby as "choosing" his classroom behaviors. His social relationships suffered, and he alienated the few friends he had since elementary school. Bobby also became the target for bullying. According to Mrs. Owens, her son spent many hours in the vice principal's office, and she was afraid Bobby would be placed in special classes.

Competency 7 a

Looking to the competency-based assessment, the advanced clinical practitioner completes a parallel assessment of a client's coping strategies that may serve to reinforce and improve adaptation. In this case story, Bobby is reported to be in good overall health, and he does not show signs of any of the other neurodevelopmental disorders or disorders such as schizophrenia. Though stressed by Bobby's explosive behavior, his family seems to love him very much and want to do whatever they can to get help for him. Aside from a recent decline in his grades, he is described as an overall good student.

ATTENTION-DEFICIT/HYPERACTIVITY DISORDER

Attention-deficit/hyperactive disorder (ADHD) is another developmental disorder that affects the areas of social skills, behavior, and communication. The key behaviors that distinguish ADHD are inattention or a lack of focus, executive functioning difficulties, impulsivity, and hyperactivity beyond what is to be expected of a person's normal developmental age. All of us at some point in our lives have blurted out something inappropriate, or perhaps we have had problems focusing or even being forgetful. For someone who struggles with ADHD, these behaviors are demonstrated to the degree that is inappropriate for that age.

Prevailing Pattern

Approximately 3 to 5 percent of children and adults are affected by ADHD (APA, 2013). It is considered a chronic disorder where 30 to 50 percent of those diagnosed in childhood will continue to have symptoms into adulthood.

Differential Assessment

The key diagnostic criteria for ADHD are inattention and/or hyperactivity-impulsivity that is present before the age of 12 years and that get in the way with the person's functioning or development. Symptoms must be present for at least 6 months. A psychotic disorder or another mental disorder (such as a mood disorder, anxiety disorder, dissociative disorder, personality disorder or substance intoxication and withdrawal) does not better explain the symptom picture.

Looking to inattention, a child must show six (or more) of the following nine symptoms. Older adolescents and adults, age 17 or older, must show at least five of these nine symptoms. They are:

- Does not pay close attention to details or makes careless mistakes.
- Has difficulty remaining focused or paying attention to tasks or lacks persistence.
- Does not seem to listen and seems "elsewhere."
- Does not follow through with instructions and fails to finish schoolwork or tasks on the job.
- Is disorganized or messy, fails to meet deadlines, or has poor time management.
- Often avoids, dislikes, or is reluctant to engage in tasks that require sustained mental effort such as schoolwork, or for adults preparing reports or completing forms.
- Often loses things needed to complete tasks or activities, such as books, school supplies, keys, eyeglasses, or mobile phone.
- Often is easily distracted by extraneous stimuli.
- Often is forgetful in daily activities such as doing chores or, for adolescents and adults, returning calls, paying bills, or keeping appointments.

A child must show six (or more) of the following nine symptoms of hyperactivity and impulsivity, while older adolescents or adults must demonstrate at least five symptoms to complete the diagnostic picture (also for 6 months' duration). Keep in mind that these symptoms are not considered as expressions of oppositional behavior, defiance, hostility, or the person's lack of understanding of what is required of them. They are:

- Excessive motor activity seen in fidgeting, tapping, or squirming.
- Often leaves his or her seat when staying seated is expected.
- Often runs around and, as an adult, seems restless.
- Often unable to play quietly or engage in leisure activities.
- Unable to sit still for an extended period of time and often seems "on the go" or acting as if driven by a motor.
- Often talks excessively.
- Often blurts out an answer before the question is completed or completes other people's sentences.

- Often has difficulty waiting his or her turn.
- Excessively interrupts others.

The DSM offers a number of specifiers. A combined presentation specifier applies when symptoms of inattention and hyperactivity-impulsivity are evident for the past 6 months. The predominately inattentive presentation specifier is used when only the symptoms of inattention are met but signs of hyperactivity-impulsivity have been absent for the past 6 months. The third specifier, predominately hyperactive/impulsive presentation, is reserved for the person who shows symptoms of hyperactivity-impulsivity without inattention for the past 6 months.

The diagnosis can be further refined by remission, specifically in partial remission. This applies when full diagnostic criteria have previously been met, but for the past 6 months the person has shown fewer than full criteria. However, struggles with social, academic, or occupational functioning remain. Severity can also be assigned ranging from mild to moderate to severe.

Louie Dessaint's story illustrates attention-deficit hyperactivity disorder.

CASE THE CASE OF LOUIE DESSAINT

Louie Dessaint was 8 years old when he was referred to the Children's Center by the school social worker. Although Louie had been attending his neighborhood school for almost a year, the social worker noticed that he was not communicating in English. The school social worker suspected that Louie might have been abused but she was not able to support her suspicions. "To be on the safe side, I think it's best to refer him for a complete workup," reflected the social worker. Ms. Dessaint did not seem to understand what was wrong with Louie's behavior in school but was receptive to the referral to the Children's Center and readily agreed to follow up on the evaluation of her son.

The intake worker at the Center noted on the referral form that Louie's classroom teacher described him as being socially isolated from the other children. Although he seemed bright, he was not progressing academically and did little work in class. He rarely listened to the teacher and did not pay attention. He needed constant reminders to stay on task. The report noted that Louie would forget to do what he was told and seemed overwhelmed if given detailed instructions. He would easily become distracted, lose his concentration, and give up. He did not stay in his seat but tended to wander around the classroom. Because of his behavior, the other children stayed away from Louie or, worse yet, they would make fun of him.

When Louie and his mother arrived at the Center for their appointment, the social worker noticed the both of them sitting in the corner of the room looking scared. Ms. Dessaint stared at her hands, and Louie was in constant motion, fidgeting in his chair next to hers. It seemed impossible for him to sit still. The Center had a corner with toys and books but nothing seemed to interest Louie. The receptionist at the front desk noticed that Ms. Dessaint would whisper something to Louie. She recognized it was in Creole and that Ms. Dessaint was telling Louie to behave—but he just didn't seem to listen. The longer he waited, the more he fidgeted. Then Louie started to leave his seat and wander around the waiting room, climbing over empty seats.

The social worker assigned to see Ms. Dessaint explained that Louie was also was being seen by another social worker during the same time as their appointment. She added that the purpose of today's session was to learn more about Louie's background in order to find out how the Center could be of help. Despite the social worker's attempts to put Ms. Dessaint at ease, she still looked uncomfortable. Reluctantly, Ms. Dessaint began, "We Haitians are a very private people but I will try to answer what you ask of me for the sake of my son. He is all I have left. The school thinks he has very big problems. Education is important to me so I will do everything I can to improve Louie's schoolwork." Though cooperative, it was clear that it was hard for Ms. Dessaint to talk about Louie's psychosocial history. "I wonder if she's just a very private person or if something else is going on. I guess maybe it's just cultural," mused the social worker.

Ms. Dessaint shared that the family had experienced a number of traumas before coming to the United States. She did not tell anyone at the school about the details because she did not want Louie to be stigmatized. Louie's father died suddenly. He had been killed in the 2010 earthquake in Haiti. "I will never forget the day it happened," said Ms. Dessaint. "At the time we lived in Jacmel, just outside of Port au Prince. I remembered the trembling but thought nothing of it. At the time Louie was in the bedroom with his father. When it started to get worse, he came out to where I was in the kitchen. Next thing I know there was darkness everywhere and all we could hear was Louie's father moaning—then it was quiet. Louie wanted to go back to his father but I said we must leave. I remember looking back and all I could see was my husband's bloody hand sticking out from under what was left of our roof. I would not let Louie look but I am sure he saw ..." Her voice trailed off, and then she resumed. "We lost many relatives. All of my sisters and their families and my parents died, too. In the nights following the earthquake we slept on the pavement. There was nowhere else to go. Everything was destroyed. The Catholic Relief Services helped us to move here to the United States. Louie was used to growing up with his cousins. Now we are here. I mean it is safe and all but we are so alone." Ms. Dessaint looked visibly shaken and I asked if she would like a drink of water. "No," she answered, "Haitians are a strong people. I will get through this for the sake of my Louie."

The psychosocial history revealed that Louie had no opportunity to learn English before entering school in the United States. Developmental milestones were unremarkable but Louie was described as having been an active and agitated child ever since he was a toddler. Some of Ms. Dessaint's family members thought that Louie's behaviors were due to evil spirits. "But the mambo helps," added Ms. Dessaint. The social worker was puzzled and said, "Ms. Dessaint, I have been asking you a lot of questions about how we can help Louie but it looks like you are already getting some help. I don't know about a mambo. Can you help me understand?" Ms. Dessaint explained that she had consulted with a mambo, a female voodoo priest, who advised her to set out a white candle with a clear glass of water and to say certain prayers on a particular saint's day to ward off the evil spirits.

The social worker who saw Louie individually noted that he easily separated from his mother and seemed cooperative throughout the interview. At first, Louie was somewhat reserved. He said very little beyond pointing to the toys in the play corner of the social worker's office. The social worker indicated it was alright for Louie to play with the toys, and his solemn demeanor brightened as he examined several of the toys. The social worker observed that Louie seemed to understand her but was unable to sustain an interest in any one item for very long. He was easily distracted, and it was hard for him to sit still. Louie lost interest in the games that required concentration and gravitated toward the soft, cuddly toy animals. At the end of the session Louie forgot the social worker's earlier instructions to put away the toys when he was finished. When reminded, he was cooperative and carefully tried to put things in their place. The task seemed to take his full attention. Though he struggled, Louie seemed eager to please. The social worker thought, "He's a likeable kid, but his behaviors somehow just seem to get in his way. I think we have some programs that can help."

The Children's Center conducted a full educational assessment and found Louie's IQ to be in the normal range; no learning difficulties were noted. A speech and language assessment also found no abnormalities. The pediatrician's report indicated Louie was in good overall health. What is your assessment of Louie Dessaint?

LOUIE DESSAINT'S DSM DIAGNOSIS IS AS FOLLOWS:

Attention-Deficit/Hyperactivity Disorder Predominately Inattentive Presentation, moderate

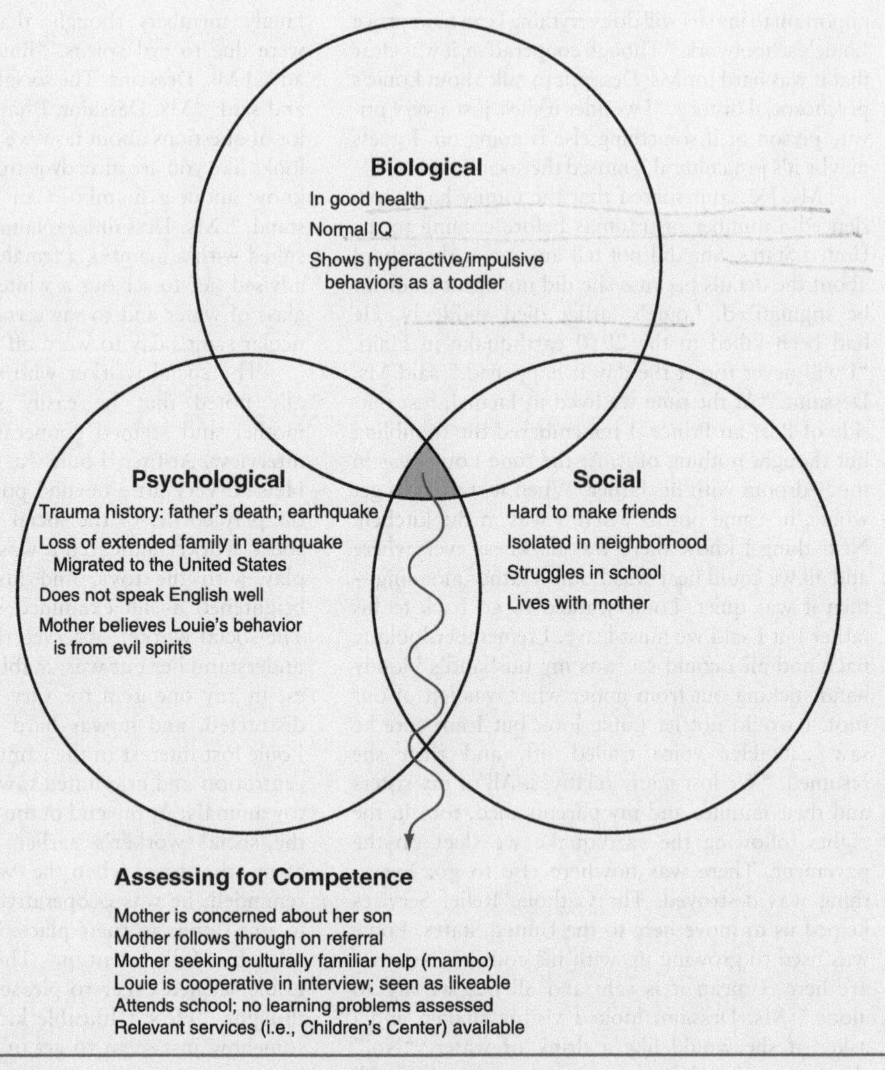

Biological
In good health
Normal IQ
Shows hyperactive/impulsive behaviors as a toddler

Psychological
Trauma history: father's death; earthquake
Loss of extended family in earthquake
Migrated to the United States
Does not speak English well
Mother believes Louie's behavior is from evil spirits

Social
Hard to make friends
Isolated in neighborhood
Struggles in school
Lives with mother

Assessing for Competence
Mother is concerned about her son
Mother follows through on referral
Mother seeking culturally familiar help (mambo)
Louie is cooperative in interview; seen as likeable
Attends school; no learning problems assessed
Relevant services (i.e., Children's Center) available

FIGURE 2.4 › ATTENTION-DEFICIT/HYPERACTIVITY DISORDER
The interactions of the biological, psychological, and social variables in Louie Dessaint's life.

Competency 5 c

ASSESSMENT SUMMARY Louie's story illustrates some of the challenges assessing ADHD, especially in a transcultural context. Beyond simply understanding diversity, the practitioner was called upon to apply her knowledge of the Haitian culture in order to fully assess his symptoms and to find ways to enhance Louie's and his mother's well-being. The competency-based assessment provides a vehicle to explore the wide range of factors as seen in this case vignette.

Competency 2 a

Ethnicity and culture affect what behaviors parents perceive as "normal" versus "abnormal" (Slade, 2004). It is important for the social worker to recognize the importance of difference in shaping the child's experiences and to be able to communicate this understanding to those who are a part of the child's life. The diagnostic process for Louie was complicated by a number of aspects, including how Ms. Dessaint saw Louie's problems (being caused by evil spirits), and a premigratory history of trauma. In particular, before coming to the United States, Louie had been exposed to the violent death of his father, the loss of his extended family, and the only home he knew in a devastating earthquake. He was currently faced with adapting to a new culture, including learning a new language. Louie was used to being surrounded by all of his cousins in his small town in Haiti, but currently he and his mother live in isolation. In addition, his mother is trying to cope with Louie's difficulties in school, but she has a limited understanding of what was causing her son's problems. Relatives attributed Louie's behavior to evil spirits and so Ms. Dessaint eventually consulted a culturally familiar source of help; specifically, a mambo (female voodoo priest) who prescribed certain rituals. Mrs. Dessaint seems to love her son and followed through with the referral to the Children's Center although she does not fully understand his problems. It was difficult for Ms. Dessaint to share family history due to her Haitian culture of being "very private." She also did not want her son stigmatized at his school, so she admitted to withholding some information.

By not fully sharing details about Louie, it was difficult for the practitioner to fully explore a symptom picture to support (or rule out) any of the trauma- and stressor-related disorders such as posttraumatic stress disorder or adjustment disorder. It is hoped that with time, Mrs. Dessaint will develop a relationship with the social worker and share additional background information. Though Louie is the identified client, the social worker also takes into account how Mrs. Dessaint is coping with the recent events in her life; for example, the death of her husband, the deaths of close relatives (her sisters), the earthquake and losing her home, migrating to the United States, and her son's behavioral problems in a foreign school.

Competency 7 b

The social worker collects, organizes, and interprets the unique features of Louie's experiences to better understand his struggles. In addition to symptoms supporting a predominately inattentive presentation of ADHD exhibited in school and at home (i.e., inattentive, distracted, not paying attention, not listening, not following through on detailed instructions, forgetful), Louie also showed a number of other problems, such as difficulties adjusting to an American school classroom and in making friends. Louie shows some symptoms of hyperactivity and impulsivity, but not to the extent of assigning the ADHD specifier of predominately hyperactive-impulsive (i.e., fidgets, leaves his seat, climbing about). Similarly, his symptoms do not fully support a "combined presentation." Louie's experiences in school seemed to further complicate adjusting to a new life in the United States. Unfortunately, this contributed to a picture of a little boy with low self-esteem, a common struggle for youngsters with ADHD (Anastopoulos, Sommer, & Shatz, 2009).

Competency 5 a

The cultural context plays a role in ascertaining Louie's diagnosis. Although Mrs. Dessaint did not describe any problems with her son as he was growing up, she did mention symptomatic hyperactive/impulsive behaviors when Louie was a toddler. The DSM cultural formulation interview (CFI) offers a format to obtain information around the client's cultural context and another version to obtain information from someone who is close to the client; for example, how Louie's mother understood his problem, her perception of what caused her son's problems, supports available to her, and past help seeking. Timmini and Taylor (2004) point to Western society's intolerance for certain behaviors and the pressure to conform academically that highlight ADHD. In this case story, it was important for the social worker to be able to assess Louie's interactions within his different social contexts. For example, while Louie's mother described him as an active and agitated child ever since he was a toddler, his behavior seemed problematic only after she migrated to the United States and her son entered the American classroom.

There are a number of disorders with a symptom picture similar to ADHD. Consider that while Louie may be a problem for the classroom teacher, he does not show the negativity, hostility, and defiance that characterize oppositional defiant disorder. As well, the serious aggression toward others characteristic of someone with intermittent explosive disorder are not seen in Louie's case vignette. A child with a specific learning disorder may be inattentive in the classroom, but it is usually due to frustrations related to academics. These symptomatic behaviors are generally not seen outside the classroom. Louie's symptoms are consistently seen in multiple contexts; that is, in the classroom and when he is at home. ADHD shares symptoms of inattention with anxiety disorders, but in ADHD the individual's lack of attention may be related to a preoccupation with an enjoyable activity or some kind of external stimuli in contrast to the worry and rumination associated with anxiety. Those struggling with depression may have difficulty concentrating, but this symptom is prominent primarily during a depressive episode. In contrast, Louie consistently struggles with concentration. Children with ADHD may show mood changes, but not of the duration (4 days or more) necessary to consider bipolar disorder. Distinguishing the symptoms of ADHD in adolescents and adults from the borderline, narcissistic, and other personality disorders can be difficult since all of these disorders share many of the symptoms of disorganization, social intrusiveness, and emotional and cognitive dysregulation. However, someone with ADHD does not show the fear of abandonment, self-injury, or extreme ambivalence that are so typical of these personality disorders.

Competency 7 a

The competency-based assessment provides a framework to take into account the broad range of factors that are continuously interacting with one another as the child develops. This case story highlights Louie's cultural identity, language, and his mother's spiritual beliefs. Risks for developing disorders are also considered; for instance, a child such as Louie, who is living in relative isolation and has experienced the trauma of losing his father and all of his relatives in a devastating earthquake before migrating to the United States. The competency-based assessment also looks to strengths and resources such as a caring parent, supportive schools, and appropriate services.

OTHER NEURODEVELOPMENTAL DISORDERS

There are a number of neurodevelopmental disorders where the social worker may not play a central role in the diagnostic process. This section provides an overview of those disorders beginning with the communication disorders. As we have already seen, one of the central features of ASD is persistent impairments in social communication. Understanding how this differs from the communication disorders advances the practitioner's understanding of the client's symptom picture. Let's begin with a brief scenario.

Imagine for a moment that you are a social worker working in the school system. One of your assignments is a nearby grammar school. Mrs. Smith, a well-respected first grade teacher, approaches you and asks for your advice about one of her students. She is not sure if he might need some kind of a speech or hearing evaluation or if he is just going through a phase. His name is Alexander, but we'll refer to him by his nickname, "Zander." She begins, "I always greet my students as they enter my classroom each morning. Most of the children wave and say 'hi' back but there is one exception. It's Zander. He just walks right past me. He never waves or greets me. Zander doesn't even look at me. Do you think there might be something is wrong with him?"

How would you respond?

COMMUNICATION DISORDERS

There are many disorders that can affect how a person speaks and communicates. What distinguishes a communication disorder is that it affects the individual's ability to communicate to the extent that it interferes with school, work, or even relationships. The DSM-5 diagnoses for communication disorders are made in a more general way and emphasize childhood onset. The communication disorders can range from the sound repetitions found in stuttering to the occasional misarticulation of words. The diagnostic categories for the communication disorders include language disorder, speech sound disorder, childhood onset fluency disorder (stuttering), social (pragmatic) communication disorder, and unspecified communication disorder.

Language disorder: The key features of language disorder are difficulties in learning and using language that involve the processing of linguistic information due to deficits in comprehension or production. The person has problems with vocabulary, grammar, and putting sentences together. Diagnostic criteria for language disorder include persistent difficulties acquiring and using language across modalities (such as spoken, written, sign language, or other) due to deficits in comprehension or production that are below what is expected of someone at that age. Symptoms can be seen in a reduced vocabulary, limited sentence structure, the ability to put words together to form a sentence, or the inability to use vocabulary and connect sentences in order to explain an event or to have a conversation. These symptoms typically appear in the child's early developmental period and are not better explained by another medical or neurological condition, such as intellectual developmental disorder.

Speech Sound Disorder: Speech sound disorder describes those who have problems with pronunciation and articulation to the extent that they interfere with being understood or prevent verbal communication. Onset is early in the developmental period. Most children are expected to make some mistakes as they learn to say new words. I remember a youngster who was almost 3 years old, and he insisted on calling his pajamas by the term "*jamammas*." No matter how many times his mother corrected him, he would just giggle and refer to his jamammas. However, when these mistakes continue past a certain age, speech sound disorder is considered. Typically, the overall speech for children at 4 years of age is understandable in contrast to children at age 2, where about half of what they say can be understood.

Producing speech sounds involves knowing the speech sounds (phonological knowledge) and the ability to coordinate the jaw, tongue, and lips (or movements of the articulation). Errors can include substitutions such as saying "wabbit" for rabbit; omission of final consonants, for example, "do" for dog or "ca" for cat; or deleting parts of blends in words, for instance, saying "poon" for spoon or "bown" for brown. In contrast, those with speech sound disorder continue to struggle with effective communication to the extent that social participation, academic achievement, or occupational performance is affected either individually or in any combination. However, before considering a speech sound disorder, the practitioner takes into account regional, social or cultural/ethnic variations. As well, the child's difficulties are not better explained by a congenital or acquired condition such as cerebral palsy, cleft palate, deafness or hearing loss, or a traumatic brain injury.

Childhood Onset Fluency Disorder (Stuttering): Childhood onset fluency disorder is reserved for frequent, persistent, and marked instances of stuttering that causes problems for the individual such as anxiety about speaking, limited effective communication, or impact on social participation or job performance (or any combination). Here, too, onset is in the child's early developmental period and can be seen as: sound and syllable repetitions; sound prolongations of consonants as well as vowels; broken words or pauses within a word; audible (or silent) blocking; substituting words that are problematic (circumlocutions); words produced with an excess physical tension; or monosyllabic repetitions, such as "I-I-I- see him." A later onset is diagnosed as adult-onset fluency disorder.

Social (Pragmatic) Communication Disorder: Social (pragmatic) communication disorder describes difficulties in social use of verbal (and nonverbal) communication that affect social participation, relationships, academic achievement, or job performance (or any combination). When considering this disorder, the practitioner looks for the "pragmatics" or the appropriate use of language in social situations in four major areas: (1) using communication for social purposes, such as knowing what to say or greeting others and sharing information; (2) how to say it, or matching communication to the needs of the listener, such as speaking differently in the classroom from on the playground; (3) when to say it, such as taking turns in a conversation, and (4) those situations where the child has problems understanding what is not explicitly stated, such as humor or something with multiple meanings that depends on the context for interpretation. This is the child who may unintentionally embarrass his or her parents by making what others view as rude comments because they lack social language skills. The difference between this disorder and ASD is that in the latter, there is also a restricted or repetitive pattern of behavior (Gleason, 2001).

Unspecified Communication Disorder: Unspecified communication disorder is reserved for those who have symptoms of a communication disorder but who do not meet all criteria and whose symptoms cause distress or impairment.

Competency 7 b

Let's return to the vignette introduced earlier, where Zander's teacher is concerned that he does not communicate like her other students. Using language includes greeting, informing, demanding, and requesting. If we consider language disorder, an important characteristic involves difficulties in learning and using language caused by problems with vocabulary, grammar, and putting sentences together. Zander simply does not return his teacher's greeting. A speech sound disorder revolves around problems with pronunciation and articulation. Zander does not verbally address his teacher like the other students. He just walks past her without the expected wave or greeting. Childhood onset fluency disorder (stuttering) is distinguished by disturbances in the normal fluency and patterning of speech. What brings Zander to his teacher's attention is his failure to acknowledge her like the rest of her students. No other communication problems are reported. A key feature of social (pragmatic) communication disorder is difficulties around the appropriate use of communication, which affects social participation and relationships. Zander's teacher's concern that he does not seem to "act" like her other students makes this disorder a likely explanation for his behavior and warrants further exploration to determine if all criteria are met. If not, an unspecified communication disorder may be considered.

Let's turn to a consideration of specific learning disorder.

Specific Learning Disorder: A specific learning disorder describes difficulties learning and using academic skills and affects a child's ability to acquire and apply reading, writing, and/or math skills. This disorder differs from intellectual development disorder in that children with a learning disorder usually have at least average intelligence and yet are still not able to acquire the academic skills expected for their age, intellectual ability, and education. This is the child who struggles with decoding words, understanding the meaning of what is read, spelling, expressing him- or herself in writing, doing calculations, and mastering mathematical reasoning. The DSM-5 groups together reading-related (dyslexia) and math-related (dyscalculia) disorders under a single diagnosis. When the child is diagnosed with learning disorder, the specific areas of impairment are designated through specifiers; for example, impairment in reading, written expression, and/or mathematics. The particular areas of impairment are then designated in the diagnostic statement.

Competency 8 c

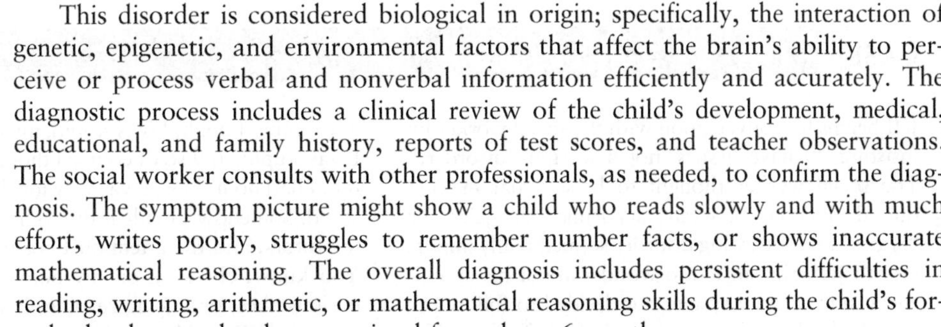

This disorder is considered biological in origin; specifically, the interaction of genetic, epigenetic, and environmental factors that affect the brain's ability to perceive or process verbal and nonverbal information efficiently and accurately. The diagnostic process includes a clinical review of the child's development, medical, educational, and family history, reports of test scores, and teacher observations. The social worker consults with other professionals, as needed, to confirm the diagnosis. The symptom picture might show a child who reads slowly and with much effort, writes poorly, struggles to remember number facts, or shows inaccurate mathematical reasoning. The overall diagnosis includes persistent difficulties in reading, writing, arithmetic, or mathematical reasoning skills during the child's formal school years that have persisted for at least 6 months.

Specific learning disorder is now a single, overall diagnosis. Rather than limiting the learning disorders to diagnoses particular to reading, written expression, and math, the DSM takes a dimensional approach to the criteria to describe shortcomings in general academic skills and provides detailed specifiers for the areas of reading, written expression, and math. Signs that a child may have a learning disorder include:

- Inaccurate or slow and effortful reading.
- Difficulty understanding the meaning of what is read.
- Difficulties with spelling.
- Difficulties with written expression.
- Difficulties mastering number sense, number facts, or calculation.
- Difficulties with mathematical reasoning.

Finally, these learning difficulties are not better accounted for by intellectual disabilities, uncorrected visual or auditory acuity, other mental or neurological disorders, psychological adversity, lack of proficiency in the language of academic instruction, or inadequate educational instruction.

The specifiers that describe the academic domains and the related impaired subskills are (APA, 2013):

- With impairment in reading—Includes possible deficits in word reading accuracy, reading rate or fluency, and reading comprehension. A note is provided for dyslexia, seen as an alternative term used to refer to a pattern of learning difficulties characterized by problems with accurate or fluent word recognition, poor decoding, and poor spelling abilities. If this term is used, any additional difficulties (such as difficulties with reading comprehension or math reasoning) are specified.
- With impairment in written expression—Includes spelling accuracy, grammar and punctuation accuracy, and clarity or organization of written expression.
- With impairment in mathematics—Includes number sense, memorization of arithmetic facts, accurate or fluent calculation, and accurate math reasoning.

Severity is also specified ranging from mild, to moderate, to severe.

Specific learning disorder is highlighted with a brief sketch of Jeff Childs's story about his struggles.

CASE The Case of Jeff Childs

Jeff begins his conversation with the social worker by insisting, "I have 'issues' not a learning disorder." The social worker thought to herself that making the distinction between academic struggles or "issues" and a learning disorder seemed really important to Jeff. She started to wonder about his experiences in the school system but decided to follow her client's lead in the conversation. Jeff continues, "Well, okay, I constantly had trouble throughout grammar school. You might say that I was different. I bet you're wondering what I mean by that. It's just that I always had different perspectives on everything. My family thought I was stupid, my teachers thought I was stupid, and so of course I thought I was stupid, too. I had no friends, I was very lonely and misunderstood. Somehow I made it through. Maybe it was all the tutors, and the attention I got from my parents. You know, checking on my homework, correcting my mistakes, practicing reading. It was like we had a routine. Come home, have a snack, start homework, a little play time, supper, and then back to the books before bed. That was my 'usual' all through grammar school. I had to go to school, so what choices did I have? So I made the best of it."

Jeff continued, "When I got to middle school, I found a teacher who actually believed I was clever. What a shock, but it was so nice to know there was somebody out there who actually had faith in me and what I could do instead of what I couldn't do! Needless to say, my parents were shocked. Their 'dumb child'"—Jeff puts his fingers up to form quotation marks for emphasis and continues—"was actually doing well. They were convinced that all my tests were mixed up. Things were perfect ... almost."

Jeff looked as if he was lost in thought at this point, paused for what seemed like a very long time to the social worker, then straightened up in his chair and continued, "For the first time I started to do okay but generally my knowledge was never reflected in my grades. I would get A+'s on my assignments but come exams, that was another story. On a good day I would get a C, but I usually flagged them." The social worker looked puzzled. Jeff added, "It means I would get the F grade. My teacher noticed this and he thought I was one of the best students in his class but my knowledge never translated well into good grades. Seems I would misread the test question or the teacher couldn't understand my answer. Those essay tests are the worst. In the end, I failed the course. Then the old frustrations came back. No matter how hard I tried to study, no matter how much I learned, I always did extremely bad on exams. I figured out the only way to get through school was to rely on my assignments for good grades. This hasn't changed but, thankfully, I got through high school and now I'm graduating from college. Would you believe it? In fact, I'm thinking of graduate school."

Jeff looked directly into the social worker's eyes and stated, "Two weeks ago I was diagnosed by a psychologist who said that I have a specific learning disability. Seems my main problem is with reading comprehension and written expression. The psychologist says I can read faster than most people but I can't seem to retain the information I read. According to him I can understand complicated concepts, but it's the simple ideas that trip me up. After all these years, I finally have a name for what's been going on with me. I'm thinking about grad school. Do you think I'll be able to make it?"

Competency 8 c

The social worker considers the ways in which social systems promote or deter people in maintaining or achieving health and well-being. As seen in Jeff Childs's story, signs of a learning disorder usually become apparent when a child begins preschool, or in Jeff's case, elementary school. Normally, the youngster encounters difficulties with one or more of the core areas of learning; that is, reading, writing, and/or math. Despite his parents' interventions (such as helping him with his homework, correcting his mistakes, and so forth), Jeff struggled with reading comprehension and clarity of written expression. Organizing his writing led to his consistent struggles with taking exams. Although these problems persisted throughout his school years, Jeff managed to somehow make it through school and to graduate college. He is now considering graduate school. Unfortunately, the long-term impact of his struggles becomes apparent when he questions his ability to be successful in graduate school.

Competency 7 a

The DSM-5 takes a different approach to learning disorders than previous editions of the manual by broadening the diagnostic criteria to incorporate the deficits that impact academic achievement. With this shift in the classification system, it may have been possible to diagnose Jeff's academic struggles much earlier. Based on his story, he was left to struggle on his own throughout most of his school years, and in his words, "somehow I made it through." Early identification of a learning disorder may have made it feasible for Jeff to receive appropriate help much sooner.

We conclude our review of specific learning disorder with a consideration of what Jeff Childs's diagnosis might look like. Consider, "Specific learning disorder, with impairment in reading and impairment in reading comprehension; specific learning disorder with impairment in writing and impairment in clarity or organization of written expression, mild."

We now turn to a review of the Motor Disorders.

MOTOR DISORDERS

The brain assigns different motor control tasks to different brain regions, and they all work together to produce the fluid and effortless body movements we all take for granted. The motor disorders result from damage to the brain's motor system and cause abnormal and involuntary movements. The classification of motor disorders is a new subcategory of the neurodevelopmental disorders and includes developmental coordination disorder, stereotypic movement disorder, and the tic disorders including Tourette's syndrome.

Developmental Coordination Disorder: Developmental coordination disorder is also known as dyspraxia or by the pejorative term, clumsy child syndrome (Gibbs, Appleton, & Appleton, 2007). The essential feature is impaired skills requiring motor coordination; for instance, it is hard for a child to use scissors, ride a bike, and/or participate in sports or team activities in school.

Competency 8 c

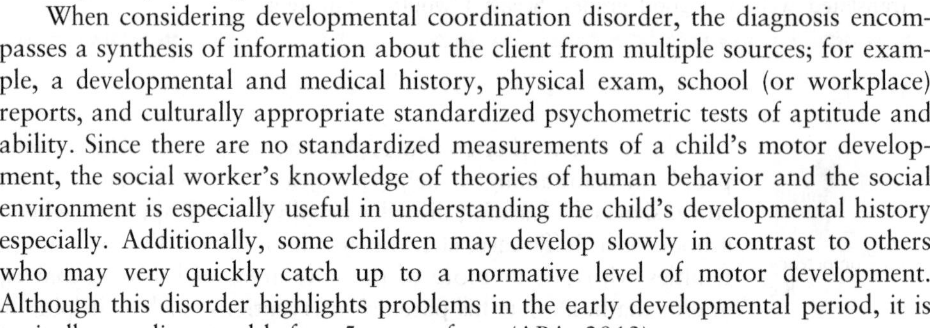

When considering developmental coordination disorder, the diagnosis encompasses a synthesis of information about the client from multiple sources; for example, a developmental and medical history, physical exam, school (or workplace) reports, and culturally appropriate standardized psychometric tests of aptitude and ability. Since there are no standardized measurements of a child's motor development, the social worker's knowledge of theories of human behavior and the social environment is especially useful in understanding the child's developmental history especially. Additionally, some children may develop slowly in contrast to others who may very quickly catch up to a normative level of motor development. Although this disorder highlights problems in the early developmental period, it is typically not diagnosed before 5 years of age (APA, 2013).

A key symptom of developmental coordination disorder specifies that the child's acquisition and performance of coordinated motor skills are substantially below what is expected of his or her chronological age and opportunities for learning and using skills. Difficulties can be seen as clumsiness. This is the individual who tends to drop or bump into things. Handwriting is illegible, or he or she may write so slowly that academic achievement is impacted. Keep in mind that the emphasis is on motor skills and not on a specific learning difficulty. These motor skills interfere with activities of daily living and impact school, academics, prevocational (and vocational) activities, leisure, and play. The symptom picture is not better explained by the presence of intellectual developmental disorder, a visual impairment or a neurological condition that affects movement such as cerebral palsy, muscular dystrophy, or a degenerative disorder.

Stereotypic Movement Disorder: Stereotypic movement disorder involves repetitive, nonfunctional motor behaviors (for example, hand waving or head banging) that markedly interferes with normal activities or can result in bodily injury.

The cause of this disorder is unknown. Symptoms typically emerge before age 3 and are often misdiagnosed as tics or Tourette's (Singer, 2009). The use of a substance or another neurodevelopmental or mental disorder does not better explain the symptom picture.

Tic Disorders: The tic disorders are distinguished by the presence of motor and/or vocal tics and organized around the categories of Tourette's disorder (also known as Gilles de la Tourette syndrome), persistent (chronic) motor or vocal tic disorder, provisional tic disorder, and other specified and unspecified tic disorders. Typically, tics occur in childhood and peak in severity early in the second decade of life followed by remission of tics and associated impairment (Roessner, Hoekstra, & Rothenberger, 2011). However, a small percentage of individuals will experience severe symptoms in adulthood (APA, 2013). Coexisting disorders seem to be the rule rather than the exception. For example, Roessner, Becker, Banaschewski, and Rothenberger (2005) observe that about 50 percent of those with a tic disorder also suffer from obsessive-compulsive disorder symptoms. Schlander, Schwartz, Rothenberger, and Roessner (2010) report attention-deficit/hyperactivity disorder in 20 percent of individuals with tic disorder.

Tics can range in presentation such as:

- Simple—Simple motor tics are of short duration (i.e., milliseconds) and include eye blinking, shoulder shrugging, and extension of the extremities; simple vocal tics include throat clearing, sniffing, and grunting.
- Complex—Complex motor tics last longer (seconds) and can include a combination of simple tics such as simultaneous head turning and shoulder shrugging. Sometimes they can appear purposeful, such as an obscene gesture (copropraxia) or a tic-like imitation of another's movements (echopraxia). Complex vocal tics can also include repeating one's own sounds or words (palilalia), repeating the last heard word or phrase of another (echolalia), or uttering socially unacceptable words including obscenities, racial slurs, and the like (coprolalia). The latter is distinguished from usual speech patterns by an abrupt, sharp bark or grunting presentation.

Onset is before 18 years of age, but presentation varies across the different tic disorders. Specifically, Tourette's disorder requires both motor and vocal tics in contrast to persistent (chronic) motor or vocal tic disorder where only motor or vocal tics are present (with the specifier to indicate motor tics only or vocal tics only). Tics can wax and wane in severity, and a one-year minimum duration is required for the diagnosis of Tourette's and persistent (chronic) motor or vocal tic disorder. Provisional tic disorder indicates single or multiple motor and/or vocal tics but present for less than one year. For other specified or unspecified tic disorders, the motor disorder symptoms are best characterized as tics but atypical in presentation, or age at onset, or the cause is unknown.

SUMMARY

Most of us remember childhood as a carefree and easygoing period in our lives. Ideally, this is a time for children to imagine, play, learn, and develop in an environment characterized by safety and love. This is the stage of life distinguished by significant social, emotional, and cognitive changes. This transformation generally follows a pattern in which the child develops one skill and then moves ahead to acquire another. For the child who struggles with a neurodevelopmental disorder, their experience is quite different. These children do not smoothly progress through life and its related challenges.

The neurodevelopmental cluster of disorders is largely characterized by strong genetic and environmental risks, a consistent course that reflects a deviation in normal development, early age of onset, a continuing course that can potentially extend into adulthood, an overlap in symptoms or within cluster comorbidity, the salience of cognitive symptoms, and increased prevalence in males (Andrews, Pine, Hobbs, Anderson, & Sunderland, 2009). The disorders reviewed in this chapter were: intellectual disabilities; communication disorders; autism spectrum disorder; attention-deficit/hyperactivity disorder; specific learning disorder; and the motor disorders. Case illustrations were included to highlight specific syndromes and the competencies that distinguish each person's unique struggle with the disorder.

As the DSM transitions from the DSM-IV-TR (APA, 2000) to the current edition of the manual, Table 2.2 provides a brief summary of the changes made to the diagnostic classifications.

TABLE 2.2 SUMMARY COMPARISON BETWEEN THE DSM-IV-TR AND DSM-5 DIAGNOSES FOR THE NEURODEVELOPMENTAL DISORDERS

Mental retardation has been renamed as "intellectual disability" (Intellectual Development Disorder)
The former phonological disorder and stuttering are now called Communication Disorders and include language disorder, speech sound disorder, childhood-onset fluency disorder (stuttering), and a new condition called social (pragmatic) communication disorder characterized by impaired social verbal and nonverbal communication
Autism spectrum disorder incorporates the formerly separate disorders of Asperger's, childhood disintegrative disorder, and pervasive developmental disorder not otherwise specified
A new subcategory, motor disorders, has been added and includes developmental coordination disorder, stereotypic movement disorder, and the tic disorders including Tourette's disorder

PRACTITIONER'S REFLECTIONS

Children with neurodevelopmental disorders experience many challenges on a daily basis and often rely on others for help. They might act out in the supermarket or movie theater, or you might be sitting next to them on an airplane. Perhaps you might be annoyed by an inappropriate remark a child may make and start to wonder why the parents do not control their child. This chapter points to the possibilities that a parent might be trying to do all they can to address their child's behavior. The next time you see a child being troublesome in public, remember the disorders discussed in this chapter and begin asking yourself what really might be the basis for this behavior.

ACTIVITIES

Competency 7 b

1. Sometimes there is a fine line between what might be considered normal behavior and those behaviors that support any one of the neurodevelopmental disorders. This underscores the practitioner's skill in collecting, organizing, and interpreting client data. Looking back at the case stories presented in this chapter, how do you think their behaviors differ from

those of a typical child? Given their life stories, can you see any behaviors that might seem normal for a child that age?

Competency 1 b

2. Children, regardless of their mental status or diagnosis, eventually grow up and mature into adulthood. Do you think persons with any of one the neurodevelopmental disorders should marry and have children of their own? Explain why or why not.
3. Explain why you think that many of the disorders discussed in this chapter are more commonly found in boys than in girls. Include in your consideration how parents (and teachers) might deal differently with boys than with girls.

Competency 5 a

4. In most instances, a child with a neurodevelopmental disorder is the proverbial involuntary client, since it is usually a parent or another adult in the child's life who identifies a problem and initiates seeking help. Unfortunately, these children may be stigmatized by their behavior and/or having a mental disorder. Access to help can be further complicated by the harsh realities of poverty, language barriers, insurance coverage, or differences in cultural values about what is a sign of mental illness. Using the case of Louie Dessaint as a platform, review with a colleague and/or your supervisor how these different contexts (relational, organizational, and community systems) may impact your clients.

Competency 6 a

5. Select any one of the case stories representing the autism spectrum disorders (Chris Wells, or Bobby Owens) and discuss with another colleague or your supervisor what challenges you might encounter developing, managing, and maintaining a professional relationship with these clients and their families. Keep in mind the competency-based perspective as you identify relationship challenges and explore the strengths found in each client's story.

Competency 1 c

6. Imagine for a moment that you have been working really hard dieting and exercising in order to lose weight and that it has been a struggle. Envision your feelings of disappointment with your lack of progress, and your sensitivity about how you look. A new client has been assigned to you with autism spectrum disorder. You introduce yourself to him in the waiting room, and in a rather loud and pretentious demeanor, he returns your greeting with, "Miss, your pants look really tight on you. You should definitely lose weight. Like big time!" You are stunned. How might you respond?

COMPETENCY NOTES

Competency 1 b—Social workers use reflection and self-regulation to manage personal values and maintain professionalism in practice situations (p. 63): Social workers recognize personal values and make the distinction between personal and professional values.

Competency 1 c—Social workers demonstrate professional demeanor in behavior, appearance, and oral/written/electronic communication (p. 63): Social workers understand how their personal experiences and affective reactions can influence their professional judgment and behavior and also understand emerging forms of technology and the ethical use of technology in practice.

Competency 2 a—Social workers apply and communicate understanding of the implications of diversity and difference in shaping life experiences in practice at the micro, mezzo, and macro levels (p. 53): Social workers understand how diversity and difference characterize and shape the human experience and that these features are critical to the formation of identity.

Competency 5 a—Social workers identify social welfare and economic policies at the local, state, and federal levels impact well-being, service delivery, and

access to social services (pp. 53, 63): Social workers understand that human rights and social justice, as well as social welfare and services, are mediated by policy and its implementation on several levels—local, state, and federal.

Competency 5 c—Social workers apply critical thinking to analyze, formulate, and advocate for policies that advance human rights and social, economic, and environmental justice (p. 52): Social workers understand their role in policy development and implementation within their practice settings and actively engage in policy practice to effect change.

Competency 6 a—Social workers apply knowledge of human behavior and the social environment, person-in-environment, and other multidisciplinary theoretical frameworks to engage with clients (and constituencies) (p. 63): Social workers understand theories of human behavior and the social environment and critically apply this knowledge to facilitate engagement with clients (and constituencies) including families, groups, organizations, and communities.

Competency 7 a—Social workers collect and organize data and apply critical thinking in order to interpret information from clients and constituencies (pp. 45, 48, 54, 59): Social workers understand that the assessment process is ongoing and conducted with, and on behalf of, diverse individuals, families, groups, organizations, and communities.

Competency 7 b—Social workers are able to apply knowledge of human behavior and the social environment, person-in-environment, and other multidisciplinary theoretical frameworks in the analysis of assessment data (pp. 39, 41, 43, 47, 53, 57, 62): Social workers understand theories of human behavior and the social environment and critically evaluate and apply this knowledge in the assessment process.

Competency 7 c—Social workers develop mutually agreed-on intervention goals and objectives based on the assessment of strengths, needs and challenges within clients and constituencies (p. 39): Social workers recognize the implications of the larger practice context in the assessment process.

Competency 7 d—Social workers select appropriate intervention strategies based on the assessment, research knowledge, and values and preferences of clients and communities (p. 35): Social workers understand methods of assessment with diverse clients (and constituencies) to advance practice effectiveness.

Competency 8 c—Social workers use interprofessional collaboration, as appropriate, to achieve beneficial practice outcomes (pp. 43, 57, 59, 60): Social workers value interprofessional teamwork and recognize the beneficial outcomes that require interdisciplinary, interprofessional, and interorganizational collaboration.

References

American Psychiatric Association (APA). (2000). *Diagnostic and statistical manual of mental disorders* (4th ed., text revision). Washington, DC: Author.

American Psychiatric Association (APA). (2013). *Diagnostic and statistical manual of mental disorders* (5th ed.). Arlington, VA: Author.

Anastopoulos, A., Sommer, J., & Shatz, N. (2009). ADHD and family functioning. *Current Attention Disorders Reports*, *1*(4), 167–170.

Andrews, G., Pine, D. S., Hobbs, M. J., Anderson, T. M., & Sunderland, M. (2009). Neurodevelopmental disorders: Cluster 2 of the proposed meta-structure for DSM-V and ICD-11. *Psychological Medicine*, *39*(12), 2013–2023.

Carulla, L. S., Reed, G. M., Vaez-Azizi, L. M., Cooper, S., Leal, R. M., Bertelli, M., … Saxena, S. (October 2011). Intellectual developmental disorders: Towards a new name, definition and framework for "mental retardation/intellectual disability" in ICD-11. *World Psychiatry*, *3*(10), 175–180.

Centers for Disease Control and Prevention (CDC). (2004, January). Economic costs associated with mental retardation, cerebral palsy, hearing loss, and vision impairment—United States, 2003. *Morbidity and Mortality Weekly Report*, *53*(3), 57–59.

Ehninger, D., Li, W., Fox, K., Stryker, M., & Silva, A. (2008). Reversing neurodevelopmental disorders in adults. *Neuron*, *60*(6), 950–960.

Gibbs, J., Appleton, J., & Appleton, R. (2007). Dyspraxia or developmental coordination disorder? Unravelling the enigma. *Archives of Disease in Childhood*, *92*(6), 534–539.

Gleason, J. B. (2001). *The development of language*. Boston: Allyn and Bacon.

Grandjean, P., & Landrigan, P. (2006). Developmental neurotoxicity of industrial chemicals. *The Lancet*, *368*, 2167–2178.

Lord, C., Risi, S., DiLavore, P. S., Shulman, C., Thurm, A., & Pickles, A. (2006). Autism from 2 to 9 years of age. *Archives of General Psychiatry*, *63*(6), 694–701.

Mash, E. J., & Barkley, R. A. (Eds.). (2002). *Child Psychopathology* (2nd ed.). New York: Guilford Press.

National Center on Birth Defects and Developmental Disabilities. (2005). *Facts about intellectual disability*. Retrieved from: http://www.cdc.gov/ncbddd/actearly/pdf/parents_pdfs/IntellectualDisability.pdf

Newschaffer, C. J., Croen, L. A., Daniels, J., Giarelli, E., Grether, J. K., Levy, S. E., . . . Windham, G. C. (2007). The epidemiology of autism spectrum disorders. *Annual Review of Public Health*, *28*, 235–258.

Roessner, V., Becker, A., Banaschewski, T., & Rothenberger, A. (2005). Tic disorders and obsessive compulsive disorder: Where is the link? *Journal of Neural Transmission, Suppl.*, *69*, 69–99.

Roessner, V., Hoekstra, P. J., & Rothenberger, A. (2011). Tourette's disorder and other tic disorders in DSM-5: A comment. *European Child & Adolescent Psychiatry*, *20*, 71–74.

Rutter, M. (2000). Genetic studies of autism: From the 1970s into the millennium. *Journal of Abnormal Child Psychology*, *28*(1), 3–14.

Schlander, M., Schwartz, O., Rothenberger, A., & Roessner, V. (2010). Tic disorders: Administrative prevalence and co-occurrence with attention-deficit/hyperactivity disorder in a German community sample. *European Psychiatry*, *26*(6), 370–374.

Singer, H. S. (2009). Motor stereotypies. *Seminars in Pediatric Neurology*, *16*(2), 77–81.

Slade, E. P. (2004). Racial/ethnic disparities in parent perception of child need for mental health care following school disciplinary events. *Mental Health Services Research*, *6*, 75–92.

Tager-Flusberg, H. (2010). The origins of social impairments in autism spectrum disorder: Studies of infants at risk. Neural Networks, 23(8–9), 1072–1076.

Timmini, S., & Taylor, E. (2004). ADHD is best understood as a cultural construct. *British Journal of Psychiatry*, *184*, 8–9.

U.S. Department of Education. (2010). *29th annual report to Congress on the implementation of the Individuals with Disabilities Education Act*, 2007, Vol. 2. Washington, DC: Author. Retrieved from: http://www2.ed.gov/about/reports/annual/osep/index.html

Zwaigenbaum, L., Bryson, S., Lord, C., Rogers, S., Carter, A., Carver, L., . . . Stone, W. (2009). Clinical assessment and management of toddlers with suspected autism spectrum disorder: Insights from studies of high risk infants. *Pediatrics*, *123*(5), 1383–1391.

CHAPTER 3

Schizophrenia Spectrum and Other Psychotic Disorders

INTRODUCTION

Dr. John Haslam, an early pioneer in the field of mental illness, wrote *Observations on Madness and Melancholy*, published in 1809. He conceptualized schizophrenia as "a form of insanity," stating:

> The sensibility appears to be considerably blunted; they do not bear the same affection towards their parents and relations; they become unfeeling to kindness, and careless of reproof. ... I have painfully witnessed this hopeless and degrading change, which in a short time has transformed the most promising and vigorous intellect into a slavering and bloated idiot. (Haslam, 1809/1976, pp. 65–67)

Almost 50 years later, in 1860 a Belgian psychiatrist named Benedict Augustin Morel (1890) standardized and formally described symptoms of schizophrenia using the French terms *demence* (loss of mind) and *precoce* (early, premature).

The use of the term *schizophrenia* began in 1896 with Emil Kraepelin, a German professor of psychiatry who brought together under one heading several types of mental abnormalities previously viewed as separate and distinct disorders even though they shared similar underlying features. Kraepelin (1919, 1971) distinguished three subtypes and included them under the Latin term *dementia praecox*:

- Catatonia (alternating immobility and excited agitation).
- Hebephrenia (silly and immature emotionality).
- Paranoia (delusions of grandeur or persecution).

Although clinical manifestations might differ, Kraepelin postulated that the central feature of the disorder was its early onset, which ultimately developed into a "mental weakness." He went on to identify several features occurring in dementia praecox, such as hallucinations, delusions, and negativism. Further, Kraepelin believed that changes in the brain were of some importance in its cause. He was the first to suggest that dementia started in early adolescence and evolved into a long-term chronic course due to brain deterioration.

In 1911, Eugene Bleuler, a Swiss psychiatrist, differed from Kraepelin's conceptualizations and described a group of "different" schizophrenias characterized by disturbances of feelings, thinking, and relationships to the outside world. Bleuler (1926, 1950) believed that underneath the person's unusual behaviors was an "associative splitting" of the basic functions of personality. He felt the most prominent feature of schizophrenia was the tearing apart of the individual's psychic functions. This, he believed, was especially evident in inappropriate behavior, in the loosening of associations between ideas, and disorganization of thought, affect, and actions. He coined the term *schizophrenia* from the Greek word *skhizein*, meaning "split," and *phren*, meaning "mind" (Fusar-Poli & Politi, 2008). This new word replaced terms such as madness, lunacy, and dementia praecox. Bleuler did not intend to suggest that "split mindedness" represented two distinct personalities (as is found in the person with dissociative identity disorder); rather that it denoted a shattered personality. Bleuler believed the split referred to the widening gap between internal and external realities. This schism between thought, emotion, and behavior established what continues to remain as the most enduring description of schizophrenia. Bleuler isolated four fundamental diagnostic features, sometimes called "the four A's," to identify the splitting of external reality:

- Associations—Logical thought processes. When thought processes are altered, speech loses its coherence (associations are loosened) and connections among ideas are absent or obscure. Communication may become highly idiosyncratic and individualized; that is, the person may create his or her own words (neologism) according to some form of special symbolism. An example of a neologism would be, "Every time I hear the clinks, snaps, and bangs on the grass, I guess, I think, I know that's where Jesus clicks and clocks."
- Affect—Observable manifestation of a person's mood or emotion. In schizophrenia this is characterized by diminished emotions (flat or blunted), feeling disconnected from surrounding events (impersonating or performing within a role), and/or emotional indifference to the surrounding world (reduction in pleasurable experiences).
- Autism—Characterized by significant impairment in social interactions, communication, and restricted patterns of behavior, interest, or activity.
- Ambivalence—Positive and negative values that exist simultaneously; they include uncertainty about taking a particular direction or vacillating between two different perspectives and/or courses of action.

In the 1930s, Kurt Schneider (1959) introduced the concept of first- and second-rank symptom, known as positive and negative symptoms. Building on Schneider's first-rank symptoms, the positive symptoms are summarized in Table 3.1.

TABLE 3.1 POSITIVE SYMPTOMS (OR THE PRESENCE OF ALTERED BEHAVIORS) ADAPTED FROM SCHNEIDER'S FIRST-RANK CRITERIA

Disorganized thinking

- Disturbances of audible thoughts.
- Voices arguing.
- Voices commenting to each other.

Disorganized behavior

- Somatic passivity experiences or inertia.

Catatonic behavior

- Muscular rigidity and immobility.
- Stupor and negativism or state of excitement.

Delusions

- Thought withdrawal (e.g., believing thoughts have been removed by an outside force).
- Thought broadcasting (e.g., believing passages from books, television, and other environmental stimuli are specifically directed at oneself).

Hallucinations

- Delusional perceptions (can occur in any of the five senses, but auditory, such as hearing voices, is the most common).

Other

- All other experiences involving avolition (inability to initiate or participate in important activities).
- Unusual motor behavior (such as rocking or pacing).
- Depersonalization (or feeling detached).
- Derealization (or loss of one's sense of reality in the external world).
- Somatic preoccupations.

Source: Adapted from the American Psychiatric Association, *Diagnostic and statistical manual of mental disorders*, 4th ed., text revision (Washington, DC: American Psychiatric Association, 2000), and from K. Schneider (M. W. Hamilton, Trans.), *Clinical psychology* (London: Grune and Stratton, 1959).

The negative symptoms, including Schneider's contribution of second-rank symptoms, are described in Table 3.2.

Researchers continued to question whether schizophrenia is actually one disorder or a combination of disorders refuting the original five subtypes that were put forward in the DSM-IV (APA, 2000; Linscott, Allardyce, & van Os, 2009). The DSM-5 characterizes schizophrenia as a heterogeneous clinical syndrome involving features characterized by abnormalities in one or more of the following five domains—delusions, hallucinations, disorganized thinking (speech), grossly disorganized or abnormal motor behavior (including catatonia), and negative symptoms. The specific DSM-5 disorders reviewed in this chapter are listed in Table 3.3.

For the most part, the schizophrenia spectrum and other psychotic disorders described in this chapter reflect the gradient of psychopathology ranking them

Table 3.2 Negative Symptoms (or the Lack of Behaviors) Adapted from Schneider's Second-Rank Criteria

Loss of feeling or an inability to experience pleasure (anhedonia)

- Disturbances of perception (the simple pleasures of life are no longer enjoyed).
- Lack of interest in social or recreational activities through failure to develop close relationships.

Poverty of speech (alogia)

- Amount of speech is greatly reduced and tends to be vague or repetitious.
- Perplexity, bewilderment, and confusion (being slow in responding to questions or does not respond at all).

Flat presentation (affective flattening)

- Depressive and euphoric mood changes.
- Unchanging facial expressions, poor or no eye contact, reduced body language, and decreased spontaneous movements.
- Stares vacantly into space and speaks in a flat, toneless voice.

Withdrawal, loss of motivation, and ambivalence (avolition)

- Feelings of emotional impoverishment or seeming lack of interest in what were usual activities.
- Inattentive to personal grooming, hygiene.
- Difficulty in persisting at work, school, or household chores.

Source: Adapted from the American Psychiatric Association, *Diagnostic and statistical manual of mental disorders*, 4th ed., text revision (Washington, DC: American Psychiatric Association, 2000), and from K. Schneider (M. W. Hamilton, Trans.), *Clinical psychology* (London: Grune and Stratton, 1959).

Table 3.3 The DSM-5 Schizophrenia Spectrum and Other Psychotic Disorders

Delusional Disorder
Brief Psychotic Disorder
Schizophreniform Disorder
Schizophrenia
Schizoaffective Disorder
Substance/Medication-Induced Psychotic Disorder
Psychotic Disorder Due to Another Medical Condition
Catatonia Associated with Another Mental Disorder (Catatonia Specifier)
Catatonic Disorder Due to Another Medical Condition
Unspecified Catatonia
Other Specified Schizophrenia Spectrum and Other Psychotic Disorder
Unspecified Schizophrenia Spectrum and Other Psychotic Disorder

from least to most severe; that is, those disorders that do not reach full criteria for a psychotic disorder or are limited to one domain of psychopathology. In this way, the diagnostic process moves away from the categorical approach; that is, either a client meets diagnostic criteria or not. In its place, the practitioner considers time-limited conditions; for example, a delusional disorder requires at least 1 month of delusions, but no other psychotic symptoms are present; brief psychotic disorder lasts more than 1 day and remits by 1 month; schizophreniform disorder very closely resembles the symptom picture of schizophrenia, except the symptoms last for less than 6 months and there is no evident decline in functioning; and the symptoms supporting a diagnosis of schizophrenia last for at least 6 months and include at least 1 month of active-phase symptoms. Schizotypal personality disorder is considered part of the schizophrenia spectrum of disorders (and you will find a complete review of this disorder in the chapter addressing the personality disorders).

Our discussion begins with schizophrenia.

SCHIZOPHRENIA

Schizophrenia is characterized by a broad range of behaviors marked by a loss of the person's sense of self, significant impairment in reality testing, and disturbances in feeling, thinking, and behavior. The individuals affected are unable to distinguish the accuracy of their own perceptions and thoughts from external reality. Persons diagnosed with schizophrenia (as opposed to other psychiatric disorders) are often unaware of their symptoms or even may contest that they have them (Lysaker, France, Hunter, & Davis, 2005). The term psychosis is often used interchangeably with schizophrenia and refers to a group of incapacitating disorders traditionally defined as the loss of reality testing and the impairment of mental functioning manifested by delusions (or irrational beliefs) and/or hallucinations (or sensory experiences in the absence of external events) as well as confusion, impaired memory, and the inability to function within the interpersonal domain.

Competency 7 a

In essence, schizophrenia is a complicated and variable condition best thought of as a syndrome or a cluster of symptoms that may or may not have related causes. While we do not know the exact cause of schizophrenia, there is growing support for neurodevelopmental, genetic, and biological factors, the early environment, and social processes associated with its origin (Thomas, 2010). Competent social work practitioners take into account the many theories that explain a client's behavior across the life span.

When considering schizophrenia, there is considerable debate among various professional disciplines regarding the validity of a schizophrenia-specific onset occurring in childhood. However, one prevalent explanation for how schizophrenia (and the other psychotic disorders) can develop is the neurodevelopmental hypothesis (Murray, Jones, Susser, van Os, & Cannon, 2003). This theory suggests that there is a subtle disease process that affects brain areas very early in life, possibly as early as the second trimester of the prenatal period, and gradually continues to the point where full-blown symptoms emerge. This hypothesis is supported by evidence that indicates early problems, and brain changes can show up as a child develops. For instance, children who show a decline in intelligence over time, lower tested intelligence scores, more repeated grades, and trouble paying attention are found to be at a higher risk for developing schizophrenia (Maki et al., 2005). Children who ultimately develop schizophrenia tend to show more withdrawn, neurotic, depressive, solitary, aggressive, and disruptive behaviors (Niemi, Suvisaari, Tuulio-Henriksson, & Lonnqvist, 2003). Each family responds differently to someone with the disorder, but these reactions in and of themselves do not cause schizophrenia (Weisman de Mamani, Kymalainen, Rosales, & Armesto, 2007). Nevertheless, if the home environment is hostile and critical this can create additional stressors that can, in turn, lead to greater struggles and possibly more relapses.

A family history of schizophrenia worsens the overall prognosis, but there is no evidence to show that a single gene causes schizophrenia. Instead, thousands of gene variances combine to produce vulnerability to having the disorder (Purcell et al., 2009; Wray & Visscher, 2010). Evidence of genetic transmission of the risk for schizophrenia has been widely accepted, and some twin and family studies further support the idea of a genetic component in schizophrenia. Studies comparing monozygotic (or identical) to dizygotic (or fraternal) twins confirm the hypothesis that genetics play a large role in the predisposition and vulnerability to schizophrenia. Several interesting findings emerged in an early definitive study begun by Fischer (1971) and continued by Gottesman (1989). Findings indicated that if one parent is an identical twin (monozygotic) with schizophrenia, then his or her child has about a 17 percent chance of having the disorder. Additionally, the child's risks for schizophrenia remained at 17 percent when the parent is the identical twin without schizophrenia (and the co-twin has the disorder). Clearly, one can have genes that predispose a diagnosis of schizophrenia and not actually have the disorder but still pass on the genes. It was also found that if one parent of fraternal twins (dizygotic) has schizophrenia, it followed that his or her child had about a 17 percent chance of having schizophrenia. Interestingly, for the parent who did not have schizophrenia but whose fraternal twin does, the child's risk for a diagnosis of schizophrenia was about 2 percent.

Gottesman (1991), in a classic analysis, looked at data from about 40 studies of schizophrenia and summarized the disorder as follows: "While the genes are necessary for causing schizophrenia, they are not sufficient or adequate by themselves, and one or more environmental contributors are also necessary for schizophrenia but they are not specific to it" (p. 164). Nevertheless, family studies indicate that the closer a person's genetic relatedness to a person with schizophrenia, the greater the likelihood of developing the disorder. The risk varies according to how many genes an individual shares with someone who actually has the disorder. There is sufficient and increasing evidence to support the fact that those with schizophrenia have a different biochemical makeup from that of the general population (Opler & Susser, 2005). More recent research suggests that genetic vulnerability to schizophrenia is multifactorial, caused by interactions of several genes (Owen, Craddock, & O'Donovan, 2005).

Paternal age is another factor in schizophrenia because of the increased chance of mutations in the chromosomes of cells that produce sperms. In contrast, women's oocytes (the female's immature egg or immature ovum) divides 23 times before the time of birth. The chance of a copying error in DNA replication during cell division (mitosis) upon fertilization of the female's egg increases with the number of cell divisions and an increase in copying errors—and an increase in copying errors may cause an accumulation of mutations that are responsible for an increased incidence of schizophrenia (Carlson, 2012).

Magnetic resonance imaging, commonly referred to by the acronym MRI, provides a way to view the structure of the brain without the use of unnecessary radiation. In principle, an MRI is a noninvasive procedure that relies upon the interactions of magnetic fields and radio frequency radiation with body tissues to provide a three-dimensional view of internal organs and structures within the body. Current research suggests significant differences can be found on brain ventricle size, with the greater majority of people with schizophrenia showing abnormally large lateral ventricles (Shenton & Kubicki, 2009). Other investigations have compared brain structure among people with schizophrenia, their same-sex siblings who did not have schizophrenia, and healthy volunteers. Both those with schizophrenia and their otherwise unaffected siblings had enlargement of the third ventricle compared to the volunteers in the study, suggesting that the enlargement of ventricles may be related to susceptibility of schizophrenia (Staal et al., 2000). However, it seems that several brain sites are associated with the cognitive dysfunction seen in those with schizophrenia, especially the prefrontal cortex, various related cortical regions, and subcortical circuits, including the thalamus and the stratum (Shenton & Kubicki, 2009). Decreased brain volume in the temporal region suggests a relationship between the severity of auditory hallucinations and disorganized language (Gur & Pearlson, 1993) as well as blunted affect and motivation (Klausner, Sweeney, Deck, Hass, & Kelly, 1992). Other variations occur in areas pertaining to cognitive competency skills, levels of concentration, memory, and perception.

In addition, neuroimaging studies of studies of victims of sexual abuse and other traumas have sometimes reported findings similar to those found in psychotic patients, such as thinning of the corpus callosum, loss of volume in the anterior cingulate cortex (the collar-like structure surrounding the frontal part or anterior section of the corpus callosum), and reduced hippocampal volume (Bentall & Fernyhough, 2008). Many practitioners continue to believe schizophrenia is a disorder of the brain; however, no evidence of brain abnormality (structure or function) has been found common to those who have schizophrenia.

Biochemical theories suggest that the presence of neurotransmitters in the brain is clearly involved in the pathophysiology of schizophrenia, but their specific role remains undetermined. To briefly review, neurotransmitters are chemical substances (such as epinephrine or dopamine) that transmit nerve impulses across synapses to either inhibit or excite a target cell. Some researchers maintain schizophrenia may be caused by alterations in these neurochemical systems resulting from some other more fundamental pathophysiologic process occurring in four areas of the brain: limbic system, frontal lobes, temporal lobes, and basal ganglia. However, the association of a single area of the brain with the cause of this disorder is unlikely—in that, the four areas are so interconnected that dysfunction in one area often causes primary pathology in another.

There is some evidence that adversities may lead to cognitive biases and altered dopamine neurotransmission, a process that has been termed "sensitization" (Collip, Mylin-Germeys, & Van Os, 2008). For instance, it has long been known that stressful life events have been found to generally precede the onset of schizophrenia. Further, living in an urban environment is seen as another contributor (van Os, 2004). Stelten, Cantor-Graae, and Kahn (2007) point to a history of migration as yet another risk factor, specifically in those situations where the individual (or his or her family) has experienced psychosocial adversity, social defeat from being considered as an outsider, racial discrimination, family dysfunction, unemployment, and poor housing conditions.

THE ROLE OF DOPAMINE

The role of the neurotransmitter dopamine (a neurotransmitter found in the brain) remains the basis for one of the foremost and enduring biochemical theories regarding the etiology of schizophrenia. Because certain antipsychotic medications work by blocking the effect of the neurotransmitter dopamine, there has been much hypothesizing about it. The following discussion is a brief overview and is intended to familiarize the practitioner with the major concepts of the role of dopamine in schizophrenia.

The central nervous system depends on neurotransmitters to communicate—they are, in essence, chemical messengers. Through their effects on specific nerve circuits, these neurotransmitters can affect a person's mood, memory, and well-being. There are hundreds of substances known or suspected to be neurotransmitters, and one of the best-understood is dopamine (Wade & Tavris, 2010). There are several types of dopamine, whose effects are either excitatory (a voltage shift in a positive direction) or inhibitory (a voltage shift in a negative direction), depending on which receptor sites are activated. The simplest formulation of the dopamine hypothesis for schizophrenia points to the possibility that somehow the dopamine system is too active (or excitatory). Excessive dopamine may mediate the symptoms of auditory hallucinations or delusions, while deficient dopamine (or inhibitory) in cortical regions of the brain may mediate the negative symptoms of schizophrenia (such as the emotional blunting, social withdrawal, apathy, and so forth). Research evidence leads us to believe that schizophrenia in certain people is partially attributable to excessive dopamine activity, especially involving the D2 receptors (the group of dopamine receptors that are typically inhibitory) (Laurelle, Kegeles, & Abi-Dargham, 2003).

Although some dopamine sites may be overactive, a second type—prefrontal D1 receptors—has captured the interest of researchers. This dopamine site is in the part of the brain used for thinking and reasoning and may account for other symptoms common in schizophrenia (Koh, Bergson, Undie, Goldman-Rakic, & Lidow, 2003). What seems clear is that dopamine's involvement in the development of schizophrenia is more complicated than once thought.

Briefly, the human brain is made up of billions of neurons (basic building blocks of the nervous system), which all send or "fire" messages back and forth between each other. These messages are received from presynaptic neurons; they continue to cross over gaps and progress toward the synapse (space at the end of the neuron), moving onto a receptor, and finally are delivered to a postsynaptic neuron. The basic dopamine hypothesis does not really elaborate on whether dopaminergic hyperactivity is due to too much release of dopamine, too many dopamine receptors, hypersensitivity of the dopamine receptors to dopamine, or some combination of those mechanisms. Regardless of its role in schizophrenia, dopamine continues to be seen as an important neurotransmitter that is involved in the regulation of cognition, sensory processes, and mood.

There are two major limitations associated with the dopamine hypothesis. First, dopamine antagonists are effective in treating virtually all psychotic and severely agitated individuals, not just those diagnosed with schizophrenia. Other clinical investigations have been looking into several other neurotransmitters suspected of being involved in the pathophysiology of schizophrenia—for example, serotonin, acetylcholine, glutamate, and gamma aminobutyric acid (GABA). There is continued debate among some practitioners about whether the impact or presence of specific neurotransmitters can alone endorse an assessment of schizophrenia. There seems to be some evidence that dopaminergic hyperactivity is not seen uniquely in individuals with schizophrenia. The second major limitation associated with the dopamine hypothesis is that some electrophysiological data suggest that dopaminergic neurons may increase their firing rate in response to long-term exposure to antipsychotic drugs. A revised theory regarding dopamine is that the neurotransmitter itself is less important than is its role in helping to control information processing in the cortex (Murray, Lappin, & Di Forti, 2008).

Other neurotransmitters have been implicated in schizophrenia, including noradrenaline, serotonin, gamma aminobutyric acid, and glutamate (Carlsson, 2006; Craven, Priddle, Crow, & Esiri, 2005). Possibly these other neurotransmitters, especially serotonin, interact with dopamine and deficits in key brain areas help produce the symptoms of schizophrenia. Others suggest that less serotonin in the frontal cortex leads to more activity in this brain area and thus more dopamine activity (Alex, Yavanian, McFarlane, Pluto, & Pehek, 2005).

KEY FEATURES DEFINING THE SCHIZOPHRENIA SPECTRUM

There are a number of key features that define schizophrenia. They are:

- *Delusions*: Delusions are false and fixed beliefs based on incorrect deductions or misrepresentations in a person's reality. These beliefs are not considered as normative within the individual's cultural or religious group. The two most common types are persecutory delusions (belief that others intend harm) and grandiose delusions (belief that one is special, famous, or important). Referential delusions (the belief that certain gestures, comments, environmental cues and the like are directed to the person), erotomanic delusions (the erroneous belief that someone is in love with the person), nihilistic delusions (or the conviction that a major catastrophe will happen, and somatic delusions (a preoccupation with one's health) are also seen. There are a number of delusions that are clearly implausible and thus seen as bizarre. These include thought withdrawal (the belief that the person's thoughts have been removed from them by some kind of outside force, thought insertion (the belief that thoughts have been put into the person's mind), and delusions of control (where the person believes his or her body is being affected by some outside force). The practitioner can explore delusions by suggesting an alternative scenario to the individual, saying, for example, "Suppose those people who followed you were not going to harm you, but rather they were just going to the same place you were." If the individual cannot acknowledge the possibility of this alternative explanation, then chances are that the practitioner is seeing a delusion at work. Delusions are of major importance in understanding schizophrenia. These delusional beliefs are firmly maintained by the individual, despite evidence to the contrary. Following is a representative sample a series of questions aimed at exploring them further.

- *Grandiose Delusions*
  - Do you think you have exceptional talents, unique powers, or mysterious abilities that no one else has?
  - (If YES) Could you describe them? Could you tell me more about this?
  - Do you possess these special abilities during special times?
- *Persecutory delusions*
  - Do you think people are against you, following you, or trying to hurt you?
  - (If YES) Could you tell me more about that?
  - Why do you think people are out to get you?
  - Are people plotting against you?
  - Do they want to hurt you?
  - (If YES) Why do you think someone would want to hurt you?
  - When you notice this happening to you, what do you think this means?
- *Referential Delusions*
  - When you are watching television, reading a newspaper, or listening to the radio, do you believe that "they" are referring specifically to you? Or that there are special messages intended just for you to see or hear?
  - (If YES) What kinds of things have you noticed?
  - What does this mean to you?
  - Do you think that strangers in stores, at the mall, or in a movie theater take special notice of you or talk about you behind your back?
  - (If YES) How do you know this? What does this mean to you?
- *Thought Insertion*
  - Are there thoughts inside your head that have been placed there by somebody from the outside? (Be sure to clarify that you are referring to thoughts inserted by others.)
  - (If YES) Could you tell me more about where these thoughts come from?
  - Have you noticed there is a special time or place when this happens?

- *Hallucinations*: Hallucinations are experiences of sensory events in the absence of environmental stimulation. For an assessment of schizophrenia, the hallucination must be considered prominent. Auditory hallucinations or hearing voices is considered the most common feature of schizophrenia. These auditory hallucinations may be present in other mental disorders, but in schizophrenia the person typically talks *about*, as well as *to*, the imagined individual. Often these voices sound so real to the person that he or she is convinced that they are coming from outside—from hidden microphones, for example. The voices are often described as abusive and critical in nature, or they command the person to perform unpleasant or harmful tasks. Somatic or tactile hallucinations are considered the least common and include sensations similar to electrical tingling or burning sensations. I remember a former client who related feeling as if "a boa constrictor was slithering down inside my body. It went around my chest, and when it split in half one part went down my arms, and the other part went down my legs." Tactile and somatic hallucinations are important in the assessment process for schizophrenia because they occur in relatively few other psychiatric disorders.

- *Disorganized Thinking (Speech)*: Disorganized speech is not governed by logic. Sometimes it is exhibited in rhymes or puns; other times it may take the form of mimicking speech patterns of those around the person—he or she may copy the tone, words, or fragments of overheard conversations (echolalia). Sometimes the person's speech can be so disorganized that it is nearly incomprehensible (incoherence or "word salad"). Two other manifestations of disorganized speech include failure to answer specific questions (going off on a tangent or tangentiality) and the random or arbitrary leaping from topic to topic (derailment—interruptions to thought and jumping from one thought to another disconnected thought or loose associations). Needless to say, these patterns of speech complicate the person's ability to communicate with others. Other examples include condensing or combining words or inventing new words (neologism). Some may continuously repeat the same words or sentence (perseveration) or use rhyme or puns (clanging). Less severe forms of disorganized thinking or speech may occur during the prodromal or residual phases of the disorder. It is important to note that only speech that is seriously disorganized and extremely difficult to understand and/or interpret should be considered a symptom of schizophrenia. However, keep in mind that disorganized speech can be seen in other disorders such as delirium or dementia, and these other conditions must be ruled out.
- *Disorganized or Abnormal Motor Behavior (Including Catatonia)*: Disorganized behavior involves physical actions that do not appear to be goal directed—for example, taking off one's clothes in public, assuming or maintaining unusual postures, pacing excitedly, or moving fingers or extremities in idiosyncratic and repetitive ways. These forms of behavior are seen as severe and create a great deal of impairment to the individual; they are not simply odd or eccentric as in a tic or compulsion. Catatonic behavior is the person's decreased ability to react to his or her environment and manifests itself in several ways, such as in negativism (the resistance to instructions), maintaining a rigid or bizarre posture, mutism and stupor (a lack of verbal and motor responses), and catatonic excitement (purposeless and excessive motor activity without an obvious cause). Similar to disorganized speech, catatonic symptoms can be seen in other disorders such as substance intoxication, and those other conditions must also be ruled out.
- *Negative symptoms*: Negative symptoms are a significant part of the symptom picture for schizophrenia and consist of those characteristics that are notably

absent even though they are normally present in people's experience. For example, someone with schizophrenia may have a blunted affect instead of the full range of emotions evident in someone without a diagnosis. Two negative symptoms are particularly prominent: one is diminished emotional expression (characterized as a reduced expression of emotions seen in the person's face, eye contact, or intonation of speech [prosody]); and the other is avolition (a loss of goal-directed behavior). Flat affect is exhibited by gazing with "vacant eyes." The individual is seemingly unaffected by what is going on around him or her and displays little change in facial expressions. Often, inappropriate affect is displayed by laughing or crying at incongruous times. Avolition involves the inability to make goal-directed choices along with the expression of little or no interest in activities. The individual is generally disorganized, behaves inappropriately, and may be excessively controlled and rigid. Avolition can be seen by the person's indifference and unresponsiveness to even the most basic everyday activities, such as maintaining personal hygiene, and the inability to independently sustain other important self-care activities. Other negative symptoms include alogia, anhedonia, and asociality. Alogia involves a speech disturbance in which there is a lack of fluency and productivity of thought and speech or poverty in its content. Anhedonia involves the decreased ability to experience pleasure or recall previously pleasurable experiences. Asociality refers to the person's lack of interest in social interactions. Unfortunately, asociality could be an indicator of the individual's limited opportunities for social interactions. Overall, negative symptoms severely reduce the singular characteristics of an individual's personality.

Competency 2 a

Complicating the practitioner's ability to understand the spectrum of schizophrenia is the fact that many of the above-mentioned domain areas *can* be found as a part of the other psychotic disorders. To better understand an individual and his or her distinctive course of schizophrenia, the competency-based assessment encourages the practitioner to look at the person's capacity for interpersonal relationships, cultural influences, environmental and social factors, and coping resources.

Competency 7 c

Despite the reality that some people with schizophrenia can function productively, the symptom picture remains misunderstood, and it becomes important for the social worker to identify and articulate a client's strengths as well as recognize vulnerabilities. Attitudes about those with mental disorders have varied throughout history, but in all eras, people with schizophrenia have been maligned. For example, someone with schizophrenia is more likely to be harassed in public than a person without the diagnosis (Tarrier, Khan, Cater, & Picken, 2007). The diagnosis of schizophrenia burdens people who have to make their way in a society that views them as different or "of a less desirable kind" (Van Dorn, Swanson, Elbogen, & Swartz, 2005, p. 152). While hostility and aggression may be a part of the symptom picture supporting the diagnosis of schizophrenia, popular books, movies, and television portrayals have exploited this illness and contribute to the misinformation about it. Newspaper headlines reading "Ex-Mental Patient Goes on Wild Shooting Spree" may be factually accurate, but they foster a false picture that all people with schizophrenia should be considered dangerous. These accounts help perpetuate a detrimental and negative picture of everyone who suffers with a mental illness.

Schizophrenia interferes with almost every aspect of a person's intrapersonal functioning and interpersonal world. Associated features may well include social cognition deficits seen in the inability to infer the intentions or others, or the person might interpret irrelevant events as meaningful. The individual may have a reduced attention span and neurological soft signs could be evident; for example, impaired coordination or sensory integration. The person may experience trouble sleeping, especially when the onset of auditory hallucinations and delusions keep him or her awake. Vocational and functional abilities may also be compromised. Schizophrenia disrupts how the person sees his or her social environment, the manner in which they think, speak, and even move.

The emotional as well as financial aspects of this diagnosis take a tremendous toll on the individual and his or her family. Schizophrenia has a chronic course, and for most people, the symptoms come and go. A complex symptom picture characterizes schizophrenia—but there are specific patterns or features that tend to appear together, which generally includes three phases indicative of the schizophrenic cycle; a prodromal phase, an active or acute phase (characterized by delusions, hallucinations, or disorganized speech), and a residual phase in which the prevailing features are in remission. They are:

1. The prodromal phase refers to the period before the features of schizophrenia become very apparent; this is the period of time during which the person's level of functioning deteriorates.
2. The active phase, wherein the disorder persists for at least 6 months with the individual exhibiting psychotic features (e.g., hallucinations, delusions, and/or grossly disorganized speech and behavior) or negative features such as flat affect or avolition for at least 1 month during that period.
3. The residual phase follows the active phase. This is sometimes considered a "filler" category because people either have been helped successfully or have improved to the point where they no longer have enough features for the practitioner to ascertain the presence of schizophrenia.

The following metaphor may be helpful in visualizing the active and residual phases. Imagine for a moment that you have a full glass of milk in front of you. Everyone can easily identify it as a glass of milk because of its color, texture, smell, and taste. This could be considered analogous to the active phase of schizophrenia; that is, the individual has all the attributes characteristic of schizophrenia. Further, imagine this glass of milk has now been emptied. Enough of a residue remains so that one can still identify its prior contents as milk. This residual phase suggests that the person has some remaining features but not to the extent that he or she could be fully assessed for schizophrenia.

CULTURAL CONSIDERATIONS

Competency 2 a

Schizophrenia is known around the world and in most cultures and socioeconomic groups. Kearney and Trull (2012) observe that the diagnosis is more common in developing countries and in immigrants and migrant workers than in developed countries. When psychosis does occur, it is not viewed as a normal phenomenon and is always seen as an indication of some profound mental process. A cultural frame of reference expands the conceptualization of mental illness and sets the stage for biases when working with those diagnosed with schizophrenia. For example, mental illness can be conceived as "bad character," the way a person is raised, or as God's will (Van Dorn et al., 2005). In some industrialized countries, researchers contend that schizophrenia is a culturally created label for those people who behave in ways that are outside accepted cultural norms (Barlow & Durand, 2012). Conversely, labeling someone may predispose them to display symptoms consistent with the disorder. Angermeyer and Schulze (2001) note that someone who was just diagnosed may withdraw from others to avoid discrimination, experience a lowered sense of self-esteem and quality of life, become depressed or angry, and act somewhat oddly. The practitioner pays attention to the extent to which the societal values may oppress, marginalize, or alienate his or her client. Additionally, as a consequence of being seen as somehow "different," clients may be misjudged and not seen for their full potential.

As part of the competency-based assessment, the practitioner should take into consideration how mental illness is perceived within the person's culture of origin as well as how it is seen in the current culture and the diverse ways of understanding a diagnosis. Also helpful is to examine the composition, structure of social and family support, and level of social communication. There are cultural variations in how families react to a member with schizophrenia, but their reactions do not contribute to the cause of the disorder (Weisman de Mamani et al., 2007). Social support, particularly attachment to others and reassurance of worth, is the best protective factor in mental health, whereas critical and hostile environments provide additional stressors that can, in turn, contribute to more relapses (Caron, Latimer, & Tousignant, 2002; Caron, Lecompte, Stip, & Renaud, 2005; van Os & Allardyce, 2009). Given the symptom picture of schizophrenia, it is easy to understand how this individual can challenge the resources of family members regardless of their culture and social structure. The case of Rudy Rosen presented later in this chapter illustrates some of these challenges.

Although at least 50 percent of individuals with schizophrenia improve significantly with treatment, some people experience the disorder as a chronic illness characterized by frequent hospitalizations and/or incarcerations—with attendant social and/or legal consequences. The overall course tends to be a progressive deterioration of functions, at least during the first few years. This includes both the exacerbations of symptoms and the partial remissions. It is this small group of chronic sufferers who often come to the practitioner's attention. The general outlook for these individuals tends to be guarded, as the disorder can be quite devastating in terms of impaired interpersonal and social functioning. Suicide, depression, substance abuse, and social withdrawal often coexist (Compton, Weiss, West, & Kaslow, 2005; Jobe & Harrow, 2005).

There are several factors that have some bearing on a person's prognosis. According to Caron, Mercier, Diaz, and Martin (2005), a negative predictor for someone's future adaptation is linked to hospitalization at a young age when the first diagnosis of schizophrenia has been made. Other factors related to a poorer prognosis are an insidious or slow onset of psychosis; a lack of awareness of or poor insight into the disorder (anosognosia); poor early adjustment; delusions; flat affect and other negative symptoms; and substantial impairment after the first episode of psychotic symptoms (Elmsley, Chiliza, & Schoerman, 2008; Ho, Nopoulos, Flaum, Arndt, & Andreasen, 2004; Malla & Payne, 2005). The outlook is brighter where the person receives effective treatment soon after an episode of strange behavior, has extensive social support, or when a person's cognitive functioning is still relatively good.

Features that suggest a chronic course with schizophrenia include an insidious onset; previous personal or family history of schizophrenia; evidence of social withdrawal; inappropriate or shallow affect; the prior assessment for schizoid or schizotypal personality disorders, or the other psychotic disorders of schizoaffective and schizophreniform disorder; and difficulties conforming to treatment regimens. Veen (2005) notes that the apparent prevalence of schizophrenia rises over time in people with other psychotic disorders, and they tend to retain the diagnosis of schizophrenia longer term.

Prevailing Pattern

The lifetime prevalence of schizophrenia is approximately 0.3 percent to 0.7 percent (APA, 2013). It has been suggested that schizophrenia affects men and women equally, but evidence indicates that it occurs slightly more often in men (Luoma, Hakko, Ollinen, Jarvelin, & Lindeman, 2008). Additionally, important gender differences are noted in relation to the age of onset. In particular, males tend to have symptoms at a younger age than females. With an earlier start, this means that men will have more severe symptoms (APA, 2013; Dickerson, 2007). It is not known why this happens. Although the disorder can occur at any age, the median age of onset is 22 years. To fully understand the symptom picture and the influence of the client's social environment, the competency-based assessment provides a framework for the social worker to take into account information about a client's biological, social, cultural, and psychological development.

Differential Assessment

Competency 7 b

When considering schizophrenia, two diagnostic criteria must be met over much of the time of a period of at least 1 month, with a significant impact on the individual's social and occupational functioning for at least 6 months. The person *has to be* suffering from delusions, hallucinations, or disorganized speech (i.e., frequent derailment). A second symptom could be negative symptoms (such as diminished emotional expression or avolition, or severely disorganized or catatonic behavior. Previous criteria giving particular weight to bizarre delusions or Schneiderian hallucinations have been removed (Tandon et al., 2013).

As a part of the assessment process, the practitioner excludes other disorders, specifically schizoaffective and mood disorder. They are ruled out because either (1) no major depressive or manic episodes have occurred concurrently with the active phase symptoms; or (2) if mood episodes have occurred during active phase symptoms, their total duration has been brief—relative to the duration of the active and residual periods. The practitioner also considers a substance/general medical exclusion. In particular, the disturbance is not due to the direct physiological effects of a substance (i.e., a drug of abuse or a medication) or a general medical condition. Keep in mind the relationship of schizophrenia to a pervasive developmental disorder. That is, if there is a history of autistic disorder or a communication disorder of childhood, the additional diagnosis of schizophrenia is made *only if* prominent delusions or hallucinations are also present for at least a month (or less, if successfully treated).

After a period of a year with the diagnosis of schizophrenia, the following course specifiers may be considered as long as they are not inconsistent with the symptom picture:

- First episode, currently in acute episode—This specifier applies to the first evidence of schizophrenia and acute episode refers to the time period where diagnostic criteria have been met.
- First episode, currently in partial remission—Partial remission is considered when there has been improvement after a pervious episode of the illness.
- First episode, currently in full remission—This specifier addresses the time period following an episode of schizophrenia when there are no symptoms present at the time.
- Multiple episodes, currently in acute episode—This applies to the presence of multiple episodes; for example, the person may have had a first episode followed by a remission and then a minimum of one relapse.
- Multiple episodes, currently in partial remission—The person has had multiple episodes of schizophrenia but there currently has been improvement after a previous episode of the illness.
- Multiple episodes, currently in full remission—Full remission is indicated when there is no evidence of schizophrenia despite a history of the illness.
- Continuous—This specifier applies when symptoms of schizophrenia remain for the majority of the course of the illness, with subthreshold symptom periods being very brief (relative to the overall course).
- Unspecified—This specifier is used when there is an underdetermined course.

Competency 8 b

The DSM-5 offers a number of emerging measures for further research and clinical evaluation (APA, 2013). Among them is the Clinician-Rated Dimensions of Psychosis Symptom Survey (CRDPSS) intended to help the practitioner with treatment planning and decision making (King, 2014). Essentially, the CRDPSS is an eight-item measure designed to assess the severity of symptoms experienced by the individual in the past 7 days across the psychotic disorders, including schizophrenia. These symptoms include: delusions, hallucination, disorganized speech, abnormal psychomotor behavior, negative symptoms (such as restricted emotional expression [avolition]), impaired cognition, depression, and mania. The practitioner rates symptoms on a five-point scale ranging from not present (0), equivocal where severity or duration is not sufficient to be considered psychosis (1), mild or little pressure to act or not very bothered by symptoms (2), moderate or some pressure to respond or somewhat bothered by symptoms (3), and severe or severe pressure to respond to voices or very bothered by voices (4).

An easy way to summarize the diagnostic criteria for schizophrenia is in terms of the presence of at least: (1) a psychotic factor such as delusions, (2) hallucinations, or (3) disorganized speech. The practitioner may also see disorganized or catatonic behavior or negative symptoms. For a significant portion of time since the onset of the disorder, one or more major areas of social functioning will have deteriorated, such as occupational, social, or self-care. Duration includes continuous signs and symptoms that must persist for at least 6 months. During this period, at least 1 month must include features of psychosis (or the active phase). Keep in mind that periods of either prodomal or residual traces are not enough to represent a full-blown episode of schizophrenia.

The following vignette provides an opportunity to become familiar with the specific features of delusions and hallucinations that are a part of schizophrenia and is intended to help practitioners differentiate among their various presentations. The case illustrates the influence of the multiple factors that help individualize a client's experience with schizophrenia. We now turn to Rudy Rosen's story, which includes details of the challenges he and his family have encountered and the effects of frequent hospitalizations, medication, and chronic relapse.

CASE The Case of Rudy Rosen

Rudy Rosen is a 76-year-old white male who is currently hospitalized because of a recent suicide attempt. Persecutory hallucinations are reflected in his statement to the social worker on admission: "My medication is poisoned by my wife." He was escorted to a large, metropolitan psychiatric hospital by a mobile crisis unit because he refused to admit himself voluntarily for observation.

During the intake process, Mr. Rosen's wife, Ruth, revealed a history that began approximately 25 years ago when her husband was first diagnosed with schizophrenia, paranoid type. "That statement changed my life," Mrs. Rosen told the social worker. At that time, Rudy had been employed as an auto mechanic. According to Ruth, 1 day he suddenly and without warning began to show some bizarre symptoms. Ruth remembered her husband saying, "Our home telephone is bugged, and the people at work tampered with it." Rudy accused some of the other mechanics of stealing his tools, and he claimed several people were following him home and plotting to harm him. His wife noted that soon after, Rudy began accusing her and their two children of plotting against him as well. However, his rationale for this blaming attitude remained vague. She went on, "Rudy ran around the house, screaming that I thought he was crazy, and that I am working with the police and his boss to put him in the 'crazy' hospital."

During Rudy's initial hospitalization 25 years ago, he had a difficult time understanding his illness or why he had been put in the "hospital for crazy people." Rudy did not believe what the psychiatrists, social workers, and his family were trying to tell him about his illness. He remained steadfastly convinced that people were plotting against him, his phone was bugged, and his medicine could not help him because "it's poisoned." Rudy began a 6-week trial course of Thorazine, his symptoms abated, and he was discharged from the hospital. Rudy did relatively well for a long period of time, although he did have several episodes of symptoms after he refused to take his medications. Whenever Rudy's symptoms became worse, his wife brought him to the hospital, where he was usually readmitted, particularly when he was actively suicidal.

The social worker reviewed Rudy's chart and found a family history noting that he was the youngest of five children. Three of his siblings are still living: a brother, Harry, aged 90; and two sisters, Natalie, 85, and Miriam, 87. The details about Rudy's oldest sister are vague; one sentence notes she died while hospitalized in a mental institution more than 50 years ago. Apparently, she had been hospitalized for what was termed "depression" following the birth of her only child. Further exploration of family history reveals that Rudy's mother was described by almost everyone in the family as being "very strange." His mother accused people of being against her and out to hurt her, and those around her reported that she "heard voices that were not heard by anyone else." Rudy's father and older siblings had raised him because the mother was considered "unfit and crazy." Of noteworthy physical importance, both of Rudy's eardrums were punctured from a serious infection when he was 5 years old. The etiology remains unknown; however, he was treated for many years, including several surgeries for chronic ear infections. This left Rudy with a very significant permanent hearing deficit. Rudy also had a history of rheumatoid heart disease as a youngster. Rudy's wife reports that one of his sisters, Miriam, exhibits "bizarre-like" behavior. However, no diagnosis has been determined, and the 87-year-old sister remains under the care of a full-time paid nursing companion.

Rudy and Ruth have been married a little over 55 years, and they have two children—a daughter who is age 54 and a son who is 50. Both children are professionals, and they live in the same community with their parents. The Rosens have six grandchildren and one great-grandchild. Rudy is retired, with no outside hobbies, interests, or friends. He is in poor cardiac health, having had a quadruple heart bypass 5 years ago. In addition, he has a pacemaker, suffers from congestive heart disease (CHD), cataracts, and chronic ear infections. Rudy experiences severe tardive dyskinesia (TD) from his many years of taking high doses of antipsychotic drugs. His symptoms include hand tremors, tongue thrusting, and unsteady gait. In addition, Rudy takes a cadre of daily medications including Coumadin (a blood thinner); Resperdal (for his psychosis); Valium (for sleep); Cogentin (for TD); Wellbutrin, Paxil, and Buspar; and Synthyroid (to treat his slow metabolism).

Ruth is a retired office manager. She looked quite tired and sad during the intake interview, and commented that she had retired to become "Rudy's full-time nurse, appointment keeper, and jailer." Although she and Rudy had a "good marriage" despite his illness, she had clung to the hope that their golden years would be filled with quality time spent together going on vacations, family activities, and fun. She always thought that if he took good care of himself and took his medications that the schizophrenia would abate. Instead, her days are spent driving Rudy from doctor to doctor, to the dentist, or to hearing aid technicians. His behavior makes it difficult for him to keep any one doctor for an extended period of time. With a sigh, Ruth explains that this is because he accuses them of "cheating, giving him the wrong medicine, or trying to kill him." Rudy changes doctors and dentists very often.

Ruth no longer allows him to take his medications without close supervision. She recently found evidence (pills on the bathroom floor) that he sometimes flushes his medications down the toilet. She is not sure how long this has been going on but suspects it is what led to this current hospitalization. He again began to have active signs and symptoms of delusions and hallucinations.

Rudy Rosen's DSM Diagnosis Is as Follows:

Schizophrenia, multiple episodes, currently in acute episode

Assessment Summary Rudy's life, as depicted in this vignette, illustrates the signs and symptoms of what schizophrenia can look like over time. Delusions and hallucinations have been a consistent part of his symptom picture. Although his initial onset occurred late in life, the course illustrated in this example is chronic. However, Rudy was able to have periods where he functioned fairly well. Rudy's interpersonal and social functioning problems have been exacerbated over his lifetime, especially when he neglects taking his medication. It is important to note the impact this disorder has had on his family. Rudy's wife has borne the emotional and financial brunt of his illness over the past 25 years. While his children were growing up, they constantly had to cope with the loss of a meaningful parental relationship, with their father's bizarre behavior, and with his frequent hospitalizations.

Table 3.4 Clinician-Rated Dimensions of Psychosis Symptom Survey for Rudy Rosen

Domain	Score
Hallucinations	4
Delusions	4
Disorganized Speech	0
Abnormal Psychomotor Behavior	0
Negative Symptoms	0
Impaired Cognition	0
Depression	0
Mania	0

If the social worker were to use the CRDPSS in Rudy's recent hospitalization, his scores might look like those shown in Table 3.4.

The scores highlight Rudy's current symptom picture as seen in the higher scores for active signs and symptoms of delusions and hallucinations leading to his recent hospitalization. While Mrs. Rosen is not clear about how long her husband had not been taking his medications, she suspects it is what has led to his current hospitalization for a suicide attempt. His CRDPSS scores indicate the highest scores in hallucinations and delusions, symptom domains that may need to be more closely monitored over the course of treatment. Ritsner and colleagues (2013) tested the CRDPSS and found that it has sound psychometric properties, making it a valuable tool to track a client's symptom changes over time. Considering Rudy's wife did not notice when he stopped his medications until his delusions and hallucinations became a problem, using the CRDPSS to track his symptom severity over time might be a useful treatment adjunct. In particular, if Rudy continued to receive high scores on these two particular domains, then the practitioner might consider further assessment and revisions to his treatment plan.

Competency 7 a

This case vignette describes how a social worker would look to accessing coping strategies that serve to reinforce and improve Rudy's (as well as the family's) adaptation to life circumstance, situations, and events. The competency-based assessment examines effective problem solving and viable alternatives. What has helped Rudy cope with such a devastating mental disorder has been the devotion shown by his wife, Ruth. They have been married for 55 years and, according to his wife, "It is a very good and satisfying marriage." In addition, Rudy is emotionally supported by his children and his grandchildren. There have been long periods of time when Rudy took his medication and experienced periods of remission. During those times, the family had a sense of cohesiveness, laying the foundation for a shared memory of "normalcy" that seemed helpful during the times when Rudy relapsed. Figure 3.1 illustrates the interaction of the biological, psychological, and social variables in Rudy Rosen's life.

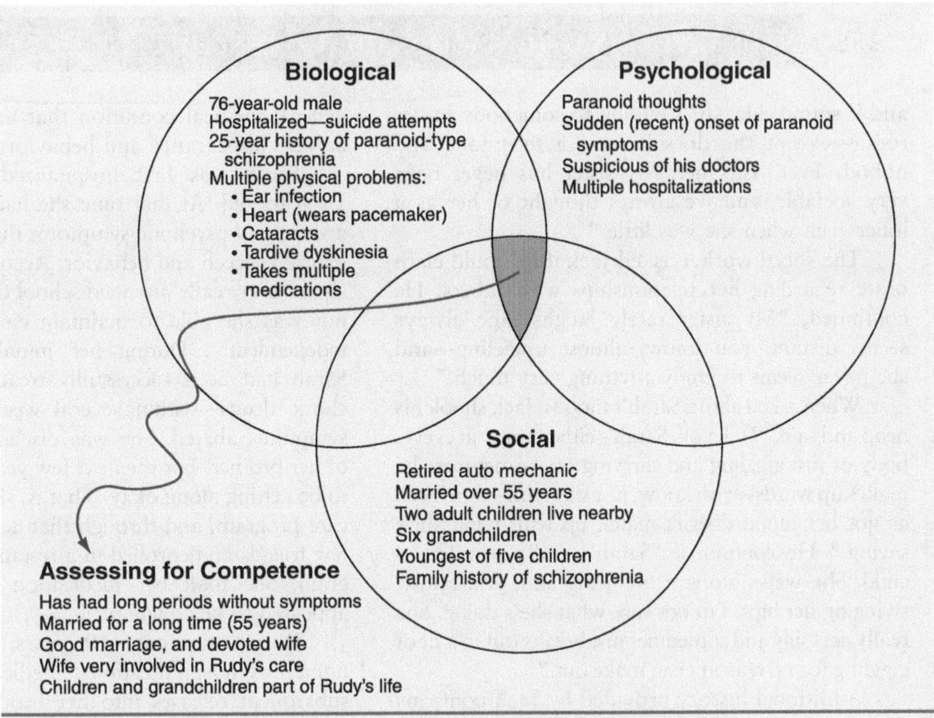

FIGURE 3.1 › SCHIZOPHRENIA
The interactions of the biological, psychological, and social variables in Rudy Rosen's life.

The following case highlights a number of other symptoms found in schizophrenia, in particular disorganized speech, disorganized behavior, and flat or inappropriate affect such as silliness or laughter without apparent reason. In this case story, hallucinations and delusions are present, but they are not organized around a central theme as they are with Rudy Rosen—they are more fragmented and disjointed. Pay particular attention to the onset and duration of symptoms. This client, Sarah MacDonald, shows early signs of difficulty with life problems and, like Rudy Rosen, the course of the illness tends to be chronic.

CASE — THE CASE OF SARAH MACDONALD

Sarah is a 30-year-old African American woman who looks a lot younger than her stated age. She was brought to the hospital emergency room by her brother, Jack, who was not sure how many times his sister had previously been admitted to the psychiatric unit, "but it's been a lot of times." Sarah has lived with her brother, his wife, and their two children during the past 10 years. Jack stated, "Most times things around the house are all right, but when Sarah starts her crazy stuff, things get pretty chaotic."

Jack added that recently he has become more fearful for the safety of his two children. He was unable to be specific, but claims that "Sarah stays in her room banging her closets and dresser drawers open and closed all day. She throws things around,

CASE The Case of Sarah MacDonald (Continued)

and it sounds like she's talking to somebody in her room—except she doesn't have a telephone and nobody ever visits her. My sister has never been very sociable, and we always thought of her as a loner even when she was little."

The social worker asked Jack if he could elaborate regarding her relationships with others. He continued, "My sister rarely laughs. She always seems distant, you know, almost unfeeling—and she never seems to enjoy anything very much."

When asked about Sarah's moods, Jack shook his head and said, "I tell you, Sarah's either angry at everybody or just giggling and carrying on. Sometimes she makes up words—you know, just silly stuff—but often as not her mood doesn't match up with what she's saying." He continued, "Sarah's really just like a child. She walks along a bouncing and, you know, swinging her hips. I'm not sure what she's doing. She really acts silly and sometimes just breaks out in a fit of giggling for no reason I can make out."

Additional history provided by Jack confirms that Sarah abruptly stopped taking her medications 6 weeks ago; her prescriptions include clozapine (Clorazil), clonazepam (Klonopin), and alprazolam (Xanax). Soon after discontinuing her medication, she began to hear voices again, act bizarre, and neglect her physical appearance. She has sometimes disappeared from the house for weeks at a time, but eventually the police pick her up "wandering the street." There is no known history of drug or alcohol abuse or other general medical condition that might account for Sarah's appearance and behavior.

Sarah was first hospitalized when she was 18 years old. At that time she had been exhibiting a variety of psychotic symptoms that included disorganized speech and behavior. According to Jack, his sister never really attended school on a regular basis, nor was she able to maintain employment or live independently. During her initial hospitalization, Sarah had been successfully treated with antipsychotic drugs—within several weeks her psychotic symptoms abated. She was discharged to the care of her brother. For the next few years, Sarah seemed to be getting along okay. That is, she attended a day care program, and through that activity she made a few friends and enrolled in a restaurant worker program. She took her medication consistently and appeared to be coping well.

During the past 10 years, Sarah has had numerous hospitalizations, medication trials, and subsequent releases into her brother's care. Once Sarah was home, she would only sporadically take her medication, ultimately becoming symptomatic and disorganized again. During this current admission, Sarah's speech made little sense and was interspersed with frequent rhyming. Sometimes she would make sounds, rather than articulate specific or meaningful words. She was involuntarily admitted for 3 days, then discharged with medications and a scheduled follow-up visit in the hospital's outpatient department.

Sarah MacDonald's DSM Diagnosis Is as Follows:

Schizophrenia, multiple episodes, currently in acute episode

Assessment Summary Nothing in Sarah's history suggests a general medical condition. Although her affect had been described as flat, she does not exhibit anything remotely similar to the severely depressed mood of a major depressive disorder with psychotic features. Sarah has never expressed suicidal ideation, nor has she had any symptoms suggestive of manic-type features. The fact that these features have persisted longer than 6 months rules out schizophreniform disorder or brief psychotic disorder. Sarah's personal appearance, social behavior, pronounced thought disorder, negative symptoms, poor hygiene, social withdrawal, poor rapport, and emotional responses are seen as inappropriate—all of which contribute to the assessment of schizophrenia. The vignette describes behaviors that include incoherent speech, inappropriate affect, auditory hallucinations, grossly disorganized behavior, and an onset that occurred at an early age (she was 18 when first hospitalized).

Competency 7 a

Despite Sarah's struggle with a serious diagnosis and the unmistakable impairment in her overall level functioning, the competency-based assessment explores potential strengths and resources evident over time. Figure 3.2 shows the interactions of the biological, psychological, and social variables in Sarah's life. The most important resource she has is her brother, who is involved actively in her life. Even though Jack is concerned for his own family's safety, he continues to take care of her. He provides her with housing, attempts to make sure she takes her medication on a regular basis, brings her to therapy appointments, and watches for possible signs of relapse.

The competency-based assessment involves a careful evaluation of the client by the practitioner and by what others in the client's social world have observed. As we have seen, the assessment carefully explores thoughts, speech, perception, affect, psychomotor activity, and interpersonal functioning. The following case of Joey Esterson provides an example of another noteworthy symptom to consider—the presence of catatonia. What distinguishes Joey's symptom picture is his abnormal and striking physical movements—or complete lack of physical movements.

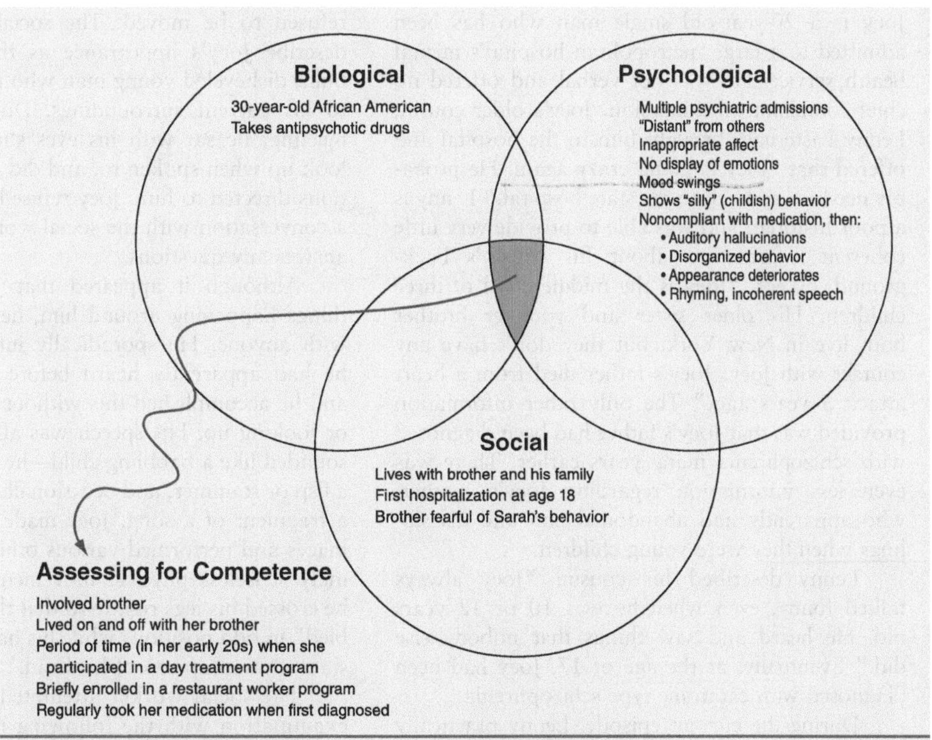

FIGURE 3.2 › SCHIZOPHRENIA
The interactions of the biological, psychological, and social variables in Sarah MacDonald's life.

The practitioner likely will easily recognize psychomotor disturbances, which alternate between the extremes of excitement and stupor. Because of this volatility, someone with the catatonic subtype may require medical supervision to prevent injury to him- or herself or to others. Clients with catatonia may be unable to eat or drink on their own—even the process of normal body elimination may require monitoring. In addition, these individuals may experience complications from untreated malnutrition, dehydration, electrolyte disturbances, or exhaustion.

At times, the person's physical motor activity may appear to be "speeded up," but the more typical catatonic behavior is a slow, retarded, or stupor-like state. The amount of activity generally ranges between extremes of seemingly driven agitation (as in an excited catatonic state) to a withdrawn and inactive state usually associated with catatonic stupor. Several characteristics usually dominate an individual's behavior. They may, for example, adopt and maintain rigid postures for hours at a time, assume bizarre positions, appear to be in a stupor, and/or become mute, which is a particularly common display. The person is seemingly oblivious to the external world, and he or she may resist being moved by others. Another pattern is rapid alternation between excitement and immobility.

CASE THE CASE OF JOEY ESTERSON

Joey is a 20-year-old single man who has been admitted to a large metropolitan hospital's mental health service. He was not verbal and offered no chief complaint on admission. Joey's older cousin, Lenny Pasternak, brought him to the hospital and offered that "Joey is going crazy again. He probably needs to go back to the state hospital." Lenny is a poor historian and was able to provide very little coherent information about his cousin's background, except, "Joey is the middle child of three children. His older sister and younger brother both live in New York, but they don't have any contact with Joey. Joey's father died from a heart attack 5 years ago." The only other information provided was that Joey's father had been diagnosed with schizophrenia many years earlier. There was even less information regarding Joey's mother, who apparently had abandoned him and his siblings when they were young children.

Lenny described his cousin: "Joey always talked funny, even when he was 10 or 12 years old. He heard and saw things that nobody else did." Eventually, at the age of 17, Joey had been diagnosed with catatonic type schizophrenia.

During the current episode, Lenny practically had to carry Joey into the hospital—Joey would only walk on the outside arches of his feet, and he refused to be moved. The social worker's notes describe Joey's appearance as that of a slightly built, disheveled young man who paid no attention to his current surroundings. During their initial meeting, he sat with his eyes shut tight, did not look up when spoken to, and did not answer questions directed to him. Joey refused to participate in a conversation with the social worker, and did not answer any questions.

Although it appeared that Joey understood things happening around him, he did not interact with anyone. He sporadically introduced phrases he had apparently heard before into his speech, and he accomplished this without opening his eyes or looking up. His speech was affected so that he sounded like a babbling child—he often spoke with a lisp or stammer, and occasionally burst forth with a fragment of a song. Joey made many facial grimaces and performed various other kinds of seemingly senseless physical movements. For example, he crossed his legs rigidly so that they were "assembled" in odd positions while his hands were in constant motion on top of his head.

The social worker attempted a mental status examination with the following results: Joey was admitted in a semi-mute state; and very little could be explored regarding his thought content, cognitive processes, insight, or judgment. Joey was retained at the hospital involuntarily for a 72-hour period. During that time, he remained essentially motionless, seated in a chair for many hours at a time. This practitioner noted that Joey showed evidence of a noticeable tremor in his extremities, a common sign of agitation. In addition, when Joey's arms or legs were placed in any position (for example, extended straight out), he maintained this position for a long period of time—even after being told he could resume his former position. If others attempted to bend Joey's extremities, he resisted. If Joey was approached from one side of his body, he gradually would turn his head away in order to look in the opposite direction. In addition, Joey wrinkled his nose, made twitching movements with his mouth, and pursed his lips for no apparent reason. These purposeless movements often lasted over several seconds and were not accompanied by any other motions of the tongue, which might be indicative of the effects of tardive dyskinesia.

Joey Esterson's DSM Diagnosis Is as Follows:

Catatonia associated with schizophrenia, multiple episodes, currently in acute episode

Competency 8 c

Assessment Summary In this case vignette, the practitioner's consultation with other medical professionals is underscored. The competency-based assessment model includes attention to ruling out general medical conditions when considering schizophrenia. In Joey's situation, there was no evidence of medical disorders (such as epilepsy and/or certain strokes) that could have produced or mimicked his catatonic behavior. The practitioner in this case referred Joey for a complete general medical and neurological evaluation to rule out other disorders. It is expected that a laboratory inquiry, including urine and blood analysis for toxic substances and drug(s) of abuse, will be conducted. There is one major source of support in Joey's social environment, his cousin Lenny. This relative not only brought Joey to the hospital, but has also cared for him for most of his life. Despite being abandoned at an early age by his mother, Joey continues to be looked after by Lenny, who expresses concern and apparently cares for his cousin. Figure 3.3 shows the interactions of the biological, psychological, and social variables in Joey Esterson's life.

Reflecting on the case of Joey Esterson, keep in mind that catatonia was used as a specifier along with his diagnosis of schizophrenia. However, catatonia can be used in the context of several other mental disorders (i.e., neurodevelopmental, bipolar, depressive disorders) or due to a medical condition. The following discussion addresses how you would differentiate among the different presentations of catatonia.

CATATONIA AS A SPECIFIER AND AS A DISORDER

In addition to symptoms supporting the diagnosis of schizophrenia, Joey Esterson demonstrates other important characteristics such as muteness, negativism, catatonic excitement, posturing, waxy flexibility, and facial grimacing. Much like Joey, the bearing and manner of the person with catatonia is often described as artificial and stilted. He or she will spontaneously pose or display bizarre, inappropriate silliness and "odd" mannerisms (for example, use facial grimaces or make silly faces).

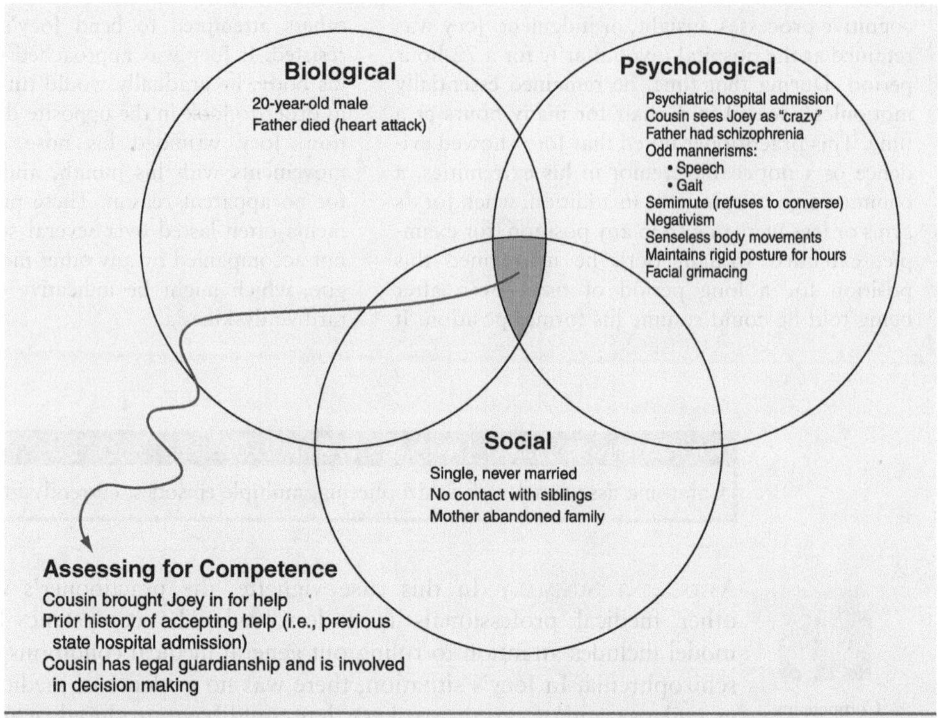

FIGURE 3.3 ❯ Schizophrenia
The interactions of the biological, psychological, and social variables in Joey Esterson's life.

These strange postures can be held for very long periods of time, making the person look like a figure in a wax museum. This behavior is referred to as **posturing**. Someone else may try to manipulate or move the individual's limbs, but once moved, the limbs can then remain fixed for hours or days. This is referred to as **waxy flexibility**. Such disturbances of volition include negativism, which is characterized by an almost mulish refusal to follow any course of action suggested or expected. This negativism is sometimes passive (e.g., if food is served to the person and they do not eat it or if someone asks a question and the person does not answer); other times it may be active.

The person's negativism is characterized as active if, for example, he or she resists being moved out of a rigid posture. The person may also repeat or mimic spoken words of others (echolalia); for example, when asked a question, he or she repeats it over and over, which can sometimes go on for an hour or more. **Echopraxia** is mimicking the physical gestures and movements of others (similar to a pantomime). This behavior is not intended to mock and may continue long after the other person has left the room. Echolalia and echopraxia are seen as involuntary and meaningless repetitions of the words and actions of others.

Certain mannerisms often have special meaning to the individual with catatonia. This may take the form of seemingly purposeless repetitive movements such as folding a piece of paper along the same creases until it disintegrates. These types of movement are referred to as stereotypy or stereotyped behaviors, and they commonly involve the entire body (the person may rock or sway, for example). Although these behaviors have some special significance to the client, the meaning is generally not discernible to others. When asked, "Why are you folding this piece of paper over and over again?" the person will offer no explanation.

An assessment for *catatonia associated with another mental disorder* (catatonia specifier) or due to another medical condition should include *at least three or more* of the following features:

- Stupor or motor immobility
- Cataplexy or a sudden and transient episode of paralysis (with no loss of consciousness) and affecting nearly all voluntary muscles
- Waxy flexibility, or a slight, even resistance to posturing by another (usually the practitioner)
- Mutism, or a deficit of communication through speech or interaction with others
- Negativism
- Posturing
- Mannerisms, or peculiar or odd behaviors evidenced by posturing, stereotypes, or mannerisms
- Stereotypy
- Agitation that is not influenced by external stimuli
- Grimacing
- Echolalia
- Echopraxia

As seen in Joey Esterson's diagnosis, the practitioner includes the name of the mental disorder. Evidence from the person's history, examination, or laboratory findings support the diagnosis of a medical condition. Here, too, the name of the medical condition is listed along with the presence of catatonia for a diagnosis of *catatonic disorder due to another medical condition.* We see no evidence of a medical condition in Joey's story. When symptoms of either a mental or medical disorder are unclear or there is insufficient evidence to support a more definitive symptom picture, the practitioner considers making the diagnosis of *unspecified catatonia.*

THE IMPACT OF SCHIZOPHRENIA: SUICIDE, DEPRESSION, AND SUBSTANCE USE

Suicide is a profoundly serious complication associated with schizophrenia. Unfortunately, these individuals see suicide as the only reasonable alternative to living with this devastating and chronic disorder. People with schizophrenia often lead lonely, isolated lives, and the disorder itself makes them highly suspicious and/or ambivalent in their relationships with others. Their behavior appears erratic and inconsistent. They have major problems relating to others and have little insight into their problems (Caron, Mercier, Diaz, & Martin, 2005). As seen in Sarah MacDonald's story, they frequently demonstrate either a strong dependency on familiar people or become bothersome, annoying, or intrusive to strangers. Real friendships rarely exist. The content of delusions and hallucinations usually frightens, estranges, or alienates others. Rudy Rosen, for instance, believes his wife is attempting to poison him. Those at a higher risk for suicide tend to be single, unemployed, and socially isolated males (Hawton, Sutton, Haw, Sinclair, & Deeks, 2005; Palmer, Pankratz, & Bostwick, 2005). Fortunately, both Sarah and Rudy have family members in their lives who mitigate the effects of their troubled interpersonal relationships.

Other disorders commonly associated with schizophrenia are mood, especially depression, and the substance-related disorders (APA, 2013; Freudenreich, Holt, Cather, & Goff, 2007). Depression may develop either before or after someone is diagnosed with schizophrenia. When depression develops before the onset of schizophrenia, it may help to trigger psychotic symptoms. Alternatively, the onset of psychotic symptoms could lead to a downward spiral in a person's functioning involving problems such as losing his or her job that later causes someone to become depressed (Rosen, Miller, D'Andrea, McGlashan, & Woods, 2006).

The presence of comorbid substance use disorders exacerbates problems already associated with the course of schizophrenia—including increased hospitalizations; homelessness; violence; family, emotional, and financial strain; and noncompliance with treatment modalities (Kaplan & Sadock, 2008). Substance abuse among those with schizophrenia symptoms is common, but whether stressful life events and drug use trigger psychotic symptoms or whether the symptoms develop afterward is not clear. What we do know is that some may use marijuana or other drugs to cope with their psychotic symptoms (Henquet, Murray, Linszen, & van Os, 2005). "Schizophrenia is a complex syndrome that inevitably has a devastating effect on the lives of the person affected and on family members. ... Society often devalues these individuals" (Barlow & Durand, 2012, p. 469). The prevailing consensus is that schizophrenia is more complicated than other disorders because of the combination of social and emotional factors that play a large role in determining its outcome.

In sum, schizophrenia seen as the more severe and longer lasting condition. We now turn to delusional disorder, where symptoms, primarily delusions, are present for 1 month or longer.

DELUSIONAL DISORDER

As the name implies, the central characteristic of delusional disorder is the person's persistent belief about something that is contrary to reality. The individual may imagine events that could be happening but, in fact, are not. At face value, the person's thoughts seem completely plausible (in that they are not bizarre). The individual with delusional disorder does not exhibit some of the other features commonly associated with schizophrenia, such as disorganized speech or negative symptoms. Compared with some other disorders, the onset of delusional disorder is relatively late in life—usually beginning when the individual is between 40 and 49 years of age (Vahia & Cohen, 2009). It is not known why this disorder has such a late onset, but there is some speculation that perhaps these individuals lead otherwise relatively normal lives and do not feel the need to seek help. In fact, apart from the subject of their delusion, people with delusional disorder often can continue to socialize and function normally. Generally, they do not behave in an obviously odd or bizarre manner. However, in some cases, someone with delusional disorder might become so preoccupied with delusions that their lives are disrupted. The person usually comes to the social worker's attention at the point when his or her symptoms become problematic and ego-dystonic (incompatible with the person's view of him- or herself).

Prevailing Pattern

Although delusions might be seen as a symptom of more common disorders the practitioner will see in practice, such as schizophrenia, delusional disorder is rather rare. The lifetime prevalence is estimated at about 0.2 percent (APA, 2013). While there are no gender differences, the jealous type is more common in males than in females. Unfortunately, as with other relatively rare disorders, little is known about the biopsychosocial influences on delusional disorder (Suvisaari et al., 2009). As you would expect, social, marital, or work problems can result from a person's delusional beliefs.

Differential Assessment

When considering an assessment of delusional disorder, the main feature is the presence of delusions lasting for at least 1 month or longer. Someone with a delusional disorder experiences non-bizarre delusions, which primarily involve situations that could occur in real life; for instance, being spied on or followed, poisoned, deceived, conspired against, or loved from a distance. If hallucinations are present (i.e., seeing, hearing, or feeling things that are really not there), they are not prominent and are related to the individual's delusional theme. For instance, as we will see in the following vignette, Scott Markam is characterized as someone who believes he has an odor problem, but he may, in fact, be smelling a bad odor. In essence, the person's delusions usually involve the misinterpretation of real-life experiences or perceptions. However, in reality these situations are either not true at all or highly exaggerated. Apart from the delusions, the person's functioning is not obviously impaired.

There are several different types of delusional disorder based on the main theme of the person's delusions, and they are specified as follows:

- Erotomanic—The individual with this type of delusional disorder believes someone else, often someone important or famous, is in love with him or her. This is where the person might attempt to contact the object of the delusion and stalking behavior is not uncommon.
- Grandiose—The person with this type of delusional disorder has an overinflated sense of worth, or a sense of having some great but unrecognized talent or insight, or has made an important discovery.
- Jealous—Someone with this type of delusional disorder believes that his or her spouse or sexual partner is unfaithful.
- Persecutory—This type of delusional disorder applies when the person believes that he or she (or someone close to them) is being mistreated, or that someone

is spying on them or planning to harm them. It is not uncommon for someone with the persecutory type of delusional disorder to make repeated complaints to legal authorities.

- Somatic—This type of delusional disorder involves bodily functions or sensations, and the person believes that she has a physical defect or medical problem.
- Mixed—People with this type of delusional disorder do not seem to have one predominant delusional theme.
- Unspecified—This type of delusional disorder applies when the individual's dominant delusional belief cannot be clearly determined or cannot be described in the specific types described above.

If the person has been suffering from delusional disorder for at least a year, the practitioner considers duration specifiers. They may be noted based on the first episode and specified as in an acute episode, currently in partial remission, or in full remission. Multiple episodes are similarly noted. If the person has experienced symptoms for the majority of the time with very brief periods of subthreshold symptoms, then the specifier continuous is assigned. Another diagnostic alternative is to note the course of the disorder as unspecified.

Delusional disorder is not separated from the shared delusional disorder (*folie à deux*), seen as situations in which there is a "significant other person" who exerts undue influence in the client's life described in earlier editions of the manual. If shared beliefs are present but full criteria for delusional disorder are not represented, then the diagnosis of "other specified schizophrenia spectrum and other psychotic disorder" is made. The practitioner must be mindful that several other disorders can cause delusions, and those should be ruled out before making an assessment of delusional disorder. One rule of thumb is to always consider the use of substances such as alcohol or/and illicit drugs prior to making a definitive assessment of delusional disorder. Major neurocognitive disorder can also manifest similar features and must be discounted. We now turn to the case of Scott Markam, who illustrates the main features of the somatic-type delusional disorder. Since little is known of his background, the biological, psychological, and social variables are not illustrated.

CASE THE CASE OF SCOTT MARKAM

Nancy Snope contacted the Counseling Center at the school where she is studying for her master's degree in social work. She is in her final semester and currently taking a required course in psychopathology. Nancy begins, "I know my professor told the class that we're not supposed to diagnose ourselves or those close to us, like as family or friends. Every week we study a different classification of disorders and I can't help but start to think that maybe I have that disorder or somebody that I know has it. I think it's called the student psychological illness syndrome or something like that. Anyway, this course has started me to worry about my uncle, Scott Markam. I mean I think he may have a delusional disorder. That's why I'm coming to see you. He's not a problem or anything like that, but for the past month or so I've noticed that he has this crazy thought. I guess I'm wondering if he'll be okay."

Nancy went on to explain that her uncle's wife, who is her mother's sister, has not complained, but tension has started to develop around Uncle Scott's behavior. "Nobody in the family knows how to deal with his behavior. No matter what we say, Uncle Scott doesn't believe us. I like to think that we're a 'normal' family but I've got to admit. My 50-year-old uncle's behavior is really a little weird. Now that I'm studying to be a social worker, I think everybody in the family is looking to me for answers."

The intake worker at the counseling center asked Nancy to further describe her concerns about her uncle. Nancy responded, "Simply put, Uncle Scott believes he smells. Trust me, he does not smell but he believes he smells of poop and he's convinced there is something wrong with his 'bum.' My aunt tells me that he's been to the doctor and had all sorts of tests. Simply put, there is nothing wrong with him. Uncle Scott's main issue is that he insists that he smells. He also believes that he can smell things that other people can't smell. Imagine what it's like when we all get together for dinner. I mean, you can smell the turkey and all the fixings, but Uncle Scott won't sit with us claiming he stinks! So my aunt opens the windows, sets a special place for Uncle Scott, tries to reason with him, whatever ... but nothing works. He's still certain that he smells of poop. There's no talking sense to him. Other than that, my uncle seems fine. I mean he doesn't drink, take drugs, or anything like that. We don't even have a history of mental disorders in our family."

Nancy continued, "Like I said, I'm taking this course in psychopathology and I've started thinking how strange his behavior has been lately, so I started researching online about delusional disorder. I never looked at this kind of stuff before taking this course. Trust me, my uncle matches all the symptoms. Everybody in the family just humors Uncle Scott, but I think he has some serious problems. My question is where do we go to get help for him ... or at the very least, who do I tell that he has a serious psychological disorder?"

Scott Markam's DSM Diagnosis Is as Follows:
Delusional disorder, somatic type

Assessment Summary Obviously, social workers do not assign a diagnosis without meeting with the client. However, this vignette is intended to illustrate the features of a delusional disorder that more than likely will bring a client to the practitioner's attention. What we can see in this vignette is the description by someone who is close to Scott Markam, a family member, who describes behavior where Mr. Markam is convinced that he smells—the most common somatic delusion—despite the reality that there is no evidence to support this delusional thought.

Competency 7 b

Integral to the assessment process, the competent practitioner understands theories of human behavior and the social environment and is able to critically evaluate and apply this knowledge when considering a diagnosis. As such, the full dimension of a client's life is explored including possible alternative explanations for Scott Markam's behavior. For instance, the practitioner might consider the possibility of stress in his life, or the impact of his delusions such as a co-occurring mood episode. On the face of it, the description of Scott Markam's delusional beliefs are unlike those with other psychotic disorders and does not automatically suggest a psychotic disorder. However, these delusional beliefs do need to be carefully evaluated in order to determine if another disorder can better account for his behavior. For example, schizophrenia and schizophreniform disorder are distinguished from delusional disorder by the absence of the other characteristic symptoms of the active phase of schizophrenia.

We now move to a review of brief psychotic disorder.

BRIEF PSYCHOTIC DISORDER

Brief psychotic disorder, also known as brief reactive psychosis, is seldom assessed in clinical practice, and therefore has received minimal attention. We include a review in this chapter to caution the practitioner to carefully explore all aspects of a client's life as a part of making the competency-based assessment. The specific cause of brief psychotic disorder is not known (Nolen-Hoeksema, 2014). One theory suggests a genetic link as the disorder is more common in those who have family members with depressive disorders, such as depression or bipolar disorder. Another theory proposes poor coping skills, as a defense against or escape from a particularly frightening situation, which may contribute to the development of brief psychotic disorder. In most cases, the disorder seems to be triggered by major stress or a traumatic event. Childbirth may be another contributing factor in that approximately one in 10,000 women experience brief psychotic disorder shortly after childbirth (Nolen-Hoeksema, 2014).

PREVAILING PATTERN

The exact incidence and prevalence of brief psychotic disorder is not known, but it generally accounts for 9 percent of cases of first-onset psychosis (APA, 2013). Internationally, it occurs twice as often in women than men and even more often in women in the United States (APA, 2013; Kaplan & Sadock, 2008). It typically appears in the late 30s and early 40s.

DIFFERENTIAL ASSESSMENT

Brief psychotic disorder is differentiated from the other related psychotic disorders in this chapter by its sudden onset, its relatively short duration, and the individual's full return to functioning. Think of it as time-limited schizophrenia; that is, it resolves within 1 month's time. Typically, brief psychotic disorder lasts more than 1 day but less than 30 days, and the individual eventually returns to his or her prior level of functioning. If these psychotic features persist beyond 30 days, the assessment would then have to suggest one of the other psychotic disorders. Depending on the specific symptoms presented, the practitioner may consider schizophreniform, delusional disorder, schizophrenia, or depressive disorder (or bipolar disorder) with psychotic features.

Features labeled brief psychotic disorder always include at least one major psychotic symptom of either delusions, hallucinations, or disorganized speech. Additionally, grossly disorganized or catatonic behavior may also be present and considered to support the diagnosis, as appropriate. Brief psychotic disorder usually occurs with an abrupt onset, but does not always include the characteristic patterns seen in schizophrenia. For example, when a person experiences some extreme, traumatic, or overwhelming situation(s), he or she may display erratic emotions, screaming, muteness, impaired memory of recent events, and/or other eccentric behaviors. Although the disturbance is brief, the person may be severely impaired and might need supervision to ensure protection from harm. Situations such as the loss of a parent, a life-threatening accident, or even the birth of a child are the kind of major life events that would cause anyone significant emotional upheaval. Thus, practitioners should consider "the event" within the context of the stress it may cause, in addition to whether or not the client might derive any type of secondary gain or benefit from illness.

There are three forms of brief psychotic disorder:

- With marked stressors—A response to a markedly stressful event or events such as such as a trauma or a death in the family.
- Without marked stressors—There is no obvious stressor.
- With peripartum onset—Usually occurs about 4 weeks after giving birth.

The practitioner may also specify catatonia when the clinical picture is characterized by a marked psychomotor disturbance and at least 3 of the 12 characteristic symptoms (i.e., stupor, catalepsy, waxy flexibility, mutism, negativism, posturing, mannerism, stereotypy, agitation, grimacing, echolalia, and echopraxia).

Take for example, a new mother who, within 4 weeks of childbirth, threatens to harm or kill her infant, experiences bizarre delusions or hallucinations, or exhibits disorganized speech or catatonic behavior; in that case, the postpartum onset should be specified. However, if the psychotic symptoms of bizarre delusions or hallucinations are culturally sanctioned (or are perceived as a normative coping response), then the practitioner would not necessarily consider using the diagnosis. For instance, in some parts of the world, cultural schemas support the idea of being possessed by an evil spirit. Castillo (1997) points out that when individuals are "possessed," they may tear off their clothes, assault others, throw things, behave incoherently, and believe that they have supernatural powers that allow them to harm or even kill people. This same behavior in modern industrialized societies is seen as deviant and bizarre, and the diagnosis of brief psychotic disorder would most likely be considered the appropriate explanation of the person's behavior.

Competency 7 a

Overall, the outcome for people diagnosed with brief psychotic disorder is good—that is, they do not generally experience long-term major psychiatric problems. For practitioners, it is useful to include information gathered from the person's friends and family as a part of the competency-based assessment, particularly exploring the individual's prior level of intrapersonal functioning, past history regarding reactions to similar stressors, and the chronological relationship between the current life stressor and the onset of symptoms. Other differential assessment distinctions should include the consideration of psychotic disorder due to a general medical condition (as in epilepsy or delirium), substance-related psychotic disorder, depressive and bipolar disorders, other psychotic disorders, malingering and factitious disorders, and psychotic episodes associated with borderline and schizotypal personality disorders.

A review of schizophreniform disorder follows.

SCHIZOPHRENIFORM DISORDER

Sometimes people display symptoms akin to schizophrenia, but not at the same level as those found in full-blown schizophrenia. Schizophreniform disorder presents, but differentiates from, the symptoms suggestive of schizophrenia—and, to complicate the clinical picture, these symptoms can disappear just as quickly as they appear, with no discernible explanation (except possibly treatment).

Prevailing Pattern

The overall global incidence of schizophreniform disorder is very likely similar to that of schizophrenia (APA, 2013). In the United States, however, rates are possibly fivefold less than that of schizophrenia.

Differential Assessment

An assessment for the presence of schizophreniform disorder requires that there be no detected organic cause of psychotic symptoms, the psychotic features must last *less than 6 months*, and the features must include prodromal, active, and residual phases. In schizophreniform disorder, it appears as if the person has schizophrenia, but he or she subsequently recovers completely with no lingering effects. A particularly useful aspect of this diagnostic category is that it helps practitioners avoid coming to premature conclusions about a person's behavior. It may also serve as a warning that the underlying cause of a specific psychosis may not yet be determined. This in itself is a valuable tool.

Some practitioners find it quite confusing that the symptoms and criteria for schizophreniform disorder are identical to those of schizophrenia. The important distinctions are in duration and intensity. An easy way to distinguish between the two disorders is to remember that the duration of schizophrenia must be longer than 6 months, whereas schizophreniform symptoms must exist for at least a substantial part of 1 month (less, if successfully treated) but *no longer* than 6 months. If an assessment must be made without waiting for the required duration interval or possible recovery (which is sometimes the case), "unspecified schizophrenia spectrum and other psychotic disorder" should be noted; if the person's recovery is complete, this diagnosis would be eliminated.

The following sample of a social work student's process recording illustrates the conversation between the intern and a client, Claudia Benjamin, who was involuntarily placed in a general medical hospital's psychiatric unit. The process recording includes both the word-for-word conversation and the student's reactions to the contents of the interaction. It is presented to demonstrate the schizophrenic-like picture a person with schizophreniform disorder may present and its subtle distinctions from schizophrenia. The biopsychosocial features are not illustrated in this case. The intent, instead, is to illustrate through the vignette how the symptom picture may emerge from the scope of the therapeutic conversation.

CASE The Case of Claudia Benjamin

Ms. Benjamin is a 23-year-old Jamaican female who was brought to the hospital by the police who found her wandering naked around 14th Street and Ocean Drive on South Beach. According to the police report, the woman appeared to be distraught and claimed, "My mother is coming from the moon to pick me up." The police officers felt the young woman was delusional and thought she was hallucinating at the time, so they decided to transport her to the hospital's emergency room. During transit, the police called their dispatcher to report their status, and they were informed of a missing person's bulletin describing the young woman they had just picked up. A social work intern was assigned to the emergency room as a part of her hospital rotation. Here is the transcript of their encounter:

Interview Content

W: "Hi, Ms. Benjamin? I'd like to introduce myself. I'm a social work intern here at General. How are you feeling now?"

CB: [The client shrugs her shoulders and begins to play with her hair and hum some kind of tune. There is no eye contact.]

W: "Are you comfortable?"

CB: "Get them away! Get them away!"

W: "I'm not sure what you want me to get away from you. Could you be clearer?"

CB: "Those things, things that are after me."

W: "Ms. Benjamin, what 'things' are you referring to? I'm not quite sure I understand what you want me to know. Could you be a bit clearer?"

CB: [The client cocked her head to one side and closed her eyes very tightly. It appeared to me that she wasn't listening to me, but to another conversation ... inside her head.]

Social Worker's Reactions to the Interview Process

I'm really nervous about working with someone who might be psychotic.

I heard that no eye contact is bad.

I'm trying to make her like me, but I don't think I'm getting anywhere with her.

Oh, boy. This isn't going the way I want it to. What should I do now?

That sounds like paranoia, but is it enough paranoia? I'm confused whether she is having delusions or hallucinations. Oh, boy.

I haven't a clue as what to do next.

At this point, I thought it was time to have a talk with my supervisor. I needed help in finding out what was going on for my client. Mary Jo Cringle, my field supervisor, suggested I talk with Claudia's family, who was sitting in the waiting room. As I spoke with the Benjamin family, the information they supplied helped to clear up some of my confusion.

According to Ms. Benjamin's mother, Claudia has been "acting this way" for only a few weeks. Her family told me that before this incident they cared for Claudia at home. After she wandered away from home today, they realized she needed more care than they could provide. Mrs. Benjamin said, "My daughter was a really good kid growing up. You know, it's very difficult to watch your own child talk to someone she thinks is there, but who really isn't. She thinks we are going to poison her food or harm her in some way." Mrs. Benjamin denied that Claudia ever experienced depressive or manic episodes, and she denied any medical problems or the use of substances ("Claudia doesn't even take aspirin"). "I just don't understand what happened to my wonderful daughter. She was all right up until just a few months ago and now this. Do you think you can help her?"

Claudia Benjamin's DSM Diagnosis Is as Follows:
Schizophreniform disorder, with good prognostic features

Competency 1 a

Assessment Summary The purpose of this vignette is to look at the social worker's process rather than an in-depth and detailed exploration of the client's life story. The transcript describes the social work intern's uncomfortable feelings about the interview and illustrates how unsettling it can be for the beginning practitioner to attempt to relate to someone who is not responding "rationally." The student's struggles to maintain a professional demeanor while interviewing the client can be seen in the transcript. The client's odd mannerisms and delusions leave the social work intern frightened and confused. While the student valiantly attempts to understand the client's "reality," Claudia Benjamin's response leaves the student feeling bewildered and inept.

The differential diagnosis of brief psychotic disorder was not considered in the above vignette since the duration of symptoms was longer than 30 days. Schizophreniform disorder is regarded to have a more hopeful outlook than does schizophrenia. Some experience the symptoms of schizophreniform for only a few months and can usually resume normal lives. Relatively few studies have been conducted on this disorder, and therefore we know very little about key aspects of how people can be affected (Barlow & Durand, 2012). However, what we do know is approximately two-thirds of those with schizophreniform disorder advance toward developing schizophrenia or schizoaffective disorder (Whitty et al., 2005).

SCHIZOAFFECTIVE DISORDER

Historically, individuals who showed symptoms of schizophrenia along with a mood disorder such as depression were grouped together under the umbrella of schizophrenia. This was often viewed as a mixed bag of problems for the practitioner who was attempting to sort through and understand these complex behaviors. Further complicating the symptom picture is the fact that depression frequently accompanies schizophrenia, making it even more difficult to distinguish schizophrenia from schizoaffective disorder and other forms of mood disorders.

Competency 7 b

The competency-based assessment is helpful in making distinctions among a person with schizophrenia, someone with a mood disorder, or someone who has both conditions. Schizoaffective disorder forms a link between psychosis and mood. In particular, practitioners should obtain pertinent intrapersonal information (including history of medical, neurological, or psychiatric problems) as well as pertinent family history. The prognosis for someone with schizoaffective disorder is better than for an individual with schizophrenia, but worse than for someone having a mood disorder.

PREVAILING PATTERN

Schizoaffective disorder appears to be about one-third as common as the diagnosis of schizophrenia with a lifetime prevalence of about 0.3 percent (APA, 2013). This disorder is higher in females than in males and principally due to the increased occurrence of the depressive disorders in females.

DIFFERENTIAL ASSESSMENT

Schizoaffective disorder revolves around the presence of a major mood episode (either major depressive or manic) that must be present after criterion for schizophrenia have been met. This approach to the assessment process takes a longitudinal perspective and makes it clear that the mood disorder must be present for the "majority of the total duration ... of the illness" (APA, 2013, p. 105).

For the practitioner to establish a diagnosis, the person must exhibit all of the following features during a single and unremitting period:

- Both a mood episode (which includes depressed mood) and the psychotic features of schizophrenia (such as social impairment and poor self-hygiene) must be present *concurrently*.

- During this same time, there must be *at least 2 (or more) weeks* of delusions or hallucinations in the absence of a major mood episode—depressive or manic.
- Symptoms of a major mood episode are present for the majority of the total duration of the active and residual portions of the illness.

The practitioner rules out the presence of substance use (such as a drug of abuse or medication) or another medical condition that might better explain the symptom picture. After a period of 1 year, the practitioner considers the following course specifiers:

- First episode, currently in acute episode—First manifestation of the disorder and seen as the time period when symptom criteria are fulfilled.
- First episode, currently in partial remission—The time when there is improvement after a pervious episode and the defining disorder criteria are only partially met.
- First episode, currently in full remission—The time period after the occurrence of a first episode during which no specific symptoms are met.
- Multiple episodes, currently in acute episode—After a minimum of two episodes, then multiple episodes are considered seen; for example, as after a first episode, there is a remission and a minimum of one relapse.
- Multiple episodes, currently in partial remission—The person experiences multiple episodes but symptoms are currently only partially met.
- Multiple episodes, currently in full remission—There are multiple episodes but currently no symptoms are met.
- Continuous—Symptoms for the disorder remain, with subthreshold symptom periods briefly seen over the course of the illness.

The following case discussion of Sydney Sutherland shows the importance of thoroughly understanding the client's presenting concerns. Clients often come to the attention of the social worker when they are disoriented and unable to provide accurate information. This underscores the importance of talking with others who are close to the client (such as family or friends) and who may be able to provide reliable factual data.

CASE THE CASE OF SYDNEY SUTHERLAND

Sydney Sutherland was rushed to the hospital after being found unconscious by her brother, Jerry Sutherland, in his home. Within her reach were an empty liquor bottle and an assortment of medicine bottles, including barbiturates, benzodiazepine-based tranquilizers, stimulants, painkillers, and a collection of unknown drugs. Sydney's condition was stabilized in the emergency room, and she was transferred to the psychiatric ward for observation.

The record room called to inform the social worker that, over the course of 10 years, Sydney had several prior admissions both to the psychiatric unit and to the acute medical hospital. The medical records also indicated Sydney had been treated for unspecified bacterial pneumonia just 3 months ago. The psychiatric records indicate she has a diagnosis of schizophrenia, and is being followed by Dr. Irene Morrell. Sydney attends the day treatment program at Bethune Shores Mental Health Agency, and Mr. Sutherland thinks the name of his sister's social worker is either Lee or Leslie Wagner. This social worker will contact Bethune Shores to find out Ms. Sutherland's current status. Her brother was asked to sign a release of information form that will enable the social worker to contact both Dr. Morrell and the day treatment program.

CASE THE CASE OF SYDNEY SUTHERLAND (CONTINUED)

"Hello, this is Martina Lopez. I'm a social worker at Regional Hospital, psych unit. Is it possible to speak with a Lee or a Leslie Wagner?"

"Lee Wagner speaking. Can I help you?"

"I certainly hope so," Ms. Lopez replied. She introduced herself and assured Ms. Wagner that she had the necessary signed permission forms allowing her to inquire about Ms. Sutherland. Martina provided some of the current information on Sydney Sutherland and then asked if Ms. Wagner might be able to fill in some gaps. "I'd really appreciate anything you can tell me that will be more relevant about Ms. Sutherland's treatment."

Ms. Wagner responded, "Of course. I've seen Sydney on and off for the past 3 years. She's been pretty unreliable throughout the time that I've known her. Most of the time, she doesn't show up for appointments—and she doesn't like to take her meds." Ms. Wagner continued, "Sydney has been diagnosed with schizophrenia and pretty much stays in the active phase, at least since I've been seeing her. You know, she'd have a fair chance to go into some type of remission—but, as I said before, she won't stay on her meds. Whenever I ask her about it, she insists that we put poison in the pills because we want to kill her."

Thoughtful, Ms. Lopez asked, "Has Sydney ever shown evidence of having a depressed, manic, or mixed episode?"

"I can't remember her ever having a mood component to the psychosis," Ms. Wagner replied, "but that sure sounds like what's going on for her right now. Is that your thinking?"

"Yes, it seems that way to me," Ms. Lopez said, "but I also need to talk with her brother to see if he's noticed any changes in her behavior recently."

Lee Wagner ended the conversation by asking if she could be kept informed as to how Sydney was doing. Martina Lopez promised she would be in touch.

Soon after this telephone conversation, Martina Lopez spoke with Jerry Sutherland. They found a quiet corner in the day room to talk. He appeared to be in shock and blurted out, "Geez! I knew Syd was having mental problems, but I didn't think she'd try to kill herself. She doesn't drink or do drugs, but then when I saw all those bottles in her room ..." He paused and ran his fingers through his hair in frustration. "Oh, man!"

Martina asked him what his impressions were of his sister's behavior over the past month or two—in particular, anything that may have been different, either worse or better than before.

"Well, you know she was always seeing things and talking to things that weren't there," Jerry said. "Sydney could never keep a job more than a day. Mostly she panhandled or hustled, you know, to earn money—but she didn't have to do that. Our parents are pretty well fixed and could easily take care of her. Mostly, she lived at Mom and Dad's, but once in a while she'd come and stay a day or two at my condo. I tried to feed her a hot meal, give her a place to take a hot shower ..." Jerry lowered his head, "... but most of the time she just came by to borrow money."

Ms. Lopez sat silently while Mr. Sutherland seemed to be deep in thought.

"The only thing I noticed different about her was that the last month or so," he began, "Syd seemed really depressed. You know. Like if she slept over my house, she couldn't drag herself out of bed until after 4:00 in the afternoon—and for her that was really unusual." He paused for a moment. "And she cried a lot ... more than I've ever seen her—Yeah, now that you're asking, she told me a few times that things were hopeless and she wanted to die. But I didn't think she meant it! Hey, do you think this suicide attempt was my fault?"

Martina offered reassurance to Jerry, explaining that his sister was pretty troubled. "You couldn't possibly follow her around 24 hours a day to make sure she was okay," she pointed out. "I'm sure we can help Sydney. Let's just stay in close touch." After saying goodbye to Mr. Sutherland, Ms. Lopez made her way back to the psychiatric unit, wishing that she felt confident in what she had just told her client's brother.

SYDNEY SUTHERLAND'S DSM DIAGNOSIS IS AS FOLLOWS:
Schizoaffective disorder, depressive type

Competency 7 b

ASSESSMENT SUMMARY As a part of the competency-based assessment, the social worker, Martina Lopez, considers several theories about human behavior and the influence of the environment in order to better understand Sidney's struggles. For instance, Sydney Sutherland had been found unconscious with numerous medications and alcohol nearby. In addition, certain organic mental disorders often have signs and symptoms resembling schizophrenia, such as hallucinations, delusions, and incoherence. Thus, the competency-based assessment must rule out factors that might otherwise explain her behavior.

As seen in Sydney Sutherland's story, an assessment of schizoaffective disorder should be made if the periods of depression or mania are in relation to the ongoing symptoms of schizophrenia. In the case vignette, Sydney has a long history of schizophrenia as reported both by her brother and by the social worker at the day care center (i.e., according to both sources, Sydney experiences auditory and visual hallucinations). However, within the last month she also began to show signs of major depression—sleeping all day, crying more than usual, confiding to her brother that things were hopeless and that she wanted to die. Because Sydney's depression is prolonged (lasting at least the past month or so), Martina Lopez concludes that a schizoaffective disorder should be considered. Figure 3.4 illustrates the interactions of the biological, psychological, and social variables in Sydney Sutherland's life.

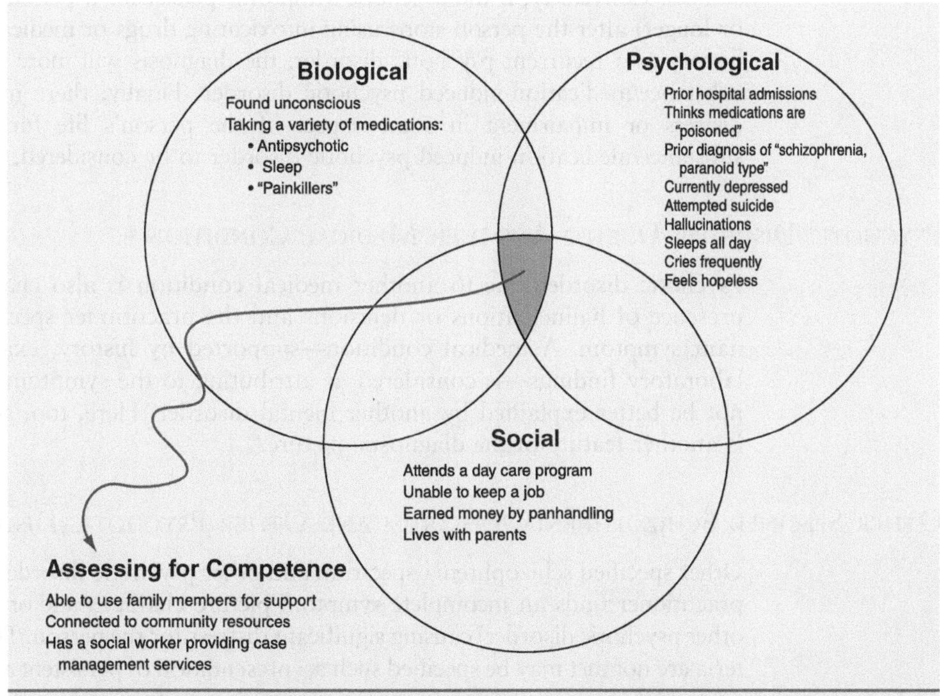

FIGURE 3.4 › SCHIZOAFFECTIVE DISORDER
The interactions of the biological, psychological, and social variables in Sydney Sutherland's life.

OTHER DISORDERS OF DIAGNOSTIC IMPORTANCE

It is not unusual for the social worker to encounter clients who do not quite "fit" the diagnostic criteria for the disorders discussed thus far in this chapter. A summary review of the following classifications is provided to round out the practitioner's understanding of the schizophrenia spectrum and other psychotic disorders. We begin with substance/medication-induced psychotic disorder.

SUBSTANCE/MEDICATION-INDUCED PSYCHOTIC DISORDER

Substance/medication-induced psychotic disorder involves the person's losing contact with reality, to a greater or lesser extent, and is most often associated with schizophrenia. While there are diagnostic similarities, substance/medication-induced psychotic disorder has two major symptoms; delusions and hallucinations. Those with substance-induced hallucinations may or may not have insight into whether they are real. The practitioner may see other symptoms, but they are not required for the diagnosis, such as abnormal psychomotor behavior and negative symptoms—particularly the lack of a normal range of emotions. As a part of the assessment, the practitioner checks to make sure that the psychosis was not there before the use of alcohol, drugs, or medications thought to be responsible. However, a person with a past history of a primary psychotic disorder can still be diagnosed with substance/medication-induced psychosis if the psychotic symptoms are better accounted for by the use of substances. Conversely, if the psychotic symptoms persist for a period of time (a month or longer) after the person stops using intoxicating drugs or medication, or there is a history of a recurrent psychotic disorder, the diagnosis will more than likely *not* be substance/medication-induced psychotic disorder. Finally, there must be significant distress or impairment in some aspect of the person's life for the diagnosis of substance/medication-induced psychotic disorder to be considered.

PSYCHOTIC DISORDER DUE TO ANOTHER MEDICAL CONDITION

Psychotic disorder due to another medical condition is also characterized by the presence of hallucinations or delusions and the practitioner specifies the predominant symptom. A medical condition—supported by history, examination, and/or laboratory findings—is considered as attributing to the symptom picture that cannot be better explained by another mental disorder. Here, too, significant distress is another feature of the diagnostic picture.

OTHER SPECIFIED SCHIZOPHRENIA SPECTRUM AND OTHER PSYCHOTIC DISORDER

Other specified schizophrenia spectrum and other psychotic disorder is used when the practitioner finds an incomplete symptom picture characteristic of schizophrenia (or other psychotic disorder) causing significant distress for the person. The reasons full criteria are not met may be specified such as: presentation of persistent auditory hallucinations; delusions with significant overlapping mood episode; attenuated psychosis syndrome (or psychotic-like symptoms that fall short of a threshold of a full psychosis); or delusional symptoms in partner of individual with delusional disorder.

Unspecified Schizophrenia Spectrum and Other Psychotic Disorder

Here, too, the practitioner may use the unspecified schizophrenia spectrum and other psychotic disorder diagnosis when the client does not meet the full symptom picture and chooses not to specify why criteria are not met. This diagnosis is most often used in acute care settings, such as an emergency room.

SUMMARY

This chapter reviewed the key features that define the psychotic disorders characterized as abnormalities in one or more of the following five domains: delusions, hallucinations, disordered thinking (speech), grossly disorganized or abnormal motor behavior (including catatonia) and negative symptoms (for example, diminished emotional expression, avolition, alogia, anhedonia, and asociality).

Next, the disorders considered part of the schizophrenia spectrum or psychotic disorders were reviewed. The key diagnoses are summarized as follows:

- *Schizophrenia:* The key symptoms required for diagnosing schizophrenia were detailed.
- *Catatonia:* The 12 symptoms that comprise catatonia were reviewed—both as a specifier for other mental disorders (for instance major depressive disorder, bipolar, and the other psychotic disorders), and as a separate diagnosis in the context of another medical condition, or as another specified diagnosis.
- *Delusional Disorder:* Delusional disorder was distinguished from schizophrenia in that it requires the presence of delusions for 1 month, and the specifiers for the types of delusions were detailed.
- *Brief Psychotic Disorder and Schizophreniform Disorder:* Both disorders share the symptom picture as schizophrenia but differ in duration.
- *Schizoaffective Disorder:* The diagnosis of schizoaffective disorder revolves around the presence of a major mood episode (either major depressive or manic) that must be present for a majority of the time and after criteria for schizophrenia have been met.
- *Other:* Completing the practitioner's understanding of the schizophrenia spectrum and other psychotic disorders, the following diagnoses were summarized: substance/medication-induced psychotic disorder, psychotic disorder due to another medical condition, other specified—and unspecified—schizophrenia spectrum and other psychotic disorders.

As the DSM transitions from the DSM-IV-TR (APA, 2000) to the current edition of the manual, Table 3.5 provides a brief summary of the changes made to the diagnostic classifications in this chapter.

Table 3.5 Summary Comparison Between the DSM-IV-TR and DSM-5 Diagnoses for the Schizophrenia Spectrum and Other Psychotic Disorders

All subtypes of schizophrenia have been deleted; specifically, paranoid, disorganized, catatonic, undifferentiated, and residual
A major mood episode is required in the DSM-5 for the diagnosis of schizoaffective disorder and for a majority of the disorder's duration after the defining criterion for schizophrenia is met—related to delusions, hallucinations, disorganized speech, disorganized or catatonic behavior, and negative symptoms (i.e., diminished emotional expression or avolition)
Diagnostic criteria for delusional disorder changed and is no longer separate from shared delusional disorder
Catatonia is now seen in the context of several disorders (i.e., neurodevelopmental, psychotic, bipolar, depressive disorders, and other medical conditions) and the clinical picture requires 3 or more of a total of 12 symptoms listed; catatonia may be part of another medical condition or unspecified when full criteria are not met

PRACTITIONER'S REFLECTIONS

Knowing the various signs and symptoms of schizophrenia is, of course, necessary, but it is also essential for the practitioner to tune in to the client's "full story." People with schizophrenia and other psychotic disorders may, at times and in many ways, function productively. At other times, they may struggle with the broad array of their symptoms. The reflections or activities provided here are designed to help you consider the full range of the person's experience with a diagnosis of the schizophrenia spectrum and other psychotic disorders.

ACTIVITIES

Competency 1 c

1. List all of the myths and reactions to people diagnosed with schizophrenia that you (or others that you know) have heard about, seen in the media, or read about in books. The professional social worker develops relationships with clients within the person-in-environment and from a strengths perspective. How might these myths and reactions challenge a strengths-based professional relationship?

Competency 1 b

2. List all of the words you can think of that are associated with the word *psychotic*. Review this list and indicate how many of them have a positive connotation and how many are negative. What does this tell you about how people with psychotic disorders are perceived? Further, imagine for a moment that you overhear several of your colleagues in the cafeteria referring to their clients in some of these negative terms. What should you do?

Competency 1 c

3. Review the case of Joey Esterson. Identify the problems related to interviewing someone who is reticent and responds the way that Joey does. Clearly, this is a client who challenges the social worker's abilities to communicate. Role-play the portion of the interview where the social worker attempts the mental status examination of Joey that illustrates your professional demeanor.

Competency 7 c

4. Look over the case vignettes discussed in this chapter, and identify some of the obstacles each person may pose in developing a therapeutic relationship. Identify and make a list of each client's strengths and vulnerabilities.
5. Imagine that an appointment was made with you and the receptionist has just told you that Rudy Rosen is in the waiting room. You greet him, help him to get settled in your office, and exchange some general pleasantries. You are now ready to begin your first interview with him.
   a. Write the first 4 to 5 minutes (8 to 10 exchanges) of your session as you imagine it to have happened. (Refer to the case of Claudia Benjamin for an example of what this process recording might look like.)

   Competency 1 a

   b. Look again at your process recording. What prompted you to say what you did and ask the questions you asked? How you were feeling at the time? Working with someone like Rudy can be frustrating at times. List the issues you would discuss with your supervisor.

Competency 1 b

6. Access the Competency-based Assessment and companion website at http://www.thomsonedu.com/social_work/gray, where the case of "Etta" is highlighted. Etta has been diagnosed with schizophrenia. In practice, she would be considered "low functioning."

She had been characterized as "very sweet" before her diagnosis, but as you will see, it is very difficult to communicate with her. The interview highlights her delusions. Note Etta's involuntary hand movements as they illustrate aspects of the body movements found in tardive dyskinesia. She also shows negative symptoms (i.e., blunted affect). Imagine that Etta is your client and describe the challenges she presents to conducting a professional interview with her.

Competency Notes

Competency 1 a—Social workers make ethical decisions by applying standards of the NASW Code of Ethics and other relevant laws, regulations and models for ethical decision-making as appropriate to context (pp. 99, 106): Social workers understand the value base of the profession and its ethical standards as well as relevant laws and regulations that may impact practice.

Competency 1 b—Social workers use reflection and self-regulation to manage personal values and maintain professionalism in practice situations (p. 106): Social workers recognize personal values and make the distinction between personal and professional values.

Competency 1 c—Social workers demonstrate professional demeanor in behavior, appearance, and oral/written/electronic communication (p. 106): Social workers understand how their personal experiences and affective reactions can influence their professional judgment and behavior and also understand emerging forms of technology and the ethical use of technology in practice.

Competency 2 a—Social workers apply and communicate understanding of the implications of diversity and difference in shaping life experiences in practice at the micro, mezzo, and macro levels (pp. 77, 78): Social workers understand how diversity and difference characterize and shape the human experience and that these features are critical to the formation of identity.

Competency 7 a—Social workers collect and organize data and apply critical thinking in order to interpret information from clients and constituencies (pp. 70, 84, 87, 97): Social workers understand that the assessment process is ongoing and conducted with, and on behalf of, diverse individuals, families, groups, organizations, and communities.

Competency 7 b—Social workers are able to apply knowledge of human behavior and the social environment, person-in-environment, and other multidisciplinary theoretical frameworks in the analysis of assessment data (pp. 80, 95, 100, 103): Social workers understand theories of human behavior and the social environment and critically evaluate and apply this knowledge in the assessment process.

Competency 7 c—Social workers develop mutually agreed-on intervention goals and objectives based on the assessment of strengths, needs and challenges within clients and constituencies (pp. 77, 106): Social workers recognize the implications of the larger practice context in the assessment process.

Competency 8 b—Social workers apply knowledge of human behavior and the social environment, person-in-environment, and other multidisciplinary frameworks in interventions with clients and constituencies (p. 81): Social workers are knowledgeable about evidence-informed interventions to achieve the goals of clients and constituencies.

Competency 8 c—Social workers use interprofessional collaboration, as appropriate, to achieve beneficial practice outcomes (p. 89): Social workers value interprofessional teamwork and recognize the beneficial outcomes that require interdisciplinary, interprofessional, and interorganizational collaboration.

References

Alex, K. D., Yavanian, G. J., McFarlane, H. G., Pluto, C. P., & Pehek, E. A. (2005). Modulation of dopamine release by striatal 5-HT2C receptors. *Synapse*, *55*, 242–251.

American Psychiatric Association (APA). (2000). *Diagnostic and statistical manual of mental disorders* (4th ed., text revision). Washington, DC: Author.

American Psychiatric Association (APA). (2013). *Diagnostic and statistical manual of mental disorders* (5th ed.). Arlington, VA: Author.

Angermeyer, M. C., & Schulze, B. (2001). Reducing the stigma of schizophrenia: Understanding the process and options for interventions. *Epidemiologia e Psichiatria Sociale*, *10*, 1–10.

Barlow, D. H., & Durand, V. M. (2012). *Abnormal psychology* (6th ed.). Belmont, CA: Wadsworth Cengage Learning.

Bentall, R. P., & Fernyhough, C. (2008). Social predictors of psychotic experiences: Specificity and psychological mechanisms. *Schizophrenia Bulletin*, *34*(8), 1012–1020.

Bleuler, E. (1926). *La schizophrenie. Rapport au Congres des medecins alienists et neurologistes de France et des pays de langue francaise. (Schizophrenia: Report to the congress of French and French-speaking alienists and neurologists)*. 30th Session. Geneva. Lausanne, Paris: Masson.

Bleuler, E. (1950). *Dementia praecox or the group of schizophrenias*. Madison, CT: International Universities Press.

Carlson, N. R. (2012). *Physiology of Behavior* (11th ed.). New York: Pearson.

Carlsson, A. (2006). The neurochemical circuitry of schizophrenia. *Pharmacopsychiatry*, *39*(Suppl. 1), S10–S14.

Caron, J., Latimer, E., & Tousignant, M. (2002). Predictors of psychological distress and quality of life in disadvantaged socioeconomic populations of Montreal. *Journal of Urban Health*, *79*(Suppl. 1), S56–S60.

Caron, J., Lecompte, Y., Stip, E., & Renaud, S. (2005). Predictors of quality of life in schizophrenia. *Community Mental Health Journal*, *41*(4), 399–417.

Caron, J., Mercier, C., Diaz, P., & Martin, A. (2005). Sociodemographic and clinical predictors of quality of life in patients with schizophrenia or schizoaffective disorder. *Psychiatry Research*, *13*(3), 203–213.

Castillo, R. J. (1997). *Culture and mental illness: A client centered approach*. Pacific Grove, CA: Brooks/Cole Thomson Learning Wadsworth.

Collip, D., Mylin-Germeys, I., & Van Os, J. (2008). Does the concept of "sensitization" provide a plausible mechanism for the putative link between the environment and schizophrenia? *Schizophrenia Bulletin*, *34*(2), 220–225.

Compton, M. T., Weiss, P. S., West, J. C., & Kaslow, N. J. (2005). The association between substance use disorders, schizophrenia spectrum disorders, and Axis IV psychosocial problems. *Psychosocial Psychiatry and Psychiatric Epidemiology*, *40*, 939–946.

Craven, R. M., Priddle, T. H., Crow, T. J., & Esiri, M. M. (2005). The locus coeruleus in schizophrenia: A postmortem study of noradrenergic neurones. *Neuropathology and Applied Neurobiology*, *31*, 115–126.

Dickerson, F. B. (2007). Women, aging, and schizophrenia. *Journal of Women and Aging*, *19*, 49–61.

Elmsley, R., Chiliza, B., & Schoerman, R. (2008). Predictors of long-term outcome in schizophrenia. *Current Opinion in Psychiatry*, *27*, 173–177.

Fischer, M. (1971). Psychoses in the offspring of schizophrenic monozygotic twins and their normal co-twins. *British Journal of Psychiatry*, *118*, 43–52.

Freudenreich, O., Holt, D. J., Cather, C., & Goff, D. C. (2007). The evaluation and management of patients with first-episode schizophrenia: A selective, clinical review of diagnosis, treatment, and prognosis. *Harvard Review of Psychiatry*, *15*, 189–211.

Fusar-Poli, P., & Politi, P. (2008). Paul Eugen Bleuler and the birth of schizophrenia (1908). *American Journal of Psychiatry*, *165*(11), 1407.

Gottesman, I. I. (1989). Dual mating studies in psychiatry: Offspring of inpatients with examples from reactive (psychogenic) psychoses. *International Review of Psychiatry*, *1*, 287–296.

Gottesman, I. I. (1991). *Schizophrenia genesis: The origins of madness*. New York: Freeman.

Gur, R. E., & Pearlson, G. D. (1993). Neuroimaging in schizophrenia research. *Schizophrenia Bulletin*, *19*(2), 337–353.

Haslam, J. (1976). *Observations on madness and melancholy*. Reprint edition. New York: Arno Press. (Original work published 1809)

Hawton, K., Sutton, L., Haw, C., Sinclair, J., & Deeks, J. J. (2005). Schizophrenia and suicide: Systematic review of risk factors. *British Journal of Psychiatry*, *187*, 9–20.

Henquet, C., Murray, R., Linszen, D., & van Os, J. (2005). The environment and schizophrenia: the role of cannabis use. *Schizophrenia Bulletin*, *31*, 608–612.

Ho, B. C., Nopoulos, P., Flaum, M., Arndt, S., & Andreasen, N. C. (2004). Two-year outcome in first-episode schizophrenia. Predictive value of symptoms for quality of life. *Focus*, *2*, 131–137.

Jobe, T. H., & Harrow, M. (2005). Long-term outcome of patients with schizophrenia: A review. *Canadian Journal of Psychiatry*, *50*, 892–900.

Kaplan, B. J., & Sadock, V. A. (2008). *Concise textbook of clinical psychiatry* (3rd ed.). Philadelphia: Lippincott Williams and Wilkins.

Kearney, C. A., & Trull, T. J. (2012). *Abnormal psychology and life: A dimensional approach.* Belmont, CA: Wadsworth Cengage Learning.

King, J. H. (2014). Deconstructing the DSM-5: Assessment and diagnosis of schizophrenia spectrum disorders. *Counseling Today*, *56*(7), 12–14.

Klausner, J., Sweeney, J., Deck, M., Hass, G., & Kelly, A. B. (1992). Clinical correlates of cerebral ventricular enlargement on schizophrenia: Further evidence for frontal lobe disease. *Journal of Nervous and Mental Disease*, *180*, 407–412.

Koh, P. O., Bergson, C., Undie, A. S., Goldman-Rakic, P. S., & Lidow, M. S. (2003). Up-regulation of the D1 dopamine receptor-interacting protein, calcyon, in patients with schizophrenia. *Archives of General Psychiatry, 60*, 311–319.

Kraepelin, E. (1971). *Dementia praecox and paraphrenia* (R. M. Barclay, Trans.). New York: Krieger. (Original work published 1919)

Laurelle, M., Kegeles, L. S., & Abi-Dargham, A. (2003). Glutamate, dopamine, and schizophrenia: From pathophysiology to treatment. *Annals of the New York Academy of Sciences*, *1003*, 138–158.

Linscott, R. J. Allardyce, J., & van Os, J. (2009). Seeking verisimilitude in a class: A systematic review of evidence that the critical symptoms of schizophrenia are taxonic. *Schizophrenia Bulletin*, *35*, 1–19.

Luoma, S., Hakko, H., Ollinen, T., Jarvelin, M. R., & Lindeman, S. (2008). Association between age at onset and clinical features of schizophrenia: The Northern Finland 1966 birth cohort study. *European Psychiatry*, *23*, 331–335.

Lysaker, P. H., France, C. M., Hunter, N. L., & Davis, L. (2005). Personal narratives of illness in schizophrenia: Associations with neurocognition and symptoms. *Psychiatry, 68*(2), 140–151.

Maki, P., Veijola, J., Jones, P. B., Murray, G. K., Koponen, H., Tienari, P., Miettunen, J., ... Isohanni, M. (2005). Predictors of schizophrenia: A review. *British Medical Bulletin*, 73–74, 1–15.

Malla, A., & Payne, J. (2005). First-episode psychosis: Psychopathology, quality of life, and functional outcome. *Schizophrenia Bulletin*, *31*, 650–671.

Morel, B. A. (1890). *Traite des maladies mentales. (Treatise on mental illness)*. Paris: Masson.

Murray, R. M., Jones, P. B., Susser, E., van Os, J., & Cannon, M. (2003). *The epidemiology of schizophrenia.* Cambridge: Cambridge University Press.

Murray, R. M., Lappin, J., & Di Forti, M. (2008). Schizophrenia: From developmental deviance to dopamine dysregulation. *European Neuropsychopharmacology*, *18*(Suppl. 3), S129–S134.

Niemi, L. T., Suvisaari, J. M., Tuulio-Henriksson, A., & Lonnqvist, J. K. (2003). Childhood developmental abnormalities in schizophrenia: Evidence from high-risk studies. *Schizophrenia Research*, *60*, 239–258.

Nolen-Hoeksema, S. (2014). *Abnormal psychology* (6th ed.). New York: McGraw Hill.

Opler, M. G. A., & Susser, E. S. (2005). Fetal environment and schizophrenia. *Environmental Perspectives*, *113*(9), 1239–1242.

Owen, M. J., Craddock, N., O'Donovan, M. C. (2005). Schizophrenia: Genes at last? *Trends in Genetics*, *21*(9), 518–525.

Palmer, B. A., Pankratz, V. S., & Bostwick, J. M. (2005). The lifetime risk of suicide in schizophrenia: A reexamination. *Archives of General Psychiatry*, *62*, 247–253.

Purcell, S., Wray, N., Stone, J., Visscher, P., O'Donovan, M., Sullivan, P., ... Morris, D. W. (2009). Common polygenic variation contributes to risk of schizophrenia and bipolar disorder. *Nature*, *460*, 748–752.

Ritsner, M. S., Mar, M., Arbitman, M., & Grinshpoon, A. (2013). Symptom severity scale of the DSM5 for schizophrenia, and other psychotic disorders: Diagnostic validity and clinical feasibility. *Psychiatry Research*, *208*(1), 1–8.

Rosen, J. L., Miller, T. J., D'Andrea, J. T., McGlashan, T. H., & Woods, S. W. (2006). Comorbid diagnoses in patients meeting criteria for the schizophrenia syndrome. *Schizophrenia Research*, *85*, 124–131.

Schneider, K. (1959). *Clinical psychopathology* (M. W. Hamilton, Trans.). London: Grune and Stratton.

Shenton, M. E., & Kubicki, M. (2009). Structural brain imaging in schizophrenia. In B. J. Sadock,

V. A. Sadock, & P. Ruiz (Eds.), *Kaplan and Sadock's comprehensive textbook of psychiatry* (9th ed., Vol. *1*, pp. 1494–1507). Philadelphia: Lippincott Williams and Wilkins.

Staal, W. G., Pol, H. E. H., Schnack, H. G., Hoogendoorn, M. L. C., Jellema, K., & Kahn, R. S. (2000). Structural brain abnormalities in patients with schizophrenia and their healthy siblings. *American Journal of Psychiatry, 157*, 416–421.

Stelten, J. P., Cantor-Graae, E., & Kahn, R. S. (2007). Migration and schizophrenia. *Current Opinion in Psychiatry, 20*(2), 111–115.

Suvisaari, J., Perala, J., Saarni, S., Juvonen, H., Tuulio-Henriksson, A., & Lonnqvist, J. (2009). The epidemiology and descriptive and predictive validity of DSM-IV delusional disorder and subtypes of schizophrenia. *Clinical Schizophrenia and Related Psychoses, 2*(4), 289–297.

Tandon, R., Gaebel, W., Barch, D. M., Bustillo, J., Gur, R. E., Heckers, S., ... Carpenter, W. (2013). Definition and description of schizophrenia in the DSM-5. *Schizophrenia Research, 150*(1), 3–10.

Tarrier, N., Khan, S., Cater, J., & Picken, A. (2007). The subjective consequences of suffering a first episode psychosis: Trauma and suicide behavior. *Social Psychiatry and Psychiatric Epidemiology, 42*(1), 29–35.

Thomas, R. (2010). Rethinking schizophrenia. *Nature*, 468(7321), 187–193.

Vahia, I. V., & Cohen, C. I. (2009). Schizophrenia and delusional disorders. In B. J. Sadock, V. A. Sadock, & P. Ruiz (Eds.). *Kaplan and Sadock's comprehensive textbook of psychiatry* (9th ed., Vol. 2, pp. 4073–4081). Philadelphia: Lippincott Williams and Wilkins.

Van Dorn, R. A., Swanson, J. W., Elbogen, E. B., & Swartz, M. S. (2005). A comparison of stigmatizing attitudes toward persons with schizophrenia in four stakeholder groups: Perceived likelihood of violence and desire for social distance. *Psychiatry, 68*(2), 152–163.

van Os, J. (2004). Does the urban environment cause psychosis? *British Journal of Psychiatry, 184*(4), 287–288.

van Os, J., & Allardyce, J. (2009). The clinical epidemiology of schizophrenia. In B. J. Sadock, V. A. Sadock, & P. Ruiz (Eds.), *Kaplan and Sadock's comprehensive textbook of psychiatry* (9th ed., Vol. *1*, pp. 1475–1487). Philadelphia: Lippincott Williams and Wilkins.

Veen, N. D. (2005). People diagnosed with schizophrenia retain the diagnosis long term. *Evidence-based Mental Health, 8*(3), 68–71.

Wade, C., & Tavris, C. (2010). *Psychology* (10th ed.). Upper Saddle River, NJ: Pearson Prentice Hall.

Weisman de Mamani, A. G., Kymalainen, J. A., Rosales, G. A., & Armesto, J. C. (2007). Expressed emotion and interdependence in white and Latino/Hispanic family members of patients with schizophrenia. *Psychiatry Research, 151*, 107–113.

Whitty, P., Clarke, M., McTigue, O., Browne, S., Kamali, M., Larkin, C., & O'Callaghan, E. (2005). Diagnostic stability four years after a first episode of psychosis. *Psychiatric Services, 36*, 1084–1088.

Wray, N. R., & Visscher, P. M. (2010). Narrowing the boundaries of the genetic architecture of schizophrenia. *Schizophrenia Bulletin, 36*(1), 14–23.

CHAPTER

Bipolar and Related Disorders

INTRODUCTION

Imagine for a moment that one day you wake up and feel oddly energized, pumped up, and ready to take on the world. Clearly, something is different. You feel like you can do anything you set your mind to and nothing will get in your way. In fact, you are so full of energy that you decide you do not need to sleep figuring that's for the lazy people. Days go by, and then they start to blend into weeks. Nothing, absolutely nothing, slows you down or gets you down. Then all of a sudden and without warning, this great feeling begins to fade. You start feeling bogged down, depressed, and even suicidal. Your life is meaningless and for weeks on end, you feel utterly hopeless. Then one day you wake up feeling ready for anything again! Does any of this sound familiar? This is the typical cycle for those who struggle with bipolar disorder.

The bipolar disorders reviewed in this chapter can cause intense, alternating episodes of mania and depression that go far beyond normal mood swings. This can be very serious and may result in employment problems, family conflict, or even heavy substance abuse. In addition to the stress these disorders can place on families and interpersonal relationships, a person with bipolar disorder is 40 percent less likely to even have a job (Cox, 2008). In addition, they are 10 times more likely than the general population to abuse alcohol or drugs (UPMC, 2005). This is unfortunate since alcohol and drugs have the potential to generate episodes of bipolar disorder. Perhaps the most alarming reality is the fact that about 15 percent of those diagnosed with a bipolar disorder succeed in committing suicide as compared to the general population, where rates are somewhere around 1 percent (Treatment Advocacy Center, 2014).

The specific DSM-5 disorders involving features characterized by alternating periods of mania and depression related to the bipolar and related disorders reviewed in this chapter are listed in Table 4.1.

TABLE 4.1 THE DSM-5 BIPOLAR AND RELATED DISORDERS
Bipolar I Disorder
Bipolar II Disorder
Cyclothymic Disorder
Substance/Medication-Induced Bipolar and Related Disorder
Bipolar and Related Disorder Due to Another Medical Condition
Other Specified Bipolar and Related Disorder
Unspecified Bipolar and Related Disorder

This chapter will pay particular attention to the two forms of bipolar disorder where sufferers either exhibit manic, euphoric, or heightened mood as well as depression, or manic episodes alone (previously known as manic depression). We will also focus on the minor (i.e., less severe) form of cyclothymic disorder. Although milder, this disorder presents many of the same symptoms as those found in the bipolar disorders.

Our discussion begins with the bipolar disorders.

BIPOLAR DISORDERS

Bipolar disorders begin more acutely than major depression (Johnson, Cuellar, & Miller, 2014). The presence of mania or hypomania (a less severe form of mania) defines a bipolar disorder. The characteristic feature of the bipolar disorders is the tendency for an individual to experience manic episodes alternating with major depressive episodes. Akin to a roller coaster, the person emotionally moves from the peaks of elation to the depths of despair (referred to as lability). Sometimes these moods alternate so quickly that both the highs and lows can be experienced on the same day. Mania is defined as a distinct period during which the predominant mood is either elevated, expansive, or irritable, and increased activity or energy with several associated symptoms such as inflated self-esteem, a decreased need for sleep, pressured speech, racing thoughts, distractibility, hyperactivity or agitation, and excessive involvement in potentially dangerous activity. In addition, the practitioner may observe impairment in functioning to the extent that hospitalization may be necessary to prevent harm to the individual or even psychotic symptoms (e.g., delusions or hallucinations and/or other perceptual disturbances).

In mania, the mood disturbance is severe and causes marked impairment; in a hypomanic episode, many of the features found in mania may be present, but overall the mood disturbance is less severe. At times it may be difficult to differentiate severe hypomania from mania. If there are psychotic features (i.e., delusions, hallucinations, and disorganization), the episode is, by definition, manic. The important determinants are psychotic symptoms or a marked impairment in normal psychosocial functioning. When hospitalization is needed, the condition has crossed an important threshold, that of mania. In conjunction with depression, the term *bipolar disorder* is a misnomer, in that a single manic episode is enough for the practitioner to make the assessment (i.e., the individual swings from the depressive pole to the manic pole).

Competency 7 b

Readers are reminded that in children, a diagnosis of disruptive mood dysregulation disorder (reviewed in the chapter addressing the depressive disorders) will generally be more appropriate than the diagnosis of bipolar disorder. Competent social workers are knowledgeable about human behavior, but how does the practitioner know when the client's depression is the result of a major depressive disorder or an aspect of bipolar disorder? For the most part, this distinction is unclear. In other words, major depressive disorder and bipolar disorder overlap, because the depression shows itself in very similar ways in both conditions. In essence, the practitioner takes a critical look at the client's behavior in order to better understand the symptom picture and the interplay with the environment. Luckily for those attempting to make an assessment, only some depressive features are the same; others are quite different. For example:

- Looking to gender, the DSM-5 notes that there is little to no evidence of gender differences for bipolar disorder, whereas major depressive disorder is more commonly seen in women (APA, 2013).
- The average age of onset for bipolar I disorder is about 18 years of age, and bipolar II disorder typically begins in the mid-20s (APA, 2013). The major depressive disorders can occur at any age, and a first onset late in life is not uncommon.
- Bipolar disorder is less affected by environmental factors in general, and seems to be more common in high-income countries (APA, 2013).
- Bipolar disorder has a greater genetic risk than major depressive disorder; in particular, a "family history of bipolar disorder is one of the strongest and most consistent risk factors for bipolar disorders" (APA, 2013, p. 130), in contrast to the major depressive disorders where risks among first-degree family members is about two- to fourfold higher than in the general population.

In bipolar disorder, manic episodes can develop within just a few hours' time. However, more typically they emerge over a period of a few days. When a person is experiencing a manic episode, it is not unusual for him or her to go without sleep for several days. The person develops inflated self-esteem (grandiosity), which can take on delusional dimensions including religious, political, financial, or sexual themes. The person's speech is often rapid and unremitting, and it has a pressured, urgent quality to it. This is the person who is "on top of the world." Children may show excessive happiness or "goofy" behavior far beyond what is normally expected for their stage of development. Additionally, racing thoughts and distractability may be seen. The person might start planning several different activities at the same time with seemingly boundless energy—you might find them sending excessive emails or text messages. During a manic episode, the person's judgment tends to be impulsive and poor—for example, the individual may go on expensive shopping sprees that they cannot afford or enter into risky business ventures. The individual may even claim to possess exceptional powers, such as having the ability to change the direction of the wind or remain impervious to harm.

Despite research into bipolar disorder, the cause remains relatively unclear. Further, Nierenberg and colleagues (2013) observe that the origins of bipolar disorder varies among individuals. In essence, there is no single cause, and it seems that many factors work together to produce the illness. What we do know is that bipolar disorder tends to be familial, meaning that it runs in families (Barnett & Smoller, 2009).

Because bipolar disorder tends to run in families, researchers have turned to searching for specific genes, the microscopic building blocks of DNA inside all cells that influence how the body and mind work. However, the largest and most recent genome-wide association study failed to find any particular locus that exerts a large effect which serves to reinforce the notion that no single gene is responsible for bipolar disorder (Craddock & Sklar, 2013). Of interest, advanced paternal age has been linked to a somewhat increased chance of bipolar disorder in offspring consistent with a hypothesis of increased new genetic mutations (Frans et al., 2008).

The current thinking is that bipolar is a predominantly biological disorder that occurs in a specific part of the brain and is due to a malfunction of the neurotransmitters (the chemical messengers in the brain). Dopamine, a neurotransmitter known to be responsible for mood cycling, has been shown to have increased transmission during the manic phase of bipolar disorder (Salvadore et al., 2010). It is hypothesized that the increase in dopamine results in secondary homeostatic down regulation of key systems and receptors. This results in decreased dopamine transmission characteristic of the depressive phase. The depressive phase ends with homeostatic up regulation potentially restarting the cycle over again (Berk et al., 2007).

Environmental factors also play a role in the development (and course) of bipolar disorder. More specifically, we are beginning to understand that environmental factors may interact with a person's genetic predispositions (Serretti & Mandelli, 2008). Recent studies have shown that recent life events and interpersonal relationships can contribute to the likelihood of the onset and recurrence of bipolar episodes (Geddes & Miklowitz, 2013). More specifically, between 30 percent and 50 percent of adults with bipolar disorder report traumatic and abusive experiences in childhood (Brietzke et al., 2012).

PREVAILING PATTERN

Competency 7 b

In order to assess for bipolar disorder, the practitioner takes a discerning look at what is known about his or her client in order to make sense of the symptom picture; specifically biological, social, cultural, and psychological development. Environmental factors are also taken into account. Looking at bipolar disorder, the 12-month prevalence among the U.S. general population for bipolar I disorder is 0.6 percent, and a rate of slightly higher prevalence of 0.8 percent for bipolar II disorder (APA, 2013).

VARIATIONS OF BIPOLAR DISORDER

As noted earlier, bipolar disorder occurs in episodes or cycles. In between, most individuals experience a "normal" (euthymic) interval during which they generally return to their usual state of psychosocial functioning. A first episode may be either depressive or manic. The presenting pattern of bipolar disorder is unpredictable—and subsequent episodes, if they occur, remain variable. It would be highly unlikely for the practitioner to find individuals who alternate between manic and depressive episodes.

Keep in mind that the bipolar and related disorders are not really separate at all, but are actually related conditions on a continuum of behavior, with some conditions reflecting mild symptoms while other conditions are much more severe. Consider the bipolar disorders as a spectrum (Youngstrom & Algorta, 2014). Individuals can present with a range of symptoms from mild (cyclothymia) to moderate (bipolar II) or more severe (bipolar I). The bipolar disorders occur in the following variations:

- *Bipolar I*—Refers to severe manic episodes accompanied by one or more periods of major depressive episodes (which can have psychotic features). In order to make the diagnosis of bipolar I disorder, the person must show at least three symptoms of mania (or four if the mood is only irritable) that last for more than 1 week. They are considered from a list of seven symptoms including inflated self-esteem, decreased need for sleep, more talkative than usual or pressured speech, flight of ideas, distractibility, and increased goal-directed activity or psychomotor activity, excessive involvement in activities that have a high potential for painful consequences such as unrestrained buying sprees (APA, 2013). In addition to manic symptoms, the manic episode may have been preceded by (or followed by) hypomanic or major depressive episodes. Depressive episodes consist of either symptoms of a depressed mood or a loss of interest in pleasure. A total of five symptoms are required for a major depressive episode, and the practitioner also looks for unusual changes in appetite or sleep, significantly decreased energy levels or fatigue, feelings of worthlessness, difficulty concentrating, and suicidal thoughts.
- *Bipolar II*—Refers to the same pattern of symptoms, but with a major distinction in the degree of severity; typically, this disorder does not lead to psychotic behavior or require hospitalization. Bipolar II disorder is generally characterized by one or more depressive episodes with at least one hypomanic episode that generally lasts approximately 4 days. Similar to Bipolar I, it also requires three symptoms (or four symptoms for those with irritable mood) from the seven characteristic symptoms required.

Bipolar Disorder Specifiers

Each type of bipolar disorder has specifiers that further clarify the diagnosis. Keep in mind that the earlier specifiers of "in full remission" and "in partial remission" have been removed from the DSM-5. The current specifiers are intended to indicate components of the disorder. The following specifiers apply to both bipolar disorders unless indicated:

Anxious distress: Anxious distress is intended to identify individuals who have symptoms of anxiety that are not part of the bipolar criteria. This specifier refers to someone who is showing anxiety symptoms that are beyond the diagnostic criteria for bipolar disorder. A minimum of two of the following symptoms must be present for most days during the current (or most recent) period of mania, hypomania, or depression—tension or feeling wound up, restlessness, an inability to concentrate due to worry, a dread of something terrible happening or fear of losing control. The practitioner indicates severity levels ranging from mild (two symptoms), moderate (three symptoms), moderate-severe (four or five symptoms), to severe (four or five symptoms with motor agitation).

Mixed features: Mixed features replaces the earlier DSM bipolar I diagnosis of "mixed episode." This specifier now applies to both bipolar disorders applied when symptoms of the opposite pole are present (i.e., symptoms of depression in mania/hypomania or, alternatively, the person shows symptoms of mania/hypomania in a depressive episode).

Rapid cycling: This specifier is indicated when the individual experiences at least four mood episodes (in any combination) within a 1-year period. In other words, the person may experience a major depressive episode and then switch to the opposite polarity of mania or hypomania, or the person may experience a full remission between episodes. Essentially these episodes are no different from the characteristic features of the bipolar disorders except that they occur more frequently.

Melancholic features: This specifier applies to bipolar I disorder, and the practitioner observes the following features in the most severe stage of the current episode:

- One of the following is present: a nearly complete loss of pleasure in all or almost all activities or a lack of a response to pleasurable stimuli; and
- Three or more of: a depressed mood characterized by profound despondency, despair and/or moroseness (or the so-called "empty mood"), depression that is consistently worse in the morning, waking up early, marked psychomotor agitation or retardation, significant anorexia or weight loss, or/and excessive or inappropriate guilt.

In other words, this specifier is reserved for a depressed mood that is considered qualitatively different from depressive episodes and for which psychomotor changes are nearly always present.

Atypical features: Also applicable only to bipolar I disorder, this specifier applies when the person's mood brightens during the most recent major depressive episode and two (or more) of the following are seen: weight gain or an increase in appetite, hypersomnia (like sleeping longer at night or napping during the day totaling at least 10 hours per day), a heavy or leaden feeling in the arms or legs (leaden paralysis), and sensitivity to rejection to the extent that it results in significant social or occupational impairment.

Psychotic features: A person may experience delusions or hallucinations at any point in a bipolar episode, but if psychotic features are present, they may be *mood-congruent psychotic features* (seen as themes of suspiciousness or paranoia along with the typical delusions and hallucinations—grandiosity, invulnerability, and so forth—seen in manic episodes); or *mood-incongruent psychotic features* (or the content of the person's delusions and hallucinations is inconsistent or a mixture of mood-congruent and mood-incongruent themes).

Catatonia: This specifier applies when the person shows catatonic behaviors during most of the episode of mania or depression.

Peripartum onset: This specifier is considered when the current or most recent episode of mania, hypomania, or major depression occurs during pregnancy or the 4 weeks following delivery.

Seasonal pattern: This specifier involves a regular seasonal pattern (within a 2-year period) for those who tend to experience at least one type of mood episode (i.e., mania, hypomania, or depression) during a particular time of year (e.g., late fall or early winter). Other episodes may not follow this pattern, in that someone may have seasonal manias but his or her depression does not occur at a specific time of the year. In general, episodes begin in the fall or winter and end in the spring. As a part of the differential assessment, it is important for the practitioner to consider obvious psychosocial stressors that may be related to seasonal work, such as being unemployed every winter, that may evoke a depressive episode. Alternatively, someone may experience a remission at a certain time of the year; for instance, a person's depression may disappear in the spring. The competency-based assessment pays attention to the client's environmental context. People who live and work in northern regions may complain about winter blues, but this kind of complaint alone is not enough to meet the specific criteria for bipolar disorder.

The practitioner may also specify the course of bipolar disorder indicated as in partial remission (where symptoms are currently present but do not fully meet criteria for the episode, or the person has gone for at least 2 months without any significant symptoms) or indicate in full remission (where there are no significant signs or symptoms for the past 2 months). Severity may also be assigned ranging from mild (few symptoms in excess of those required for diagnosis), moderate (the number of symptoms is between mild and severe) to severe (symptoms present are in excess of those needed for a diagnosis along with marked interference in social or other important areas of functioning).

Review of the literature suggests that bipolar has a poorer prognosis than major depressive disorder (Youngstrom & Algorta, 2014). Comprehensive follow-up studies have shown that 16 percent of individuals with bipolar disorder recover in contrast to 52 percent who experience multiple relapses. One study noted that 8 percent had committed suicide (Angst & Sellaro, 2000). Another longitudinal study indicated higher rates, with 11 percent of those with bipolar disorder having committed suicide (Angst, Angst, Gerber-Werder, & Gamma, 2005).

Up until the 1980s, the term bipolar II was little known. However, the sequence of mood cycles in bipolar disorder has become the single most important feature in distinguishing it from other mood disorders. Those individuals assessed as having either bipolar I or bipolar II disorder manifest very similar features. An important distinction between the two is the degree of impairment and discomfort in intrapersonal and interpersonal (and especially occupational) functioning. The following case discussion illustrates the shifts in mood common to those who experience bipolar disorder. It is important to note that because Carol Bishop's pattern of symptoms does not lead to psychotic behavior, and because she does not require hospitalization, she is assessed as having bipolar II disorder.

CASE THE CASE OF CAROL BISHOP

I first met 14-year-old Carol when she sometimes stayed in the waiting room while her parents, Francine and Gerald, came for marriage counseling. I am not sure they ever really had any hope of saving their 15-year marriage—and looking back I guess counseling was really just lip service for them. It was a way to tell themselves, their child, and their respective families, "we tried." About a year after the Bishops stopped coming, they contacted me again.

I have been affiliated with a private practice group made up of other licensed social workers for more years than I want to acknowledge. Several of us old-timers wanted to keep our daytime agency jobs, but also branch out into private work. We decided to share office expenses and subsequently put up our respective shingles. Private practice isn't what it used to be; however, it makes a nice departure from working for someone else. While my private practice doesn't generally necessitate checking my messages daily, if a client needs to speak with me or has an emergency, the office can always reach me. The other day, coming in for a regularly scheduled office session, I found a message from Francine Bishop asking me to call her. She had made a point of saying it was "nothing urgent."

I called Francine, and after a few minutes of chitchat and catching up on what had been happening, Francine shared with me that she and Gerald had divorced two months ago. He has a girlfriend, the house is up for sale, yadda, yadda. Francine finally got around to telling me the reason for her call.

"It's Carol, she's been driving me crazy for the last six or eight months. I mean, I don't want to sound like one of those horrible mothers that you see in the movies, but she's really gone off the deep end." Francine didn't wait for me to say anything before continuing. "Get this, she went to Macy's and charged $3,000 worth of cosmetics and designer purses. Can you imagine how many purses and lipsticks that is?" Sensing that she didn't really expect me to answer, I remained silent.

"What is she going to do with all that stuff?" Francine asked, rhetorically again. "What could she have been thinking? I told her I wasn't going to give her the money. To top it off, she won't take anything back. How is she going to pay for everything? She only earns minimum wage—I should say she 'used to earn minimum wage.' I found out she just lost her afterschool job. I tried to get her boss to rehire her, but he told me Carol hasn't shown up for work in 3 weeks. He just had to let her go. I guess I can't blame him." Francine paused, and I could tell she was getting closer to telling me why she called me.

"Carol's boss also told me, 'When she did show up for work, she was either higher than a kite or deader than a doornail.' He said he never knew what to expect when she came to work. He told me he didn't think Carol uses drugs, but he couldn't be sure. He said, 'A lot of the customers complain about Carol because sometimes she talks so fast they can't understand her—either that or she looks like she's falling asleep in the middle of a transaction.'"

Francine continued, "You know, I feel really guilty now, because I've been so wrapped up in my own troubles that I've ignored what's been going on in Carol's life. I always suspected something wasn't quite right, but I guess I just didn't want to deal with it. Is there any chance that I could bring her in to see you sometime soon?"

An appointment was scheduled for the next afternoon. I was left with the impression that Francine was terribly overwhelmed. I also realized I hadn't gotten in a word edgewise; that in itself was unusual.

When I did see Carol, I was somewhat surprised by the difference I saw in the youngster I had seen only a year ago. Although she looked more mature, she also appeared to be under a great deal of distress. Initially, I saw Francine and Carol together and gathered relevant family history. Francine related that her oldest brother, Henry, has been treated for bipolar disorder since he was 18. She was uncertain as to whether one of his daughters had the same kind of problem. Francine continued, "When Henry was a kid, he'd do all sorts of wacky stuff. You know, in a way it sounds a lot like what Carol has been up to. As I recall, Henry never needed much sleep. He would talk nonstop and did some wild and crazy things. Then, just like somebody flipped a switch, all the energy would go out of Henry. You couldn't drag him out of bed—all he wanted to do was sleep. My poor parents had a real hard time with him. They were glad when he joined the Army and moved out."

I spent the remainder of the session with Carol. Currently, she is enrolled in the 11th grade and wants to attend a local community college after she graduates. Carol admits that her grades could be a lot better than they are—she is "only failing a couple of classes." She is an attractive young woman, of average height and slender build. My sense of her was that she was restless. I noticed she tapped her fingers on the arm of the chair, and her crossed leg was in a constant motion.

"Carol, why do you think you are here?" I asked.

"I don't know what the problem is," she replied, "because I feel just fine. Maybe the problem is my mother. Now that Daddy is out of the house, she doesn't have anything else to keep her busy, so she's putting her nose into my business. She thinks I have a mental problem, but I don't. Just because I don't need as much sleep as she does, she gets all bent out of shape. I mean, come on!"

"What about that, Carol? Were you ever so energetic that instead of sleeping you did household chores or worked throughout the night?"

"Sure," she replied. "Look, I just feel happy, that's all. I don't like wasting my time sleeping, all right? Everybody makes such a big deal out of it. I can sleep when I'm old. Right now I'd rather spend my time on the computer. Did you know they have some fabulous 24-hour chat lines? I mean you can talk to hundreds of people all night long. It's really cool."

I asked, "When you are up all night on the computer, don't you feel tired the next day?"

"Heck no! Even if I don't sleep a wink, I feel GREAT. Why should I worry about sleeping if I don't need it?"

I asked Carol to describe those times when she felt really happy. Her reply was enthusiastic.

"It's the best! It's wonderful! It's great! It's terrific! It's like being on top of the world! I love it because I can do anything and everything." Carol is positively gleeful. "Did I tell you that someday I'm going to be a famous movie star?"

I was very aware of how pressured her speech had become and asked her about it. "Yeah, I've been told I'm pretty talkative—but hey, I guess I just have a lot to say."

I asked Carol if there were times in the past few months or year when she felt the opposite of being happy. "Do you ever feel really sad or tired—or feel like crying? You know, do you ever have feelings that are different from the ones you are describing today?"

Carol appeared thoughtful for a moment, and responded slowly nodding her head. "Yeah, there are some times when I just don't want to get up in the morning. I can't lift my head off my pillow or wake up." Carol looked puzzled. "Sometimes I'm on top of the world—then other times I'm totally down. That's weird, huh? ... And for a couple of months I didn't want to eat, so my clothes started to just sort of hang on me. Mom kept bugging me about being anorexic. There were a few times I couldn't wake up for school or work. I didn't care about anybody or anything—but that's all changed now!"

Carol denies using drugs or alcohol. She says she likes to have fun and sometimes spends too much money. She likes to go out and have a good time with her friends. Carol is currently sexually active with four boys, none of whom knows about the others. She admitted she doesn't always use protection but her attitude is, "Nothing bad has happened, so why bother?"

We set up several appointments for the following week, and I gave her a couple of referrals: One is to Dr. John Wojcik, an internist I've worked with before for a medical evaluation to rule out a possible general medical condition such as multiple sclerosis, hyperthyroidism, or AIDS. The other referral is for a psychiatric consultation with Dr. David Macy to consider medication intervention.

Carol Bishop's DSM Diagnosis Is as Follows:
Bipolar II disorder, current episode hypomanic, moderate severity

Competency 7 b

Assessment Summary Professional practice requires the social worker to carefully organize and interpret data from this case vignette illustrating Carol Bishop's symptoms. To begin, a manic episode must always be distinguished from schizophrenia. Although difficult, a differential assessment is possible with a few clinical guidelines. Merriment, elation, an infectiousness of mood are more commonly seen in manic episodes than in schizophrenia. The practitioner considers the presenting combination of a manic mood, rapid speech, and hyperactivity to tip the scale in the direction of a manic episode. Individuals who are currently undergoing an acute exacerbation of schizophrenia are able to sit quietly, whereas individuals who present with acute mania are hyperactive and their conversation takes on a pressured quality.

The specifier of catatonia can be found in several disorders, including the neurodevelopmental, psychotic, depressive, and bipolar disorders. However, when considering the catatonia, the essential feature is a marked psychomotor disturbance that may involve decreased activity and detachment (no matter how agitated the behavior), and the individual generally maintains limited interaction with others around them. Catatonia applies to the bipolar disorders if features are present during most of the manic or depressive episodes. By comparison, those individuals experiencing primarily a manic episode (no matter how fragmented their behavior) want to be involved with others.

In Carol's situation, her mother was the first to notice something unusual. Often, it is a close family member who notices a change in the client's behavior or personality. Carol herself had no insight into her behavior and the difficulties she caused. She explained away her inability to sleep, time spent chatting on the computer, incessant talking, and feelings of invincibility as typical teenage behaviors. The task before the social worker is to differentiate among a manic episode, a hypomanic episode, mixed episode, major depression, or a cyclothymic disorder. As well, the differential diagnosis considers the symptoms found in the personality disorders, attention/deficit-hyperactivity, panic, or other anxiety disorders.

The competency-based assessment helps to carefully examine the multiple influences in a person's life and to distinguish between a depressive episode and a bipolar episode. The practitioner assessed Carol's behavior this way. At least one manic and one depressive episode characterized her presentation. Carol exhibited bipolar features by cycling up into a manic episode, returning to her normal behavior, and then cycling down into a depressive episode. Carol's period of major depression, as described in the vignette, was evident when she could not get out of bed to go to work. For a short while after, she "bounced back"—and, if nothing else had occurred, the social worker could probably consider only the presence of major depression. However, common to bipolar disorder, especially in the first episode, is the unexpected arrival of manic features. At this juncture, the social worker pays particular attention to Carol's shopping spree at Macy's and considers bipolar disorder (the shorthand for all mood disorders that include at least one manic episode). Because of the severity of her behavior, the social worker did not consider the diagnosis of cyclothymia. Figure 4.1 illustrates the interactions of the biological, psychological, and social variables in Carol Bishop's life.

Competency 7 c

The competency-based assessment highlights the many strengths in Carol's context and social support networks. Her mother is concerned about her and very involved. Carol has many friends in school and has been able to work, though sporadically. Finally, Carol followed through with the appointment, has a past positive relationship with the social worker (who knows her family history), and is willing to continue treatment.

We now shift to the related bipolar disorders beginning with cyclothymic disorder.

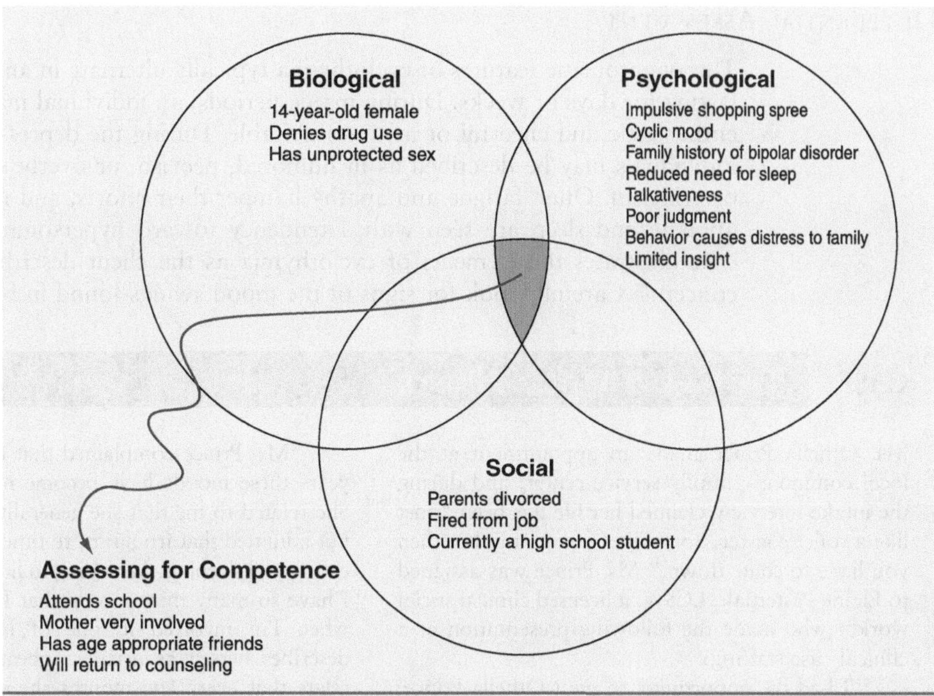

FIGURE 4.1 › Bipolar I Disorder
The interactions of the biological, psychological, and social variables in Carol Bishop's life.

CYCLOTHYMIC DISORDER

Cyclothymic disorder refers to a chronic or cyclic mood disturbance that has many of the same features found in major depressive episodes. For example, the individual may exhibit low mood, lethargy, despair, problems eating and sleeping, and trouble concentrating. Those with cyclothymia will be in one mood state or the other for years with relatively few periods of a neutral mood (Youngstrom & Algorta, 2014). When considering the diagnosis, this pattern must last for a 2-year period (1 year for children and adolescents), and the individual is not free of its specific manifestations for more than 2 months. Typically, the person regards his or her chronic low mood as normal or just the way they have always been. Cyclothymia is considered a milder form of bipolar II disorder; that is, the hypomanic phase alternates with mild depressive phases. Cyclothymia often begins early in life and represents a risk factor for the eventual development of bipolar I or bipolar II. Unfortunately, this disorder often goes unrecognized—and the person is simply thought to be high-strung, explosive, moody, or hyperactive.

Prevailing Pattern

In the general population, cyclothymia occurs equally among male and females. The lifetime prevalence is about 0.4 to 1 percent (APA, 2013).

DIFFERENTIAL ASSESSMENT

The symptomatic features of cyclothymia typically alternate in an irregular fashion, lasting for days or weeks. During manic periods, an individual may be described as enthusiastic and cheerful or at times irritable. During the depressive periods, these individuals may be described as ill humored, peevish, or overly sensitive to slights or criticism. Often fatigue and apathy hamper their efforts, and modest changes in appetite and sleep are seen with a tendency toward hypersomnia. The following case illustrates the elements of cyclothymia as the client describes her presenting concerns. Carefully look for signs of the mood swings found in bipolar disorder.

CASE THE CASE OF OTHELLA PRINCE

Ms. Othella Prince made an appointment at the local community family service center, and during the intake interview claimed her life has been " just like a roller coaster. Sometimes you go up, but then you have to come down." Ms. Prince was assigned to Elaine Pasternak, LCSW, a licensed clinical social worker who made the following presentation at a clinical case staffing:

"I had the opportunity to meet Othella Prince, who is a 33-year-old married woman and the mother of a 4-year-old son. She is an attractive, African American woman. Her medical history reveals that she has had diverticulitis of the colon for the past 10 years. This condition has responded well to dietary restrictions. Currently, Ms. Prince is employed as a waitress at a local deli. The reason she gave for coming to the agency involves her mood swings.

"Ms. Prince complained that over the past five years these moods have become more problematic. She related to me that she generally feels pretty well but admitted that from time to time she has difficulty eating and sleeping. According to her, 'That's because I have so many things to do that I can't stop to eat when I'm involved in one of my projects.' She describes herself as usually upbeat but goes on to relate that every few months she experiences a few weeks of not really wanting to do much of anything. She went on to say, and I quote, 'It's just like being on a roller coaster. I don't mean one of those monster things when you go way up and then rush way down. No, it's more like a hill and valley thing.' She denies having medical and/or substance-related problems or suicidal ideation—and has never been hospitalized for these moods."

OTHELLA PRINCE'S DSM DIAGNOSIS IS AS FOLLOWS:

Cyclothymic disorder

Competency 7 b

ASSESSMENT SUMMARY This case history offers another opportunity for the practitioner to organize and interpret client data to discern the diagnosis of cyclothymic disorder. The vignette illustrates Othella's prevailing mood. Note that the characteristics of cyclothymia include a hypomanic episode that is similar to a manic episode, except that the disturbance is less intense and not severe enough to cause marked impairment in interpersonal functioning. Analogous to a "hill and valley" roller coaster ride, Ms. Prince described a dysphoric mood, but it was not serious enough to qualify as a bipolar disorder. In contrast to bipolar disorder, cyclothymia is characterized by numerous fluctuations (up and down) of hypomanic and depressive features that persist for at least two years without intervals in a normal mood range. Figure 4.2 shows the interactions of the biological, psychological, and social variables in Othella Prince's life.

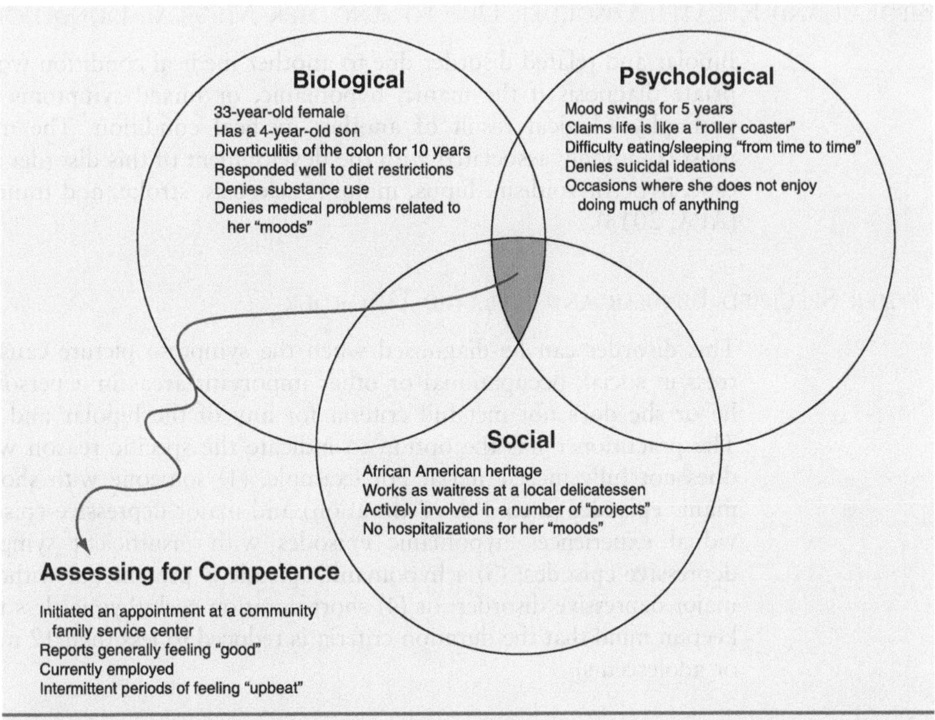

FIGURE 4.2 › Cyclothymic Disorder
The interactions of the biological, psychological, and social variables in Othella Prince's life.

OTHER BIPOLAR AND RELATED DISORDERS

There are many variations of bipolar disorder. To complete the practitioner's understanding of the bipolar and related disorders, a summary review of the related bipolar disorders follows beginning with substance/medication-induced bipolar and related disorder.

Substance/Medication-Induced Bipolar and Related Disorder

Substance/medication-induced bipolar and related disorder is characterized by elevated or expansive mood—there may or may not be evidence of a depressive mood episode. This disorder is considered when it is clear that there is evidence that the symptoms of bipolar disorder have occurred during or soon after substance intoxication or withdrawal, or after the exposure to a medication that is known to produce the symptoms of bipolar disorder. In such situations, the substance ingested would be listed along with a specifier indicating whether onset was during intoxication or during withdrawal.

BIPOLAR AND RELATED DISORDER DUE TO ANOTHER MEDICAL CONDITION

Bipolar and related disorder due to another medical condition would be the appropriate diagnosis if the manic, hypomanic, or mixed symptoms occur as a direct pathophysiological result of another medical condition. The medical conditions most commonly associated with the development of this disorder are Cushing's disease, hyperthyroidism, lupus, multiple sclerosis, stroke, and traumatic brain injury (APA, 2013).

OTHER SPECIFIED BIPOLAR AND RELATED DISORDER

This disorder can be diagnosed when the symptom picture causes significant distress in social, occupational or other important areas in a person's life. However, he or she does not met full criteria for any of the bipolar and related disorders. The practitioner has the option to indicate the specific reason why the individual does not fully meet criteria. For example: (1) someone with short-duration hypomanic episodes (2 to 3 days' duration) and major depressive episodes; (2) the individual experiences hypomanic episodes with insufficient symptoms and major depressive episodes; (3) a hypomanic episode is present but without any history of major depressive disorder; or (4) short-duration cyclothymia (less than 24 months—keep in mind that the duration criteria is reduced to less than 12 months for children or adolescents).

UNSPECIFIED BIPOLAR AND RELATED DISORDER

This diagnosis refers to the presentation of symptoms of a bipolar disorder that do not meet the full criteria, but distress in social, occupational, or other areas of functioning are present. Insufficient information may be available or the clinician may choose not to specify the reason the criteria were not met.

SUMMARY

Formerly known as manic-depressive illness where one's mood and affect are seen as maladaptive, bipolar disorder is characterized by alternating periods of mania and depression. The symptoms of the manic type of bipolar disorder are hyperactivity, euphoria, distractibility, pressured speech, and grandiosity. The depressive symptoms can include deep sadness, apathy, sleep disturbance, poor appetite, low self-esteem, and slowed thinking. The DSM provides a number of specifiers to better distinguish among the bipolar and related disorders.

This chapter reviewed bipolar I disorder, which is characterized by a single manic episode or, more commonly, by recurrent manic episodes or hypomanic episodes often immediately preceded or followed by a major depressive episode. Hypomanic symptoms are identical to the manic episode except that they are not as severe and do not include the possibility of delusions or hallucinations. Bipolar II disorder is characterized by one or more depressive episodes and at least one hypomanic episode.

Also reviewed was cyclothymia, which is comprised of chronic, fluctuating mood disturbance with numerous periods of hypomanic symptoms and numerous periods of depressive symptoms lasting for at least 2 years in adults (1 year for children and adolescents). This diagnosis is similar to bipolar disorder except that the symptoms are not as severe; for example, there are no major depressive, manic, or mixed episodes.

The bipolar disorders have been separated from the depressive disorders in the DSM-5 and placed between schizophrenia spectrum and other psychotic disorders and the depressive disorders (reviewed in the following chapter). This sequencing in the DSM was done in order to create a bridge among the disorders and to better see the overlap of the symptom picture (Paris, 2013). As well, the symptoms from one disorder are also relevant for another. A visual summary of the differential course of the bipolar and depressive disorders is presented in Figure 4.3. Take note of the differential course of these disorders.

As the DSM transitions from the DSM-IV-TR (APA, 2000) to the current edition of the manual, the following table provides a brief summary of the changes made to the diagnostic classifications in this chapter.

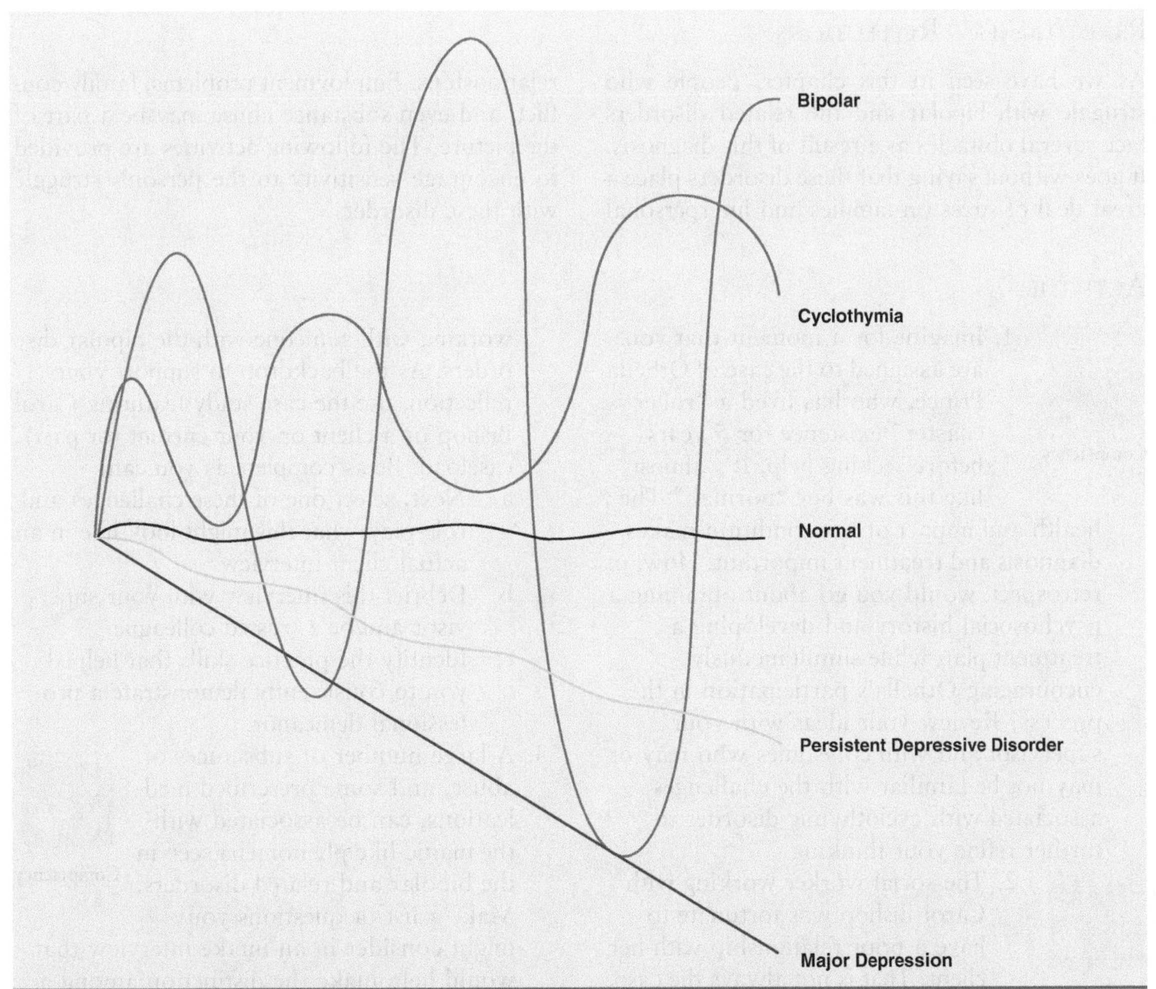

FIGURE 4.3 › VISUAL SUMMARY OF THE DIFFERENTIAL COURSE OF THE BIPOLAR AND RELATED DISORDERS AND DEPRESSIVE DISORDERS

TABLE 4.2 SUMMARY COMPARISON BETWEEN THE DSM-IV-TR AND DSM-5 DIAGNOSES FOR THE BIPOLAR AND RELATED DISORDERS

A new specifier "with mixed features" has been included that can be applied to bipolar I disorder, bipolar II disorder, and bipolar and related disorder due to another medical condition
When the person does not meet full criteria for any of the disorders in the bipolar and related disorders diagnostic class, the manual now allows for the diagnosis of other specified bipolar and related disorder for particular conditions
Anxiety symptoms are included as a specifier to highlight the anxiety that is not a part of the bipolar diagnostic criteria

PRACTITIONER'S REFLECTIONS

As we have seen in this chapter, people who struggle with bipolar and the related disorders face several obstacles as a result of this diagnosis. It goes without saying that these disorders place a great deal of stress on families and interpersonal relationships. Employment problems, family conflict, and even substance abuse may be a part of the picture. The following activities are provided to encourage sensitivity to the person's struggle with these disorders.

ACTIVITIES

Competency 7 c

1. Imagine for a moment that you are assigned to the case of Othella Prince, who has lived a "roller coaster" existence for 5 years before seeking help. It's almost like this was her "normal." The health and impact of her condition makes diagnosis and treatment important. How, in retrospect, would you go about obtaining a psychosocial history and developing a treatment plan while simultaneously encouraging Othella's participation in the process? Review your ideas with your supervisor and with colleagues who may or may not be familiar with the challenges associated with cyclothymic disorder to further refine your thinking.

Competency 1 b

2. The social worker working with Carol Bishop was fortunate to have a prior relationship with her client. That is not always the case. Develop a list of challenges you might potentially encounter working with someone with the bipolar disorders. As the backdrop to support your reflection, use the case study featuring Carol Bishop or a client on your current (or past) caseload. Be as complete as you can.
   a. Next, select one of these challenges and role-play what this might look like in an actual client interview.
   b. Debrief this interview with your supervisor and/or a trusted colleague.
   c. Identify the practice skills that helped you to consistently demonstrate a professional demeanor.

Competency 7 a

3. A large number of substances of abuse, and some prescribed medications, can be associated with the manic-like phenomena seen in the bipolar and related disorders. Make a list of questions you might consider in an intake interview that would help make the distinction among a substance abuse disorder, the bipolar disorders, or a substance/medication-induced

bipolar disorder. As a part of your consideration, consider any ancillary sources of information you would include to make the differential diagnosis.

Competency 8 b

4. Peripartum-onset mood episodes in bipolar disorder can occur with psychotic features and infanticide, characterized by command hallucinations to kill the infant or delusions that the infant is possessed can occur. It tends to be more common in primiparous women (women who have given birth only once). Imagine that you are working in a setting such as a hospital or health department, where you routinely see mothers who have recently given birth. As a part of outreach and prevention planning, your supervisor has asked you to develop a brochure aimed at providing information better understand the features of peripartum-onset in order to facilitate the mother's transition to caring for the infant at home. What kind of information do you think would be helpful to include? Target information for the first-time mother.
5. Access the Competency-based Assessment and Companion web site at http//www.thomsonedu.com/social_work/gray. There you will find the case about Mary, who is struggling with bipolar disorder. There are illustrations of her in the depressive and manic phases of her diagnosis. The manic phase highlights Mary's symptoms of hyperactivity, pressured speech, racing thoughts, and distractibility. In addition, we see evidence of her psychotic symptoms. As you review her interview, make a list of Mary's strengths and the limitations related to her diagnosis.

Competency 7 c

Competency Notes

Competency 1 b—Social workers use reflection and self-regulation to manage personal values and maintain professionalism in practice situations (p. 126): Social workers recognize personal values and make the distinction between personal and professional values.

Competency 7 a—Social workers collect and organize data and apply critical thinking in order to interpret information from clients and constituencies (p. 126): Social workers understand that the assessment process is ongoing and conducted with, and on behalf of, diverse individuals, families, groups, organizations, and communities.

Competency 7 b—Social workers are able to apply knowledge of human behavior and the social environment, person-in-environment, and other multidisciplinary theoretical frameworks in the analysis of assessment data (pp. 113, 114, 119, 122): Social workers understand theories of human behavior and the social environment and critically evaluate and apply this knowledge in the assessment process.

Competency 7 c—Social workers develop mutually agreed-on intervention goals and objectives based on the assessment of strengths, needs, and challenges within clients and constituencies (pp. 120, 126, 127): Social workers recognize the implications of the larger practice context in the assessment process.

Competency 8 b—Social workers apply knowledge of human behavior and the social environment, person-in-environment, and other multidisciplinary frameworks in interventions with clients and constituencies (p. 127): Social workers are knowledgeable about evidence-informed interventions to achieve the goals of clients and constituencies.

References

American Psychiatric Association (APA). (2000). *Diagnostic and statistical manual of mental disorders* (4th ed., text revision). Washington, DC: Author.

American Psychiatric Association (APA). (2013). *Diagnostic and statistical manual of mental disorders* (5th ed.). Arlington, VA: Author.

Angst, A., Angst, F., Gerber-Werder, R., & Gamma, A. (2005). Suicide in 406 mood disordered patients with and without long-term medication: A 40 to 44 years' follow-up. *Archives of Suicide Research*, 9, 279–300.

Angst, J., & Sellaro, R. (2000). Historical perspectives and natural history of bipolar disorder. *Biological Psychiatry*, *48*(6), 445–457.

Barnett, J. H., & Smoller, J. W. (2009). The genetics of bipolar disorder. *Neuroscience*, *164*(1), 331–343.

Berk, M., Dodd, S., Kauer-Sant'Anna, M., Malhi, G. S., Bourin, M., Kapczinski, F., & Norman, T. (2007). Dopamine dysregulation syndrome: Implications for a dopamine hypothesis of bipolar disorder. *Acta Psychiatrica Scandinavica*, 116 (Suppl. s434), 41–49.

Brietzke, E., Kauer-Sant'Anna, M., Jackowski, A., Grassi-Oliveria, R., Bucker, J., Zugman, A., ... Bressan, R. A. (2012). Impact of childhood stress on psychopathology. *Revista Brasileria de Psiquiatria—Official Journal of the Brazilian Psychiatric Association*, *34*(4), 480–488.

Cox, L. (2008, March 3). Support or stigma: Bipolar in the workplace. *ABC News*.

Craddock, N., & Sklar, P. (2013). Genetics of bipolar disorder. *Lancet*, *381*(9878), 1654–1662.

Frans, E. M., Sandin, S., Reichenberg, A., Lichtenstein, P., Lansgtrom, N., & Hultman, C. M. (2008). Advancing paternal age and bipolar disorder. *Archives of General Psychiatry*, *65*(9), 1034–1040.

Geddes, J. R., & Miklowitz, D. J. (2013). Treatment of bipolar disorder. *Lancet*, *381*(9878), 1672–1682.

Johnson, S. L., Cuellar, A. K., & Miller, A. D. (2014). Risk factors for bipolar disorders. In I. H. Gotlib & C. L. Hammen (Eds.), *Handbook of depression* (3rd ed., pp. 315–334). New York: Guilford Press.

Nierenberg, A. A., Kansky, C., Brennan, B. C., Shelton, R. C., Perlis, R., & Iosifescu, D. V. (2013). Mitochondrial modulators for bipolar disorder: A pathophysiologically informed paradigm for new drug development. *Australian and New Zealand Journal of Psychiatry*, *47*(1), 26–42.

Paris, J. (2013). *The intelligent clinician's guide to the DSM-5*. New York: Oxford University Press.

Salvadore, G., Quiroz, J. A., Machado-Vieira, R., Henter, I. D., Manji, H. K., & Zarate, C. A. (2010). The neurobiology of the switch process in bipolar disorder: A review. *Journal of Clinical Psychiatry*, *71*(11), 1488–1501.

Serretti, A., & Mandelli, L. (2008). The genetics of bipolar disorder: Genome "hot regions," genes, new potential candidates and future directions. *Molecular Psychiatry*, *13*(8), 742–771.

Treatment Advocacy Center. (2014). How many people with schizophrenia and bipolar disorder commit suicide? Retrieved on January 4, 2015 from: http://www.treatmentadvocacycenter.org/resources/briefing-papers-and-fact-sheets/159/463

University of Pittsburgh Medical Center (UPMC). (2005, January 3). *Anticonvulsant drugs cuts drinking in bipolar alcoholics, shows University of Pittsburgh research*. Pittsburgh, PA: Author.

Youngstrom, E., & Algorta, G. P. (2014). Features and course of bipolar disorder. In I. H. Gotlib & C. L. Hammen (Eds.), *Handbook of depression* (3rd ed., pp. 142–162). New York: Guilford Press.

CHAPTER 5

Depressive Disorders

INTRODUCTION

Almost everyone at some time in his or her life has had the experience of feeling depressed. Moodiness is almost universal, and these experiences are common. Almost half of the population, and maybe even more, will experience mood changes that meet the DSM criteria for a major depressive episode at some point in their life (Moffitt et al., 2010). You might say that depression is the common cold of psychiatry. Depression can be a symptom, a syndrome, or a disorder. Even if depression is seen as the "common cold," a cold should not be confused with pneumonia. How does sadness differ from the kind of depression seen in the depressive disorders?

The specific DSM-5 disorders involving features of sadness, emptiness, or irritable mood accompanied by somatic and cognitive changes related to the depressive disorders reviewed in this chapter are listed in Table 5.1.

The chapter begins with a disorder found in children, disruptive mood dysregulation disorder.

DISRUPTIVE MOOD DYSREGULATION DISORDER

Studies have been conducted exploring the amygdala (the part of the brain that plays a role in forming emotional memories) and its response in processing emotions among children with severe mood dysregulation as well as those with bipolar disorder and attention deficit hyperactivity disorder (Brotman et al., 2010). Preliminary findings point to deficits in emotion processing and hyperarousal symptoms among youths with these disorders. **Disruptive mood dysregulation disorder (DMDD)**, a relatively new diagnosis to the DSM, is included to capture children with frequent temper tantrums and irritability and prevent the overdiagnosis of other closely related disorders such as bipolar disorder or oppositional defiant disorder (Copeland, Angold, Costello, & Hegger, 2013). A number of children with DMDD were previously diagnosed with bipolar disorder, even when they did not have all the signs and

TABLE 5.1	THE DSM-5 DEPRESSIVE DISORDERS
	Disruptive Mood Dysregulation Disorder
	Major Depressive Disorder
	Persistent Depressive Disorder (Dysthymia)
	Premenstrual Dysphoric Disorder
	Substance/Medication-Induced Depressive Disorder
	Depressive Disorder Due to Another Medical Condition
	Other Specified Depressive Disorder
	Unspecified Depressive Disorder

symptoms (Axelson et al., 2012). However, they are more likely to develop problems with depression or anxiety in adulthood. Therefore, DMDD is placed in the depressive disorders of the DSM-5 since studies indicate that children with severe mood dysregulation are understood to go on to develop depression later in life (Brotman et al., 2006; Liebenluft, 2011; Liebenluft, Uher, & Rutter, 2012).

PREVAILING PATTERN

DMDD is relatively uncommon after early childhood (Axelson et al., 2012). The disorder is more frequently seen among children presenting to pediatric mental health clinics with the overall 6-month to 1-year prevalence among children and adolescents falling in the 2 percent to 5 percent range (APA, 2013).

DIFFERENTIAL ASSESSMENT

Almost any parent will agree that occasional temper tantrums and bad moods are considered a normal part of a child's behaviors while growing up. From time to time, children can be irritable, upset, or moody. DMDD should not be confused with the regular tantrums that most toddlers will experience, often referred to as the "terrible twos." When frequent temper tantrums disrupt peer and family relationships and cause difficulties in school and problems in maintaining relationships, then DMDD is considered. The defining characteristic of this disorder is chronic, severe, and persistent irritability in children older than 6 years of age. Between these outbursts, children with DMDD show a persistently irritable or angry mood, most of the day and nearly every day that can be seen by parents, teachers, or peers.

This irritability can be displayed as temper tantrums, or a temper outburst that occurs frequently (three times a week). When the child is not having a temper tantrum, he or she (though prevalence is more common in males) seems to be persistently angry or irritable. In other words, DMDD is distinguished by severe and recurrent temper outbursts that are out of proportion in intensity or duration of the child's situation. Onset of symptoms must occur before age 10 (and not diagnosed before age 6 or after age 18). These are children (6 to 18 years of age) who commonly show dangerous behaviors such as aggression, suicide attempts, and self-harm. The following should be taken into consideration when formulating a diagnosis of DMDD:

- Temper outbursts/rages—Severe (and recurrent) temper outbursts shown verbally (such as verbal rages) and behaviorally (such as physical aggression toward people or property) that are out of proportion to the situation. These outbursts are not consistent with the child's developmental level; that is, you would not expect the child of this age to have a temper tantrum.
- Frequency—The temper outbursts occur on the average of three or more times per week.
- Mood fluctuations—Between these outbursts, parents (and teachers or peers) see the child most of the day and nearly every day as irritable or angry most of the time.
- Duration—During this duration of time, the child has not been without a relief period of symptoms for longer than 3 months, and these symptoms are present for a year or more;
- Setting—The child has trouble functioning in more than one place, such as at home, school, and/or with friends.
- Exclusions—These behaviors do not occur exclusively during an episode of major depressive disorder and are not better explained by another disorder.

Like all of the mental disorders seen in children, these symptoms cannot be better explained by a medical or neurological condition or the effects of a substance.

Additional behaviors the practitioner can expect to see in a child with DMDD are an exaggerated self-esteem, flight of ideas, a decreased need for sleep, distractibility, pressured speech, enhanced goal-directed motions and activity, and involvement in those activities that can pose a threat to the child's life or health.

The case of John Laughlin provides a thumbnail sketch of the key features of DMDD. As such, the interactions of the biological, psychological, and social features of his life are not presented. However, the competencies in his life are clearly evident. For instance, despite frequent temper outbursts that seem to overwhelm his mother, she recognizes the need for help and contacted the mental health clinic. Mrs. Laughlin continues to maintain the hope for a positive change in her son's behavior. The vignette summarizes the social worker's conversation with Mrs. Laughlin. John was seen by the psychologist on the evaluation team who found him to be of average intelligence. The psychologist's overall impression of John was one of an irritable and minimally cooperative youngster. When frustrated with portions of the test, the psychologist observed a temper outburst confirming Mrs. Laughlin's description of her son's behaviors.

CASE THE CASE OF JOHN LAUGHLIN

John Laughlin is a 6½-year-old boy who lives with his mother, stepfather, and younger sister. His mother began, "To look at him, you would never know why we brought John to the mental health clinic. He looks like an angel ... those blue eyes, his freckles, and that tousled blonde hair of his. But in reality, he's more like the devil reincarnated. Don't get me wrong. I love my son but any parent can tell you that the problems we're having with him are just not normal. John's not defiant or

CASE THE CASE OF JOHN LAUGHLIN (CONTINUED)

anything like that. It's just his temper. Plain and simple. This has been going on for well over a year and I don't know how much more we can handle. He's our son so we just can't give him up or anything like that." The reason the Laughlins are seeking counseling is for John's severe temper outbursts, both verbal and behavioral, and usually when "things don't go his way," which is just about all the time.

Mrs. Laughlin added, "My mother kept a scrapbook for each of her grandchildren. After she died, I came across John's scrapbook. She had scribbled in the margin, 'This one is the "wild child."' I was shocked but...." Tears filled her eyes and she continued, "Sadly, I have to admit that mother was right. I love my son but each day is getting harder and harder. I just don't know what to do anymore. That's why I'm here."

Mrs. Laughlin continued, "John throws things, stamps his feet, hits himself, and sometimes he lashes out at others. It's awful. He doesn't have friends anymore. I think they're afraid of him." Mrs. Laughlin added that her son's disruptive behavior can last anywhere from 10 minutes to up to 2 hours or "until he just gets tired." She looked somewhat overwhelmed as she described her son's behavior and added that his outbursts happen almost daily and "sometimes several times a day." Just about every day John comes home with a behavior report from school. When he is doing something he likes, his attention span is not impaired. "When he plays his favorite video games he's fine, so I know there's hope for a change," stated Mrs. Laughlin.

John's overall behavior is characterized as angry and irritable. His tantrums or "meltdowns," as his mother calls them, started when he was just a little over 2 years of age. The family had hoped he would outgrow the "terrible twos" but that didn't happen. John is in good overall health and there is no known family history of bipolar disorder.

JOHN LAUGHLIN'S DSM DIAGNOSIS IS AS FOLLOWS:
Disruptive mood dysregulation disorder

ASSESSMENT SUMMARY As seen in John Laughlin's story, his temper outbursts are clearly out of proportion in intensity or duration to the situation (Dickstein et al., 2005). His mother describes a symptom picture that goes beyond a child who is temperamental to one with an impairment so severe that it prompted her to seek professional help. Far beyond temper tantrums, John's behavior is characterized by recurrent temper outbursts that are grossly out of proportion in intensity or duration to the situation, and they occur, on average, several times a week. This has been going on for at least 1 year. He no longer has any friends, he comes home on an almost daily basis with behavior reports in school, and his mother seems overwhelmed. The mood symptoms of bipolar disorder and oppositional defiant disorder are not seen in Mrs. Laughlin's description of her son's behavior. When doing things he likes, John seems well behaved and on task.

Competency 7 a

There are a number of disorders that closely resemble DMDD and may co-occur such as attention-deficit/hyperactivity disorder, major depressive disorder, and/or anxiety disorder. In fact, it is rare for DMDD to occur alone (APA, 2013). As a part of the assessment process, the practitioner carefully considers the symptom picture. For instance, if the child's irritability is *one aspect* of the symptoms for a major depressive disorder (or the persistent depression that characterizes dysthymia), then DMDD is ruled out. Further, if the child's irritability is seen in the context of an anxiety disorder, then the relevant anxiety disorder is assigned. Some children with an autism spectrum disorder can become irritable when their routine is interrupted. When that happens, then the diagnosis of DMDD is not assigned.

If symptoms of bipolar disorder are evident, such as a change in mood that occurs during a manic episode that is quite different from the typical symptoms of DMDD, then only the diagnosis of bipolar disorder is made. Oppositional defiant disorder involves problems with emotional and behavioral regulation and is characterized by a persistent pattern of an angry irritable mood, and argumentative defiant behavior or vindictiveness. Clearly, these symptoms very closely resemble DMDD. However, unlike DMDD, these behaviors are confined to only one setting. If the child meets criteria for both oppositional defiant disorder and DMDD, only the diagnosis of DMDD is assigned.

A review of major depressive disorder follows.

MAJOR DEPRESSIVE DISORDER

Depression has been described throughout the ages, and accounts of what are currently referred to as the depressive disorders can be found in many ancient documents. The DSM-IV (APA, 1994) expanded in size by approximately 50 percent from its predecessor DSM-III-R (APA, 1987), and the space allocated to what is now referred to as the depressive disorders tripled in size.

In practice, the social worker may hear the person with a major depressive disorder say, "I just can't seem to get myself out of bed," or "When I try to remember anything, it's like trying to fight through a thick fog." The person's reduced interest, energy, and motivation begin to adversely have an impact on his or her interpersonal life. The person may have difficulty making normal everyday decisions, lose interest in pleasurable activities, have difficulty sleeping, and/or show decreased interest in sexual activities.

Negative ideation and low self-esteem characterize the intrapersonal or personal domain; they view themselves as worthless and valueless. Individuals with a major depressive disorder are generally pessimistic and possess little or no sense of hope for themselves or their future. They tend to "forget" about their accomplishments while fixating on their present failures, misdeeds, and flaws. The person may experience somatic ailments such as weight loss or gain or a loss of appetite. If left on their own, they may not bathe or change their clothing for days at a time. As a result, major depressive episodes often lead to interpersonal difficulties such as unemployment, scholastic failure, divorce, and social isolation.

There are a number of problems related to defining who is depressed and how depression is shown. For example:

- Not all clients, especially children, can accurately describe how they feel.
- Presenting symptoms can vary greatly—one person might sleep too much, whereas another sleeps too little; or one eats too much, and another cannot touch food.
- Practitioners may not fully appreciate the impact that culture plays on the expression of depression.
- Depressive disorders commonly occur as presenting features in a wide variety of other syndromes such as a mood disorder due to another medical condition or substance/medication-induced depressive disorders.

PREVAILING PATTERN

The prevalence of major depressive disorder in the U.S. population is approximately 7 percent over a 12-month period (APA, 2013). While the disorder can occur at any age, differences can be seen according to age, with incidence three times higher in those 18 to 29 years of age compared to individuals 60 years and older. Rates are 1.5- to 3-fold higher for females than for males beginning in early adolescence.

Major depression can start at any age, presents itself in a variety of ways, and exhibits itself in varying degrees of severity. The first episode usually develops gradually—commonly beginning during adolescence and becoming more prominent during the individual's mid-20s. Overall, the prevalence of mood disorders in pre-pubertal children occurs less often than in adults but rises dramatically in adolescence (Gelder, Andreasen, Lopez-Ibor, & Geddes, 2012). In rare instances, it may occur in early childhood or among children ages 2 to 5 (Garber et al., 2009).

DIFFERENTIAL ASSESSMENT

Individuals diagnosed with major depressive disorder usually report experiencing a dampening or lowering of mood. Many of us experience an occasional bad day, when for no apparent reason we feel glum, irritable, grumpy, or out of sorts; however, what is considered clinical depression lasts for more than a day or two. People who live with major depression do not bounce back; this down feeling consumes their entire lives to the extent that nothing is interesting or fun anymore.

Experiences that would ordinarily be expected to raise someone's mood (e.g., spending a fun evening with a friend) do not seem to have any impact on the person with major depressive disorder. A client once described his depression in the following way:

> I just don't enjoy eating food, making love to my wife, sleeping, or spending time with friends anymore. I always feel either sluggish or restless. I can't concentrate, and making the smallest decision tends to paralyze me into inaction. Sometimes it takes me all day just to get out of bed, and then I sit out on the couch watching TV until it's time to go back to bed. That's no life.

The language of the client may reflect other expressions of depression such as feelings of worthlessness, loss of energy, and a marked loss of ability to experience pleasure (anhedonia). Although all of these are important in assessing for depression, the presence of physical changes, referred to vegetative features, are critical to a determination of mood disorder, often serving as warning signals in the form of changes in sleep patterns, energy levels, or appetite fluctuations (Gelder et al., 2012). The vegetative features occur along with a person's behavioral and emotional shutdown.

Competency 7 b

The competency-based assessment provides a framework for a systematic review of the various theories of human behavior and environmental influences to help the practitioner distinguish between what could be considered an expected sad reaction from the symptoms of depression. The core issue in looking for the presence of major depressive disorder is evaluating whether the presenting characteristics are the primary problem or are related to another disorder. This distinction is complicated by the fact that both situations tend to create problems in living for the individual. Almost everyone at some point in his or her life experiences feeling depressed—but the low that comes from a setback (e.g., losing one's job) is very different from having major depression. The competency-based assessment recognizes that getting a new job or moving on in life does not necessarily eliminate the feelings of sadness. Assessment of a major depressive episode requires the presence of either a depressed mood or a loss of interest or a loss of pleasure. The practitioner considers major depressive disorder when five (or more) of the following features have been present over a 2-week period of time and represent a change from the client's earlier ways of coping:

- Despondent mood most of the day, nearly every day—in children or adolescents, this can be an irritable mood.
- Markedly diminished interest or pleasure in most activities.
- Significant changes in weight (either gain or loss).
- Vegetative features such as insomnia (cannot sleep) or hypersomnia (sleeping too much).
- Psychomotor agitation or retardation (either hand wringing and restless pacing or slowness in activities such as walking or talking).
- Fatigue and/or loss of energy.
- Feeling worthless or experiencing excessive guilt.
- Inability to concentrate or think.
- Recurring thoughts of death, or suicidal ideation.

The depressive episode is not caused by street drugs, medication, physical illness, or alcohol.

A person's responses to a significant loss, such as bereavement, can include the symptoms that define a major depressive episode. Grief is a complicated process that does not automatically end after two weeks, and it is important for the practitioner to distinguish between the symptoms of grief and loss and the presence of a major depressive episode. The practitioner is cautioned against diagnosing a major depressive disorder even if prolonged grief best accounts for symptoms. The DSM cautions, "The presence of a major depressive episode in addition to the normal response to a significant loss should also be carefully considered" (APA, 2013, p. 161).

In summary, practitioners can differentiate between a person's experience of moods as a part of everyday life and the presence of a depressive disorder in the following ways:

- The depressed mood is not temporary or easily shaken off, and it typically persists for weeks, months, or years.
- The depressive disorder is significant and severe enough to impair important areas of a person's interpersonal functioning.
- Depressed individuals exhibit both physical and behavioral signs and symptoms, such as sleep disturbance, loss of interest in pleasurable pursuits, and changes in appetite.

Major depression generally occurs in specific episodes; that is, individuals cycle down into and then back up from periods of depression. The course of major depressive disorder varies and exceptions do occur, but for the most part this periodic depressive process (or cycling) is what you can expect to see in clinical practice. Individuals with a major depressive episode have a higher probability of recurrence, and each new episode carries renewed risks of psychosocial difficulties and suicide. In severe cases where an episode can last for 5 years or even longer, only about 35 percent of these individuals can be expected to eventually recover (Barlow & Durand, 2014). The length of each episode may vary from as little as 2 weeks to several years in severe cases—with the average duration of the first episode being 4 to 9 months if not treated. The greater clinical uncertainty is whether an individual will experience new episodes, since there is no way to reliably predict the influence of the biological, psychological, and social factors in a person's life.

The DSM-5 provides a number of specifiers to identify different pathways to the depressive disorders:

- With anxious distress—Involving at least two of the following five symptoms: feeling tense or keyed up; feeling unusually restless; difficulty concentrating; fearing that something bad may happen; and the person feels he or she might lose control of themselves.
- With mixed features—Involving at least three of the following seven symptoms: an elevated, expansive mood; inflated self-esteem or grandiosity; more talkative than usual; flight of ideas or the person talks quickly jumping from one topic to another; increased energy; involvement in high-risk activities like unrestrained buying sprees or sexual indiscretions; and a decreased need for sleep.
- With melancholic features—Includes at least one of the following: loss of pleasure or a lack of reactivity (for example, the person does not feel better even if something good happens to them). Next, the person experiences three (or more) of the following six symptoms: a depressed mood characterized by feeling profoundly despondent; depression that is usually worse in the morning; waking up early; agitation (or retardation); weight loss; and feeling excessively guilty;
- With atypical features—Involving mood reactivity or the person's mood improves in response to positive events and two or more of the following four symptoms: significant weight gain or increase in appetite; hypersomnia or excessive daytime sleepiness; leaden paralysis or severe body exhaustion, particularly feeling that arms or legs are too heavy to move; and sensitivity to rejection.
- With psychotic features—Where delusions and/or hallucinations are present and the specifier mood-congruent psychotic features specifies delusions and hallucinations consistent with typical depressive themes (i.e., personal inadequacy, guilt, disease, death, **nihilism** [a viewpoint that traditional values or beliefs are unfounded and that existence is senseless or useless], or deserved death) in contrast to the specifier of mood incongruent psychotic features where the person's delusions and hallucinations do not involve typical depressive themes.

- With catatonia—Applies if catatonic features are present during most of the episode.
- With peripartum onset—This specifier can be applied if onset of mood symptoms occur during pregnancy or in the 4 weeks following delivery.
- With seasonal pattern—Applies if there is a relationship between major depressive episodes and a particular time of the year such as fall or winter.
- Severity—Based on the number of symptoms and ranges from mild (2 symptoms), to moderate (3 symptoms), to moderate-severe (4 or 5 symptoms) to severe (4 or 5 symptoms with motor agitation); and
- Remission—Seen as partial (symptoms of the previous major depressive episode are present, but full criteria are not met or the person has gone for less than 2 months without significant symptoms) or full remission (no symptoms present for at least 2 months).

Thoughts about killing oneself (or suicidal ideation) are almost always present, and often the risk is greatest when the individual begins to recover from the depression. While coming out of depressive fatigue, the person may acquire enough energy to carry out a suicide strategy. Suicide is often associated with other disorders, and some people may experience panic attacks or other problems such as obsessions or compulsions. In fact, more than 80 percent of people who actually kill themselves have a depressive or other disorders such as substance use or impulse control disorders (Nock, Millner, Deming, & Glenn, 2014; Joe, Baser, Breeden, Neighbors, & Jackson, 2006).

Complications typically center on interpersonal difficulties related to employment, relationships with others, marital discord, and substance abuse—thus, the practitioner should consider a client's use of any drug when assessing for a mood disorder (Sadock & Sadock, 2010). The following two cases illustrate different pictures of depression. The first vignette introduces Anita Richards, who experiences recurring episodes of major depression. In contrast, the subsequent case describes Alice Jackson, who is experiencing her first episode.

CASE The Case of Anita Richards

Anita Richards was admitted to the hospital psychiatric unit after being brought in by the Mobile Crisis Unit (MCU), which responded to her suicide threat made over the telephone. The intake report notes that she threatened to slash her wrists with a razor blade. Anita Richards is a 38-year-old Hispanic divorced mother of four (ages 15, 12, 11, and 9). Ms. Richards has been hospitalized on three previous occasions. According to her medical records, she has been diagnosed with major depressive disorder, recurrent episode, severe. Here is a partial account of the practitioner's interview.

The social worker enters Ms. Richards's hospital room and immediately notes her disheveled and unkempt appearance. Ms. Richards's hair is tousled and wild—her eyes are puffy and swollen. When she sees the social worker, Ms. Richards jumps right in.

"I've got lots and lots of problems that just don't seem to go away. My boss fired me six months ago and I haven't been able to find work since. Every time somebody calls him about me, he tells them not to hire me because I was always late to work. Sure I overslept a few times, but that's not enough to ruin my getting another job, is it? Because of him, I can't

CASE THE CASE OF ANITA RICHARDS (CONTINUED)

support my four kids. The oldest two live with their father out in Arizona, and I never see them. My younger two live with my mother. I'm going to get them back as soon as I can."

The social worker asks gently, "What happened to bring you back to the hospital this time?"

Ms. Richards begins to sob quietly. "I don't know what gets into me. I get into these crying jags, and I just can't seem to stop."

"Are you still taking the antidepressants prescribed during your last hospitalization?" the practitioner asks. Ms. Richards closes her eyes and becomes silent as she twists a tissue into shreds.

"I hated being so constipated all the time," she responds. "I gained 15 pounds and none of my clothes fit me.... I know I should take those damn pills! But after a while I just didn't think they helped."

When Ms. Richards appears to have calmed down somewhat, the social worker asks, "What happens when you have one of those crying jags?"

"Oh, you know ... I feel really rotten." Ms. Richards begins to cry again. "I hate myself, and I don't feel like I deserve to live anymore. I hate the way I look, hate the way I feel, I hate ... [sobbing harder] ... I hate ... hate ... I hate all of this. I just want it all to end." She dabs at her eyes with a new tissue and sniffles quietly.

The social worker leans over and gently suggests, "Perhaps you really don't want to end it all." (She is very aware that this is a tenuous moment in the interview. She knows she can't talk Anita out of wanting to commit suicide—that would be like just ignoring her feelings. Instead, at this point the practitioner decides to focus on Anita's other options for living and getting help.) She points out to Ms. Richards, "Deep down inside you want someone to help you find a way to get better. After all, you did reach out and make that phone call to MCU." There is a long pause, then the social worker asks, "What do you think about what I just said?"

The client nods her head slightly and says, "I just don't think anything in my life is ever going to get better. Jeez, you have no idea how tired I am of fighting life." She seems lost in thought and then continues, "I got busted by the cops 2 days ago for selling crack. I spent the whole night in jail because I didn't have the money to post bail. I called my mother, but she wouldn't help—some mother, huh? I used my one phone call just to hear her tell me I got into trouble one too many times. She said, 'I hope the judge throws the book at you, and you rot in jail for 10 years.' I tried to tell her the whole deal wasn't my fault. How was I supposed to know the kid was a narc? He looked like he was about 12 years old, you know what I mean? He set me up. I don't use drugs, but I got to eat, don't I?" Anita continued, "My mother didn't want to tell my kids that I was in jail so she just took the easy way out and finally came up with the money to bail me out. I know I'll never hear the end of it. You know, what a screw up I am!" Anita looks intently at the tissue in her lap and whispers almost as if she was talking to herself, "I'll never get my kids back."

The social worker asks about her suicidal call to MCU, and Ms. Richards responds, "Well, what do you expect? I don't have a job, I can't ever seem to get caught up, my no-good ex and my lousy mother are raising my kids—and, and, I can't eat, can't sleep, can't ... [she is sobbing],"

When she calms down, the social worker asks her to describe what has been happening to her. "Well, it's just like the other times," Ms. Richards goes on. "I can't force myself to eat anything. I guess I've lost weight—at least my clothes fit me again." She tugs at the waist band of her jeans. "Actually, they kind of hang on me now, you know, sorta baggy."

The social worker smiles at this, and then asks, "What about other problems? Is anything else going on?"

"I feel down in the dumps ALL the time," Ms. Richards replies. "I cry all the time, fall asleep for hours on end, but then I wake up feeling like I never slept at all. I just feel really blah.... I'm just tired of life, that's all there is to it. It's hopeless. I have nothing going for me. I'm a real loser. You know, there's absolutely nothing I like about living. I've tried to just hang on until the kids are grown up and independent; then there won't be anything to hold me here." She relates this with a wistful half smile and tears streaming down her face.

"Anita, aren't there any times when you feel good? Do you ever feel up in the clouds or just really happy and full of energy?"

"No, but I wish I did," she replies. "Maybe then I'd feel like there was at least something to keep me going."

As the conversation continues, Ms. Richards denies experiencing manic or psychotic behavior, and she has trouble accurately recounting when her last depressive episode occurred. Her hospital chart shows three previous admissions for major depressive disorder—all within the last 3 years. Her most recent admission was noted 5 months earlier.

The social worker tries to explore further. "What about your other relationships? Can you tell me what they are like?"

"I used to have a boyfriend, but he left me stranded." The client looked sadly at the floor. "Said I was a cold fish—just because I didn't want to have sex all the time. He's a jerk."

The social worker asks if Ms. Richards has any hobbies or special things she enjoys doing.

"When I was a kid I used to like to read," Anita offers. "Now I can't seem to concentrate—I can't get through two pages before I forget what I read. I guess that's why I don't watch much TV either."

As the interview continues, they discuss several questions about Ms. Richards's past and present medical history. She denies any medical or neurological problems—and she denies using alcohol or drugs. "I just sell them, I don't use them," Anita says. The practitioner notes this response and plans to explore this issue further.

Anita Richards was subsequently hospitalized for observation.

Anita Richards's DSM Diagnosis Is as Follows:

Major depressive disorder, recurrent episode, moderate-severe

Assessment Summary In this case vignette, the social worker needs to decide if Anita is currently experiencing a normal reaction to a series of life events (such as losing her job, being arrested, her boyfriend breaking up with her, her mother's reluctance to help) or if the onset of her latest depressive episode has nothing to do with those events. This requires the ability to organize and interpret data from the case history in order to better understand Anita's symptom picture. The worker may never know causality, but a competency-based assessment provides the foundation for the worker to fully explore the client's world as well as to look for Anita's strengths in coping with what she describes as a hopeless situation. It is important to discern what can normally happen in a person's life from unfortunate circumstances—especially losses, humiliation, and social rejection—because they are often followed by depressive symptoms (Monroe, Slavich, & Georgiades, 2014). As well, Anita did not provide evidence to the worker that her depression was related to bereavement issues.

Competency 7 c

Despite numerous interpersonal difficulties, Anita has shown much strength in coping with recurring major depression. She has been able to maintain employment for a period of time (5 years). Despite the distasteful side effects associated with antidepressant medications, such as constipation and weight fluctuations, Anita realizes the importance of taking them on a regular basis. Perhaps most important, she wants to be reunited with her children, who currently reside with her mother and her former husband. Figure 5.1 illustrates the interactions of the biological, psychological, and social variables in Anita Richards's life.

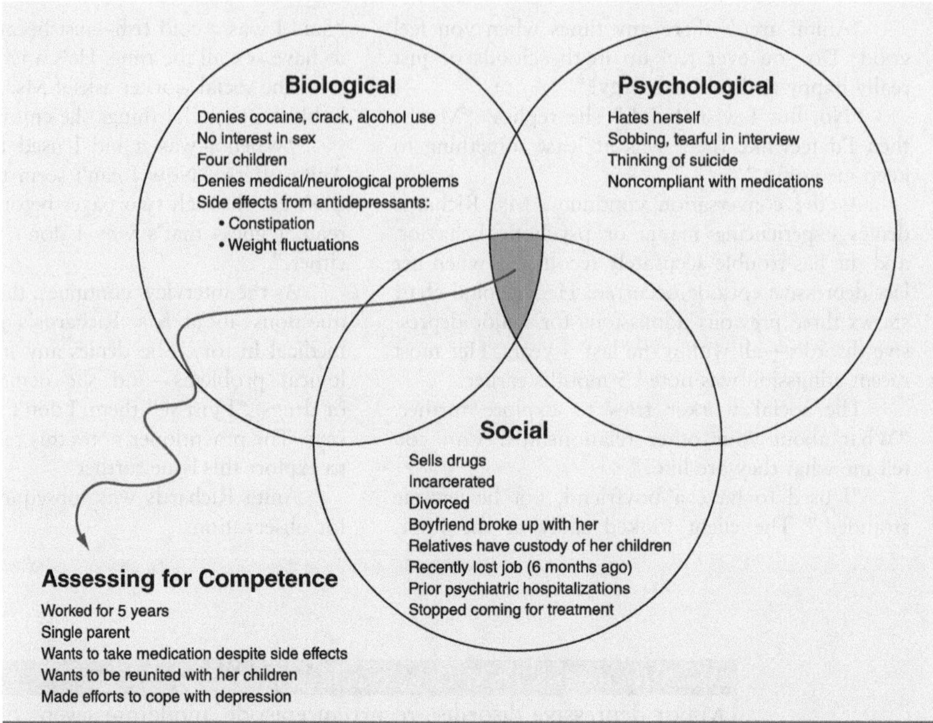

FIGURE 5.1 › MAJOR DEPRESSIVE DISORDER
The interactions of the biological, psychological, and social variables in Anita Richards's life.

The following vignette recounts the story of Alice Jackson, who experiences her first episode of depression.

CASE THE CASE OF ALICE JACKSON

Alice Jackson, age 19, gave birth to her second child almost 3 weeks ago, and since then she has been experiencing a "depressed mood" (according to her husband). Mark Jackson brought his wife into the emergency room because "She won't stop crying, and I didn't know what else to do."

I was the social worker on duty, so I introduced myself to Mr. and Mrs. Jackson. He appeared quite upset, and I asked him to have a seat. He slumped into a nearby chair, and I had the impression he had been crying shortly before I saw him. Mrs. Jackson was having her vital signs taken by a nurse in an examining room nearby. I began the interview by asking Mr. Jackson to describe what brought them to the emergency room. He inhaled, ran his hands through his hair, and then over his face. Exhaling loudly, he said, "I just don't know what to do with Alice anymore. She's got everything going for her, so I don't know what the problem is. I mean, why would she want to hurt herself? How could she not love our new baby? We have 2 beautiful and healthy kids but she thinks she's worthless. Can you imagine that?"

I asked Mr. Jackson to go back and tell me something about the incident or circumstances when he felt his wife first began to experience these problems.

"Well, let's see. We were childhood sweethearts and all that, and she never gave any sign of being anything but rock solid. Sure, we married young—I was 19 and she was 17—but most of our friends married young, too. We both got jobs right outta high school. I got a job working at Sweeny's Auto Repair Shop, and Alice got a job as a cashier at Kmart. Things were going real good for us. We were making good money, rented a nice apartment, and then—bam—our first kid's on the way. Hell, we didn't really care, except maybe it was a little too soon, that's all. Well, I'll tell you what, Alice was beside herself happy when Ben was born. She fussed and spoilt him like nobody's business. Of course, it was a little rough on her having to adjust to working part time and staying home with Ben—but you never saw a prouder mother."

I asked Mr. Jackson if his wife had ever exhibited any "baby blues" after Ben was born. He replied, "I didn't notice anything unusual, 'cept maybe she was tired more." He sat and thought for a moment and then continued.

"Everything was going along fine. Ben was growing fat and sassy and was the apple of our eye. We had so much fun showing him off and all. Alice's mother doesn't live too far from us, and she helps out babysitting and stuff every once in a while, but we try not to trouble her too much 'cause she's got her own problems." When asked to elaborate, Mr. Jackson replied, "Well, I don't like to tell tales outta school you know, but if you think it'll help Alice ... Her mother had some mental problems in the past. I don't know much about it, but she tried to kill herself a few times using some pills and washing it down with a bottle of liquor. Don't that beat all? Damn fool thing to do. She stayed in the hospital for a while. Getting treated for depression or something, Alice said. You know, come to think of it, Alice's two sisters had some trouble like that, too—but I don't know what all that has to do with us."

I asked him to tell me more about Alice. "Well, when Ben was about 6 months old, we found out we were gonna have another one. We were glad, you know, but we knew it was gonna put a big dent in our lives. We had to move to a bigger trailer, and of course the rent went up, so I started working more hours at the body shop. Toward the end of this pregnancy, Alice had some problems carrying the baby. She gained a lot of weight and her fingers and toes really swole up. She's never been much of a complainer, but she did have lots of aches and pains this time. She had to quit her job, and let her mom take care of Ben most of the day."

"I understand she gave birth just about 3 weeks ago, now," I interjected.

"That's right. His name's Josh, after my Dad. Anyhow, once we got home from the hospital, Alice got so...." He struggled to name it. "So ... down. She doesn't want to hold the baby or take care of him. She loved nursing Ben, but with Josh she just sits there rocking and crying—with great big tears running down her face. It breaks my heart to see her like that." He looks sad, and afraid for his wife. "She doesn't want to eat, won't pay any attention to Ben at all, says she's tired, and just wants to go back to bed. Nothing gets done around the house, either. It's like she can't focus on anything. What gets to me the most is when she says that she doesn't deserve to have two such beautiful sons. It's like she sees herself as totally useless. I didn't know what else to do but bring her to the hospital. She was never like this before. Alice said she didn't deserve to live anymore and was gonna do something about it. I think she needs some help, don't you?"

I asked Mr. Jackson if Alice ever used any type of substances, and he answered with a definitive "No"—he also indicated that she did not have any other medical problems. She did not exhibit any psychotic symptoms, nor had she had any manic, or mixed, episodes. Alice Jackson was admitted to the psychiatric unit at the hospital for observation.

Alice Jackson's DSM Diagnosis Is as Follows:

Major depressive disorder, single episode, moderate-severe, with peripartum onset

Competency 7 a

ASSESSMENT SUMMARY In this case vignette, the practitioner is called upon to interpret client data to differentiate the mood disorder diagnosis. Clearly, both Anita and Alice struggle with symptoms of depression, but because Alice has had only one major depressive episode and has never exhibited a manic feature, her assessment is major depressive disorder, single episode. Unfortunately, Alice's single episode described in this vignette may very well lead to another occurrence either months or years from now. If (or when) that happens, her assessment will be changed to major depressive episode, recurrent, as in the case of Anita Richards.

In summary, the practitioner should consider the following points to make a differential assessment between a single episode of major depression and recurring episodes of major depression:

- What are the individual's particular symptoms? Further, are those symptoms "out of proportion" to the precipitating event?
- What is the duration and intensity of the depressive features?
- Is the individual's mood "reactive" to changes in life—in other words, is the individual likely to "perk up" when something good happens? (Those with a depressive episode are not likely to do so.)
- Is there a family history of major depression?

A wide range of other life problems and/or stressful events are associated with the onset of a major depressive disorder and are important for the practitioner to consider (Hammen, 2005; Monroe et al., 2014; Monroe & Reid, 2009). In addition, the practitioner must determine whether or not the individual has had episodes of manic-like behaviors, which would indicate a bipolar disorder or cyclothymic disorder.

Competency 7 c

The competency-based assessment helps carefully examine the multiple influences in a person's life and to distinguish between a depressive episode and other closely related disorders. The competency-based assessment, for example, considers medical conditions (such as epilepsy, cerebrovascular diseases, and certain tumors) that manifest depressive features. Other conditions that can complicate making an assessment include psychotic disorders commonly associated with depression such as schizophrenia, attention-deficit/hyperactivity disorder, adjustment disorder with depressed mood, and periods of sadness that are simply an inherent part of life experiences.

The task of considering Alice Jackson's diagnosis of a major depressive disorder, single episode, with peripartum onset may confound the practitioner because the depressive episode occurs shortly after childbirth (about 4 weeks immediately following childbirth) and does not occur at any other times. As we can see in Alice's situation, fathers are not immune to the emotional consequences either. Ramchandani and colleagues (2005) underscore the importance of evaluating the father for depressive symptoms as well. Figure 5.2 shows the interactions of the biological, psychological, and social variables in Alice Jackson's life.

The practitioner should pay careful attention to situations of postpartum onset because of the increased likelihood of maternal harm to the infant. In Alice's case,

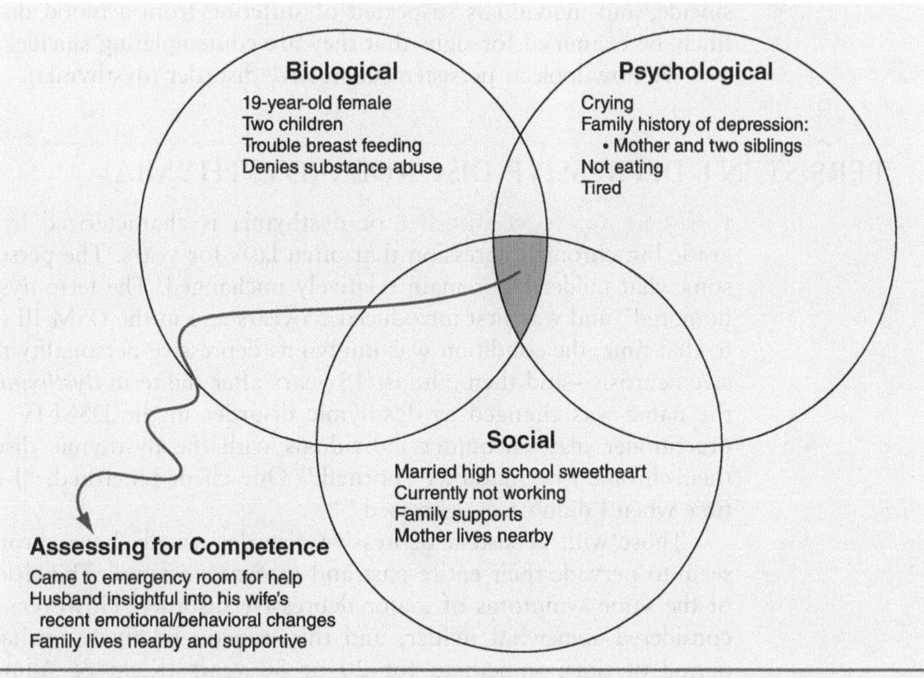

FIGURE 5.2 › Major Depressive Disorder
The interactions of the biological, psychological, and social variables in Alice Jackson's life.

her husband Mark reacted quickly to the changes in her behavior, underscoring the importance of collateral contacts.

Schizoaffective disorder can be distinguished from major depression in that it has a defined element of psychosis along with a mood disorder lasting more than 2 weeks. The relative absence of the symptoms of a major depressive episode, such as fatigue, loss of interest, and insomnia, help the practitioner differentiate from the sadness that is a part of life or an adjustment disorder with depressed mood. As well, distractibility is a key aspect of attention-deficit/hyperactivity disorder (ADHD), which can be interpreted as the inability to concentrate seen in major depressive disorder. However, someone with ADHD most likely presents with irritability rather than the sadness or loss of interest seen in depression. However, the two disorders can co-occur, and the practitioner is encouraged to be cautious when considering a co-occurring major depressive disorder (APA, 2013). Major depressive disorder more frequently co-occurs with the substance-related disorders, panic disorder, obsessive-compulsive disorder, anorexia nervosa, bulimia nervosa, and borderline personality disorder.

The most common emotional change associated with major depression is not the depressed mood per se but rather the pervasive loss of interest and pleasure in everyday living. Major depressive episodes are associated with a significant risk of suicide, and individuals suspected of suffering from a mood disorder should routinely be examined for signs that they are contemplating suicide.

We now look at persistent depressive disorder (dysthymia).

PERSISTENT DEPRESSIVE DISORDER (DYSTHYMIA)

Persistent depressive disorder or dysthymia is characterized by a relatively low-grade but chronic depression that often lasts for years. The person's symptoms are somewhat milder but remain relatively unchanged. The term *dysthymia* means "ill humored" and was first introduced 25 years ago in the DSM-III (APA, 1980). Prior to that time, the condition was known as depressive personality disorder or depressive neurosis—and then (almost 15 years after the term *dysthymia* was introduced) the name was changed to dysthymic disorder in the DSM-IV (APA, 1994). The practitioner may encounter individuals with the dysthymic disorder who regard their chronic low mood as "normal." One client remarked, "I don't remember a time when I didn't feel depressed."

Those with persistent depressive disorder usually have chronic symptoms that seem to pervade their entire past and present existence. This disorder shares many of the same symptoms of major depressive disorder. However, the symptoms are considered somewhat milder, and they remain relatively unchanged over a long period of time; sometimes for 20 or 30 years (Klein & Allmann, 2014; Klein, Shankman, & Rose, 2006). It seems that most people suffering from persistent depressive disorder eventually experience a major depressive episode. However, differences between the two disorders appear to be in their levels of severity and chronicity; dysthymic symptoms are milder but more chronic than those of major depression.

PREVAILING PATTERN

Persistent depressive disorder is a consolidation of chronic major depressive disorder and dysthymia noted in the DSM-IV (APA, 2000, 2013). Its prevalence is reported to be about 0.5 percent in the general U.S. population.

DIFFERENTIAL ASSESSMENT

Persistent depressive disorder is considered when an individual presents with a chronic depressed mood that lasts at least 2 years or longer (or in children and adolescents presenting with an irritable mood for 1 year), is evident more days than not, and is not severe enough to fit the picture of someone with a major depressive episode. For the practitioner to consider this diagnosis, the person has never been without symptoms and must exhibit at least two (or more) of the following:

- Increased or decreased appetite.
- Increased or decreased sleep.
- Low energy.
- Low self-esteem.

- Poor concentration or decision-making ability.
- Hopelessness.

In addition, the practitioner should rule out manic or hypomanic bipolar episodes as well as cyclothymic disorder.

There has been a great deal of discussion within the professional community about whether persistent depressive disorder represents a disorder *sui generis* (unique or singular) or whether it is merely a milder form of major depression. A small percentage of individuals with persistent depressive disorder never experience a full depressive episode. However, at some point, a large majority of these individuals will experience a depressive episode. Typically, the persistent depressive disorder develops first, and then one or more major depressive episodes subsequently occur (Klein & Allmann, 2014; Klein et al., 2006). It may be important for the practitioner to discern this particular patterning of depression, because it is associated with more severe problems in living and a more problematic future outlook.

Persistent depressive disorder (dysthymia) typically has an insidious onset beginning in the childhood or adolescent years. It is less common to find symptoms emerging in adulthood. Persistent depressive disorder in children and adolescents can be considered after a 1-year period of a depressed or irritable mood. Those individuals with an onset on or before the age of 21 are characterized as early onset, and those after the age of 21 are considered late onset. The age when a person first begins to experience the symptoms of persistent depressive disorder may influence the course and outcome. Unless the practitioner has known a client for a period of time, persistent depressive disorder may be hard to identify. For instance, if the practitioner notices a sudden or gradual worsening of the client's symptoms, then persistent depressive disorder might be considered.

A person's mood is characterized as brooding, complaining, sorrowful, gloomy, somber, and nihilistic (or a sense of one's existence that is senseless and useless). Everything seems to be taken very seriously, and life is perceived as a constant struggle that brings little happiness or satisfaction. The biological domain may reflect an assortment of somatic (or physical symptoms) or neuropsychological features, which can include fatigue, lack of energy, difficulty thinking, and problems eating and sleeping. Persistent depressive disorder is not characterized by episodes but by the perpetual waxing and waning presence of symptoms. As a consequence, the individual often feels deficient, unlovable, inferior, and unable to appreciate their value to others. Because of this self-concept, they often experience difficulties in interpersonal domains of their life; for example, marriages and friendships tend to suffer. The combined effects of dysphoria (or a state of feeling unhappy or unwell), low sense of self, and poor interpersonal relationships frequently contribute to the individual's vulnerability.

There are no universally accepted precipitants for what causes this disorder, but predisposing factors may include a history of childhood psychiatric illnesses, chronic psychosocial stressors, or a family history of major depressive disorder. The following vignette illustrates persistent depressive disorder (dysthymia) and how it influences Mario Delucca's life. Note that he sought help not for the symptoms associated with this disorder, but for other problems like his relationship with his wife and getting along on the job.

CASE The Case of Mario Delucca

Mario Delucca is a 56-year-old married father of three grown daughters. He is a well-respected college professor. Dr. Delucca called my office last week saying he was concerned about how things were going for him at the university. When I saw him, he looked older than his stated age; he carried himself in a stooped and hunched-over manner. While he had what I would characterize as the "rumpled, disheveled, absentminded professor look," there was an air about him that made him look depressed and tired. His gray hair looked to me like a haircut was long overdue—in fact, overall, his personal appearance could be characterized as sloppy: he hadn't combed his hair, and clearly he needed a shave.

He entered my office in a subdued manner and quietly took a seat in the farthest corner possible. I initiated the conversation. "Dr. Delucca, what has been happening that made you decide to come in today?"

He replied, "Things are, well, not so good. I know I should have come in to see you before now, but I got caught up in some family stuff. Well, you know, after a while things just went downhill. I feel embarrassed just having to talk about it."

"Well, you are here now," I responded, "and that's important." I commented that he appeared tired.

Dr. Delucca sighed and stated, "I just don't seem to have very much free time. When I'm not teaching, I'm grading papers, presenting at conferences, or writing. I guess I don't have many opportunities for leisure." He smiled sadly and continued, "I know I should have come in sooner, but things were going all right for a while—for about a month—but then everything just went right back to the way it used to be."

I asked Dr. Delucca to elaborate.

"I just feel sad and tired all the time," he responded. "I never want to do anything, and I'm having some trouble eating and sleeping. I can't say I've lost any weight because my clothes still fit me. Well, mostly. I saw my doctor last week for a physical, and she wanted to give me a prescription for some sleeping pills ... but I told her I'd rather tough it out. You know, I really can't remember a time when I didn't feel this way. Maybe this's just the way I am—or maybe it's my job. I don't know."

We spoke a while longer. After he left, I made the following summary of our discussion:

- Manages to work, but is experiencing problems at the university. Should have been promoted to full professor (according to him) 3 years ago (but admits he does not have publications to warrant tenure). Claims his department chair has hinted it's time for him to look for another position elsewhere.
- His third wife (of 5 years)—Rosemary—recently filed for divorce. He says that's more evidence he's a loser. Feels he just can't do anything right.
- Denies any periods of elevated mood or increased energy.
- Was told by his physician to reduce his stress and salt intake due to hypertension and (mild) congestive heart failure.
- Denies alcohol or drug use—has an occasional beer on the weekends.
- He has gone through recurring depressed moods, lasting 1 to sometimes 2 months at a time.
- Denies any psychotic features (no hallucinations, delusions, or bizarre thoughts or ideas).

Mario Delucca's DSM diagnosis is as follows:

Persistent depressive disorder (dysthymia), late onset with intermittent major depressive episodes, with current episode, moderate severity

Competency 7 b

Assessment Summary This case vignette offers yet another opportunity to organize and interpret case data to develop the competency-based assessment for Mario Delucca. Looking for differences between persistent depressive disorder (dysthymia) and major depressive disorder can be very complex, because the symptoms are nearly identical. In addition, some individuals can also meet criteria for major depressive disorder. When that happens, as seen in the case of Dr. Delucca, the practitioner assigns the diagnosis of persistent depressive disorder and then specifies the presentation of major depressive disorder. All in all, the duration of persistent depressive disorder tends to be longer, and its depressive symptoms can vary; that is, there can be periods of time when full criteria for major depressive disorder are not met. Looking carefully at Dr. Delucca's story, his mood symptoms can be described as chronic rather than acute or recurrent; that is, he has never been without these features for longer than a few weeks at a time, and they are present more days than not for him, so this is his "normal." Dr. Delucca's presentation characterizes someone who is depressed at the time he came to see the social worker, and he describes a poor self-image, fatigue, difficulty sleeping, decreased appetite, and what could be considered a gloomy outlook on life. Impaired social and occupational functioning can be seen in his social relationships; particularly, his third wife has recently filed for a divorce, and there are "hints" that his job may be in jeopardy. Dr. Delucca considers his wife's actions as evidence that he's worthless or "a loser," which is what prompted him to seek help.

Many times the practitioner will work with individuals who experience reversals in life, may have life-threatening illness, or sustain other misfortunes which, in the context of chronic depression, seem understandable. For most people, however, life is not always filled with misfortune. Through careful questioning, the practitioner can usually find a period of time where misfortune did not occur, which helps differentiate a general state of unhappiness from persistent depressive disorder. In the case of Dr. Delucca, even if he did experience a reversal of his misfortunes, he would more than likely still remain sad and gloomy.

Depressive symptoms may occur in individuals with Cluster B and C personality disorders and the anxiety disorders, placing them at a higher risk for a co-occurring persistent depressive disorder. Those with a chronic psychotic disorder, such as schizoaffective disorder, schizophrenia, or delusional disorder, may also experience depressive symptoms, but they are differentiated from persistent depressive disorder if the symptoms are seen only during the course of the psychotic disorder (or in the residual phase). In addition, dysthymia can be automatically ruled out at the appearance of any manic episode, a feature of bipolar I disorder.

Competency 7 c

It might be considered a challenge to look for Dr. Delucca's coping strategies in this case vignette. However, learning about intrapersonal and interpersonal functioning provides a more complete clinical picture of what is going on for Dr. Delucca and helps identify the competencies within his life that can be later expanded upon in counseling. In this way, the emphasis shifts to the positive behaviors and events rather than examining so-called defects. Dr. Delucca's sense of himself is poor, and it would be important to point out the reality that he has had a successful career. Additionally, he is well respected in his profession and needs to focus his concern on ways to achieve tenure and become more productive. His willingness to seek professional help should be viewed as another of his strengths. Figure 5.3 illustrates the interactions of the biological, psychological, and social variables in Mario Delucca's life.

There are several additional conditions that are a part of the depressive disorders. They are briefly reviewed in this chapter, highlighting the common threads in

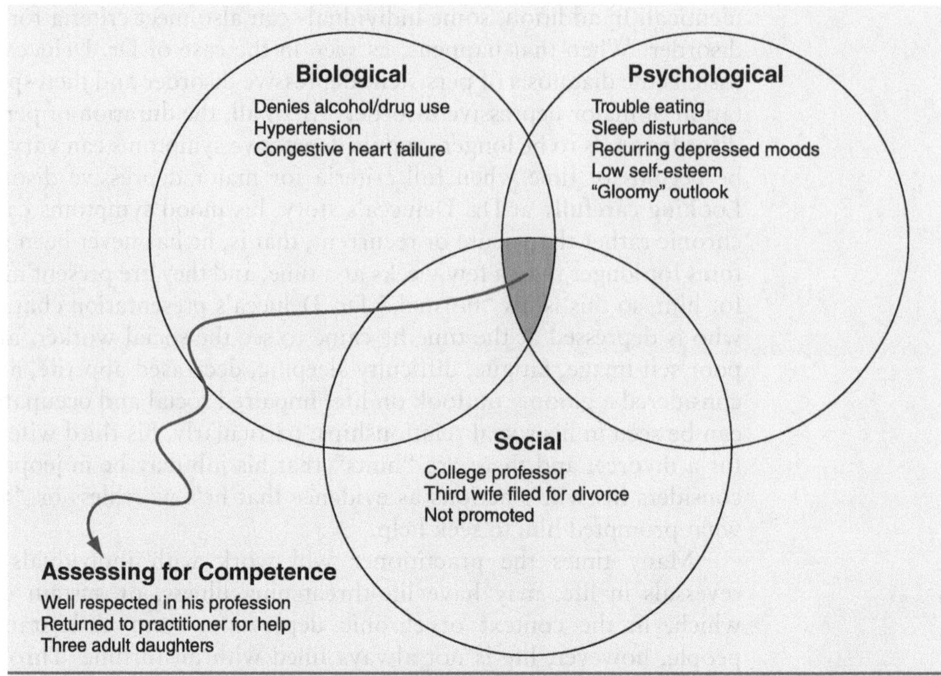

FIGURE 5.3 › PERSISTENT DEPRESSIVE DISORDER (DYSTHYMIA)
The interactions of the biological, psychological, and social variables in Mario Delucca's life

the symptom picture. We begin with an introduction to premenstrual dysphoric disorder, new to the DSM-5.

THE MINOR DEPRESSIVE DISORDERS

PREMENSTRUAL DYSPHORIC DISORDER

Premenstrual dysphoric disorder is a premenstrual syndrome associated primarily with the latter phase (or luteal phase) of the menstrual cycle, consisting of a cluster of affective, behavioral, and somatic symptoms (Rapkin & Lewis, 2013). Considered a severe form of premenstrual syndrome (PMS), the disorder affects between 1.8 percent and 5.8 percent of menstruating women (APA, 2013). Symptoms follow a predictable, cyclic pattern and end shortly after menstruation begins. On average, the symptoms last 6 days, with the most intense symptoms happening in the 2 days before and through the day of the start of menstrual blood flow (Biggs & Demuth, 2011). Emotional symptoms are generally present, and mood symptoms are dominant. In the words of a client:

> When I get my period, I get very extreme mood swings but if you look at me, no one can tell. That's because I feel like I would lose my friends if I let these ridiculous moods show. I can go from smiling to holding back tears in what feels like an instant. I'm one of those people who is always happy, but when

I'm like this, I can get incredibly angry or cry over nothing. Absolutely nothing! I also get bad pain. So far, the doctors haven't found anything yet.

A substantial disruption to personal relationships is typical. The main symptoms include: affective liability (or mood swings), anger or irritability, depressed mood, and marked anxiety. At least one or more must of these symptoms be present for at least a year to support the diagnosis. One or more of the following symptoms, and totaling five to reach a diagnosis, must also be present: decreased interest in daily activities and relationships; trouble concentrating or focusing; tiredness or low energy; change in appetite, seen as food cravings or overeating; trouble sleeping or sleeping all the time; feeling out of control; and/or physical symptoms, such as bloating, breast tenderness, headaches, and joint or muscle pain. The diagnosis is confirmed by daily ratings during at least two symptomatic menstrual cycles. If not, the diagnosis is assigned as provisional.

Substance/Medication-Induced Depressive Disorder

Substance/medication-induced depressive disorder is the diagnostic category reserved for depression that is induced by alcohol or drugs. When a substance/medication-induced depression hits, unlike the transient feelings of sadness that are normal and that everyone experiences—or even the temporary hangover that often affects people the morning after excessive alcohol or drug use—it feels considerably worse and lasts for much longer. For some people, it can mean a complete loss of interest or enjoyment in life. Ironically, most people take drugs to feel better, and yet it is those same drugs in substance/medication-induced depressive disorder that make them feel worse. For this reason, people sometimes do not realize that the alcohol, drugs, or medications are causing the way that they are feeling, because they only associate those substances with positive emotions.

To confirm the diagnosis, it is important to check and make sure that the person's depression was not there before the use of alcohol, drugs, or medications thought to be responsible. Generally, the diagnosis is not considered if the person has a history of depression without substance use, or if the symptoms continue for more than a month after the person becomes abstinent from alcohol, drugs, or medication. Finally, there has to be a significant impact that the change in mood is having on the person's life, either by causing a great deal of distress or by impairing some aspect of social relationships, work, or other parts of life important to them.

Depressive Disorder Due to Another Medical Condition

Certain medical conditions can lead to a state of depression. For example, there are clear associations of depression with Huntington's disease, Parkinson's disease, or traumatic brain injury. Hypothyroidism can also induce clinical depression (Duntas & Maillis, 2013). A principal diagnostic characteristic of depressive disorder due to another medical condition is that it is not the result of a mental disorder per se but, instead, is the consequence of medical conditions, and even some that are not always linked to depression. To confirm the diagnosis, the practitioner must establish that the individual's mood disturbance is related to the medical condition. Additionally, the disturbance does not occur during delirium.

Consider, for example, the practitioner who works in an acute care medical setting like a hospital or nursing home, and may see a patient who has experienced a stroke (a cerebrovascular accident [CVA], which is the sudden death of some brain cells due to a lack of oxygen when blood flow to the brain is impaired by a blocked vein or artery) that is accompanied by depression. In particular, over 30 percent of stroke patients are affected by depression, making it the most common disorder—commonly referred to as post-stroke depression (Espárrago Llorca, Castilla-Guerra, Fernández Moreno, Ruiz Doblado, & Jiménez Hernández, 2015). Hallmarks include social isolation and sleep complications. These individuals are at a higher risk of mortality than those post-stroke patients who have no post-stroke depression.

Other Specified and Unspecified Depressive Disorders

These disorders are reserved for when the person shows symptoms characteristic of a depressive disorder but do meet full criteria for any specific diagnostic class. The other specified depressive disorder is reserved for situations when the practitioner may indicate the specific reason criteria are not fully met, such as a recurrent brief depression, a short-duration depressive episode (lasting 4 to 13 days), or a depressive episode with insufficient symptoms. Unspecified depressive disorder is assigned when the practitioner chooses not to specify when criteria is not met, such as a client seen in an emergency room setting.

COMPLICATIONS ASSOCIATED WITH MAJOR DEPRESSIVE DISORDERS

Competency 1 a

Of all the complications associated with depressive disorders, the risk for suicide is a major concern for the practitioner. All major mental illnesses carry an increased risk for suicide but the affective state of hopelessness, a key feature of major depressive disorder, is a powerful predictor. The lifetime risk of suicide among those with untreated depression ranges from a little over 2 percent to 15 percent (American Association of Suicidology, 2014). No one really knows why people choose to end their lives—nor does anyone know how to predict those who will try. The social work profession's Code of Ethics is very clear about the practitioner's responsibilities to clients who are at risk of harming themselves. In these instances, the importance of acting in the client's behalf is clearly spelled out in the Code. In particular, "Social workers may limit clients' right to self-determination when, in the social workers' professional judgment, clients' actions or potential actions pose a serious, foreseeable, and imminent risk to themselves or others" (National Association of Social Workers, 1999, p. 7). At all times, the practitioner strives to promote clients' well-being and to protect them from harm. Despite this clear professional mandate, the reasons for someone considering suicide are complex, and there are many features for the practitioner to consider.

The competency-based assessment helps explore those factors that may help identify individuals who have a high risk for suicide. Within the depressive disorders cohort, attempted and completed suicide is very common in individuals who experience depression because of the heightened feelings of hopelessness and helplessness. In 2014, the American Association of Suicidology reported that those suffering from depression are 25 times at greater risk for suicide than the general population. More specifically, depression is present in at least 50 percent of all suicides. This translates into major depressive disorder being the diagnosis most commonly associated with suicide.

Sources used to develop the following discussion include the American Association of Suicidology (2014); Gotlib and Hammen (2014); James and Gilliand (2012); Kanel (2014); and Wade and Tavris (2013). We begin with a review of the numerous myths about suicide. It is important for the practitioner to be able to distinguish myth from reality in order to avoid misunderstanding suicidal behavior. Consider the following:

1. *If suicide is discussed with a client, that client will be more likely to attempt suicide.* In practice, it will be a sense of relief for an individual to talk about suicide with someone like the practitioner who is accepting and not judgmental. Simply put, for thoughts about suicide to be addressed, they need to be discussed. This kind of conversation will not cause harm to the individual who is really not suicidal.
2. *Clients who threaten suicide will actually not do it and the practitioner does not need to take them seriously.* A large percentage of people who kill themselves have often previously threatened or disclosed their intent to others beforehand.
3. *Suicide is an irrational act.* If suicide is viewed from the suicidal person's perspective, it makes sense to them.
4. *Individuals who commit suicide are insane.* There is evidence of an association between suicide and mental illness; principally bipolar disorder, major depression, schizophrenia, or the personality disorders, particularly borderline personality disorder. Comorbidity increases suicide risk, especially the anxiety disorders or panic attacks. A history of alcohol abuse and dependence is commonly found among people with commit suicide and intoxication at the time of the suicide attempt is an all too common pattern. Unfortunately, most individuals who are suicidal are normal people who are acutely depressed, lonely, hopeless, helpless, newly aggrieved, shocked, deeply disappointed, jilted, or otherwise overcome by an emotionally charged situation.
5. *Suicide is an inherited tendency that tends to run in families.* Although more than one family member has been found to commit suicide, the genetic risk for suicide has not been established. However, one may learn self-destructive tendencies, or they may be situational, or even linked to depression or other life conditions.
6. *Once a person thinks about suicide, the thought does not go away.* While a person at one point in life may contemplate suicide, he or she may recover from the original threat and related painful feelings that led to the suicidal thought. Additionally, that individual may learn appropriate responses and controls, and go on to live a productive life free of the threat of self-inflicted harm.
7. *When the individual has attempted suicide and moves through it without self-harm, the danger is over.* In reality, most suicides occur within 3 months after the person begins to "improve." A clue the practitioner ought to look for is when the person seems euphoric (or elated) following a depressed or suicidal episode; in essence, the person has everything settled and planned and is at peace with the idea of committing suicide.
8. *One sign of recovery for the person who was suicidal is when he or she shows generosity and shares personal possessions.* Many suicidal individuals begin to

give away their most prized possessions once they have enough energy to make a definite (suicide) plan. Giving away personal effects is equivalent to acting out a last will and testament.

9. *Suicide is an act that is always impulsive.* There are several types of suicidal acts ranging from impulsive actions to others that are very carefully planned and carried out.
10. *Suicide affects only the wealthy and privileged members of society.* Unfortunately, suicide can affect people at all levels of society.
11. *Suicide happens without warning.* Suicide is usually preceded by a warning and in most cases, the person will show symptoms of suicidal thinking or provide clues to his or her intent.

The following questions are helpful to keep in mind when considering a person's potential risk for suicide:

- *Is there anything in the client's history that generates the suicidal thoughts/behavior*, such as a family history of a first-degree relative that committed suicide, adverse childhood experiences (parental loss; emotional, physical, and sexual abuse; isolation; and other acute psychosocial stressors)?
- *What precipitated the client's current crisis and is it different from other life events?* Consider, for example, recent adverse life events such as a recent lob loss, financial stress, unemployment and a drop in socioeconomic status, domestic partner violence, separation and divorce, bereavement, poor relationship with family, and family instability. Also ask your client about current health factors, such as the presence of acute and chronic health problems or diagnoses of conditions such as HIV or cancer.
- *What does the client feel during the crisis?* For instance, consider feelings of hopelessness, helplessness, despair, or in other words a sense that nothing will ever get better.
- *How does the client think about suicide?* For example, are they frightened by the idea of self-harm, or is this a welcoming thought?
- *What active (or planned) suicidal behaviors have occurred or are occurring?* A suicide plan may include the following: timing, availability of method, setting, and actions made toward carrying out the plan (such as having access to medicines, poisons, rope, or a weapon), choosing and checking out a setting for suicide, and rehearsing the plan. Keep in mind that the more detailed and specific the person's suicide plan, the higher the level of risk for carrying out self-harm through suicide.

Competency 4 a

Social workers are often called upon to apply critical thinking skills to inform their professional judgment about the potential for a client's suicide. In practice, there are a number of evidence-based inventories and research-based questionnaires that are helpful tools to determine a person's suicide risk. Unfortunately, because of the emergency nature of suicide, the practitioner often does not have the luxury of time to administer a test, or the client may not be interested in sitting down with a paper-and-pencil assessment. Therefore, the practitioner is usually left to rely on his or her clinical judgment and practice wisdom to assess suicide risk. Each client is different and there is no stereotypical behavioral pattern for people who commit suicide. Although it is beyond the scope of this book to offer specific guidelines for a risk assessment, the following offers a mnemonic for identifying the key warning signs for suicide called, "Is path warm?" They are:

I	Ideation	The person will often express thoughts of suicide or threaten suicide before an attempt. Is he or she looking for ways to kill him- or herself by seeking access to firearms, pills, or other means? Are they threatening to hurt or kill themselves? Are they talking (or writing) about death, dying, or suicide— and are these actions really out of the ordinary for them?
S	Substance abuse	Is the person suddenly increasing substance use? This includes alcohol, which can sometimes be easily overlooked.
P	Purposelessness	The person may start talking about having no purpose or meaning in life. This may be communicated indirectly, and the practitioner listens for comments like, "Life is not worth living," or "There is no reason to go on."
A	Anxiety	The person may show signs of anxiety or agitation. They might appear to be "on edge" just about all the time. They may be unable to sleep or sleep all the time.
T	Trapped	The person may feel like there is "no way out" of their situation. They may talk about not seeing any solution to their problem.
H	Hopelessness	Suicidal persons may express feeling hopeless; that is, they may talk about how things will not change and may even seem desperate.
W	Withdrawal	The individual may withdraw from family, friends, and even society. This sense of isolation can be gradual or rather dramatic and sudden. Low self-esteem may be a factor, and the person may feel worthless, guilty, shameful, or unworthy of being around other people.
A	Anger	The person may show signs of rage, uncontrolled anger, and/or seek revenge. Behavior might be erratic and may include hurting others in addition to themselves.
R	Recklessness	The person may engage in high-risk activities or behaviors, seemingly without thinking.
M	Mood changes	Dramatic changes in the person's personality, mood, or behavior are seen.

Additional warning signs the practitioner may look for are:

- Changes in appetite.
- Speaking or moving with unusual speed (or slowness).
- Unusual neglect of one's physical appearance.
- Difficulties concentrating.
- Giving away prized or valued possessions.

- Saying goodbye to family and/or friends.
- Involvement in destructive or abusive relationships.
- Younger children or adolescents may be bullied or bully others.

Competency 1 b

When exploring suicide with a client, the practitioner's goal is to begin to construct alternatives to suicidal behavior and minimize the short-term reinforcements that happen when suicidal ideation and behavior begin to develop. The practitioner initiates the discussion by taking all threats of suicide seriously, not overreacting, being aware of his or her own feelings especially around the emotional content of suicidal ideation (or countertransference), and remaining calm and listening to the client's "story" with empathy (or compassion). The practitioner will:

- Be available and have backup support.
- Obtain consultation or supervision as appropriate.
- Fully explore the client's reasons for considering suicide.
- Minimize opportunities for self-harm.
- Deal with the client's lethality.
- Involve others in the client's life when appropriate.
- Obtain a positive commitment from the client (including a contract agreement not to commit suicide if needed).
- Develop a specific plan with the client for continued follow-up care.
- Revisit the client's issues related to suicide, especially as the depression lifts.
- Document the work in the patient's chart.

MEDICATIONS COMMONLY ASSOCIATED WITH THE DEPRESSIVE DISORDERS

Antidepressant medications have been linked with suicide. Of interest, people who are taking antidepressants may entertain thoughts of committing suicide about 1 to 2 weeks after starting to take an antidepressant. Unfortunately, many people fail to recognize their depression, figuring that's "just way it is," but there are a number of biological therapies for treating the depressive disorders, ranging from medication to electroconvulsive therapy, that can dramatically affect brain chemistry. According to the American Association of Suicidology (2014), the treatment of depression is effective 60 to 80 percent of the time.

As mentioned in Chapter 1, we are only now beginning to better understand the neurological features of mental disorders. To expand this understanding, we turn to a brief overview of the latest medical approaches, beginning with a general idea of how the central nervous system works and the related effects of four basic types of antidepressants. We conclude with a synopsis of electroconvulsive therapy, an approach commonly used when medication does not appear to work.

As considered in Chapter 1, the function of the central nervous system (brain and spinal cord) is to gather and process information, produce responses to stimuli, and to coordinate the workings of different cells. This is accomplished by the transmission of messages in the brain—primarily across neurons—through a complicated process of electrical and chemical reactions. As we have seen, the neuron is a basic building block of the nervous system that processes and transmits information by electrical and chemical signaling. Responding to a neural impulse, the brain must get its message across the synaptic cleft to another cell. The neurotransmitters can affect behavior such as mood or emotion through their effect on specific nerve circuits. Three things can happen to the neurotransmitter:

- They can bind to a specific site on the postsynaptic cell membrane of the next neuron.
- They can be reabsorbed into the presynaptic cell to be stored until the next release of transmitter.
- They can be broken down and metabolized by enzymes (such as monoamine oxidase or a cholinesterase).

Four basic types of antidepressant medications are commonly associated with treating the depressive disorders; selective-serotonin reuptake inhibitors (SSRIs), mixed reuptake inhibitors, monoamine oxidase (MAO) inhibitors, and tricyclic antidepressants. The SSRIs are the class of drugs considered the first-line choice of treatment for depression. They work by selectively inhibiting or blocking the presynaptic reuptake of serotonin (the neurotransmitter that can have either an excitatory or inhibitory effect associated with sleep, mood, anxiety, and appetite) in the brain. This serves to temporarily increase levels of serotonin at the receptor site. The best-known medication in this class is fluoxetine (or its brand name of Prozac). There are concerns about the increased risk for suicide when taking this drug, particularly among children and adolescents, and research in this area continues. There are side effects to taking the SSRIs, and the most common are physical agitation, sexual dysfunction, low sexual desire, insomnia, and gastrointestinal upset.

The newer antidepressant medications are the mixed reuptake inhibitors. They act in a slightly different manner by blocking reuptake of norepinephrine (which affects the neurons that are involved in increased heart rate, the slowing of intestinal activity associated with stress, and the neurons involved in learning, memory, dreaming, waking from sleep, and emotion) as well as serotonin. Some of the more common medications are bupropion (Wellbutrin), venlafaxine (Effexor), and duloxetine (Celexa). Nausea, vomiting, insomnia, headaches, and seizure are typical side effects.

The MAO inhibitors work by blocking the enzyme MAO that breaks down neurotransmitters such as norepinephrine and serotonin. Because they are blocked and not broken down, the neurotransmitters gather in the synapse, leading to a down regulation. The MAO inhibitors are known to be slightly more effective than the tricyclics but are used far less often. This is because of the side effects of tyramine-rich foods that can lead to severe hypertensive episodes and even death, such as eating aged cheese (i.e., Camembert or Edam), sauerkraut, aged meat, sausages, cold cuts, chocolate, yogurt and sour cream, pickled herring or smoked fish, sardines, anchovies, and yeast extracts (various forms of processed yeast products commonly used as food additives or flavorings) or drinking alcohol (most notably beer and red wine, especially Chianti) as well as caffeinated beverages. Even cold medications are dangerous. Additional side effects include constipation, dizziness, dry mouth, hypotension, insomnia, nausea, sexual difficulties, skin reaction, weakness, and weight gain. The MAO inhibitors tend to be prescribed only when the other antidepressants do not seem to work.

Before the introduction of the SSRIs, the tricyclic antidepressants were more widely used. While researchers do not know exactly how this class of drugs works, it seems they block the reuptake of certain neurotransmitters, allowing them to collect in the synapse and desensitize or down-regulate the transmission of that particular transmitter—at least initially. That way, less of the neurochemical is transmitted. These drugs seem to have the greatest effect by down-regulating norepinephrine. However, other neurotransmitter systems are also affected, particularly serotonin. The best-known drugs are imipramine (Tofranil) and amitriptyline (Elavil). The side effects are somewhat severe, causing many individuals to stop taking the drug. They include blurred vision, dry mouth, constipation, difficulty urinating, drowsiness, weight gain, and sometimes sexual dysfunction. The SSRIs are preferred because of their fewer side effects (Arroll et al., 2005).

One alternative to antidepressants that has become increasingly popular is the natural herbal extract St. John's wort (hypericum). It has few side effects and is relatively easy to produce. Currently available in health food stores, drugstores, and similar outlets, there is no guarantee that St. John's wort may contain the appropriate ingredients. Different brands may have different concentrations of the active substance.

In those instances where a person does not respond to medication, electroconvulsive therapy (ECT) may be considered. In this instance, an electric shock is administered directly through the brain for a very brief period of time (less than a second), producing a seizure and a series of brief convulsions. These treatments are usually given once every other day in a series of 6 to 10 administrations; fewer if the person's mood returns to normal. Side effects include temporary short-term memory loss and confusion that disappears after a week or two. Some individuals may experience longer-term memory problems.

SUMMARY

This chapter began with a review of the key features of disruptive mood dysregulation disorder, new to the depressive disorders in the DSM-5. Though the key diagnostic feature is irritability, it is placed in this chapter as it is believed to place the individual at a higher risk for a depressive disorder later in life. The common features of the depressive disorders are a sad, empty, or irritable mood accompanied by somatic and cognitive changes that significantly impact the individual's ability to function socially, occupationally, or in other important areas of life. This theme is evident in the disorders addressed in this chapter, such as major depressive disorder, persistent depressive disorder (or dysthymia), premenstrual dysphoric disorder, and substance/medication-induced depressive disorder. To complete the practitioner's understanding of the depressive disorders, the chapter briefly reviewed the diagnoses of depressive disorder due to another medical condition and the specified and unspecified depressive disorders. As we have seen, the depressive disorders can cause persistent feelings of sadness and loss of interest. A person may feel as if life is not worth living, thus increasing the risk of suicide. The chapter concluded with an overview of suicide risks and medications commonly used to treat depression and the additional therapeutic approach of electroconvulsive therapy (ECT).

As the DSM transitions from the DSM-IV-TR (APA, 2000) to the current edition of the manual, the following table provides a brief summary of the changes made to the diagnostic classifications in this chapter.

TABLE 5.2 SUMMARY COMPARISON BETWEEN THE DSM-IV-TR AND DSM-5 DIAGNOSES FOR THE DEPRESSIVE DISORDERS
A new disruptive mood dysregulation disorder (DMDD) was introduced for children from 6 years up to 18 years of age
The DSM-IV bereavement exclusion was removed
Specifiers were added for mixed symptoms and for anxiety along with extended discussion for suicide
The term *dysthymia* is now termed *persistent depressive disorder*
Premenstrual dysphoric disorder was removed from the DSM-IV
Appendix for Further Study and introduced in the DSM-5 as a new disorder

PRACTITIONER'S REFLECTIONS

A variety of biopsychosocial factors are correlated with the onset of depression. The competency-based assessment examines all aspects of the client's life. Competent practice takes into account the varying degrees of depression, euphoria, or irritability found in mood disorders. The following activities are aimed at helping us better understand our clients' experiences.

ACTIVITIES

Competency 1 b

1. Persons with a mood disorder present unique challenges for the practitioner. The case of Anita Richards, who struggles with major depression, can evoke many feelings in the practitioner such as incompetence, worry, or anxiety. From the case vignettes presented in this chapter, select a situation reflecting a problem that is (or could be) a potential struggle for you or someone that you know. As a strategy to practice personal reflection and self-correction to assure your continued professional development, ask your supervisor (or a colleague) or to role-play the first minute or two of the interview with you. Take turns assuming the role of the client and the social worker, then provide each other with feedback about this experience. Pay attention to the times when your own feelings might potentially get in the way of your therapeutic relationship.

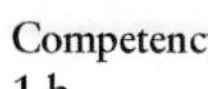

Competency 1 b

2. Can you remember a time in your life when you felt down or depressed? Write down in as much detail as you can remember what this experience felt like. For example, consider how you felt during this time, what kinds of thoughts you may have had, your level of energy, whether you experienced any sleep and/or appetite changes, how you related to others who are (or were) important in your life, and what helped you feel better. Make a list of these insights and discuss with your supervisor how you can use these insights to improve your professional use of self with clients.

Competency 7 c

3. Reflect back on the cases presented in this chapter. Consider the interpersonal and/or social obstacles these clients experienced in coping with their mood disorder. Then assess the client coping strategies available to these clients used to reinforce and improve adaption to living with a mental health diagnosis. Make a list of what else might be needed to improve each client's adaptation to life situations, circumstances, and events related to living with their specific diagnosis.

Competency 7 a

4. Think back to the clients you have seen in your own clinical practice who were feeling sad or down in the dumps but you felt did not qualify for assessment as having a mood disorder. What went into making that determination?

Competency 7 c

5. The competency-based assessment determines the influence of contextual events in a person's life and the unique meaning of those events to him or her. Interview several people who have shared the same kind of stressful life events (e.g., divorce, serious illness, or a death of a loved one). During these conversations, inquire how they felt about the *event*. Be aware of how each person assigns different meanings to the same type of event.

6. Access the Competency-based Assessment and Companion web site at http//www.thomsonedu.com/social_work/gray. You will find the case of Barbara, who typifies someone diagnosed with major depression that is characterized as severe and long lasting. Her feelings of worthlessness, loss of energy, and a marked loss of ability to experience pleasure are prominent in the interview. As your review her interview, make a list of her strengths and the limitations related to her diagnosis.

Competency 7 c

Competency Notes

Competency 1 a—Social workers make ethical decisions by applying standards of the NASW Code of Ethics and other relevant laws, regulations and models for ethical decision-making as appropriate to context (p. 150): Social workers understand the value base of the profession and its ethical standards as well as relevant laws and regulations that may impact practice.

Competency 1 b—Social workers use reflection and self-regulation to manage personal values and maintain professionalism in practice situations (pp. 154, 157): Social workers recognize personal values and make the distinction between personal and professional values.

Competency 4 a—Social workers use practice experience and theory to inform scientific inquiry and research (p. 152): Social workers understand both quantitative and qualitative research methods and their respective roles in evaluating their practice.

Competency 7 a—Social workers collect and organize data and apply critical thinking in order to interpret information from clients and constituencies (pp. 132, 142, 158): Social workers understand that the assessment process is ongoing and conducted with, and on behalf of, diverse individuals, families, groups, organizations, and communities.

Competency 7 b—Social workers are able to apply knowledge of human behavior and the social environment, person-in-environment, and other multidisciplinary theoretical frameworks in the analysis of assessment data (pp. 134, 146): Social workers understand theories of human behavior and the social environment and critically evaluate and apply this knowledge in the assessment process.

Competency 7 c—Social workers develop mutually agreed-on intervention goals and objectives based on the assessment of strengths, needs, and challenges within clients and constituencies (pp. 139, 142, 147, 157, 158): Social workers recognize the implications of the larger practice context in the assessment process.

References

American Association of Suicidology. (2014). Know the warning signs of suicide. Retrieved on January 15, 2015 from: http://www.suicidology.org/resources/warning-signs

American Psychiatric Association (APA). (1980). *Diagnostic and statistical manual of mental disorders* (3rd ed.). Washington, DC: Author.

American Psychiatric Association (APA). (1987). *Diagnostic and statistical manual of mental disorders* (3rd ed., revised). Washington, DC: Author.

American Psychiatric Association (APA). (1994). *Diagnostic and statistical manual of mental disorders* (4th ed.). Washington, DC: Author.

American Psychiatric Association (APA). (2000). *Diagnostic and statistical manual of mental disorders* (4th ed., text revision). Washington, DC: Author.

American Psychiatric Association (APA). (2013). *Diagnostic and statistical manual of mental disorders* (5th ed.). Arlington, VA: Author.

Arroll, B., Macgillivray, S., Ogston, S., Reid, I., Sullivan, F., Williams, B., & Crombie, I. (2005). Efficacy and tolerability of tricyclic antidepressants and SSRIs compared with placebo for treatment of depression in primary care. *Annals of Family Medicine*, *3*, 449–456.

Axelson, D., Findling, R. L., Fristad, M. A., Kowatch, R. A., Youngstrom, E. A., McQue Horwitz, S., ... Birmaher, G. (2012). Examining the proposed disruptive dysregulation disorder diagnosis in children in the longitudinal assessment of manic symptoms study. *Journal of Clinical Psychiatry*, *73*(10), 1342–1350.

Barlow, D. H., & Durand, V. M. (2014). *Abnormal psychology: An integrated approach* (7th ed.). Belmont, CA: Wadsworth Cengage Learning.

Biggs, W. S., & Demuth, R. H. (2011). Premenstrual syndrome and premenstrual dysphoric disorder. *American Family Physician*, *84*(8), 918–924.

Brotman, M. A., Rich, B. A., Guyer, A. E., Lunsford, J. R., Horsey, S. E., Reising, M. M., ... Liebenluft, E. (2010). Dysregulation versus ADHD or bipolar disorder amygdala activation during emotion processing of neutral faces in children with severe mood. *American Journal of Psychiatry*, *167*(1), 61–69.

Brotman, M. A., Schmajuk, M., Rich, B. A., Dickstein, D. P., Guyer, A. E., Costello, E. J., ... Liebenluft, E. (2006). Prevalence, clinical correlates, and longitudinal course of severe mood dysregulation in children. *Biological Psychiatry*, *60*, 991–997.

Copeland, W. E., Angold, A., Costello, E. J., & Hegger, H. (2013). Prevalence, comorbidity, and correlates of DSM-5 proposed disruptive mood dysregulation disorder. *Psychiatry*, *170*(2), 173–179.

Dickstein, D. P., Rich, B. A., Binstock, A. B., Pradella, A. G., Towbin, K. E., Pine, D. S., & Leibenluft, E. (2005). Comorbid anxiety in phenotypes of pediatric bipolar disorder. *Journal of Child and Adolescent Psychopharmacology*, *15*, 543–548.

Duntas, L. H., & Maillis, A. (2013). Hypothyroidism and depression: Salient aspects of pathogenesis and management. *Minerva Endocrinologica*, *38*(4), 365–377.

Espárrago Llorca, G., Castilla-Guerra, L., Fernández Moreno, M.C., Ruiz Doblado, S., & Jiménez Hernández, M.D. (2015). Post-stroke depression: An update. *Neurologia*, *30*(1), 23–31.

Garber, J., Clarke, G. N., Weersing, V. R., Beardslee, W. R., Brent, D. A., Gladstone, T. R., ... Iyengar, S. (2009). Prevention of depression in at-risk adolescents: A randomized controlled trial. *Journal of the American Medical Association*, *301*(21), 2215–2224.

Gelder, M. G., Andreasen, N. C., Lopez-Ibor, Jr., J. J., & Geddes J. R. (Eds.). (2012). *New Oxford textbook of psychiatry* (2nd ed., Vol. 1). Oxford, UK: Oxford University Press.

Gotlib, I. H., & Hammen, C. L. (Eds.). *Handbook of depression* (3rd ed.). New York: Guilford Press.

Hammen, C. (2005). Stress and depression. *Annual Review of Clinical Psychology*, *1*, 293–319.

James, R. K., & Gilliand, B. E. (2012). *Crisis intervention strategies* (7th ed.). Belmont, CA: Cengage Learning.

Joe, S., Baser, R., Breeden, G., Neighbors, H., & Jackson, J. (2006). Prevalence of and risk factors for lifetime suicide attempts among blacks in the United States. *Journal of the American Medical Association*, *296*, 2112–2123.

Kanel, K. (2014). *A guide to crisis intervention* (5th ed.). Belmont, CA: Cengage Learning.

Klein, D. N., & Allmann, E. S. (2014). Course of depression: Persistence and recurrence. In I. H. Gotlib & C. L. Hammen (Eds.). *Handbook of depression* (3rd ed., pp. 82–102). New York: Guilford Press.

Klein, D. N., Shankman, S., & Rose, S. (2006). Ten-year prospective follow-up study of the naturalistic course of dysthymic disorder and double depression. *American Journal of Psychiatry*, *163*, 872–880.

Liebenluft, E. (2011). Severe mood dysregulation, irritability, and the diagnostic boundaries of bipolar disorder in youths. *American Journal of Psychiatry*, *168*, 129–142.

Liebenluft, E., Uher, R., & Rutter, M. (2012). Disruptive mood dysregulation with dysphoria disorder: A proposal for ICD-11. *World Psychiatry*, *11*(Suppl. 1), 77–81.

Moffitt, T. E., Caspi, A., Marrington, H., Milne, B., Melchior, M., Goldberg, D., ... Poulton, R.

(2010). Generalized anxiety disorder and depression: Childhood risk factors in a birth cohort followed to 32 years of age. In D. Goldberg, K. S. Kendler, P. J. Sirovatka, & D. A. Reiger (Eds.). *Diagnostic issues in depression and generalized anxiety disorder: Refining the research agenda for DSM-V* (pp. 217–240). Washington, DC: American Psychiatric Press.

Monroe, S. M., & Reid, M. W. (2009). Life stress and major depression. *Current Directions in Psychological Science, 18*(2), 68–72.

Monroe, S. M., Slavich, G. M., & Georgiades, K. (2014). The social environment and depression. In I. H. Gotlib & C. L. Hammen (Eds.). *Handbook of depression* (3rd ed., pp. 296–314). New York: Guilford Press.

National Association of Social Workers. (1999). *Code of ethics*. Washington, DC: Author.

Nock, M. K., Millner, A. J., Deming, C. A., & Glenn, C. R. (2014). Depression and suicide. In I. H. Gotlib & C. L. Hammen (Eds.). *Handbook of depression* (3rd ed., pp. 448–468). New York: Guilford Press.

Ramchandani, P., Stein, A., Evans, J., O'Connor, T., & the ALSPAC Study Team. (2005). Paternal depression in the postnatal period and child development: A prospective population study. *Lancet, 365*, 2201–2205.

Rapkin, A. J., & Lewis, E. I. (2013). Treatment of premenstrual dysphoric disorder. *Women's Health (London England)*, 9(6), 537–556.

Sadock, B. J., &. Sadock, V. A (2010). *Kaplan and Sadock's pocket handbook of clinical psychiatry* (5th ed.). Philadelphia: Lippincott Williams and Wilkins.

Wade, C., & Tavris, C. (2013). *Psychology* (11th ed.). Upper Saddle River, NJ: Prentice Hall.

CHAPTER 6

Anxiety Disorders

INTRODUCTION

Anxiety disorders are considered the most common and frequently occurring mental disorders. Often chronic in nature, these disorders are associated with severe impairments across interpersonal and social domains. The neurotransmitter systems that use serotonin (5-HT) through other neurotransmitters and neuro-hormones have been implicated in anxiety disorders. Early animal studies have advanced our understanding of stress and the role of genetics and the environment in susceptibility to the risk of anxiety and related disorders (Stein, Schork, & Gelernter, 2008). Increasingly, we have come to understand that early life experiences and genetics may interact to produce alterations in stress responsiveness.

Many anxiety disorders begin in childhood and tend to persist if not treated. They primarily affect females more than males by a ratio of 2:1 (APA, 2013). Anxiety is regarded as a warning signal that helps alert a person to impending or imminent danger and enables him or her to deal with the threat of harm. Fear is a similar warning signal but is markedly different from anxiety. Fear is seen as a response to a definite and/or known hazard, whereas anxiety is a response to an unknown or unspecified threat. The predominant difference between the two is that fear is considered an acute reaction, while anxiety is considered chronic.

A practitioner considers whether or not anxiety is a normal response to something going on in a person's life, or if anxiety is excessive or out of proportion. In particular, a competency-based assessment investigates a person's (1) physical resources (physical arousal), (2) cognitive responses and distortions, and (3) coping strategies (Barlow, 2004). An anxiety disorder should be considered if the person's response is exaggerated in at least one of these three areas.

Anxiety is a mood state wherein a person anticipates future danger or misfortune with apprehension. This response causes a markedly negative effect consisting primarily of tension and somatic features (Barlow, 2004). Clients often experience anxiety as a vague feeling of apprehension manifested as worry, unease, or dread. Everyone experiences anxiety from time to time. One might feel a sense of discomfort, "butterflies in the stomach," a rapid heart rate, or "nervous" fidgeting (Barlow & Durand, 2014). Experiencing some anxiety is considered normal, even adaptive, and a certain amount of anxiety can motivate a person toward taking appropriate actions that ward off a threat. Some anxiety is good, but having too much, as we will see in this chapter, is not.

Anxiety is a normal reaction to anything that might be threatening to a person's lifestyle, values, self, or loved ones. Some degree of anxiety can appear when things go wrong—and (perversely) when things go right or change. To illustrate, when you study and prepare yourself for an exam, you are attempting to reduce anxiety in a good way. When you make adequate preparations, you are taking steps to avoid the anxiety you would experience if you did not study and subsequently failed the exam. Your anxiety about taking an exam becomes an "early warning system" that motivates you to take anticipatory action by studying hard to pass the test.

Competency 7 c

Those who are adversely affected by anxiety are plagued by a sense of having no control over challenging life situations and of being unable to predict them. Anxiety becomes problematic when it begins to significantly interfere with the demands of daily living, particularly in social and occupational functioning. A major problem in understanding anxiety is its subjective nature—anxiety can mean many different things to different people. The competency-based assessment begins by distinguishing between what is considered a normal or adaptive response to life stressors. Anxiety rarely occurs in isolation, and other features such as depression, suicidal ideation, or somatic complaints are commonly noted alongside it (Brown & Barlow, 2009; Clark, 2005; Wilamowska et al., 2010).

The disorders found in this chapter are arranged developmentally beginning with the typical age of onset. The specific DSM-5 disorders involving features of fear and excessive anxiety related to the anxiety disorders are listed in Table 6.1.

Our review begins with separation anxiety, a disorder that tends to begin in childhood and declines as the child moves through adolescence and adulthood.

SEPARATION ANXIETY DISORDER

Separation anxiety is a normal part of a child's development, but when it persists past a certain age or significantly impacts activities, then it can be a problem. Most children tend to be minimally affected by separation anxiety when they reach about 5 years of age. The author remembers a close friend complaining that her 2-year-old would not fall asleep unless she was nearby. Every night their routine was to check the closet and under the bed for monsters. My friend added that she just couldn't wait for her little one to outgrow these night fears and be able to go to bed like everyone else in the house. Unlike the mild worries a child may feel at times of separation, SAD affects the child's ability to engage in ordinary activities. This is the child who, when faced with separation, shows anxiety or tantrums well beyond what is expected for him or her age.

Table 6.1	The DSM-5 Anxiety Disorders
Separation Anxiety Disorder	
Selective Mutism	
Specific Phobias	
Animal	
Natural environment	
Blood-injection-injury	
Situational	
Social Anxiety Disorder (Social Phobia)	
Panic Disorder	
Agoraphobia	
Generalized Anxiety Disorder	
Substance/medication-induced Anxiety Disorder	
Anxiety Disorder due to Another Medical Condition	
Other Specified Anxiety Disorder	
Other Unspecified Anxiety Disorder	

While the cause of separation anxiety disorder (SAD) is unknown, a number of risk factors contribute to its development. For example, children and adolescents who have experienced some form of significant stress such as a stay in the hospital, the death of a loved one or even a pet, or a change in environment are at a higher risk for developing the disorder. Even moving to another house or a change of schools can lead to separation anxiety. Trauma, such as physical or sexual assault, can also be a contributing factor. This disorder is often seen in children when they first begin attending school, but can occur at all ages and in many situations.

Prevailing Pattern

The lifetime prevalence of childhood SAD is estimated to be 4.1 percent of the general population and is equally distributed between boys and girls (Shear, Jin, Ruscio, Walters, & Kessler, 2006). The 12-month prevalence among adults in the United States is reported as 0.9 to 1.9 percent, approximately 4 percent among children, and 1.6 percent in adolescents (APA, 2013).

Differential Assessment

Competency 7 b

SAD should not be confused with the normally occurring separation anxiety seen in children between 18 months and 3 years of age, or stranger anxiety, which is typically seen at 7 to 11 months of age. Being able to differentiate between normal age-appropriate behavior and the symptoms of SAD underscores the social worker's skill in collecting, organizing, and interpreting client data. The main differences between healthy separation anxiety and SAD are the intensity of the child's fears, and whether these fears keep him or her from normal activities, and these fears are well beyond what is considered developmentally appropriate. Children with SAD may become agitated at just the thought of being away from a parent, and may complain of sickness to avoid playing with friends or attending school.

SAD is characterized by an extreme fear and significant distress about being away from home and family to the extent that it affects a child's ability to function socially and academically. For example, they may worry about being kidnapped or getting lost. These are the children who have a great need to stay home or be close to their parents and worry excessively when they are apart.

To reach the diagnostic threshold for this disorder, the child's anxiety or fear must cause distress or affect social or academic functioning and last, at a minimum, 4 weeks for children and adolescents, and 6 months or longer in adults. Children with separation anxiety may cling to their parent and have difficulty falling asleep alone at night. They may be afraid to go out or even refuse to leave the house. The most common fear a child with SAD experiences is the worry that harm will come to a loved one when separated from one another. The individual worries that some unpredicted event may happen that would lead to permanent separation. When separated, a child may be afraid that his or her parent will be involved in an accident, become gravely ill, or in some other way be "lost" to them forever. They may also worry about being kidnapped or getting lost. The need to stay close to their parents or at home may make it difficult for the child to attend school or camp, stay at friends' houses, or even to be in a room alone. Some children may even have repeated nightmares or scary dreams about separation. The child may complain of headaches or stomachaches. An intense fear of separation can lead to dizziness, nausea, or palpitations (Gallo, Thompson-Hollands, Pincus, & Barlow, 2012).

Patty Nemeth's vignette highlights the behaviors that illustrate the symptom picture for SAD. Since we do not know the details of her family life, the competency-based assessment is not included.

CASE The Case of Patty Nemeth

Patty Nemeth is a 7-year-old girl who lives with both of her parents. She has two older sisters, Myra and Kimberly. Ever since kindergarten, Patty has missed several days of school each month. Mrs. Nemeth had not experienced any of these problems with her other two daughters, and she hoped Patty would grow out of this behavior. Unfortunately, Patty's fears about going to school only seem to have gotten worse. For the past month, Patty has become even more upset about going to school. Patty tells her mother that she is afraid "something bad" will happen to her family if she leaves them. Her mother wonders if all the recent news on the television about the tornadoes in the Midwest has something to do with Patty's fears.

At any rate, Patty has temper tantrums and screams to be allowed to stay home. It's hard for Mrs. Nemeth to see her daughter so upset, and she struggles not to give in. This behavior usually happens on a Monday. On the other days when Patty does go to school, she insists that her mom stay close by for at least an hour. Mrs. Nemeth worked out an arrangement with Patty's teacher to leave the classroom door open so Patty can see her. After about an hour of checking the door, Patty seems okay with her mother leaving. After Mrs. Nemeth leaves, the school counselor checks in on Patty just before lunch; more often if the teacher notices if Patty starts to worry that something bad has happened to her mother on the way home. Mrs.

Nemeth stays near her cell phone just in case the school calls. Patty insists that her mother be either on time or early in picking her up after school. If Mrs. Nemeth is even a little late, Patty threatens not to go to school the next day.

To make matters worse, Patty started having nightmares about being kidnapped by strangers who would come in her bedroom window to get her and take her away. She even refused to go on a recent school trip unless her mother went along. When she is at home, Patty wants her mother in sight at all times. Patty also worries about her mother having a terrible accident.

Patty Nemeth's DSM Diagnosis Is as Follows:
Separation anxiety disorder

Assessment Summary The most outstanding feature of Patty Nemeth's behavior is her persistent reluctance to go to school starting as early as kindergarten. Patty's mother had hoped her daughter would outgrow this behavior, but for the past month it has only gotten worse. The fears of separating from mother are beyond what could be reasonably expected for a 7-year-old. Patty's refusal to go to school typically starts on a Monday. When she does go to school, Mrs. Nemeth, along with the teacher's assistance, developed an elaborate plan to separate Patty from her mother; that is, Mrs. Nemeth stays outside the classroom door for at least an hour, allowing Patty to check on her mother. After Mrs. Nemeth leaves, the school counselor checks in on Patty. At the end of the school day, Patty insists that her mother pick her up early or on time. Patty also expresses the fear that something "bad" will happen to her family. In addition, Patty has started to have nightmares, and refused to go on a recent school trip unless her mother went along. When she is at home, Patty insists on keeping her mother in sight at all times.

Competency 7 b

Integral to a differential assessment, the social worker considers a number of alternative diagnostic possibilities. For example, if Patty had a number of worries in addition to separation anxiety, the practitioner might consider the diagnosis of generalized anxiety disorder. If Patty's separation from her mother led to extreme anxiety and panic, a diagnosis of panic disorder may be more appropriate. As well, agoraphobia may be seen if Patty showed a fear of being trapped in places with no viable escape. Those with a conduct disorder are also frequently absent from school, but unlike Patty, the absences are usually related to truancy and not a fear of being separated from a loved one. Similarly, someone with social anxiety disorder may also be absent from school, but this avoidance comes from a fear of being judged by others. It is not uncommon for children to worry about separation from loved ones after a traumatic event such as a disastrous hurricane or tornado, and posttraumatic stress disorder may be seen when symptoms revolve around memories associated with the event itself. Likewise, illness anxiety disorder is evident when the individual's worries revolve around specific illnesses. Bereavement is distinguished by an intense longing for the deceased. Some people with depressive and bipolar disorders may be afraid to leave home, but what differentiates their experiences from those of Patty Nemeth is a diminished level of motivation and energy to engage with the outside world. Patty was certainly oppositional if her mother arrived late to pick her up from school as seen in her threats to be absent the following day, but this differs from oppositional defiant disorder in that Patty's behaviors revolved around separation anxieties rather than a pattern of opposition. Individuals with dependent personality rely on others, and clearly 7-year-old Patty Nemeth is dependent on her mother. However, what distinguishes individuals with a dependent personality disorder from Patty is the fear of abandonment by loved ones. By the same token, Patty's dependence on her mother is developmentally appropriate. Without a doubt, Patty's mother will return each day to pick up her daughter from school, despite Patty's fears to the contrary. Those with a psychotic disorder experience unusual perceptual experiences (hallucinations), which are quite unlike Patty's misperception of her mother's behavior.

It is interesting to note that the vignette makes no reference to the Nemeth family seeking counseling for Patty's behaviors. Unfortunately, this is typical for a number of families struggling with a child with SAD. Instead, Mrs. Nemeth worked out an elaborate plan with the teacher to facilitate her being able to leave Patty at school. The school counselor intervenes only to check on the status of Patty's fears and call Mrs. Nemeth to pick up her daughter, if needed.

In summary, all children experience some anxiety around separation from significant caregivers to some extent, but this fear usually diminishes as the child grows older. Separation anxiety, as seen in Patty Nemeth's vignette, qualifies as a diagnosis when these fears are greater than would be expected of a child of her age. Unfortunately, there is evidence that separation anxiety, if not treated, can extend into adulthood in about a third of cases (Shear et al., 2006).

A review of selective mutism, a relatively rare disorder, follows.

SELECTIVE MUTISM

Children with selective mutism may also be anxious, but what distinguishes these youngsters is a lack of communication with others in selected settings.

PREVAILING PATTERN

Selective mutism is considered a rare disorder and, as such, has not been included in epidemiological studies of the prevalence of childhood disorders (APA, 2013). However, it is considered to occur more frequently in children and usually seen before 5 years of age.

DIFFERENTIAL ASSESSMENT

Selective mutism, formerly known as elective mutism, is characterized by the child's inability to speak in certain settings where speaking is expected while they are able to speak in other settings. For instance, the child may not talk at school but speak freely at home. In some instances, the child may not speak to specific people. These children are often extremely shy. The pattern is serious enough to interfere with school or with social communication, lasting for at least a month but not limited to the first month of school. In addition, this inability to speak is not due to a lack of knowledge of or discomfort with the language required in a social situation.

Since selective mutism is considered to be extremely rare and more than likely will not be seen in the average social worker's mental health practice, a brief snapshot of what this behavior looks like can be seen in the following vignette of Nathaniel "Nate" Sella.

> When Nate turned 4, he just stopped talking. That is, he simply would not talk with anyone at the daycare center. He seemed to understand what people were saying, but he just didn't speak. This had been going on after he was there for about a month and came on for no apparent reason. If he wanted something, Nate would simply point. When he was at home, his mother indicated that Nate seemed just fine. Mrs. Sella was at a loss to understand her son's behavior. She saw him as bright and inquisitive so she was puzzled by his refusal to speak at the daycare center.

We now examine another anxiety-based disorder—specific phobia and the four related specifiers.

SPECIFIC PHOBIA

The term phobia is derived from Phobos, the name of the much feared Greek deity whose father, Ares, was the god of war. Thus, we use the word *phobia* to describe an extreme and irrational fear of simple things or social situations. Most of us have the usual kinds of fears that may include ordinary events like going to the doctor or dentist for a checkup. However, these fears do not rule our lives to the point where we completely avoid such activities. Rather, they tend to be considered inconvenient nuisances that we somehow adapt to and try to work around. In contrast, a person who becomes engulfed in a phobic episode usually feels inundated by overwhelming terror that literally obscures almost all other experiences. In its severest form, a phobia becomes extremely incapacitating. Examples of phobic features include profuse sweating, racing heart, a feeling described as choking or smothering, dizziness (or lightheadedness), and trembling, to name a few.

Prevailing Pattern

The prevalence of fears strong enough to qualify as a phobia during a 1-year period is 8.1 percent of the general population, making this disorder one of the most commonly seen in the United States (Arrindell et al., 2003; Kessler, Berglund, Demler, Jin, & Walters, 2005). Prevalence rates in children are approximately 5 percent, increasing to a rate of 16 percent in the adolescent years seen as ages 13 to 17, and dropping to about 3 to 5 percent in older individuals (APA, 2013).

Differential Assessment

A specific phobia is defined as any persistent, unreasonable, and irrational fear of a specific object (dogs or cats) or situation (flying, heights, animals, receiving an injection, or seeing blood) that causes intense distress. In children, their fears may be seen by crying, tantrums, freezing, or clinging behaviors. The specific object or situation provokes an immediate response, is actively avoided (or somehow endured) with a lot of fear or anxiety and out of proportion to the actual dangers posed. Specific phobias typically last for about 6 months or longer and markedly interfere with a person's capability to function well. They result in the individual's compelling desire to avoid the feared object.

More than 100 specific phobias have been identified—and although enumerating them seems to add little to understanding this disorder, it does highlight the extent of the named phobias. The best recognized specific phobias are specified as the following four major types—animal, natural environment, blood-injection-injury, and situational—plus one category labeled as "other." This other category includes those fears that do not fit into of the four major specifiers; for instance, situations that may lead to choking, vomiting, or in children, a fear of loud sounds or costumed characters often seen at entertainment parks.

Competency 4 a

In practice, the practitioner can expect to see someone who suffers from multiple phobias of several different types. Given the number of phobias, the importance of collecting, organizing, and interpreting data from the client's story are key skills for the conducting the assessment of phobia. However, the practitioner should not consider such a diagnosis unless the person is truly impaired by fears and there is marked distress or interference with usual routines, employment, or other areas of interpersonal functioning.

While the "other" category does not receive very much attention, parents of toddlers can recognize the viability of its existence. It originates when a child is startled—either by a loud noise (fireworks or marching band) or by a costumed cartoon-type character (familiar or not). The usual scenario involves the child being very eager to get away from the cause. Even if the character is one of the child's favorites (e.g., Cinderella or Mickey Mouse), the child becomes quite distressed and fearful—perhaps crying or even screaming in the desire to get away. Children eventually outgrow such reactions—but until they do, parents generally avoid situations that are potentially upsetting.

The following vignettes provide a brief picture of each of the four specified phobias. In general, it is helpful to remember that the phobias cause a great deal of intrapersonal (or personal) and interpersonal distress for people, and the competency-based assessment is helpful for understanding each client's unique source of anxiety and stress.

Animal Phobia: Excessive or unreasonable fear of animals and insects defines animal phobia. While these are common fears, they are considered to be a phobia when a person's functioning is severely impaired. Young children are especially susceptible to animal phobias and age of onset usually peaks at 7 years of age (LeBeau et al., 2010) as is illustrated in the following vignette:

> Shortly before he turned age eight, Kyle Spector was playing in his grandmother's backyard when the dog from next door broke away from his chain restraint and lunged at Kyle, scratching him on the arm. The scratch was not serious, but Kyle's grandmother put a small bandage on it to appease him. For the past 10 years (since the incident), Kyle has not approached another dog, nor has he visited his grandmother's home.

Natural Environment Phobia: At a very early age some children develop fears of situations or events occurring in nature. These fears are specified as natural environment phobias. Common examples include heights, storms, and water—and here too, these fears sometimes seem to cluster together (Antony & Barlow, 2011). Here is a brief example of natural environment phobia:

> When Miles Halley was 6 years old, he accidentally fell out of his family's fishing boat during a camping trip and almost drowned. Miles states, "My dad put his mouth on top of mine and performed CPR. After I was revived, everybody told me I had stopped breathing and had turned blue. I guess you could say I was dead." Since that incident, Miles refuses to go anywhere near a large body of water. His parents recently announced their plans to celebrate their 35th wedding anniversary by taking the family on a cruise to the Caribbean Islands. Miles, who is now 28 years old, absolutely refuses to go.

Fear of water, as described in Miles's story, is only one of the natural environment phobias. Almost any situation or event out of doors that traumatizes a person (e.g., thunderstorms, lightning, or water) could potentially become a specific phobia.

Blood-Injection-Injury: Those with blood-injection-injury phobias fear needles or invasive medical procedures. These individuals almost always differ in their physiological reaction from persons with other types of phobias. The source of this difference is not known, but this specifier tends to run in families (Hofmann, Alpers, & Pauli, 2009). The average onset is at about 9 years of age (LeBeau et al., 2010). The following illustrates blood-injection phobia.

> Ralph Tyler, a 29-year-old, Hollywood, Florida, policeman, came in for a complete medical examination. Before he was even seated in an exam room, he stated, "I have been in excellent health my whole life, so I don't need any in-depth tests." Mr. Tyler recently moved to the South Florida area and was told he could not get medical insurance with the police department unless he had a medical examination. Only under great duress had Mr. Tyler agreed to the exam—and he canceled six previously scheduled appointments before showing up today.
>
> His physical health was noted as "unremarkable." When he was escorted into the laboratory area, he asked the technician, "Can I get you to donate some of your blood to substitute for mine? I can't stand the sight of needles. I mean I really freak out. Maybe you don't understand, but I can't stand to even think about blood. My mom is the same way. I can't even watch television shows having to do with medicine. Do you know the doctor program that shows people being treated in the hospital? I can't remember what it's called but I can't even watch it! Yuk."
>
> After a great deal of reassurance and trying to convince Mr. Tyler that I am the best drawer of blood he was ever going to meet, I jokingly told him that I had won many awards for being South Florida's "most painless lab tech." He finally settled his 6-foot-3-inch, 240-pound frame into one of the lab chairs. I laid out the usual row of tubes, needles, cotton, and alcohol swabs. I tightened the tourniquet on his arm, and began feeling around for a nice juicy vein. As I made preparations to draw his blood, Mr. Tyler said weakly, "I don't feel so good," and then fainted dead away. After he was revived, Mr. Tyler revealed that he always fainted whenever he saw a needle or blood, especially his own. When

questioned why he didn't say something to me in the first place, he admitted, "Look at me. I'm supposed to be this big tough cop and look what happens when I see a little tiny needle. Hey, would you tell anybody?"

Situational Phobia: People who have a situational phobia would have difficulty using public transportation (e.g., buses, trains, and airplanes), or being in enclosed places such as elevators. These features may sound very similar to agoraphobia, but there is a key difference: Individuals with situational phobia never experience a panic attack outside the context of their phobic object or situation (Barlow & Durand, 2014). The following vignette is an example of a person with a situational-type phobia:

> Upon reporting for jury duty a number of years ago, the author was sitting in the jury box being asked the typical prospective juror-type questions. "I remember I had just finished answering a series of questions when I happened to glance sideways. I noticed a middle-aged woman in obvious distress. I leaned over and whispered to her, 'Are you alright?'"
>
> She whispered back, "I have to get out of here. I mean, I really have to get out of here. Can you see an exit door from here?" I told her I couldn't, and she said, "Oh, I knew this was a bad mistake, this always happens to me." I raised my hand, and a very surprised judge asked, "What seems to be the problem madam?" I suggested that the woman sitting next to me was in need of some immediate attention. The judge quickly took in the situation, and ordered a 15- minute recess. After several minutes of discussion between the woman, the attorneys, and the judge, she was excused from jury duty.
>
> As she left the courtroom, she leaned over and said to me, "Thank you so much for helping me out. I always have problems whenever I'm in a place where I can't get out." Then she laughed and added, "You should consider yourself lucky that we weren't in an elevator together."

SOCIAL ANXIETY DISORDER (SOCIAL PHOBIA)

Undoubtedly, there are a lot more people who are shy, but not to the extent of being diagnosed with social anxiety disorder. The essential feature of this disorder is an intense fear or anxiety of social situations where the person may be scrutinized by others.

PREVAILING PATTERN

In a given 1-year period, the prevalence of social anxiety disorder is about 7 percent or as many as 12.1 percent of the general population in the United States (Kessler, Berglund, et al., 2005; Kessler, Chiu, Demler, & Walters, 2005). In other words, more than 35 million people struggle with social anxiety. The disorder generally begins during early adolescence, and decreases with age with a 12-month prevalence reported for adults in the U.S. population at 2 to 5 percent (APA, 2013). Social anxiety disorder tends to be more prevalent in young adults (18 to 29 years of age) who are undereducated, single, and of low economic status (Kessler, Berglund, et al., 2005). When making the competency-based assessment, it should not surprise the practitioner to discover interpersonal problems in a client's life—such as problems sustaining employment, suspended educational pursuits, lack of career promotion, and severe social restrictions.

Differential Assessment

Social anxiety disorder, also known as social phobia, is commonly referred to as performance anxiety, a condition in which a person fears performing publicly lest he or she be revealed as inept, foolish, or inadequate thereby suffering disgrace, humiliation, or embarrassment (Heimberg & Magee, 2014). For children, this fear occurs in interactions with peers as well as with adults. Even though the person who feels this way readily admits the fears are baseless and illogical, he or she nevertheless becomes severely anxious (and almost always in social situations) and often goes to great lengths to avoid being in these situations. In children, this anxiety can be seen in tantrums, crying, freezing, clinging, shrinking, or a failure to speak in social situations.

Several famous stage, screen, and recording artists no longer perform publicly because they fear they will forget song lyrics or their lines in the script, their voice will crack, or they will suffer some other embarrassment. Social anxiety is more than a matter of being overly shy. Apparently, it is not the "act" of doing something in and of itself that is feared; rather, it is the "doing of the act" and making a mistake in public that exacerbates their fear (Bogels et al., 2010). However, if the person performs in private, he or she may experience little or no anxiety. In addition to the preoccupation with the fear of embarrassing oneself in public, the fear is out of proportion to the actual situation, and typically lasts 6 months or longer. The practitioner considers if the effects of drugs, medications, or another medical condition (such as disfigurement from burns, or Parkinson's disease) may better explain the person's behavior. As well, other disorders, such as panic disorder, body dysmorphic disorder, or autism spectrum disorder, are ruled out. If the fear is restricted to speaking or performing in public, then the specifier "performance only" is considered.

Fear of speaking in public is considered the most common form of social anxiety disorder (Barlow & Durand, 2014). Other situations that may evoke anxiety are having a conversation, meeting unfamiliar people, a fear of trembling when writing in public (e.g., signing one's name on a charge receipt in front of a salesperson), worrying about choking on food when eating in a public place, or being unable to urinate when others are present (known as bashful bladder or paruresis). For example, men with this problem often must wait until a stall in a public bathroom becomes available—which can be quite inconvenient depending on the circumstances. Many persons with a social anxiety disorder avoid being in almost all social situations. Sometimes they are able to endure their discomfort and go through with the "performance situation." Other times they may refuse to perform, and in extreme cases, they may have a panic attack. The fear that others will detect their nervousness and see signs of their somatic distress—such as trembling hands or erythrophobia (blushing)—adds to the symptom picture. As a consequence, important areas of a person's life are adversely affected.

The following vignette illustrates social anxiety disorder with the performance-only specifier.

CASE THE CASE OF HERBERT WILKS

I received a referral from a social work colleague who was concerned that a personal friend, Herbert Wilks, was beginning to experience problems whenever he had to speak publicly. The following is a brief description of my first session with Mr. Wilks.

I walked into the waiting room and identified myself to Mr. Wilks. We shook hands and introduced ourselves. I told him, "I like to be called Marie," and he said, "I like to be called Herb. My mother is the only one that still calls me Herbert." We made our way down to my office. After a few moments, Herb began to explain the difficulties that brought him in.

"Well, to tell you the truth, this is sort of embarrassing, but I've been having problems doing my job for the past four years," he said. I asked Herb what he does for a living, and he replied, "Well, actually I do several things. To make financial ends meet, I drive an 18-wheel tractor-trailer rig on the weekends, but I only take the short hauls so I can be home with my wife and kids. It's a little different from my other jobs but I like it because I have the chance to just chill and be alone. It's easy money. I also teach a language arts course over at the community college a few days a week, just about every semester. But I guess what you'd call my regular job is being a motivational speaker for big corporations. I've always liked what I do—it's just that, for about the last year or so, I simply can't get up and talk in front of a bunch of people. That's the kiss of death for somebody who has three jobs and two of them involve speaking to big groups of people. It's gotten so bad now, that I'm afraid I'll have to quit those two jobs."

"Let me see if I understand," I ventured. "Is it that you fear being watched or being embarrassed in front of other people?"

Herb replied, "Exactly! That's exactly right! I am just so afraid of being humiliated by giving the wrong answer or not being able to finish my lecture." I asked Herb what happens when this occurs. He continued, "I get all sweaty, my hands shake, sometimes my voice cracks—and a few times I blushed bright red. It's terrible. I worry I'll get tongue-tied. Now mind you, I know this is what you might call an irrational fear, and I've always somehow gotten my words out, but ..." Herb pauses, and then continues. "Well, it's gotten to the point where I actually canceled six speaking engagements that were for really high-profile companies. I just couldn't perform." Herb seemed very frustrated with himself. He went on, "A few times, I hid out in the men's room before I had to present. I just didn't want to come out. Several times, I literally had to force myself to do the presentations. I have to tell you, it's just awful. I'm so anxious that, even when I do make it through the talk, my clients aren't getting their money's worth. I'm sure some of them think I'm stupid—they must wonder how in the world I gained a reputation for being such an expert motivational speaker. I can't stand the humiliation." Herb sounded really defeated. "Now I've started canceling some of my classes because I just can't teach feeling this way. Of course, the students are thrilled when the class is canceled, but if news ever gets back to the dean, my job is toast—you know, I'll be finished."

I asked Herb why he thought he had these problems. He shook his head slowly, "You know, I'm a clean and decent fella. I try to help out at my church when I can. I don't use drugs. I don't smoke. I don't drink alcohol. I'm a dedicated family man.—I don't think I mentioned my wife. She's a stay-at-home mom.... We were childhood sweethearts ... have three great kids." Herb seems truly puzzled. "I have no history of any medical problems. I just don't know how to explain what's going on."

When I asked if there are any other kinds of distress connected to his public speaking, Herb replied, "Yes. I think about this all the time. My wife, Dora, has been giving me a hard time. She tells me just to snap out of it—like I ought to have some control over it. Don't you think I would, if I could? I mean, I realize I'm blowing this out of proportion, but what can I do? Do you think you can help me?"

HERB WILKS'S DSM DIAGNOSIS IS AS FOLLOWS:
Social anxiety disorder, performance only

Assessment Summary Herb has some insight into his fears of public speaking and teaching. He did not provide any indication of experiencing panic disorder, nor did he show evidence of anxiety due to a medical condition or substance-induced anxiety disorder. His anxiety focuses on performance, so a generalized anxiety or separation anxiety disorder can be ruled out. While Herb is aware of his tendency to blush when having to speak in public, he does not show the preoccupation with perceived bodily imperfections seen in body dysmorphic disorder. Selective mutism restricts one's speaking, but they do not show the anxiety around a negative evaluation as evident in Herb's situation. Those with oppositional defiant disorder may refuse to speak, but the motivation stems from an opposition to authority in contrast to Herb, who is anxious about how others would evaluate him. Other mental disorders are not evident, such as a delusional disorder, autism spectrum disorder, an avoidant personality disorder, or schizophrenia. Ultimately, Herb's assessment boils down to the differences among the phobias.

Competency 7 b

None of the features of a specific phobia, or agoraphobia, are manifested in this case. Further, social anxiety disorder could be difficult to ascertain in people who are naturally shy and retiring. Discerning among the disorders underscores the practitioner's ability to collect, organize, and interpret data from the client's story. Many people at some time or another will worry about or feel uncomfortable when involved in social situations; thus, unless the person is significantly affected occupationally, socially, or in other interpersonal areas, he or she should not be considered as having social anxiety. Herb's excessive fears of speaking and teaching certainly fit with a diagnosis of social anxiety disorder.

Competency 7 a

Using the competency-based assessment model, the practitioner is more interested in finding out about what is right about Herb than what is wrong. Questions to Herb about how he manages to get through all of the challenges throughout the day will provide the opportunity to shift the focus away from deficits and toward his own competency. Herb presents himself as a very hardworking, well-educated man. He is married to his childhood sweetheart, and he works very hard at three jobs to keep his family together. He also somehow finds the time to stay active in his church community. His insight and willingness to change—and his decision to seek help are additional strengths. Figure 6.1 shows the interactions of the biological, psychological, and social variables in Herb Wilks's life.

We now look at panic disorder and the specifier of a panic attack.

PANIC DISORDER

The DSM-5 differentiated the diagnosis of panic disorder from agoraphobia. As we will see in the following story featuring Jada Wu, a panic attack is largely unexpected and not related to any obvious trigger. In other words, someone can be calm one minute and in the next will experience an abrupt surge of intense

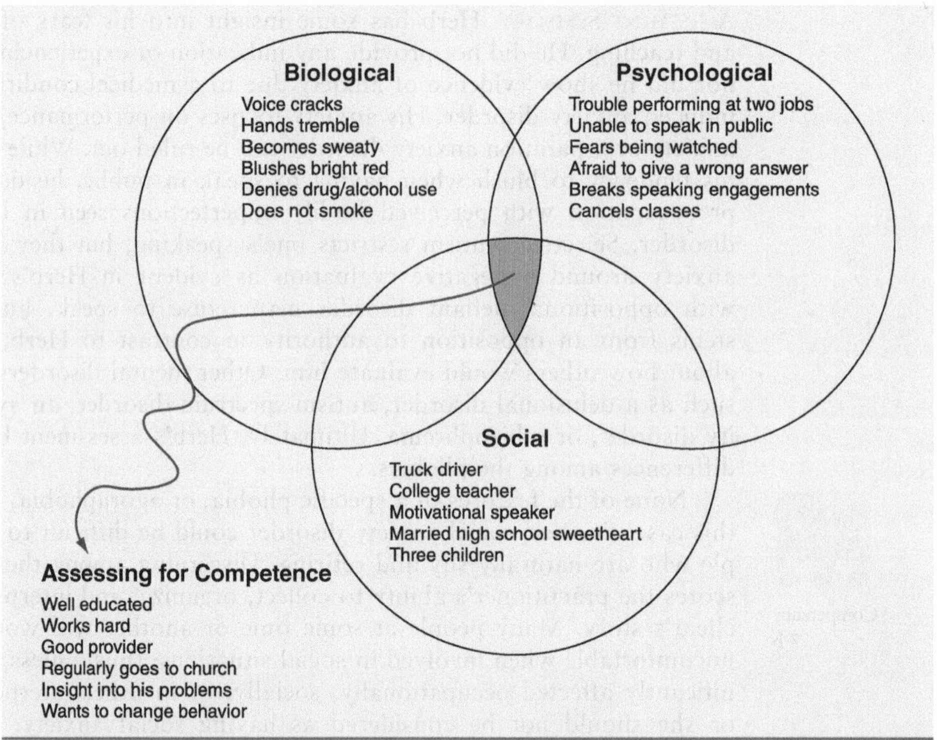

FIGURE 6.1 › SOCIAL ANXIETY DISORDER (SOCIAL PHOBIA)
The interactions of the biological, psychological, and social variables in Herb Wilks's life.

fear or discomfort that can peak within a very short period of time, usually within minutes.

People will sometimes go out of their way to avoid having another panic attack, doing things like avoiding strenuous physical activities to completely reorganizing their daily life. Most of what is known suggests that agoraphobic avoidance behavior seems to be a complication of severe unexpected panic attacks (Barlow, 2004; Craske & Barlow, 2014). In other words, if someone experiences an unexpected panic attack, they are usually afraid they will experience another one. What the individual wants to do is stay in a place considered safe or surrounded by people that can help out, just in case another episode occurs.

Many youngsters are seen by a general medical practitioner with symptoms that resemble a panic attack, such as shortness of breath or smothering, but are too young to report other symptoms characteristic of a panic attack; for instance, losing control or a fear of dying (Barlow & Durand, 2014). If left untreated, panic attacks can endure for years with a chronic relapsing course. Obviously, remission cannot occur as long as the panic attacks remain. Due to the physical symptoms or discomfort (somatization) that often occurs for those suffering panic attacks, the practitioner may find clients frequently using the health care system.

Prevailing Pattern

The rates of panic disorder gradually increase during adolescence and peak during adulthood. In the general U.S. population, the estimates for panic disorder are about 2 to 3 percent in adults and adolescents but significantly decline in older individuals (or over age 64) to about 0.7 percent (APA, 2013). This decline could be understood by the reality that older adults might explain their panic attacks as related to specific (and stressful) situations; for example, a medical procedure (Barlow & Durand, 2014). The median age of onset for a panic disorder is 20 to 24 years of age. While considered rare in childhood, the practitioner may find a report of "fearful spells" from those who are close to the child.

Differential Assessment

The defining feature of panic disorder is recurrent and unexpected panic attacks that last for a very short time, usually within minutes, accompanied by intense fear or discomfort. The frequency of these attacks varies ranging from once a week to intervals of over many years. A person may experience four or more of the following:

- Palpitations or a pounding heart rate (or increased heart rate).
- Sweating.
- Trembling or shaking.
- Sensation of shortness of breath (or a feeling of smothering).
- Feelings of choking.
- Chest pain or discomfort.
- Nausea or abdominal distress.
- Feeling dizzy, unsteady, light-headed, or faint.
- Chills or heat.
- Paresthesias (numbness or tingling).
- Derealization (feelings of unreality) or depersonalization (detachment from oneself).
- Fear of "going crazy."
- Fear of dying.

The number of symptoms a person may experience can differ from one panic attack to the next. Culturally specific symptoms, such as the uncontrollable screaming or crying seen in ataque de nervios, are not considered. Keep in mind that the person may worry about having another panic attack and/or engage in (maladaptive) behaviors to ward off another attack.

The following vignette of Jada Wu highlights panic disorder. You will see that she does not abuse substances, nor does she have any co-occurring medical or mental condition that may better explain her behaviors; for example, hyperthyroidism, or social anxiety disorder, specific phobia, or posttraumatic disorder, to list a few.

CASE The Case of Jada Wu

Jada Wu, a 27-year-old flight attendant, was referred to the social worker at the Employee Assistance Program (EAP) 2 weeks ago. The only information known is what Ms. Wu noted in her pre-intake form: "I suffer from feelings of nervousness." This is our first session, and we are meeting in my office near the airport concourse where Ms. Wu is employed.

Jada is a very attractive woman of Chinese descent, who appears her stated age of 27. She is of medium height, is slim figured, and wears her long hair in a braid hanging down her back. She has a ready smile and appeared comfortable meeting me for the first time.

As for her relevant background history, her parents were originally from Beijing and immigrated to South Florida 25 years ago (when Jada was 2 years old). She remembers growing up in cramped living quarters with several other family members who had also immigrated to the United States around the same time. She says that, although there was not a great deal of money for material things, her family always celebrated traditional festivals and holidays. She remembers especially the Chinese New Year, "sweeping of the grave," and mid-autumn festivals. In addition, her family started one of the first Chinese restaurants in their neighborhood. She has fond memories of helping the family business thrive. She describes herself as being social and gregarious—she waited on tables, took orders, and joked with the customers.

Jada is the first woman in her family to complete college, which seems to have caused a great deal of controversy among family members, because it represents to them a pull away from family unity. In her family, if a child attempts to act independently, he or she is labeled as "inconsiderate, ungrateful, and self-indulgent." The family believes in sticking together. In addition, when Jada started her job with the airline, she was the first to work outside of the family business. Although they seem proud of her, she senses that her parents simply tolerate her career accomplishments—consequently, Jada says that there is now a certain degree of tension at family gatherings.

When Jada settles in her chair, I ask, "Ms. Wu, why do you think you are here?" After a moment's hesitation, she states, "Please call me Jada. ... I guess it's about what's been happening to me lately." She is quiet for a moment and seems to need a bit of direction. I suggest she explain to me what has been happening. Then she continues, "Well, everything was going along just fine until one day I was on a routine flight in-bound from Dallas to San Antonio. All of a sudden—I mean really out of the blue—I know that sounds like a joke," she laughs nervously, "but it wasn't meant to be. Anyway, I began to feel dizzy. One of other attendants sat me down in an empty first-class seat so I wouldn't topple over. I felt nauseous, I was freezing cold, my heart was beating so fast it felt like it was going to pop out of my chest. I felt short of breath, and I thought I was going to die right there on the plane."

Jada seems to be reliving every sensation as she describes it to me, but she goes on, "The captain made an overhead announcement asking if there was a physician on board. We didn't have a doctor, but the nicest social worker came forward and offered to help. She took one look at me, and asked lots of medical kinds of questions like was I taking any medication, has this ever happened before, did I have a history of heart disease? I told her I had just passed my annual physical examination. As a rule, I've always been a very healthy person. I keep my weight down, I'm a vegetarian. Don't drink. I told her all that sort of stuff. The social worker was really nice. She held my hand, and reassured me that what she thought might be happening was something called a panic attack. She said I'd be all right and suggested I try to breathe into an airsickness bag for about 10 minutes. That helped calm me down—but before the social worker left the plane she suggested I seek some counseling and go see my doctor again."

"Do you have any idea what precipitated this incident?" I ask.

Jada responds, "I can't actually tell you."

I ask her a series of questions aimed at exploring whether or not Jada experiences agoraphobia. "Do any of the following make you feel very fearful, nervous, or anxious? Being away from your home; being in a closed or small room (like an elevator); being on a bridge; in a crowd of people like at a concert hall?"

Jada answers right away, "Well, yes, I worry if I might get dizzy or something when I'm away from home. You know, for the last several months my sister has started to go grocery shopping with me—but I didn't make a connection between that and any problems I've been having." As soon as the words are out of her mouth, she says, "Oh, wait a minute! I just remembered, there were a few times when I felt like I was getting nauseous. I was shopping at the mall. It was really weird, you know, like I needed to get as far as I could from the food mall. You know ... all those smells. Eventually it went away once I got outside and somehow I managed to get myself home. Since then, I do most of my shopping on the Internet. Did you know you can even get groceries online?"

I comment that it does indeed sound as if she is having episodes of panic, and I ask her how long they've been happening.

Jada replies, "You know, ever since that first time it happened when I was in flight. I've had a lot more. Sometimes they happen every day. They aren't always the same, but they are always scary. They start like that," Jada snaps her fingers, "Then they develop really fast—but they are over in 30 or 40 minutes. That doesn't matter, though, because when you are responsible for several hundred people like I am you have to always be ready to help them, not the other way around. Several times I had a panic attack when I was walking out of my house to leave for the airport—and twice they happened during a layover when I went out to dinner with the crew. Of course, I didn't tell them anything was wrong with me. I made up a story that I might be getting a fever, and tried to hide it from them. I don't know if they bought my story or if they could see me shaking, breathing hard, and sweating—but no one said anything. You know, it's not a good thing to have a flight attendant who looks like she's falling apart."

When I ask how she is currently doing, she replies, "Well, I'm always worried about when it's going to happen again. It's like I'm constantly worrying. It's the losing control that's the biggest problem for me. If I have problems leaving my house for work, I ask my mother or my sister to drive me to the airport—but they can't hold my hand forever, can they? I'm thinking about changing my job. The airline offered me a spot as a reservation clerk, and I'm seriously thinking about it. I'm just too afraid to go through one of these panic attacks while flying but I can't imagine my life without flying. Flying is my life, and I will really miss traveling."

I ask where she has traveled. She looks down at her hands resting in her lap and replies, "Pretty much everywhere: Mexico, Japan, China, Thailand, Hong Kong, Bali, Australia, Papua New Guinea, Egypt, Israel, Russia, all of Europe and Scandinavia. I guess that's going to be a thing of the past, huh?"

Jada Wu's DSM Diagnosis Is as Follows:

Panic disorder

Competency 8 c

Assessment Summary Jada's panic attack was quite typical; it began suddenly, escalated rapidly, and included heart palpitations, shortness of breath, lightheadedness, and nausea. Jada experienced the same fear that most people do during an attack: that she was going to die. There are times when the practitioner may need to consult with medical professionals to confirm the diagnosis. Although a number of general medical conditions can mimic panic attacks, the social worker should note that Jada recently passed her annual physical examination and was found to be in good health. Jada does not drink, and there is no evidence she may have a mental disorder that could better explain her panic attacks, like generalized anxiety disorder, for instance. Making an assessment of specific or social phobia is not likely, because the focus of

Jada's anxiety was not directed toward a single situation or to a social situation. Major depressive disorder can accompany panic disorder with or without agoraphobia; however, Jada did not describe a past history of depression.

Competency 7 a

Understanding Jada's functioning on all levels helps provide a more complete clinical picture and helps highlight the coping strategies she can tap into in order to reinforce and improve her adaptation to life situations, circumstances, and events. The competency-based assessment requires the practitioner to discern Jada's medical status, intrapersonal factors, and the influence that culture plays in her life. The vignette reveals Jada's insight that her problem is interfering with her work, and she has an employer who is supportive. Her family, although only "tolerant" of Jada moving outside of the family system, are supportive of her independence. When she had fears of having another panic attack away from home, her sister helped with shopping chores. Finally, Jada has followed through on the counseling referral and is motivated to work on her problems. See Figure 6.2 for an illustration of the interactions of the biological, psychological, and social variables in Jada Wu's life.

Panic Attack Specifier: The DSM-5 presents the symptom picture for a panic attack, which mirrors the symptoms for panic disorder in order to help the practitioner to accurately determine when someone is having a panic attack. Keep in mind that having a panic attack in and of itself is not considered a mental disorder. However, when the person begins to avoid social situations like Jada Wu did when

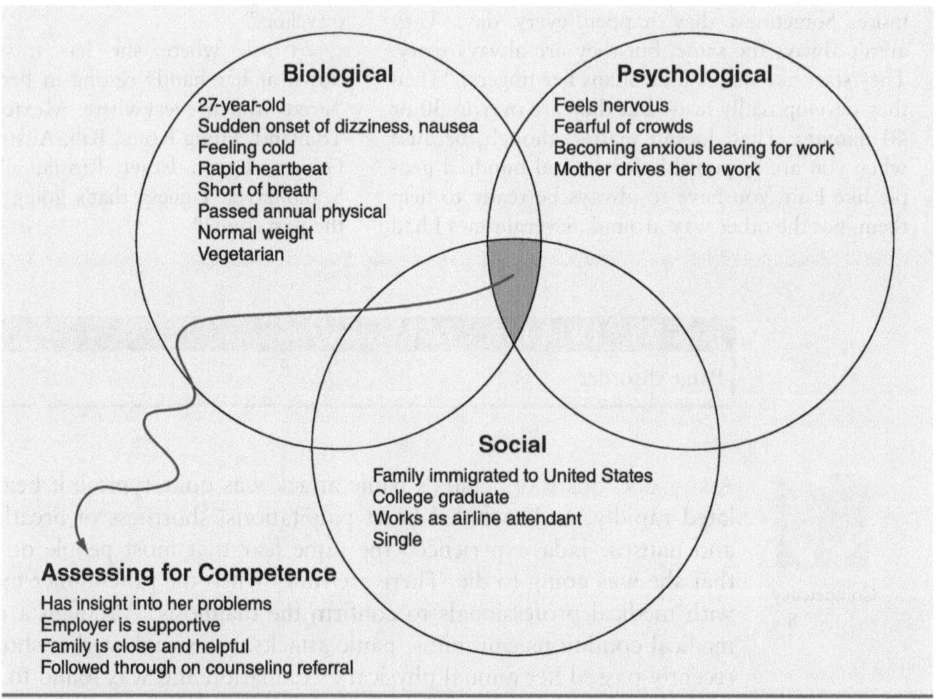

FIGURE 6.2 › PANIC DISORDER
The interactions of the biological, psychological, and social variables in Jada Wu's life.

she started shopping online and began to worry about additional unexpected attacks, then a panic disorder is considered.

A panic attack can accompany other mental disorders; for example, the depressive disorders, posttraumatic stress disorder, or the substance use disorders. In addition, a number of medical conditions may evoke a panic attack; like someone who is having a heart attack, for instance. In those situations, the practitioner may consider adding the specifier, panic attack, to the individual's diagnosis.

AGORAPHOBIA

Taken from the Greek language, the term agoraphobia literally means "fear of the marketplace." When the practitioner begins to explore the presence of anxiety, what becomes quite apparent is not the fear of being in a particular place or situation, but rather the likelihood of suddenly becoming ill, not being able to escape, or not being able to receive immediate help. The person is afraid of being incapacitated or embarrassed.

There is some research supporting the existence of more than one kind of agoraphobia, but the most common type almost always provokes a panic-like symptom (Craske & Barlow, 2014; Perugi, Frare, & Toni, 2007). The research notes a small minority of cases in which people deny ever having panic-like symptoms—they simply experience the dread that "something might happen." In these instances, they are considered to have agoraphobia but without the ensuing panic component (Kikuchi et al., 2005). Interestingly, two-thirds of those who have panic-like symptoms along with agoraphobia are women (Kessler, Berglund, et al., 2005). Somehow it seems more culturally acceptable for women to be fearful and to avoid situations where men, in contrast, are expected to be strong and just tough it out (Wolitzky-Taylor, Castriotta, Lenze, Stanley, & Craske, 2010).

Prevailing Pattern

The age of onset is typically during the person's early adult life, ranging from mid-adolescence to about 40 years of age with no reported differences in age of onset or duration between men and women (Kessler, Berglund, et al., 2005). Approximately 1.7 percent of adolescents and adults are reported each year to have a diagnosis of agoraphobia (APA, 2013).

Differential Assessment

There are a number of situations or places the person with agoraphobia generally avoids, such as subways, airplanes (using public transportation); parking lots, shopping centers, grocery stores (being in open spaces); being in movie theaters, elevators, in tunnels or over bridges, or riding in the backseat of a two-door car (being in enclosed spaces); waiting in a line (or being in any type of a crowd); or even driving (being outside of home alone). Some individuals with agoraphobic avoidance also show another cluster of avoidant behaviors known as interoceptive avoidance

(Wald & Taylor, 2007). In this type of avoidance, the person removes him- or herself from situations or activities that might evoke the physiological arousal that resembles the beginnings of a panic attack. For instance, the person might avoid strenuous exercise because it increases their heart rate or they start breathing faster, and this reminds them of panic attacks, which then makes them think this might be the beginning of one.

The different agoraphobic situations almost always provoke feelings of fear and anxiety for the person that are out of proportion to the actual dangers posed, lasting for at least 6 months or longer. As the person begins to take steps to avoid these agoraphobic situations, such as avoiding public transportation or struggling to leave home as we will see in the following case story of Matilda Suarez, this only serves to cause significant social and interpersonal distress. In extreme situations, the individual fears being anywhere except in the safety of his or her own home. For example, the prospect of walking outside to pick up the morning paper may fill the person with debilitating fear. Some people become so incapacitated they refuse to venture out of their homes, which may last for years. Other mental conditions or medical disorders do not better explain these puzzling behaviors.

The case of Matilda Suarez highlights the key features of agoraphobia.

CASE THE CASE OF MATILDA SUAREZ

Matilda Suarez, age 58, has not walked outside of her home for the past 15 years. Her parish priest, Father Michael Krane, has referred Ms. Suarez to the Homebuilders' Social Service Agency. He became quite concerned because of her failing health and dwindling financial resources. Father Michael recently learned that Ms. Suarez's apartment complex is going to be demolished to make room for a "neighborhood improvement project." A home visit was scheduled by the social worker, and Ms. Suarez was seen the following week.

Ms. Suarez was born in Havana, Cuba, and immigrated to South Florida during the Mariel boatlift of the early 1980s. She has two daughters, aged 22 and 25, both of whom live in South Florida as well. Ms. Suarez divorced her husband almost 20 years ago and has had no further contact with him. She thinks he may have returned to Cuba.

During the first visit with the social worker, Ms. Suarez indicated that she is quite lonely. "My daughters have their own lives, but I wish they'd visit me more often. Sometimes I don't see anybody for 2 or 3 weeks at a time."

The social worker prompted, "Can you tell me more about why you don't see anyone for weeks at a time?"

Ms. Suarez looked up from under her eyebrows and said, "Well, did Father Michael tell you I haven't been able to leave my house in years?" The social worker nodded to indicate that she knows something about the situation. Ms. Suarez continued, "I mean I don't even go outside to pick up my morning newspaper. The paperboy knows he has to lean the newspaper right up against my front door or else I don't get to read the paper that day. I hate to even open up my front door because I'm afraid I'll get an attack. I know it's no way to live—but what choice do I have?"

The worker asked Ms. Suarez several other questions. The following is a composite of her responses. Ms. Suarez has no contact with anyone other than Father Michael, her daughters, and a visiting nurse. She is completely dependent on her girls to do all shopping and basic household maintenance. She used to do her own errands—not alone, of course, but with at least one of her daughters accompanying her. Ms. Suarez says that she is afraid to go out alone, and that she used to get especially nervous if she had to be around a lot of people. She's not so much afraid of the people, but she does not like closed-in spaces. The last time she went to her doctor's office, she walked out because "the waiting room got too crowded and cramped."

A visiting nurse comes to see Ms. Suarez once or twice a year to follow her medical needs. She suffers from varicose veins in her lower extremities, making it difficult for her to walk. She is also monitored for hot flashes associated with being postmenopausal. She denies using alcohol or drugs, and denies depression, hallucinations, delusions, or suicidal ideation. Ms. Suarez earns a living as a medical transcriber, which she is able to do from her home. Ms. Suarez says of her situation, "I have no friends in this world that care about me. I'm a prisoner in my own world." Gesturing expansively, she continues, "My constant companions are these four walls and my television. Year after year, month after month, day after day—nothing ever changes." She sighs. "I can't leave my house because I don't feel safe, and now the County Reclamation Agency is going to tear my world down. Where can I go from here? Don't they understand I can't walk out of my house? What am I going to do?"

Matilda Suarez's DSM Diagnosis Is as Follows:
Agoraphobia

Assessment Summary Because of her anxiety and fears, Ms. Suarez completely avoids going to different places and being in situations where she does not feel safe. Even with the companionship of her daughters, she still feels unable to leave her home. She is not able to explain to the social worker exactly what might happen if she leaves the house, but she is able to recognize that she would feel very afraid.

Competency 7 b

Distinguishing the diagnosis of agoraphobia requires the practitioner to collect, organize, and interpret the data in Ms. Suarez's story. The features illustrated in the vignette are too varied to be specific phobia, situational type or social anxiety disorder (social phobia). The overriding distinction for assessing agoraphobia is the danger Ms. Suarez perceives from her environment—social phobia, in contrast, would involve the perception of danger from her relationship with others, and social anxiety disorder revolves around being negatively evaluated. Ms. Suarez does not have separation anxiety disorder because she does not have a problem being left alone. Her diagnosis would not be posttraumatic stress disorder, as she does not claim to have experienced any traumatic situations such as being mugged or raped. There are no features suggesting a major depressive disorder, nor did she show evidence of having a panic disorder. While the visiting nurse comes to see Ms. Suarez twice a year to monitor her medical needs, we do not see any medical condition that would better explain her avoidance of situations outside her home. Despite a severely restricted life, there are a number of competencies in Ms. Suarez's life. Figure 6.3 illustrates the interactions of the biological, psychological, and social variables in Matilda Suarez's life.

We turn to a disorder seen twice as often in women than in men, generalized anxiety disorder.

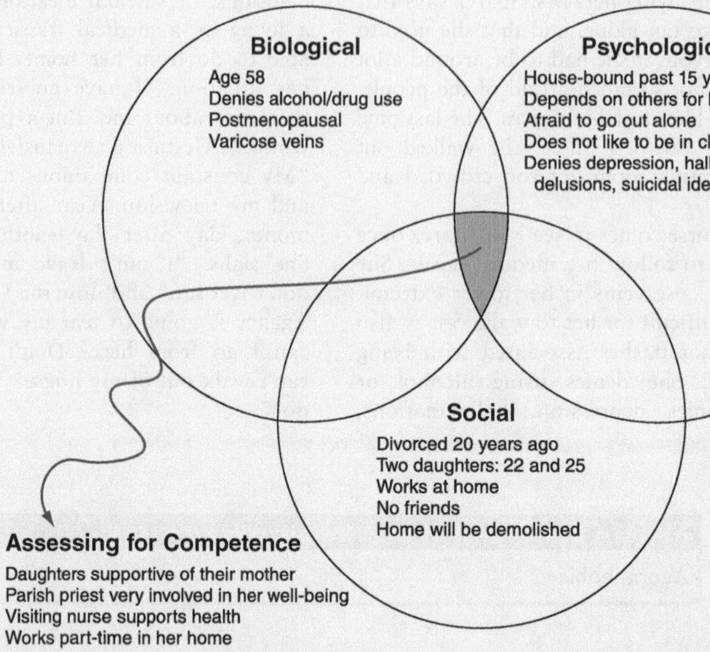

FIGURE 6.3 › AGORAPHOBIA
The interactions of the biological, psychological, and social variables in Matilda Suarez's life.

GENERALIZED ANXIETY DISORDER

In contrast to people with the anxiety disorders already discussed, individuals with generalized anxiety disorder (GAD) do not focus on any particular object, situation, or person. Rather, the anxiety they suffer pervades their entire lives and significantly interferes in all aspects of life functioning. Most of us understand that experiencing some worry is part of the normal human condition, but those with GAD are considered incessant worrywarts—they worry about everything, even when there is nothing obvious going on in their lives to provoke their concerns. This uncontrollable worry is the most salient feature of GAD.

PREVAILING PATTERN

The 12-month prevalence for GAD is 0.9 percent for adolescents and almost 3 percent (2.9 percent) for adults in the U.S. general population (APA, 2013). At some point in their lifetime, 9 percent will be affected, making it one of the most common anxiety disorders (APA, 2013). Although GAD can occur at any age, it peaks in middle age and begins to decline in the later years.

Differential Assessment

GAD refers to what used to be termed free-floating anxiety, or the kind of anxiety experienced but not attached to any specific situation. If you were to ask someone with GAD, "Do you find yourself worrying a lot about minor things?" do not be surprised by a "Yes" answer. In essence, the person with GAD focuses his or her anxiety and worry (seen as apprehensive expectation) on minor everyday events as well as major life events on more days than not for at least 6 months. The focus of these worries are associated with three or more of the following six symptoms:

- Feeling restless or keyed or on edge.
- Being easily fatigued.
- Difficulties concentrating or one's mind goes blank.
- Irritability.
- Muscle tension.
- Sleep disturbances such as difficult falling or staying asleep, restlessness, or unsatisfying sleep.

These symptoms differ with age, and only one symptom is required to diagnose children. These are those individuals who find it hard to control his or her worry and to keep worrisome thoughts from interfering with the tasks at hand. Typically, children center their worry on competence in sports, academics, or social skills (Albano & Hack, 2004; Ayers, Thorp, & Weatherell, 2009; Furr, Tiwari, Suvey, & Kendall, 2009). Adults center their worries on potential misfortunes that may happen to their children, health, job responsibilities, and minor problems such as being on time for appointments. As might be expected, older adults focus on health concerns, and muscle tension can bring about muscle aches and soreness along with feeling shaky, and twitching or trembling.

The etiology of GAD is not clear, and unfortunately little is known about its cause and predisposing features. It is not unusual for the practitioner to hear clients report, "I've felt this way for as long as I can remember." The disorder tends to take a chronic course over the life span where symptoms can wax and wane. It goes without saying that excessive anxiety and worry cause significant problems in one's social, work, and interpersonal life.

The symptom picture is not better explained by substance use or another medical condition, such as hyperthyroidism. There are a number of disorders with an element of worry but not to the degree they could account for the level of anxiety and worry that typifies GAD. For instance, someone with a panic disorder may develop anticipatory anxiety, but the anxiety in panic disorder is over the anticipation of having another attack.

Individuals with the symptoms of generalized anxiety disorder generally tough it out on their own—if help is sought, it is usually from a primary care physician rather than from a social worker or other mental health practitioner. The following case vignette illustrates the symptoms and effects of generalized anxiety disorder.

CASE THE CASE OF BARBARA "BARBIE" CHAPMAN

Barbara Chapman is a 34-year-old married woman with two daughters (ages 5 and 7). Barbie (as she is called) and her husband Jeffrey have come for marital counseling because her excessive anxiety, worry, and physical complaints are "destroying their 12-year marriage."

This is their first session, so I am seeing them together (as is typical). I begin by asking them what brought them to my office. Barbie answers first. "Jeffrey overstates the problem. He thinks I worry too much—he calls me a worrywart, and Mrs. Misgiving. I guess I do tend to worry a little, but he calls me names—and, well, it does cause tension between us."

Jeffrey rejoins. "Barbie understates the problem. She is in fact overly concerned about absolutely everything. Now, I'm not just talking about being worried if it will rain, for example, and whether or not she should take an umbrella to work. I'm talking about worrying that she'll get the girls to school late, have an accident along the way, run a yellow light, run out of gas, or maybe the windshield wipers won't work—I mean, I could go on and on, but you get the picture."

Barbie breaks in, "Hey, it's not a crime to take care of your family's safety, is it?"

Jeffrey responds, "Yeah, but you are always restless and edgy. You have trouble falling asleep, and when you wake up you're always tired. It's because you worry so much. You know, I could recite a litany of things that you worry about. You worry about something bad happening to you, to the girls or me, you worry about your job, you worry about driving, the weather, your mother's health, the Brazilian rain forest, and—just absolutely everything. You even call me 10 times a day to make sure I'm okay. Your own mother put in caller ID just so she could screen out your calls. You worry about things even before they happen. Do you remember that presentation you had to do at work? You fretted about that for weeks and weeks beforehand."

I ask if Barbie is generally a nervous person.

She responds, "Well, I guess I do tend to ruminate about stuff, but I can't seem to stop, no matter how hard I try. I get so nervous. Maybe I am just a worrywart like Jeffrey says. You know, I try to maintain a tight control over all aspects of my life. If I can stay alert to anything that could go wrong, then I can prevent mistakes."

I inquire if Barbie ever experiences any physical problems.

She replies, "Well, I do feel fidgety and jittery, you know, like I'm keyed up or something. I mean, this has been going on for years. It's nothing new. Sometimes my mind goes blank, and I have trouble concentrating. That's not so good when you're making a presentation in front of your boss. I sometimes worry so much that I can't fall asleep, so of course I wake up tired. I always seem to have neck and back aches, and I just about live on Tylenol because of muscle tension. I tried using a heating pad, you know, for the muscle aches. But then I worried the heating pad would short out and cause an electrical fire and burn the house down."

I ask, "Barbie, how have these worries changed your life?"

"Oh man, it's affected my job performance," she replies, "my relationship with Jeffery and the girls, and our social life. With all my worrying, we only have one couple who are still our friends—that's Kenny and Sue. We try to go to a movie with them at least once a month, but we don't see much of our other friends anymore."

BARBARA "BARBIE" CHAPMAN'S DSM DIAGNOSIS IS AS FOLLOWS:

Generalized anxiety disorder

ASSESSMENT SUMMARY Generalized anxiety disorder is difficult to assess, because worry is a part of everyone's life. Although worry and physical tensions are very common experiences for most, the kind of severe anxiety experienced by Barbie is above and beyond what would be considered normal. Her worry is chronic and excessive, and it greatly diminishes the overall quality of her life.

Competency 7 b

Distinguishing the symptom picture of GAD calls on the practitioner's skills to collect, organize, and interpret data from the client's story. Unlike acute stress disorder, which lasts about a month, GAD is often pervasive and does not diminish over time. The quality of Barbie's worrying is very different. The focus of Barbie's constant worry is her husband, her children, and her job performance. If the target of her concerns revolved around a fear of becoming contaminated, the practitioner might begin thinking about obsessive-compulsive disorder. This vignette does not illustrate any struggles with depressive, bipolar, and psychotic disorders, so they would not be a viable consideration. Barbie complains about the aches and pains of muscle tension but shows no worries about having a serious illness. Therefore, the practitioner would not consider illness anxiety or somatic symptom disorder. Similarly, we do not see evidence supporting a social anxiety disorder (social phobia), which typifies fears of a negative evaluation; a separation anxiety disorder that provokes anxiety around separation from attachment figures; or a posttraumatic disorder that evokes reminders of traumatic events. Barbie has no concerns about her appearance so the diagnoses of anorexia nervosa, which centers on worries about gaining weight, and body dysmorphic disorder that typifies perceptions of serious body flaws are not considered.

The competency-based assessment looks at the wide range of factors influencing Barbie's life. Among them, the practitioner inquires about medications or drugs Barbie is taking because they could produce side effects that might mimic generalized anxiety features (e.g., taking certain antidepressants can cause similar symptoms). GAD is far more problematic than the symptoms found in an adjustment disorder; in the latter, symptoms tend to be milder. Adjustment disorder is distinguished by the stresses one normally encounters in daily life, but its symptoms are not sufficient to cause the clinically significant impairment seen in the diagnosis of GAD. While we can concede that Barbie's worries are excessive, they do not take on the qualities of the delusional beliefs seen in schizophrenia or delusional disorder.

On the surface, Barbie's concerns about her family, husband, and job might not warrant professional intervention, but her husband describes a much different scenario. He experiences his wife's multiple excessive worries along with her inability to control them as problematic. Additionally, her ongoing and minor physical complaints have now become a burden for him. As illustrated in the vignette, family members tend to feel the brunt of Barbie's worries, but they remain supportive of her. In addition, this couple is able to maintain a relationship with each other as well as with another couple and socializes with them on a regular basis. Figure 6.4 shows the interactions of the biological, psychological, and social variables in Barbie Chapman's life.

The following discussion reviews the remaining anxiety disorder diagnoses beginning with substance/medication-induced anxiety disorder.

OTHER ANXIETY DISORDERS

Substance/Medication-Induced Anxiety Disorder: There is not much information related to the prevalence of substance/medication-induced anxiety disorder. However, it is undeniable that that this disorder is most likely to occur in people who frequently abuse alcohol and drugs. While it is normal to have some feelings of

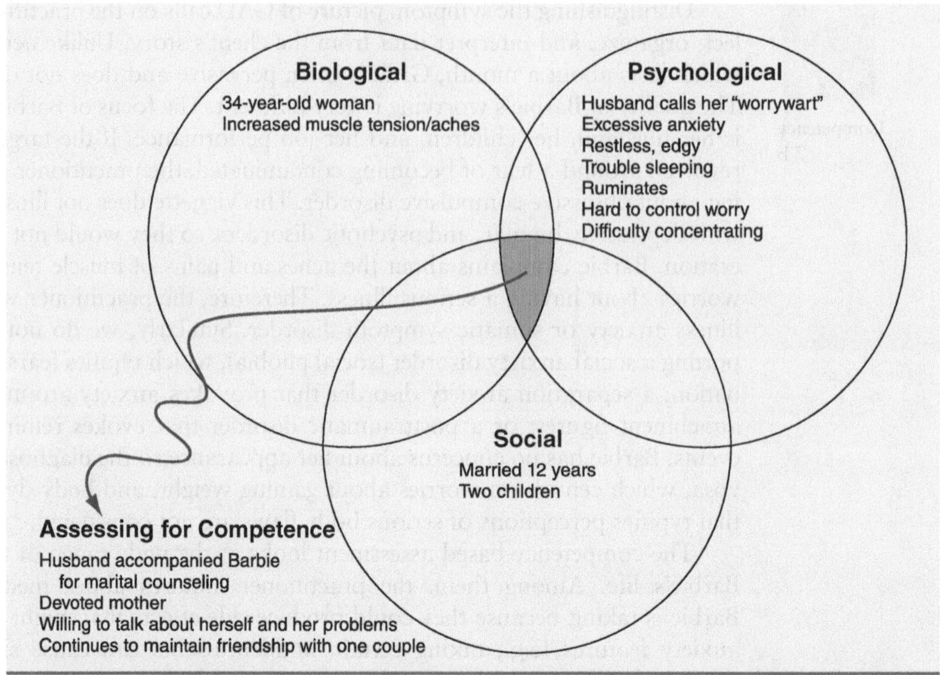

FIGURE 6.4 › GENERALIZED ANXIETY DISORDER
The interactions of the biological, psychological, and social variables in Barbara "Barbie" Chapman's life.

anxiety in stressful situations, the same drugs that people use to help them to relax and lower their inhibitions are the ones most likely to cause substance/medication-induced anxiety disorder. When making the diagnosis, it is important to make sure that the anxiety was not there before the use of alcohol, drugs, or medications thought to be responsible. If the anxiety symptoms were present before the use of substances, then substance/medication-induced anxiety disorder is not considered.

In some cases, the anxiety or panic can occur right away or when the person is drunk or high on the drug. It can also occur during withdrawal, when the symptoms of anxiety are more common. However, when anxiety is primarily a symptom of withdrawal, these symptoms will usually resolve within a few days of discontinuing the use of alcohol or drugs. In contrast, substance/medication-induced anxiety disorder can start during withdrawal, and may even get worse as the person moves through the detox process; that is, the substance/medication-induced anxiety feels much worse and goes on for a lot longer. Substance/medication-induced anxiety disorder is mainly induced by the action of various drugs, which include excessive alcoholism, toxins, and medication. Finally, for the diagnosis to be considered, symptoms have to be adversely affecting the person's work, social life, or other important areas of functioning.

Anxiety Disorder due to Another Medical Condition: There are a number of medical conditions associated with anxiety; for example, endocrine diseases such as hyperthyroidism, cardiovascular disorders like congestive heart failure or arrhythmias, and respiratory illnesses such as chronic obstructive pulmonary disease or asthma, to list a few. The first step in making the diagnosis is to determine the presence of a medical condition that is etiologically related to a person's anxiety symptoms. Here, too, the disturbance must be causing significant social or work distress in important areas of functioning.

Other Specified (and Unspecified) Anxiety Disorder: The diagnosis of other specified anxiety disorder is reserved for when clients do not meet full criteria for an anxiety disorder and the practitioner elects to offer a reason such as: limited-symptom attacks, generalized anxiety not occurring more days than not, Khyal cap (wind attacks), or ataque de nervios (attack of the nerves). Unspecified anxiety disorder is used when the practitioner chooses not to indicate why criteria are not met for a specific anxiety disorder, and when there is not enough information available to make a more specific diagnosis such as in an emergency room.

SUMMARY

As we have seen in this chapter, the anxiety disorders include a range of conditions that all share the common features of fear and anxiety. Panic attacks are prominent among these disorders, but it is important to note that panic attacks are not limited to the anxiety disorders. A panic attack per se is not a mental disorder but can occur in the context of other mental disorders. When that happens, it can be added as a specifier to the relevant diagnosis.

Apropos of the developmental perspective organizing the DSM-5, the chapter begins with a review of the anxiety disorders commonly found in young children—separation anxiety disorder, followed by selective mutism and the specific phobias. Next, social anxiety disorder, formerly social phobia, seen in individuals with a predominant fear of performance, is reviewed followed by panic disorder, and generalized anxiety disorder which highlights excessive anxiety and worry. The chapter concludes with a summary of substance/medication-induced anxiety disorder, anxiety disorder due to another medical condition, and the other specified and unspecified anxiety disorders.

As the DSM transitions from the DSM-IV-TR (APA, 2000) to the current edition of the manual, Table 6.2 provides a brief summary of the changes made to the diagnostic classifications in this chapter.

TABLE 6.2 SUMMARY COMPARISON BETWEEN THE DSM-IV-TR AND DSM-5 DIAGNOSES FOR THE ANXIETY DISORDERS
Separation anxiety disorder and selective mutism have been classified as anxiety disorders in the DSM-5 and moved from the Disorders in Infancy, Childhood or Adolescence chapter in the DSM-IV
For the different forms of the phobias and anxiety disorders, the requirement that the person "must recognize that their fear and anxiety are excessive or unreasonable" has been removed; in addition, the symptom duration of at least 6 months now applies to everyone and not just to children
The specific types of phobias became specifiers but have not otherwise changed from the DSM-IV
The generalized specifier for social anxiety disorder (or social phobia in the DSM-IV) changed in favor of a performance-only specifier; for example, public speaking or performance
Panic disorder and agoraphobia are now two separate disorders in the DSM-5
Panic attack is listed as a specifier for all DSM-5 anxiety disorders

Practitioner's Reflections

Most people function every day with some form of anxiety generated by life stresses, upheavals, or challenges. Anxiety is considered a normal part of one's internal signaling system that alerts us to changes in our bodies and the world around us. Anxiety may be either adaptive or maladaptive. Some degree of anxiety is experienced not only when things go wrong in life but also when things simply change or happen unexpectedly. The purpose of the following activities is to help the practitioner differentiate among normal anxiety and the various types of anxiety disorders.

Activities

Competency 7 b

1. Reflect back on the cases presented in this chapter. Select one of them, and find a partner to role-play the details of the case with you. Assume the role of either the client or the social worker. After you have finished the role-play, identify the point in the exchange when you determined the presence of an anxiety disorder. Keep in mind that the focus is to practice collecting, organizing, and then interpreting client data in order to ascertain the client's diagnosis and related competence. Then describe how you were able to distinguish between normal worry and the client's symptoms.

Competency 6 b

2. Reflect back on selected cases in this chapter, such as Jada Wu, Matilda Suarez, or Herb Wilks. It might be hard to offer reassurance around their anxiety and worry. What challenges can you anticipate in developing a relationship with these clients (and their families)? Next, share your challenges with your supervisor and brainstorm how they might be addressed.

Competency 6 b

3. Imagine that you are the social worker in the school where Patty Nemeth is enrolled as a student. On your way to the school library, you notice Mrs. Nemeth outside her daughter's classroom and stop to talk with her. You are left with the impression that Mrs. Nemeth is worried about her daughter and seems a bit stressed herself. However, she does not ask for help and, in fact, seems to be in a hurry to be on her way. What next steps, if any, do you think you should take? Review the National Association of Social Work Code of Ethics and identify the sections of the Code that would inform your behavior.

Competency 1 a

4. Let's adjust the details of Patty Nemeth's vignette a bit further. Imagine that Patty's teacher is concerned about Patty's behavior and shared these concerns with you. Here, too, neither Patty nor her mother have reached out to you. How would you respond to Patty's teacher?

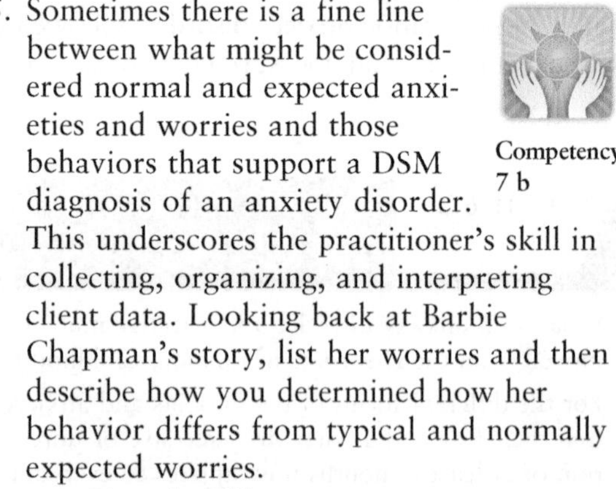

Competency 7 b

5. Sometimes there is a fine line between what might be considered normal and expected anxieties and worries and those behaviors that support a DSM diagnosis of an anxiety disorder. This underscores the practitioner's skill in collecting, organizing, and interpreting client data. Looking back at Barbie Chapman's story, list her worries and then describe how you determined how her behavior differs from typical and normally expected worries.

Competency 4 a

   a. Given her life story, can you see any worries and anxieties that might seem normal? Explain why or why not.

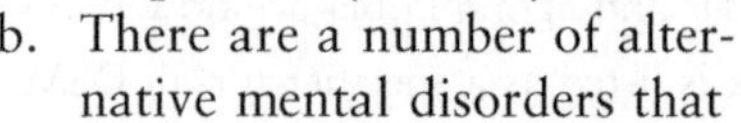

   b. There are a number of alternative mental disorders that

closely resemble GAD. Imagine that you are consulting with the social worker hearing Barbie's story. What tips can you offer to help another colleague to carefully consider and then rule out those other disorders that might potentially explain her behavior (for example, panic disorder, social phobia, obsessive-compulsive disorder, separation anxiety, posttraumatic disorder, somatic symptom disorder, body dysmorphic disorder, schizophrenia or delusional disorder, to list a few)?

Competency Notes

Competency 1 a—Social workers make ethical decisions by applying standards of the NASW Code of Ethics and other relevant laws, regulations and models for ethical decision-making as appropriate to context (p. 188): Social workers understand the value base of the profession and its ethical standards as well as relevant laws and regulations that may impact practice.

Competency 4 a—Social workers use practice experience and theory to inform scientific inquiry and research (pp. 168, 188): Social workers understand both quantitative and qualitative research methods and their respective roles in evaluating their practice.

Competency 6 b—Social workers use empathy, personal reflection, and interpersonal skills effectively to engage clients (and constituencies) (p. 188): Social workers value the importance of human relationships.

Competency 7 a—Social workers collect and organize data and apply critical thinking in order to interpret information from clients and constituencies (pp. 173, 178): Social workers understand that the assessment process is ongoing and conducted with, and on behalf of, diverse individuals, families, groups, organizations, and communities.

Competency 7 b—Social workers are able to apply knowledge of human behavior and the social environment, person-in-environment, and other multidisciplinary theoretical frameworks in the analysis of assessment data (pp. 163, 165, 173, 181, 185, 188): Social workers understand theories of human behavior and the social environment and critically evaluate and apply this knowledge in the assessment process.

Competency 7 c—Social workers develop mutually agreed-on intervention goals and objectives based on the assessment of strengths, needs and challenges within clients and constituencies (p. 162): Social workers recognize the implications of the larger practice context in the assessment process.

Competency 8 c—Social workers use interprofessional collaboration, as appropriate, to achieve beneficial practice outcomes (p. 177): Social workers value interprofessional teamwork and recognize the beneficial outcomes that require interdisciplinary, interprofessional, and interorganizational collaboration.

References

Albano, A. M., & Hack, S. (2004). Children and adolescents. In R. G. Heimberg, C. I. Turk, & D. S. Mennin (Eds.). *Generalized anxiety disorder: Advances in research and practice* (pp. 383–408). New York: Guilford Press.

American Psychiatric Association (APA). (2000). *Diagnostic and statistical manual of mental disorders* (4th ed., text revision). Washington, DC: Author.

American Psychiatric Association (APA). (2013). *Diagnostic and statistical manual of mental disorders* (5th ed.). Arlington, VA: Author.

Antony, M. M., & Barlow, D. H. (Eds.). (2011). *Handbook of assessment and treatment planning for psychological disorders* (2nd ed.). New York: Guilford Press.

Arrindell, W.A., Eisemann, M., Richter, J., Oei, T. P. S., Caballo, V. E., van der Ende, J., ... Hudson, B. L. (2003). Phobic anxiety in 11 nations. Part I: Dimensional constancy of the five-factor model. *Behavior Research and Therapy*, 41, 461–479.

Ayers, C. R., Thorp, S. R., & Weatherell, J. L. (2009). Anxiety disorders and hoarding in older adults. In M. M. Antony & M. B. Stein (Eds.), *Oxford handbook of anxiety and related disorders* (pp. 625–635). New York: Oxford University Press.

Barlow, D. H. (2004). *Anxiety and its disorders: The nature and treatment of anxiety and panic* (2nd ed.). New York: Guilford Press.

Barlow, D. H., & Durand, M. V. (2014). *Abnormal psychology: An integrative approach* (7th ed.). Stamford, CT: Wadsworth Cengage.

Bogels, S. M., Alden, L., Beidel, D. C., Clark, L. A., Pine, D. S., Stein, M. B., ... Voncken, M. (2010). Social anxiety disorder: Questions and answers for the DSM-V. *Depression and Anxiety*, 27 (2), 168–189.

Brown, T. A., & Barlow, D. H. (2009). A proposal for a dimensional classification system based on the shared features of the DSM-IV anxiety and mood disorders: Implications for assessment and treatment. *Psychological Assessment*, 21 (3), 256–271.

Clark, L. A. (2005). Temperament as a unifying basis for personality and psychopathology (Special Issue). *Journal of Abnormal Psychology*, 114, 505–521.

Craske, M. G., & Barlow, D. H. (2014). Panic disorder and agoraphobia. In D. H. Barlow (Ed.), *Clinical handbook of psychological disorders: A step-by-step treatment manual* (5th ed., pp. 1–61). New York: Guilford Press.

Furr, J. M., Tiwari, S., Suvey, C., & Kendall, O. C. (2009). Anxiety disorders in children and adolescents. In M. M. Antony and M. B. Stein (Eds.), *Oxford handbook of anxiety and related disorders* (pp. 636–656). New York: Oxford University Press.

Gallo, K. P., Thompson-Hollands, J., Pincus, D. B., & Barlow, D. H. (2012). Anxiety disorders. In I. B. Weiner, G. Strickler, & T. A. Widiger (Eds.). *Handbook of psychology, clinical psychology* (Vol. 8, pp. 147–170). New York: John Wiley & Sons.

Heimberg, R. G., & Magee, L. (2014). Social anxiety disorder. In D. H. Barlow (Ed.), *Clinical handbook of psychological disorders: A step-by-step treatment manual* (5th ed., pp. 114–154). New York: Guilford Press.

Hofmann, S. G., Alpers, G. W., & Pauli, P. (2009). Phenomenology of panic and phobic disorders. In M. M. Antony & M. M. Stein (Eds.), *Oxford handbook of anxiety and related disorders* (pp. 34–46). New York: Oxford University Press.

Kessler, R. C., Berglund, P., Demler, O., Jin, R., & Walters, E. E. (2005). Lifetime prevalence and age of onset distributions of DSM-IV disorders in the National Comorbidity Survey Replication. *Archives of General Psychiatry*, 62, 593–602.

Kessler, R. C., Chiu, W. T., Demler, O., & Walters, E. E. (2005). Prevalence, severity, and comorbidity of 12-month DSM-IV disorders in the National Comorbidity Survey Replication. *Archives of General Psychiatry*, 62, 617–627.

Kikuchi, M., Komuro, R., Oka, H., Kidani, T., Hanaoka, A., & Koshino, U. (2005). Panic disorder with and without agoraphobia: Comorbidity within a half-year of the onset of panic disorder. *Psychiatry and Clinical Neurosciences*, 59, 639–643.

LeBeau, R. T., Glenn, D., Liao, B., Witchen, H. U., Beesdo-Baum, K., Ollendick, T., & Craske, M. (2010). Specific phobia: A review of DSM-IV specific phobia and preliminary recommendations for DSM-V. *Depression and Anxiety*, 27 (2), 148–167.

Perugi, G., Frare, F., & Toni, C. (2007). Diagnosis and treatment of agoraphobia with panic disorder. *CNS Treatment*, 21, 741–764.

Shear, K., Jin, R., Ruscio, A. M., Walters, E. E., & Kessler, R. C. (2006). Prevalence and correlates of estimated DSM-IV child and adult separation anxiety disorder in the National Comorbidity Survey. *American Journal of Psychiatry*, 163, 1074–1083.

Stein, M. B., Schork, N. J., & Gelernter, J. (2008). Gene-by-environment (serotonin transporter in childhood maltreatment) interaction for anxiety sensitivity, an intermediate phenotype for anxiety disorders. *Neuropsychopharmacology*, 33 (2), 312–319.

Wald, J., & Taylor, S. (2007). Efficacy of interoceptive exposure therapy combined with trauma-related exposure therapy for posttraumatic stress disorder: A pilot study. *Journal of Anxiety Disorders*, 21, 1050–1060.

Wilamowska, Z. A., Thompson-Hollands, J., Fairholme, C. P., Ellard, J. K., Farchione, T. J., & Barlow, D. H. (2010). Conceptual background, development, and preliminary data from the unified protocol for transdiagnostic treatment of emotional disorders. *Depression and Anxiety*, 27 (10), 882–890.

Wolitzky-Taylor, K. B., Castriotta, N., Lenze, E. J., Stanley, M. A., & Craske, M. B. (2010). Anxiety disorders in older adults: A comprehensive review. *Depression and Anxiety*, 27 (2), 190–211.

CHAPTER

Obsessive-Compulsive and Related Disorders

INTRODUCTION

As children, most of us carefully tiptoed down sidewalks in an effort not to step on the cracks. If someone did happen to step on a crack, friends joyously chanted, "Stepped on a crack, broke your mother's back." This same process of rituals and superstitions is what drives people with obsessive-compulsive disorder. Even though we weren't sure why we were supposed to avoid "the cracks," we felt that in some way we were protecting our mothers from harm. Most of us can identify with this example, simplistic as it is.

What if everyone we know spent their entire lives trying to avoid stepping on cracks—or if they were driven to counting rituals because of being so totally afraid that their every impulse would bring disaster to them or their families? At the very least, it certainly wouldn't feel like a game anymore. People who are considered obsess*ive* or compuls*ive* are not the same as those who have obsess*ions* or perform compuls*ions*. The difference between the two is more than just the word endings. Obsession is a personality style (with some adaptive features), while obsessive represents a mental disorder often considered debilitating.

Obsessive-compulsive disorder and related conditions within this spectrum include syndromes where symptoms tend to cluster together (Hollander, Kim, Braun, Simeon, & Zohar, 2009; Hollander, Zohar, Sirovatka, & Regier, 2010). Obsessive-compulsive disorder describes a picture of obsessions and compulsions that lead to significant dysfunction in a person's life while the other related disorders are distinguished by preoccupations and by repetitive behaviors or mental acts as a response to these preoccupations. Still others are primarily recurrent body-focused repetitive behaviors, like hair pulling or skin picking.

There is increasing evidence that these disorders are related to one another, and there is a great deal of overlap among these conditions (Fineberg, Saxema, Zohar, & Craig, 2010). In order to distinguish between the behaviors representative of the

TABLE 7.1 THE DSM-5 OBSESSIVE-COMPULSIVE AND RELATED DISORDERS
Obsessive-Compulsive Disorder
Body Dysmorphic Disorder
Hoarding Disorder
Trichotillomania (Hair-Pulling) Disorder
Excoriation (Skin-Picking) Disorder
Substance/Medication-Induced Obsessive-Compulsive and Related Disorder
Obsessive-Compulsive and Related Disorder due to Another Medical Condition
Other Specified Obsessive-Compulsive and Related Disorder
Unspecified Obsessive-Compulsive and Related Disorder

obsessive-compulsive and related disorders, it is important for a social worker to collect, organize, and carefully interpret data from the client's social history. These disorders are somewhat easy to diagnose and will more than likely be seen by practitioners working in the mental health field (Stein & Feinberg, 2007).

Specific DSM-5 disorders involving features of obsessions and/or compulsions related to the obsessive-compulsive disorders are listed in Table 7.1.

This chapter begins with a review of obsessive-compulsive disorder.

OBSESSIVE-COMPULSIVE DISORDER

Persons with obsessive-compulsive disorder (OCD) are plagued with unwanted, recurrent obsessions or compulsions (or both). Most of us have experienced, at some time or another, a temporary obsession; for example, when you cannot seem to get the lyrics to a song or an advertising sales pitch out of your mind. It just spins around and around, over and over again. Have you ever gone out for the evening and worried whether you locked your front door or turned off the oven? Sound familiar? Sometimes these thoughts can be initiated by others—say, a coworker asks you the name of an actress in a movie; you know the answer, it's on the tip of your tongue, but you just can't think of it. It starts to bother you. In fact, it bothers you a lot. You might even stop thinking about everything else while you struggle to remember the name of "that" actress. Although you might not recognize it, you are experiencing a mild form of an obsession. The "not knowing" is certainly irritating and bothersome—but after a while you either remember the name of the actress or your need to know diminishes. This is considered perfectly normal because it stops, and does not take over your entire life.

Consider the person who has OCD and fights battles like these every minute of every hour of every day, day after day for most of their lives. Those with clinical obsessions are different from others because they suffer recurrent obsessions and/or compulsions that take over their lives; these obsessions or compulsions are severe enough to be time consuming, cause marked distress, or result in significant impairment in life functioning.

Prevailing Pattern

OCD occurs in 1.2 percent of the U.S. population within a 12-month period, with females slightly more affected than males (APA, 2013). However, incidence in childhood is somewhat higher in males.

Differential Assessment

OCD has two components: obsession (which involves thinking, doubts, ideas) and compulsion (which involves doing, acting out, performing), and the disorder is characterized by obsessive, distressing, intrusive thoughts and the related compulsive actions that attempt to neutralize them. The DSM-5 (APA, 2013) notes that a person's obsessions or compulsions must be time consuming (e.g., taking up more than one hour per day), and they must cause distress or impairment in social, occupational, or school functioning. A diagnosis of OCD requires the presence of either obsessions or compulsions alone or obsessions and compulsions together.

Obsession involves "the thinking aspect" or the thoughts and ideas that the person cannot stop thinking about. The thoughts, impulses, or images are not simply excessive worries about real-life problems. Obsessions are typically automatic, frequent, distressing for the person, and difficult to control or extinguish. According to the DSM-5 (APA, 2013, p. 237), obsessions are distinguished by:

- Recurrent and persistent thoughts, impulses, or images that are experienced, at some time during the disturbance, as intrusive and inappropriate and that cause marked anxiety or distress.
- The person attempts to ignore or suppress such thoughts, impulses, or images, or to neutralize them with some other thought or action.

There are several types of obsessions (Mathews, 2009). The most prevalent is associated with symmetry. This includes impulses such as having things aligned in a particular order; for example, pictures on the wall, fringes on a rug, or articles on a desk, or doing something in a specific way. The second most frequent obsession is characterized by forbidden thoughts or actions. This can be seen as repeated ideas such as injuring someone while driving an automobile (e.g., a bump in the road translates into thoughts about running over a body even though it has never actually occurred). There are also aggressive or forbidden obsessive impulses characterized by a fear of shouting obscenities, insults, antireligious thoughts, or sexual thoughts. The third most commonly occurring obsession is cleaning and a fear of contamination that often leads to washing rituals (Rachman, 2006).

If obsessions are about the thinking, then compulsions are about the doing. Compulsions refer to the specific actions that the person performs, usually repeatedly, in an attempt to try to make the obsession go away. The DSM-5 (APA, 2013, p. 237) defines compulsions as:

- Repetitive behaviors or mental acts that the person feels driven to perform in response to an obsession, or according to rules that must be applied rigidly.

- The behaviors or mental acts are aimed at preventing or reducing distress or preventing some dreaded event or situation; however, these behaviors or mental acts are not connected in a realistic way with what they are designed to neutralize or prevent or they can be considered clearly excessive.

Competency 7 a

The repetitive behaviors that comprise compulsions may include physical or mental acts like hand washing, checking, counting objects a precise number of times, or silently repeating words over and over. The goal of the compulsive behavior is to prevent or reduce anxiety or distress—not to provide the person with pleasure or gratification while performing the act. The lack of pleasure associated with compulsive behavior, and the fact that it is performed in response to obsessive thoughts, help differentiate OCD from other behaviors thought to be compulsive in nature (e.g., gambling and/or substance use).

Compulsions may manifest in a variety of ways; that is, the person may feel compelled to count, to touch, to check, to wash, to buy, and/or to have everything lined up in a perfect symmetrical order. Some compulsions are relatively simple, such as speaking or thinking a word or phrase to protect against an obsessive thought. Other types of compulsions can be exceedingly elaborate—for example, the person may insist on washing in a certain way, dressing in specific clothes, or placing items around the room in exact and complex patterns. These tasks often take many hours to perform, and they can be highly debilitating. People with a contamination obsession and its companion washing compulsion might in fact wash their hands 200 times a day. Hand washing, as shown in the case of Maddy Yarborough in this chapter, has been known to continue even when the skin has been rubbed raw.

If the person manages to resist performing a compulsion (even for a short time), he or she experiences a great deal of anxiety that is relieved only by giving in to the compulsion. Unfortunately, this method of trying to cope becomes a revolving door consisting of obsessions/compulsions that force their way into the person's mind. The process becomes one of thinking → doing → action → relief → thinking → doing → action → relief (and on and on and on). The individual experiences extreme distress, especially when these obsessions and compulsions interfere with his or her normal routine, work, and other interpersonal activities. The severity of these obsessions can vary, ranging from spending a few hours a day to the more severe and incapacitating levels as seen by constant intrusive thoughts or compulsions.

Symptoms of OCD the practitioner may look for include:

- A need for both sides of the body to feel even.
- A need to do everything perfectly so that terrible things will not happen.
- A need to prevent contamination (usually by dirt or germs) by repeated hand washing; this cleaning is in lieu of something bad happening.
- A need for specific counting systems or methods of checking—behaviors generally ruled by magical thinking.
- A strict need for order and symmetry, fueled by superstitions that require, for example, perfectly aligning objects at precise right angles.
- A need to banish sexual thoughts because sex is perceived as "indecent" or as a lewd act; the person may obsess over whether he or she is genuinely aroused by these thoughts.

A number of specifiers are offered to allow for a distinction among individuals struggling with OCD. The specifiers are also used for body dysmorphic disorder and hoarding disorder. They are detailed as follows:

- With good or fair insight—The person is able to recognize that obsessive-compulsive disorder beliefs are definitely (or probably) not true or that they may not be true.
- With poor insight—The person thinks obsessive-compulsive disorder beliefs are probably true.
- With absent insight/delusional beliefs—The person is completely convinced that obsessive-compulsive disorder beliefs are true.

Also included for obsessive-compulsive disorder is a tic-related specifier that pertains to individuals with a current or past history of a tic disorder.

In summary, the person suffering from OCD generally experiences a range of responses when confronted with situations that trigger obsessions and compulsions. However, the practitioner can anticipate a number of common themes including those of cleaning, symmetry, taboo thoughts, and harm. Some may even be afraid to throw something away because it might somehow be important. This could include useless items like old magazines or even used sanitary napkins (Steketee & Frost, 2007a, 2007b). As seen in hoarding disorder, these are the people you hear about in the news where their house is filled from floor to ceiling with junk leaving just a small path to navigate from room to room. The obsessions are automatic because they come and go on their own accord. Although the person obsesses and may try to resist, ultimately he or she is unable to stop the thoughts (impulses or images) from occurring.

Maddy Yarborough's vignette highlights the behaviors that illustrate the symptom picture for OCD.

CASE The Case of Maddy Yarborough

I had a message to return the call of Nelson Roberts, M.D., a board-certified dermatologist who often referred clients to me. The following is an account of our telephone conversation.

"Hi, Dr. Roberts, I got the message that you called."

"Hey, I'm really glad you called me back so quickly. The reason for my call is I have a very interesting patient I would like to refer to you. Your social work expertise is always right on target. Her name is Maddy Yarborough. She's 22, a single mother of two small children. I first saw her about a month ago for a severe case of excoriation (denuding the skin) that was complicated by a superficial infection. She had come in to see me complaining that her hands, knuckles, and elbows were raw and bleeding. Apparently, this young woman has been washing—no, I take that back—she wasn't washing, she was scouring her hands and arms with surgical soap and scrub brushes, sometimes more than 100 times a day. Maddy told me that she sometimes spends 6 hours a day washing. She's afraid of being contaminated by some antibiotic-resistant flesh-eating bacteria she heard about on television."

All I could think of to say was, "Oh ... my ... God."

Dr. Roberts went on, "I treated her with a course of topical antiseptic ointment for 10 days, but that didn't really help. I saw her back in the office after that, and she had even more inflammation, with an early cellulitis. I started her on oral antibiotics and saw her back in the office about a week later, only to

CASE The Case of Maddy Yarborough (Continued)

find a persistent and progressive cellulitis. I realized that if I didn't get her to stop washing her hands so much, she would continue to get even worse. So at that point I applied an occlusive dressing to both of her hands." Dr. Roberts took a deep breath. "Finally, I saw signs of significant improvement by the next visit—now she's back with the same symptoms. That's why I'm calling you. I don't think the antibiotic medication treating her skin infection alone is going to make a significant difference. I hope you can help her. She's going to need more help than I can give her."

I told him I'd do my best and thanked him for the referral. I met with Maddy a few days later. She appeared to be in obvious distress about something. I had barely introduced myself when she blurted out, "I can't remember if I locked the front door of my house."

I asked if she had ever actually left home without locking her front door before. She answered, "Well, I haven't—yet—but I know I did this time. I can't stop worrying about it until I get home and can check on it."

I mentioned that I had spoken with Dr. Roberts, and asked her, "How does it feel when you have these worries?"

"Oh, I can't stop thinking about getting diseases from people," she replied. "That's why I wear a surgical mask and gloves all the time. I took them off just before coming in. Didn't want to scare you. Anyway, that's why I wash my hands all the time, too. I can't stop worrying about germs. I know all about how antibiotics can't treat infections anymore because the germs are mutating so fast that everything is becoming resistant to bacteria. Pretty soon we are going to have a plague on our hands, like the one that caused millions of deaths back in the Middle Ages." The whole time we had been talking, Maddy had been looking around my office and fidgeting. At this point, she leaned over and began to straighten up some books lying on top of my desk. Then she moved on to tidying up my pencils and errant social work journals. Our eyes met, and she smiled sheepishly.

"Sorry. I'm always doing that, and I don't even realize it. My mom is always telling me our kitchen floor is cleaner than a hospital operating room." I asked her to tell me more about that. "Oh, ever since I was, what, maybe 15 or 16, I've been a cleaning nut. I just can't help it. I don't like it when anything is out of place. I guess part of it is because I don't like to throw anything away, so I have to keep it neat."

I asked Maddy a series of questions to explore the difficulties she has been experiencing—questions like:

> What does she do to get rid of these thoughts in order to put them out of her mind?
>
> Does she try to ignore the thoughts?
>
> Are these her own thoughts, or does she believe they're put in her head by someone or something outside of herself?
>
> Are there any other things she worries about?

Changing the focus slightly, I asked Maddy if she was employed. She replied, "I used to work as a restaurant hostess at a really nice place, but sometimes I had to pitch in and bus tables when it got busy. I guess one of the customers was freaked out by the scabs on my hands and complained to the manager.... and then there were a few times when a line formed at the hostess desk while I was in the ladies' room washing my hands. That job only lasted a couple of days, thank goodness. Arrgh, I was disgusted having to handle some stranger's dirty dishes—ugh, nasty, nasty job!"

I asked Maddy to tell me more about her washing—whether it was a ritual that she always had to do in a particular order. When she described the sequence of her ritual, I also explored what happened if the order of washing was changed. Would she have to start all over again? Maddy looked surprised and said, "Yes. How did you know that?"

After a bit more discussion, I asked again about her employment status, in particular if she had any other jobs in addition to the work as a restaurant hostess. She replied, "I once worked as a salesperson, but the manager wouldn't let me wear gloves when I handled money. The stupid manager told me [mimicking a singsong voice], 'Maddy, you spend entirely too much time rearranging the money drawer and all the clothes on display. You are supposed to *sell* clothes, not fuss over whether they're hanging straight on the hanger.'" Shifting back to her natural voice, she continued, "After that, I looked for jobs where I didn't have to have direct public contact. The only one I've found so far is telemarketing. It meets all my needs, and I don't have to put up with anybody telling me what to do or when to do it. Hey, I'm not getting rich, but it's putting food on my table."

When I asked Maddy about her friends, she answered, "I don't have much time or money to party with people. I'm really lucky that my best friend from high school, Melissa, still hangs out with me. Sometimes, though, she can be just like my mother—constantly nagging me not to be so clean." Maddy looks down at her hands and picks idly at a thread on her bandage. She continued softly, "I think I'm a nice person, but some people see me as strange. I used to have a boyfriend, but he got fed up because he said I always spent more than half our date in the bathroom washing my hands."

"What do you think might happen if you didn't wash your hands?" I asked.

Maddy replied, "Well, first of all, something bad might happen to him. See, he didn't understand that if I didn't wash my hands I couldn't protect him. I know it probably sounds crazy to you—and in a way it sounds crazy to me—but I get so unstrung if I don't wash." Maddy paused for a moment and then added a little testily, "Why does anybody care if I do this? It's not like I'm hurting anybody."

I asked if her difficulties had affected her children at all. She replied, "Did I tell you both of my babies were potty trained before they were a year old? Thank goodness, I live with my mother—I couldn't stand changing dirty diapers, so she took care of that job. Yuk!" With a look of complete distaste, she continued. "I have a hard time just touching my babies—never mind actually holding them—the only way I can do it is if Mom does 'the cleansing ritual' first. Otherwise, forget it. They're dirty, you know?"

I asked if she knew why she felt compelled to wash her hands. Maddy looked pensive for a moment and answered, "I know it sounds really strange, but a part of me just has to wash all the time; otherwise, the pressure just builds up inside me until I have to wash—I wash, I feel better—but it only lasts for a little while. Then the thoughts start up again, and, well, you know ... I end up at Dr. Roberts's office."

Maddy denied depression, suicidal ideation, and eating or sleeping problems.

Maddy Yarborough's DSM Diagnosis Is as Follows:
Obsessive-compulsive disorder with good to fair insight

Assessment Summary Maddy Yarborough experiences some short-lived relief from obsessive tension but finds no pleasure or gratification from the hand-washing ritual itself. She recognizes her obsessive thoughts as somewhat irrational and senseless (unlike someone with schizophrenia who has delusional thoughts). For Maddy, her rigidity around washing seems quite reasonable to her. Someone with the eating disorder of anorexia may "obsess" about food and gaining weight, but for someone with OCD, their concerns extend beyond these areas.

The terms *obsessive-compulsive disorder* and *obsessive-compulsive personality disorder* sound similar, but there are several notable distinctions between the two conditions. People with obsessive-compulsive personality disorder (refer to the chapter on the personality disorders) rigorously defend following rules and regulations—but their rigid compulsive perfectionism gets in their way; things have to be done so correctly that they rarely get tasks completed to their total satisfaction. Although there once may have been a degree of perfectionism that was adaptive or encouraged by parents or teachers, the pattern now has become self-defeating.

As well, the person with obsessive-compulsive personality disorder shows behaviors that are punctual, precise, dependable, and conscientious. At the same time, their behavior often wears friendships thin because of the compulsive rigidity. In contrast, Maddy never attempts to justify her behavior, nor does she adhere to the rigidity that influences those with obsessive-compulsive personality disorders. The likelihood that Maddy has social or specific phobias, however, must be taken into consideration because of her (almost phobic) concern about contamination. The fear of humiliation in those with social phobias and the need to avoid particular things seen in those with specific phobias constitute significant differences from OCD. Note that the patterns of the phobias do not hold true in Maddy's situation.

Competency 7 b

The practitioner's struggle is in shifting the lens away from Maddy's pathology. The competency-based assessment considers all of the various environmental influences in Maddy's life. Despite what could be a potentially debilitating condition, she truly is coping relatively well. Maddy followed through on the physician's referral, and she complies with medical treatment recommendations. Similarly, she works cooperatively with the social worker. Maddy's mother and Melissa (Maddy's high school friend) provide a support system. In addition, Maddy has found gainful employment that allows her to work at home—a rather clever way to cope with her fear of germs in the workplace. Figure 7.1 illustrates the interactions of the biological, psychological, and social variables in Maddy Yarborough's life.

We now look at body dysmorphic disorder.

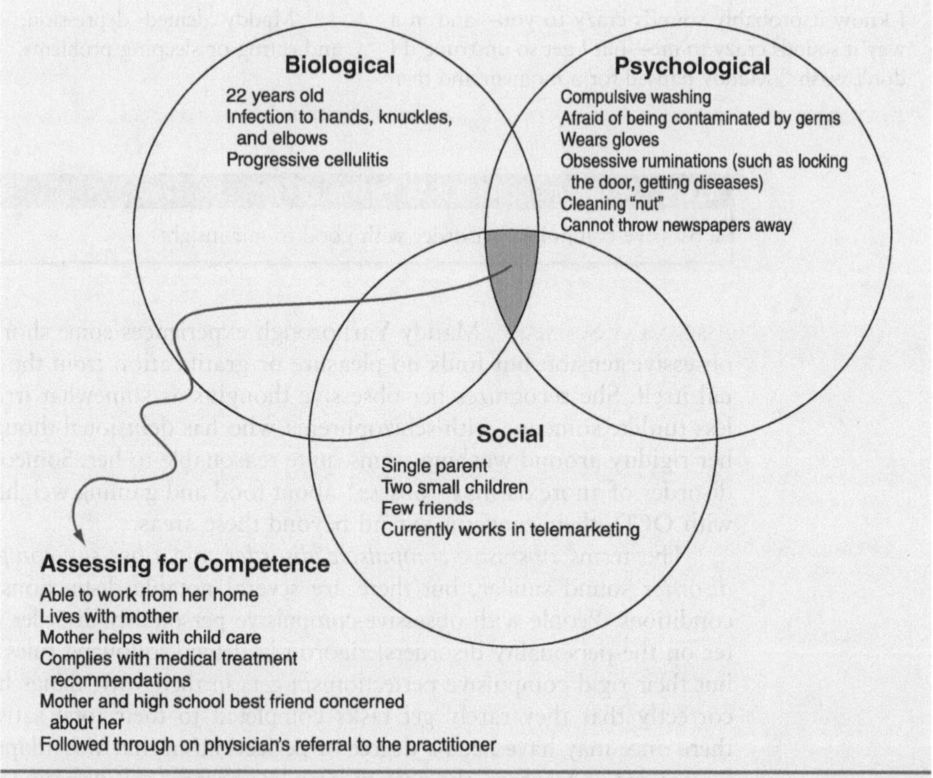

FIGURE 7.1 › OBSESSIVE-COMPULSIVE DISORDER
The interactions of the biological, psychological, and social variables in Maddy Yarborough's life.

BODY DYSMORPHIC DISORDER

The initial formulation of the clinical category of dysmorphophobia (which literally means fear of being ugly) resulted from a term coined by Enrico Morselli during the late nineteenth century. Dysmorphophobia referred to specifiable behaviors that described having an "attitude" toward parts of oneself and/or one's body and often referred to as an imagined ugliness. Dysmorphophobia disorder has been depicted for more than a century and has been reported to exist around the world. This concept was commonly referenced in European literature during the 1960s and 1970s, but not formally introduced in the United States until its appearance in DSM-III-R (APA, 1987). As an interesting aside, the DSM-IV editors felt the term *dysmorphophobia* is somewhat misleading and inaccurately suggests the presence of phobic avoidance. Consequently, they decided to relabel dysmorphophobia as body dysmorphic disorder (BDD) in order to avoid any clinical confusion.

Prevailing Pattern

Body dysmorphic disorder tends to develop around 16 to 17 years of age with the median age of onset at 15 years (APA, 2013). A person may begin to have concerns about his or her appearance as early as age 12 or 13, and these concerns usually evolve to meet full diagnostic criteria. Some individuals may experience an abrupt onset of BDD. The disorder is slightly more prevalent in females (2.4 percent) than in males (2.2 percent) and the overall occurrence in the U.S. adult population is 2.4 percent.

Differential Assessment

A central feature to remember about BDD is the person's preoccupation about some imagined defect in their body. Virtually any body part can be the focus of concern—that is, the individual is greatly preoccupied with the notion that something is very wrong with the shape, size, or appearance of some part of his or her body. Many people become fixated on mirrors, frequently checking for some presumed ugly feature to see if any change has taken place or they might avoid reflective surfaces altogether (Veale & Riley, 2001). If there happens to be some slight physical defect present, the concern is grossly exaggerated and well in excess of what is considered normal. Although the individual with BDD is continually distressed about appearance, he or she appears perfectly normal to others. This preoccupation with physical appearance includes extreme self-consciousness and embarrassment, excessive importance given to appearance in self-evaluation, avoidance of activities, body camouflaging, and a pattern of constant body checking or even picking at their skin. Keep in mind that body dysmorphic disorder does not refer to persons who are grossly disfigured or have a deformed appearance and realistically need multiple plastic surgeries (Anderson, 2003).

Body dysmorphic disorder includes the following features:

- The individual is preoccupied with an imagined defect in their appearance or is excessively concerned about a slight physical anomaly.
- At one time or another, the person is engaged in repetitive behaviors (such as seeking reassurance, checking in the mirror, excessive grooming) or mental acts (for instance, comparing how one looks with someone else) in response to concerns about appearance.
- The individual's preoccupation causes significant distress or impairs several important areas of interpersonal functioning (e.g., family, social relationships, or at work).
- The individual's preoccupation is not better explained by concerns with body fat or weight seen in someone with an eating disorder (e.g., anorexia nervosa) (APA, 2013).

A number of people are more uniquely focused on muscle defects and body building known as muscle dysmorphia, a diagnostic specifier. They may spend many hours in the gym working out in lieu of both social and occupational pursuits, often causing severe subjective distress and creating the potential for abuse of anabolic steroids or other body-building substances (Pope & Brower, 2009).

The most common symptoms of body dysmorphic disorder that social workers will encounter in practice involve facial flaws such as wrinkles, spots and/or the texture of the skin, excessive facial hair, and the shape of certain features (e.g., the nose, jaw, mouth, eyes, or eyebrows). It is common for individuals to be concerned about four different body areas, but the focus on a particular "flawed" body part will sometimes change from one site to another. For example, someone who is worried about wrinkles on their face may have plastic surgery and afterwards "discover" that his or her lips are not full enough and therefore appear grotesque. They may also go to great lengths to camouflage a "flawed" appearance by using excessive amounts of makeup, clothing, or hats. Still others can be found tanning themselves excessively to hide skin defects (Phillips, Menard, Fay, & Weisberg, 2005). In sum, their lives are significantly affected, as they tend to withdraw from most social and occupational activities. In severe cases, the person may become house-bound to hide the perceived deformity.

To give you an idea of the desperation those who struggle with BDD have about their perceived distorted appearance, Veale (2000) describes several cases where individuals performed their own "DIY" surgery in which they attempted to alter their appearance dramatically after they were either turned down or could not afford surgery. For instance, one man was so concerned about the loose skin around his face that he took a staple gun to both sides of his face to tighten his skin. Needless to say, the results were disastrous. The staples fell out after a couple of minutes and he almost damaged a facial nerve. Another woman who was unable to afford liposuction for what she saw as ugly parts of her body cut open her thighs and attempted to squeeze out the fat.

The following vignette introduces Barry Roger and describes his concerns about his thinning hair. This case can help practitioners recognize the pathologic uneasiness associated with BDD.

CASE The Case of Barry Roger

"Oh, please, whoever you are just shut that door. You're letting in all the light."

I started to poke my head inside my office, when the voice once again demanded, "Please, just come on in and close that door."

Somewhat taken aback, I said to the voice, "I know I'm in the right room, because this is my office."

The voice said, "Who are you looking for?"

"I have an appointment to see Barry Roger," I replied. "Is that you?"

The voice answered somewhat wearily, "Yeah, that's me all right. I guess the staff was pretty freaked out when they saw me walk into the waiting room."

"Oh? Why is that?" I inquired.

Mr. Roger replied, "Well, you have to admit I'm pretty ugly looking. Hey, I don't blame anybody getting grossed out when they see my ugly and grotesque baldness. I mean, come on, I can't even look. Yuk! Anyway, that's why your staff hustled me in your office real quick because they didn't want me scaring the other people. Don't get me wrong or anything—they were real nice to me, but I could see 'that look' in their eyes."

By a bit of dim light afforded me from a small separation between the window shades, I was able to see Mr. Roger sitting on a chair in the corner of my office. When I approached, he turned his face away, apparently trying to hide from my gaze. I was able to see that he had covered the top part of his head with something that looked like a cross between a baseball cap and something worn by the French Foreign Legionnaires.

As I sat down in my usual spot, I asked Mr. Roger why he had made an appointment to come see me.

He replied, "I want to have another hair transplant."

I pointed out that as a social worker, "I'm not allowed to do hair transplants."

"Very funny," he retorted. "I used to go to old Doc Connolly," he said, getting down to business. "But he retired last year. So I found this new plastic surgeon, Dr. Frick. He told me that I wasn't bald, and he refused to do any more surgery because he said I didn't need it. I don't know what his problem is. He told me that I was lucky because I had a nice full head of hair—he said I might have the slightest bit of thinning but that was normal for a guy 27 years old. Personally, I think he needs glasses."

I noted that Mr. Roger's overall health was excellent except for episodic hemorrhoid inflammation. I gently reminded him that he hadn't answered my question about his reasons for coming to the agency.

"Dr. Frick told me I didn't have a hair problem," he said rather petulantly, "but a problem about the way I see myself. He said he absolutely wasn't going to do a hair transplant, and that I should go talk to a professional."

"I see," I said before asking my next question. "Well, could you describe for me what you think you look like?"

He responded with a deep sigh. "Yeah, it's obvious that I look gross, ugly, and disfigured. I mean look at this." He snatched his hat off. "What do you think about this, huh?"

I was a bit startled, but managed to answer, "Well, actually I see a very full head of hair."

He responded quietly, "That's what everyone says."

After a moment, I continued. "I was wondering—may I call you Barry?" He nodded, and I went on. "I was wondering how much time you spend thinking about your hair?"

"Oh, all the time," he said. "I can't seem to get my mind off my baldness. If only I didn't have this problem, everything else would be terrific."

"Have you discussed this with anyone in your family or perhaps with your friends?" I asked.

He replied, "Yeah, but all they do is say the same thing that you just did. They don't see what I'm talking about. You know, it's funny—well, not really funny—but my girlfriend, Sharon, broke up with me a few months ago. She told me she was damn tired of always hearing about my hair. I mean, what's her problem? If she doesn't love me enough, well then good riddance to her. It just proves how ugly I really am without much hair." When I asked how long he's been troubled by his "baldness," he said, "I can't really say exactly when I started worrying about my hair. Maybe it started 3 years ago when I was 24. I started to notice that I was picking more and more hairs out of my hairbrush. Whenever I asked my family or friends if

CASE **THE CASE OF BARRY ROGER (CONTINUED)**

they noticed I am going bald, they just told me I had enough hair on my head for three people."

I asked Barry if his "baldness" caused him any difficulties other than feeling ugly.

He responded, "I can't leave my house or do anything outside. I know I disgust people because I can see it in their eyes. I notice it more when I don't wear my hat, because people point at me and laugh. I hate living like this. I'm a salesman, and I have to be able to interact with people—but I can't do it as a bald man."

Barry admitted that he felt unhappy but denied feeling depressed or having any thoughts about suicide. He stated he was eating and sleeping well and felt no loss of energy. I asked if there were other parts of his body that concerned him. He reported that when he was a teenager he had a few plastic surgeries, including a rhinoplasty, his ears flattened, and a "huge" mole removed from the right side of his nose.

He continued, "I had a hard time convincing my parents to let me have those surgeries. You know how parents are. They always think their child looks perfect, even when they are ugly and deformed."

He admitted to regularly working out at a gym near his home. Last year he opted to have bilateral chest muscle implants "because my chest looked so sunken in." He insists, "I know my life would be absolutely perfect if I could only get another hair transplant. Is that so terrible?"

BARRY ROGER'S DSM DIAGNOSIS IS AS FOLLOWS:

Body dysmorphic disorder with poor insight

ASSESSMENT SUMMARY The practitioner carefully organizes data about a client's symptoms in order to interpret the diagnostic picture in view of the fact that body dysmorphic disorder is comorbid with a wide range of disorders—from obsessive-compulsive disorder, to social anxiety disorder (social phobia), to major depressive disorder. Depression and substance-related disorders are commonly seen (Phillips et al., 2010). The practitioner must carefully assess a client's thoughts about him- or herself and how those perceptions influence interpersonal relationships.

Gender differences occurring in body dysmorphic disorder are just beginning to emerge, and particularly about the way physical defects are seen. Women tend focus on more varied areas of the body such as the size of their hips and the texture of their skin, and they are more likely to be diagnosed with an eating disorder. Women also pay significant attention to their breast size and shape of their legs. Men are found to be significantly preoccupied about their genitals, body height or build, and either excess hair or thinning hair (Pope et al., 2005). Most often, both men and women seek out plastic surgery or dermatological interventions—but these procedures, while physically and clinically successful, are not able to change perceptions about the defect.

Competency 7 a

Focusing on deficiencies is an especially unhelpful approach for a practitioner to use with the client who has BDD. Concentrating on negative characteristics often reinforces the client's belief in the defect, and may encourage him or her to continue picking out negative qualities—not only in him- or herself, but also in life and in significant others. It is helpful to assess the client's coping strategies and to reinforce and improve adaptation to life situations, circumstances or events. It is of

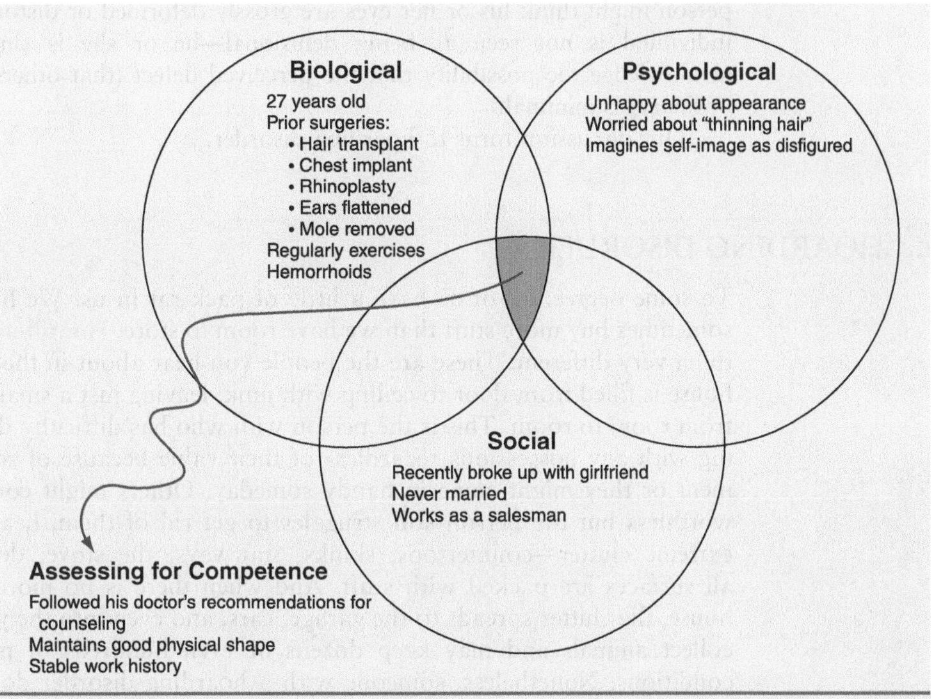

FIGURE 7.2 › Body Dysmorphic Disorder
The interactions of the biological, psychological, and social variables in Barry Roger's life.

utmost importance that Barry Roger be helped to identify and focus on his positive assets, which include following up on the referral for counseling and maintaining a healthy lifestyle. The interactions of the biological, psychological, and social variables in Barry Roger's life are illustrated in Figure 7.2.

If we look at Barry Roger's difficulties in relation to other types of disorders, we see that individuals with illness anxiety disorder (like Carl Beacher) might be overly concerned about having blotches or blemishes on their body, but their primary fear is one of being diagnosed with a serious disease. Those with anorexia nervosa are characterized by a pervasive concern with the shape and size of their bodies—their goal is to be successful in the pursuit of absolute thinness rather than in the quest to maintain a normal weight. Those with the obsessive-compulsive disorder of excoriation pick at their skin, but when this happens in an attempt to improve one's appearance, then BDD would be the more appropriate diagnosis. A notable difference for Barry Roger, however, is that he sees himself as ugly in an interpersonal world that does not view him in the same way. He is generally satisfied in other aspects of his life, but Barry's thinning hair and the "gross" appearance he imagines creates a great deal of distress for him.

In contrast to Barry's body dysmorphia, some people develop **monohypochondriacal paranoia** (delusional disorder, somatic type) and harbor delusional beliefs in which one particular part of their bodies play a part. (For example, a person might think his or her eyes are grossly deformed or distorted.) In BDD, the individual is not seen as being delusional—he or she is simply unwilling to acknowledge the possibility that the perceived defect (that others may consider as ordinary) is minimal.

Our discussion turns to hoarding disorder.

HOARDING DISORDER

To some degree, all of us have a little of pack rat in us. We hoard, collect, and sometimes buy more stuff than we have room to store. Hoarding disorder is something very different. These are the people you hear about in the news where their house is filled from floor to ceiling with junk, leaving just a small path to navigate from room to room. This is the person with who has difficulty discarding or parting with any possessions regardless of their value because of sentimental attachment or they might come in handy someday. Others might consider these items worthless but the person still struggles to get rid of them, heading for living in extreme clutter—countertops, skinks, stairways, the stove, desk, and virtually all surfaces are packed with stuff. And when there is no more room inside the house, the clutter spreads to the garage, cars, and even into the yard. Some people collect animals and may keep dozens or even hundreds of pets in unsanitary conditions. Nonetheless, someone with a hoarding disorder does not see this as a problem. Hoarding was previously considered a subtype or symptom dimension of obsessive-compulsive disorder or obsessive-compulsive personality disorder (Mataix-Cols et al., 2010).

Brain imaging studies using PET (positron emission tomography) scans have detected cerebral glucose metabolism patterns that differ for those diagnosed with OCD and hoard from those with OCD but do not hoard (Saxena et al., 2004). The most notable difference was the decreased activity of the (anterior) cingulate gyrus; the part of the brain responsible for focus, attention, and decision making (Grisham, Brown, Savage, Steketee, & Barlow, 2007). Other neuropsychological factors associated with hoarding behaviors include slower and more variable reaction times, increased impulsivity, and decreased spatial attention. However, later brain lesion studies involved in hoarding behaviors suggest the implication of these brain structures still remains unclear (Pertusa et al., 2010).

PREVAILING PATTERN

Hoarding is the fourth most common obsession (Bloch, Landeros-Weisenberger, Rosario, Pittenger, & Leckman, 2008). Symptoms usually start with clutter and a difficulty discarding things, which often shows up during adolescence and, on average, at about age 13 (Nordsletten et al., 2013). Hoarding begins to interfere with daily functioning in the mid-20s, and significant clinical impairment becomes apparent by the mid-30s. By middle age, symptoms are often quite severe. Nationally available prevalence studies are not available, but what we do know is that hoarding symptoms are about three times more prevalent in older adults; specifically in the age range of 55 to 94 years (APA, 2013). Community surveys among

U.S. populations estimate hoarding rates to be about 2 to 6 percent, and equally involves both males and females.

Differential Assessment

Hoarding disorder affects a person's emotions, thoughts, and behavior. The defining feature of hoarding disorder is the individual's persistent difficulties discarding or parting with possessions regardless of their actual value because of a perceived need to save them or sentimental attachment. These individuals may even feel safer when surrounded by things they love. Some may consider an item too big of a bargain to simply throw it away. Just the idea of letting things go or having someone touch or borrow them can cause discomfort. This provides a trajectory for living in cluttered spaces, and making areas of the home unusable for the intended purpose, such as not being able to cook in the kitchen or use the bathroom tub to bathe. The author remembers a client who could not decide where to put something so she decided it was better just to keep it and found a place for it in her bathtub.

The practitioner may see a person keeping stacks of newspapers, magazines, or junk mail. Food or trash can build up to remarkably unsanitary conditions. Some items may seem useless, such as napkins or old menus from a restaurant. It goes without saying that things can get lost in the clutter, and organization becomes a challenge. Items tend to get moved from one pile to another, but nothing is discarded. Fire hazards, tripping hazards, and health code violations can inadvertently be created. Hoarding disorder impairs social, occupational, and other important areas in a person's life. In addition, the person may have difficulty managing daily activities because of procrastination and/or trouble making decisions. They may feel ashamed and embarrassed about how they live and not want anyone to enter their home, thus limiting social interactions. They are often in debt. Hoarding can also lead to family strain and conflict, isolation, and loneliness. The obsessions are automatic because they come and go on their own accord. Although the person obsesses and may try to resist, ultimately he or she is unable to stop the thoughts (impulses or images) from occurring.

People with hoarding disorder often do not see it as a problem, which makes the assessment challenging. The following story of Melody Bryant is intended to provide a snapshot of the struggles associated with hoarding disorder in order to highlight key features of the symptom picture. Since we do not know the details of her family life, the competency-based assessment is not included.

CASE The Case of Melody Bryant

My first impression of Melody Bryant was one of a polite, reserved, soft-spoken, and articulate woman. She is a 37-year-old single mother who lives in a one-story ranch-style home in a quiet middle income neighborhood with her son and her boyfriend of the past 4 years. The police had been called to Ms. Bryant's house because of a foul-smelling odor. After one look around, the police called in the health department. As soon as the garbage on the back porch was removed, the smell stopped. I was asked to see Ms. Bryant to determine what community services might be indicated.

CASE THE CASE OF MELODY BRYANT (CONTINUED)

Most of the rooms in the house were cluttered and some were even unusable, so I spoke to Ms. Bryant on her front porch. We had to stand up, though, since junk—newspapers, tools, even an obviously broken lawn mower—were strewn everywhere.

She started, "My boyfriend, Mark, is upset and we're starting to get into these horrible fights. Yelling and screaming at each other. Yes, we've had our disagreements, who doesn't? But it was never this bad between us until the police came knocking on the door." Melody drew a deep breath and continued, "We were going to get engaged the end of this year, but now Mark is not sure he can commit what with all the attention we're getting from the clutter. Now I'm scared when he threatens to leave me. My son doesn't even invite his friends over anymore. I feel so guilty that the clutter makes them upset. But I get so anxious just thinking about throwing something away. For as long as I can remember, I always had trouble throwing things away. I keep thinking that I might need them someday. The stuff in the house keeps growing. I'm always bringing more home figuring I'll somehow find a place for it. Don't know if you noticed, but there's no place to sit down and I can't get to the back bedroom any more. I have carved out paths, though. Now I'm just living around piles and the piles that I need to get rid of. I'm so embarrassed by all this attention we've been getting. It's a good thing I have no health issues what with all that's been going on. Do you think there's something wrong with me," Ms. Bryant paused, averted her eyes, and resumed, "Like am I crazy?"

MELODY BRYANT'S DSM DIAGNOSIS IS AS FOLLOWS:

Hoarding disorder with excessive acquisition and with good to fair insight

ASSESSMENT SUMMARY Melody Bryant shows typical symptoms of hoarding disorder in her difficulty discarding possessions that look as if they are of little value; for example, newspapers, tools, and even a broken lawn mower on the front porch. Her home is cluttered and had been smelling so badly that the neighbors called the police to investigate. She lives in fear that her boyfriend threatens to leave, and lately the couple has started to argue. Plans for an engagement have been put on hold. Melody's son does not invite his friends over anymore.

In essence, Melody Bryant is experiencing significant distress and impairment in important areas of her life. She is embarrassed, worried, and living in isolation. However, she is cooperative in the interview and presents herself as very insightful. Though quiet and reserved, the full symptom picture for another mental disorder that might better explain Melody Bryant's hoarding behavior is not evident, such as major depression, schizophrenia, or another psychotic disorder. As well, Ms. Bryant states that she is in good physical health, thus eliminating any medical conditions, such as a brain injury or cerebrovascular disease, that could be attributed to her hoarding. Of note, people with hoarding may also experience other disorders including depression, anxiety disorders, attention-deficit/hyperactivity disorder, or alcohol use disorder. A stressful life event, such as the death of a loved one (and possibly inheriting the loved one's possessions), can also trigger or aggravate hoarding symptoms (Tolin, Meunier, Frost, & Steketee, 2012).

Hoarding disorder is different from collecting. Those who are "collectors" will deliberately search for items, categorize them, and carefully display the collection. Although some collections can be large, they are not cluttered nor do they cause the distress and impairment seen in hoarding disorder. Hoarding can also be a symptom of another disorder and is most often is associated with obsessive-compulsive disorder (OCD). For example, the accumulation of things that can be seen in OCD might really be the result of the person trying to avoid time-consuming rituals—that is, if something is not discarded, then the person avoids endless washing or checking rituals. Someone with schizophrenia spectrum and other psychotic disorders may accumulate items, but this behavior can be attributed to the person's delusions or negative symptoms.

To complete the practitioner's diagnostic understanding of the obsessive-compulsive and related disorders, the following section reviews two disorders the practitioner will rarely see in practice; trichotillomania (hair-pulling disorder) and excoriation (skin-picking) disorder. The discussion concludes with an overview of substance/medication-induced obsessive-compulsive and related disorder, obsessive-compulsive and related disorder due to another medical condition, and other specified (and unspecified) obsessive-compulsive and related disorders.

OTHER OBSESSIVE-COMPULSIVE AND RELATED DISORDERS

Trichotillomania (Hair-Pulling) Disorder: Trichotillomania includes the name hair-pulling disorder and involves the recurrent pulling out (or twisting) of one's own hair, resulting in hair loss. Hair may be targeted from just about any part of the body where hair grows, and the more common areas are the scalp, eyebrows, and eyelids. The hair-pulling sites may vary over time, and less common areas affected are facial, pubic, and rectal regions. As well, patterns may vary, ranging from brief episodes of hair pulling throughout the day or for more sustained periods that can last for hours. This can go on for months and even years. When the loss of hair is visible, the person may try to cover it up or camouflage the hair loss by wearing a wig or makeup. Individuals may feel ashamed, embarrassed, or unable to control the hair pulling. The disorder causes significant distress or impairment in important areas of a person's life. The 12-month prevalence for trichotillomania among the general population in adults and adolescents is 1 to 2 percent, with females more likely affected than males by a ratio of 10:1. The disorder may occur with other mental disorders and is most commonly seen with major depressive disorder, excoriation (skin-picking) disorder, and repetitive body-focused symptoms—other than hair pulling or skin picking (such as nail biting).

Excoriation (Skin-Picking) Disorder: Recurrent skin-picking, most commonly on the arms, face, and hands resulting in skin lesions, characterizes excoriation (skin-picking) disorder. Most people pick at their skin with their fingernails but excoriation may also involve using tweezers, pins, or other objects. The skin may be rubbed, squeezed, lanced, or bitten. Much like trichotillomania, the person may try to conceal or camouflage lesions with makeup or clothing. The disorder affects 1.4 percent of the general U.S. population and is more common in individuals with obsessive-compulsive disorder and their first-degree family members. Excoriation disorder is highly gender specific, with females constituting 75 percent of those affected. While onset may occur at any age, it most frequently coincides with the onset of puberty and may begin with a dermatological condition such as acne, and may increase the time spent in picking. There can be associated rituals, such as looking for a particular kind of scab to pull, and/or examining, playing with, mouthing, and swallowing the skin. The individual may feel unable to control his or her behavior, embarrassed, and ashamed. Significant impairment in important social, academic, or occupational areas of one's life may be affected, in part due to avoiding social situations. This disorder is highly comorbid with OCD, trichotillomania, and major depressive disorder. It may also co-occur with other specified obsessive-compulsive and related disorders such as body-focused repetitive behavior disorders (nail biting, lip chewing).

Substance/Medication-Induced Obsessive-Compulsive and Related Disorder and Obsessive-Compulsive and Related Disorder due to Another Medical Condition: Both of these disorders reflect the reality that some medications, substances, or medical conditions can induce symptoms similar to obsessive-compulsive and related disorders. The disturbances do not occur during the course of a delirium. First and foremost, the practitioner checks to make sure that the person's obsessions or compulsions were not there before using the drug, medication, or medical condition thought to be responsible for the symptom picture. Both disorders cause significant distress or impairment in important social, occupational, or other areas of functioning.

Unlike the transient feeling and intrusive thoughts we all experience from time to time, especially when stressed, the substance/medication-induced obsessive-compulsive and related disorder behaviors are considerably serious and more difficult for the person to control. While considered rare, the consequences can be severe. The specifier "with onset during intoxication" may be used when the obsessive compulsive episode actually begins when the individual is high on the substance. The specifier "with onset during withdrawal" is applied when symptoms develop during or shortly after withdrawal. If symptoms appear after the initiation of a medication or after a medication or a change in use, the specifier "with onset after medication use" is used. Unlike many of the other substance/medication-induced disorders, the number of substances seen as causing the obsessive-compulsive type is quite limited. They are: amphetamine (or other stimulant), cocaine, or other (or unknown) substances.

If obsessive-compulsive and related disorder due to another medical condition is diagnosed, the following specifiers are considered: with OCD-like symptoms; with appearance preoccupations; with hoarding symptoms; with hair-pulling symptoms, or with skin-picking symptoms.

Other Specified (and Unspecified) Obsessive-Compulsive and Related Disorder: Other specified obsessive-compulsive and related disorder diagnosis is used in situations in which the symptoms do not meet all of the criteria of an obsessive-compulsive or related disorder and the clinician does not have sufficient information to make a more specific diagnosis. The practitioner may indicate the reasons for using this diagnosis such as:

- Bodydysmorphic-like disorder with actual flaws, a preoccupation with real flaws in physical appearance, in which the preoccupation becomes obsessive and interferes with daily functioning;

- Body dysmorphic-like disorder without repetitive behaviors, which is self-explanatory;
- Body-focused repetitive behaviors (nail biting, lip biting, self-pinching, cheek chewing), which have resulted in failed attempts to extinguish or reduce the behaviors;
- Nondelusional obsessional jealousy, which involves a preoccupation with thoughts that one's partner is involved in infidelity. These beliefs may lead to the performance of repetitive behaviors (checking, calling, etc.) that cause clinically significant distress and disrupt the person's life;
- Koro, an intense anxiety that the penis will recede into the body (in females, the belief is about the vulva or nipples);
- Shubo-kyofu, intense fear of having a deformity (similar to body dysmorphic disorder); or
- Jikoshu-kyofu (olfactory reference syndrome), an intense fear of having a foul body odor.

The unspecified designation is used when full diagnostic criteria are not met and the practitioner chooses not to specify the reason criteria are not met for the diagnosis.

SUMMARY

This chapter reviewed obsessive-compulsive disorders (OCD) and related conditions in the OCD spectrum. The overall definition of OCD describes a symptom picture of obsessions and compulsions, and most who struggle with the disorder have both. The symptom picture describes individuals who can spend hours on rituals, making this syndrome relatively easy to diagnose, although some persons with severe symptoms may present with signs that seem very close to the picture of a psychosis. Body dysmorphic disorder (BDD), a syndrome that has a lot in common with OCD, was reviewed next. BDD characterizes those who perform excessive, repetitive behaviors or have recurring mental thoughts due to a perceived or actual defect in their appearance. BDD stands apart from the more typical insecurities about appearance in that the person is obsessed and chronically anxious about his or her "defect" to the extent that the quality of life is impaired.

Subsequently, hoarding disorder was examined. Just about all of us have had the moment where we just could not bear to part with something and throw it away. But as a disorder, hoarding is characterized by persistent difficulty in discarding or parting with possessions regardless of the value others may see in these items. The accumulation of possessions causes clinically significant distress or functional impairment.

An overview of trichotillomania (hairpulling), a disorder that features symptoms of the recurrent pulling out of one's own hair, was also included in this chapter. Next, excoriation (skin-picking) disorder, which is characterized by the urge to pick at one's own skin to the extent that it brings about skin lesions, was considered. The key features of substance/medication-induced obsessive-compulsive and related disorder, and obsessive-compulsive and related disorder due to another condition, were described, and the chapter concluded with the distinctions between other specified and unspecified obsessive-compulsive and related disorders.

As the DSM transitions from the DSM-IV-TR (APA, 2000) to the current edition of the manual, Table 7.2 provides a brief summary of the changes made to the diagnostic classifications in this chapter.

TABLE 7.2 SUMMARY COMPARISON BETWEEN THE DSM-IV-TR AND DSM-5 DIAGNOSES FOR THE OBSESSIVE-COMPULSIVE AND RELATED DISORDERS
The DSM-5 adds a new chapter on obsessive-compulsive and related disorders, which includes four new disorders: hoarding disorder, excoriation (skin-picking) disorder, substance/medication-induced obsessive-compulsive and related disorder, and obsessive-compulsive and related disorder due to another medical condition
Trichotillomania (hair-pulling disorder) was moved from "impulse-control disorders not elsewhere classified" in the DSM-IV to the DSM-5 classification as an obsessive-compulsive disorder
Continuing with attempts to avoid an "either-or" approach to diagnosis, a specifier was expanded and added to body dysmorphic disorder and hoarding disorder to allow for good or fair insight, poor insight, and absent insight/delusional (or when the person is convinced that the obsessive-compulsive disordered beliefs are true)
Criteria were added to body dysmorphic disorder to describe repetitive behaviors or mental acts that may surface with perceived defects of flaws in physical appearance
The specifier "with obsessive-compulsive symptoms" was moved from the anxiety disorders to the DSM-5 category of obsessive-compulsive and related disorders
There are two added diagnoses: (1) other specified obsessive-compulsive and related disorder, which applies when diagnostic criteria are not met but the practitioner can stipulate reasons why; and (2) unspecified obsessive-compulsive and related disorder, used when there is insufficient information to make a diagnosis

PRACTITIONER'S REFLECTIONS

The obsessive-compulsive and related disorders present with a range of obsessions and compulsions that vary among individuals. The symptom picture includes a variety of challenges as the individual struggles to cope with thoughts, urges, and even intruding, unwanted images. The following activities are intended to highlight these struggles.

ACTIVITIES

1. Rent the popular, award-winning film *As Good as It Gets*, featuring the actors Jack Nicholson and Helen Hunt. Describe how Nicholson's character depicting compulsive behaviors affects everyday life. Pay particular attention to how he was able to cope, and notice those supportive interpersonal and social factors in his environment.

Competency 2 b

2. Discuss (with another colleague or with your supervisor) how superstitions are perceived in our society versus how compulsions are viewed. Describe how you would engage a superstitious client as an informant to help you to learn more about their cultural beliefs in order to make the distinction between superstitions and the compulsions found in obsessive-compulsive disorder.
3. In many instances, the practitioner's first contact with a client is over the telephone, which (because of the lack of visual stimuli) can help the practitioner to better focus on the client's concerns. This activity is designed to help you learn to focus, as sharply as

possible, on the client's concerns. Review the case of Barry Roger.

Competency 1 a

a. With a colleague or your supervisor, role-play how you would proceed in the first 5 minutes of conducting a telephone interview with him. Imagine this is your first contact. Make an effort to screen out all visual stimuli (e.g., sit in a darkened room, wear a blindfold when playing the role of the practitioner, or sit with your back to your partner).
b. After you have completed the role-playing exercise, exchange with each other the "cues" you were able to pick up on that helped you recognize you were speaking with someone with body dysmorphic disorder.

Competency 7 a

c. Ask yourself the following questions: At what point did you begin to consider that Mr. Roger is someone with body dysmorphic disorder? When did you decide that he met the criteria for body dysmorphic disorder? How does he cope? What strengths does Mr. Roger have?

4. Persons with body dysmorphic disorder tend to focus their attention on the defects found on their breasts, face, neck, or genitals. Using the format described above, conduct a role-play of someone who is concerned about a mole on his or her chin (or use another example), but who does not have a body dysmorphic disorder.

Competency 6 b

5. Develop a list of the advantages and disadvantages of undergoing plastic surgery. Taking your own personal values into consideration as a means to acknowledge the professional values to guide practice, imagine how a person with body dysmorphic disorder would critique your listing.

6. Considering the increase of cosmetic surgeries, how do you feel about individuals who have multiple surgical procedures to improve "defects" that no one else can see? Develop a list of the ethics related to the desire to having a "perfect" body.

Competency 4 a

7. Hoarding disorder has been around for quite some time. Read the fascinating historical novel entitled *Homer and Langley* written by E. L. Doctorow in 2009 and published by Random House. The book fictionalizes the real-life Collyer brothers based on the newspapers found in their home after their death. The book provides a captivating version of the Collyer brothers' life in New York City and follows their eccentricities—including the habit of compulsive hoarding. As you read the book, identify the strengths and competencies in their lives. Also consider the social context of the Collyer brothers' struggles. How would the context of their lives compare to today's contemporary society? That is, note what is different and identify the similarities.

Competency 5 a

8. Access the Competency-based Assessment and Companion website at http://www.thomsonedu.com/social_work/gray. The case of Chuck is highlighted on the website. He is someone who describes himself as "a little bit compulsive." For example, once he has a thought, he can't put it out of his head. He's also a "checker," meaning that he has to repeatedly check things. Another case introduces Steve, who is diagnosed with agoraphobia with panic disorder. He talks about his panic attacks and how they have changed his behavior in a way that indicates the distress that these attacks have caused him. Imagine that either one (or both) of these individuals was assigned as your client. Describe how you would develop empathy for their behaviors and concerns.

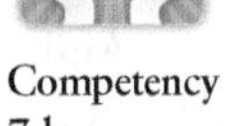

Competency 7 b

COMPETENCY NOTES

Competency 1 a—Social workers make ethical decisions by applying standards of the NASW Code of Ethics and other relevant laws, regulations, and models for ethical decision-making as appropriate to context (p. 211): Social workers understand the value base of the profession and its ethical standards as well as relevant laws and regulations that may impact practice.

Competency 2 b—Social workers present themselves as learners and engage clients (and constituencies) as experts of their own experiences (p. 210): Social workers recognize the dimensions of diversity are understood as the intersectionality of multiple factors.

Competency 4 a—Social workers use practice experience and theory to inform scientific inquiry and research (p. 211): Social workers understand both quantitative and qualitative research methods and their respective roles in evaluating their practice.

Competency 5 a—Social workers identify social welfare and economic policies at the local, state, and federal levels impact well-being, service delivery, and access to social services (p. 211): Social workers understand that human rights and social justice, as well as social welfare and services, are mediated by policy and its implementation on several levels–local, state, and federal.

Competency 6 b—Social workers use empathy, personal reflection, and interpersonal skills effectively to engage clients (and constituencies) (p. 211): Social workers value the importance of human relationships.

Competency 7 a—Social workers collect and organize data and apply critical thinking in order to interpret information from clients and constituencies (pp. 194, 202, 211): Social workers understand that the assessment process is ongoing and conducted with, and on behalf of, diverse individuals, families, groups, organizations, and communities.

Competency 7 b—Social workers are able to apply knowledge of human behavior and the social environment, person-in-environment, and other multidisciplinary theoretical frameworks in the analysis of assessment data (pp. 198, 211): Social workers understand theories of human behavior and the social environment and critically evaluate and apply this knowledge in the assessment process.

REFERENCES

American Psychiatric Association (APA). (1987). *Diagnostic and statistical manual of mental disorders* (3rd ed., revised). Washington, DC: Author.

American Psychiatric Association (APA). (2000). *Diagnostic and statistical manual of mental disorders* (4th ed., text revision). Washington, DC: Author.

American Psychiatric Association (APA). (2013). *Diagnostic and statistical manual of mental disorders* (5th ed.). Arlington, VA: Author.

Anderson, R. C. (2003). Body dysmorphic disorder: Recognition and treatment. *Plastic Surgical Nursing*, *23*, 125–129.

Bloch, M. H., Landeros-Weisenberger, A., Rosario, M. C., Pittenger, C., & Leckman, J. F. (2008). Meta-analysis of the symptom structure of obsessive-compulsive disorder. *American Journal of Psychiatry*, *165*(2), 1532–1542.

Fineberg, N. A., Saxema, S., Zohar, J., & Craig, K. J. (2010). Obsessive-compulsive disorder: Boundary issues. In E. Hollander, J. Zohar, P. J. Sirovatka, & D. A. Regier (Eds.). *Obsessive-compulsive spectrum disorders: Refining the research agenda for DSM-V* (pp. 1–32). Washington, DC: American Psychiatric Association.

Grisham, J. R., Brown, T. A., Savage, C. R., Steketee, G., & Barlow, D. H. (2007). Neuropsychological impairment associated with compulsive hoarding. *Behaviour Research and Therapy*, *45*, 1471–1483.

Hollander, E., Kim, S., Braun, A., Simeon, D., & Zohar, J. (2009). Cross-cutting issues and future directions for the OCD spectrum. *Psychiatry Research*, *170*, 3–6.

Hollander, E., Zohar, J., Sirovatka, P. J., & Regier, D. A. (2010). *Obsessive-compulsive behavior spectrum disorders: Refining the research agenda for DSM-5*. Arlington, VA: American Psychiatric Association.

Mataix-Cols, D., Frost, R. O., Pertusa, A., Clark, L. A., Saxena, S., Leckman, J., ... Wilhelm, S. (2010). Hoarding disorder: A new diagnosis for DSM-V? *Depression and Anxiety*, *27*, 556–572.

Mathews, C. A. (2009). Phenomenology of obsessive-compulsive disorder. In M. M. Antony & M. B. Stein (Eds.), *Oxford handbook of anxiety and related disorders* (pp. 56–64). New York: Oxford University Press.

Nordsletten, A. E., Reichenberg, A., Jatch, S. L., Fernandez de la Cruz, L., Pertusa, A., Hotopf, M., & Mataix-Cols, D. (2013). Epidemiology of hoarding disorder. *British Journal of Psychiatry*. Retrieved on February 28, 2015 from: http://bjp.rcpsych.org/content/early/2013/10/17/bjp.bp.113.130195.full-text.pdf+html

Pertusa, A., Frost, R. O., Fullana, M. A., Samuels, J., Steketee, G., Tolin, D., ... Mataix-Cols, D. (2010). Refining the boundaries of obsessive compulsive hoarding: A review. *Clinical Psychology Review*, *30*, 371–386.

Phillips, K. A., Menard, W., Fay, C., & Weisberg, R. (2005). Demographic characteristics, phenomenology, comorbidity, and family history in 200 individuals with body dysmorphic disorder. *Psychosomatics*, *46*, 317–325.

Phillips, K. A., Wilhelm, S., Koran, L. M., Didie, E., Fallon, B., Feusner, J., & Stein, D. K. (2010). Body dysmorphic disorder: Some key issues for DSM-V. *Depression and Anxiety*, *27*(6), 573–591.

Pope, C., Pope, H., Menard, W., Fay, C., Olivardia, R., & Phillips, K. (2005). Clinical features of muscle dysmorphia among males with body dysmorphic disorder. *Body Image*, *4*, 385–400.

Pope, H. G., & Brower, K. J. (2009). Anabolic-androgenic steroid related disorders. In B. J. Sadock, V. A. Sadock, & P. Ruiz (Eds.), *Kaplan and Sadock's comprehensive textbook of psychiatry* (9th ed., Vol. *1*, pp. 1419–1431). Philadelphia: Lippincott Williams and Wilkins.

Rachman, S. (2006). *Fear of contamination*. New York: Oxford University Press.

Saxena, S., Brody, A. L., Maidment, K. M., Smith, E. C., Zohrabi, N., Katz, E., ... Baxter, L. R., Jr. (2004). Cerebral glucose metabolism in obsessive-compulsive hoarding. *American Journal of Psychiatry*, *161*(6), 1038–1048.

Steketee, G., & Frost, R. O. (2007a). *Compulsive hoarding and acquiring: Client workbook*. New York: Oxford University Press.

Steketee, G., & Frost, R. O. (2007b). *Compulsive hoarding and acquiring: Therapist guide*. New York: Oxford University Press.

Stein, D. J., & Feinberg, N. (2007). *Obsessive-compulsive disorder*. New York: Oxford University Press.

Tolin, D. F., Meunier, S. A., Frost, R. O., & Steketee, G. (2012). Course of compulsive hoarding and its relationship to life events. *Depression and Anxiety*, *27*, 829–838.

Veale, D. (2000). Outcome of cosmetic surgery and "DIY" surgery in patients with body dysmorphic disorder. *Psychiatric Bulletin*, *24*(6), 218–221.

Veale, D., & Riley, S. (2001). Mirror, mirror on the wall, who is the ugliest of them all? The psychopathology of mirror gazing in body dysmorphic disorder. *Behavior Research and Therapy*, *39*, 1381–1393.

CHAPTER 8

Trauma- and Stressor-Related Disorders

INTRODUCTION

This chapter organizes those disorders where symptoms occur after exposure to a traumatic or stressful event. The sequence of this chapter in the DSM-5 reflects the close relationship between these diagnoses and the disorders found in the preceding chapters on the anxiety disorders, obsessive-compulsive and related disorders, and the following chapter of the dissociative disorders. Creating a separate chapter for trauma- and stressor-related disorders is based on strong evidence around how a person shows psychological distress following exposure to a traumatic or stressful event.

Trauma- and stressor-related symptoms can be understood within an anxiety- or fear-based context. Anxiety is regarded as a warning signal that helps alert a person to impending or imminent danger and enables them to deal with the threat of harm. Fear is a similar warning signal but is markedly different from anxiety. Fear is seen as a response to a definite and/or known hazard, whereas anxiety is a response to an unknown or unspecified threat. The predominant difference between the two is that fear is considered an acute reaction, while anxiety is considered chronic.

However, exposure to stress or trauma is marked by a range of symptoms depending on the person's age, previous exposure to trauma, temperament, and environmental factors. Usually, some combination anxiety (internalizing symptoms) or anger (externalizing symptoms) is a part of the symptom picture. There are two disorders included in this chapter that share a common etiology of social neglect—understood as the absence of adequate caregiving during childhood. One of these disorders is reactive attachment disorder, where the more prominent features are expressed as an internalizing disorder (anxiety) with withdrawn behavior and depressive symptoms. The other disorder is disinhibited social engagement disorder, marked by externalizing angry and aggressive behavior and expressions of disinhibition. As children with

TABLE 8.1	THE DSM-5 TRAUMA- AND STRESSOR-RELATED DISORDERS
	Reactive Attachment Disorder
	Disinhibited Social Engagement Disorder
	Posttraumatic Stress Disorder
	Acute Stress Disorder
	Adjustment Disorders
	Other Specified Trauma- and Stressor-Related Disorder
	Unspecified Trauma- and Stressor-Related Disorder

inhibited or disinhibited attachment behaviors grow older, they may develop relationship problems with just about everyone.

The conditions reviewed in this chapter are characterized by anxiety and fear and by behavior calculated to ward it off. The specific DSM-5 disorders involving the trauma- and stressor-related disorders are listed in Table 8.1.

We now turn to a review of the specific trauma- and stressor-related disorders beginning with reactive attachment disorder.

REACTIVE ATTACHMENT DISORDER

Children who have experienced various types of adverse environments are at risk for reactive attachment disorder (RAD), sometimes known as attachment disorder. This is a fairly new diagnosis to the DSM. These are children who lack attachments despite the developmental capacity to form them. RAD was first formally defined as a disorder in the DSM-III (APA, 1980) and criteria were subsequently revised in later editions. The DSM-5 revisions are the first to be made supported by relevant research data (Gleason et al., 2014). RAD is rare, and there are no accurate statistics on how many babies and children have this condition in the general population.

In essence, RAD results from inadequate caregiving environments in early childhood and encompasses a distinct pattern of a child who is emotionally withdrawn and inhibited. The symptom picture may lead to controlling, aggressive, or delinquent behaviors; trouble relating to peers; and other problems. While treatment can help children and adults cope with reactive attachment disorder, the changes that occur during early childhood are permanent, and the disorder is a lifelong challenge (Ferguson, Follan, Macinnes, Furnivall, & Minnis, 2011).

PREVAILING PATTERN

The actual prevalence of RAD is unknown. However, in rare occasions the practitioner may encounter the disorder in clinical settings, particularly among children placed in foster care or raised in institutional settings (APA, 2013).

DIFFERENTIAL ASSESSMENT

The core features of RAD include failure to seek and respond to comforting when distressed, including social and emotional disturbances seen as at least two of the following: minimal emotion regulation, reduced positive affect, and episodes of unexplained fearfulness and anxiety. Children at a higher risk for developing this disorder show a history of living in settings that limit attachment opportunities such as being separated, ignored, or neglected by their birth parents (or primary caretakers), placed in multiple foster homes, or raised in settings where there is minimal individualized care (Zeanah, Berlin, & Boris, 2011).

Symptoms begin before the age of 5, and usually can be seen while still an infant (Boris, Zeanah, & Work Group on Quality Issues, 2005). The child has not bonded to an adult and is unable to trust, and thus must have a developmental age of at least 9 months. Essentially, the child has learned that the adults in his or her life are untrustworthy. Basic needs for comfort, affection, and nurturing have not been met, and loving, caring attachments with others were never established. The child may show markedly disturbed and developmentally inappropriate ways of relating socially in most contexts. This is the child who may watch others closely but not engage in social interactions, or may withdraw from others.

As a part of the assessment, the practitioner rules out autism spectrum disorder, which may better explain these behaviors. The specifier of "persistent" can be applied when the disorder has been present for at least 1 year. The severity specifier of "severe" is used when the child exhibits all symptoms of the disorder—and at relatively high levels.

The case of Annie Marozas illustrates the symptom picture for RAD.

CASE THE CASE OF ANNIE MAROZAS

Karen Callaghan wanted to be a social worker for as long as she could remember and she always knew she wanted to work with children. Karen was thrilled, at long last, to be a graduate social work student. This was her first internship and she was placed at the Children's Home. Her first week was consumed by orientation and, finally, she had her first case assignment, Annie Marozas.

After reading her client's case record in preparation for their first visit, Karen was surprised by her reaction. She felt confused and overwhelmed. Karen was now questioning her career choice and didn't think she wanted to work with children, either. Karen wondered if she should give the placement a little more time, ask the school for a change in her field placement, or just drop out of school altogether. Karen always thought social workers make a difference in people's lives, but she felt this case was hopeless. "What's wrong with me?" Karen wondered as she absently tapped her fingers on Annie's case file.

Karen thought that even the case notes sounded detached and clinical. Her client, Annie Marozas, didn't sound like anybody's child. Maybe that's part of the problem, she mused. Annie really belongs to nobody.

The case record indicated that Annie was born to a 16-year-old single mother with a history of drug and alcohol use. She had multiple sex partners and so the biological father was unknown. Annie's mother lived at home with her mother, also a single unmarried mother. It was reported that the grandmother was extremely disappointed in her daughter's pregnancy, and this disappointment transferred to how she related to Annie—noted in the chart as cold and distant. When Annie was almost a year old, her mother was reported to have gone out for a pack of cigarettes and never returned. The maternal grandmother subsequently assumed custody of Annie. A heavy smoker, the grandmother experienced numerous health problems. When Annie was 3, the grandmother died suddenly of a heart attack.

Annie was placed in the care of the grandmother's sister, described as a distant relative who did not know Annie. The case notes subsequently recorded the aunt's observations of what she characterized as Annie's "odd behavior." She reported Annie as detached, distant, and hard to console. Annie never seemed happy or positive about anything. She rarely responded to the aunt's efforts to reach out to her, especially when upset. At times, Annie was described as irritable and for no apparent reason. The aunt had raised four sons and thought Annie's emotional responses were highly unusual. Much like Annie's grandmother, the aunt had numerous health problems. After a year of surgeries, radiation, and chemotherapy, she died of cancer when Annie was 4 years of age. Annie was subsequently placed in foster care.

A psychological report in the chart offered no supporting evidence for a diagnosis of autism spectrum disorder. Intellectual functioning was noted as average. Karen noticed a pattern to Annie's foster care placements. She would remain in each home for anywhere from a few months to several weeks. Each time, the foster family requested removal due to Annie's behavior, typically described as inhibited and emotionally withdrawn. Overall, Annie seemed like an unhappy and fearful child who was hard to approach. Although each placement presented adjustment challenges, she did not respond to reassurance and comforting from the fostering parents. Annie was seen as minimally responsive and mostly kept to herself; usually retreating to her room. Consequently, the fostering parents felt inept and unable to appropriately care for Annie. The most recent case note recorded aggressive and unprovoked behavior toward the foster mother. Annie fell off her bike and the foster mother picked her up and attempted to console her. Much to her surprise, Annie lashed out and started pushing her away. The foster family also had a special needs infant placed in the home, and they were frightened by Annie's aggressiveness. The family requested immediate removal. Unfortunately, the chart noted that there are currently no openings in therapeutic foster care and so Annie remains in this family's home. It has been 3 weeks.

Karen wondered what it must be like for this 5-year-old child to be living in a home where she is not wanted while waiting to be sent to yet another strange place to live. Karen recalled one of the lectures in her human growth and development course at school. She remembered that early childhood attachment disorders result from inadequate caregiving environments. Children like Annie show no focused attachment behaviors toward a preferred caregiver, and do not respond to comforting when distressed. They also cannot reciprocate in relationships and later on struggle regulating emotions—including unexplained fearfulness or irritability. Much like Annie, she mused. Karen thought to herself, "With a history of such severe neglect, how can I develop a relationship? If I fail with my very first client, then what?"

Karen's thoughts were abruptly interrupted when she heard her field educator's voice. "I'm making a pot of tea," said the field educator, "Would you like to join me?"

Annie Marozas's DSM Diagnosis Is as Follows:
Reactive attachment disorder, persistent, severe

Assessment Summary Understandably, RAD is a disorder commonly seen in settings by those who come in close contact with children such as the agency where Karen Callahan is starting her internship working with challenging children. As seen in Annie Marozas's story, it is often problematic to obtain a full history from the parents' perspective. Therefore, it is difficult to fully understand Annie's lived experiences of neglect. The chart carefully details numerous foster care placements lasting for several months to weeks before replacement. Each time, Annie's behaviors demonstrate what can be considered as the impact of early neglect. Specifically, she is insecure, is emotionally withdrawn, and struggles with social and emotional reciprocity; for example, Annie fails to seek out and respond to comforting at times of distress. Further, the chart describes Annie as a fearful and unhappy child. While children with a reduced level of positive effect can be considered for depressive disorders, they do not have the attachment problems seen in Annie's case.

Further, her emotion regulation is disturbed. For example, Annie is seen as a negative child who shows unexplained episodes of irritability—when she pushed the most recent foster mother away from her after she fell off her bike. Children with inhibited behavior may avoid relationships and attachments to just about everyone. It goes without saying that a person's diagnosis is not made based solely on chart notes, and seeing the client directly is key. However, the notes can serve as supplemental sources of information to the practitioner. Annie's case vignette serves to highlight key symptoms supporting a picture of RAD.

Symptoms of autism spectrum disorder can closely resemble RAD. However, a history of severe social neglect distinguishes children with RAD. In addition, the restrictive interests and repetitive behaviors characteristic of autism spectrum disorder are not seen in children with RAD. Children with either disorder may have a range of intellectual functioning. The psychological evaluation in Annie's case notes do not point to any intellectual disability, so this diagnosis can be ruled out.

Competency 7 b

Since Annie was not yet seen by the practitioner, the interaction of the biological, psychological, and social variables in her life will not be reviewed. However, a number of competencies are apparent. Her case notes do not show evidence of any physical illness, and co-occurring disorders of autism spectrum disorder, mood disorder, and intellectual disability are not supported in her symptom picture. Although not yet re-placed, arrangements have been made for a transfer to a therapeutic foster home.

A review of disinhibited social engagement disorder follows.

DISINHIBITED SOCIAL ENGAGEMENT DISORDER

Competency 7 b

A child's ability to form attachments is seen as important in the development of self-esteem, self-efficacy, and his or her ability to cope in stressful situations (Weinfield, Stroufe, & Egeland, 2000). This extends to the ability to form interpersonal relationships in adulthood (Stroufe, 2005). A lack of stimulation and interaction that might be typical in situations of neglect is associated with developmental problems in children, such as difficulties with impulse control (Gunnar, 2001; Gunnar, Bruce, & Grotevant, 2000). The strength and security of the parent-infant attachment, characterized as the child's confidence in the primary attachment figure being available and responsive when needed, is to some extent dependent on parenting style characterized as consistent, sensitive, and emotionally available. While attachment theory does not fully explain the features of disinhibited social engagement disorder (DSED), it does play a big part in the diagnostic criteria.

DSED is a disorder of a child's social relatedness and the central feature is that the child has experienced serious neglect or pathogenic care (such as severe parental neglect, abuse, or mishandling) very early in life.

PREVAILING PATTERN

DSED is exclusively a disorder found in childhood and is not diagnosed before the age of 9 months or after the age of 5 (Boris, Zeanah, & Work Group on Quality Issues, 2005). Infants and very young children are at risk if they receive inconsistent or insufficient care from a primary caregiver. As with RAD, prevalence is unknown (APA, 2013). In high-risk populations, understood as children who have been severely neglected and subsequently placed in foster care or raised in institutions, prevalence is estimated to be about 20 percent.

DIFFERENTIAL ASSESSMENT

Core diagnostic features of DSED seen in a child's behavior include an inappropriate approach to unfamiliar adults, a lack of wariness of strangers, and a willingness to wander off with strangers. For example, they will readily sit on someone's lap, or go off with an unfamiliar person. In other words, they do not discriminate between parents and strangers (APA, 2013). Children with disinhibited behavior will seek attention from just about everyone, including strangers. These behaviors are not limited to the impulsivity seen in attention-deficit/hyperactivity disorder, but also includes the quality of socially disinhibited behavior.

The child who has experienced extremes of insufficient care such as being separated, ignored, or neglected by their birth parents (or primary caretakers), or placed in multiple foster homes, or raised in settings where there is minimal individualized care that limits attachment opportunities, is placed at a higher risk for developing this disorder. The diagnosis is not considered before the child is developmentally able to form attachments, so he or she must be at least 9 months of age. DSED occurs in children, and most notably during early childhood. Minnis and colleagues (2013) observe that the disorder is more common in developmentally disabled infants because they are more likely than healthy children to be mistreated or institutionalized. It seems likely the disorder can persist into middle childhood and adolescence (Zeanah, Gunnar, McCall, Kreppner, & Fox, 2011) and has not been described in adults.

The case of Jimmy John Clark illustrates the symptom picture for reactive attachment disorder.

CASE THE CASE OF JIMMY JOHN CLARK

Marion Clark looked a little uncomfortable in the social worker's office. She began, "I've never been to see a counselor before so please just ask me your questions and I'll do my best to answer them. My pastor thought it might be a good idea for us to come here." The social worker, Nan Walker, attempted to put Mrs. Clark at ease and explained the intake process. Marion seemed relieved and continued, "It's just that my husband and I are so worried about our little Jimmy John. Chuck—

CASE **THE CASE OF JIMMY JOHN CLARK (CONTINUED)**

that's my husband—had to work today, but he told me to tell you that he will make the time to come in, if you need to see him. It's just that he had this meeting scheduled for months and couldn't change it. Please don't think he's not worried about our little Jimmy John, because he is. People always told me that being a mother would change your life. Well, believe me, it did ... but not in the way I expected."

Marion Clark looked up and asked, "Am I talking too much? Is this what you want to know?" Nan Walker offered reassurance and encouraged Marion to elaborate her concerns.

Marion continued, "Jimmy John is four-and-a half-years old now but we adopted him very early on. He was about 16 months old. The agency assured us that he was in excellent physical health, and he was! He was an active toddler and curious about everything. I can't remember how many times he got into my kitchen cabinets. There wasn't a day when my pots weren't scattered all over the floor!"

Marion looked thoughtful as she reminisced about her early experiences with her son and continued, "He was so adorable and he still is a cute little boy. But as time went on things began to change. It was like we weren't connecting or something. We adopted Jimmy John from an agency connected to our church, so I trusted everything was fine. But now I'm beginning to wonder. I've done a little research about behavior problems in very young children like my Jimmy John. Although he was in good physical health when we got him, I'm starting to wonder about his mental health. I don't know if he was exposed to any neglect, abuse, or some kind of trauma. I wonder if his mother drank or took drugs, was she depressed, or was she under any kind of stress when she was pregnant. You know, domestic violence and things like that. I now know this can affect a child's behavior." Marion Clark sighed and added, "I just trusted the agency report on Jimmy John's background and didn't ask any questions. Maybe I should have but who knew?"

Marion continued, "After Jimmy John came into our home I devoted all of my attention to him. Like getting to know him and bonding. Chuck and I didn't go out or socialize much, but we always had a lot of kids over. You know, play dates and things like that. Jimmy John was the center of my world. He was never sick and not clingy like some of those other kids."

Marion's eyes began to fill with tears and she quickly wiped them away. She went on, "At first there were little things but I thought Jimmy John would outgrow them. Like when we would go to Sunday school. On our way there he would tell me that I couldn't be with him and that I had to go away. Seems like he didn't want me there. I thought maybe it was his way of showing his independence. You know, the 'terrible twos.' So I would leave him and he seemed happy. But then he would fuss when I came back to pick him up. Things came to a head when Jimmy John started preschool last month. Same behavior, but now he runs away as soon as we get there. Never looks back and not so much as a 'good-bye.' And when I pick him up, he tells me he hates me. How could a little boy be filled with such contempt? Breaks my heart. The teachers tell me that Jimmy John will approach anyone, even people he doesn't know. He'll hold their hand, sit on their lap, ask if he could have their watch, whatever. The teachers have to keep a close eye on because they're afraid he'll wander off. It's so discouraging to hear these reports. When Jimmy John is at home, he is just the perfect angel. But the preschool experiences are totally different."

"Come to think of it," added Marion Clark, "just a couple of months ago we went to Ohio to visit my sister. She had never seen Jimmy John. We were so busy catching up that it took about an hour before we noticed Jimmy John was missing. Apparently wandered over to the neighbor's house and we found him on their porch sitting on the neighbor's lap. And he doesn't even know the guy! I'm so scared this kind of behavior will get worse when he gets older."

Marion turned to the social worker and asked, "Do you think there's something wrong with Jimmy John or is this just a phase he's going through?"

JIMMY JOHN CLARK'S DSM DIAGNOSIS IS AS FOLLOWS:
Disinhibited social engagement disorder, persistent

ASSESSMENT SUMMARY There are a number of similarities in the criteria for children with reactive attachment disorder and disinhibited social engagement disorder. Both are linked to a history of social deprivation, neglect, abuse, or abrupt separation from caregivers and are readily identified among children raised in institutional settings. Both diagnoses appear to be relatively stable over time and seen in infants with a developmental age of at least 9 months. Diagnostic criteria are evident before the age of 5 years. Since Jimmy John was adopted, this information is not available to the Clarks.

Jimmy John seems to show the most obvious symptom of DSED around his absence of normal fear or discretion when approaching strangers. In fact, he seems unusually comfortable with strangers, even to the point of leaving with them or sitting on a stranger's lap. The vignette describes how Jimmy John will approach anyone in preschool, hold their hand, or inappropriately ask someone he does not know for their watch. His teachers now watch him closely, and his mother is afraid this behavior will get worse. It is not uncommon for caregivers like Marion Clark to feel frustrated and discouraged that her son is not developing an appropriate attachment (Oliveria et al., 2012).

At this point in his case story, Jimmy John's behavior meets criteria for DSED, but the diagnosis is not considered "final" until he is seen. As well, the diagnostic criterion of a history of extreme social neglect or deprivation in his early care (and prior to his adoption) cannot be documented. With large pieces of his history missing, the interaction of the biological, psychological, and social variables in his life will not be illustrated. Until recently, Jimmy John's mother has been able to manage his behavior. The turning point seemed to be when Jimmy John started preschool. Marion Clark began to worry that her son's inappropriate social behavior would get worse. Accordingly, the specifier of "severe" is not assigned.

Jimmy John's behaviors are not described as a part of attention problems or other issues that might be associated with impulsive behavior such as attention-deficit/hyperactivity disorder (ADHD). According to Zeanah and Smyke (2008), DSED can be distinguished from ADHD by the following symptoms, which occur far less or not at all in ADHD: cuddliness with strangers, seeking comfort from strangers, unpredictable responses when reunited with a caregiver, and frozen watchfulness (or sitting as if frozen).

Table 8.2 highlights key differences between reactive attachment disorder and disinhibited social engagement disorder.

We turn to a review of posttraumatic stress disorder.

POSTTRAUMATIC STRESS DISORDER

Competency 4 a

Interest in returning war veterans helped focus clinical research efforts on trauma leading to the emergence of the posttraumatic stress disorder (PTSD) diagnosis, which was first named in the DSM-III (APA, 1980). Historically, social workers have recognized the impact of stressful life events and the challenges they place on a client's life. Longitudinal studies suggest PTSD can become a chronic problem, often persisting for

TABLE 8.2 KEY DIFFERENCES BETWEEN REACTIVE ATTACHMENT AND DISINHIBITED SOCIAL ENGAGEMENT DISORDER

A lack of comfort-seeking behavior is characteristic of reactive attachment disorder, while a lack of capacity for self-regulation in social situations is a key feature of disinhibited social engagement disorder
Reactive attachment disorder symptoms typically highlight a limited interest in interaction with unfamiliar adults, while disinhibited social engagement disorder shows an interest in, and willingness to interact with, unfamiliar adults
The symptom presentation of reactive attachment disorder in childhood and later in adolescence is less clear in contrast to disinhibited social engagement disorder, where social and verbal intrusiveness and attention-seeking are more often seen during childhood, and there are superficial peer relationships along with enhanced peer conflicts that can be more noticeable in adolescence
Those with reactive attachment disorder are more vulnerable to internalizing disorders (such as a depressed mood), while disinhibited social engagement presents a greater risk for developing externalizing disorders (for example, attention-deficit/hyperactivity disorder, oppositional defiant disorder, or conduct disorder)
Reactive attachment disorder is more likely to be confused with the diagnosis of autism, whereas disinhibited social engagement disorder is more likely to be confused with attention-deficit/hyperactivity disorder

decades and sometimes lasting a lifetime (Op Den Velde, Deeg, Hovens, Van Duijn & Aarts, 2011).

The major reference points for PTSD include the reaction to catastrophic events, such as:

- Witnessing a homicide or suicide.
- Traffic accidents.
- Combat.
- Natural disasters.
- Sexual assault.
- Victimization (such as sexual molestation, robbery, aggravated assault).
- Survivors of holocausts.
- Life events such as domestic violence or a diagnosis of HIV.

Competency 7 b

The competency-based assessment takes into account each person's individualized response to overwhelming stress. Some people can simply walk away from a terrible automobile accident in which they have been pried out with the "jaws of life." They never give the incident another thought, other than perhaps the details about getting their car replaced. Others re-experience the automobile accident in their dreams and waking thoughts (daydreaming), endure a numbing of responsiveness, and evade or shun everything that reminds them of the accident. Their lives may become centered exclusively on the traumatic event and accompanied by somatic complaints and chronic anxiety, to the extent that difficulties arise in interpersonal functioning. Some people may not react until years afterward, and why this happens is not yet clear.

Competency 4 a

What we do know is that different levels of stress and trauma appear to influence memory in different ways. Specifically, excessive amounts of stress can cause significant memory impairment (Siegel, 1998). When exposed to this kind of stress, the body's physiological responses culminate in the release of steroid hormones, most notably cortisol from the adrenal glands. Chronic exposure to these stress hormones can damage neurons, especially those comprising the hippocampus and lead to memory abnormalities indicative of hippocampal dysfunction. Brain-imaging studies have revealed that chronic exposure to traumatic circumstances seen in people with PTSD reduces the volume of the hippocampus (Bremmer & Narayan, 1998, as cited in Siegel, 1999).

Those suffering from PTSD may not make the connection between the traumatic event and feeling depressed and/or anxious, abusing substances, cognitive difficulties (memory problems or poor concentration), domestic violence, or marital problems. The practitioner must incorporate into the competency-based assessment specific questions about either a traumatic event or a series of traumatic events experienced over time.

PREVAILING PATTERN

The National Comorbidity Survey Replication (NCS-R), conducted between February 2001 and April 2003, indicated the lifetime prevalence of PTSD was 3.6 percent among men and 9.7 percent among women (National Comorbidity Survey, 2005). Looking at the rates of PTSD among adolescents between the ages of 12 and 17, Kilpatrick and colleagues (2003) found that the 6-month prevalence was estimated to be 3.7 percent for boys and 6.3 percent for girls Within a 12-month period, the overall prevalence among the U.S. adult population is estimated to be about 3.5 percent (APA, 2013). Rates are higher among veterans and those whose job increases the risk of traumatic exposure, such as police, firefighters, or emergency medical personnel. The highest rates are found among survivors of rape, military combat and captivity, and ethnically or politically motivated captivity and genocide. The relationship between gender and PTSD suggests that women tend to be more vulnerable to traumatic events than men.

DIFFERENTIAL ASSESSMENT

Competency 4 c

Keep in mind that close exposure to the trauma seems to be a main aspect of developing PTSD (Friedman, 2009). Combat experiences and sexual assault are the most common traumas associated with PTSD (Barlow & Durand, 2014). The plight of war veterans and the aftereffects of their experiences suggest that certain types of war events are empirically connected with longer-term problems. For example, among Vietnam veterans, 18.7 percent developed PTSD with prevalence rates related to combat exposure where the soldier experienced the horrors of dying, death, and direct attack (Dohrenwend, Turner, & Turse, 2006). Another example is the now infamous 9/11 tragedy. Among those who lived close to the site of the World Trade Center, 20 percent were diagnosed with PTSD (Galea et al., 2002). We now know that posttraumatic stress disorder can affect not only the "survivors," but also their families, significant others, those who witnessed the event, first responders, and society as a whole.

The central feature of PTSD that applies to those 6 years of age and older is exposure to actual or threatened death, serious injury, or sexual violence. The practitioner considers, for example, whether the event was experienced directly, witnessed, or experienced indirectly. This expands diagnostic possibilities; for example, recurrent exposure could apply to police officers who investigate numerous incidents of sexual violence. Simply learning about a traumatic event that has happened to a family member or close friend can be another contributor to PTSD. Ordinarily, this does not include something seen on TV, movies, or in pictures unless the exposure is work related.

Next, the practitioner considers four symptom clusters. They are characterized as follows:

- Re-experiencing the event—One or more of the following intrusion symptoms associated with the traumatic event(s) of (1) spontaneous memories of the traumatic event (Note: children older than 6 years of age may engage in repetitive play showing themes of the trauma); (2) recurrent dreams related to it (Note: children may have frightening dreams where the content is vague or indistinguishable); (3) flashbacks (Note: children may reenact trauma through play); (4) other intense or prolonged psychological distress; and/or (5) marked physiological reactions.
- Avoidance—One or both of the following symptoms of (1) distressing memories, thoughts, feelings, or external reminders of the event; and (2) efforts to avoid external reminders that provoke distressing memories thoughts or feelings associated with the traumatic event(s).
- Negative thoughts and mood or feelings—Two or more of the following symptoms of (1) an inability to remember key aspects of the event; (2) negative thoughts about oneself, others, or the world such as "I am bad" or "No one can be trusted"; (3) feelings that may vary from a persistent and distorted sense of blame of self or others; (4) a persistent negative emotional state such as fear, horror, anger, guilt, or shame; (5) a markedly diminished interest in activities to estrangement from others; (6) feelings of detachment or estrangement from others; and/or (7) to an inability to experience positive emotions such as happiness or loving feelings.
- Heightened arousal—As seen by two or more of the following: (1) aggressive angry outbursts; (2) reckless or self-destructive behavior; (3) hypervigilance; (4) exaggerated startle response; (5) problems concentrating; and/or (6) sleep disturbances.

For an assessment of PTSD, symptoms must last for more than 1 month and significantly affect important interpersonal areas of the person's life such as family interaction and employment. The symptom picture is not reflective of another medical condition or the effects of a substance such as medication or alcohol.

Competency 7 a

The competency-based assessment should take into account coping strategies and adaptations to stressful life events. When there is a history of trauma such as physical battering or child sexual abuse, the pain from the abusive experience may surface later in life as an additional or different disorder such as:

- Anxiety disorders and obsessive-compulsive disorder.
- Major depressive disorder.
- Personality disorders.
- Dissociative disorders.
- Conversion disorder (functional neurological symptom disorder).

PTSD can occur at any time and to anyone. Sometimes those exposed to a traumatic event may not exhibit PTSD features until years afterward (as seen in the following case of Buddy Jackson). When that happens, the diagnosis is specified with delayed expression. The person may also experience dissociative symptoms. This can be applied when PTSD can be either experiences of feeling detached from one's own mind or body (depersonalization), or experiences in which the world seems unreal, dreamlike, or distorted (derealization).

Reflective of the developmental approach to diagnosis, the DSM-5 also addresses diagnostic thresholds for PTSD for children 6 years of age and younger. The central feature of exposure to the traumatic event applies with the exception that witnessing does not include events seen only in electronic media, television, movies, or pictures. Obviously, repeated exposure through one's occupation also does not apply. Specific modifications to the major symptom clusters for children are described as follows:

- Re-experiencing the event—One or more of the following intrusion symptoms associated with the traumatic event(s) of (1) spontaneous memories of the traumatic event (Note: for the child younger than 6 years of age, these memories may not necessarily appear distressing and may primarily be expressed through play); (2) recurrent dreams related to the event (Note: it may not able possible for the practitioner to determine if the child's dreams are related to the traumatic event); (3) flashbacks, which may be reenacted in the child's play; (4) other intense or prolonged psychological distress; and/or (5) marked physiological reactions.
- Avoidance—One (or more) of the following symptoms of (1) persistent avoidance of stimuli seen as (a) avoiding (or efforts to avoid) activities, places, or reminders that arouse memory of the traumatic event(s), or (b) to avoid people, conversations, or interpersonal situations that arouse recollections of the trauma; and/or (2) negative changes in thoughts, seen as (a) increasingly negative emotional states such as fear, guilt, sadness, shame, or confusion, (b) diminished interest (or participation) in activities, including limited play, (c) withdrawn, or (d) reduced positive emotions.
- Heightened arousal—As seen by two or more of the following (1) aggressive angry outbursts, typically expressed as tantrums; (2) hypervigilance; (3) exaggerated startle response; (4) problems concentrating; and/or (5) sleep disturbances.

We now turn to the case of Buddy Jackson, who experienced a delayed onset of PTSD when he was in a situation that closely resembled the original traumatic event.

CASE THE CASE OF BUDDY JACKSON

"I just don't know where to begin. I mean everything in our lives has been turned upside down. I'm at a loss as to where to go from here," said a tearful Margaret Jackson. I asked her to start at the beginning so I could understand what had happened to bring her to my office.

"I guess I should start by telling you something about Buddy and me," she began again. "We met in 1945, at the USO. I don't imagine you know what I'm talking about, because you seem much too young. But there were literally hundreds of these service clubs in the states and around the world

CASE The Case of Buddy Jackson (Continued)

during the war. Servicemen went there for food, dancing, and you know, R & R. The fellas really loved the USOs because, no matter where they were transferred, just about, they knew there would be a place for them to go and relax and meet people—especially young ladies, I guess. Well, my girlfriends and I attended the club in Philly, where I lived then. My cousin, Wynne, and I went at least once a month."

I could tell by the look on her face that Mrs. Jackson was remembering a magical time in her life.

"You know it's kinda funny, but I remember the night I met Buddy as if it were yesterday. I saw him from across the room; he was so handsome in his Navy uniform. So tall, so ... I don't know, I guess it was love at first sight for me. Anyway, he was due to be discharged soon, and one thing led to another. He found a job as a bookkeeper for a small company in Philadelphia, and the rest is history. We were married a year later, and then the kids started coming. I used to laugh that our life was just like that rhyme from grade school: 'First comes love, then comes marriage, then comes Maggie with a baby carriage.'" Mrs. Jackson smiled broadly and stared into the distance, as if transported.

"We had three boys. We named the boys after the saints—you know, Christopher, Patrick, and Anthony. Buddy thought the names would help keep the boys out of trouble, but it didn't work. I don't know, maybe Buddy was too strict with them. Oh, he didn't abuse them or anything like that, but he did have a heavy hand sometimes. Once in a while he used to take a belt to them, just to keep them in line. I'm sure you can imagine what a handful three boys can be." Mrs. Jackson sat quietly for a moment before continuing.

"Looking back, I guess you might say Buddy was kind of isolated from the boys. Don't get me wrong, he was always a good father, and a good husband and provider—but every once in a while he'd go on what I'd call a bender. I kinda feel bad telling you this, but Buddy really liked to tie one on every now and then. He never missed much work or anything—he'd just go on what I would call a lost weekend. It was just alcohol, you know. Back then, nobody had heard of all these drugs and things they have now. He doesn't drink anymore, though."

I asked Mrs. Jackson where her boys are now.

"Oh, the boys are all grown and out of the house. I guess they are doing as well as can be expected. Christopher, our oldest, has had his fair share of setbacks in his life. He's divorced twice and has a lot of financial troubles. His ex-wife never lets up on him about making alimony payments. Did you know that Saint Christopher is the patron saint of travelers, but then later lost his sainthood status? Well, almost. Seems back in the late 1960s the church started to raise questions about whether he really even existed in the first place. In spite of all that, St. Christopher hangs in there. I guess it's all somehow fitting when I tell you more about my Christopher." Mrs. Jackson seemed oblivious to the non sequitur and continued, "Somehow our Christopher seems to have gotten lost in life—and Patrick, the middle son, unfortunately has been in and out of jail since he was a teenager. I don't know what Patrick's problem is. Buddy has just about stopped letting Patrick come visit me at the house. It's not always Patrick's fault— his boss stole money and blamed the whole thing on Pat. What a scoundrel! ... the boss, I mean."

Mrs. Jackson brightened a little. "Our youngest son, Anthony, is a good boy. He's never been married, and we call him the playboy of the family. He's got a good job, but he lives in California, so we never see him. I'm still waiting to be a grandmother, but I don't think it's going to happen anytime soon." I remained silent, curious to see where the conversation would go next. After a moment, she went on.

"Anyway, this year Buddy and I have been married 50 years. Some of our friends went to Hawaii to celebrate their anniversary, and they suggested we do the same. Buddy and I have never really traveled anywhere past Teaneck, New Jersey. I guess we're just two country bumpkins. I know Buddy didn't want to go to Hawaii, so I told him the trip was free—actually, I lied and told him I won the trip in the San Pedro church raffle. I had some money set aside, and I really wanted to go."

I couldn't help but admire her feisty spirit, but she didn't wait to hear whether or not I was going to pass judgment on her. Instead, she asked if she could have a glass of water. After a rather long swallow, she continued. "The trip was supposed to be the thing dreams are made of. You know ... a second honeymoon?" I nodded my head encouragingly; she proceeded. "Hawaii in December, what could be better? Well, maybe I'm getting ahead of myself. I guess I should go back and tell you that Buddy was stationed in 1941 at Pearl Harbor, on December 7th. You know, people call it The Day of Infamy—but, in 50 years' time, Buddy never talked about that day, or about the war, for that matter. It was an unwritten rule in our house; you just didn't talk about Pearl Harbor or what happened in the war. Even when our boys were growing up, they weren't allowed to ask him any questions. If a documentary came on television about the war, Buddy either turned it off or walked out of the room. After a while, we just got used to the way he was about it. All I ever knew was that Buddy was hospitalized for a few weeks after Pearl Harbor with some kind of shrapnel injury. He has this big old scrape on the side of his body. But he never talked about it, and I didn't want to be too nosy, you know—so I really don't know for sure what happened."

Maggie was quiet for what seemed like a very long moment. I asked how she was doing. "Oh, I'm alright. It's just difficult to tell you about this part," she replied.

"I can understand that," I said.

She blew her nose and began once more. "Well, there we were in Oahu. We couldn't have asked for a nicer flight over to Hawaii, nicer weather, or a nicer hotel. In fact, we met several couples on the airplane who were flying to Hawaii for their wedding anniversaries, too. Anyway, Buddy and I met this one couple, Gert and Abe, sitting next to us on the plane. Get this, Abe was a gunnery officer in Pearl Harbor—such a small world, isn't it? Well, Gert told me all about how Abe shot down some enemy airplanes and earned a Bronze Star. She said they planned this trip so Abe could have a reunion with the guys he served with. When I realized that our trip coincided with the 55th anniversary of Pearl Harbor, well you could have knocked me over with a feather. Imagine, of all the lousy timing. I had been so caught up in the idea of Hawaii and luaus and leis—I never once thought about Pearl Harbor even being there! Now, with it being the 55th anniversary, how could we not go?" Maggie had become somewhat tearful and she reached for several more tissues. After another sip of water, she continued.

"I can't remember when I've talked so much about this. I can't seem to stop now that the floodgates are opened. Are you sure you're okay listening to me go on and on?"

I replied, "It sounds as if you have a lot to say."

Maggie looked surprised and said, "Why, yes, I guess I do. Well, we did some sightseeing and everything was fine—or I should say I thought everything was fine. I found Buddy walking the floor at night at the hotel. When he did sleep, he seemed so restless and agitated, almost like he was having a bad dream. I figured he might be feeling the effects of jet lag, you know, the difference in time? Me, I'm fine. No problems eating, sleeping, or anything. I'm soaking up the sun and having lots of fun. I'm busy being a tourist and having a ball. Buddy was more quiet than usual, but I didn't think much of it. I noticed he took a few extra blood pressure pills, but he said not to worry about it." I noticed that Mrs. Jackson was beginning to "worry" the tissue she was holding. But she went on.

"One day we met Abe and Gert leaving the hotel. They were on their way to visit the Pearl Harbor Naval Shipyard. On the spur of the moment, Abe asked us if we wanted to go with them. They were going to visit the memorial dedicated to the USS *Arizona* battleship. I said yes right away, but Buddy was quiet a long time. He asked Abe if he'd be willing to wait an extra minute so he could get something from our hotel room. Everybody got cozy in the taxicab, and we're waiting for Buddy to join us. Well, out of the front door of the hotel comes Buddy, and he's wearing a flak jacket—something I never saw before. It looked burned in several places and was ripped up pretty good, too." She looked up at me and said with a kind of wonder, "You know what I thought? All that went through my mind was that that jacket could use a really good cleaning."

I couldn't help laughing out loud, but she continued with her story.

"Buddy settled into the taxi, and everything seemed to be all right. When we got to the Memorial Visitor Center, Abe and Buddy sort of wandered off together, and Gert and I got interested in

CASE The Case of Buddy Jackson (Continued)

one of the National Park Service rangers detailing the battle that took place. We saw a 20-minute film documenting some of the actual footage of the attack, went through a small library, and found a few things to buy in the gift shop. I thought the memorial was a wonderful tribute to the men and women who died there, and it was done in really nice taste. Gert and I got to see some dioramas that explained exactly what happened that day. So many of our people were killed—and so many ships and planes were destroyed. I remember thinking about how the ex-servicemen, like Buddy and Abe, were dealing with the Japanese visitors who were also there. I started to wonder what it must have been like at that day for Buddy.

"Well, anyway, when the 'boys' came back, we took a shuttle boat out to where the USS *Arizona* sank after it was hit. The tour people pointed out all the interesting areas like Battleship Row and Ford Island—that's where the beginning battle took place. Did you know that seven of those enormous battleships were destroyed? I remember, I kept peeking over at Buddy to see if he was okay. He didn't acknowledge me. He seemed like he was in his own world."

She went on, "One thing that impressed me was how quiet everyone was when we were riding over to the USS *Arizona*. It was so eerie. You could hardly believe there was a bustling city not more than 10 minutes away. Anyway, we walked up the gangplank, and, I have to tell you, I had heard people complain about the memorial being too plain. Well, I don't agree—it isn't plain—I thought it was a perfect balance between respect, serenity, and dignity. We were really lucky because when we got there the earlier crowds had already thinned out, and only about 30 people were walking around taking pictures. Buddy immediately walked away from me, and I guessed he wanted to be alone. I drifted over to the memorial railing, you know, to look over the side. It's true what they say; you can still see evidence of an oil slick floating on top of the water. Imagine that—after all these years. Anyway, I was wearing the lei the hotel gave me when we first arrived. I was so touched about being there that I took the lei off, dropped it in the water, and said a prayer for the dear souls who had died that day. I watched my lei float off on the oil slick and the current."

"That was a nice thing to do," I offered.

"I realized that it must be very hard for people to come back here and deal with what happened during the war. I started thinking that maybe I should be with Buddy, so I started looking around for him. He was at the far end of the memorial in what's called the Shrine Room. I could see he was reaching up to touch some of the names of people who died. I started to walk over to him, when all of a sudden a loud commotion happened exactly where I last saw him. I thought Oh, Lord, no! But I felt in my bones that something was wrong with Buddy. It could not have been more than 20 seconds, but by the time I got to him I had to push my way through a small crowd of people. He was lying on the floor, sort of wrapped into a tight ball. He was rocking side to side, and screaming, 'Get down, hurry up, and get over here! The planes are coming, hurry, hurry, hurry! John, Harry, Paul, Billy, get over here. Help me with this. We've got to undo the ties on the planes or they'll be destroyed just sitting on the field. Hurry, hurry, hurry. No! No! No! Get away from there. No! No! Nooooooo! Oh, nooooooooo!'"

As tears trickled down her cheeks, Maggie said, "I can still hear Buddy's tormented screams. One of the Service Park rangers gently asked me if Buddy had seen military action here. I told him, yes, that Buddy had been at Pearl. The ranger said he'd seen this reaction a lot of times over the years. He said it's posttraumatic stress disorder, and of course I'd heard of it with the boys from Vietnam and that Desert Storm war—but how on earth could it happen after more than 50 years? The ranger didn't know much about that, but he told me, 'Ma'am, your husband should get some kind of counseling once you get him home.'"

Maggie reached for more tissues and kept going. "Somehow we got Buddy stabilized, but he refused to leave the ship, saying he had something he had to do. Buddy took two small boxes from the pocket of his flak jacket. When he opened up the boxes, I saw two beautiful Purple Heart medals nestled in the white silk lining. He walked over to the railing of the memorial and silently dropped each medal into the water. I saw him salute, turn on his heel, and we walked away. He never once looked back. We left for home the next day."

"He hasn't talked much about what happened at Pearl Harbor, except to say that he saw his four best friends die—and he was stranded for hours guarding their dead bodies. Apparently, he saved the lives of several people when he erected a temporary shelter from flying debris. He also saved a man's leg by tying off a severed artery." Mrs. Jackson dabbed at her eyes and looked at me. "You think you know somebody after 50 years, but I guess you never know. Buddy was a war hero, and no one knew about it. It just breaks my heart to think how scared he must have been—just a 20-year-old boy in the middle of a raging battle. Buddy just hasn't been the same since we returned from our trip. Do you think you can help him?"

I was a little overwhelmed by how much Mrs. Jackson had to say. It seemed like she'd been holding all of this in for a long time—but the significant facts of Buddy's PTSD seemed pretty clear to me. In an effort to reassure her, I looked squarely at Ms. Jackson and said, "Let's begin with your husband's reactions to the war memorial. Later we can work on how all of this has affected the family. How does that sound?"

Buddy Jackson's DSM Diagnosis Is as Follows:
Posttraumatic stress disorder, with delayed expression with dissociative symptoms

Competency 7 b

Assessment Summary In general, posttraumatic stress disorder must be differentiated from other mental disorders through careful questioning by the practitioner about the presence of previous traumatic experiences. In this vignette, Mrs. Jackson shares a great deal of information about her "life story," and the practitioner's challenge is to listen for the indicators of Buddy's diagnosis of PTSD. Of course the diagnosis of PTSD will not be formally assigned until the practitioner sees Buddy firsthand. Although the 50-year delay of Buddy Jackson's symptoms is quite atypical, his traumatic episode is typical. The fact that Buddy experienced the severe trauma of combat and the death of several of his closest friends, coupled with his avoidance of talking about these experiences, contributes to the diagnosis of PTSD. There is no evidence to suggest Buddy was experiencing an anxiety, obsessive-compulsive, or a major depressive disorder, because his life history is not consistent with those symptoms. Further, we see no evidence to support a personality disorder. Although Buddy experienced combat, there is no reference to a traumatic brain injury. Although Buddy seemed "out of it" to warrant the specifier of dissociative symptoms, the full symptom picture for the dissociative disorders was not evident. Similarly, while Buddy's flashbacks made him look detached from reality, a diagnosis for the psychotic disorders is not warranted. Adjustment disorder was not considered a factor because it is more often associated with ordinary stressors, such as the impending birth of a child, a divorce, or even going back to graduate school.

However, PTSD may go undetected, because substance abuse frequently masks the debilitating symptoms, as seen in Buddy's early postwar history (Sadock, Sadock, & Ruiz, 2014). Acute stress disorder (ASD) can be considered when all the elements of PTSD are present, but for less than 1 month. If symptoms persist beyond that time, the disorder is no longer considered acute. The practitioner begins by listening for the full spectrum of symptoms that last much longer, as seen with Buddy Jackson. In Buddy's situation, a true war trauma occurred. He attempted to deal with his experiences by not talking about them—so, when he and his wife visited the site of the trauma, his memories emerged.

In contrast to people with PTSD or ASD, those with malingering disorder cannot sustain their symptoms when there is no secondary material gain (e.g., insurance or disability claims). The avoidant behavior seen in people with phobias may be similar to that seen in PTSD. However, people with phobias usually acknowledge the senselessness of their behavior—Buddy Jackson's behavior was readily understandable.

Competency 7 a

Assessing Buddy's condition solely in terms of whether or not he meets the DSM criteria fails to appreciate the ways in which he has coped with life's challenges. Competency-based practice emphasizes the importance of investigating Buddy's competencies and focuses on his assets rather than his defects. Buddy has had a long-term and stable marriage, and his wife is very devoted to him. Additionally, he made an effort to be a parent to his sons and sustained long-term employment. Though troubled by the symptoms of PTSD, he is very proud of his military service record. In fact, he proved himself a war hero at a very young age. Figure 8.1 shows the interactions of the biological, psychological, and social variables in Buddy Jackson's life.

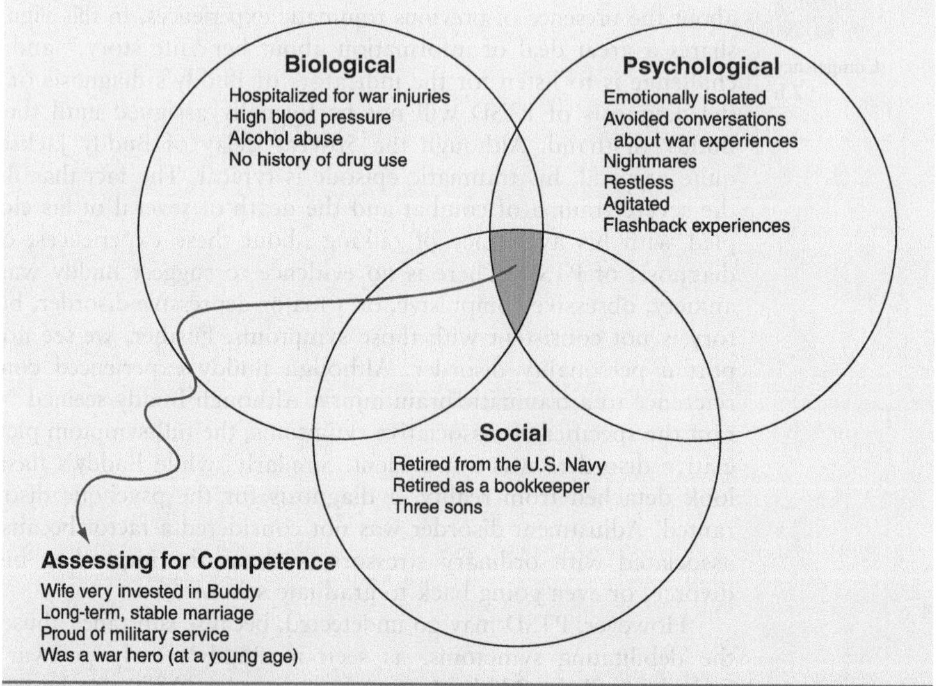

FIGURE 8.1 › POSTTRAUMATIC STRESS DISORDER
The interactions of the biological, psychological, and social variables in Buddy Jackson's life.

ACUTE STRESS DISORDER

Aspects of acute stress disorder (ASD) were identified in the DSM-I under the category entitled "gross stress reaction." Specific characteristics of this disorder were initially covered under the diagnosis of PTSD in the DSM-III (APA, 1980). Being relatively new to the DSM-IV-TR, the symptom picture of ASD looks a lot like PTSD (APA, 2000). The only difference is the emphasis on the severe reaction that some people have within the first month immediately following a trauma. There is some debate over whether the diagnostic criteria (especially its emphasis on dissociation) accurately reflect the aftereffects of someone's traumatic experience (Harvey & Bryant, 2002). The inclusion of ASD in the DSM-5 in many ways parallels the symptom changes made to PTSD, but there is a greater emphasis on dissociative symptoms (APA, 2013).

Competency 4 a

The practitioner's skill in distinguishing and evaluating multiple sources of knowledge, including research-based knowledge and practice wisdom, is a key part of the diagnosis of ASD. For instance, there have been studies identifying the presence of ASD in survivors in several different types of events such as motor vehicle accidents, typhoons, industrial accidents, violent assaults, burn victims, or those who have experienced a robbery or a mass shooting, to list a few (see, for example, Elklit, 2002; Holeva, Tarrier, & Wells, 2001). The practitioner must determine that the symptom picture emerges shortly after the trauma and dissipates within a month for a diagnosis of ASD. If the person does not recover within that 1-month time frame, then the diagnosis changes to PTSD. The individual with ASD is more likely to have the enduring symptoms associated with PTSD when the traumatic event evokes feelings of intense fear, helplessness, or horror.

While we cannot predict when a traumatic event will happen, we can predict that there will be an emotional impact. For some people, simply learning that such a traumatic event has happened to a loved one or close friend can cause problems. Likewise, just witnessing a horrific event may trigger symptoms. It has become clear that the effects of trauma are not limited to the people directly affected by the experience (Marcus & Dubi, 2006). Exposure to the traumatic event is through "witnessing, hearing, and connecting—time and time again—with the painful material of others" (Knight, 2004, p. 82). Those who seem to be the most affected are closest to the survivors (Morrissette, 2004). This includes family members, rescue workers, and other helpers. Clearly, those who work with people suffering from the aftermath of traumatic events suffer themselves because of the work.

Extreme distress, no matter what its source, is associated with adjustment problems for both survivors and helpers (Halpern & Tramontin, 2007). Growing recognition of transient and normative stress reactions has paved the way for the conceptualization of ASD and its ultimate inclusion in the DSM. Our country's recent experiences with disasters, both natural and man-made, have further highlighted acute stress disorder, which is the most common psychiatric problem following a traumatic event. A person has a greater risk of developing problems when faced with manmade trauma. For example, the terrorist attacks in

New York City and Washington, DC, on September 11, 2001, injured and killed thousands, and many more felt their traumatic impact. This tragedy will forever be a part of a nation's memory and characterized as a day of violence and disaster. For numerous individuals and their families, life will never be the same.

PREVAILING PATTERN

The prevalence of ASD varies according to the nature of the event and the context in which it is assessed (APA, 2013). In particular, in U.S. (and non-U.S.) populations, disorder can be seen in less than 20 percent of instances following traumatic events that do not involve interpersonal assault, 13 to 21 percent of motor vehicle accidents, 14 percent of mild traumatic brain injury, 19 percent of assault, 10 percent of severe burns, and 6 to 12 percent of industrial accidents. Higher rates (20 to 50 percent) are reported for interpersonal and traumatic events such as rape, assault, and witnessing a mass shooting.

DIFFERENTIAL ASSESSMENT

Acute stress disorder in the DSM-5 has been updated correspondingly to PTSD criteria. In particular, the central feature requires being explicit as to whether qualifying traumatic events were experienced directly, witnessed, or experienced indirectly. The key distinction between PTSD and acute stress disorder is the development of symptoms lasting from 3 days to 1 month after trauma exposure. Acute stress disorder may progress to PTSD after 1 month. If the person's response to stress remits within 1 month, the diagnosis of PTSD is not considered. However, it should be noted that approximately half of those who eventually develop PTSD initially present with acute stress disorder.

Individuals are considered for ASD if they show any 9 of 14 symptoms specified in the following categories:

- Intrusion—As seen by: (1) recurrent, involuntary, and intrusive distressing memories of the traumatic event(s) (Note: children may engage in repetitive play where themes or aspects of traumatic event(s) are communicated); (2) the content and/or affect of recurrent, distressing dreams related to traumatic event(s); (3) dissociative reactions, such as flashbacks, that can range on a continuum, with the most extreme reaction being a complete loss of awareness of one's surroundings (Note: children may reenact trauma-specific themes in play); (4) intense or prolonged reactions (either psychological or physiological) in response to cues that resemble (or may symbolize) an aspect of the traumatic event(s).
- Negative mood—Persistent inability to experience positive emotions such as happiness, satisfaction, or loving feelings.
- Dissociation—Understood as (1) an altered sense of reality of one's surroundings or oneself, much like being in a daze or time has slowed or seeing oneself from another's perspective; or (2) being unable to remember important features of the traumatic event(s) and typically not due to dissociative amnesia or a head injury, alcohol, or drug use.

- Avoidance—Considered to be (1) efforts to avoid distressing memories, thoughts, or feelings about (or closely associated with) the traumatic event(s); and (2) trying to avoid external reminders such as avoiding people, places, conversations, activities, or situations that provoke distressing memories, thoughts, or feelings about (or closely associated with) the traumatic event(s).
- Arousal—Regarded as (1) sleep disturbances, (2) irritability or angry outbursts typically seen as verbal or physical aggression toward others or objects, (3) hypervigilance, (4) difficulty concentrating, or (5) an exaggerated startle response.

The following case of Louise Ann Brown illustrates acute stress disorder.

CASE The Case of Louise Ann Brown

Louise Ann Brown is a single mother of two children and she was feeling "blessed." After Hurricane Katrina, Louise Ann, her daughter Vernika, age 14, and son Darius, age 11, had lost a lot ... the house, her job and ... well, everything. Even the kids' school was gone, destroyed in the storm. She felt very lucky to relocate to Paris, Tennessee, a small town in the western part of the state just due north of Memphis. Everybody there was so helpful. Louise Ann admitted that she missed the familiar sights, smells, and sounds of her home in New Orleans. She especially remembers the smell of chicory-roasted coffee ... and those beignets! She smiled to herself remembering how one of her new neighbors had called them "big nets." Paris is the home of the world's biggest fish fry, so she reckons she'll have to get used to the local delicacies. "Whatever," she thought. "I feel safe here, and folks are just so nice." The warm welcome offered by the people of Paris made missing home just a little easier.

After all, her memories of the storm were not particularly pleasant. Louise Ann and Darius had gone out for last-minute hurricane supplies, so they were not even at home when Vernika was rescued. As Louise Ann went out the front door, she remembered turning to wave at her daughter, who was talking on her cell phone with her best friend. No one anticipated how fast the water would come up—and the flooded streets made it impossible to get back to the house.

When Vernika tells the story of how she was rescued, her fingers absentmindedly fiddle with strands of her braided hair. She remembers going up to the attic, and when the water continued to rise, she climbed out a small window on the side of the house. Somehow she managed to get up on the roof. Vernika tried to get her cell phone to work so she could call her mother. All she got was a busy signal. "Next thing you know," Vernika said, "two men came floating by my house in a boat. That was so weird, seeing somebody float by the roof of your house. One of the men had a hatchet, and he had to cut a hole in the side of the house to reach me," she added. "I kept hearing a voice calling, 'Vernika, Vernika' over and over, and finally I realized that the other man in the boat was one of our neighbors—it was him, calling to me." Vernika seemed as if she were simply recalling a dream. "He's a fireman, and somehow he knew where Mama and Darius were, so he took me right over to them. I didn't realize how lucky that was until I saw all the news later on about missing people and stuff." She kept wrapping one of her braids around her finger. "Mostly, we just hung out on the streets with the folks from our church. It was so hot—that's what I remember—how hot it was. No electricity, no water, and piles of junk and garbage everywhere! The hard part was not being able to take a shower and not having food and water unless we went out hunting for it."

Vernika went on to explain that, while all this was happening to her, her best friend was also trapped on the roof of her house. "I heard she's in Springfield now with 12 of her aunts, uncles, and cousins, all in one house." Vernika pauses. "I feel lucky that me and Mama and Darius can be in our own apartment instead of being crammed in with

CASE The Case of Louise Ann Brown (Continued)

relatives. Some people from our church knew this family, here in Paris, who had a place where we could stay." Vernika had overheard Louise Ann telling somebody that they were able to stay rent-free in the apartment until they could get settled. "I didn't know folks could be so nice, but I guess you pull together when something like this happens," added Vernika. "To tell you the truth, I usually zoned out at church when the preacher was giving his sermon—but now, after how good people have been to us, I think I finally know what he means about doing good works."

Louise Ann had taken small steps to get her little family relocated to Tennessee. "Making a game plan and being proactive really helped," she stated proudly. Her first item of business was to enroll the kids in school. She worked hard to keep to a regular daily routine with normal times for sleeping and eating—that way she felt she could cut down on the stress of relocating on the kids. She also found a wonderful church community at Fairview Baptist, and the members there were a great support. Next, she wanted to get Darius registered to play baseball. He had been on a team back home, so Louise Ann thought it would be important for Darius to be able to keep doing something he enjoyed. She marveled at Vernika's adjustment—her daughter loved her new school and made several new friends right away. "Planning for our future and taking small steps made things so much easier for us," Louise Ann remarked.

The best part of living in Paris was Louise Ann's new job. She had worked for a bank in New Orleans, but her new position was a step up to head teller. The benefits were great and the pay raise sure came in handy. Actually, she had been at her new job just about a week when the tornado hit.

"It was Tuesday, November 15, 2005—but I remember it like it was yesterday. Well, I remember parts of the day really well—other parts are just a blur," said Louise Ann. "I was busy helping with the cash tally, and before I knew what was happening it hit. It was such a surreal moment. My hand was shaking so much I could hardly hold on to things. All at once, there was a huge roar outside and the wind really started blowing. The windows creaked and rattled. Then the building actually started to groan. I was so scared." Louise Ann was almost rigid in her chair as she recounted the experience. "I had almost lost Vernika in Katrina, and this time I didn't think I was going to get out. All I could think about was that I would never see my kids again. It was so hard to wrap my brain around what was happening. The tornado watches were issued throughout the morning and on the news they talked about how dangerous tornadoes are—but they also said how unusual tornadoes are for mid-November, so I just didn't think much about it." Louise Ann looked down and shook her head slowly. "You know, you can prepare for a hurricane. It's on the news for days ahead ... but a tornado? It hits all of a sudden. I don't know which is worse. I guess it's a tornado 'cause you never know when it will hit. I tried to stay calm through it all—and at the time everybody applauded me for handling the situation—but after that I just couldn't cope. Heck, I can't even remember how I got home that day."

Even though the event ended safely for Louise Ann, physically at least, she no longer felt competent or able to return to work. She couldn't seem to shake the emotional burden precipitated by her close involvement in the tornado. She even stopped calling the friends she made at work. "All they want to talk about is the storm," said Louise Ann, "and that's more than I can handle. I really don't want to remember the details anyway." The bank building she was in survived intact—but at least 30 nearby houses were completely destroyed, and severe damage was widespread throughout the surrounding area. There were constant reminders of the storm everywhere. "Even the Henry County emergency management center took a direct hit from one of the tornadoes and was forced to relocate," Louise Ann recalled.

After the tornado, Louise Ann constantly felt on the alert, would get upset whenever she tried to return to work, and would have flashbacks of the fateful day. Even though the incident was over, she was convinced that her family was in danger. The slightest gust of wind would startle Louise Ann and if it rained, she would start checking and rechecking the windows. It was like Louise Ann was on constant alert for the next storm. Just before the tornado hit, she remembered hearing on the radio at work that some high school sports games were canceled that day, but the seriousness of it all didn't seem to hit until a few days later. She stopped watching the news on TV altogether.

When Louise Ann saw all the devastation caused by the tornado, she just couldn't believe this had really happened to her. She became irritable, and the least little thing seemed to set her off. Though Louise Ann always had a good relationship with her children, she started finding fault and yelling at them for the smallest thing. All of the positive feelings seemed to go out of her, and Louise Ann just felt numb. Then she began to have trouble concentrating—but the nights were the worst; after the kids were in bed and asleep, the trembling started. For the first few days after the tornado, she would sleep for only 2 hours a night because, "my heart was pounding, thump, thump," she recounted. "I kept remembering the tornado. Then there were the nightmares." All Louise Ann could think about was her narrow miss with the tornado.

Luckily, within the first 3 weeks following the tornado, a conscientious human resources manager at the bank recognized the symptoms of acute stress disorder and referred Louise Ann to the Employee Assistance Program for crisis counseling. Louise Ann subsequently saw a social worker who specialized in the treatment of the emotional aspects of trauma. "I thought I'd try it out—and I found it really useful. I had only one really long session with the social worker, and then I spoke to her on the phone a couple of times as well. She told me my response is normal. She said strong reactions are common during and in the days and even weeks following these kinds of disasters. When she told me that I had good reasons to be upset, I really felt a lot better—that was encouraging. It wasn't a magical cure or anything like that, but it was really helpful." Louise Ann has made a full recovery and is once again back on the job and enjoying her new life in Paris, Tennessee.

Louise Ann Brown's DSM diagnosis Is as Follows:
Acute stress disorder

Assessment Summary Prior to the tornado, Louise Ann enjoyed a close relationship with her kids, her new friends, and colleagues at work. She was enjoying success at her job and was involved in her church community. You could characterize Louise Ann as "well adjusted," especially considering that she had just been through the displacement caused by Hurricane Katrina. Under the circumstances, her response to the tornado was an understandable (and common) reaction to an abnormally disturbing event. Louise Ann had no prior history of substance use or depression, nor had she taken any medications for a medical condition that could better explain her symptoms.

For an accurate assessment for ASD, symptoms must develop within 1 month of a traumatic event. In this situation, Louise Ann's symptoms emerged almost immediately after the tornado—her hands started shaking uncontrollably, and she had difficulty grasping the enormity of the event. As she said, "It was so hard to wrap my brain around what was happening." She worried about never seeing her children again and began to feel numb. She hardly remembers driving home after the storm. Shortly thereafter, Louise Ann experienced difficulty concentrating, experienced recurrent thoughts of the tornado, and felt increasingly irritable toward her children. In addition, she felt unable to cope with work, avoided friends, and was not sleeping well. She refused to watch the news on TV, and her thoughts were preoccupied with the tornado. Any signs of a storm, even a light rain, startled Louise Ann, and she would go around the house checking windows. Her responses clustered around symptoms of intrusion,

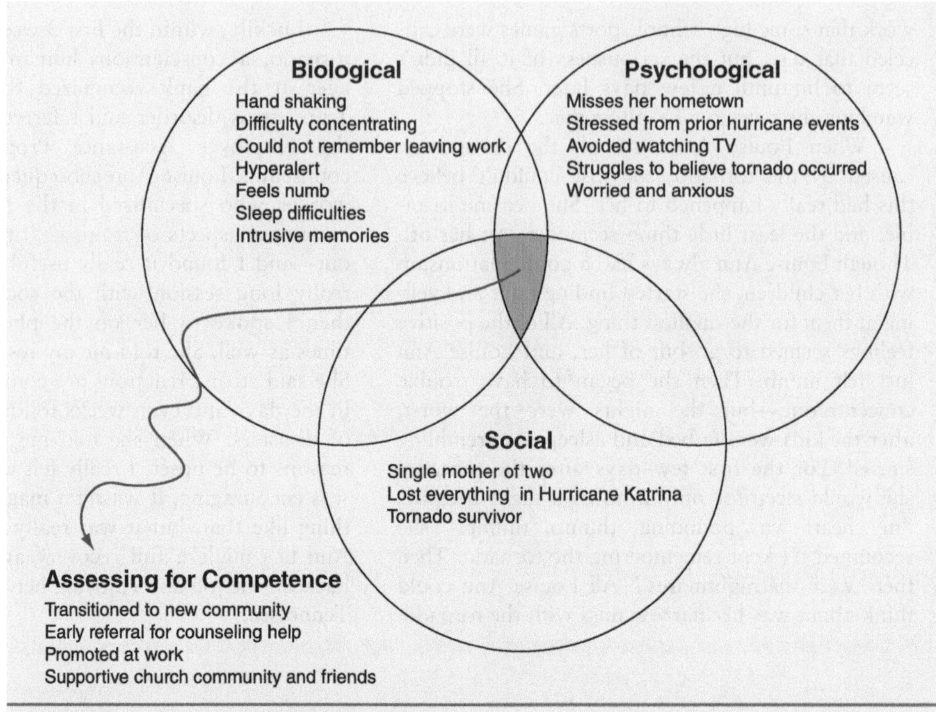

FIGURE 8.2 › ACUTE STRESS DISORDER
The interactions of the biological, psychological, and social variables in Louise Ann Brown's life.

negative mood, dissociative, avoidance, and arousal. Fortunately, her symptoms abated within a month's time, thus confirming the diagnosis of ASD.

Competency 7 a

The competency-based assessment looks to a client's coping strategies to reinforce and improve adaptation to life situations, circumstances, and events. Fortunately, Louise Ann's employer was able to recognize the symptoms of acute stress and made a timely referral to an appropriate practitioner. In addition, Louise Ann had survived Hurricane Katrina and was making a smooth transition to a new community. In fact, Louise Ann received a job promotion. She was also attentive to helping her children make the transition from a familiar home in New Orleans to her new community in Tennessee. Figure 8.2 summarizes the interactions of the biological, psychological, and social variables in Louise Ann Brown's life.

ADJUSTMENT DISORDERS

The adjustment disorders were seen as a residual diagnostic category in the DSM-IV and reserved for individuals who exhibited clinically significant distress but did not meet diagnostic criteria for a more discrete disorder (APA, 2000). The adjustment disorders are reconceptualized in the DSM-5 as a stress-response syndrome that occurs after exposure to a distressing (traumatic or non-traumatic) event.

Prevailing Pattern

Adjustment disorders are considered to be a common problem, although prevalence may vary considering the population studied. For instance, Fernandez and colleagues (2012) point to the low recognition of the disorder in primary care settings by general practitioners, with only 2 of 110 cases being recognized. In contrast, outpatient mental health treatment settings report a principal diagnosis of adjustment disorder ranging from approximate 5 to 20 percent of those seen. In hospital psychiatric settings, the disorder is often the most common diagnosis, reaching 50 percent (APA, 2013).

Differential Assessment

Adjustment disorders differ from PTSD in that PTSD generally occurs as a reaction to a life-threatening event and tends to last longer. On the other hand, the adjustment disorders are short term, and symptoms generally resolve within 6 months after the stressor or its consequences have ended.

However, adjustment disorders usually interfere with social functioning and performance arising in the period of adaptation (within 3 months) to a significant life change or stressful life event. The stressor may have affected the individual's social network (such as bereavement or separation experiences), or a wider system of social supports and values (such as migration, refugee status), or may be represented by a major developmental transition or crisis (such as going to school, becoming a parent, failure to attain a goal or retirement). Adjustment disorder may be related to a single event or multiple stressors. The individual, the family, or even the larger community may be affected. Many diagnoses of medical disorders are comorbid with adjustment disorders. Unfortunately, adjustment disorders often go unrecognized by the general practitioner and instead are mistaken for depression (Fernandez et al., 2012).

For diagnostic purposes, the person's distress is out of proportion to the severity or intensity of the stressor(s). Once the stressor or its consequences have ended, symptoms do not persist for more than an additional 6 months. Adjustment disorders are not considered when the symptom threshold for another condition is met.

Onset can be specified as acute (lasting for less than 6 months) or chronic (if stressors last for 6 months or longer). The practitioner also considers six specifiers:

- With depressed mood—low mood, tearfulness, or feelings of hopelessness are prevalent.
- With anxiety—nervousness, worry, jitteriness, or separation anxiety are predominant.
- With mixed anxiety and depressed mood—a combination of depression and anxiety.
- With disturbance of conduct—when disturbed conduct is predominant.
- With mixed disturbance of emotions and conduct—both emotional symptoms (such as depression, anxiety) and a disturbance of conduct are present.
- Unspecified—for maladaptive reactions that are not seen as one of the specific subtypes of adjustment disorders.

The adjustment disorders remain as a place to consider a diagnosis when an individual does not otherwise meet the criteria for another disorder in the DSM-5; for example, the distinguishing features of a major depression (Casey et al., 2006).

Nevertheless, an adjustment disorder may be seen along with the diagnosis of another mental disorder. For instance, someone diagnosed with obsessive-compulsive disorder may lose their job and subsequently meet the symptom picture for the additional diagnosis of adjustment disorder. It goes without saying that cultural considerations should be taken into account and the practitioner should only make the diagnosis of adjustment disorder when a person's response to stress is greater than what would normally be expected.

A brief snapshot of what happened to Jeannette Hutton when she learned some devastating news about her sister highlights adjustment disorder.

CASE THE CASE OF JEANNETTE HUTTON

Jeannette Hutton is a 23-year-old young woman who recently graduated college and started her first job as an elementary school teacher. She always loved working with children starting when she was a summer camp counselor in high school. She and her longtime boyfriend had just gotten engaged and planned for their wedding in the following year. Things were going well for Jeannette, and in one day she felt like her life was falling apart.

That was the day Jeannette learned that her older sister was diagnosed with breast cancer and would start a protocol of radiation and chemotherapy after surgery. From that point on, Jeannette found her life had irrevocably changed. "I don't know what came over me. It was like my life just stopped. I was really close with my boyfriend and I just lost interest in seeing him. We used to be inseparable," said Jeannette. She added there was now a great deal of tension in their relationship.

Ordinarily Jeannette could be characterized as upbeat and optimistic. Since the news about her sister, she comments, "This has been going on for the past 2 months and I just feel so down. I know my boyfriend is really worried, and we seem to argue all the time now. I just can't stand another minute of knowing what my sister is going through and not being able to do anything about it. Anyway, from the instant I heard about her condition, my whole life changed." Jeannette adds that there is a strong history of breast cancer in her family going back to her grandmother. She faithfully has yearly checkups and passed her most recent with a clean bill of health.

Jeannette started to withdraw from her friends, does not enjoy her job anymore, and finds it harder to get the energy to devote to her classes. She added. "I just feel so down. I cry at the drop of a hat, and feel so hopeless about things getting back to normal."

JEANNETTE HUTTON'S DSM DIAGNOSIS IS AS FOLLOWS:

Adjustment disorder, with depressed mood

ASSESSMENT SUMMARY A diagnostic challenge for the practitioner is to differentiate adjustment disorders from normal stress responses. Looking at Jeannette's story, she seemed to be at an exciting place in her life—a new job, recently engaged, and planning a wedding—when devastating news about her sister changed her life. Given the context of a strong family history of cancer, one can appreciate Jeannette's response. However, when interpersonal relationships were adversely impacted, and her mood shifted to one characterized by sadness and feelings of hopelessness, the symptom picture for adjustment disorder emerges. Her response does not look like normal loss and bereavement, and criteria for another mental disorder are not seen in this vignette.

The chapter concludes with an overview of other specified and unspecified trauma- and stressor-related disorders. The specified trauma- and stressor-related disorder applies when the person's symptom picture does not meet full criteria for any of the disorders in this chapter. The practitioner has the option to communicate the specific reason that the person's symptom presentation does not meet criteria. Examples are:

- Adjustment-like disorders with delayed onset of symptoms that occur more than 3 months after the stressor.
- Adjustment-like disorders with prolonged duration of more than 6 months without prolonged duration of stressor.

Competency 5 c

- Ataque de nervios, which is generally reserved for individuals of Latino descent, and characterized by symptoms of intense emotional upset including acute anxiety, anger, or grief; screaming and shouting uncontrollably; attacks of crying; trembling; heat in the chest rising to the head; and becoming verbally and physically aggressive.
- Other cultural syndromes as listed in the DSM-5 "Glossary of Cultural Concepts of Distress."
- Persistent complex bereavement disorder, characterized by severe and persistent grief and mourning reactions.

Unspecified trauma- and stressor-related disorder applies to those who present with symptoms characteristic of a trauma- and stressor-related disorder. It can also be used in situations when the practitioner elects not to specify the reason that diagnostic criteria are not met and includes presentations in which there is insufficient information to make a more specific diagnosis.

SUMMARY

This chapter reviewed those disorders where symptoms occur after exposure to a traumatic or stressful event. Posttraumatic stress disorder, acute stress disorder, and adjustment disorders can be understood by symptoms within an anxiety- or fear-based context. Also included is a review of two disorders—reactive attachment disorder and disinhibited social engagement disorder—that share a common etiology of social neglect characterized by the absence of adequate caregiving during childhood. Reactive attachment disorder is understood where the more prominent features are expressed as anxiety with withdrawn behavior, and depressive symptoms. In contrast, disinhibited social engagement disorder is marked by externalizing angry and aggressive behavior and expressions of disinhibition.

As the DSM transitions from the DSM-IV-TR (APA, 2000) to the current edition of the manual, Table 8.3 provides a brief summary of the changes made to the diagnostic classifications in this chapter.

PRACTITIONER'S REFLECTIONS

The core emotions of anxiety and fear serve as an alarm to escape danger or harm. Essentially, they warn the person to take extra precautions or to galvanize protective behaviors. The behaviors a person uses to manage his or her anxiety or fear shows in very different ways. Included in this chapter are two disorders marked by early childhood experiences of

TABLE 8.3 SUMMARY COMPARISON BETWEEN THE DSM-IV-TR AND DSM-5 DIAGNOSES FOR THE TRAUMA- AND STRESSOR-RELATED DISORDERS
Reactive attachment disorder and disinhibited social engagement disorder are two new disorders in the DSM-5 that were formerly subtypes in the DSM-IV—they are included in the chapter on trauma- and stressor-related disorders
Posttraumatic stress disorder (PTSD) is included in the DSM-5 chapter of entitled trauma- and stressor-related disorders
The symptom clusters of PTSD were reorganized and expanded from a total of three clusters found in the DSM-IV to the current four clusters
Additional and separate criteria were added to PTSD for children age 6 years and younger
The stressor criterion (or Criterion A1 in the DSM-IV) for PTSD was modified, and the subjective reactions to the traumatic event or Criterion A2 (for example, intense fear, helplessness, or horror) have been eliminated
Adjustment disorders were moved to the trauma- and stressor-related disorders chapter and reconceptualized as stress-response syndromes
The DSM-IV subtypes of the adjustment disorders of depressed mood, anxious symptoms, and disturbed conduct remain unchanged in the DSM-5

neglect and abuse. Unfortunately, when these children grow older, they continue to experience relationship problems. The competency-based assessment helps to tease out the critical differences around these very different trauma- and stressor-related disorders.

ACTIVITIES

Competency 6 a

1. Select one of the case stories representing either reactive attachment disorder or disinhibited social engagement disorder (Annie Marozas or Jimmy John Clark) and discuss with another colleague and/or your supervisor what challenges you might encounter developing, managing, and maintaining the professional relationship with these clients and their family. Keep in mind the person-in-environment and strengths perspectives as you identify these relationship challenges.

Competency 1 a

2. Review the case of Annie Marozas representing reactive attachment disorder. Imagine that you are Karen Callahan's supervisor. How would you introduce this case assignment to your supervisee? Conversely, imagine that the case of Annie Marozas has been assigned to you. After you review the case notes, what questions will you have for your supervisor?

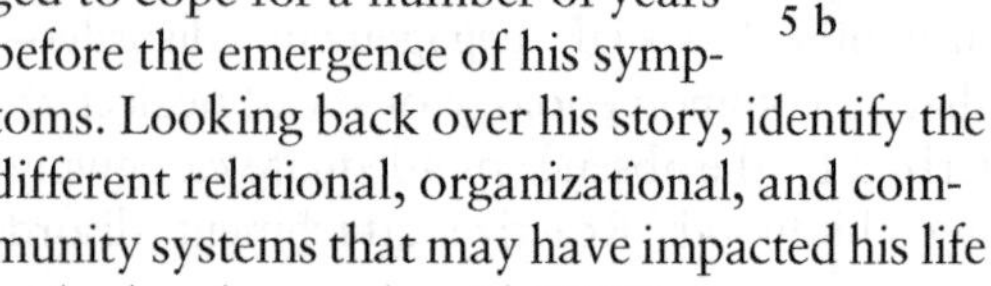

Competency 5 b

3. Reflect back on the case of Buddy Jackson representing acute stress disorder. Despite experiencing the traumatic events of war, he managed to cope for a number of years before the emergence of his symptoms. Looking back over his story, identify the different relational, organizational, and community systems that may have impacted his life and related struggle with PTSD.

Competency 7 c

4. Imagine for a moment that you are the social worker newly assigned to Louise Ann Brown. Find a partner to role-play the intake interview using the details of this case.

Assume the role of either the social work practitioner or the client, Louise Ann Brown. At what point in the exchange did you determine the presence of acute stress disorder? Keep in mind that the focus of this activity is to try to fully understand the interplay of this client's biological, social, cultural, psychological, and spiritual development with her diagnosis of ASD. Then describe how you made the distinction between what would be considered a normal reaction to stress and Louise Ann Brown's symptom picture.

Competency Notes

Competency 1 a—Social workers make ethical decisions by applying standards of the NASW Code of Ethics and other relevant laws, regulations, and models for ethical decision-making as appropriate to context (p. 240): Social workers understand the value base of the profession and its ethical standards as well as relevant laws and regulations that may impact practice.

Competency 4 a—Social workers use practice experience and theory to inform scientific inquiry and research (pp. 221, 222, 231): Social workers understand both quantitative and qualitative research methods and their respective roles in evaluating their practice.

Competency 4 c—Social workers use and translate research evidence to inform and improve practice and service delivery (p. 223): Social workers understand the processes for translating research findings into effective practice.

Competency 5 b—Social workers assess how social welfare and economic policies impact delivery of and access to social services (p. 240): Social workers recognize the multiple influences affecting social policy and are knowledgeable about policy formulation, analysis, implementation, and evaluation.

Competency 5 c—Social workers apply critical thinking to analyze, formulate, and advocate for policies that advance human rights and social, economic, and environmental justice (p. 239): Social workers understand their role in policy development and implementation within their practice settings and actively engage in policy practice to effect change.

Competency 6 a—Social workers apply knowledge of human behavior and the social environment, person-in-environment, and other multidisciplinary theoretical frameworks to engage with clients (and constituencies) (p. 240): Social workers understand theories of human behavior and the social environment and critically apply this knowledge to facilitate engagement with clients (and constituencies) including families, groups, organizations, and communities.

Competency 7 a—Social workers collect and organize data and apply critical thinking in order to interpret information from clients and constituencies (pp. 224, 230, 236): Social workers understand that the assessment process is ongoing and conducted with, and on behalf of, diverse individuals, families, groups, organizations, and communities.

Competency 7 b—Social workers are able to apply knowledge of human behavior and the social environment, person-in-environment, and other multidisciplinary theoretical frameworks in the analysis of assessment data (pp. 218, 222, 229): Social workers understand theories of human behavior and the social environment and critically evaluate and apply this knowledge in the assessment process.

Competency 7 c–Social workers develop mutually agreed-on intervention goals and objectives based on the assessment of strengths, needs, and challenges within clients and constituencies (p. 240): Social workers recognize the implications of the larger practice context in the assessment process.

References

American Psychiatric Association (APA). (1980). *Diagnostic and statistical manual of mental disorders* (3rd ed.). Arlington, VA: Author.

American Psychiatric Association (APA). (2000). *Diagnostic and statistical manual of mental disorders* (4th ed., text revision). Washington, DC: Author.

American Psychiatric Association (APA). (2013). *Diagnostic and statistical manual of mental disorders* (5th ed.). Arlington, VA: Author.

Barlow, D. H., & Durand, M. V. (2014). *Abnormal psychology: An integrative approach* (7th ed.). Stamford, CT: Wadsworth Cengage.

Boris, N. W., Zeanah, C. H., & Work Group on Quality Issues. (2005). Practice parameter for the assessment and treatment of children and adolescents with reactive attachment disorder of infancy and early childhood. *Journal of the American Academy of Child and Adolescent Psychiatry*, *44*(11), 1206–1219.

Casey, P., Maracy, M., Kelly, B. D., Lehtinen, V., Ayuso-Mateos, J. L., Dalgard, O. S., & Dowrick, C. (2006). Can adjustment disorder and depressive disorder be distinguished: Results from ODIN. *Journal of Affective Disorders*, *92*, 291–297.

Dohrenwend, B. P., Turner, J. B., & Turse, N. A. (2006). The psychological risks of Vietnam for U.S. veterans: A revisit with new data and methods. *Science*, *313*, 979–982.

Elklit, A. (2002). Acute stress disorder in victims of robbery and victims of assault. *Journal of Interpersonal Violence*, *17*, 872–887.

Ferguson, L., Follan, M., Macinnes, M., Furnivall, J., & Minnis, H. (2011). Residential childcare workers' knowledge of reactive attachment disorder. *Child and Adolescent Mental Health*, *16*(2), 101–109.

Fernandez, A., Mandiva, J. M., Salvador-Carulla, L., Rubio-Valera, M., Luciano, J. V., Pinto-Meza, A., ...The DASMAP Investigators. (2012). Adjustment disorders in primary care: Prevalence, recognition, and use of services. *British Journal of Psychiatry*, *201*, 137–142.

Friedman, M. J. (2009). Phenomenology of posttraumatic stress disorder and acute stress disorder. In M. M. Antony and M. B. Stein (Eds.), *Oxford handbook of anxiety and related disorders* (pp. 65–72). New York: Oxford University Press.

Galea, S., Ahern, J., Resnick, H., Kilpatrick, D., Bucuvalas, M., Gold, J., & Vlahov, D. (2002). Psychological sequelae of the September 11 terrorist attacks in New York City. *New England Journal of Medicine*, *346*(13), 982–987.

Gleason, M. M., Fox, N. A., Drury, S., Smyke, A. T., Egger, H. L., Nelson, C. A., ... Zeanah, C. H. (2014). The validity of evidence-derived criteria for reactive attachment disorder: Indiscriminately social/inhibited and emotionally/withdrawn/inhibited types. *Journal of the American Academy of Child and Adolescent Psychiatry*, *50*, 216–231.

Gunnar, M. (2001). Effects of early deprivation. In C. Nelson & M. Luciana (Eds.), *Handbook of developmental cognitive neuroscience* (pp. 671–629). Cambridge, MA: MIT Press.

Gunnar, M., Bruce, J., & Grotevant, H. (2000). International adoption of institutionally reared children: Research and policy. *Development and Psychopathology*, *12*(4), 677–693.

Halpern, J., & Tramontin, M. (2007). *Disaster mental health: Theory and practice*. Belmont, CA: Brooks/Cole Thomson Learning.

Harvey, A. G., & Bryant, R. A. (2002). Acute stress disorder: A synthesis and critique. *Psychological Bulletin*, *128*(6), 886–902.

Holeva, V., Tarrier, N., & Wells, A. (2001). Prevalence and predictors of acute stress disorder and PTSD following road traffic accidents: Thought control strategies and social support. *Behavior Therapy*, *32*, 65–83.

Kilpatrick, D. G., Ruggiero, K. J., Acierno, R., Saunders, B. E., Resnick, H. S., & Best, C. L. (2003). Violence and risk of PTSD, major depression, substance abuse/dependence, and comorbidity: Results from the National Survey of Adolescents. *Journal of Consulting and Clinical Psychology*, *71*(4), 692–700.

Knight, C. (2004). Working with survivors of childhood trauma: Implications for clinical supervision. *The Clinical Supervisor*, *23*(2), 81–105.

Marcus, S., & Dubi, M. (2006). The relationship between resilience and compassion fatigue in counselors. In G. R. Walz, J. Bleuer, & R. Yep (Eds.), *Vistas: Compelling Perspectives on Counseling 2006* (pp. 223–225). Alexandria, VA: American Counseling Association.

Minnis, H., McMillan, S., Prichett, R., Young, D., Wallace, B., Butcher, J., ... Gillberg, C. (2013). Prevalence of reactive attachment disorder in a deprived population. *British Journal of Psychiatry*, *202*, 342–346.

Morrissette, P. J. (2004). *The pain of helping: Psychological injury of helping professionals*. New York: Brunner/Routledge.

National Comorbidity Survey. (2005). NCS-R appendix tables: Table 1. Lifetime prevalence of DSM-IV/WMH-CIDI disorders by sex and cohort. Table 2. Twelve-month prevalence of DSM-IV/WMH-CIDI disorders by sex and cohort. Retrieved July 17, 2011 from: http://www.hcp.med.harvard.edu/ncs/publications.php

Oliveria, P. S., Soares, I., Martins, C., Silva, J., Marques, S., Baptista, J., & Lyons-Ruth, K. (2012). Indiscriminate behavior observed in the strange situation among institutionalized toddlers: Relations to caregiver support and to early family risk. *Infant Mental Health Journal*, *33*(2), 187–196.

Op Den Velde, W., Deeg, D. J., Hovens, J. E., Van Duijn, M. A., & Aarts, P. G. (2011). War stress and late-life mortality in World War II male civilian resistance veterans. *Psychological Reports*, *108*(2), 437–448.

Sadock, B. J., Sadock, V. A., & Ruiz, P. (2014). *Kaplan and Sadock's synopsis of psychiatry: Behavioral sciences/clinical psychiatry* (11th ed.). Philadelphia, PA: Wolters Kluwer.

Siegel, D. J. (1998). The developing mind: Toward a neurobiology of interpersonal experience. *The Signal: Newsletter of the World association for Infant*, 6, 1–10.

Siegel, D. J. (1999). *The developing mind: Toward a neurobiology of interpersonal experience.* New York: Guilford Press.

Stroufe, L. A. (2005). Attachment and development: A prospective, longitudinal study from birth to adulthood. *Attachment and Human Development*, 7, 349–367.

Weinfield, N. S., Stroufe, L. A., & Egeland, B. (2000). Attachment from infancy to early adulthood in a high-risk sample: Continuity, discontinuity and their correlates. *Child Development*, *71*, 695–702.

Zeanah, C. H., Berlin, L. J., & Boris, N. W. (2011). Practitioner review: Clinical applications and research for infants and young children. *Journal of Applied Psychology, Psychiatry and Allied Disciplines*, *52*, 819–833.

Zeanah, C. H., Gunnar, M. R., Mc Call, R. B., Kreppner, J. M., & Fox, N. A. (2011). Sensitive periods. *Monograph for the Society for Research in Child Development*, *76*(4), 147–162.

Zeanah, C. H., & Smyke, A. T. (2008). Attachment disorders in relation to deprivation. In M. Rutter, D. V. M. Bishop, D. S. Pine, S. Scott, J. Stevenson, E. Taylor, & A. Thapar (Eds.), *Rutter's child and adolescent psychiatry* (5th ed., pp. 906–915). London: Blackwell.

CHAPTER 9

Dissociative Disorders

INTRODUCTION

When the DSM-I was first published in 1952, only one dissociative disorder, the dissociative psychoneurotic reaction, was described (APA, 1952). Fifteen years later, the second edition noted two dissociative disorders: depersonalization neurosis and dissociative type of hysterical neurosis (mentioning multiple personality disorder as a symptom). The DSM-III (APA, 1980) and the later revised version DSM-III-R (APA, 1987) included four dissociative disorders: psychogenic amnesia, psychogenic fugue, depersonalization disorder, and multiple personality disorder. In the DSM-IV (APA, 1994), all of these dissociative categories underwent a name change, and the role dissociation plays in each disorder was highlighted. Currently, the existing categories are (1) dissociative identity disorder, (2) dissociative amnesia (with dissociative fugue included as a specifier), and (3) depersonalization disorder/derealization disorder (APA, 2013).

All of these conditions have in common a dysfunction in the memory and/or awareness processes. What happens when we cannot remember why we are in a certain place or who we are? What happens if we lose our sense that our surroundings are real? These are examples of disintegrated experience—or alterations in our relationship to our self, to our world, and/or to our memory processes (Gleaves, May, & Cardena, 2001). Many of us experience minor sensations of dissociation that may temporarily help to handle stress by keeping it at an arm's length. However, once we are feeling calmer and able to adjust to the stressful situation the dissociation usually goes away. For instance, you might be faced with taking your licensure exam. Your career as a professional social worker is on the line at this point, and passing means everything to you. At the very moment you sit down in the testing room, you might have the sensation that the whole situation is unreal (or you dissociate from your surroundings). However, once you start the test and feel good about your answers to the first few questions, your confidence returns, and you begin to work on completing the test. You are back on task and in touch with what's going on around you. Keep in mind that you are at a higher risk for this kind of dissociative experience if you stayed up all night cramming for the exam and you were tired or did not get enough sleep beforehand (Giesbrecht, Smeets, Leppink, Jelicic, & Merckelbach, 2007). The dissociative disorders are quite different. The person's separation from self can be severe. This class of disorders is quite controversial, and most practitioners find them difficult to understand. Could a person be faking these symptoms or pretending to be more troubled than they really are? This question becomes particularly relevant in situations where a person is charged with a serious crime, and he or she pleads not guilty by reason of insanity.

Competency 7 b

The causes of the dissociative disorders are not really known, but if a person experiences a traumatic event, between 31 and 66 percent will experience dissociation (Keane, Marx, Sloan, & DePrince, 2014). Dissociative experiences seem to be triggered by unexpected trauma or severe emotional threats—however, the connection between trauma and dissociation is controversial (Giesbrecht, Lynn, Lilienfeld, & Merckelbach, 2008). In fact, the majority of people who have experienced trauma do not suffer a dissociative disorder—which underscores the importance of a competency-based assessment in avoiding premature conclusions about what happens in the client's life along with carefully collecting, organizing, and interpreting assessment data. Often, the most salient points in a client's life history reside in what is not said. The person may have large gaps of time for which he or she cannot account—or the individual may relate many inconsistencies about his or her past. Rather than acknowledge these discrepancies, the person may try to make up the details or shift the subject away from a conversation about him- or herself. As you attempt to determine the presence of dissociative disorder, consider using a set of questions evocative of the competency-based assessment, such as those presented in Table 9.1.

Barlow and Durand (2014) review several variables that are related to a person's vulnerability to a dissociative disorder. They are:

1. Childhood trauma—A history of physical and/or sexual abuse as a child is involved.
2. Suggestibility—Considered a personality trait, some people are more suggestible than others. In particular, people who are suggestible may use dissociation to defend against extreme trauma. However, the exact nature of this intrapersonal process and its relationship to the etiology of dissociative disorders remains unclear.
3. Biological factors—Traits that are inherited, such as tension and responsiveness to stress, may increase a person's vulnerability to the dissociative disorders. Head injury, seizure disorders, and sleep deprivation increase the likelihood of dissociative experiences.

The dissociative disorders are characterized by "a disruption of and/or discontinuity in the normal integration of consciousness, memory, identity emotion, perception, body representation, motor control and behavior" (APA, 2013, p. 291). To qualify as a dissociative experience, discrepancies in the person's experiences cannot be the product of other forms of conscious deception (e.g., in the case of malingering, where the person intentionally attempts to produce symptoms).

TABLE 9.1 QUESTIONING PROTOCOL FOR THE PRESENCE OF DISSOCIATIVE DISORDERS USING THE COMPETENCY-BASED ASSESSMENT MODEL

Interpersonal Relationships:

- Do others seem to know you, and yet you do not know them?
- Are you unable to figure out how you got from one place to another?

Social Environment:

- Have you ever found things and not known how you happened to have them?
- Have you ever had things missing and you have no idea how this happened?

[After the therapeutic relationship has been established and the presence of alters is suspected, begin to explore the following areas.]

Intrapersonal (or Personal) Domain:

- Are you unable to remember significant periods of time?
- Are there periods of time in your life (especially during early childhood) that you cannot remember?
- Do you sometimes hear voices and when no one else is physically present?
- Are there other people who are inside of you and who take charge of you at times?
- Do you think that one of the individuals (inside of you) takes charge for any particular period of time?
- Do any of these people have a special occupation, behavior, or social relationship that the others (inside of you) do not?
- Are all of the persons (inside of you) of the same age or gender?
- Do these people have names?
- How often do you notice these changes in your personality?

Dissociation refers to a state in which the person experiences unprompted intrusions into awareness and behavior accompanied by losses of continuity in these subjective experiences, or an inability to control or access mental functions such as amnesia (APA, 2013). In other words, dissociation allows the mind to separate or compartmentalize selected memories (or thoughts) from normal consciousness. These "split-off" mental contents are not erased from the person's mind—they may resurface spontaneously or be triggered by something in the person's environment. Symptoms are experienced as a loss in connections—parts of his or her identity are relegated to a separate compartment (or buried)—but they may reemerge suddenly and unexpectedly. One group of normal mental processes becomes separated from the rest; that is, the person's sense of identity changes along with a particular set of memories, feelings, and perceptions. Some individuals experience a sudden onset with temporary symptoms, whereas others experience a gradual onset and a chronic course.

The dissociative disorders are listed in Section II of the DSM-5 after the trauma- and stressor-related disorders but are clearly not a part of them. However, there is a close relationship between these two diagnostic classes. For instance, both acute stress disorder and posttraumatic stress disorder share dissociative symptoms such as amnesia, flashbacks, numbing, and depersonalization/derealization. There has been a resurgence of interest in dissociative disorders, especially in view of its association with posttraumatic stress disorder and its correlation with severe childhood sexual abuse. Unfortunately, the bulk of the published literature in the field consists of anecdotal experience, poorly conceived studies (suffering from lack of adequate controls, selection bias, and/or unwarranted conclusions from data), and controversial arguments. What we do know is that social and cultural factors strongly influence the dissociative disorders (Barlow & Durand, 2014).

Competency 7 a

The competency-based assessment, which considers all of the systems affecting the client's life, is most helpful in understanding the client's experience of traumatic life events and how each person struggles to make sense of these events while concurrently looking for those strengths that enable them to cope with life situations and events. This shifts the emphasis away from a standardized description of dissociation toward those skills integral to assessing each person's unique response to trauma.

Not all dissociative experiences are pathological, and to some extent, most of us have experienced dissociative events at one time or another. Daydreaming is a common experience of how people can switch states of consciousness. To do this, a person's sets of memory and attitudes must also switch. We know (all too well) what it is like to be listening to a lecture or presentation, and suddenly become aware that we have "tuned out" what is being said. To others, it appears that we are still listening intently, when in fact we are on automatic pilot. Usually these incidents are brief and do not interfere with our normal functioning.

The dissociative disorders entail a more complicated process wherein people forget who they are, where they are, and what they have been doing. One might begin to think of these disorders as the "elsewhere disorders"; that is, part of the person's present memory or identity is elsewhere and not available. In dissociative states, people "lose" their identity. For example, they may wander away from their home (as seen in a fugue state) or lose their memory without wandering away from their home (as seen in dissociative amnesia). In extreme cases of dissociation, people may acquire one or more distinct identities, each of which is typically referred to as alter (the shorthand term for a different identity or personality). Each one of these alternate identities represents a cohesive character with his or her own unique memories, attitudes, habits, facial expressions, gestures, and personal histories that are clearly different and apart from the "host" individual they share. Typically, these "personalities" differ from each other along any number of dimensions, including race, gender, age, and intelligence. As the individual's alter emerges, the host appears to become a different person.

Because all humans are capable of experiencing dissociation, there is a dissociative continuum on which we are all placed. The normal end of this dissociative continuum includes daydreaming and culture-specific manifestations, while the dysfunctional end of the spectrum is represented by the dissociative disorders. For instance, people in many different cultures have dissociative experiences in the course of religious or other group ceremonies that induce a trancelike state. The essential feature of a dissociative disorder is disruption in the client's intrapersonal domain—specifically of the mental functions of consciousness, memory, emotion, perception, body representation, motor control, and behavior. The dissociative

TABLE 9.2 THE DSM-5 DISSOCIATIVE DISORDERS
Dissociative Identity Disorder
Dissociative Amnesia
Depersonalization/Derealization Disorder
Other Specified Dissociative Disorder
Unspecified Dissociative Disorder

disorders share several common features: they generally end suddenly; a profound disturbance of memory is noted (except in depersonalization/derealization disorder); and episodes are precipitated by psychological conflicts. There are five key symptoms found in most dissociative disorders:

1. Amnesia—Losing memory of one's own identity or the loss of periods of time in one's past. (It is more than simple forgetfulness, such as where the car is parked.)
2. Depersonalization—Feeling detached from oneself or as an outside observer of one's own self.
3. Derealization—Sensing that objects in one's world are strange, unreal, or have suddenly changed dimension, appearance, or location (e.g., one's own home feels unfamiliar).
4. Identity confusion—Being unsure of one's own identity, who one is.
5. Identity alteration—Behaving in a way that suggests one has assumed a new identity.

The specific DSM-5 disorders involving the dissociative disorders are listed in Table 9.2.

CULTURAL PERSPECTIVES AND THE DISSOCIATION EXPERIENCE

Competency 2 a

The individual's social and cultural context is fundamental to the consideration of the dissociative disorders. The practitioner's skill in recognizing and communicating his or her understanding of the importance of "difference" in shaping the person's experiences is underscored when attempting to assess for pathology associated with dissociation. Throughout history and across many cultures, examples of dissociation have been described. Dissociative experiences such as trance states, speaking in tongues, or spirit possession are widely accepted and practiced in many present-day cultures—and such experiences are not considered to be disorders within the culture. Specific characteristics of these dissociative experiences are generally determined by the culture within which they occur. The symptoms may appear to outsiders as evidence of dissociation, but insiders view the personality changes as attributable to a spirit or some other aspect of their belief system.

Within the environmental or cultural context, trances or possession states are not simply culturally sanctioned, they are seen as normative and adaptive. For example, in regions of Thailand, Phii Pob (a common type of spirit possession) temporarily takes over a person's body. Afterward, the individual has no memory of what took place during the event. Other cultures have shamans or healers who induce trancelike states in order to communicate with spirits or with the "other world." In the highland region of Papua New Guinea, dissociative states are an intrinsic part of religious ceremonies. Only men participate in ceremonies in the spirit house (a place of worship), where they speak with their ancestors through the "crocodile spirit" who intercedes and interprets ancestors' responses. Women are expressly forbidden to enter a spirit house or practice any form of "ancestor" religion.

In light of these types of cultural differences, a systematic review of a person's cultural background before making the diagnosis of dissociative disorder is a part of the competency-based approach to the assessment process. The role of culture in the expression of symptoms and level of dysfunction is considered with attention to:

- *Cultural identity of the individual*—Explore the individual's ethnic or cultural orientation.
- *Cultural explanations of the person's illness*—Pay attention to the predominant phrases or behaviors through which symptoms are communicated (i.e., do not automatically assume the presence of a dissociative disorder).
- *Cultural and psychosocial environment*—Look for all culturally relevant explanations of the person's level of functioning and the influence of social stressors, and/or available supports.
- *Cultural aspects of the relationship between the individual and the practitioner*—Consider the impact culture may have on formulating a diagnosis, noting that some behaviors unfamiliar to the practitioner are regarded as normative in a different culture.

The DSM-5 includes cultural concepts of distress in the manual's appendix. The types of culture-bound syndromes that would be consistent with a diagnosis of dissociative disorder are numerous. The following examples are intended to add familiarity with the impact of diverse cultural influences. One example is amok, a trance syndrome—common in Southeast Asia—characterized by a sudden outburst of unrestrained violent and aggressive behavior, usually of a homicidal nature, preceded by a period of anxious brooding and followed by exhaustion. Similar patterns of behavior are found in Puerto Rico (where it is referred to as mal de pelea), and among the Navajo (who call it iich'aa). Amok is often accompanied by ideas of persecution, automatism, amnesia, and exhaustion, but following the episode, the person returns to his or her premorbid level of functioning.

Another culturally accepted dissociative experience is ataques de nervios, a commonly noted response to acute stress in Latin American and Hispanic cultures. Features include uncontrollable crying, screaming, shouting, seizure-like behaviors, and a failure to remember the episode afterward. The event is usually brief, leaves no evidence of any residual difficulties, and is perceived within the culture to be a beneficial and adaptive way to cope with and relieve distress. Lopez and Guarnaccia (2000) characterize ataques de nervios as not really "a cultural syndrome or clinical entity that resides within individuals, but as a common illness that reflects the lived experience largely of women with little power and disrupted social relations" (p. 581). Latah, primarily thought of as a Malay-Indonesian syndrome, is another set of trancelike symptoms that occur in response to startling stimuli. It is characterized by the person's attention becoming highly focused, increased anxiety, and trance-like behaviors (e.g., violent body movements, striking out, dropping objects, or mimicking others' movements). Again, the competency-based assessment dictates that the individual's cultural context be taken into account, which may result in the practitioner finding that this client's "dissociation" is actually adaptive.

Falling out (blacking out) is characterized by the individual's collapsing, sometimes without warning, in a trance. The person's eyes are usually open, but the individual claims an inability to see. It can be preceded by feelings of dizziness or a sensation of swimming in the head. The person is not able to move, yet they are able to hear and understand what is going on around them. This culture-bound syndrome occurs primarily among Caribbean groups or in the southern United States. A similar syndrome, called indisposition, occurs in Haitians. Here, too, the person falls to the ground in a trance—the difference is that they are not able to understand anything that is said or done around them.

Pibloktoq, sometimes called arctic hysteria, is a Polar Eskimo trance syndrome seen as an abrupt dissociative episode accompanied by extreme excitement of up to 30 minutes' duration and frequently followed by convulsive seizures and coma lasting up to 12 hours. Before the attack, the person may be irritable or withdrawn for several hours or days. During the episode, the person may rip off his or her clothes and go running into the snow or across the ice, shout obscenities or scream incoherently, eat feces, become violent, or do something seen as dangerous or irrational. The individual has no memory of his or her actions. Interestingly, this behavior has also been described as resulting from the sexual exploitation of Inuit women by explorers. Although this syndrome is seen primarily in arctic and subarctic Eskimo communities, it can also be found among the Miskito Indians of Central America, where it is referred to as grisi siknis.

A Korean syndrome known as shin-byung involves initial feelings of anxiousness, somatic complaints (such as weakness, dizziness, fear, anorexia, insomnia, or gastrointestinal problems) followed by dissociation and possession by ancestral spirits. Zar, another term that refers to the experience of spirits possessing an individual, is found in Ethiopia, Somalia, Egypt, Sudan, Iran, and other North African and Middle Eastern societies.

The dissociative disorders were previously thought to be extremely rare. When the dissociative episode does occur, it is transient in nature and disappears within a few hours or days. As a result, most practitioners have few opportunities to witness an episode firsthand. Relying on client accounts of their experiences complicates the understanding of dissociative disorders. The two most common dissociative disorders are dissociative amnesia and depersonalization/derealization disorder, but dissociative identity disorder (DID) attracts the most research and clinical attention. On the dissociative continuum, dissociative identity disorder is considered the most severe.

We begin with dissociative identity disorder.

DISSOCIATIVE IDENTITY DISORDER

Dissociative identity disorder (DID), formerly known as multiple personality disorder (MPD), is considered the most severe of all the dissociative disorders because the most common and fundamental alteration includes the presence of more than one discrete identity. Most research studies indicate the average number of personalities exhibited by those who suffer from DID is 15. However, some question the presence of multiple personalities and describe them as differences in representations of different emotional states (Merckelbach, Devilly, & Rassin, 2002). However, DID is a viable diagnosis. Unfortunately, once the disorder is established, it tends to last a lifetime (in the absence of treatment). It is usually traceable to traumatic events that occurred during childhood. There are several reasons that can cause symptoms to emerge. One is when the individual removes him- or herself from the traumatizing situation, such as running away from home. Another can be when the affected individual's children reach the same age as when he or she was originally abused or traumatized. Later traumatic experiences, even something as inconsequential as a fender-bender auto accident, can provoke symptoms. As well, DID symptoms can develop when the abuser dies or becomes terminally ill.

Competency 7 a

A competency-based assessment that pays attention to life situations, circumstances, and events will set the stage for the practitioner's skill aimed at uncovering environmental factors that lead to the development of dissociative identity disorder. The client's life history, in at least one aspect, may contain terrible and frequently indescribable instances of physical or sexual abuse, most often incest. Multiple, long and painful early-life medical procedures may also be reported. In the author's practice experiences, all too often, clients relate childhood incidents of being locked in basements or closets, brutally tortured, burned, cut, beaten, or tormented in a variety of ways far too horrible to recount in detail here. In all such cases, the important thing to remember is that the individual learns as a young child to survive by fleeing into the dissociative process. This process includes a psychobiological mechanism that allows the mind to escape what the body is experiencing; that is, the child exists in a fantasy world where these brutal experiences are blunted. Each time the child endures an abusive episode, he or she "learns" better how to escape by recreating the haven of safety and "switching" into his or her fantasy world. On some level, the child learns there is no limit to the variety of identities he or she can construct for protection from the abusive situation.

Looking to the neurobiology of childhood stress, several kinds of biological changes occur that serve as important signals that may help a child to mobilize adaptive coping responses. Reflecting back on the limbic system of the brain (reviewed in Chapter 1), these changes occur in the amygdala, hippocampus, and hypothalamus as well as in the pituitary gland (or master gland that controls or influences all of the other endocrine glands that release a variety of hormones; this system includes the hypothalamus) and adrenal cortex (which produces hormones to initiate or control stress reactions) causing biological responses to stress. These changes are typically associated with the fight-or-flight response. Research has shown that early traumatic experiences can affect aspects of brain structure; for example, the volume of the hippocampus—the part of the brain associated with the capacity to integrate memories into a coherent narrative and sense of self (Pollak, Cicchetti, Klorman & Brumaghim, 1997; Stein, Hanna, Vaerum & Koverola, 1999). A compromised neurobiological capacity that occurs in response to unresolved stress increases the child's vulnerability in several ways (Hofer, 1995; Perry, Pollard, Blakley, Baker & Vigilante, 1995). Some children who have been exposed to trauma early in life develop a dissociative pattern of coping or an extreme version of the fight-or-flight response that then becomes engrained in their neurobiological makeup.

The process of switching seems to decrease with age, and over time one of the personalities becomes more dominant than the others. Although the use of dissociation as a defense mechanism begins in childhood, the presence of a dissociative identity disorder is often undetected until adulthood. By this time, the dissociation is well entrenched as a way of coping.

The developmental disruptions that accompany child sexual abuse and neglect set into motion events that increase the likelihood of future maladaptation. It should be pointed out that not all children who experience maltreatment will later develop serious problems in living. However, they are at a much greater risk for problems—for example, aggression and violence; chronic impairment in self-concept and self-esteem; emotional and behavioral self-regulation, and depression and posttraumatic stress disorder. In adulthood, the developmental impairments stemming from those childhood experiences often lead to more pervasive and chronic intrapersonal and interpersonal difficulties and comorbid disorders such as the depressive disorders, trauma- and stressor-related disorders, personality disorders (especially avoidant and borderline personality disorders), conversion disorder (functional neurological symptom disorder), somatic symptom disorder, eating disorders, substance-related disorders, obsessive-compulsive disorder, and sleep disorders. Keep in mind that the dissociative alterations in a person's identity, memory, and consciousness may well influence symptom presentation of these disorders.

There is emerging opinion that dissociative identity disorder is a very extreme subtype of posttraumatic stress disorder (PTSD) (Barlow & Durand, 2014). In both conditions, strong emotional reactions are commonly associated with experiencing a severe trauma. When PTSD was first identified, the specific reference points were catastrophic events—for example, war, rape, torture, natural disasters (hurricanes or floods), and disasters of human origin (airline or train crashes). A distinction should be made between trauma and other extremely stressful life events such as a family breaking up due to a divorce. The traumatic experiences associated with PTSD are likely to exceed and overwhelm the person's abilities in coping. Interestingly, children who experience sexual abuse show many of the same symptoms previously identified in adults who experienced combat situations, torture, or natural disasters; that is, what they share in common are nightmares, fears, and panic attacks for many years following the traumatic experiences. Although it happened almost 25 years ago, as many as 30 percent of the children who experienced the natural disaster of Hurricane Andrew were reported to have severe levels of PTSD symptoms for almost 2 years afterward (La Greca, Silverman, Vernberg, & Prinstein, 1996).

Prevailing Pattern

Prevalence patterns for DID are very small. The 12-month prevalence among adults in a small U.S. community study was slightly over 1 percent (1.5 percent) (APA, 2013).

Differential Assessment

The distinguishing feature of dissociative identity disorder is the presence of two or more distinct personality states that can be described in some cultures as an experience of possession. This disruption in the individual's identity involves an obvious discontinuity in the person's sense of self accompanied by alterations in affect, behavior, consciousness, memory, perception, cognition, and sensory-motor functioning. In children, these symptoms are not better explained by an imaginary playmate or other fantasy play activities. Most people with dissociative identity disorder are generally not forthcoming about their various personalities, even when they learn that they have them. They often fear they will be regarded as an exhibitionist or worse, as a freak. The signs and symptoms of DID can be observed by others or reported by the individual.

The various personalities tend to be distinctive and dominate or control the behavior of the person; often there is a sense of struggle for dominance among alters. Sometimes there may be a shifting importance in the role of each personality over time, which is reflected in the amount of time spent in each identity. The person has trouble remembering everyday events, important personal information, or even traumatic events in a way that is very different from ordinary forgetting.

The "host" identity, that is, the person who comes in (or is referred) for counseling, is usually overwhelmed by efforts to hold various fragments of these personalities together. The person may not be aware of the presence of these alters and may be confused about what is happening. A fundamental question is whether these fragmented identities are real or if the individual is just faking symptoms to avoid some responsibility or to get relief from stress. Similar to conversion disorder, this question is very difficult to answer. Clearly, the symptoms cause significant distress or impairment in social occupational or other important areas of a person's functioning.

Evidence indicates that those diagnosed with DID tend to be suggestible (Giesbrecht et al., 2008). Another possibility is that the person's alters may be created in order to respond to leading questions from practitioners. For instance, the practitioner who believes that a history of childhood abuse is a primary cause of dissociative identity disorder will probably be more likely to ask clients leading questions and to use interview techniques that encourage a report of symptoms that might not otherwise be offered. Admittedly, although some individuals may enact dissociated identities, and some practitioners may reinforce these enactments, not all cases of dissociative identity disorder are fabrications. Both the practitioner and the client are best served if the practitioner completes a competency-based assessment that carefully explores all domains of the client's life—and remains open-minded to all manner of possibilities that explain client behavior. For instance, the practitioner considers accepted cultural or religious practices and whether the symptom picture differs from these customs and traditions.

Competency 7 b

Since dissociative disorder symptoms can resemble other diagnoses, the practitioner's skill in collecting, organizing, and interpreting the client's "story" is underscored. For example, dissociative disorder must be differentiated from other general medical conditions, particularly neurological conditions like seizures, and the effects of psychoactive substances that can lead to impaired memory. Individuals with certain neurological disorders, especially seizure disorders, experience an increase of dissociative features (Barlow & Durand, 2014). Dissociative features must also be distinguished from other diagnoses such as the substance use disorders. For example, a person may experience memory loss associated with substance intoxication (e.g., blackouts), and behave in a way that is very uncharacteristic. Although the person may have no memory of the blackout, he or she maintains the same identity during that episode. Thus, a neurological examination is essential to rule out other factors that might produce symptoms of dissociation. With malingering disorder, any reasons the client might have for inventing other personalities must be ruled out, and the practitioner has to be alert to any type of gain, financial or otherwise, that a person might obtain by virtue of having these symptoms.

The following case introduced Emily Samuels, who suffers from dissociative identity disorder.

CASE THE CASE OF EMILY SAMUELS

Emily Samuels was referred by one of the author's colleagues for a consultation. The colleague called and said, "Susan, I've seen Emily three times, and I'm more confused than ever. While she presents herself in sessions with some depression, I'm not sure what is going on for this young woman. I only know it might be something very serious. Could you please see her for me?"

The first thing I noticed about Emily was how she entered my office. She was very subdued and approached the session in a tentative, hesitant manner. I felt she was watching and waiting for me to make the first move. Her voice was barely above a whisper as she introduced herself. Once she was settled, I asked her why she thought she was referred to me.

Emily responded, "Well, I don't want you to think I'm crazy or anything, but sometimes I get into trouble using my MasterCard."

Her answer took me a little by surprise, so I asked her to elaborate on what she meant by that.

"Well, I know it sounds really strange, but the MasterCard company claims I've charged over $22,000 this year on three different cards." Emily was looking directly at me now, and her voice was a little louder than the whisper she started out with. "I don't know anything about that. I think they are a bunch of crooks trying to rip me off. I wanna know one thing. If I spent that much money, where is all the stuff I'm supposed to have bought? They don't want to tell me anything. They are taking me to court in 2 months. They said I applied for three different credit cards in three different names and now I have to pay up. Where would I get that kinda money? Besides, I can prove I didn't spend that money. Those cards aren't in my name, and on top of it all the handwriting on the charge receipts isn't mine either."

I asked her, "Has anything else happened like this before where you didn't remember things?"

"Sometimes, people I don't even know call me by other names," she replied. "Like last week, I was in Wal-Mart, and this lady I've never laid eyes on was calling me 'Harriet.' She just about ran me down yelling, 'Yoo-hoo, Harriet, Harriet where are you going? Why didn't you answer me?' I was so humiliated because she was creating such a scene."

I asked Emily, "What did you think about that?"

She shrugged her shoulders to indicate she was not sure, and looked slightly uncomfortable. "She's the one who made an idiot out of herself."

"No," I said, "I meant what did you think about her mistaking you for someone else?" I thought I saw a momentary look of fear in her eyes, but then she averted her gaze away from mine. I continued, "Has this ever happened to you before?"

She responded, "Well, yeah. Now that you mention it, some guy I didn't know before called me 'Beth Ann' when I was grocery shopping. I thought he was a 'nut job,' you know, a stalker or something. I complained to the store manager, and he said he'd take care of it. Only he came back and told me that that guy claimed to be my husband." Emily's face flushed with embarrassment. "I guess that's why Mary Jo asked you to see me. I don't think she's ever heard of anything like this before."

I asked Emily, "What do you think happened to you when you were in the grocery store?"

She sort of giggled and said, "The lighting musta been bad, and I didn't recognize my husband, that's all." She refused to answer any further questions along that line.

I asked Emily a series of questions regarding her interpersonal experiences as a child—specifically about school and whether she had any difficulties with her peer group or with her family. She acknowledged problems with poor grades, truancy, and having only a few friends. She also mentioned her parents were very strict with her; she was their only child. She said she had never been hospitalized for anything other than having her tonsils out. Emily also said that she doesn't take any medications.

At this point in the interview, she looked pensive. After a moment, she quietly asked, "When you say hospitalized, is that the same as being in a mental institution?"

"Well, that depends on how you think about it," I answered cautiously.

Emily cleared her throat. "My parents put me in a mental hospital a coupla times when I was a kid 'cause I used to have terrible nightmares all the time. I would try to stay awake all night. I guess I was afraid to go to sleep." When asked about what happened at this time in her life, she replied, "I don't really remember much except that I had these terrible, terrible dreams that somebody was really hurting me."

After some gentle prodding, Emily recounted that the nightmares usually had a pattern and that they were connected to her father coming into her room at night and touching her in secret places. "I told my mother about my dreams," she continued, "but she just laughed and said, 'Emily, you *do* have a vivid imagination. You know I'd never let anybody hurt you.' She used to tell me, 'That's why we put you in a mental institution—because you remembered things that never happened.' I wish she would have believed me." Emily denied currently feeling depressed or suicidal.

Shifting the subject, I asked Emily if she ever found items of clothes, jewelry, or other things that she didn't recognize.

She looked at me as if to say, how did you know that? She replied, "Yeah, once I found some motorcycle stuff in my closet at home. It was really weird stuff, too." Gently, I asked her to elaborate. "Well, you know, some of the stuff looked like it shoulda belonged to a guy. It sure didn't belong to me."

She sounded a bit scared and uncertain at this point. Then she went on, "I mean, what would I be doing with a pair of black leather pants, boots, and some bracelets with those spikey things sticking out? The only thing I can think of is, I musta found them and brought them home or something," she replied twisting in her chair.

I decided to ask Emily a series of questions about time and memory. I asked, "Have you ever experienced any gaps in time? You know, time that you just could not account for?" and "Have there been large periods of time when you were growing up that you could not remember?"

Quite abruptly, Emily sat up and began to stare at me in a way that she had not done before. I observed almost immediately that her posture, facial expressions, and mannerisms also changed. Her voice became gruff and raspy.

"Hey, bitch, you leave the kid alone. You hear what I'm saying? She's had enough trouble from you shrinks, so back off."

I responded that I had been asking Emily about time gaps in her life. Then I decided to take a direct approach. "What did I say that brought about such a change?"

"Well, first of all, I ain't Emily, I'm Rick. I bet you weren't expecting me, huh?" I began to wonder about several inconsistencies in what Emily had told me earlier. I replied, "Okay, Rick, I wonder if you could tell me something about who you are."

CASE THE CASE OF EMILY SAMUELS (CONTINUED)

"Emily doesn't know about us, but we know all about her. We don't get in her face too often, but every once in a while we like to get out and have fun. She's much too fussy, you know what I mean? Anyway, there are four of us and ...," she continued.

"Hey, Bozo, you don't have to talk for me, I can talk for myself. I'm Frenchy, and I love sex." She laughs hysterically. "That Emily's always been such a rigid little piece of work. She used to really freak out when her old man made her do him. You know," mockingly, 'Boo hoo, Daddy, don't. It hurts. Boo, hoo, hoo.' So I take over for her—'cause I don't care. It don't bother me as much, so it don't hurt, right?" The interview continued.

"Where was I?" continued Rick, **"Oh yeah, I was telling you how we protect Emily—always have. So butt out."**

At this point, Emily flexed her neck and head from side to side, and looked at me in the way I first remembered meeting her. She smiled shyly, raised her eyes, and asked, "Did something happen I should know about?" Before answering her, I immediately remember thinking that I needed to call Mary Jo and discuss this interesting turn of events.

EMILY SAMUELS'S DSM DIAGNOSIS IS AS FOLLOWS:

Dissociative identity disorder

ASSESSMENT SUMMARY The most striking feature about Emily is her sudden shift during our session among three distinct personalities: Emily (the host), Rick, and Frenchy. It should be pointed out that the phenomenon of "switching" is rare and a relatively unusual occurrence in practice. Each distinct personality struggles for dominance, and this shift from one to another can initially confuse the practitioner. As Emily's "story" unfolds, she is relating to me as a shy, soft-spoken, and demure young woman. Then I notice there are some indications of other personalities. Rick emerges in the interview at a time when I am beginning to explore potentially sensitive material, specifically whether or not Emily ever experiences blocks of time she can't explain. It turns out that Rick, who is a different gender, seems quite protective of Emily. He is brusque and controlling. Then Frenchy emerges as I attempt to understand Rick and his relationship to Emily. It is Frenchy who functions as Emily's protector, and becomes clear as the content of childhood sexual abuse is again introduced. (The first reference to abuse is made when Emily talks about being institutionalized in a mental hospital.)

Emily is considered the "host" personality, and it is the host who usually seeks help from a practitioner. Although Emily is unaware of her alters, they are aware of each other—however, they only revealed themselves one at a time during the interview. The transition from one personality to another occurred during stressful points in the session. Both alters expressed protectiveness toward Emily, especially during the most stressful times in Emily's life.

Emily's history of childhood sexual abuse by her father set the stage for the development of her dissociative identity disorder. This fantasy world is, in fact, very closely associated with posttraumatic stress disorder in that both are strong reactions to the experience of childhood trauma. Emily's escape into the dissociative realm blunted her physical and emotional pain.

Assessment conversations should always involve the client, no matter what the source of the referral. During the initial meeting, I encouraged Emily to share personally relevant material, and helped her to explore situations of concern, their meanings, and related feelings. Sometimes people will immediately bring up topics for discussion, and at other times, like Emily, they are reserved and hesitant. Figure 9.1 illustrates the interactions of biological, psychological, and social variables in Emily Samuels's life.

The dissociative disorder is often misconstrued as being a thought disorder similar to schizophrenia or other psychotic disorders (in which the individual exhibits delusions, hallucinations, bizarre behavior, and/or disorganized speech). However, dissociative identity disorder is the result of "switching" back and forth between one personality entity and another. The symptoms are usually transient and related to a cycling of personality entities as they struggle for control over the person's core identity. Dissociative amnesia, fugue, and depersonalization/derealization disorder are not characterized by the experience of multiple, discrete identities. People suffering from dissociative identity disorder may initially be misdiagnosed as having a bipolar disorder because the mood swings are confused with the switching personalities in DID. However, the individual with DID usually does not feel depressed for any length of time—and, if mood swings exist, they are typically of short duration. The person may also appear depressed, but upon closer assessment, the depressed mood and thoughts fluctuate as they are experienced in some identity states but not in others.

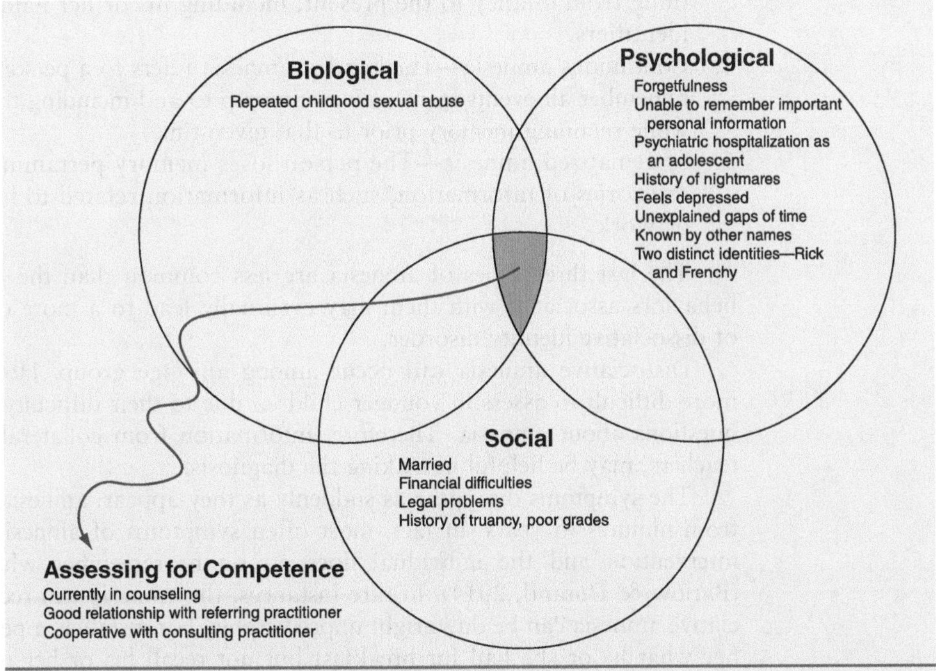

FIGURE 9.1 › DISSOCIATIVE IDENTITY DISORDER
The interactions of the biological, psychological, and social variables in Emily Samuel's life.

DISSOCIATIVE AMNESIA

Dissociative amnesia was formerly known as psychogenic amnesia. This is a completely reversible amnesia that is associated with some form of emotional, traumatic, or psychological stress. While the person's generalized fund of life knowledge remains intact, he or she cannot remember important personal information, such as his or her name, age, or marital status. This cannot be attributed to ordinary forgetfulness or absentmindedness. Dissociative amnesia is different from the permanent amnesias associated with neurobiological damage or toxicity that interferes with memory storage; that is, in dissociative amnesia, the memory has been successfully stored and thus the amnesia is potentially reversible.

There are several different patterns of dissociative amnesia:

1. Localized (or circumscribed) amnesia—The person is unable to recall events that occurred during a particular time or followed a profoundly disturbing event, such as combat.
2. Selective amnesia—The person can bring to mind patchy recollections of an event, but other portions of time are forgotten (for example, a woman might not remember giving birth to her child, but she might remember various aspects of being in labor events after the actual birth).
3. Generalized amnesia—This is a disorder that encompasses all of the experiences during a person's entire lifetime. The person cannot remember anything from infancy to the present, including his or her name and other identifiers.
4. Continuous amnesia—This type of amnesia refers to a person's inability to remember all events from a given time up to and including the present time, while retaining memory prior to that given time.
5. Systematized amnesia—The person loses memory pertaining only to certain categories of information, such as information related to his or her family or work.

The last three types of amnesia are less common than the first two, and the behaviors associated with them may eventually lead to a more complex diagnosis of dissociative identity disorder.

Dissociative amnesia can occur among any age group. However, it may be more difficult to assess in younger children due to their difficulty in understanding questions about amnesia. Therefore, information from collateral sources, such as teachers, may be helpful in making the diagnosis.

The symptoms disappear as suddenly as they appear; amnesia events can range from minutes to years. In fact, most often symptoms of amnesia resolve without intervention and the individual does go on to remember what was forgotten (Barlow & Durand, 2014). In rare instances, the amnesia can recur. In fact, dissociative amnesia can be downright unpredictable. For instance, a person may remember what he or she had for breakfast but not recall his or her name. In contrast, those with Alzheimer's-type neurocognitive disorder usually remember their names, but not what they ate for breakfast. Memory loss associated with abusing substances, taking medications, or a general medical condition (such as seizures) should be distinguished from the symptoms of dissociative amnesia.

Prevailing Pattern

Dissociative amnesia has been poorly studied, and consequently not much is known about family prevalence, demographic data, or etiology. The 12-month prevalence of dissociative amnesia among adults in a small U.S. community showed a rate of almost 2 percent (1.8 percent) (APA, 2013).

Differential Assessment

A single episode of dissociative amnesia is the most common pattern; however, multiple episodes are possible in situations where there are repeated experiences of extreme stress or trauma (e.g., physical and/or sexual abuse). The person who suffers from dissociative amnesia experiences at least one episode where he or she is either partially or completely unable to retrieve important memories and personal information. It most often consists of the selective type (or being unable to recall a specific event or events) or generalized (inability to recall identity and life history). The information usually is about the trauma or stress, and the amnesia is more extensive than what could be explained by ordinary forgetfulness.

These symptoms cause significant distress and interpersonal difficulties, including, for example, problems with employment and in social relationships. The symptoms cannot be attributed to the effects of alcohol and/or drugs (including prescribed medications) or a neurological or general medical condition. As well, they are not better explained by dissociative identity disorder, posttraumatic stress disorder (PTSD), acute stress disorder, somatic symptom disorder, or major or mild neurocognitive disorder.

The assessment is not made if the loss of recall is only around childhood memories; it must involve events that are more current, usually those following a psychologically traumatic event. The correlation between dissociative amnesia and traumatic events is not clear, and the practitioner is encouraged to proceed cautiously when evaluating the onset of dissociative amnesia in a client's life. However, individuals who have had one episode of dissociative amnesia may be more vulnerable to developing amnesia in reaction to a subsequent trauma (Barlow & Durand, 2014). A competency-based assessment that thoroughly explores the interactions of biological, psychological, and social factors in a person's life greatly decreases the possibility of coming to the wrong conclusion about how a person copes with and adapts to traumatic life events.

People with dissociative amnesia usually suffer their first bout of amnesia at a young age—but, most important, they are eventually able to recall what happened. Dissociative amnesia is coded "with dissociative fugue" if the person's memory gaps occur exclusively during fugue states—which involve unexpected travel and confusion about personal identity. Feigned dissociative amnesia indicates either malingering or factitious disorder.

The following vignette introduces Margarethe Jean-Baptiste, whose case depicts dissociative amnesia as it is typically encountered by practitioners.

CASE The Case of Margarethe Jean-Baptiste

[Voice from the hospital intercom system] "Paging Doctor Gray. Doctor Susan Gray, please call operator number three."

I grabbed the nearest house telephone and asked for operator three. "This is Susan Gray, you're looking for me?"

The voice on the other end of the line responded, "Hi, Susan, it's Terry in the ER. Look, I don't have time to go into a lot of detail, but could you please come down here right away?"

"Sure, I'm on my way," I replied and headed into the stairwell for the two-flight descent. Terry Holcomb, an ER nurse on duty in admitting, was waiting for me. "Terry, what's up?"

"Well, we have a situation here," she said as she gestured me into a quiet corner. "Did you hear about the group of Haitian rafters the Marathon Police picked up this morning?" I shook my head no. She continued, "Well, it's the same old story—the police found five men and two women beached in what was left of a homemade wooden raft out near the Seven Mile Bridge. One of the men told me that 10 of them set out 8 days ago, but they started having trouble with the raft almost right away. There was a bad squall, and three people were swept overboard, along with most of their water and supplies. It's nothing short of a miracle that the rest of them made it at all—and they're not in too bad shape. You know, aside from exhaustion and sunburn."

"So, you want me to check for PTSD, or what?" I asked.

"No, I really need you to talk with a young woman—they call her Margarethe Jean-Baptiste—but you couldn't prove it by her. She can't remember anything about the last 8 days. We asked her the usual questions, you know, 'Who are you? Where are you? What's today's date? yadda, yadda ... nothing! It's like time just stopped for her. Margarethe does not remember what happened to the other people, and it's my guess she experienced some pretty bad emotional stuff on that raft—more than likely, one of those who didn't make it was a family member, or something. She doesn't know where she is, even though I've reminded her several times that she's safe and sound in the hospital here in the Florida Keys."

I asked Terry, "What about her physical exam?"

She responded, "Everything checks out fine. Margarethe doesn't appear to be suffering from any kind of problem other than being sunburned and having some mild dehydration. She's some lucky lady, considering what she's been through. Just to cover all my bases, I brought in Malcolm Renaldo. Do you know him? No? Well, he just started his neurology rotation here from the University of Miami and seems like a sharp fellow. Anyway, I spoke to him before I called you. On his physical exam he found no evidence of any head trauma or anything else that could explain her memory loss. Margarethe's labs just came back—nothing remarkable there either, you know, like drugs or whatever. So it appears, medically at least, she's all right. I guess, the next look-see is in your department. I'll be waiting to hear from you."

I introduced myself to Margarethe through an interpreter who spoke Creole and asked what I could do to be of help. Her English was pretty good, but I used the interpreter as a backup. I also wanted to reduce any additional stresses in our conversation, with English being Margarethe's second language.

"I want to call my family back home and let them know I'm all right," she replied. "They will be worried about me." I sensed that Margarethe was a bit uneasy at this point and gently inquired about how she managed to survive the last few days. Tears welled up in her eyes as she spoke to me. She said (sobbing softly), "I remember leaving my country to make a new life. Since the storm, I, I, I ... I do not know the rest."

I reassured Margarethe that I would try to help. After a few days in the hospital, Margarethe was discharged with a referral to the Middle Keys Guidance Clinic and another to legal aid, to deal with her immigration status.

Jean Margarethe-Baptiste's DSM Diagnosis Is as Follows:
Dissociative amnesia

Assessment Summary Margarethe Jean-Baptiste's amnesia was the chief concern for hospital staff. Aside from being sunburned and dehydrated, she was in good overall medical health. Nonetheless, she was under a great deal of physical exhaustion and emotional stress from a tortuous and traumatic boat trip, which could have provided the stimulus for her dissociative amnesia. When found, Margarethe was brought to the local hospital, where she received a complete medical evaluation. The findings of her tests and examination were all within normal limits and provided no basis to support any biological cause for her state of amnesia. Additionally, there was no indication of head trauma, epilepsy, or substance abuse, and it would seem that Margarethe's health was generally good before the boat trip. She was not faking her symptoms, as would be seen in factitious disorder, nor was there any secondary gain to warrant a consideration of malingering. Ultimately, Margarethe's dissociative amnesia was attributed to the traumatic experience of leaving her country and the resulting voyage.

Competency 7 b

The competency-based assessment looks at environmental factors as well as intrapersonal ones that include a person's thoughts and feelings about what happened to them. In Margarethe's case, her immigration from Haiti was complicated by a perilous boat journey that ended in the death of several of her companions. This traumatic incident was the capstone of events causing her memory loss. Figure 9.2 shows the interactions of the biological, psychological, and social variables in Margarethe Jean-Baptiste's life.

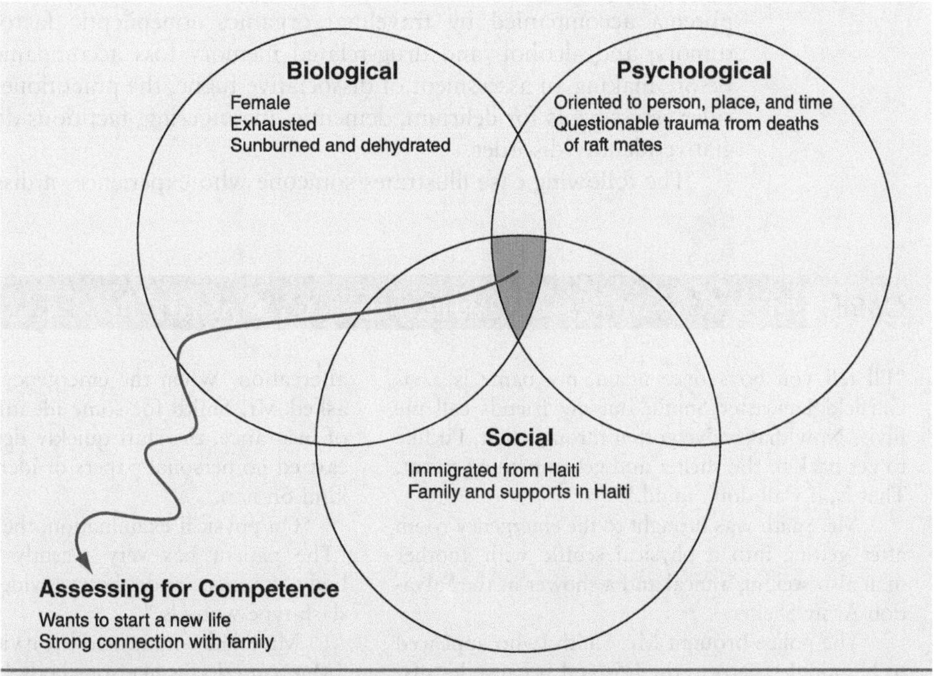

FIGURE 9.2 › Dissociative Amnesia
The interactions of the biological, psychological, and social variables in Margarethe Jean-Baptiste's life.

DISSOCIATIVE AMNESIA WITH DISSOCIATIVE FUGUE

People with dissociative fugue, a specifier for dissociative amnesia, experience unexpected travel away from their home or work, suffer an inability to recall their past, assume a new identity, and cannot remember important personal details about their past. Mostly, the person with this curious disorder just takes off and loses the ability to recall his or her entire previous identity. While in a fugue state, the person does not remember his or her prior life—after the fugue, the episode may or may not be remembered. The stimulus for a fugue state usually involves the individual leaving behind some kind of difficult and troubling situation that (on some level) he or she finds intolerable. For example, traumatic memories, financial crises, and/or marital problems have triggered fugue states. In some cases, the individual assumes an entirely new identity along with traveling to another geographical location.

Competency 7 b

Dissociative fugue is far more common in movies and television programs than in clinical practice. The person with this disorder usually comes to the practitioner's attention as a John or Jane Doe, who is lost or confused about who he or she is and where he or she comes from. A competency-based assessment helps practitioners avoid being overly vigorous in assigning "pathology" and looks to strengths and coping. This orientation to the assessment helps the practitioner to discern the more serious conditions with similar symptoms. The symptoms associated with dissociative fugue are the same as those for dissociative amnesia except for the sudden travel component. Other diagnostic categories to consider are episodes of schizophrenia accompanied by traveling; organic, nonepileptic factors such as brain tumors; and alcohol- and drug-related memory loss accompanied by wandering. Before making an assessment of dissociative fugue, the practitioner should also consider assessments for delirium, dementia, malingering, factitious disorder, and dissociative identity disorder.

The following case illustrates someone who experiences a dissociative fugue.

CASE THE CASE OF "ELVIS GARFIELD LANCASTER SMITH"

"I'll tell you boys once again, my name is Elvis Garfield Lancaster Smith, but my friends call me Elvis. Now that we've gotten through that, I'd like to get back to the shelter and get something to eat. That is, if y'all don't mind."

Mr. Smith was brought to the emergency room after getting into a physical scuffle with another man also seeking a meal and a shower at the Salvation Army Shelter.

The police brought Mr. Smith (who appeared to be middle-aged) to the hospital because he sustained a head wound during the physical altercation. When the emergency room physician asked Mr. Smith for some identification or proof of insurance, the staff quickly determined that he carried no personal papers or identification of any kind on him.

On physical examination, the physician noted, "The patient has very recently sustained severe body trauma, and shows evidence of multiple slash-type wounds."

Mr. Smith commented when viewing his injuries, "Man, sure looks like somebody beat me up pretty good—I just don't remember nothing about it."

As the interview progressed, Mr. Smith offered that he was new to the Miami area, and he could not recall where he had worked or lived before he came here. He was unable to provide the names of friends or family members who could be contacted to help. The police began an investigation to see if they could find out anything further about Mr. Smith, who was kept overnight for observation.

During the night, the police were able to piece together his identity and what had happened to him. Mr. Smith, as it turned out, was really Mr. Edgar Edelstein, who lived in Orlando. Three days before the physical altercation at the homeless shelter, Mr. Edelstein was involved in an automobile accident that killed his wife, Margie, and his mother-in-law, Sheila. The Orlando police had been looking for Mr. Edelstein, who apparently wandered away from the scene of the accident.

Elvis Garfield Lancaster Smith's (Edgar Edelstein's) DSM Diagnosis Is as Follows:
Dissociative amnesia with dissociative fugue

Competency 7 b

Assessment Summary The competency-based assessment serves as a tool to organize the data collected. This case is a classic example of dissociative fugue in that "Mr. Smith" Edelstein was unable to provide any biographical facts about his identity. He traveled away from home and set about seeking shelter. There is no evidence that Mr. Edelstein switched to any other personality entities, which rules out making the assessment of dissociative identity disorder—dissociative fugue and dissociative identity disorder cannot coexist. There is no evidence in Mr. Edelstein's history of a cognitive disorder (other than the obvious amnesia) that would support an assessment of dementia.

Figure 9.3 shows the interactions of the biological, psychological, and social variables in Mr. Smith's (Edgar Edelstein's) life.

We now turn to depersonalization/derealization disorder.

DEPERSONALIZATION/DEREALIZATION DISORDER

Depersonalization seems to be one of those disorders that capture the imagination of filmmakers and tabloid headline writers. Consider the popular comic-book character, Superman, who adopts a different personality to hide his true self from the world. On the one hand, there is the invincible persona who flies around wearing a cape and doing good; on the other hand, there is the meek and mild-mannered news reporter, Clark Kent. Other popular characters—like Spider-Man and the Incredible Hulk—also capture people's imaginations because they suggest the idea that an individual may harbor more than one personality. Steinberg and Schnall's popular book (2001), *Stranger in the Mirror*, explores the extent of dissociation in society. In reality, depersonalization/derealization disorder remains poorly studied and is rarely seen in clinical practice. It is included in this chapter to remind the practitioner that, even though they are unlikely to encounter a client who has these experiences, a competency-based assessment will help to ensure that premature or incorrect conclusions are not reached about the person's biopsychosocial history.

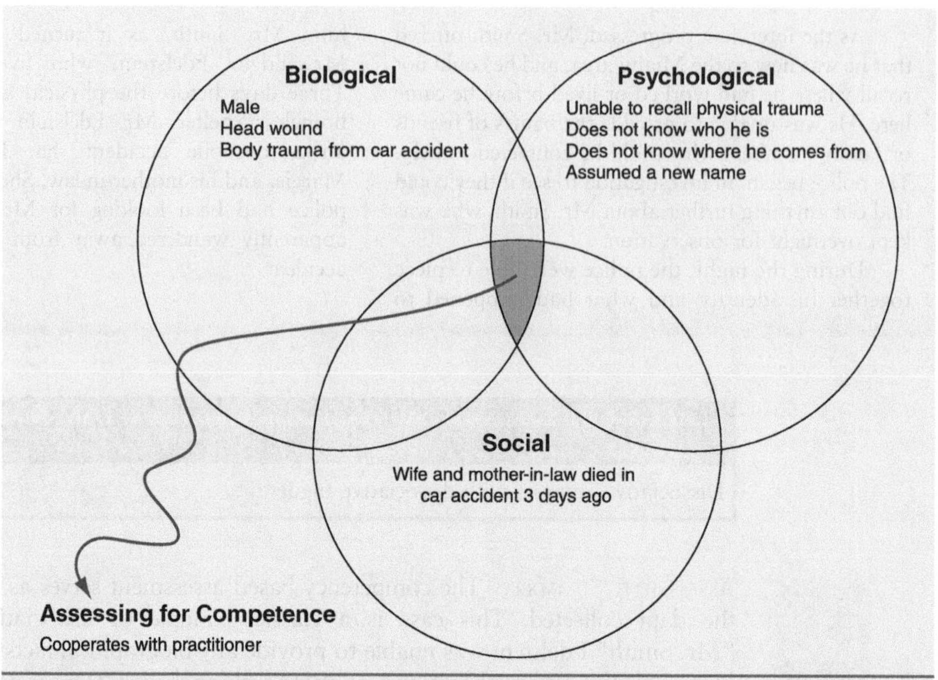

FIGURE 9.3 › DISSOCIATIVE AMNESIA WITH DISSOCIATIVE FUGUE
The interactions of the biological, psychological, and social variables in Mr. Smith's (Edgar Edelstein's) life.

PREVAILING PATTERN

Symptoms of depersonalization/derealization disorder lasting for hours to days are common in the general population, although precise estimates are unavailable (APA, 2013). For those individuals who meet the full symptom picture, the lifetime prevalence in the United States (and in non-U.S. countries) is approximately 2 percent.

DIFFERENTIAL ASSESSMENT

The people with depersonalization/derealization disorder experience themselves or their surroundings as strange or unreal in some way. The depersonalization experience is highly subjective. The individual reports feeling detached from his or her body and more like an observer. With derealization, they might feel detached from their surroundings, as if someone else is "in control," or like they are living in a dream or moving in slow motion. Although the individual remains in touch with reality, his or her symptoms may be persistent, recurrent, or seriously impair functioning—only then should an assessment of depersonalization/derealization disorder be considered.

Often the first episode of depersonalization occurs during late adolescence or early adulthood and generally begins without warning. The person finds him- or herself "detached" but able to continue doing what he or she was already doing (e.g., eating, working, or talking). The individual seems to be observing things rather than actually participating in them. One client described the experience as, "I'm on automatic pilot and watching myself looking at seeing myself from outside my body." The following case discussion illustrates how these symptoms may emerge in the therapeutic conversation.

CASE The Case of Jean Redhorse Osceola

"Listen, I don't want to be here. I want to go home. I don't want somebody to lock me up and tell me that I'm crazy or something," Jean Redhorse cried.

She had come to the attention of the school social worker when it was reported that the 17-year-old Native American told one of her teachers she "felt like a robot," and "I can see myself standing outside my body." Jean Redhorse's mother was called at work and was asked to come to the school immediately.

"My daughter had this thing several times before," Mrs. Osceola said, "but it doesn't amount to much of anything. It's just her crazy talk—I have way too much to do at work to be wasting my time coming down to school when she gets into one of her spells. I just wish she would eat a good breakfast, ya know?"

The social worker replied, "Can either you or Jean Redhorse tell me anything more about this?"

"Well," Jean Redhorse replied, "sometimes it looks like my arms and legs get really big or really small. Sometimes I feel like I'm floating up in the air—you know, like floating outside my body and above my head. It's not like I'm crazy or anything, because I know it's happening ... but the first time it was so weird. Now, it's getting a little scary. I feel like I have no control over it. It just sorta happens."

Jean Redhorse denies experiencing any blackout spells, convulsions, headaches, dizziness, or trauma to her head. She also denies hearing voices or having hallucinations. She denies feeling that other people plot against her, and never feels suicidal or depressed. She claims she is alcohol and drug free—and, though some of her friends tried pot once or twice, she never did.

Mrs. Osceola interjected with a note of pride in her voice, "It is unacceptable for us Navajos to drink."

Jean Redhorse just had a physical examination by their family physician. Other than her spells, nothing appears to be wrong with Jean Redhorse Osceola.

Jean Redhorse Osceola's DSM Diagnosis Is as Follows:

Depersonalization/derealization disorder

Assessment Summary Jean Redhorse appears to be a typical teenager in every way except for the "spells" she experiences. These episodes are typical depersonalization experiences wherein Jean Redhorse reports feeling as if a part of her body is detached from the rest of her. Doctors have found no physical or neurological bases for these sensations. Although Mrs. Osceola dismisses them as teenage exaggerations, Jean Redhorse seems to be increasingly concerned by their recurrence.

Competency 5 b

The practitioner in this case is not Native American. Therefore, in order to make an accurate competency-based assessment, the worker needs to have a better understanding of the client's cultural environment. This approach to the assessment process underscores the importance of being able to assess the quality of a client's interactions within their social contexts. For instance, when Mrs. Osceola comments that the Navajo do not use alcohol, the worker notes this as a reflection of her culture's beliefs about drinking. When considering depersonalization/derealization disorder, the practitioner should not be confused by the presence of their client's culture and its interplay with coping behaviors. In other words, individuals need to be placed in their sociocultural context before their behavior can be judged to be pathological. Another example can be found among the Hindu Yogis who, through yogic meditation, experience a voluntary form of derealization. This deliberately induced trance practice should not be confused with depersonalization/derealization disorder.

Figure 9.4 illustrates the interaction of the biological, psychological, and social variables in Jean Redhorse Osceola's life.

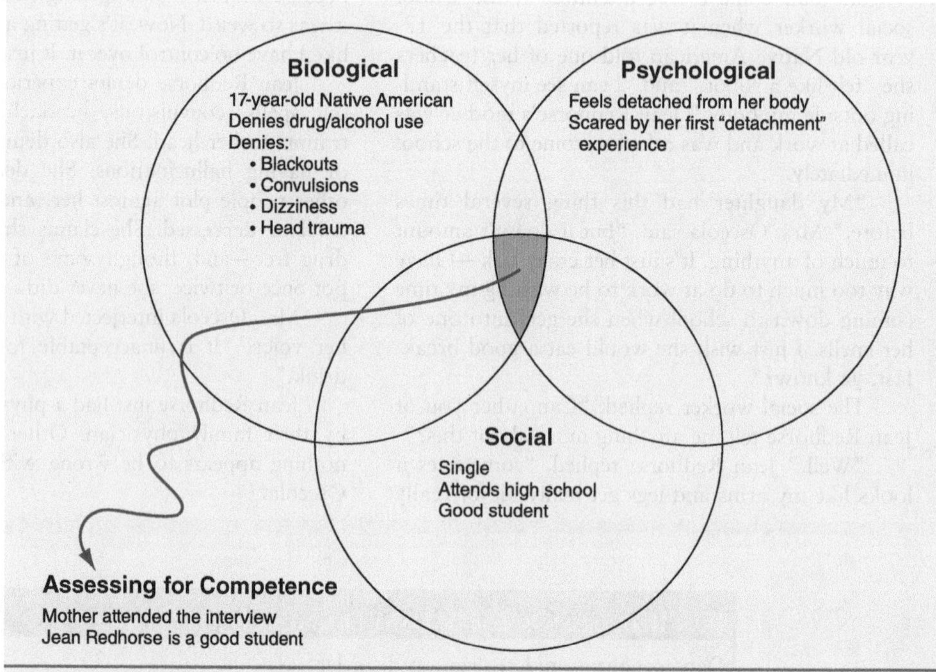

FIGURE 9.4 › DEPERSONALIZATION/DEREALIZATION
The interactions of the biological, psychological, and social variables in Jean Redhorse Osceola's life.

SUMMARY

The competency-based approach to assessment explores the full spectrum of a client's life. In this way, the practitioner not only considers the overt, troublesome, or difficult behaviors but also pays attention to the influence of interpersonal and sociocultural factors underpinning the dissociative experience. The dissociative disorders continue to be mired in controversy. The symptoms are not easily seen, and many people do not seek counseling help. Many may even have another disorder. Mueller and colleagues note that about 17 to 25 percent of people with

TABLE 9.3	SUMMARY COMPARISON BETWEEN THE DSM-IV-TR AND DSM-5 DIAGNOSES FOR THE DISSOCIATIVE DISORDERS
Criteria for dissociative identity disorder was expanded in the DSM-5 to now include possession-form phenomena and functional neurological symptoms; in addition, the person's "transitions" in identity may be observed by others, or self-reported; gaps in recall include not only trauma but are also extended to everyday events	
Dissociative fugue became a specifier in the DSM-5 criteria for the diagnosis of dissociative amnesia	
Depersonalization disorder is now termed depersonalization/derealization disorder	

another psychiatric disorder also have a dissociative disorder, most commonly depersonalization disorder (Mueller, Moergeli, Assaloni, Schneider, & Rufer, 2007). Perhaps the dissociative disorders are more common than they used to be.

As the DSM transitions from the DSM-IV-TR (APA, 2000) to the current edition of the manual, Table 9.3 provides a brief summary of the changes made to the diagnostic classifications in this chapter.

PRACTITIONER'S REFLECTIONS

Dissociation is a common phenomenon, and it is not necessarily considered pathological. The practitioner must listen carefully to the client's story, especially when the individual experiences alterations in his or her perception and a temporary loss of reality—which is generally viewed as pathological. By paying close attention to the client's symptoms, the practitioner can distinguish the dissociative disorders from other less serious disorders or normal behavior.

ACTIVITIES

Practitioners often encounter clients who come from different cultural backgrounds, as evidenced in the cases of Margarethe Jean-Baptiste and Jean Redhorse Osceola. The following activity is aimed at helping you increase your sensitivity to a client's cultural background while integrating that sensitivity into developing a full understanding of presenting concerns.

Competency 5 b

1. Imagine that you are the social worker assigned to Margarethe Jean-Baptiste or Jean Redhorse Osceola. Briefly summarize your knowledge about the language, customs, and values found in the Haitian and Native American cultures.
   a. What could be some of Margarethe's motives for coming to the United States illegally?
   b. What immigration problems might she encounter?
   c. What difficulties could she encounter in locating other family members who live here while she gets settled?
   d. Describe some of the residuals of either Margarethe's or Jean Redhorse's culture that they may try to maintain, such as family traditions, religious ceremonies, or folklore sayings.
2. Sometimes dissociation is a normal experience (e.g., I hesitate to admit, but a good example might be something like tuning out a boring lecture or having a conversation with a colleague who only talks about him- or herself). Reflect back on those situations (or other similar situations) where this may have happened to you. How does your experience compare with someone who has a dissociative disorder?
3. Rent the video (or read the book) *The Three Faces of Eve*. How closely does this portrayal fit the classification of dissociative identity disorder?

Competency 7 b

COMPETENCY NOTES

Competency 2 a—Social workers apply and communicate understanding of the implications of diversity and difference in shaping life experiences in practice at the micro, mezzo, and macro levels (p. 248): Social workers understand how diversity and difference characterize and shape the human experience and that these features are critical to the formation of identity.

Competency 5 b—Social workers assess how social welfare and economic policies impact delivery of and access to social services (pp. 265, 267): Social workers recognize the multiple influences affecting social policy and are knowledgeable about policy formulation, analysis, implementation, and evaluation.

Competency 7 a—Social workers collect and organize data and apply critical thinking in order to interpret information from clients and constituencies (pp. 247, 251): Social workers understand that the assessment process is ongoing and conducted with, and on behalf of, diverse individuals, families, groups, organizations, and communities.

Competency 7 b—Social workers are able to apply knowledge of human behavior and the social environment, person-in-environment, and other multidisciplinary theoretical frameworks in the analysis of assessment data (pp. 245, 254, 261, 262, 263, 267): Social workers understand theories of human behavior and the social environment and critically evaluate and apply this knowledge in the assessment process.

REFERENCES

American Psychiatric Association (APA). (1952). *Diagnostic and statistical manual of mental disorders*. Washington, DC: Author.

American Psychiatric Association (APA). (1980). *Diagnostic and statistical manual of mental disorders* (3rd ed.). Washington, DC: Author.

American Psychiatric Association (APA). (1987). *Diagnostic and statistical manual of mental disorders* (3rd ed., revised). Washington, DC: Author.

American Psychiatric Association (APA). (1994). *Diagnostic and statistical manual of mental disorders* (4th ed.). Washington, DC: Author.

American Psychiatric Association (APA). (2000). *Diagnostic and statistical manual of mental disorders* (4th ed., text revision). Washington, DC: Author.

American Psychiatric Association (APA). (2013). *Diagnostic and statistical manual of mental disorders* (5th ed.). Arlington, VA: Author.

Barlow, D. H., & Durand, M. V. (2014). *Abnormal psychology: An integrative approach* (7th ed.). Stamford, CT: Wadsworth Cengage.

Giesbrecht, T., Lynn, S. J., Lilienfeld, S., & Merckelbach, H. (2008). Cognitive processes in dissociation: An analysis of core theoretical assumptions. *Psychological Bulletin, 134*(5), 617–647.

Giesbrecht, T., Smeets, T., Leppink, J., Jelicic, M., & Merckelbach, H. (2007). Acute dissociation after one night of sleep loss. *Journal of Abnormal Psychology, 116*(3), 599–606.

Gleaves, D. H., May, M. C., & Cardena, E. (2001). An examination of the diagnostic validity of dissociative identity disorder. *Clinical Psychology Review, 21*, 577–608.

Hofer, M. (1995). Hidden regulators: Implications for a new understanding of attachment, separation, and loss. In S. Goldberg, R. Muir, & J. Kerr (Eds.), *Attachment theory: Social, developmental and clinical perspectives* (pp. 580–592). Hillsdale, NJ: Analytic Press.

Keane, T. M., Marx, B. P., Sloan, D. M., & DePrince, A. (2014). Trauma, dissociation, and posttraumatic stress disorder. In D. H. Barlow (Ed.), *Handbook of clinical psychology* (pp. 3364–391). New York: Oxford University Press.

La Greca, A. M., Silverman, W. K., Vernberg, E. M., & Prinstein, M. J. (1996). Symptoms of posttraumatic stress in children after Hurricane Andrew: A prospective study. *Journal of Consulting and Clinical Psychology, 64*, 712–723.

Lopez, S. R., & Guarnaccia, P. J. J. (2000). Cultural psychopathology: Uncovering the social world of mental illness. *Annual Review of Psychology, 51*, 571–598.

Merckelbach, H., Devilly, G. J., & Rassin, E. (2002). Alters in dissociative identity disorder: Metaphors or genuine entities? *Clinical Psychology Review, 22*, 481–497.

Mueller, C., Moergeli, H., Assaloni, H., Schneider, R., & Rufer, M. (2007). Dissociative disorders among chronic and severely impaired psychiatric outpatients. *Psychopathology*, *40*, 470–471.

Perry, B., Pollard, R., Blakley, T., Baker, W., & Vigilante, D. (1995). Childhood trauma, the neurobiology of adaptation, and "use-dependent" development of the brain: How "states" become "traits." *Infant Mental Health Journal*, *16*(4), 271–289.

Pollak, S., Cicchetti, D., Klorman, R., & Brumaghim, J. (1997). Cognitive brain ERP and emotional processing in maltreated children. *Child Development*, *68*(5), 773–783.

Stein, M., Hanna, C., Vaerum, V., & Koverola, C. (1999). Memory functioning in adult women traumatized by childhood sexual abuse. *Journal of Traumatic Stress*, *12*(3), 527–534.

Steinberg, M., & Schnall, M. (2001). *Stranger in the mirror*. New York: HarperCollins.

CHAPTER

Somatic Symptom and Related Disorders

INTRODUCTION

In the days of Hippocrates and in the Egyptian era before him, the word *hysteria* implied that the source of certain disorders (occurring primarily in women) could be traced to a "wandering uterus." Centuries later, Greek physicians still believed that the event called wandering uterus resulted from the uterus being displaced so that it would float about the body, dislocating other vital organs and causing multiple physical symptoms. The treatment for this unfortunate condition consisted of attracting and redirecting the wayward uterus to its proper place in the womb, by using aromatic substances placed near the vagina (Alexander & Selesnick, 1966).

In the ninth century, hysteria was considered a purely physical disorder—but by the Middle Ages, the perspective had shifted away from conceiving of hysteria as a medical condition to thinking of it as a spiritual disorder emerging from evil and demonic possession, as in the case of witchcraft. Hysteria applied to a state of mind characterized by unmanageable fear or emotional stress. The fear often centered on one part of the body. In the seventeenth century, Thomas Sydenham, an English physician, observed that hysteria could disguise almost any medical disease (North & Guze, 1997). Because hysteria was thought of as a disease for so long, its various definitions became blurred over time. For example, a century after Sydenham, Dr. William Cullen adapted the term *neurosis* to describe a type of "nervous energy" or "nervous force" that he thought played an important part in the etiology of certain illnesses having medical, neurological, or psychiatric underpinnings.

In 1859, the noted French physician, Pierre Briquet studied 430 of his patients for over a decade and was able to provide the first formal description of the disorders with prominent somatic symptoms. Briquet focused on describing people who had seemingly endless lists of complaints, but did not have a supporting medical basis. His observations advanced the notion that individuals were usually afflicted early in life, and their symptoms were manifested by recurrent, unexplained, somatic complaints noted in many organ sites. Women were primarily affected. The affliction seemed to be incurable; individuals would return time and again with a new batch of symptoms. The most common complaints noted by Briquet's patients included vomiting, aphonia (inability to create sounds or speak), painful limbs, muscle weakness, dizziness, painful menstruation, a burning sensation in reproductive organs, and paralysis. Because of his initial observations, this "hysterical" disorder became known as Briquet's syndrome, and remained so called for over 100 years. In 1980, the disorder was renamed somatization disorder and was included for the first time in the DSM-III (APA, 1980).

The DSM-5 includes a chapter for somatic symptom and related disorders that feature prominent somatic symptoms. These disorders are distinguished by the prominence of somatic symptoms associated with significant distress and impairment. They may be accompanied by actual medical disorders. These are individuals who generally show up in medical settings and primary care facilities, and less so in mental health settings. The social worker should not underestimate the genuine discomfort experienced by the client and recognize the person's need to address somatic complaints. Instead of talking about what is physically wrong with the client, focus the conversation on how symptoms limit functioning. People with somatic symptom and related disorders really believe they have something seriously wrong with them, and this often causes enormous anxiety, distress, and impairment.

Competency 2 a

There may be some instances in which making an assessment is not clear cut. It is during those times that the practitioner must be especially savvy about the multiple factors influencing the client's life and especially the cultural influences play an important role in understanding a person's manifestation of physical illness. Vague complaints (often labeled as an unconscious psychological conflict) may in fact be culturally acceptable and adaptive behavior.

The specific DSM-5 disorders involving the somatic symptom and related disorders are listed in Table 10.1.

Competency 7 b

The competency-based assessment is a way to help practitioners rethink the category of somatic symptom and related disorders. This assessment model encourages

TABLE 10.1 THE DSM-5 SOMATIC SYMPTOM AND RELATED DISORDERS

Somatic Symptom Disorder
Illness Anxiety Disorder
Conduct Disorder
Conversion Disorder (Functional Neurological Symptom Disorder)
Psychological Factors Affecting Other Medical Conditions
Factitious Disorder
Other Specified Somatic Symptom and Related Disorder
Unspecified Somatic Symptom and Related Disorder

the practitioner to avoid some of the invalidating, negative attitudes, and stigmatization that affect clients with these disorders. From the competency-based perspective, the assessment pays attention to the client's biological domain and calls upon the practitioner to consider the influence of medically unexplained symptoms in the person's life when formulating the assessment. We begin with what is regarded as the major diagnosis in this diagnostic class, somatic symptom disorder.

SOMATIC SYMPTOM DISORDER

Somatic symptom disorder emphasizes the individual's experiences of distressing somatic symptoms plus abnormal thoughts, feelings, and behaviors in response to these symptoms rather than the absence of a medical explanation for these somatic symptoms. The disorder is characterized by recurrent, multiple bodily or physical somatic complaints. It goes without saying that those with somatic symptom disorder will overuse and perhaps misuse the health care system. A distinctive feature of this disorder is not the somatic symptoms in and of themselves, but how they are presented and interpreted by the person who struggles with this disorder.

Most of us have endured annoying physical symptoms or ailments at one time or another. We all have probably suffered from headaches, nausea, muscle aches, or just feeling blah—and, when we do, we usually try to "tough it out" or ignore the discomfort. For the individual with somatic symptom disorder, this is generally not true. For almost every ache or pain, the person will seek medical attention, which may include an office visit to a physician—with a workup that involves extensive laboratory tests, X-rays, or other diagnostic procedure—and will more than likely emerge with prescriptions to "cure" the medical complaint. It is incumbent upon the practitioner to be mindful of the client who describes a pattern of recurring, multiple, clinically significant physical complaints.

The practitioner should listen carefully when the client talks about his or her medical history. It may be helpful to ask about the extent to which someone who is suffering from somatic symptom disorder wants to get better—and what it would mean to give up the physical symptoms. The individual tends to be somewhat inaccurate, vague, and uncertain about when symptoms first started. They may also tend to exaggerate or dramatize symptoms. For example, a backache is never described as "a mild ache that will pass." I can remember a client with somatic symptom disorder who described her backache as "the worst backache anyone in the entire world could possibly have—it feels like red-hot pokers jammed up inside my spine." Some individuals may assume an opposite emotional stance, showing inappropriate indifference in the face of seemingly tragic and overwhelming medical events; known as la belle indifference (Stone, Smyth, Carson, Warlow, & Sharpe, 2006). This blasé attitude toward illness is sometimes shown by people with actual physical disorders as well. Practitioners should be cautioned, however, that neither the presence nor the absence of la belle indifference is an accurate measure of whether the individual has somatic symptom disorder.

After repeatedly recounting descriptions of complaints, the individual with somatic symptom disorder might begin to reinvent or create changes regarding the intensity, duration, severity, or the level of impairment in his or her health and medical problems. Ultimately, these symptoms become a never-ending way of life. If the person manages to gain some relief, there are always new complaints waiting to emerge. The person's symptoms may come and go, but the accompanying sick role and related complaints seem to provide meaning and organization to an otherwise chaotic life.

Competency 7 b

Certain red flags in a client's medical history should alert the practitioner to begin thinking about somatic symptom disorder. Often, the first clue is the medical history itself—it is complicated and fraught with multiple diagnoses, failed treatments, and voluminous medical records. Hardly a year will pass without the person experiencing some intense physical discomfort, and the medical "story" is further complicated by other features, such as a history of multiple allergies or medication intolerance. None of these signs by itself is pathognomonic (indicative of a disease). However, each is important to consider when combined with other signs and symptoms. They include complaints for which no well-integrated structural or pathophysiologic models are known, or for which the individual does not fit the definition of the syndrome.

Prevailing Pattern

Those with somatic symptom disorder have a number of both medical and physical complaints. Individuals considered to be primarily emotionally distressed frequently utilize medical services instead of using mental health services. For instance, the median prevalence in samples of a large number of patients in primary care settings was 16.6 percent (Creed & Barsky, 2004).

Competency 8 c

It seems that a fine line exists between those who have psychologically related concerns and those who struggle with somatic complaints. The prevalence of those with somatic symptom disorder is unknown (APA, 2013). In practice, it seems as if those with somatic symptom disorder tend to be shuffled back and forth between medical and mental health settings. The practitioner might consider recommending a thorough physical examination to identify those physical symptoms that cannot be explained by the accompanying physical findings.

In the United States, women who are unmarried and from lower socioeconomic groups are most likely to be assessed as having somatic symptom disorder (Creed & Barsky, 2004). Somatic symptoms may be a way disenfranchised women can express their discontent or disappointment with their social situation without incurring the negative consequences of acting out in other, more inappropriate ways. It is estimated that somatic symptom disorder in the adult population may be about 5 to 7 percent (APA, 2013), and females tend to report more somatic symptoms than males.

Further, those without social support may be driven to seek out medical or clinical attention as a substitute for the lack of a social network. Although these individuals tend to focus on physical complaints, they also report a wide spectrum of psychological symptoms and are often assessed with mood and anxiety disorders.

Differential Assessment

The symptom picture for somatic symptom disorder is multiple, current, somatic symptoms that cause distress or result in significant disruption in the person's daily life. Sometimes only one severe symptom, commonly pain, can be present. These symptoms can be specific (such as located pain in one area) or relatively nonspecific (such as fatigue). As we will see in Helene Martin's story, she went to the emergency room for the vague complaint of having "trouble breathing." Sometimes the somatic symptoms are normal bodily sensations of discomfort that do not generally indicate a serious disease.

The person's suffering is genuine regardless of whether they have a medical explanation for their symptoms or not. Someone may have a medical condition and somatic symptom disorder, but what distinguishes somatic symptom disorder are the thoughts, feelings, and excessive time and energy devoted to health concerns. The person's symptom picture is present for at least 6 months (APA, 2013). These are people who tend to worry a lot about having an illness, even when there is no supportive evidence. Health concerns play a central role in their lives. Going to the doctor, or even several doctors, and having numerous tests and procedures are a big part of life and nothing seems to work. Some might describe being unusually sensitive to medications. Others may feel that they have received inadequate treatment. Any reassurance by the doctor tends to be short-lived, and the person might react with surprise when referred to mental health counseling.

The following vignette illustrates how someone who has somatic symptom disorder may come to see a social worker.

CASE: THE CASE OF HELENE MARTIN

Helene Martin, 24, is a single, attractive African American woman. She came into the emergency room with her best friend, Jessica Leah, because she was "having trouble breathing." She thought she might be starting to have a heart attack. Helene also complained to the emergency room physician that she was experiencing terrible swelling in her knees.

Helene and Jessica have been friends since grade school and have shared many "troubles" together. Their friendship is extremely important to her. During the physical examination, Helene related that she had had many health problems over the years. She always considered herself to be a sickly child, but she started having "serious" physical problems when she was a teenager. (According to Helene, her mother was sickly as a child, too.) She related that she was raised in a family who was usually demanding and critical—unless she was ill. Then her parents seemed to be loving and caring.

As a part of her medical history, Helene revealed that her father tended to rule the family with an iron hand, and a heavy belt. The physician noted in the medical history that Helene was overly dramatic when talking about herself, had a strong need to be the center of attention, and expressed emotion in a shallow and rapidly shifting way. In addition, Helene described an excessive concern with her physical appearance and that her relationships with men were fraught with sexually provocative behavior.

The physician considered Helene to be very bright, yet she never finished high school. Helene stated that she wants to go back to night school to earn her GED. Her lack of formal education seemed to keep her locked into low-paying and menial jobs, causing feelings of discontent and disappointment. Before the physician could go further in her examination, Helene took out a large sheaf of papers, and handed them over.

"Here," she stated. "Instead of me rattling off all the problems I've had, I'll give you a copy of my records. It'll save you some time figuring everything out."

Helene's personal 300-page "health diary" documented 10 years of her past medical history. The following highlights a partial, limited accounting of her most recent and current problems:

> ***January 10*** **(3:30 p.m.)** I had a terrible period, with lots of horrible cramps and bleeding. I stayed in bed 4 days; had to miss work. I saw Dr. Able, and she gave me a prescription, but it didn't help very much.
>
> ***January 31*** **(3:00 a.m.)** I had pain during intercourse (again). I went to see Dr. Baker today, but she wasn't very helpful. She told me to "relax more." What a joke!
>
> ***February 9*** I had a urinary tract infection, and it burned a lot when I tried to pee. I saw Dr. Carter, but he wouldn't give me a prescription (said it wouldn't help). He said that I complained about urinary burning three times last year, and I didn't have anything wrong then, and I didn't have anything wrong today. I won't go back to him again!
>
> ***March 7*** I had another seizure. I was admitted to the hospital, but the EEG didn't show anything. I was hospitalized at Mercy Baptist for 2 days and had lots of tests. Dr. Dankin said, "There is really good news, you don't have a brain tumor." I told him that I felt really dizzy a lot this week and lost my balance four times. He told me not to worry about anything and said my problems would probably disappear if I forgot about them.
>
> ***April 11*** **(8:00 p.m.)** My knee and hip joints are really painful and swollen. I lost 3 days of work because I can hardly sit or walk. Mom came over to cook dinner. Dr. Evans was on vacation, but her associate (I don't know her name) was on emergency call. The doctor said that since she didn't know me well enough, she couldn't give me a prescription over the telephone. She told me to go the emergency room and she would meet me there to examine me. I don't think I'm gonna use Dr. Evans anymore.
>
> ***May 21*** I had several really bad episodes of diarrhea, bloating, and vomiting the past few days. I went in for an appointment with Dr. Frankel, and he admitted me to the hospital. He said that I needed a complete workup. I had every test you could think of (upper and lower barium enema, sigmoidoscopy, colonoscopy, X-rays of my stomach, MRI, lots of blood work). Dr. Frankel called it the VIP treatment. After all that, he said, "Absolutely nothing is wrong with you," and suggested that maybe "it was just an upset stomach." Dr. Frankel added that I should watch my diet for a couple of days after I got home. He also suggested that I make an appointment to see a social worker. I think he wants to blame this on a mental condition, but he's wrong.
>
> ***May 25*** I had terrible diarrhea again at midnight; also think I'm allergic to eggs, because I had a serious case of heartburn.
>
> ***June 1*** The diarrhea is finally gone, but now I'm so constipated I feel very bloated. My rectum is swollen and it hurts to have a bowel movement. Being constipated has irritated my hemorrhoids into acting up. I called Dr. Graystone, but she's no longer in practice, so I guess I'll find another doctor (someone who can finally help me). I went to the emergency room, and they agreed with me that I was constipated. I wanted a prescription for my condition, but they told me to go out to the drug store and buy some milk of magnesia. They promised it would work.
>
> ***June 15*** I have both a terrible headache and backache, but I don't have the money to go see a doctor, so I used some of the medicine I once got from Dr. Carter, but it didn't help. I'm in a tremendous amount of pain. I have to miss work again.
>
> ***June 17*** **(2:00 a.m.)** My headache and backache continue to cause me terrible pain. I finally went to the emergency room, and they admitted me for observation. I had several tests, but the doctors think that whatever I had went away, and that I shouldn't have any more trouble. The ER doctor gave me the name of some social worker, but I told him, "I'm not a head case." They are just trying to pass me off because they can't find out what's wrong with me.
>
> ***July 15*** I'm having a lot of trouble swallowing. I saw a new doctor, Dr. Herrold, and he referred me to Dr. Isaac, an ear, nose, and throat specialist. Dr. Isaac stuck some tubes down my throat, and said he couldn't find anything wrong. He told me not to think about it, and that it would go away. I got a peek at my insurance form, and saw that the doctor called my swallowing trouble,

CASE THE CASE OF HELENE MARTIN (CONTINUED)

"Globus hystericus." I looked up that diagnosis as soon as I got home. I think that Dr. Isaac doesn't know what he's talking about. Globus hystericus doesn't sound like "nothing" to me. In the meantime, Mom prepares soft foods and milk shakes for me to eat.

August 13 I can't tolerate eating any dairy products because I have had lots of stomach bloating recently. I found out from my mom that when I was a teenager I had lots of "intolerances to foods and certain medications."

September 22 I'm having burning when I urinate. I went to see Dr. Jankowski and she told me, "Helene, you don't have any evidence of a urinary tract infection. There is nothing to treat you for." I don't agree with her. Later in the day, I made an appointment to see Dr. Kaye (who came highly recommended by another secretary who used her). Dr. Kaye said she thought I might have a bladder problem. I had all sorts of "procedures" done. She told me, "Your laboratory tests were unremarkable and didn't support any findings that would lead me to believe that you have any kind of urinary or bladder problem going on right now." She told me to drink more fluids.

October 5**(11 p.m.)** I'm feeling really very, very nauseated. I know that I'm not pregnant (have my period, too). I threw up lots of times. I don't know what's wrong. Fred went to get me something from the drug store. I didn't work yesterday or today.

November 15 I went to see Dr. Baker (again). My period is causing me a lot of discomfort. She said that if I still have problems by tomorrow, she'll do another D&C, but she said she was not happy to be performing a fourth procedure on me. She said I should go to a specialist after this.

November 22 Today, I went to the outpatient facility for a D&C. The doctor said that maybe I should seek out some counseling. I told her I'd think about it, but I really won't. How come they don't realize how much pain I'm in?

December 15**(6:00 a.m.)** I'm really having problems breathing. I can't catch my breath or take a deep breath. I'm worried that I might be having a heart attack because my heart feels like its fluttering. Jessica's coming to take me to the emergency room. Maybe they can help me.

On December 16, Helene was hospitalized because of her cardiac symptoms and breathing complaints. During the current hospitalization, she had both a comprehensive physical and medical examination, and laboratory tests (to rule out any viable medical condition). Helene was given a clean bill of health and subsequently referred to a social worker for counseling and support.

HELENE MARTIN'S DSM DIAGNOSIS IS AS FOLLOWS:

Somatic symptom disorder, persistent, severe

ASSESSMENT SUMMARY Irrespective of the underlying motives, all possible explanations for somatization encourages a thorough medical examination and an inquiry into Helene's biopsychosocial history. Helene's behavior should be explored in the context of existing medical complaints and the extent to which her symptoms might be helping to resolve her life problems or represent psychological conflicts. The extent of Helene's complaints, the degree to which she suffers, and her inability to engage in her usual level of activities are noteworthy.

Individuals with major depressive disorder, generalized anxiety disorder, delusional disorder, and body dysmorphic disorder might present somatic complaints, but eventually their symptoms override the somatic complaints. Although there is a strong association between panic attacks and somatic symptom disorder, the person diagnosed with panic disorder is generally not bothered by somatic symptoms between panic attacks. In factitious disorder, the person derives great satisfaction from being considered ill. Recurrent ideas about somatic symptoms or illness are less intrusive for those with somatic symptom disorder than for those with obsessive-compulsive disorder. As well, the person does not engage in the repetitive behaviors aimed at reducing anxiety typical of obsessive-compulsive disorder. In contrast, Helene's physical discomfort is genuine, in that she truly believes she is ill. She also exhibits a long-standing pattern of excessive emotionality and attention seeking behavior that seeps into all areas of her life.

Competency 7 a

When beginning to understand Helene's total functioning, the practitioner must first make an assessment that includes all aspects of her life history and life experiences. Helene's suffering is authentic, whether or not it is medically explained. Helene's worker, first and foremost, must find out if she has any medical conditions that may offer added insight into her symptoms. Unlike individuals with illness anxiety disorder, who excessively "doctor shop" and who are preoccupied with the false belief that they have a specific disease or have a fear of a specific disease, Helene focuses more heavily on the symptoms of disease. In conversion disorder (discussed later in this chapter), symptoms are usually limited to only one, typically involving the central nervous system—for example, the individual becomes "blind," "paralyzed," or "mute." In contrast, Helene's "health diary" reveals a wide variety of symptoms occurring over a period of time. When one complaint is addressed, another one emerges.

Competency 7 a

The competency-based assessment provides a framework for assessing Helene's strengths. In particular, an assessment of interpersonal factors notes that she has a good relationship with her mother. She also has a close childhood friend who is supportive of her. Additionally, Helene wants to return to school for her GED. Figure 10.1 shows the interactions of the biological, psychological, and social variables in Helene Martin's life.

A review of illness anxiety disorder follows.

ILLNESS ANXIETY DISORDER

The person with illness anxiety disorder is characterized as having physical complaints that are without a clear cause. These physical symptoms become an overwhelming and unrelenting preoccupation that is deeply rooted in some unrealistic apocalyptic interpretation or somatosensory amplification; that is, the tendency to experience their own bodily sensations as being unusually intense, aversive, and distressing. This is the individual who not only strongly suspects but actually believes he or she is suffering from a very serious and life-threatening

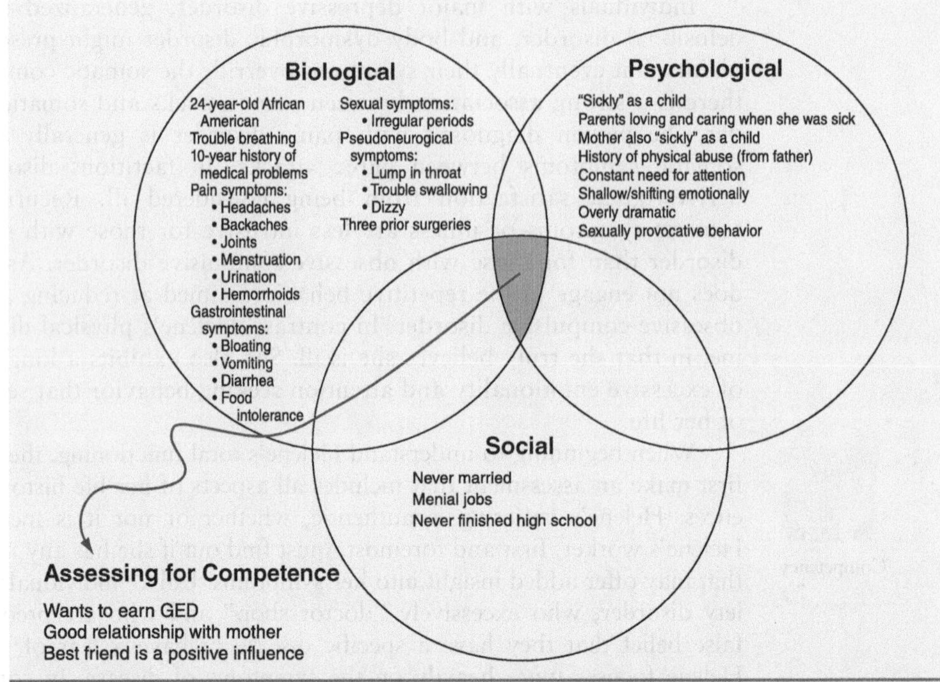

FIGURE 10.1 › SOMATIC SYMPTOM DISORDER
The interactions of the biological, psychological, and social variables in Helene Martin's life.

condition. Often the illness process begins when the person notices a lump, bruise, or blemish.

From that humble beginning, he or she starts to assume with a great degree of certainty, and considerable anxiety, that a serious illness has taken root—the more they ruminate about it, the lump becomes a tumor, the bruise becomes hemophilia, and the blemish becomes skin cancer. As the process unfolds, the individual begins to constantly fret about "the illness," often to the point that his or her normal occupational activities and relationships with others are dramatically disrupted. The world of someone with illness anxiety disorder becomes filled with unrealistic and dire interpretations of disease symptoms and his or her subsequent reactions to them. These individuals remain steadfast in their concern for themselves, and convinced that something is very wrong with them.

PREVAILING PATTERN

Prevalence for illness anxiety disorder is based on DSM-IV-TR (APA, 1980) estimates for the diagnosis of hypochondriasis. In community surveys and population-bases samples prevalence ranges from a little over 1 percent (or 1.3 percent) to 10 percent (APA, 2013). In ambulatory medical populations, prevalence rates are 3 to 8 percent. There is no difference in the rates between males and females.

Differential Assessment

Someone who struggles with hypochondriasis can be classified as having a somatic symptom disorder, specifically illness anxiety disorder. The clinical course of illness anxiety disorder is the preoccupation with having or getting a very serious and undiagnosed illness. The person does not have any somatic symptoms, but if they do, they are very mild. However, a medical exam fails to identify any medical condition to explain the person's concerns. It is the anxiety around having something physically wrong that is the source of the person's distress. So this is someone who repeatedly checks for signs of the illness or even avoids going to the doctor to check things out. To confirm the diagnosis, symptoms must be present for at least 6 months, but symptoms may wax and wane for years. Often symptoms flare up during times of stress. The individual's conclusion is always on the side of having a grave, life-threatening condition versus a transient or minor disease. If medical care is rarely used, the person is deemed to be the care-avoidant type, in contrast to someone who constantly goes to the doctor for even the slightest complaint. In that case, the specifier, "care avoidant type," is assigned.

The following case illustrates how someone with illness anxiety disorder typically presents in social work practice.

CASE The Case of Carl Beacher

Carl Beacher is a 53-year-old white male. He has been married to his high school sweetheart, Sally, for 30 years. Although they have no children of their own, the couple is involved actively in the lives of their many nieces, nephews, and godchildren.

Carl's initial complaint was of anxiety and stress due to his high-pressured job as a manager in used car sales. During our first contact, it didn't take long for me to realize that his principal concern is about health issues. Whenever he experiences some minor physical problem, say a cough or headache, Carl immediately concludes that the coughing symptoms are lung cancer, or a headache means a malignant brain tumor. When experiencing other (benign) physical sensations, he quickly transforms them into life-threatening medical conditions.

With considerable frustration, Carl relates, "Going to all these doctor appointments cuts into my commissions and my time off. I really can't afford to be away from work anymore. As it is, the big bosses are starting to watch me like hawks. I don't know how long I can keep doing this. Even Sally has started calling me her disease-of-the-month husband—which, I might add," he says testily, "I don't really appreciate. You know, I don't think she takes my medical concerns seriously."

He admits that his constant worrying about having a serious disease has caused a lot of tension, not just in his relationship with Sally, but with other family members as well. "They don't want to listen to me anymore." Carl says he finds himself absorbed by reading medical books or medical journals. In fact, he admits to subscribing to several of them. "Sometimes, when I have a problem I look up my physical symptoms—that's when I really start worrying." Interestingly, Carl brags about having an extensive and valuable collection of vintage medical books and antique surgical instruments purchased at a local flea market.

"He lives in fear of being diagnosed," Sally confirms. "Just in the last 6 months alone, Carl has complained of chest pain, stomach problems, dizziness, muscle spasms, bruises on his arm—I could go on and on."

Carl adds somewhat defensively, "Even hearing about a friend or family member's illness is enough to incapacitate me for days." He explains that his fears developed about 5 years ago, around the time he was trying to start up a new trucking business. "I had a bad cough that just wouldn't go

CASE THE CASE OF CARL BEACHER (CONTINUED)

away, so first I went to our family doctor, Dr. Vasquez, who couldn't find anything wrong with me. Dr. Vasquez sent me to a specialist, but he couldn't find anything wrong with me either." Carl had continued to see a succession of physicians despite the fact that each one assured him that he was in excellent health. "So, after all this time, I still haven't found out what's really going on with me," he concluded.

I ask Carl how it feels to be constantly reassured that no medical condition exists. He answers, "The doctors just keep missing it—but somebody's going to figure it out. I know they will." When asked if he ever felt a sense of relief when reassured that he didn't have cancer, Carl said, "At first, I feel some relief, but it only lasts a few days. When my symptoms start up again, I start worrying all over again."

The next question, I ask somewhat cautiously. "Carl, when the doctors tell you that they haven't found anything wrong, can you say what it is that gets in the way of you believing them?"

He answered with complete conviction, "You know, laboratories are always making mistakes. They aren't infallible. Suppose they mixed up my results with somebody else's? Can you absolutely tell me that that doesn't happen? Well, I say it's hard to feel reassured when so many people have the opportunity to mess up."

I ventured a step further and asked him if he thought it was at all possible that he didn't have cancer.

"Absolutely not!" he replied. "The only reason they haven't diagnosed me yet is because they have to do a few more tests. The last time I had a workup was 6 months ago. I'm sure between then and now something has had time to develop."

I asked Carl about his car sales job—whether this was having any impact on his ability to work (other than the time he takes off to visit doctors).

He allowed that his concerns about his medical "condition" sometimes takes his mind away from business at the office. "I get so distracted that every once in a while I lose a customer. I won't lie to you, things could be better in the money department," he said.

Carl denies thoughts about suicide, says he doesn't have delusions or hallucinations, and shows no symptoms of a major depressive episode. His appetite and sleep habits are no cause for concern, except for every once in a while, "when I can't stop worrying about my cancer." He denies a history of problems related to alcohol or recreational drug use. Although he has experienced quite a lot of anxiety about having cancer, he has never had symptoms suggestive of a panic disorder.

CARL BEACHER'S DSM DIAGNOSIS IS AS FOLLOWS:

Illness anxiety disorder, care-seeking type

Competency 7 a

ASSESSMENT SUMMARY The most important diagnostic consideration for the diagnosis of illness anxiety disorder is the presence of an underlying medical condition and the person's persistent preoccupation with his or her medical status—despite appropriate medical evaluation and/or reassurance. When necessary, the practitioner may consult with medical professionals to understand the medical underpinnings of a client's concerns. Somatic symptoms are more commonly found in children (e.g., stomach pain) and would be diagnosed as illness anxiety disorder if the child is concerned about having a more serious illness than a stomachache. Some people with a major depressive episode may be preoccupied about their health. Illness anxiety disorder in not considered if these health concerns occur only during the major depressive episode. When depression occurs secondarily to illness anxiety disorder, then the more appropriate diagnosis would be illness anxiety disorder.

The person with illness anxiety disorder takes a better-safe-than-sorry approach to dealing with even a minor physical symptom by getting it checked out as soon as possible. A central feature of this disorder is the person's faulty interpretation of physical signs and sensations as evidence of having an actual physical illness. The anxiety and mood disorders, especially with panic disorder, often co-occur with illness anxiety disorder (Creed & Barsky, 2004). In contrast to the anxiety disorders, someone struggling with illness anxiety disorder is preoccupied with bodily symptoms and sees them as indications of a serious illness despite reassurance from others that they are fine. Any relief they might get from being reassured about their medical condition is generally short-lived. In time, they once more begin to focus on their symptoms, and the cycle of worry begins anew. The anxiety is focused on the possibility of disease or illness, referred to as a disease conviction (Woolfolk & Allen, 2014). This preoccupation with minor symptoms, the persistent conviction that they suffer from a deadly disease and the futile inadequacy of medical reassurance can cause friendships to wear thin, especially when the sufferer's every ache or pain is recounted in minute detail. Easy access to medical and diagnostic information via the Internet has spawned a mutation of this phenomenon known as cyberchondria (Gray, 2006).

As a part of the diagnostic picture for illness anxiety disorder, the person constantly seeks reassurance about his or her medical condition. This preoccupation may resemble symptoms of an obsessive-compulsive disorder; however, the diagnosis would be obsessive-compulsive disorder only when the obsessions or compulsions include concerns other than those related to illness (e.g., the person is also concerned if he or she left the house and the door is unlocked). For those struggling with body dysmorphic disorder, the concern is limited to the individual's personal appearance. Specific phobia is considered when the person is fearful of developing or being exposed to a disease in contrast to illness anxiety disorder, where the person is preoccupied with the idea that they actually have the disease. For those with illness anxiety disorder, the conviction that one has a disease does not reach the delusional proportions found in the psychotic disorders.

The distinction between illness anxiety disorder and somatic symptom disorder essentially rests on the significance of the symptoms; that is, somatic symptom disorder is considered when significant somatic symptoms are present. Carl's complaints are typical of the person experiencing illness anxiety disorder—his initial concerns revolve around worrying about having a serious disease despite the lack of supportive findings. In this case, Carl continues to question his physicians' expertise. His world is filled with anxiety and constant worry. He is absolutely convinced that it is not a matter of if he is going to be diagnosed with cancer, a tumor, or a serious disease, but when he is going to be diagnosed. To Carl, every symptom is the precursor of a life-threatening condition.

The individual with somatic symptom disorder complains because it hurts when he or she coughs. However, when Carl coughs, he concludes it is another sign that he has cancer; this time it may be lung cancer. Phobic individuals who are afraid they might develop a disease usually take steps to avoid being in situations exposing them to risks. People with panic disorders might fearfully overreact to physical symptoms, but their reaction is generally confined to the experience of having a panic attack—and they do not consult physicians to verify or disprove their health status. In contrast, Carl consults physicians, one after the other, hoping to find the right one, the one who will confirm his "disease." Carl truly believes he experiences these physical symptoms rather than inventing or maintaining them as found in persons with factitious and malingering disorders.

Competency 7 b

Practitioners may be tempted to diagnose first and then ask questions to support that clinical picture. The competency-based assessment helps to stifle that impulse by encouraging an exploration of the multiple influences in the client's life—i.e., intrapersonal issues, patterns of interpersonal relationships, social context, and support networks. The core elements of this assessment framework encompass knowledge about human behavior across the life span, the social systems in which the client lives, and the ways social systems affect health and well-being.

Competency 7 a

Rather than sustaining the focus on Carl's "illness," the competency-based assessment allows the social worker to identify his adaptive coping skills. Paying attention to such skills serves a preventive function in that Carl learns to anticipate (and thereby prevent) further problems from arising. He has a long-term and stable marriage, is actively involved in the lives of extended family members, and is seeking counseling. Figure 10.2 summarizes the biopsychosocial features in Carl Beacher's life.

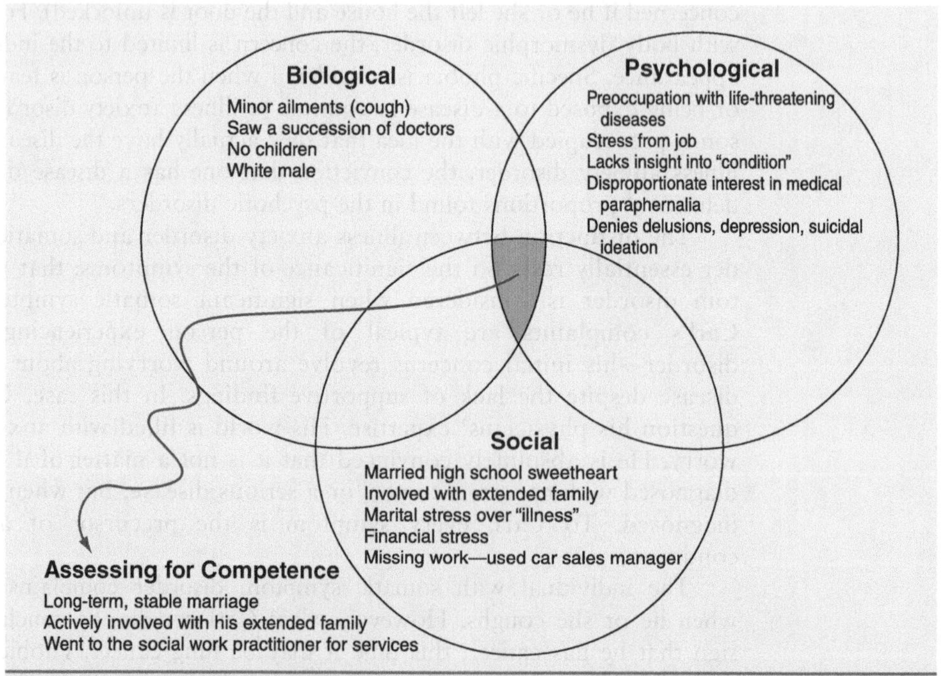

FIGURE 10.2 › ILLNESS ANXIETY DISORDER
The interactions of the biological, psychological, and social variables in Carl Beacher's life.

CONVERSION DISORDER (FUNCTIONAL NEUROLOGICAL SYMPTOM DISORDER)

The symptoms of conversion disorder, a type of somatic symptom disorder, have been described since antiquity. The affected individual experiences a loss or change in physical functioning that suggests the presence of a physical disorder but cannot be explained on the basis of any known physiologic mechanism. In other words, this loss or change does not exist outside the individual's own personal experience.

Sigmund Freud believed the anxiety that was the product of unconscious conflicts needed to find expression and was somehow "converted" into physical symptoms. He believed that this transformation, or conversion, allowed the individual to "get rid" of some of their anxiety without actually having to experience it as such (Barlow & Durand, 2014). Freud is credited with coining the term conversion in conjunction with one of his most famous cases, that of Anna O (Freud, 1894). However, he was not the actual originator of the term—he borrowed it from the Middle Ages.

Conversion disorder is one of the most intriguing types of behavior a practitioner will encounter in his or her entire professional practice. What could possibly account for a person going blind when their optic functions are perfectly normal? What could cause a person to experience a seizure when there is no viable neurological explanation? (Barlow & Durand, 2014). Consider the following historical account from the 1677 Bargarran witchcraft trial:

> Seven people were condemned in Paisley, Ireland, for allegedly using witchcraft against Christina, favored daughter of the powerful Laird of Bargarran. As the story unfolds, seven months after several disgruntled servants placed a "spell" on Christina, she began having bizarre seizures. During these episodes, she claimed to see the devil. She believed that invisible assailants forced strange and foreign materials into her mouth, and she herself had no real understanding of why she experienced fits [seizures] or why she ate strange things. The notable Glasgow physician, Matthew Brisban, was consulted, and he later gave evidence at the trial against the servants. Dr. Brisban admitted he could find no natural explanation for Christina's seizures or for her eating strange substances.
>
> Christina subsequently recovered, and later married a minister from Kilmours. After her husband's untimely death (no information is known about what happened), Christina established a highly prosperous spinning business that later led to the beginning of the famous Paisley cotton industry. (McDonald & Thom, 1996)

The case of Christina is a good example of pseudoneurological symptoms. Her conversion symptoms resemble genuine sensory or motor symptoms, but do not conform to anatomical patterns expected for a condition with a well-defined physical cause—and they developed suddenly, after what anyone would agree was a stressful event (in this case, being cursed by disgruntled servants).

PREVAILING PATTERN

The DSM-5 observes that "transient conversion symptoms are common," but the prevalence of conversion disorder is unknown (APA, 2013, p. 320). However, estimates report incidence of individual persistent conversion symptoms are between 2 and 5 per 100,000 persons per year. As well, the disorder seems to be more common in females (APA, 2013).

DIFFERENTIAL ASSESSMENT

If Christina found herself in similar circumstances today, she would more than likely be diagnosed with a conversion disorder, the essential feature of which is the presence of symptoms that affect voluntary motor or sensory function, suggesting a neurological or other general medical condition. The assessment criteria for conversion disorder include the presence of one or more symptoms affecting a person's voluntary motor or sensory functions, suggesting a neurological or another general medical condition.

Competency 7 a

Conversion disorder is characterized by the occurrence of certain signs and symptoms that are clearly inconsistent with what is actually known about recognized neurological or medical conditions. As well, a general medical condition, or another mental disorder, cannot fully explain these symptoms. It goes without saying that the person's distress impairs social, occupational, or personal functioning or calls for medical evaluation. Actual manifestations of symptoms are quite varied and specific symptoms can be specified from among the following:

Motor symptoms:

- Weakness or paralysis.
- Abnormal movement (such as tremors or dystonic movements or involuntary slow repetitive movements).
- Gait abnormalities.
- Abnormal limb posturing.

Sensory symptoms:

- Altered, reduced, or absent skin sensation, vision, or hearing.
- Abnormal generalized limb shaking with apparent impaired (or loss of) consciousness that may resemble epileptic seizures.
- Unresponsiveness resembling syncope (or fainting) or a coma.

Other symptoms such as:

- Speech problems (such as dysphonia or difficulty in speaking usually evidenced by hoarseness, slurred speech).
- Altered articulation (dysarthria or slurred speech).
- Sensation of having a lump in the throat (globus).
- Diplopia (double vision).

The person may experience one or more symptoms of several types. Although the symptoms of conversion disorder are temporarily disabling, the diagnosis requires that the symptom is not explained by a neurological disease. In other words, the symptoms typically do not conform to known anatomical pathways, disease processes, or physiological mechanisms. For example, a person who is actually paralyzed cannot move certain parts of his or her body, whereas in conversion disorder, the individual is able to move his or her "paralyzed" arm if needed to scratch an annoying itch. However, the person does not realize that movement is possible. This is not to say that these symptoms are consciously constructed or intentionally faked.

There is some risk of actual physical and long-term impairment if certain conversion symptoms persist over an extended period of time. Those who do not regularly use their muscles often experience muscle atrophy (or damage). This disuse of muscles may also result in the demineralization of the skeletal system.

The DSM-5 includes "functional neurological symptom disorder" to the diagnosis of conversion disorder since there is no clear (or very little) research evidence to support the reasons for a person's symptoms. Including the term functional is intended to add more diagnostic clarity by characterizing symptoms as lacking an organic cause (Stone, LaFrance, Levenson, & Sharpe, 2010). All in all, the diagnosis should be based on the person's overall clinical picture and not on a single symptom presentation. Conversion disorder can appear at any age. Some individuals may have a history of many similar somatic symptoms. As we will see in the following case of Jenny Webber, onset may be associated with stress or trauma. However, if there is no stress or trauma, the diagnosis of conversion disorder can still be made.

Competency 7 b

It is possible that a person might be faking his or her symptoms. Nonetheless, making this distinction is not required for diagnosing conversion disorder. In some instances, there might be a secondary gain from being sick; for instance, the person may be excused from confronting or dealing with difficult life situations, they may be able to control other people, or they might even receive support and help that might not otherwise be given. Here, too, assessing secondary gain is not specific to conversion disorder. However, if the person is faking symptoms and clearly there is secondary gain, the practitioner might consider factitious disorder, especially if the person's apparent aim is to assume the sick role. Malingering could be considered if the aim is to obtain some kind of an incentive such as money.

We now turn to the case of Jenny Webber to illustrate symptoms of conversion disorder.

CASE The Case of Jenny Webber

Jake Webber rushed his wife, Jenny, to the emergency room of a rural hospital that was two towns away from their home. During the 75-mile drive, he was extremely worried about his wife. Jenny Webber is 34 years old and the mother of three children. She has been employed as a secretary for the past 8 years at a local accounting firm. She is involved in her church, where she teaches Sunday school—and through work and church she has cultivated many friends.

In the emergency room, Jake tells the resident physician on duty, "We were just standing in line buying some soda at Duncan's General Store when all of a sudden some guy pulls out a gun and says, 'This is a holdup.' Then he tells us to get down on the floor." He continues, "The robber grabs some money out of the cash register, runs to a waiting car, and heads for the hills. I mean, the whole thing didn't take more than 15 seconds. The next thing I know, the police are all over the place, and

CASE The Case of Jenny Webber (Continued)

they're asking people to describe the thief. One of the cops comes over to Jenny and me and asks us if we'd come downtown to the station and go through some mug shots. Of course, I said sure, anything to help out," Jake said. "But the next thing I know, Jenny stumbles and falls—she's in a panic, telling me she can't see anything."

The physician began his physical examination. He noted that, although Mrs. Webber complained of blindness, her pupils constricted when he directed his penlight in her eyes. And when he made a sudden movement toward her face, she blinked involuntarily.

Mrs. Webber was examined for signs of neurological or other general medical conditions that may account for her inability to see. Her laboratory results indicated that she was not under the influence of drugs or alcohol. The physician consulted the other (more senior) doctor in town, who suggested treatment with a placebo. The emergency room physician assured Mrs. Webber that the "special injection" he was going to administer would restore her vision back to normal. Within 10 seconds of having this special shot, Mrs. Webber's vision returned, much to her delight. She was discharged from the hospital with a follow-up referral to evaluate the risk for any longer-term adjustment problems at the North Bismarck Mental Health Center.

Jenny Webber's DSM Diagnosis Is as Follows:

Conversion disorder, with special sensory symptom, acute episode, with psychological stressor—witnessing an armed robbery

Assessment Summary Conversion disorder generally refers to some type of physical problem without any underlying physical pathology. Hurwitz (2004) points to a psychodynamic explanation wherein a person experiences a trauma that is too difficult to bear and, as a consequence, the distress is converted into a sensory motor disability that is easier to tolerate. This supports Jenny Webber's experience. As seen in Jenny's story, conversion disorders have an uncanny resemblance to neurological problems. Formulating a differential assessment is critical, and the practitioner should refer the client to a physician in order to rule out neurological diseases.

In somatic symptom disorder, most of the somatic symptoms are not clearly incompatible with pathophysiology. In contrast, there was no medical support for Jenny Webber's symptoms of blindness; for example, when the physician saw her in the emergency room, her pupils constricted in reaction to light, and she blinked when the doctor made a sudden movement. Her frightening experience witnessing the general store holdup set the foundation for the underlying psychological struggle to cope with her fears and the associated loss of sight. Her blindness occurred suddenly; that is, just when the police officer asked her and her husband to come to the station to look at mug shots of potential suspects. While stress and trauma are not essential for the diagnosis, clearly Jenny was traumatized by witnessing a robbery.

Someone with body dysmorphic disorder is excessively concerned about a perceived defect in their appearance but does not complain of symptoms of sensory or motor functioning in the affected body part. Conversely, Jenny experienced (medically unsupported) symptoms of blindness and she was not at all concerned about the appearance of her eyes.

The Webbers were unwilling participants in this criminal and potentially violent event. Despite her trauma, Jenny manifested none of the features of panic disorder, where neurological symptoms are typically transient and acutely episodic with characteristic cardiorespiratory symptoms.

Jenny was given a placebo injection, and she experienced a spontaneous remission of her blindness. In fact, she made a complete recovery. Prompt recovery is the rule with treatment of conversion disorder, and especially when the individual, like Jenny Webber, is surrounded by supportive family members. It is not uncommon for the practitioner to see someone similar to Jenny in an ambulatory or emergency room setting where the individual responds to almost any therapeutic intervention that offers the suggestion of a cure. In this case story, the key strategy for recovery was to identify and attend to Jenny Webber's traumatic life event.

Competency 7 a

Although the relevant information in this case focuses on deficits and blindness, the competency-based assessment provides a framework for the practitioner to look at the whole person and take into consideration Jenny's strengths as an integral part of the assessment. For example, she is very active in her rural community and committed to church functions. A number of friends seem to care about Jenny. In addition, she has worked in the same position for 8 years. Finally, her husband, Jake, is very devoted to her. The social worker's focus was short term and crisis oriented. She also took into account the possibility of risk factors that may potentially affect Jenny's long-term recovery. The referral to the mental health center for further evaluation was made as a preventative measure to further ensure Jenny's continued recovery.

The following conditions are not often seen in practice but are reviewed to enhance the practitioner's understanding of the somatic symptom and related disorders. We begin with a disorder new to the DSM-5, psychological factors affecting other medical conditions.

PSYCHOLOGICAL FACTORS AFFECTING OTHER MEDICAL CONDITIONS

A number of psychological factors ranging from mood, the personality disorders, and responses to stress or pain, to name a few, can have adverse effects on the body's physical condition. Therefore, it becomes important for the practitioner to address both the physiological and psychological factors that can influence the course, treatment, or outcome of an existing medical condition. The diagnosis of psychological factors affecting other medical conditions is supported by a growing body of research and diagnosed when psychological or behavioral factors adversely affect the course or outcome of an existing medical condition (Fava, Fabbri, Sirri & Wise, 2007).

DIFFERENTIAL ASSESSMENT

Psychological factors affecting other medical conditions is considered when the individual has a symptom (or actual medical condition) as well as significant psychological or behavioral factors that adversely affect the medical condition. This becomes evident in several ways, such as a delayed recovery, poor adherence to treatment, increasing health risks, or exacerbating symptoms. These effects can range from acute and requiring immediate attention to occurring over a long period of time. Severity can range from mild to severe.

We take a look at Kathy Hood's experiences with anxiety-exacerbating asthma, one of the more common clinical examples of this diagnosis.

CASE THE CASE OF KATHY HOOD

Kathy Hood was referred to the social worker for counseling by her physician, who was treating her for her asthma symptoms that were out of control. Her physician prescribed the oral steroid prednisone, which can cause mood swings as a side effect, adding fuel to the anxiety she was experiencing. She was also referred to the local mental health center for counseling.

At first, Kathy looked a little uneasy but somehow relieved to see the social worker. She began, "You might say we were the picture-perfect family ... and I really think we were. I think that's why it is so hard for me to understand what I'm going through. We were all very close. My sisters are still my best friends. Growing up I can remember my dad taking us out on special field trips every weekend. Gosh! We went to so many interesting places and saw such great things. Mom always had a great dinner waiting for us when we came home, and we would share our adventures with her. It was always such a fun day. I still remember our conversations. I went to the same school. We never moved around. After high school went straight to college. On a scholarship, of course. And yes, I went to the same college that my older sister went to. With her there, I had a great built-in network so it was real easy to make friends."

Kathy paused and continued, "Sorry, I hope I'm not boring you. You see, I've never had counseling before so I'm not sure if you want to hear all this." The social worker, Diane Laughlin, responded that hearing about Kathy's background was helpful and encouraged her to ask any questions if she was unsure about the counseling process or feels uncomfortable. Diane encouraged Kathy to continue and wondered if she could share some of the details around what led up to her doctor's referral.

Kathy looked relieved. Diane thought to herself that it seemed like Kathy had no one that understood exactly what she was going through right now. Apparently her sisters saw her anxiety as a "passing phase" and seemed consumed with their own lives; her younger sister was newly married and the older one just had her first child.

Kathy resumed, "I think it started after I graduated college. I got this really great job here on the West Coast. It was the perfect position to launch my career but I had to move across country leaving my friends and family behind. I always had asthma and it seemed living out here with all the fresh air and sunshine was great for me. Then after a few months I got laid off. What was I going to do next? To top it off, I got news that my mother was killed in a car accident. And then the bills started piling up."

Kathy looked visibly upset and tears started to roll down her cheeks. She reached across the social worker's desk for a tissue, blew her nose, took a really deep breath, and continued, "That's when things started to go downhill for me. I have to live with the reality that my family will never be the same. My mom was really the heart of our family ... and now she's gone."

Kathy stopped and stared off into space looking lost. Diane waited for Kathy to collect her thoughts. Kathy then asked, "Where was I? Oh I remember. You wanted to know when the asthma got worse. I felt battered by the recent layoff. Then there were the high-stakes job interviews. They were really taxing on my nerves. As my financial worries built up, so did my attacks of shortness of breath, coughing, and wheezing. I got so anxious never knowing when or where I would have another attack."

At this point in the interview, Diane noticed that Kathy looked physically overpowered. Kathy shifted nervously in her chair and asked, "Do you think there's a connection between asthma and stress?"

Diane responded, "Asthma can get worse, and it sounds like you've had a lot going on lately—the recent loss of your mother, a layoff, intense job interviews, mounting bills. During periods of stress and anxiety, asthma attacks can occur more frequently and controlling them becomes more difficult. Sometimes during periods of stress and anxiety, people forget to take their asthma medications, making an attack more likely."

Kathy interrupted, "How did you know! That's exactly what's been happening to me. This makes so much sense. Now that I think of it, I have been forgetting to take my medications. Then when the wheezing and coughing gets worse, my health is another reason to worry. I feel like I'm in a vicious circle ... and spiraling downward really fast. I think I finally understand why my doctor asked me to see you but do you think you can help me get back on track?"

Kathy Hood's DSM Diagnosis Is as Follows:
Psychological factors affecting other medical conditions, moderate

Assessment Summary Kathy's story features the psychological aspects of increased stress and anxiety and their interplay with exacerbating her asthma, a key feature of the diagnosis of psychological factors affecting other medical conditions. Her increased anxiety causes her to forget taking her asthma medications, thus increasing her asthma symptoms. Stress is an inescapable part of life, but when Kathy's stress levels started to creep up, her asthma symptoms seemed to also increase. As her asthma symptoms got worse, her health became yet another source of anxiety, setting the stage for a vicious cycle. Additionally, Kathy's medication was adjusted, and because her symptoms seemed out of control, she was prescribed an anti-inflammatory, prednisone. The problem is that this medication can cause mood swings with the potential of adding fuel to Kathy's anxiety.

While a mental disorder due to another medical condition is also associated with symptoms of a mental disorder and those of a medical condition, Kathy's experiences are just the opposite in that her medical condition came first and was aggravated by the psychological features of anxiety and stress. If Kathy had anticipatory anxiety around having an asthma attack, she would meet criteria for an adjustment disorder with anxiety. Kathy's symptom picture describes the anxiety and how it affects her asthma. Somatic symptom disorder is another closely associated diagnosis, but its distinction from psychological factors affecting other medical conditions is that the person may or may not have a medical disorder. Kathy reports that she "always had asthma." Those with illness anxiety disorder are characterized by high illness anxiety that is distressing and can disrupt a person's daily life—even with the most minimal symptoms. In most cases, the person actually has no medical serious disease. In Kathy's situation, her asthma is a relevant factor. She was referred for counseling by her doctor since her anxiety was adversely affecting her medical condition.

Competency 7 a

While we know little of Kathy Hood's life history (thus the interaction of the biological, psychological, and social variables will not be detailed), several competencies are evident as she struggles with asthma. Her family, though geographically distant and confronting the recent loss of their mother, remains a consistent source of support. Kathy graduated from college and despite a recent layoff was able to obtain what she described as a great job to launch her career. She is also actively interviewing for another job. Kathy also sought medical help when her asthma symptoms worsened and followed up with her physician's referral for counseling. During the session with the social worker, Kathy seemed insightful around the connection between her stress and asthma symptoms. As well, she appeared motivated to seek help.

A consideration of factitious disorder follows.

FACTITIOUS DISORDER

Another puzzling set of conditions is factitious disorder; something that is not real, genuine, or natural. Here, the person displays physical and psychological symptoms that are intentionally produced and are completely under the person's voluntary control (as with malingering), but there is no obvious reason for voluntarily producing the symptoms except, possibly, to take on the sick role and receive increased attention. As a part of the competency-based assessment, the practitioner will find it helpful to explore the person's level of social and occupational functioning. Clues to this disorder include records of hospitalizations, medical appointments, and being sick—all of which may impair relationships and job performance. These individuals often have distorted perceptions of justice as well as a sense of entitlement, which further justify their sick role. They are also prone to see themselves as victims.

A prototypical factitious disorder is Munchausen syndrome. In the eighteenth century, Baron Karl Friedrich Hieronymous von Munchausen, a German cavalry officer, had a reputation for being a colorful raconteur who spun outrageous stories and wandered about the countryside to find audiences. (As a character, he was committed to history in Raspe's [1948] book, *Baron Munchausen's Narrative of His Marvelous Travels and Campaigns in Russia*.) There is no evidence that the real Baron von Munchausen ever believed the stories he fabricated, tried to deceive his listeners, or sought out unneeded medical treatment. Nevertheless, his name continues to be linked to a term that represents a syndrome considered the most extreme example of factitious disorder. In 1951, Richard Asher, an English physician, wrote an article entitled "Munchausen's syndrome" in *The Lancet*. The first sentence in his article stated, "Here is described a common syndrome which most doctors have seen, but about which little has been written" (Asher, 1951, p. 339). He borrowed Munchausen's name and applied it to people who demonstrated a triad of features: (1) the recurrent simulation of disease, (2) pathological lying (pseudologia fantastica), or (3) wandering (peregrination). The individual so afflicted will travel extensively in order to receive medical care where his or her previous medical history is unknown. It has been suggested that if Asher had been less self-effacing, the syndrome might have been named after him. However, Asher's article served to bring the syndrome to public attention. The disorder has been called various names, including polysurgical addiction, hospital addiction, and professional patient syndrome.

PREVAILING PATTERN

The prevalence of factitious disorder is unknown (APA, 2013). However, it is estimated that the disorder can be found in about 1 percent of individuals in hospital settings.

DIFFERENTIAL ASSESSMENT

The literature available for understanding this disorder is still evolving. IsHak and colleagues (2010) recommend large descriptive and longitudinal studies with adequate diagnostic workups, including medical, neurologic, neuropsychological, and personality testing evaluations aimed at developing a clearer understanding of factitious disorder. Unfortunately, these kinds of studies are difficult due to the reality that those struggling with factitious disorder try not to be "discovered." These are the clients who will provide misleading information about themselves and who represent themselves to others as sick, injured, or impaired. This level of deception is obvious even in the absence of obvious external rewards. It is not clear which presentation of factitious disorder is most common, but the symptom picture of physical symptoms seems higher than for psychological symptoms (Krahn, Li, & O'Connor, 2003).

Munchausen by proxy is a variant of the factitious disorder, but this disorder typically occurs within the context of a relationship between the parent and child. The diagnosis is assigned to the perpetrator, not the victim. This condition occurs when the parent or caregiver deliberately falsifies the child's (or another adult's or pet's) medical history and subjects the child to unnecessary medical procedures (including unnecessary surgeries) and unneeded hospitalizations. The deception can involve contaminating laboratory samples, providing false medical history, initiating an injury, or actually causing sickness (e.g., by poison) of the child. Munchausen by proxy is considered a form of child abuse and is mandated by law reportable if suspected. Detection of this disorder is extremely difficult.

Those involved with Munchausen by proxy tend to be mothers who are married, educated, middle-class women in their early 20s. Females who are employed in medical fields such as nursing or medical technology where there are opportunities to learn about diseases and easy access to equipment to produce them (syringes or chemicals) have a high incidence of factitious disorder (Todd & Ahmed, 2001).

The practitioner may find someone with factitious disorder displaying feelings of victimization, a sense of entitlement, and usually some "righteous indignation." The following vignette illustrates how a client with factitious disorder might present his or her concerns.

CASE THE CASE OF NAN FINKELHORN

Nan Finkelhorn is a 27-year-old female who is currently in her 35th hospital admission. She works as a nurse in the dialysis unit of the hospital, and her supervisor is wondering if Nan may have some kind of rare infection. Recently, Nan was diagnosed with chronic fatigue, and since that time her job performance has been sporadic. It has been difficult for the supervisor to know how to respond, because

CASE THE CASE OF NAN FINKELHORN (CONTINUED)

Nan is vague about the details of her condition. It seems that when the unit is hectic and there is much work to be done, Nan loudly announces to her coworkers that she needs a coffee break. As a result, there is growing tension between Nan and her supervisor around performance expectations.

Nan's presenting problems during this current admission include chronic headaches, fevers, lupus-like symptoms, vomiting, inability to walk, and numbness in her left hand and her right foot. She came to the emergency room last evening asking for narcotic medication for pain. During her examination by the attending physician on duty, Nan doubled over and said she felt a terrible pain in her left kidney area. The physician felt it was prudent to admit Ms. Finkelhorn for observation. Nan's reaction was, "I hate hospitals, especially this one—my mother died here, and no one ever bothered to take care of her."

After a complete set of laboratory tests and additional physical examinations, Nan was given a clean bill of health. Just a few minutes after she was discharged and declared fit to return to her full responsibilities at work, Ms. Finkelhorn began to complain loudly. "Are you people nuts? I am an extremely ill person. All of you doctors are incompetent—I'm going to report all of you, and my stupid supervisor, to Employee Assistance. Looks like that's the only way I'll ever get any justice from this place." As she continued down the corridor, Nan muttered, "When I end up dead, it'll be on your heads."

CLOSING OBSERVATIONS ABOUT NAN FINKELHORN

There is no assessment summary discussion for the case presentation of Nan Finkelhorn because the intention is to show how clients with a diagnosis of factitious disorder might present themselves to the practitioner. The important distinction when making this diagnosis is that Nan's symptoms are not better explained by a true general medical condition or by an apparent mental disorder. Instead, Nan describes a vague set of symptoms, such as headaches, fevers, lupus-like symptoms, vomiting, inability to walk, and numbness in her left hand and her right foot, that bring her to the emergency room for some kind of relief. On the face of it, none of these complaints seems to justify her request for a narcotic medication. While the attending physician is examining her, Nan inexplicably doubles over in pain. However, the physical examination and related lab tests do not support her physical "complaints."

Competency 1 c

Interestingly, when Nan's job gets hectic and much work needs to be done, she announces that she needs a coffee break, creating tension with her supervisor. Nan's vague illnesses, righteous indignation, and veiled threats about getting justice certainly shift the focus away from her work performance. As a matter of fact, her supervisor is beginning to wonder if Nan might have some kind of rare infection that might better explain her behavior. Clients like Nan can be difficult to work with and can certainly challenge the practitioner's ability to maintain a professional demeanor and to communicate respectfully in the face of such overt hostility.

Somatic symptom disorder can involve multiple treatment seeking, but there is no evidence that the individual is deceptively providing information about their condition. Malingering involves falsification of symptoms, but the individual is motivated by personal gain, such as a monetary reward for their "injury" or "illness." Conversion disorder involves neurological symptoms, and someone with this diagnosis, unlike Nan, does not deceptively falsify their symptoms. Someone with a borderline personality disorder may deliberately physically harm themselves. Nan, however, inflicts her injury in association with deception.

SUMMARY

This chapter reviewed the various somatic symptom and related disorders with a focus on the most prevalent diagnoses. The development of somatic symptom disorder revolves around symptoms that are distressing or result in significant disruption in the person's life. Illness anxiety disorder centers on an individual's excessive preoccupation with his or her health—even when there are no identifiable medical conditions to support these complaints. Conversion disorder characterizes symptoms that are not explained by neurological disease. Psychological factors affecting other medical conditions highlight those psychological or behavioral factors that adversely affect a person's medical condition. Factitious disorder is characterized by the intentional feigning of physical symptoms to assume the sick role. This contrasts to malingering disorder, which includes external motivations for sustaining such behavior (for example, seeking economic gains through litigious actions).

In conclusion, the other specified somatic symptom and related disorder and unspecified somatic symptom and related disorder are reserved for those situations when the practitioner does not have full information about the person's disorder.

Competency 7 b

The competency-based assessment facilitates an emphasis on the client's concerns by:

- Evaluating symptom presentation in the context of both current and past interpersonal, social, cultural, and environmental factors.
- Encouraging the practitioner to include a conversation about how well clients are functioning in terms of their interpersonal relationships and their social and family support systems.
- Keeping the focus on intrapersonal, interpersonal, and/or social problems, not the physical or somatic symptoms. (This is not to say that new signs or symptoms are not carefully evaluated.)
- Reminding the practitioner that, to the clients, their symptoms are very real and quite distressing.
- Recognizing early on the need for a comprehensive medical evaluation, especially for those individuals who have chronic symptoms, severe psychological consequences, or morbid types of illness behavior.

From the competency-based perspective, the practitioner:

- Thoroughly explores the client's medical history;
- Provides reassurance, as appropriate, to the client that he or she does not have a serious illness.
- Suggests to the client that symptoms will eventually resolve themselves.
- Encourages the client to return to normal activities.
- Follows the client for a period of time and inquires about medical status on subsequent visits.

As the DSM transitions from the DSM-IV-TR (APA, 2000) to the current edition of the manual, the following Table 10.2 provides a brief summary of the changes made to the diagnostic classifications in this chapter.

Table 10.2 Summary Comparison Between the DSM-IV-TR and DSM-5 Diagnoses for the Somatic Symptom and Related Disorders

Somatoform disorders are called somatic symptom and related disorders in the DSM-5
To reduce the overlap across the DSM-IV somatoform disorders, the number of diagnoses have been reduced; specifically, the diagnoses of somatization disorder, hypochondriasis, pain disorder, and undifferentiated somatoform disorder were deleted in the DSM-5
Individuals with chronic pain can now be diagnosed with somatic symptom disorder with predominant pain or psychological factors that affect other medical conditions (or with an adjustment disorder)
Somatization disorder and undifferentiated somatoform disorder are combined in the DSM-5 to become somatic symptom disorder; this new diagnosis no longer requires a specific number of somatic symptoms
Somatic symptom and related disorders are defined by positive symptoms (such as distressing somatic symptoms plus abnormal thoughts, feelings, and behaviors in response to these symptoms), and medically unexplained symptoms are minimized except in the cases of conversion disorder and pseudocyesis (or false pregnancy)
Criteria for conversion disorder (functional neurological symptom disorder) were changed
The DSM-5 includes a new diagnosis—psychological factors affecting other medical conditions; this was in the DSM-IV under "Other Conditions That May Be a Focus of Clinical Attention"

Practitioner's Reflections

Somatic symptom disorders have earned a reputation of being very difficult to assess. As a practitioner, remember that even though the client may have excessive thoughts, feelings, or behaviors about an "illness," he or she is still ill. The client's concerns must be taken seriously rather than dismissed as playing games or pretending an illness that they do not have.

The following activities are intended to help practitioners better understand these disorders.

Activities

Competency 6 a

1. This activity focuses on understanding the individual with illness anxiety disorder.
   a. Keep a log of your bodily sensations for three or four days. Be as detailed as you can in your recording. Include, for example, headaches, backaches, muscle aches, stomach grumblings, perspiration, fatigue, and so forth.
   b. Reflect back on your log and compare how your own body sensations differ from those in the case of Carl Beacher. Be as specific as you can.
   c. Imagine for a moment that you are having a conversation with Carl Beacher. How would he respond to your listing of your body sensations?
   d. Remember the last time you had a common cold? Write down your experiences. Be sure to include how you felt, how long it lasted, and what you did to minimize your discomfort.
   e. Look over this list, and imagine how a person diagnosed with illness anxiety disorder would describe his or her own experience with having a cold.
2. Factitious disorder is very uncommon. To better understand the symptom picture of someone with this disorder, imagine that you have some-

Competency 6 a

one on your caseload with factitious disorder and describe what you think their experiences of a common cold would be like. What challenges can you identify that would affect your ability to develop manage, and maintain a therapeutic relationship within the person-in-environment and strengths perspectives?

Competency 1 c

3. Imagine that you are a social worker in an acute medical care hospital. A patient that you have been seeing over several admissions has just died after a long and courageous struggle with cancer. She had painful procedures done on several prior admissions but never complained and seemed to be a source of strength and inspiration not only for her family but also for other patients on the floor. After the death, you went to see Helene Martin in the emergency room on her December 16 visit. After reviewing her medical chart, you recognize several negative feelings about Helene's "illness" experiences. Describe what you might do to address these reactions.
   a. Make a list and be as specific as you can. Hopefully, you will be able to better able to manage your feelings and strong reactions to Helene and accept her without judging her.

Competency 1 a

   b. As a next step, review your list with your supervisor and together discuss what you learned; further, consider how your experiences and reactions to Helene Martin can be generalized to future clients who may provoke hostile reactions.
   c. You know that it is not ethical to judge your clients negatively. Research the National Association of Social Workers Code of Ethics for further guidance on how to ethically respond to clients who may provoke negative reactions.

Competency 6 b

Competency Notes

Competency 1 a—Social workers make ethical decisions by applying standards of the NASW Code of Ethics and other relevant laws, regulations, and models for ethical decision-making as appropriate to context (p. 295): Social workers understand the value base of the profession and its ethical standards as well as relevant laws and regulations that may impact practice.

Competency 1 c—Social workers demonstrate professional demeanor in behavior, appearance, and oral/written/electronic communication (pp. 292, 295): Social workers understand how their personal experiences and affective reactions can influence their professional judgment and behavior and also understand emerging forms of technology and the ethical use of technology in practice.

Competency 2 a—Social workers apply and communicate understanding of the implications of diversity and difference in shaping life experiences in practice at the micro, mezzo, and macro levels (p. 271): Social workers understand how diversity and difference characterize and shape the human experience and that these features are critical to the formation of identity.

Competency 6 a—Social workers apply knowledge of human behavior and the social environment, person-in-environment, and other multidisciplinary theoretical frameworks to engage with clients (and constituencies) (p. 294): Social workers understand theories of human behavior and the social environment and critically apply this knowledge to facilitate engagement with clients (and constituencies) including families, groups, organizations, and communities.

Competency 6 b—Social workers use empathy, personal reflection, and interpersonal skills effectively to engage clients (and constituencies) (p. 295): Social workers value the importance of human relationships.

Competency 7 a—Social workers collect and organize data and apply critical thinking in order to interpret information from clients and constituencies (pp. 277, 280, 282, 284, 287, 289): Social workers understand that the assessment process is ongoing and conducted with, and on behalf of, diverse individuals, families, groups, organizations, and communities.

Competency 7 b—Social workers are able to apply knowledge of human behavior and the social environment, person-in-environment, and other multidisciplinary theoretical frameworks in the analysis of assessment data (pp. 271, 273, 282, 285, 293): Social workers understand theories of human behavior and the social environment and critically evaluate and apply this knowledge in the assessment process.

Competency 8 c—Social workers use interprofessional collaboration, as appropriate, to achieve beneficial practice outcomes (p. 273): Social workers value interprofessional teamwork and recognize the beneficial outcomes that require interdisciplinary, interprofessional, and interorganizational collaboration.

REFERENCES

American Psychiatric Association (APA). (2000). *Diagnostic and statistical manual of mental disorders* (4th ed., text revision). Washington, DC: Author.

American Psychiatric Association (APA). (2013). *Diagnostic and statistical manual of mental disorders* (5th ed.). Arlington, VA: Author.

Alexander, F. G., & Selesnick, S. T. (1966). *The history of psychiatry: An evaluation of psychiatric thought and practice from prehistoric times to the present*. New York: Harper and Row.

Asher, R. (1951). Munchausen's syndrome. *Lancet*, *1*, 339–341.

Barlow, D. H., & Durand, V. M. (2014). *Abnormal psychology: An integrative approach* (7th ed.). Stamford, CT: Wadsworth Cengage.

Creed, F., & Barsky, A. (2004). A systematic review of the epidemiology of somatization disorder and hypochondriasis. *Journal of Psychosomatic Research*, *56*, 391–408.

Fava, G. A., Fabbri, S., Sirri, L., & Wise, T. N. (2007). Psychological factors affecting a new medical condition: A new proposal for DSM-5. *Psychosomatics*, *48*(2), 103–111.

Freud, S. (1894, 1962). The neuropsychoses of defense. In J. Strachey (Ed.), *The complete psychological works*: Vol. 3 (pp. 45–62). London: Hogarth Press.

Gray, S. W. (with Zide, M. R.). (2006). *Psychopathology: A competency-based treatment model for social workers*. Pacific Grove, CA: Brooks/Cole.

Hurwitz, T. A. (2004). Somatization and conversion disorder. *Canadian Journal of Psychiatry*, *49*, 172–178.

IsHak, W. W., Rasyidi, E., Saah, T., Vasa, M., Ettekal, A., & Fan, A. (2010). Factitious disorder: Case series with variations of psychological and physical symptoms. *Primary Psychiatry*, *17*(9), 40–43.

Krahn, L. E., Li, H., & O'Connor, M. K. (2003). Patients who strive to be ill: Factitious disorder with physical symptoms. *American Journal of Psychiatry*, *160*(6), 1163–1168.

McDonald, S. W., & Thom, A. (1996). The bargarran witchcraft trial—A psychiatric reassessment. *Scottish Medical Journal*, *41*(5), 152–158.

North, C. S., & Guze, S. B. (1997). Somatoform disorders. In S. G. Guze (Ed.), *Adult psychiatry*. St. Louis, MO: Mosby-Year Book.

Raspe, R. E. (1948). *Singular travels, campaigns, and adventures of Baron Munchausen*. London: Cresset Press.

Stone, J., LaFrance, W. C., Levenson, J. L., & Sharpe, M. (2010). Issues for DSM-5: Conversion disorder. *American Journal of Psychiatry*, *167*, 626–627.

Stone, J., Smyth, R., Carson, A., Warlow, C., & Sharpe, M. (2006). La belle indifference in conversion symptoms and hysteria: Systematic review. *British Journal of Psychiatry*, *188*, 204–209.

Todd, E., & Ahmed, I. (2001). Factitious disorder. *eMedicine Journal*, *2*(1). Retrieved on November 1, 2014 from: http://emedicine.medscape.com/article/291304-overview#showall

Woolfolk, R. L., & Allen, L. A. (2014). Somatoform and physical disorders. In D. H. Barlow (Ed.), *The Oxford handbook of clinical psychology: Updated edition* (pp. 339–363). New York: Oxford University Press.

CHAPTER

Feeding and Eating Disorders

INTRODUCTION

Eating disorders have been recognized throughout history, beginning with the ancient past, through the early Christian era, the Dark and late Middle Ages, early Renaissance, the twentieth century, and now continuing into the twenty-first century. Each historical period has influenced the frequency and appearance of eating disorders, and cases of bulimia have been described for thousands of years (Parry-Jones & Parry-Jones, 2002). For example, incidents of bingeing (or excessive eating) and purging (vomiting) of food were considered socially acceptable during the Roman era—when banquets serving 20 or more different courses were a common occurrence. Societal, cultural, or religious beliefs have always affected people's eating patterns. During the Dark Ages, a person could rid themselves of sin and/or sexual desire through acts of purging. During the Middle Ages, according to well-documented accounts, women known as "the sainted women" starved themselves for their religious beliefs; such episodes of starvation as these are referred to as *anorexia mirabilis* or holy anorexia. At the time, this practice was not considered pathological because the women's fasting practices were seen as culturally accepted expressions of their religious devotion.

In 1689, Dr. Richard Morton described a self-starving 18-year-old woman who looked like a "skeleton only clad with skin." He referred to her condition as "nervous consumption" (Hersen, Turner, & Beidel, 2007; Kilgus, Maxmen, & Ward, 2009). Other examples of starvation involved the notorious fasting girls of the sixteenth and seventeenth centuries. Certain young women adopted this eating pattern as a visible demonstration of their virtuous lifestyle and zealous commitment to the church. Some societies allowed or sanctioned starvation, while others encouraged women to have a well-fed or plump appearance to indicate that a father or husband was a good provider and could afford to feed his family well.

Anorexia nervosa was first described in the early 1860s and 1870s by the French physicians Marcé (1860) and Lasegué (1873) and by the English physician Sir William Gull (1873). Gull characterized this disorder of eating as a "want of appetite," which he saw as being characteristic of a "morbid mental state." Marcé eloquently describes the ravages of starvation and the curious mental state that often accompanies it:

> Whatever the duration of their abstinence, they experience a distaste for food which the most pressing want is unable to overcome.... Deeply impressed, whether by the absence of appetite or by the uneasiness caused by digestion, these patients arrive at a delirious conviction that they cannot or ought not to eat. In one word, the gastric nervous disorder becomes cerebro-nervous. (pp. 264, 266)

Lasegué notes the frustration encountered by families and caregivers:

> The delicacies of the table are multiplied in the hopes of stimulating the appetite, but the more the solicitude increases, the more the appetite diminishes. What dominates in the mental condition of the hysterical patient is, above all, the state of quietude.... Not only does she not sigh for recovery, but she is not ill-pleased with her condition. (pp. 385, 403)

The age-old question of what drives so many into a dangerous and life-threatening eating pattern of semistarvation or purging remains unanswered. There are a number of risk factors that can play a role in an individual's judgments about his or her body, such as cognitive, affective, cultural, and attitudinal variables (Hill, 2006; McGee, Hewitt, Sherry, Parkin, & Flett, 2005; Sassaroli et al., 2008; Stice, 2002; Utter, Neumark-Sztainer, Wall, & Story, 2003). Being overweight, dieting and dissatisfaction with one's body, and status in a higher social class seem to be increasingly recognized as the primary risk factors for developing an eating disorder (Polivy & Herman, 2002; Stice, Ng, & Shaw, 2010). Less understood are those feeding or eating disturbances that may include but are not limited to eating nonnutritive substances, the repetitive regurgitation of undigested food, and the decreased interest in food or eating in general.

Although the majority of eating disorders are first noticed during late childhood and early adolescence, they often continue well into adulthood (Gonzalez, Kohn, & Clarke, 2007). Looking to all of the feeding and eating disorders, none appear to be specific to a certain culture. For instance, Anderson-Frye (2009) found anorexia nervosa and bulimia nervosa in a number of immigrant populations who have recently moved to Western countries, including the United States (Goel, McCarthy, Phillips, & Wee, 2004). While the eating disorders can be found around the world, they seem more prevalent in Western cultures, in contrast to those countries where food is scarce.

The range of diagnostic classifications related to ingesting an adequate variety and amount of food are dichotomized into the feeding or eating disorders in the DSM-5 and depend on the need for affected persons to eat on their own or to be fed. This chapter focuses on those disorders applied to feeding/eating disturbances as seen in pica, rumination disorder, and avoidant/restrictive food intake disorder. Also addressed are the disorders associated with behaviors related to weight control or self-concept strongly influenced by body weight or shape, as seen in anorexia nervosa, bulimia nervosa, and binge-eating disorder.

TABLE 11.1 THE DSM-5 FEEDING AND EATING DISORDERS
Pica
Rumination Disorder
Avoidant/Restrictive Food Intake Disorder
Anorexia Nervosa
Bulimia Nervosa
Binge-Eating Disorder
Other Specified Feeding or Eating Disorder
Unspecified Feeding or Eating Disorder

Table 11.1 lists the specific feeding and eating disorders listed in the DSM-5.

It should be noted that there are several significant coexisting disorders associated with the feeding and eating disorders, including: the depressive disorders; anxiety disorders; personality disorders; obsessive-compulsive and related disorders, particularly obsessive tendencies; substance abuse, including both alcohol and drugs; and suicide (Agras, 2001; Hudson, Hiripi, Pope, & Kessler, 2007). Underlying traits of emotional instability and novelty seeking are also found in some individuals (Wade, Bulik, Prescott, & Kendler, 2004).

We now turn to a review of pica.

PICA

The term *pica* is derived from the Latin word for magpie, a bird reputed for its unusual eating behaviors. These birds are known to eat almost anything. As a part of exploring the world around them, it's not unusual for children to put things in their mouth. They are naturally curious about their environment and, as an example, you might find them eating some of the dirt in the sandbox. Those with the diagnosis of pica go far beyond this harmless level of exploration.

After Novak Djokovic defeated former champion Roger Federer and won the 2014 Wimbledon tennis championship, he knelt down and ate some of the grass on the court. Afterward, he reportedly said, "That was the best meal I ever had." Do you think Djokovic has pica? After all, the DSM-5 disorder of pica is characterized by a person's appetite for substances that are largely nonnutritive. Some of the nonfood items people with pica frequently crave are shown on Table 11.2.

The most commonly ingested substance is ice. Unfortunately, it is associated with a high risk of tooth cracking, deterioration of tooth enamel, and jaw joint strain. It can also affect the digestive tract, causing the peristalsis (a wave-like movement that propels food particles through the digestive track) to move more slowly or even temporarily stop. When this happens, gaining weight is easier and, conversely, losing weight becomes much harder or even impossible. Pica can also lead to surgical emergencies due to an intestinal obstruction as well as nutritional deficiencies or even malnutrition (Blinder & Salama, 2008).

TABLE 11.2 NONFOOD ITEMS FREQUENTLY CONSUMED BY INDIVIDUALS WITH PICA
Dirt
Clay
Paint chips
Plaster
Chalk
Cornstarch
Laundry starch
Baking soda
Coffee grounds
Cigarette ashes
Burnt match heads
Cigarette butts
Feces
Ice
Glue
Hair
Buttons
Paper
Sand
Toothpaste
Soap

PREVAILING PATTERN

The prevalence for pica is difficult to establish because of the different ways it is defined and the reluctance of individuals to admit to abnormal cravings and ingesting nonnutritive substances (Blinder & Salama 2008). Pica is more commonly seen in women and children affecting all ages in these subgroups (Rose, Porcerelli, & Neale, 2000). It is also commonly seen in individuals with neurodevelopmental disorders, particularly autism spectrum disorder and intellectual disabilities (Young, Wilson, Miller, & Hillier, 2008). Prevalence seems to increase with the severity of the diagnosis (APA, 2013).

DIFFERENTIAL ASSESSMENT

Pica is typically defined as the persistent ingestion of nonnutritive substances for a period of at least 1 month and occurs at an age where this behavior is considered to be developmentally inappropriate; for example, eating nonnutritive substances is common for the child who is 18 months to 2 years of age, but not for someone who is much older. Additionally, the individual's eating behavior is not considered to be part of a culturally sanctioned practice. If the eating behavior occurs along with another mental disorder (for example, intellectual disability [intellectual developmental disorder], autism spectrum disorder, or schizophrenia), or a medical condition (such as pregnancy), it must be sufficiently severe enough to warrant clinical attention. The practitioner may add the specifier "in remission" if criteria have been present but currently not met for a sustained period of time (APA, 2013). Going back to the earlier question about tennis champion Djokovic, if we assume that he was overcome with the joy of winning the Wimbledon title, and savored the moment by eating the court's grass this one time, then he would not meet diagnostic criteria for pica.

Because pica can occur in people who have lower-than-normal nutrient levels and poor nutrition (malnutrition), it is helpful to conduct blood tests for levels of iron and zinc. In some situations, bowel obstructions or an intestinal obstruction such as that resulting from a bezoar (a hard, indigestible mass trapped in the gastrointestinal system, usually the stomach), intestinal perforations, or infections resulting from ingesting feces or dirt, or poisoning from ingesting certain substances, for instance lead paint, are evident (APA, 2013). Very often, pica is discovered only after a health problem; for example, someone who suffers from an intestinal perforation, poisoning, and/or parasitic infection. Not surprisingly, these individuals may have severe tooth abrasion, small cracks or notches on the teeth, or surface tooth loss (Johnson, Shynett, Dosch, & Paulson, 2007).

The case of Mary Ellen Creamer illustrates her struggles with pica.

CASE The Case of Mary Ellen Creamer

After she graduated from college with her degree in education, Mary Ellen Creamer, now 24 years old, took a high school teaching job in the town where she grew up. She was doing well, popular with her students, and glad to have her family nearby. Midway through the spring term, Mary Ellen learned that the gym teacher was doing a special program on the feeding and eating disorders. Mary Ellen thought to herself, "You know, I have a story of my own to tell," so she asked if she could participate in the program and share her story. The gym teacher was glad to include one of the teachers who had such great rapport with the students and scheduled Mary Ellen as one of the program's featured speakers.

After she was introduced to the students, she began her presentation with, "I first began eating weird things when I was about 4 years old. I guess you could call them 'non-foodables.' I started with dirt and rocks. At the time, I thought it was pretty normal but I remember my Mom constantly telling me that I should stop." She paused and asked the students, "So what do you think I did?" Most of the students thought her behavior was "weird" and guessed that she stopped. Mary Ellen continued, "No. I refused, and kept it up. I think my Mom referred to this as my 'stubborn period.' Anyway, by the time I went to the first grade it just went away. Or rather I think I just forgot about it."

Mary Ellen thought she would be nervous talking about such a personal experience in a public forum, but when she saw how interested the students were, she knew she had an important story to tell. She silently reflected, "I wonder how many kids out there have had the same experience as I did but are afraid to talk about it. After all, the stuff I ate was nothing to be proud of, and I mostly remember thinking nobody would believe me anyway." She continued her talk, "Well, you guessed it. When I was 6, I started to crave grass. Then it was

CASE The Case of Mary Ellen Creamer (Continued)

dust, sand, and different forms of paper such as candy wrappers or books. I remember that once I ate a whole book! Occasionally I would eat bugs." Mary Ellen could hear a few groans in the audience. She continued, "But it faded. Then it came back with a vengeance when I was around 15."

"I guess you might say by then I was a connoisseur," added Mary Ellen. She heard a few giggles in the audience and added, "I craved mud. I remember when it would rain and I could smell it. Oh how my mouth would water. I'd go outside and scoop up the mud and pile it up in the palms of my hands. Then I would slowly put my hands up to my lips and suck the mud into my mouth. It was so delicious. I couldn't stop. Needless to say, I ate this stuff when I was alone and got really good at hiding it. Lucky for me the cravings would come and go and nothing really bad happened to me. Believe it or not, my health was pretty good all throughout all of this. By the time I got to college, I decided I couldn't go on like this, so I started doing some Internet research and discovered what I had." She looked directly at the students and asked, "Have any of you ever heard of pica? Once I had a name to it, I started experimenting with vitamins and minerals to see if they could help stop the cravings. I learned that this is a disorder that's hard for the doctors to diagnose. I finally had some blood tests and they showed low levels of iron and zinc. Sure signs of not getting the right nutrients. But all is good now. Once you get treated for anemia, the craving disappears. Now I eat healthy foods."

Mary Ellen continued, "The reason I'm sharing my story today is to encourage you to find out whatever your body lacks and give it what it needs." She added with emphasis, "and in healthy ways. Don't starve yourself. Don't overeat. Don't eat nonfood things. Don't eat just one or two things all the time. It's not good for you. The sooner you realize, the better you are going to be."

At the end of her talk, Mary Ellen was surprised by the number of questions from the students. She decided that sharing her story was the right thing to do.

Mary Ellen Creamer's DSM Diagnosis Is as Follows:
Pica, in remission

Competency 7 b

Assessment Summary Pica can occur in childhood, adolescence, or adulthood. As seen in Mary Ellen's story, her persistent eating of nonnutritive and nonfood substances support the symptom picture of pica. It started in childhood when she was 4 years old, reappeared when she was 6 years of age, and her eating pattern returned again in adolescence, clearly exceeding the diagnostic criterion of lasting for at least 1 month (APA, 2013). Although pica is associated with other mental disorders, Mary Ellen's story shows that the disorder can also occur in otherwise normally developing individuals. As clients share the details of their life story, it becomes important for the social worker to organize and interpret data to support (or rule out) the presence of a psychological disorder.

Mary Ellen ingested a variety of nonnutritive substances, beginning with dirt and rocks when she was about 4 years old, and later as an adolescent included ingesting grass, dust, sand, and different forms of paper such as candy wrappers or books. She would occasionally consume bugs. However, Mary Ellen found mud to be "so delicious."

Those with anorexia nervosa may ingest nonnutritive substances, but it is done in an attempt to control appetite. What distinguishes this pattern from the way

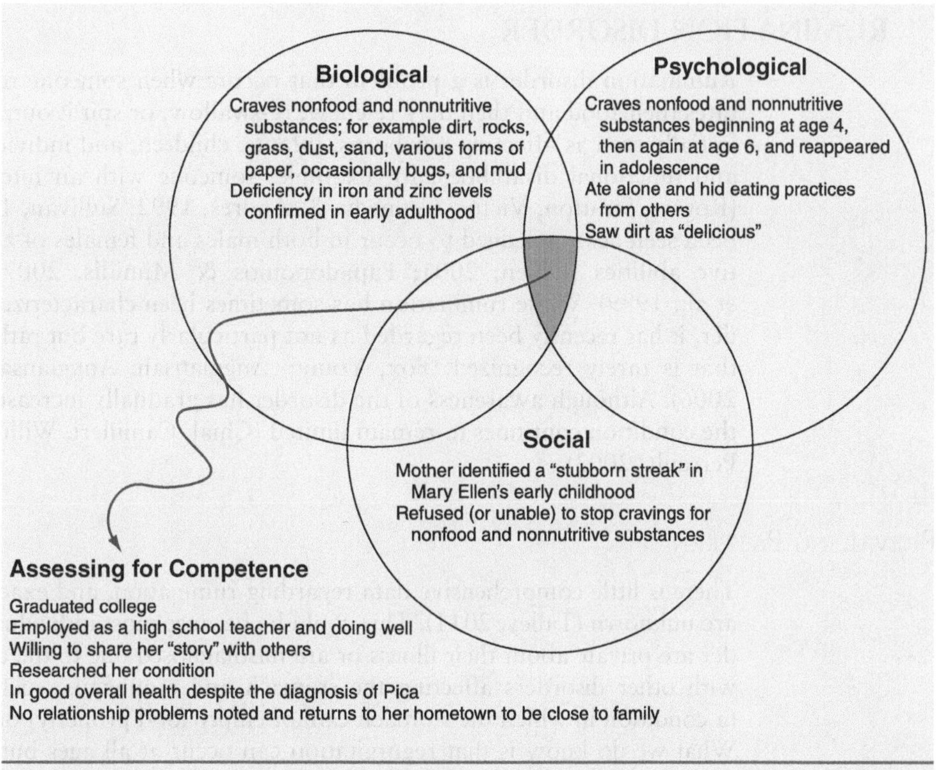

FIGURE 11.1 › PICA
The interactions of the biological, psychological, and social variables in Mary Ellen Creamer's life.

Mary Ellen was eating is that she did not try to control her weight. For those with factitious disorder, the person may ingest foreign objects, but this is done to deceive others about his or her health and to fake physical symptoms. Individuals diagnosed with a personality disorder may deliberately swallow pins, needles, or even knives in an attempt to self-harm. What distinguished Mary Ellen was her persistent pattern of eating nonnutritive substances. Mary Ellen does not describe any medical complications as a result of the substances she ingested over time.

Competency 7 c

The competency-based assessment considers the resources and strengths in a person's struggle with a disorder. Mary Ellen did try to learn more about her diagnosis and began experimenting with vitamins and minerals to help stop her cravings. She was apparently successful. Later blood tests confirmed a deficiency in iron and zinc levels. Although those who struggle with pica tend to be secretive about their eating patterns, Mary Ellen decided she had an important story to tell and shared her experiences by participating in a local high school program about the feeding and eating disorders. By doing so, she was able to reach out to a group most vulnerable to these disorders, adolescents. Hopefully, Mary Ellen helped someone in the audience with a similar struggle. Figure 11.1 illustrates assessing for competence.

We now review rumination disorder.

RUMINATION DISORDER

Rumination disorder is a problem that occurs when someone repeatedly regurgitates their food and then may re-chew, re-swallow, or spit it out. The disorder was initially seen as affecting newborns, infants, children, and individuals with mental and functional disabilities; for example, someone with an intellectual disability (Rogers, Stratton, Victor, Cennedy, & Andres, 1992; Sullivan, 1997). It has since been seen acknowledged to occur in both males and females of all ages and cognitive abilities (Olden, 2001; Papadopoulos & Mimidis, 2007; Rasquin-Weber et al., 1999). While rumination has sometimes been characterized as a rare disorder, it has recently been regarded as not particularly rare but rather as a syndrome that is rarely recognized (Fox, Young, Anggiansah, Anggiansah, & Sanderson, 2006). Although awareness of the disorder has gradually increased, understanding the condition continues to remain limited (Chial, Camilleri, Williams, Litzinger, & Perrault, 2003).

Prevailing Pattern

There is little comprehensive data regarding rumination, and exact prevalence rates are unknown (Talley, 2011). This could be because most individuals with the disorder are private about their illness or are misdiagnosed due to the clinical similarities with other disorders affecting the stomach and esophagus, such as gastroparesis (a condition in which the stomach cannot empty food properly) or bulimia nervosa. What we do know is that regurgitation can occur at all ages but is reported to be higher in people with intellectual disability (APA, 2013; Chial et al., 2003). The typical age of onset for children is from 3 to 12 months of age, while adolescent onset is at about 12 years of age (Olden, 2001).

Differential Assessment

Rumination disorder involves the repetitive regurgitation of undigested food (or rumination) from the stomach back up into the mouth. In the affected person, rumination usually occurs 1 to 2 hours after most meals for at least 1 month. It is considered a chronic condition in that the regurgitation typically happens after every meal (Talley, 2011). Infants may characteristically assume the position of straining and arching their back and, with the head held back, make sucking movements with their tongue. Sometimes the child spits food out, and in other cases it is re-chewed and re-swallowed. Adolescents may try to disguise regurgitation by putting a hand over their mouth or coughing. Still others will avoid eating with others because of their behavior (APA, 2013). While the number and severity of symptoms varies, the repetitive regurgitation of undigested food (rumination) after a meal is always present (Chial et al., 2003).

Symptoms are not the result of some type of medical condition such as an obstruction or gastroesophageal reflux disease (GERD) (a condition in which the stomach contents [food or liquid] leak backwards from the stomach into the esophagus or the tube from the mouth to the stomach) or pyloric stenosis (a problem with a baby's stomach that causes forceful vomiting, which happens when the baby's narrowed [stenosed] pylorus that connects the stomach and the small intestine swells and thickens, keeping food from moving into the intestine). As well, the symptoms do not occur during the course of anorexia nervosa, bulimia nervosa, binge-eating disorder, or avoidant/restrictive intake food disorder. If someone with another mental disorder such as intellectual disability or another neurodevelopmental disorder repeatedly regurgitates food, the symptoms must be severe enough to warrant the additional diagnosis of rumination disorder. The practitioner may add the specifier "in remission" if diagnostic criteria have previously been met but are currently not present for a sustained period of time.

The case of Brad Highers illustrates rumination disorder.

CASE The Case of Brad Highers

The social worker first met Brad Highers when he self-referred to the college counseling center for a "checkup." Brad shares that he had seen a psychologist before and described his experience as helpful. This is his first year in college and living away from home. He's worried about making the adjustment, given his "problem," and thought the social worker would be the best person to talk with about his concerns.

Brad begins, "You see, I have this problem that that most folks don't understand so I thought you would be the best person to talk to." He looks down at his hands and resumes, "It's the way I eat. Bottom line is that since I've been here I started eating alone because of my problem. Who knew? I always loved going out with my friends but now I'm making excuses because of my problem. Everything else in my life is going fine, so you might wonder why such a big deal about food."

Brad continues, "I've had this thing for as long as I can remember but at long last I finally have a diagnosis. You see, it's a condition called rumination disorder but it's not very well understood yet. Anyway, I've had this thing for as long as I can remember and it took a couple of years for the doctors to finally diagnose me. I'm 19 now and, like I said, this is my first year in college. Never been away from home, either. I sure hope I can make it through. My grades are okay but things in the social department are not so great."

The social worker encouraged him to continue. He said, "My eating problem developed very slowly but right now it's starting to act up again. When it first started, I would unexpectedly spit up food. Seemed like it would happen only if I ate something very rich or very heavy. It happened every now and then. Then it progressed to almost every time I eat. It's not like I was puking over the toilet or anything like that. In fact, it wasn't unpleasant at all, and what came up tasted normal. I remember I worried that this couldn't be good for my teeth. Then, when the food filled my mouth it tasted just like the food I ate so I just swallowed hard and sent it back down. I tried to stop it, but it didn't work. Seems it was not a matter of willpower. It just happened automatically. Then it became an everyday struggle just to eat. It would also happen if I burped, but in smaller amounts. I literally regurgitated every time I ate anything or drank anything. I couldn't predict when it would happen, but I could expect that it would happen. Sometimes I had this feeling that the food was stuck in my esophagus and then it would come right back up into my mouth. Other times I had absolutely no problems swallowing but, predictably, it would eventually come back up. It could take up to a minute or an hour after eating. Never had any heartburn, stomach pain, nausea, or anything like that."

Brad added, "Then I started to pay attention to what I was eating and found that there are some foods that agree with me, or mostly agree with me. I rarely have trouble with cereal, yogurt, or oatmeal." Brad added that as a youngster he was considered a picky eater, but he somehow managed until his symptoms worsened his last year of high school and resumed now that he is in college.

He continued, "The doctors I saw were always really nice and helpful. I did tests for upper-GI, endoscopy." Brad paused and then resumed, "You know, where they take a good look at your stomach,

CASE THE CASE OF BRAD HIGHERS (CONTINUED)

and everything came out fine. I tried taking antacids like Mylanta, Tums, and Tagament, but no relief. Then I thought some of those waste enhancers they sell at the gym would work, so I started with Crystal Light then switched to Vitamin Water. No success there either. Seems they would work for a while, but then it all came back. Finally, my regular doctor who's known me for just about all my life suggested to my parents that they take me to one of those big medical clinics that have doctors who specialize in what I have. In the end, I got some answers. They were real thorough. First, the docs asked me and my parents a lot of questions about my medical history. They asked a lot of questions about my symptoms, too. Then they did a complete physical exam."

Brad stopped and seemed a little self-conscious. He turned to the social worker and said, "I'm sorry. Am I boring you with all these details? It's just that after struggling for so long I was so glad to finally get some answers." The social worker responded, "No, you're not boring me. It sounds like you've been through a lot and for quite some time, too." (Brad nodded in agreement.) "As a matter of fact, I would like your permission to contact your doctors for the details, if that's okay with you." Brad agreed, and the social worker made a mental note to be sure to ask Brad sign the necessary consent forms before the interview ended. Brad continued, "Well to make a long story short, the clinic doctors watched me eat and then took more tests. I'm sure the names of those tests will be in my medical report, but basically they looked at my esophagus again, another look at my stomach, the upper part of my small intestine, and afterwards they tested the muscles involved in digestion and gastric emptying. No ulcers on my esophagus or anything like that. Finally I had some answers and I was referred to a psychologist for behavior therapy. At last! There was something I could do about and it worked. He taught me breathing techniques ... from the diaphragm ... that prevent abdominal contractions and so I don't regurgitate. Finally ... success! But that's where you come in."

Brad relates, "When you're at the cafeteria it's pretty hard when you eat like I do, so I pretty much sit by myself. Sometimes I feel kinda awkward doing those breathing exercises and I think some of the other students are starting to wonder what's going on with me. I haven't told anybody about my eating problems because it's so embarrassing. Around here, the guys I've made friends with like to go out for a beer after a long week of studying. Me? Forget about anything carbonated. Soon as I take a sip, I'm spitting up foam. Everybody's on a budget, so food like hot dogs is a big thing. Highly processed foods will do me in. I'll spit them up immediately. I have to pay attention to what I eat. When I eat real slow and concentrate on my breathing exercises after each bite, I can manage to keep things down. But what with having a mental disorder and all, I'm starting to feel like I was some sort of freak." He added, "That's where you come in. Do you have any suggestions for me?"

As the social worker listened to Brad, she was impressed by his insight, perseverance over the years, and his ability to deal with a disorder that affects an everyday activity that most people take for granted—eating.

BRAD HIGHERS'S DSM DIAGNOSIS IS AS FOLLOWS:

Rumination disorder

Competency 7 b

ASSESSMENT SUMMARY Although he refers to himself as a "picky eater" in childhood, the onset of Brad's rumination symptoms are unclear. From his story, the repeated regurgitation of food that he would re-swallow seemed to start when he was in high school. Brad had some unspecified medical tests and tried a number of remedies on his own (for example, GERD-supporting medications such as Mylanta, Tums, Tagament, and waste enhancers such as Crystal Light and Vitamin Water) but without success. He also began to pay careful attention to the kinds of foods that seemed to exacerbate

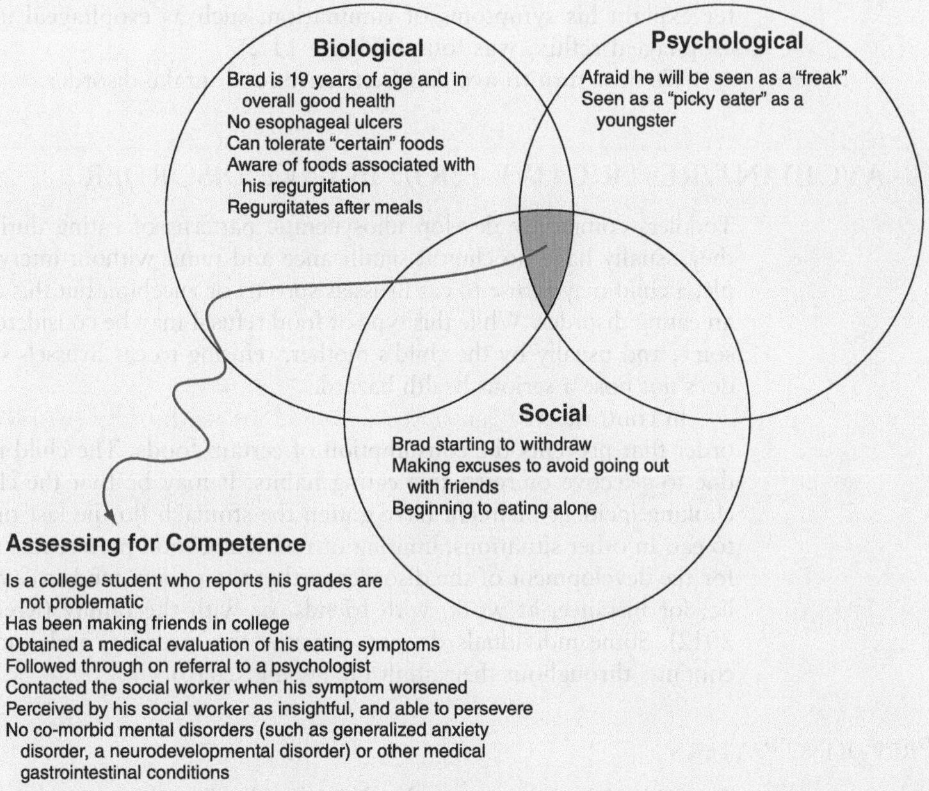

Biological

Brad is 19 years of age and in overall good health
No esophageal ulcers
Can tolerate "certain" foods
Aware of foods associated with his regurgitation
Regurgitates after meals

Psychological

Afraid he will be seen as a "freak"
Seen as a "picky eater" as a youngster

Social

Brad starting to withdraw
Making excuses to avoid going out with friends
Beginning to eating alone

Assessing for Competence

Is a college student who reports his grades are not problematic
Has been making friends in college
Obtained a medical evaluation of his eating symptoms
Followed through on referral to a psychologist
Contacted the social worker when his symptom worsened
Perceived by his social worker as insightful, and able to persevere
No co-morbid mental disorders (such as generalized anxiety disorder, a neurodevelopmental disorder) or other medical gastrointestinal conditions

FIGURE 11.2 › RUMINATION DISORDER
The interactions of the biological, psychological, and social variables in Brad Highers's life.

his symptoms. Still, within a few minutes to about an hour after eating, Brad would, as he sees it, involuntarily and automatically regurgitate food, typically on a daily basis. When clients like Brad are unclear about the onset of symptoms of a disorder, the social worker's knowledge about the different theories of human behavior and the influence of the social environment is underscored.

There were no other medical conditions found to support Brad's symptom picture. Additionally, he also did not show signs of another mental disorder, such as bulimia. In Brad's own words, "It's not like I was puking over the toilet or anything like that."

Competency 8 c

There are a number of competencies seen in Brad's struggle with rumination disorder. Despite struggling since high school, Brad was somehow able to manage. However, his symptoms were starting to affect his adjustment to college and were the central focus of his decision to see the social worker at the college counseling center. Brad's symptom picture of rumination disorder was eventually confirmed by a medical evaluation. According to Brad, this medical evaluation consisted of a medical history, observations of his eating behavior, and what was described as a detailed series of medical tests. With Brad's consent, the social worker plans to obtain the full report. No other medical condition that could better explain his symptoms of rumination, such as esophageal ulcers or a gastroesophageal reflux, was found (Figure 11.2).

We now turn to avoidant/restrictive food intake disorder.

AVOIDANT/RESTRICTIVE FOOD INTAKE DISORDER

Toddlers commonly develop idiosyncratic patterns of eating during childhood, but they usually have no clinical significance and remit without intervention. For example, a child may refuse to eat Brussels sprouts or zucchini, but this does not constitute an eating disorder. While this type of food refusal may be considered manipulative by some, and usually by the child's mother, refusing to eat Brussels sprouts or zucchini does not pose a serious health hazard.

In contrast, avoidant/restrictive food intake disorder (ARFID) is an eating disorder that prevents the consumption of certain foods. The child is severely harmed due to selective or restrictive eating habits. It may be that the child experienced a choking incident or might have gotten the stomach flu the last time he or she tried to eat. In other situations, limiting or restricting food preferences may be the reason for the development of the disorder in that the person tends to avoid eating in public; for instance, at work, with friends, or with the family (Kreipe & Palomkaki, 2012). Some individuals do not outgrow the disorder, and symptoms of ARFID continue throughout their adult life (Wang, 2010).

PREVAILING PATTERN

The DSM-5 has reconceptualized the avoidant/restrictive food intake disorder from the prior DSM-IV disorder of "feeding disorder of infancy and early childhood," a diagnostic category that was very rarely used (APA, 2013). As a consequence, there is almost no information on the characteristics of those who have it.

However, Fisher and colleagues (2014) studied those with avoidant/restrictive food intake disorder and found that these individuals are demographically and clinically different from those with other restrictive eating disorders such as anorexia nervosa or bulimia nervosa. The authors found that they are more likely to be male, be picky (or selective) eaters since early childhood, experience gastrointestinal symptoms, have a history of vomiting/choking, and have food allergies.

DIFFERENTIAL ASSESSMENT

The first critical element in the DSM-5 definition of ARFID is feeding or eating disturbances, which may include but are not limited to: the decreased interest toward food or eating in general; avoidance, which is associated with the sensory characteristics of food; and increased concern toward the various consequences or disadvantages of eating, manifested by the repeated failure or inability to meet the ideal energy and nutritional requirement and needs. This is related to one or several of the following:

- Considerable amount of weight loss (which may also be associated with the failure to gain weight, or irregular growth and weight in the case of children).

- Presence of different nutritional deficiencies in the person.
- Enteral feeding dependency (tube feeding) or oral nutritional supplements.
- Interference or disturbance of psychosocial functioning.

Three additional criteria in the DSM-5 are intended to exclude individuals who have a clinically significant problem that is better described in some other way. For example, if the person's nutritional problems are better explained by the lack of available food or a cultural practice (for instance, religious fasting), or if the person has substantial and irrational dissatisfaction with body shape or weight (as seen in anorexia nervosa or bulimia nervosa), or if the clinical problem is better explained by an existing medical condition or another mental disorder. The practitioner can further specify the diagnosis of ARFID as in remission when the criteria have previously been met but have not currently been met for a sustained period of time.

To illustrate avoidant/restrictive food intake disorder, the following summarizes the experiences of Amber Scott, who appeared on the popular television show *20/20* on February 7, 2014. The segment was entitled "My Strange Affliction," and highlights her struggles with ARFID. The details of Amber's psychosocial history were not featured, so you will not find a review of the interactions of the biological, psychological, and social variables in her life.

CASE The Case of Amber Scott

Amber Scott, a young single mother in her early 30s with an 11-year-old daughter, eats only French fries. Occasionally she will have pizza or pasta. The French fries must be skinless, hand-cut, and fried in canola oil with a touch of salt. She does not eat fish, vegetables, or any proteins, adding, "I don't know why." Beverages are limited to milk, soda, and red wine. Despite her restrictive diet, she reports being in good health, and the program shows a young woman who appears to be in good physical shape. When asked about her diet, Amber responds, "I've heard it all. I've heard I am going to have a heart attack any day now. I've heard I wouldn't make to age 40." She went on to say that she has faced anger and scorn from people who think her eating pattern is unhealthy and she is just being stubborn. Amber adds that she does not date because she is afraid of what her date might think of her.

During the program, Amber was asked to eat something outside of her customary diet, white rice. As the plate was placed before her and she tentatively filled her fork with a few grains of rice, the show clearly displays Amber's distress. Tears roll down her cheeks, and after 7 minutes, she manages to eat a few grains. Amber nearly vomited at the thought of eating the rice and shared that she would not try it again. She remembers once trying shredded carrots and comments that she could feel every shard of carrot in her mouth. Amber remembers that her eating problems started during her childhood. She describes facing a plate of peas and just could not eat them. Her mother was interviewed and remembered that she did not want to force her daughter. Instead, she made French fries, which subsequently became the staple for all of Amber's meals. Amber added during the interview, "It's a very old-fashioned kind of mentality to tell your children you'll eat what I made or you'll starve." Amber's daughter shows no signs of restrictive/avoidant eating.

A few years ago Amber learned that she is not the only one affected with ARFID and now has a podcast that provides the forum to share experiences with other adults characterized as "picky eaters."

AMBER SCOTT'S DSM DIAGNOSIS IS AS FOLLOWS:

Avoidant/restrictive food intake disorder

ASSESSMENT SUMMARY The course of illness for those with ARFID is, at this time, relatively unknown (Mascola, Bryson, & Agras, 2010). As seen in Amber's situation, her long-standing avoidance of most foods due to their sensory characteristics lasted into adulthood. At the outset, she remembers a childhood encounter with a plate of peas and refusing to eat them. In response, her mother fixed a plate of French fries for her daughter that ultimately became the mainstay of Amber's diet. She once tried eating carrots and describes feeling every fragment of carrot in her mouth. In some cases, individuals will exclude whole food groups from their diet, and Amber does not eat fish, vegetables, or foods with proteins. Others may exclude foods based on color, temperature, and/or texture.

Competency 7 b

Amber's experiences provide an added dimension to the term "picky eater." At one point in the show, Amber was asked to try what was a new food for her, white rice, and the viewer can see her anxiety and panic. Although Amber does not show further symptoms to support another diagnosis, the presence of other disorders can be risk factors for ARFID, such as the anxiety disorders, obsessive-compulsive disorder, and the neurodevelopmental disorders of attention-deficit/hyperactivity disorder, autism spectrum disorder, and intellectual disability (intellectual developmental disorder) (APA, 2013; Timimi, Douglas, & Tsiftsopolou, 1997). Other disorders with symptoms of a restricted food intake can include major depressive disorder, schizophrenia, and factitious disorder (or factitious disorder imposed on another). However, the central focus for Amber was her eating habits that caused clinical impairment for her.

Competency 8 c

Additionally, Amber appeared to be of a normal weight for her size and there was no mention of concerns about body weight or shape, thus ruling out a consideration of anorexia nervosa. According to Nicholls, Christie, Randall, and Lask (2001), there are no outward appearances associated with ARFID. Similarly, individuals with a history of gastrointestinal conditions, as gastroesophageal reflux, may develop ARFID. Although she nearly vomited at the thought of eating rice, Amber's symptom picture did not reflect any concurrent medical condition and centered on her painful emotional and physical reactions to certain foods. In fact, Amber mentioned that she is in good overall health despite her restricted diet of French fries. Her story shows no evidence of any neurological or neuromuscular or congenital disorders that may cause eating problems for her, such as tongue protrusion or unsafe swallowing. Amber's diagnosis underscores the importance of consulting with medical professionals to ascertain a comprehensive understanding of a person's symptom picture.

Competency 7 c

Amber highlighted the anger and scorn she faces from people who think she is unhealthy and just a stubborn "picky eater." She does not date because she's afraid of what others may think of her. Despite her struggles, Amber does not indicate any desire to change her eating behaviors. Her competence in struggling with such an unknown and poorly understood disorder is highlighted in her efforts to start a podcast aimed at sharing difficult eating experiences with other adults.

The next section examines anorexia nervosa.

ANOREXIA NERVOSA

The most striking feature of anorexia is the marked distortion in the way the individuals experience their body size and shape. Often they have no concept of how they appear to others and distort what they see in the mirror; that is, even though they are emaciated, they often see themselves as fat and express concerns about gaining weight. The author recalls a conversation with a client diagnosed with anorexia nervosa; she remarked, "Every time I looked in the mirror I hated my body. My reflection only exposed my imperfections." This client would elaborate her fears of developing a double chin and seeing fat cells "just about everywhere" despite her gaunt, wasted appearance. These individuals are generally dissatisfied with their weight. Losing weight every day and for months on end is seen as satisfactory. Although the person is usually hungry and preoccupied with thoughts of food, they will not eat (or eat very little) because of their relentless obsession to be thinner.

Looking to causal factors associated with anorexia nervosa, a woman's perception regarding ideal body size is greatly influenced by television commercials, magazines, and/or beauty pageants. The media promotes being thin as the ideal standard for beauty, and many impressionable young women (and men) hold unreasonable expectations about how thin they should be in order to be attractive (Andrist, 2003).

Competency 7 c

Work has been done to prevent the prevalence of the disordered eating behaviors, unhealthy dieting practices, and distorted body image seen in anorexia nervosa, but with mixed success (Stice, Shaw, & Marti, 2007). In general, peer pressure, media influence, and the perception that extreme dieting strategies are harmless motivate disordered eating behaviors. These realities underscore the importance of looking at the whole person and exploring symptoms in their social context. The competency-based assessment model organizes the social worker's consideration of the multiple social and environmental factors found in a person's life.

By the time individuals with anorexia nervosa come to the social worker's attention, they usually weigh even less than the 15 percent below what is considered a healthy weight. These individuals often weigh between 25 and 30 percent below their normal weight. Unfortunately, there is no clear boundary between the "thinness" of anorexia nervosa and that of an individual who is considered naturally slender. Here, too, the social worker's careful evaluation of the multiple influences in a person's life is essential when considering an eating disorder, and underscores the person/environment perspective. Many individuals are naturally thin, and others diet to remain slim, while still others are in occupations where low body weight is mandated, such as a jockey, fashion model, or ballet dancer (Tiggerman & Slater, 2001). The difference between someone who is of low weight and someone with anorexia nervosa revolves around intrapersonal factors, whereby the individual refuses to maintain a normal body weight and is extremely fearful of becoming fat.

Competency 7 b

As a part of the competency-based assessment, the practitioner might explore biological issues by asking about the individual's target weight; dieting, nutritional, or exercise patterns; and use of laxatives. Nonverbal communication should be observed carefully by the practitioner when asking about a client's eating habits—some individuals may withhold information or minimize the extent of their disturbed eating behaviors. Using a courteous but direct approach, the practitioner

TABLE 11.3	QUESTIONS TO ASK TO FURTHER EXPLORE ANOREXIA NERVOSA

Have people (either friends or others) ever given you a hard time about being too thin or losing too much weight?

Have you ever weighed a lot less than others thought you should weigh?

If the answer is yes to either question, follow with:

- How old were you when this first happened?
- Is this still true?
- What was the lowest amount you have ever weighed?
- What do you weigh right now? How do you feel about that?
- What do you think about your body size and shape?
- What do you think about how much you weigh?
- Are you on a diet right now?
- Do you ever feel the urge to binge or purge? What happens when you do?
- How often do you diet?
- Have either you or anyone in your family ever had a history of anorexia, bulimia, binge- eating, or obesity?

should ask questions, highlighted on Table 11.3, aimed at specifically exploring the person's eating patterns, history, and attitudes toward food.

In general, most individuals with an eating disorder do not exhibit a prodromal phase—that is, they are usually characterized as being normal and healthy prior to the actual onset of the eating disorder. Occasionally, going off to college, experiencing a death in the family, or some other major life cycle event will immediately precede the onset. At other times, the precipitating factor may be so integrated into a "decision to begin dieting" that the onset seems almost immaterial. For example, in the following case discussion, Joy Walker wants to lose weight so she can fit into her prom dress. Joy begins to diet simply by reducing her total daily food intake and only later begins to restrict all high-calorie foods. Eventually, her eating pattern is so severely limited, and Joy ingests very few foods. She dreaded being fat, but her weight loss did not alleviate this fear. In addition, she underestimates the extent of her thinness—she believes she is "fat and ugly"—when in reality, she appears skeletal to her family and friends.

In essence, individuals with anorexia nervosa have two faulty perceptions regarding their own body: (1) the way they view their body—or body image distortion (BID), and (2) body image concerns involving a delusional misperception, referred to as "body dysmorphophobia." The key feature in each of these views is the misperception of body size and shape. Body image or the overinvestment in the way one appears is primarily a perceptual phenomenon (Grabe & Hyde, 2006). Those with body dissatisfaction are more than just concerned about their weight (Thompson & van den Berg, 2002).

PREVAILING PATTERN

The 12-month prevalence rates for the presence of anorexia nervosa in young females is approximately 0.4 percent (APA, 2013). It is more common in females, with a female-to-male ratio of 10:1. Unfortunately, we know relatively less about why the eating disorders are not as prevalent in men. However, some interesting findings have emerged. For instance, the eating disorders are on the rise among male athletes, especially where a lean appearance may lead to a competitive advantage such as wrestling, rowing, boxing, and possibly ski jumping (Glazer, 2008; Sudi et al., 2004).

DIFFERENTIAL ASSESSMENT

Individuals with eating disorders manifest abnormal attitudes about their body shape and maladaptive attempts to control their body weight. The symptoms that distinguish anorexia nervosa include:

- Restricting one's energy intake, leading to a significantly low body weight considering one's age, sex, developmental course, physical health, and life circumstances. The DSM defines significantly low body weight as weight that is less than minimally normal or, in the case of children and adolescents, less than that minimally expected (e.g., a woman who should weigh 100 pounds by age and height but weighs less than 85 pounds) (APA, 2013). You will notice that the DSM-5 no longer includes the word "refusal" in terms of weight maintenance seen in earlier editions of the manual and, instead, focuses on "restriction" of calorie intake.
- Desperately fearful of gaining weight or becoming "fat," even though already severely underweight.
- Disturbance in the perception of body weight or body shape, or denial that present low weight is seriously dangerous.

Competency 7 b

Anorexia nervosa is divided into two subtypes based on the method used to limit calorie intake. They are referred to as the restricting type and the binge-eating/purging type, and have significantly different clinical presentations and characteristics. Differentiating between these subtypes highlights the importance of carefully collecting and organizing data to ascertain the applicable symptom picture.

During an episode of the restricting type of anorexia nervosa, the individual severely limits caloric intake (for at least the past 3 months), but does not regularly engage in binge eating or purging behavior. These individuals are described as highly controlled, rigid, and obsessive. Various techniques are used to help enhance control over food intake; for example, the person might eat very slowly, make food less attractive, or garnish food with unappetizing spices. She or he can also be found to diet, fast, and or excessively exercise to lose weight. Additionally, the person often feels a great deal of satisfaction about controlling or regulating calorie intake.

Individuals with the binge eating/purging type of anorexia nervosa regularly engage (minimally for at least the past 3 months) in weight control behaviors such as self-induced vomiting and/or misuse of laxatives, enemas, or diuretics. The person alternates between periods of perfectionism (with rigid control) and impulsive binge-eating behavior (APA, 2013). Binge eating is defined as an episode in which the individual eats "out of control" and is unable to resist the temptation to consume certain foods.

A binge is seen as ingesting a much larger amount of food than most people would eat under similar circumstances in a limited period of time (Kearney & Trull,

2012). Although there can be a wide variation in the quantity of calories ingested, a very large amount of food is consumed during a binge episode. Some binges occur in time-limited situations, such as over the lunch hour; while others can take up most of the day, where the individual eats small amounts of food almost continuously. The latter is sometimes referred to as grazing. On the average, binge episodes last about two hours. Binge eating is usually performed in private because the individual does not want to be discovered or interrupted.

Binge episodes should be distinguished from those overeating incidents that occur during special occasions such as birthday celebrations or holiday events. Perhaps the most notable culturally sanctioned time for overeating for Americans is the Thanksgiving holiday dinner. How many of us have indulged in that plate full of turkey and all the fixings?

Binge eating is often followed by depressive moods, feelings of guilt, and self-deprecating thoughts. However, when overeating is sanctioned (along with little or no long-lasting guilt for eating a large meal), the person does not have the sense of "losing control," and the individual perceives the amount of food eaten to more closely resemble a normal meal rather than the quantity of food consumed during a binge episode.

Purging is defined as any activity aimed at ameliorating the perceived negative effects of a binge on body shape and weight. This includes self-induced purging (vomiting); the misuse of laxatives, enemas, or diuretics; and/or excessive exercise. When exercise and diet are used for weight loss rather than to counteract the effects of a particular episode of excessive bingeing, they should be regarded as compensatory behaviors—but with eating disorders, the individual continues to use weight loss techniques or purging in the desperate hope that they will somehow "work." Figure 11.3 illustrates the cycle of anorexia nervosa.

It is not uncommon for individuals with anorexia nervosa to cross over between the two subtypes over the longer term of the illness, and therefore the social work practitioner should describe the current symptom picture rather than delineate the overall progression. The practitioner also specifies if the individual is in "partial remission"; that is, when full criteria for the diagnosis have previously been met, but at this point in time, low body weight has not been met for a prolonged period. However, the individual still has the intense fear of gaining weight that hinders gaining weight or continues to see her- or himself as "fat." The specifier "in full remission" is assigned when none of the diagnostic criteria have been met for an extended period of time.

Current severity is also considered and calculated by body mass index (BMI) (a measure of one's weight calculated in kilograms in relationship to height calculated in meters) and specified as mild, moderate, severe, or extreme. The level of severity based on the BMI is:

- Mild—BMI greater than or equal to 17 kg/m.
- Moderate—BMI 16 to16.99 kg/m.
- Severe—BMI 15 to 15.99 kg/m.
- Extreme—BMI less than 15 kg/m.

For example, let's take a 20-year-old woman who is 5 feet 7 inches tall and weighs 140 pounds. Her BMI would be 21.9, which is considered within the

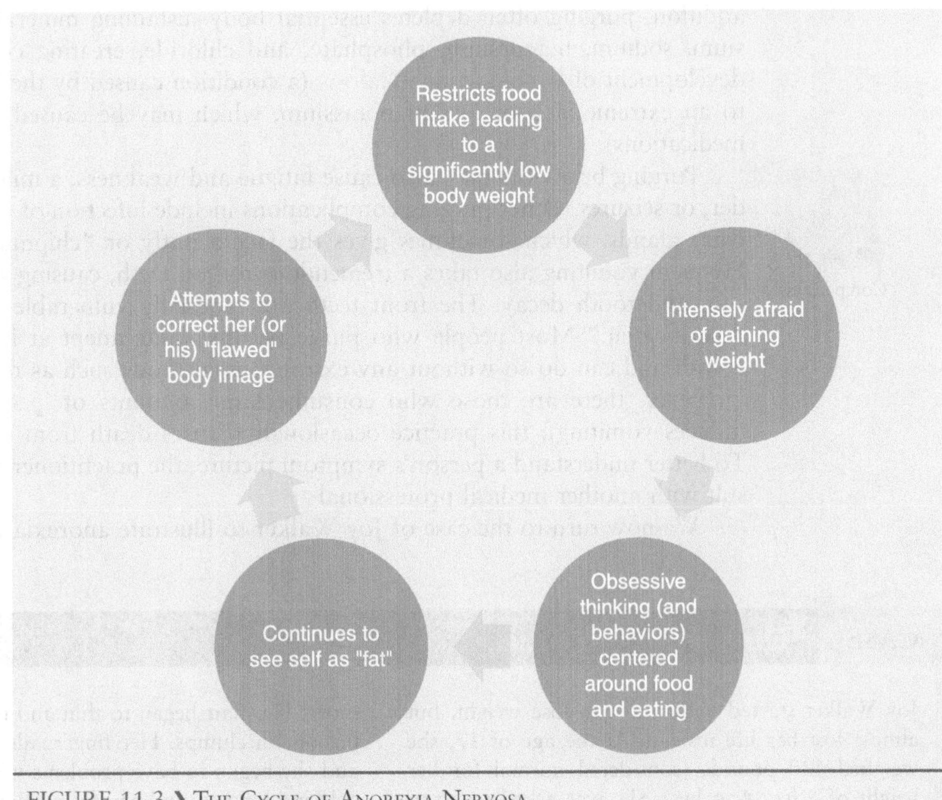

FIGURE 11.3 › THE CYCLE OF ANOREXIA NERVOSA

healthy range. Let's assume she restricts her food intake and loses roughly 22 percent of her body weight, or 31 pounds. She now weighs 109 pounds. Her BMI of would calculate as 17.1, which falls within the DSM-5 severity rating of "mild."

Considering that children and adolescents grow at different rates, a BMI-for-age percentile is a more useful measure to calculate BMI. However, the practitioner is cautioned against solely using numerical guidelines and should also take into account the child's body build, weight history, and the presence of any physiological disturbances (APA, 2013).

Competency 6 a

The biological component, an integral part of the competency-based assessment, helps serve as an objective physical index of the degree of food restriction. One of the unfortunate aspects of this eating disorder is that it is entirely possible for an individual to starve to death in the midst of plenty. There are a number of additional medical complications associated with the starvation that characterizes the advanced state of anorexia, including osteoporosis (caused by loss of calcium from the bones), constipation, and swollen joints (Rome & Ammerman, 2003). When purging behaviors are suspected, the practitioner should be mindful of a number of cardiovascular or renal problems that may be present, including hypotension (chronically low blood pressure); bradycardia (slow heartbeat); cardiac arrhythmia (irregular heartbeat); and an increased risk of kidney failure. In addition, purging often depletes essential body-sustaining minerals such as potassium, sodium, magnesium, phosphate, and chloride, creating concern about the development of hypokalemic alkalosis (a condition caused by the kidneys' reaction to an extreme lack or loss of potassium, which may be caused by some diuretic medications).

Competency 8 c

Purging behaviors may also cause fatigue and weakness, a mild cognitive disorder, or seizures. Other purging complications include infection of the parotid or salivary glands, which sometimes gives the face a puffy or "chipmunk" appearance. Frequent vomiting also takes a tremendous toll on teeth, causing severe dental erosion and tooth decay. The front teeth are especially vulnerable and may appear "moth-eaten." Most people who purge become quite adept at inducing vomiting at will and can do so without any extraneous methods such as the use of emetics. However, there are those who consume large amounts of ipecac (solution that induces vomiting); this practice occasionally causes death from overdose toxicity. To better understand a person's symptom picture, the practitioner may elect to consult with another medical professional

We now turn to the case of Joy Walker to illustrate anorexia nervosa.

CASE The Case of Joy Walker

Joy Walker started with a diet to lose weight, but almost lost her life instead. At the age of 17, she weighed 130 pounds (considered normal for her height of 5 feet 4 inches). She was asked to go to the senior prom by her boyfriend, Kenneth, but he warned her in advance, "You'd better lose some weight, because I don't want to be seen dancing with a fat blimp."

Joy made up her mind to lose some weight and started by skipping breakfast. A few days later, she stopped eating lunch. Dinner time with her family became problematic, because she did not eat anything. She was served regular portions, but ended up moving the food around on her plate to make it appear she was eating. She told her parents that she ate "a huge lunch" so she was not very hungry.

Most of the time, Joy secretly dropped food to the family dog, who conveniently positioned himself under the table. Other times, she would hide food in her pockets and later throw it away. Within a month, Joy lost almost 30 pounds. She began to receive a lot of positive attention, especially from her boyfriend, and compliments on how nice she looked. By now her daily food intake included eating some lettuce leaves or an apple, but nothing more. Her hair began to thin and then started falling out in clumps. Her fingernails started to split, and she began to have problems with constipation, cold intolerance, and painful swelling of her fingers, knees, and elbows.

After 5 months of dieting, Joy weighed 85 pounds. She had gone from a size nine to a size zero. Her friends started telling her that she looked "like a skeleton" and was "way too thin." Joy's response was, "I just want to lose a few more pounds because my thighs are way too fat, and my stomach pouches out too much." She added, "I'm so disgusting." Joy hadn't had a normal menstrual period for the past 3 months, which pleased her.

While dancing with Kenneth at the senior prom, Joy fainted. She was taken by ambulance to a nearby emergency room, where the attending physician expressed shock at Joy's physical condition and state of emaciation. The doctor immediately contacted Joy's parents and explained that their daughter was in serious trouble. Joy was admitted to the hospital and diagnosed with anorexia nervosa. The hospital social worker spoke to Joy and referred her and her family to an eating disorder clinic.

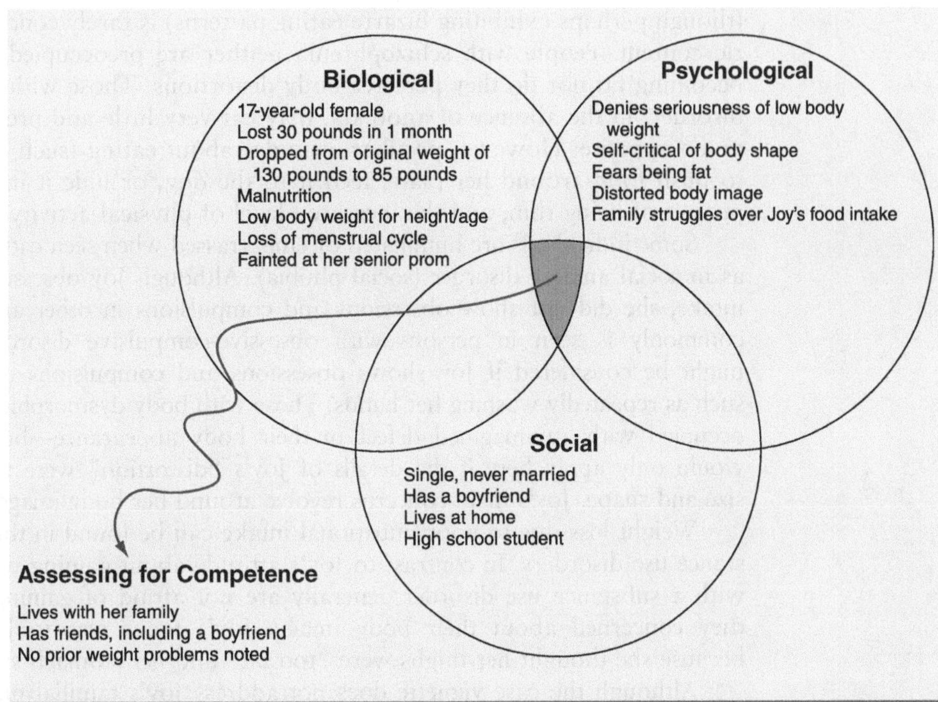

FIGURE 11.4 › Anorexia Nervosa
The interactions of the biological, psychological, and social variables in Joy Walker's life.

Joy Walker's DSM Diagnosis Is as Follows:
Anorexia nervosa, restricting type, extreme

Competency 7 b

Assessment Summary The differential assessment of anorexia nervosa is complicated by Joy's denial of symptoms and her unwillingness to seek help. In addition, she has been extremely secretive about her eating patterns and methods of weight control. Joy's caloric intake, consisting of an apple or lettuce leaves, is typical of someone with anorexia nervosa. Even though Joy is 35 percent underweight, she continues to express unrealistic concerns about being fat. She has a distorted view of her body (also characteristic of those with anorexia nervosa), seeing her thighs as too fat and her stomach as bulging.

Competency 8 c

A referral to a physician is appropriate and critical in determining whether or not there are other processes going on that can better account for the weight loss; for example, hyperthyroidism, diabetes mellitus, Crohn's disease, acquired immunodeficiency syndrome (AIDS), neoplasms, or tuberculosis. The important distinction between the eating disorder illustrated in the Joy Walker vignette versus a general medical condition is that individuals with general medical conditions usually do not have a distorted body image (DBI), or the desire for further weight loss.

Schizophrenia might look very similar to anorexia, especially if the person refuses to eat. However, upon closer examination, the person with schizophrenia (though perhaps exhibiting bizarre eating patterns) is rarely concerned about caloric content. People with schizophrenia neither are preoccupied with the fear of becoming fat nor do they perceive body distortions. Those with major depressive disorder, in the absence of anorexia, may eat very little and profess to have little or no appetite. However, peculiar attitudes about eating (such as Joy's tendency to push food around her plate, feed it to the dog, or hide it in her pockets; the pursuit of being thin; and the increased level of physical activity) are absent.

Some individuals are humiliated or embarrassed when seen eating food in public, as in social anxiety disorder (social phobia). Although Joy obsessed about her food intake, she did not show obsessions and compulsions in other areas of her life as commonly is seen in persons with obsessive-compulsive disorder (OCD). OCD might be considered if Joy shows obsessions and compulsions unrelated to food, such as repeatedly washing her hands. Those with body dysmorphic disorder are preoccupied with an imagined defect in their body appearance—but this assessment would only apply here if the details of Joy's "distortion" were unrelated to body size and shape. Joy's main concerns revolve around her body image.

Weight loss due to poor nutritional intake can be found in those with the substance use disorders. In contrast to Joy's attitude about gaining weight, individuals with a substance use disorder generally are not afraid of gaining weight nor are they concerned about their body image. Joy's focus was to lose more weight because she thought her thighs were "too fat" and her stomach sticks out.

Competency 7 b

Although the case vignette does not address Joy's familial picture and related interpersonal processes, the competency-based assessment looks at the full range of factors affecting Joy's life, how she copes with life challenges, and the supports available to her. From this perspective, the person is not the problem, but the problem is the problem. What is known from her case story is that Joy lives at home with her family who are concerned about her, she has many friends, and she has not experienced prior eating difficulties (Figure 11.4).

Competency 2 a

Joy Walker's story highlights the importance of considering culture-related issues when assessing for anorexia. For example, when looking to dissatisfaction with one's body, African American adolescent girls are found to have fewer concerns about their weight and a more positive self-image compared to Caucasian adolescent girls (Celio, Zabinski, & Wilfley, 2002). This could be related to the cultural norm where American women are socialized to be more independent and self-reliant than other women of color, thus making the latter less susceptible to the thin ideal promoted by popular media (Grabe & Hyde, 2006). These influences underscore the importance of applying a competency-based assessment that thoroughly examines all aspects of an individual's life. Some of the broad social factors that can potentially influence the eating disorders include a cultural emphasis on the desirability of being thin; and concerns with attractiveness, self-concept, body concept, and sexuality. The practitioner's competency-based assessment also carefully evaluates the possible coexistence of other mental disorders (e.g., anxiety, affective, or personality disorders).

The course and outcome of anorexia nervosa varies; some individuals recover after a single episode, whereas others continue to vacillate between trying to restore their normal weight and/or relapsing. As seen in Joy's situation, she is steadfast in her commitment to losing weight. Those who struggle with a fluctuating pattern may require hospitalization to reinstate their weight and address fluid and electrolyte imbalances. Anorexia nervosa is considered a potentially fatal disease, with a mortality rate that ranges somewhere between 5 and 10 percent (Keel et al., 2003; Zipfel, Lowe, Deter, & Herzog, 2000). The mortality rate from the eating disorders, and particularly anorexia, is the highest of any psychological disorder (Vitiello & Lederhendler, 2000). The cause of death is usually associated with starvation, suicide, infection, or electrolyte imbalance. Joy Walker's restricted eating highlights the importance of assessing suicide risk.

Those who suffer from anorexia nervosa tend to conceal their symptoms, and it behooves the practitioner to look for "clues" to disturbances in eating patterns. Just by observation, practitioners may detect the following signs of the disorder:

- Dry or scaly (yellowed) textured skin.
- Lanugo ("peach fuzz" or baby fine hair found on the trunk, face, and extremities).
- Intolerance of cold temperatures or hypothermia. (It is not uncommon to find a person wearing a heavy sweater on a hot summer day.)
- Extensive weight loss that has affected the skeletal structure. When there is a tremendous loss of body fat and muscle mass, the individual takes on a stooped or hunched-over appearance.
- Dull, lifeless hair, a pale complexion, poor posture, and extreme thinness hidden under loose, baggy clothing.

After dieting for 5 months, Joy Walker lost an extreme amount of weight, going from 130 pounds to 85 pounds. At that point, her friends began to remark about her emaciated appearance, but no one intervened until she fainted at her senior prom. Like many with anorexia nervosa, she was secretive about her eating habits, thus underscoring the importance of paying attention to the unspoken signs pointing to the presence of the disorder.

We now turn our attention to a review of bulimia nervosa.

BULIMIA NERVOSA

Bulimia nervosa is characterized by repeated dietary restriction alternating with uncontrollable binge eating and desperate measures to prevent weight gain. In order to counteract the effects of eating, the person will either vomit or use compensatory methods (e.g., using large amounts of laxatives to purge their bowels) in the struggle to control their weight. The use of fasting is often a misguided method for controlling a binge—the process usually backfires, causing increased hunger and leading to greater overeating.

The characteristic feature of bulimia nervosa is eating a larger amount of food (typically junk food such as potato chips, candy bars, doughnuts, or cookies) than most people would or could eat under similar circumstances (Fairburn, Cooper, Shafran, & Wilson, 2008). However, the actual caloric intake varies from person to person (Franco, Wonderlich, Little, & Herzog, 2004).

While anorexia is less common than bulimia, there is a great deal of overlap between the two disorders. Fairburn and colleagues (2008) observe that many individuals with bulimia have a history of anorexia. These individuals report a history of having used fasting as a way to reduce their body weight below desirable levels. The practitioner should begin by evaluating how often the individual engages in the purging/bingeing behaviors.

Prevailing Pattern

The person with bulimia nervosa is usually a young woman. The 12-month prevalence among women who meet the assessment criteria ranges from 1 to 1.5 percent (APA, 2013). Less is known about the prevalence among males. However, Kearney and Trull (2012) observe the rate of occurrence in males is approximately one-tenth of that found in females.

Differential Assessment

The person with bulimia nervosa generally has a normal or slightly above-normal weight. They exhibit a pattern of sequential binge eating in addition to inappropriate compensatory weight loss responses that include self-induced purging (vomiting), misuse of laxatives or enemas, and excessive exercise. Although the majority of eating disorders are first noticed during late childhood and early adolescence, they often continue well into adulthood.

An important distinction between anorexia nervosa and bulimia nervosa is that the person with bulimia does not have the extreme distortion of self-image characteristic of those with anorexia. A majority of individuals with bulimia never have had anorexia. However, it is not uncommon to find a history that includes many anorexic features. The symptom picture for bulimia nervosa includes:

- Recurrent episodes of binge eating, which are characterized by both of the following:
    1. Eating occurs during a discrete period of time (e.g., within 2 hours); the amount of food consumed is definitely larger than most other individuals would eat during a similar period of time and under similar circumstances.
    2. The individual experiences a lack of control over eating during the episode; for example, they cannot stop eating or control what they are eating.
- Recurrent, inappropriate compensatory methods are used to prevent weight gain (e.g., self-induced vomiting; misuse of laxatives, diuretics, or other medications; fasting; or excessive exercise).
- Both the binge eating and inappropriate compensatory methods occur, on average, at least once a week for 3 months.
- Body shape and weight unduly influence the way a person sees her- or himself.
- The disturbance does not occur exclusively during episodes of anorexia nervosa.

The practitioner may specify if the individual is in "partial remission"; that is, when full criteria for the diagnosis have previously been met, but at this point in time some, but not all, of the criteria have been met for a sustained period of time. The specifier "in full remission" is assigned when none of the diagnostic criteria have been met for an extended period of time.

Current severity is also considered and calculated by the number of episodes of inappropriate compensatory behaviors per week and specified as mild, moderate, severe, or extreme. The level of severity based on episodes of inappropriate compensatory behaviors is:

- Mild—an average of 1 to 3 episodes per week.
- Moderate—an average of 4 to 7 episodes per week.
- Severe—an average of 8 to 13 episodes per week.
- Extreme—an average of 14 or more episodes per week.

Generally, for practitioners who struggle with sorting through a person's symptom picture to arrive at this diagnosis, it is helpful to remember that the major features of this disorder tend to "cluster together" (Fairburn et al., 2003; Franco et al., 2004). Figure 11.5 illustrates the cycle of bulimia nervosa.

It is not unusual to find other disorders co-occurring with bulimia. For example, because of the low self-esteem related to binge eating, a feeling of a lack of control, and the use of compensatory behaviors to prevent weight gain, the practitioner may find an increased frequency of depressive symptoms and the bipolar and depressive disorders. The person may also be worried about eating in social situations and show signs of anxiety or an anxiety disorder. One may use stimulants to

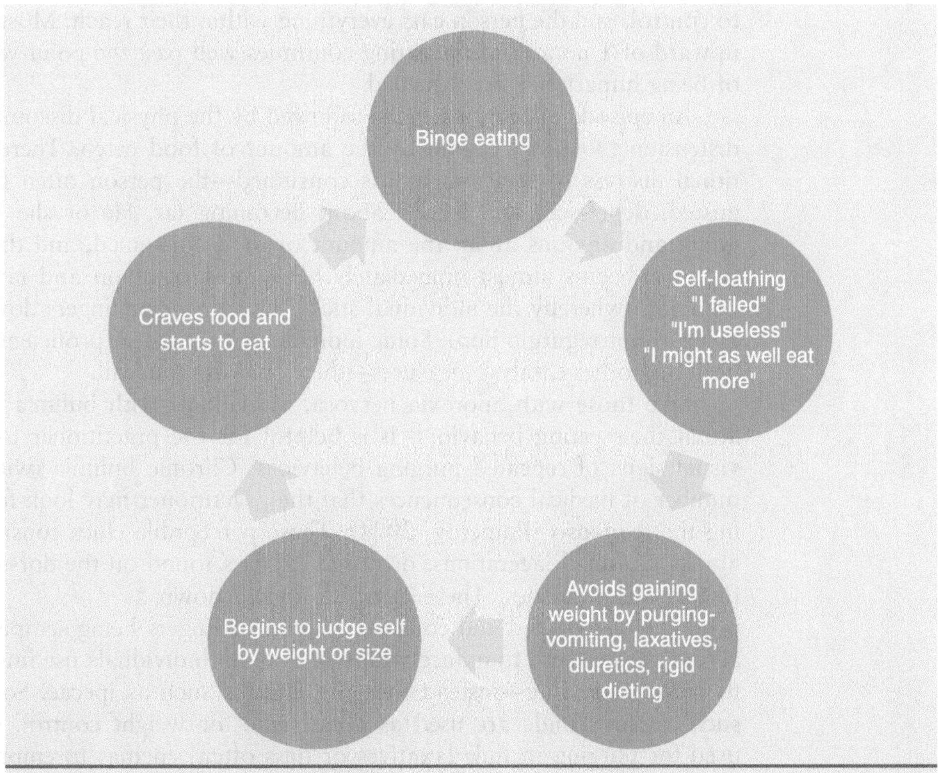

FIGURE 11.5 › THE CYCLE OF BULIMIA NERVOSA

control appetite evocative of a substance-related and addictive disorder. Bulimia may or may not begin in the context of another disorder (e.g., depression, anxiety, or substance abuse).

The onset of symptoms occurs fairly innocuously during late adolescence or the early 20s when an attempt to diet is closely followed by purging behaviors. At first, purging may serve as a convenient method of overeating without gaining the resultant weight, but it quickly becomes a destructive process that cannot be easily controlled. Over time, the binge/purge cycle escalates and becomes more dominant in the individual's thoughts and behaviors, often causing a multitude of difficulties such as impaired interpersonal relationships, which then leads to isolation, shame, helplessness, and lowered self-esteem.

Bulimia appears to run a chronic and episodic course whereby the occurrence of bingeeating may either have a gradual or acute presentation. Sometimes the individual can sense a binge starting, whereas other times he or she has no forewarning. They may or may not report feeling hungry preceding a binge; and a binge is often precipitated by the simple presence of something to eat. Psychologically stressful circumstances can often trigger a binge, because for that individual, food becomes a temporary fix to soothe and reduce emotional tensions.

The individual often reports episodes in which they eat large amounts of food in a short period of time, once or twice a week or several times a day. Generally, high-calorie sweets are the food of choice, but once a binge begins it is very difficult to control, and the person eats everything within their reach. Most often, binges last upward of 1 hour, and the eating continues well past the point when the sensation of being hungry has been quelled.

An episode of binge eating is followed by the physical discomfort of abdominal distension (bloating) caused by the amount of food eaten. There is also the emotional distress of how much was consumed—the person often feels helpless, disgusted, depressed, and fearful about becoming fat. He or she usually feels very guilty and anxious about the amount of food consumed, and the planning to get rid of it begins almost immediately. The most common and favored "action" is vomiting (whereby the individual sticks their finger or fingers down their throat to bring about regurgitation). Some individuals become so proficient that they do not need any other catalyst measures—they can vomit at will.

Like those with anorexia nervosa, individuals with bulimia are very secretive about their eating behaviors. It is helpful for the practitioner to look for telltale visual signs of repeated purging behaviors. Chronic bulimia (with purging) has a number of medical consequences that the practitioner may look for when considering the diagnosis (Pomeroy, 2004). These perceptible clues consist of skin lesions, abrasions, small lacerations, or raised calluses found on the dorsal (top) surface of fingers and knuckles. These dorsal lesions, known as Russell's signs, are the byproducts of repeated and constant friction of fingers being scraped back and forth across incisor teeth to induce vomiting. Not all individuals use finger manipulations to induce vomiting—instead they use emetics such as ipecac. Sometimes diuretics such as furosemide are used as a cathartic for weight control. Other maneuvers used for purging include laxatives or (less often) enemas to empty the bowel. Still other techniques involve using coat hangers, wadded paper, or pens that are stuck down the throat.

As noted in the previous discussion of anorexia nervosa, purging behaviors can produce negative health complications. The chemical stimulation of vomiting by ingesting ipecac can lead to serious heart damage. Excessive laxative abuse often causes constipation or permanent damage to the colon. Perhaps one of the most serious medical complications is electrolyte abnormalities (low potassium levels), which not only can disrupt signals to the heart causing irregular conduction, but also can cause kidney failure.

Competency 7 b

Impulsivity is a personality feature associated with bulimia nervosa, and persons with bulimia nervosa are more likely to engage in impulsive behaviors such as shoplifting and/or substance abuse (Stice, 2002). In addition, the eating disorders may co-occur with the personality disorders; for example, borderline personality disorder or avoidant personality disorder. Depression and the anxiety disorders can also co-occur with bulimia.

While child maltreatment is not necessarily specific to the eating disorders, many people with a major mental disorder report significantly higher rates of child abuse or trauma (Jacobi, Hayward, deZwan, Kraemer, & Agras, 2004; Stice, 2002). Those who have experienced such abuse are more likely to have more serious and chronic eating disorder symptoms. Childhood sexual abuse appears to be more strongly associated with bulimia, especially purging behaviors, than with the restricting type of anorexia (Carter, Bewell, Blackmore, & Woodside, 2006). However, the brutality of the person's history of abuse does not appear to correlate with the severity of bulimia. Family variables, interpersonal skills, and emotional reactions following sexual abuse serve to buffer the negative effects of these adverse life events. A past history of sexual abuse is not a specific risk factor for an eating disorder, but rather a risk factor for intrapersonal (or personal) difficulties in general. However, as a part of the competency-based assessment, consider the possibility of prior sexual or physical abuse when an eating disorder is diagnosed. Those individuals who report recent episodes of abuse tend to show greater body image disturbance.

The tragic pull of a binge/purge episode is depicted in the following vignette as Mary McDaniel struggles with her eating disorder. This case focuses on a typical day of bingeing and purging rather than on the full range of intrapersonal, interpersonal, and sociocultural variables that may be at play.

CASE THE CASE OF MARY MCDANIEL

"I eat a tremendous amount of food—and I don't even care what the food is. You know, like milk and orange juice usually sour the stomach? I don't care about anything like that. I eat whatever is in the pantry. The best way I can explain it is that it's sorta like a feeding frenzy. I gulp food down, and most of the time I don't even taste it."

Mary continues, "A typical day for me starts after my kids go off to school and my husband leaves for work. I usually have an extra hour before I have to leave the house. During that time, I usually eat anything I can stuff in my mouth. I start with some ice cream, and when I'm done with that, I munch on bags of cookies. They are much easier to put in my mouth while I'm getting dressed. I always try and eat soft things, because they're easier to vomit up. I don't like to eat stuff like pretzels or hard candies. I also don't like to eat spicy stuff, you know, hot peppers, garlic, and onions. They are terrible to bring up!

"Before I leave for work, I have just enough time to vomit up everything I just ate. I'm pretty good at it—most of the time, I don't even need to stick my

CASE THE CASE OF MARY MCDANIEL (CONTINUED)

fingers down my throat anymore. All I have to do is just start thinking about throwing up, and the next thing I know, I start gagging and I just vomit. I usually vomit within 20 minutes after I've eaten, because after that it's started digesting, and then it's too late. The food is already being absorbed.

"When I'm driving to work, I always have a bag of M&Ms or cookies in the car; or else I stop and buy a dozen Dunkin Donuts. You know, its stuff I can eat without taking my eyes off the road. Usually, I throw up before I get to work—I always keep a couple of mason jars under the front seat of my car for that. I prefer not to do it that way because it smells up everything, and I can't always rinse my mouth out right afterward. I do keep a can of air freshener in the glove compartment, though.

"When I'm at work, I don't eat much in front of other people. They mean well, I guess, but they're always so critical of me. They'll say things like, 'You eat like a bird, but you never lose any weight on all your different diets.' I always eat lunch by myself—and most of the time, I go out. I either get a couple of hamburgers, fries, and a large shake, or I'll find a drive-in fast-food place to get something. I always eat in my car, and I always throw up before I go back to work. If things are rushed at work and I don't have a full lunch hour, I'll grab a bunch of laxatives. Only problem with that is going to the bathroom all afternoon. Good thing my office is away from everybody and down the hall near the restrooms.

"After work, I eat stuff in the car on the way home, but as soon as I get home I hit some of my secret stashes—I have 'em all over the house. There's food hidden in the bottom of the laundry hamper. That's a great hiding place 'cause you know nobody but me is going to be emptying it out to do the wash! I have candy stuffed inside my shoes and shoeboxes ... inside the pockets of my winter clothes ... under my mattress. I used to hide food under the kid's cribs, but they sleep in beds now. Once, I put a huge bag of M&Ms in the dog's dry food bin, and my husband found it. I had a hard time explaining that one. So I stopped putting stuff in there. Now, I have to get real creative, like when I wrap up ice cream bars in aluminum foil so they look like frozen hamburger patties. I'm always saving empty cereal boxes so I can put food back inside them and then put them back in the pantry.

"My husband complains sometimes about our food bills, but he doesn't know why we go through so much. I tell him that prices are really terrible, but most of the time I clip coupons to help with the cost. During dinner I eat like everybody else. But then as soon as dinner is over I start eating again right up until the time I go to bed. I usually can put away half of an apple pie and a quart of ice cream, but I have to be quiet when I throw up because everybody is home and they might hear me. Sometimes, when it's late at night and everyone is in bed, I'll treat myself to a nice enema.

"Most of the time I eat in the bathroom, because it's the only place that gives me any privacy. Did you know that mothers only get about 42 minutes a day to themselves? I've got to be creative. The hard part is throwing up so no one hears me. I usually run the shower to hide my gagging noises.

"I hate to admit it but this is my typical routine. I used to pride myself on being a nice person, but now I'm just this horrible pig. I feel terrible, but I don't know how to stop. I've tried stopping so many times. I just can't give up the food—and if I don't vomit, use laxatives, or enemas, I start putting on the pounds. This is no way to live."

MARY MCDANIEL'S DSM DIAGNOSIS IS AS FOLLOWS:

Bulimia nervosa, severe

Competency 8 c

ASSESSMENT SUMMARY Consistent with bulimia nervosa, Mary McDaniel's behaviors leave little doubt that she has all the salient features, including binge/purge cycles, use of laxatives, diuretics, and enemas, and no control over how much she eats. The physical complications associated with bulimia highlight the importance of consulting with medical professionals. Mary comments that she cannot give up the food she eats and expresses the fear that if she does not vomit or use laxatives or enemas, she will gain weight. Clearly, Mary is dissatisfied with her body seeing herself as a "horrible pig." This picture closely resembles the struggle of anorexia, specifically the fear of gaining weight, the desire to lose weight, and dissatisfaction with one's body. For a small minority of individuals (about 10 to 15 percent), there is a crossover to anorexia, but they will revert back to bulimia (APA, 2013). Some will experience multiple occurrences of crossovers between the two disorders. However, bulimia nervosa should not be diagnosed when the disturbance occurs only during episodes of anorexia nervosa. Keep in mind the individual's current (or for the past 3 months) symptom picture when considering the diagnosis.

In contrast to the symptoms of anorexia, Mary is unable to stop her pattern of eating despite feeling unhappy about herself. In fact, she believes she has no control over her eating behaviors. For Mary, her struggles around food are never ending. It is an all-or-nothing perspective; that is, she is either completely in control or completely out of control. Likewise, food is seen as either all good or all bad. With this pattern, the practitioner might begin to be on the lookout for depressive symptoms like low self-esteem, or symptoms of anxiety such as a fear of social situations. She's already eating lunch by herself at work. Looking to the future, Mary might start using stimulant medications in order to control her weight by dieting or begin drinking alcohol. If that happens, the social worker might take into account the co-occurrence of a substance-related disorder. The lifetime prevalence of substance use, especially stimulants or alcohol, is at least 30 percent for those diagnosed with bulimia (APA, 2013).

We now turn to a review of binge eating

BINGE-EATING DISORDER

It should come as no surprise that people put on weight when they consume more calories than they burn. There is no question that Americans are heavier than ever before. Meengs, Roe, and Rolls (2012) conducted a study of eating habits, and according to the authors, "previous research has shown that increasing the variety of foods leads to increased consumption" (p. 1211). Apparently the appeal of the same food declines while you are eating, but if there are other foods on your plate with different tastes, aromas, shapes, and textures, instead of stopping you will be stimulated to shift to another food—and eat more. Remember this the next time you stand in the all-you-can-eat buffet line. An increase in the variety of foods on your plate can lead to an increase in consumption.

We live in a society that thinks that large portions are customary, eating throughout the day is customary, eating late at night is customary, and eating in the car is customary. Food is everywhere and available at any time. Recent studies have found that the food cues activated in the brain also activate the same brain areas as those who are addicted to drugs or alcohol. Gearhardt and colleagues (2011) report that the most addictive response can be found in foods that are higher in sugar, fat, and salt.

Competency 8 c

Although only recently recognized as a distinct diagnosis, binge-eating disorder (BED) is the most common eating disorder among adults in the United States (Hudson, Hiripi, Pope, & Kessler, 2007; Iacovino, Gredysa, Altman, & Wilfley, 2012). This disorder is most like bulimia, except that there is no self-induced vomiting or laxative misuse. In essence, individuals with binge-eating disorder show different eating behaviors from those exhibited by Mary McDaniel in the earlier vignette. BED is characterized by recurrent binge eating, but without subsequent purging episodes that are part of the bulimic picture. Therefore, binge-eating disorder involves none of the medical complications attributable to purging behaviors. However, the practitioner may consult with medical professionals as needed to confirm the diagnosis.

Binge-eating disorder was moved from the DSM-IV section "Other Conditions That May Be a Focus of Clinical Attention" to status as a disorder in the DSM-5. The disorder is characterized by the consumption of large quantities of food whether the person is hungry or not.

PREVAILING PATTERN

The prevalence of BED over a 12-month period for adults (over 18 years of age) in the United States is 1.6 percent for females and 0.8 percent for males (APA, 2013). About 1.6 percent of adolescents may be affected (Swanson, Crow, Le Grange, Swendsen, & Merikangas, 2011). The lifetime prevalence has been observed in studies to be 3.5 percent for women and 2 percent for men (Westerburg & Waitz, 2013). The DSM-5 notes that the disorder is as prevalent "among females from racial or ethnic minority groups as has been reported for white females" (APA, 2013, p. 351). Further, the disorder is more prevalent among those seeking weight-loss treatment than in the general population.

DIFFERENTIAL ASSESSMENT

Individuals with BED have some of the same concerns about body shape and weight as those with anorexia nervosa and bulimia nervosa. However, people with BED consume large quantities of food, and they also report disorganized and even chaotic eating habits. Anywhere from 5,000 to 15,000 calories are consumed within a binge (MentalHealth.gov, 2015). Most people who binge feel ashamed and try to hide their problem. They can become so good at hiding binges that even family members and close friends may not know of their loved one's eating behaviors.

In a pattern similar to that of bulimia, individuals with BED alternate between episodes of binge eating and then attempts to control their food intake on their own, but are not successful in the longer term. Although dieting is related to binge eating, it is not clear if dieting causes the disorder. For some, skipping a meal, not eating enough food each day, or avoiding certain kinds of foods may lead to binge eating.

People with BED frequently eat large amounts of food beyond the point of feeling full. Most of us have overeaten on occasion. However, what differentiates BED is the ongoing habit of consuming large amounts of food in a short period of time.

This ultimately leads to weight gain and obesity, but keep in mind that BED is a disorder distinct from obesity (Westerburg & Waitz, 2013).

The main consequences of BED are brought on by the person's weight gain resulting from the bingeing process. The criteria to consider a person's behavior as a binge-eating disorder include recurrent episodes of binge eating characterized by:

- Each binge consists of eating, in a discrete period of time (such as within any 2-hour period) an amount of food that is definitely larger than most people would eat in a similar period of time under similar circumstances, and it is accompanied by a feeling of loss of control; that is, the feeling that they cannot stop eating, cannot control what they are eating, and how much they are eating.
- Also, the person must have three or more of the following:
  1. Eats much more quickly during binge episodes than during normal eating episodes;
  2. Eats until physically uncomfortable and nauseated due to the amount of food consumed;
  3. Eats large amounts of food (far more than a regular person would eat) even when not really hungry;
  4. Often eats alone during periods of normal eating, owing to feelings of embarrassment about food; and
  5. Feels disgusted, depressed, or guilty about binge eating or very guilty afterward.
- The person is distressed about the binge eating.
- The binge eating occurs, on average, at least once a week for 3 months.
- The binge eating is not associated with the recurrent use of inappropriate compensatory behavior as seen in bulimia, and does not occur exclusively during the course of bulimia nervosa or anorexia nervosa.

Figure 11.6 illustrates the cycle of binge-eating disorder.

Competency 6 a

No one knows for sure what causes BED and little is known about its development, thus highlighting the importance of the practitioner's understanding the different theories of human behavior. For example, genetic inheritance may be a factor associated with a person's greater risk for the disorder along with a higher incidence of co-occurring disorders; for example, bipolar disorders, depressive disorders, anxiety disorders, and, to a lesser degree, the substance use disorders (APA, 2013). The social worker may also find kleptomania, body dysmorphic disorder, irritable bowel syndrome, or fibromyalgia as a part of the symptom picture (Marazziti, Corsi, Baroni, Consoli, & Catena-Dell'Osso, 2012; Westerburg & Waitz, 2013). Hudson and colleagues (2007) observed that 78.9 percent of individuals with BED have a co-occurring psychiatric disorder.

Bingeing episodes typically consist of foods that are high in sugar, fat, and/or salt but low in vitamins and minerals. As such, those who have BED, and are obese, are at risk for those health conditions commonly associated with obesity, such as type 2 diabetes mellitus, high blood pressure, heart disease, gastrointestinal issues, high cholesterol levels, musculoskeletal problems, and obstructive sleep apnea (Iacovino et al., 2012; Westerburg & Waitz, 2013).

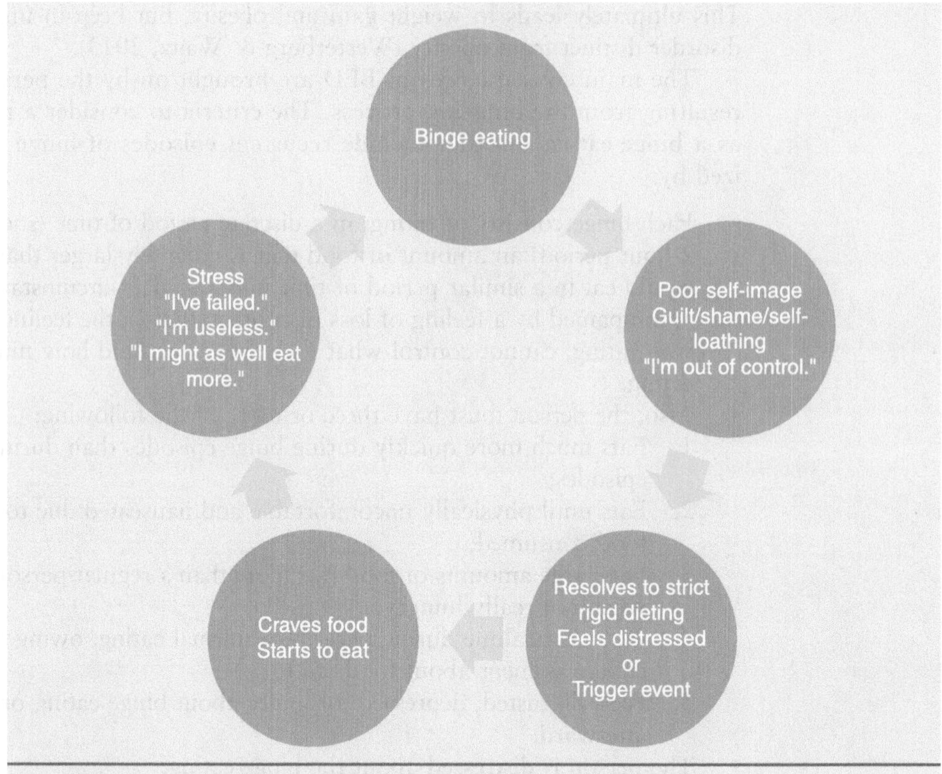

FIGURE 11.6 › THE CYCLE OF BINGE-EATING DISORDER

Many of those who struggle with BED use food as a way to cope with uncomfortable feelings and emotions. They may have never learned how to deal well with stress and, instead, find comfort in eating. Unfortunately, they end up feeling guilty and unhappy about not being able to control their eating, which leads to more stress and more binge eating.

We now turn to the case of Cindy Dalton to illustrate binge-eating disorder.

CASE — THE CASE OF CINDY DALTON

"I am a compulsive overeater and an adult child of what I could best describe as a set of crazy parents. If I were writing a book about what I've gone through, you could call my story, 'Who Is in Control?' The one thing I learned is that I'm not in control, and never was. The real deal is that I'm a binge eater. For as long as I can remember, I had a distorted relationship with food. I'm not making any excuses here, but you might say that my childhood sucked. You see, both of my parents were stinking drunks. They were always drinking something. Then my mom would start screaming and my dad would get passive-aggressive. I could pretty well predict when my parents would act out.

Dinner time usually turned into a real scene; mostly yelling and screaming. Me? I would fly under the radar comforting myself with food. I had the perfect relationship with food. Simply put, it made me feel safe. My favorites were mac and cheese, plain pizza, white bread, and canned ravioli. When things got really bad between my parents, there was candy, anything chocolate, and ice cream. You might say I saved the best for the worst. Like I said, I could predict when my parents would act out and I could always depend on the comforting taste of that mac and cheese. What a combination! I was pretty thin back then and I don't think I overate."

Cindy looks lost in thought for a moment and picks up again, "Ultimately divorce came into the picture and my parents went their separate ways. I was in the seventh grade at the time. I remember the night they broke the news. I locked myself in my room and ate a whole box of those Little Debbie snacks. What with my dad out of the house and my mom working a second job to meet expenses, I was alone a lot. You might say it was a tough time for me what with my parents wrapped up in their own problems. Nobody was available to help me, and here I was, starting middle school. It was a huge leap from elementary school. I was thrown in with the older kids, had to find out where to go, and figure out how to switch classes. I felt so lonely. I remember when I broke up with my first boyfriend, I ate a whole pizza, large one fully loaded, and two bags of barbecue potato chips washed down by a liter of Coke, and not that pansy diet kind either. By then I was eating for comfort, started sneaking into the kitchen at night, and eating whatever I could find. I put together some of the most interesting things. How does cheese whiz with sweet pickles nuked in the micro slathered over white bread sound? Sometimes it was bread with butter and peanut butter and then I would finish that off with two bags of Doritos or a box of pretzels. Gotta admit though, chips were my favorite, especially the barbecue. I would eat whatever I could get my hands on. I started to think I was some kind of weirdo because I couldn't stop this uncontrollable eating. By then I was eating compulsively, and my body started maturing. Not only was I developing a woman's body but I was also gaining weight. The kids in school started calling me 'chubbs,' short for chubby. That only caused me to eat more and get fatter. Did I cut down on what I was eating? No. Or I should say 'hell no!' I started wearing big baggy tops and jeggings to hide my body. The night I ate two boxes of Oreo cookies in about 10 minutes flat I knew something was terribly wrong."

Cindy continues, "Yeah, I've had counseling before. It doesn't take a highly trained clinical social worker to help me figure out that I found 'safety' in familiar foods and it has a lot to do with my environment at home when I was growing up." Cindy looks to the social worker. "Sorry, I didn't mean to offend you. Anyway, the only difference between then and now is back then I didn't eat as much junk food like I do now."

Cindy adds, "Somehow I made it through high school and went off to college. Things only got worse. I had no time for exercise and started eating even more. Then I started buying jumbo sizes and, you guessed it, I gained more weight. Periodically I would go on diets to lose the weight I had gained, only to relapse. I put the weight back on and then some. When I couldn't stop eating once I started, I made myself not eat anything during the day. Of course that was ridiculous, so when nobody was around I'd start bingeing again. Then I would start eating nonstop. First something sweet, then salty, then back to the sweets and so on. I could easily consume at least 5,000 calories in one sitting. Sometimes I would wake up with half-eaten food still in my mouth. I got fatter and fatter. Never thought about purging.

"Right after I graduated college with my degree in business I got a job as a cost estimator with a small company. I thought it would be the perfect job, but it turned out to be really boring. All you do is go to job sites and measure things. If there is a construction change, then you're back on site and re-measuring." Cindy turned to the social worker and asked, "I'm sorry. Am I boring you?" The social worker found Cindy's conversation to be quite engaging and was surprised by her question. She began to think that Cindy did not think much of herself. The social worker commented that she was interested in Cindy's experiences and encouraged her to continue.

Cindy continued, "I do have some great friends, though. Some even go back to high school and a great boyfriend. So here I am, 26 years old and weigh in at

CASE THE CASE OF CINDY DALTON (CONTINUED)

210. Keep in mind I'm 5 feet and 6½ inches tall. Some days it doesn't feel too bad and my health is not in any immediate danger, at least that I know about. It's just that I hate myself and I hate the way I eat. I eat all the time; when I'm sad, when I'm lonely, when I'm bored, when I feel bad about myself, which is just about all the time. Seems like there's always a time to eat. My binges go for four to five times a day, on average. So that's where you come in."

Cindy turned to the social worker and added, "For years I was so proud of myself that I survived my neurotic childhood. I don't drink, never did drugs, and graduated with honors from college, have a steady job, my own apartment, and good friends. In fact, one of them gave me your name. Seems you were real helpful when she had 'issues' with her ex. I gotta tell you. When I called and you told me you could see me the next day it made me feel that maybe I really am worth something. That I'm not a total failure. I know that I'm the one who has to stop bingeing, but do you have any suggestions to help me?"

CINDY DALTON'S DSM DIAGNOSIS IS AS FOLLOWS:

Binge eating disorder, severe

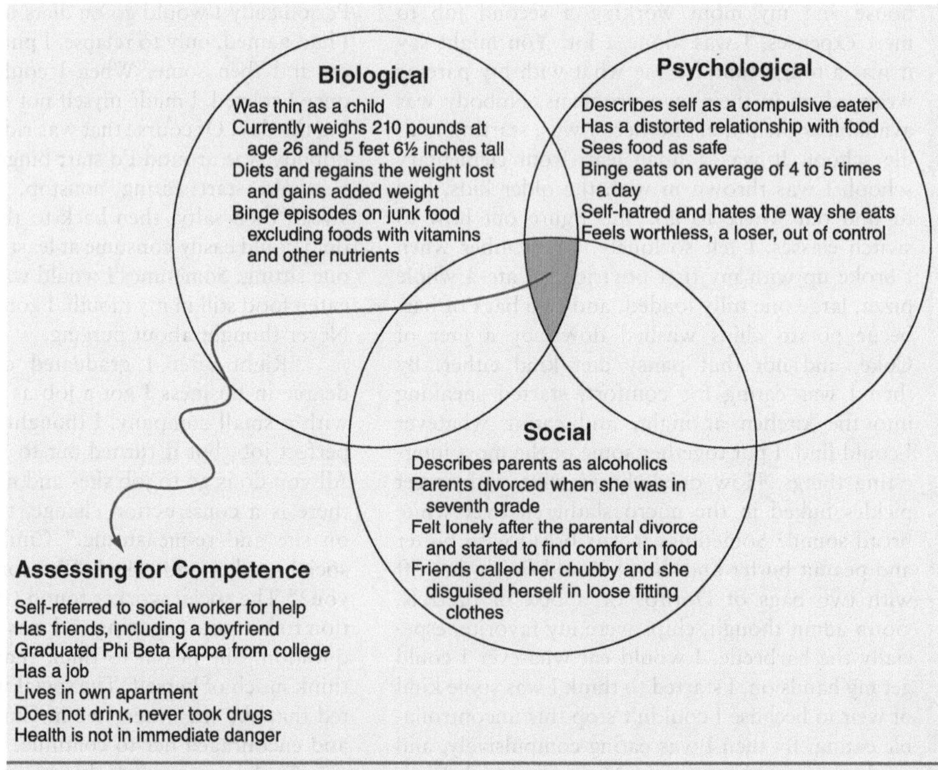

FIGURE 11.7 › BINGE-EATING DISORDER
The interactions of the biological, psychological, and social variables in Cindy Dalton's life.

Assessment Summary Cindy's story illustrates the three essential features of binge-eating disorder. First, she has been binge eating. This has been going on for some time, and clearly for a lot longer than the past 3 months required to make the diagnosis. Her eating pattern can be seen as eating an amount of food that is more than most people would eat in a similar period of time and under similar circumstances. For example, Cindy talks about eating bread with butter and peanut butter and then finishing this off with two bags of Doritos chips. She comments that she can consume at least 5,000 calories in a single sitting. In fact, she once woke up with uneaten food still in her mouth. Second, Cindy feels that her eating is out of control. In the beginning of her story, Cindy comments that she would characterize her life story with the title of "Who Is in Control," adding that it certainly would not be her. The third key feature of Cindy's eating pattern is that she is clearly distressed over how much she eats. She adds that she feels bad about herself most of the time. Cindy told the social worker that she hates herself and she hates the way that she eats.

Binge eating is associated with obesity. Concerns about her weight and health were a part of Cindy's decision to seek help for her eating patterns. While Cindy tried to diet and lose weight, her symptom picture is distinguished from bulimia nervosa in that she does not continually use inappropriate measures to lose weight, such as purging or excessive exercise. While Cindy is unhappy with how she eats, we do not see the full symptom picture supporting a depressive disorder in her story.

Competency 7 b

Despite her struggles, there are a number of competencies that can be seen in Cindy's circumstances. Although her parents were characterized as alcoholics, Cindy comments that she does not drink and never took drugs. She graduated with honors from college and found a job where she is able to support herself. She is also able to maintain her own apartment. Additionally, Cindy has several friends, some from high school, and a boyfriend. Although Cindy is overweight, she seems to be in good overall health. Additionally, Cindy is insightful about her eating struggles and sought out the social worker's help (Figure 11.7).

OTHER FEEDING OR EATING DISORDERS

There are two additional disorders to complete our review that are used when the social worker finds symptoms characteristic of the eating and feeding disorders reviewed in this chapter but does not have enough information for a full diagnosis. The supplementary disorders are:

Other Specified Eating or Feeding Disorder

Other specified eating or feeding disorder is used when the person shows symptoms of an eating and feeding disorder, and experiences distress or impairment, but does not meet full criteria for any of the other disorders reviewed in this chapter. The practitioner may indicate the specific reason that the client does not meet criteria. Examples include:

1. Atypical anorexia nervosa—Used when all criteria for anorexia nervosa are met except that while the person may have lost a great deal of weight, their overall weight is within (or above) normal range.
2. Bulimia nervosa (of low frequency and/or limited duration)—Used when all of the criteria for bulimia nervosa are met, except that the binge eating and inappropriate compensatory behaviors do not meet the required time criterion; that is, less than once a week and/or for less than 3 months.
3. Binge-eating disorder (of low frequency and/or limited duration)—Used when all criteria for binge-eating disorder have been met except the required time criterion is not met; that is, the person's binge-eating occurs, on average, less than once a week and/or for less than 3 months.
4. Purging disorder—The individual engages in recurrent purging behavior to effect weight or shape (for instance, self-induced vomiting, misuse of laxatives, diuretics, or other medications) in the absence of binge eating.

Unspecified Feeding or Eating Disorder

Unspecified feeding or eating disorder is assigned when the individual does not meet full criteria for any of the feeding and eating disorders, can be applied in situations when the social worker chooses not to specify the reason full criteria are not met, and can include presentations where there is insufficient information to make a definitive diagnosis (such as the client who shows up in emergency situations).

We now turn to a consideration of obesity and how it differs from the eating and feeding disorders.

THE ROLE OF OBESITY

While not physically healthy, obesity is not considered a psychiatric disorder (APA, 2013). However, it is generally lumped together with eating or weight disorders. Unfortunately, this only serves to stigmatize those who are portly. As researchers continue to examine the role of biological influences, particularly neurotransmitters and genetic predisposition, perhaps society will begin to view obesity differently; that is, as a complex metabolic disorder, rather than an emotional or behavioral problem. It would seem that as our society advances technologically, we are simply getting fatter (Henderson & Brownell, 2004). We are seen as living in a toxic environment where people are constantly exposed to inexpensive fatty foods that have low nutritional value combined with an increasingly inactive life style (Schwartz & Brownell, 2007). The promotion of an inactive, sedentary lifestyle and consuming a high-fat diet seem to be the major contributors to obesity (Caballero, 2007; Levine et al., 2005). How many times have you been to a fast food restaurant and were asked, for a small sum (usually less than a dollar), if you would like to "supersize" your meal? Then there are the restaurants that serve jumbo portions, and as they say in New York City slang, "fuhgeddabout" those endless all-you-can-eat buffets.

Nevertheless, being overweight and obese does pose major public health challenges. These conditions place a person at a higher risk for various cardiovascular diseases, hypertension, and high blood cholesterol (National Center for Health Statistics, 2005). The prevalence of obesity or a body mass index (BMI) of 30 or greater among adults of all gender, age, and racial/ethnic groups in the United States in 2000 was 30.5 percent of the general population and steadily increased to 33.8 percent in 2008 (Flegal, Carroll, Ogden, & Curtin, 2010). While this increase seems to be leveling off, the problem of obesity in our society continues. Flegal and colleagues (2010) note that 5.7 percent of the adult population have a BMI over 40, or 10 million people in the United States alone. The numbers for children and adolescents are even worse. Obesity rates for children ages 2 to 19 years of age (or above the 95th percentile for sex-specific BMI for that age) increased from 13.9 percent in 2000 to 16.9 percent in 2008 (Ogden, Carroll, Curtin, Lamb, & Flegal, 2010).

The term obesity (or excess body fat resulting from the long-term excess of energy intake relative to energy expenditure) does not appear in the DSM as a mental disorder because a consistent association has not been established between obesity and a psychological or behavioral syndrome (APA, 2013). The DSM reads, "However, there are robust associations between obesity and a number of mental disorders (e.g., binge-eating disorder, depressive and bipolar disorders, schizophrenia)" (APA, 2013, p. 329). In the section listing "Other Conditions That May Be a Focus of Clinical Attention," the DSM-5 notes that "overweight or obesity" may be specified when there is evidence of nonadherence to medical treatment (APA, 2013, p. 726).

SUMMARY

This chapter outlined the major characteristics of the feeding and eating disorders. The risk factors that may precede these disorders can be summarized to include gender, ethnicity, early childhood gastrointestinal problems, elevated weight and shape concerns, negative self-evaluation, sexual abuse, and other adverse experiences. Principally, pica centers around eating nonnutritive substances; rumination involves the repetitive regurgitation of undigested food; avoidant/restrictive food intake disorder prevents the consumption of certain foods; anorexia nervosa refers to an individual's refusal to eat anything but minimal amounts of food resulting in extremely low body weight; bulimia nervosa describes uncontrolled binge-eating episodes followed by self-induced purging; and binge-eating disorder characterizes marked distress due to binge eating without compensatory behaviors.

To highlight the distinctions among the eating disorders, individuals with anorexia nervosa differ in one very important way from those with bulimia; they are (much to their detriment) extremely successful at losing weight. Granted, the individual with bulimia is not trying to achieve low weight. The motivating force is to avoid becoming fat. Someone with anorexia wants to be extremely thin, even when they have lost a significant amount of weight. Although these two conditions frequently coexist, the individual with bulimia usually does not meet the criterion of being at least 15 percent underweight as seen in those with anorexia. Those with BED do not attempt to compensate for gaining weight by vomiting, using laxatives, or exercising excessively. Although no weight range is currently noted for diagnostic purposes, these individuals do tend to be obese. Refer to Table 11.4 for a summary of the major features of anorexia nervosa, bulimia nervosa, and BED.

As the DSM transitions from the DSM-IV-TR (APA, 2000) to the current edition of the manual, the following Table 11.5 provides a brief summary of the changes made to the feeding and eating diagnostic classifications.

TABLE 11.4 OVERVIEW OF THE MAJOR FEATURES OF ANOREXIA, BULIMIA NERVOSA, AND BINGE EATING

	Anorexia Nervosa	Bulimia Nervosa	Binge Eating
Weight	BMI of less than 17.5 or significantly underweight	Weight varies but is usually normal weight or overweight	Usually overweight
Body Image	Obsessed with weight and appearance Sees self as fat even when underweight	Preoccupied with weight and appearance	May be overly focused on weight and appearance
Eating Practices	Takes in very few calories May eat a limited variety of foods May have odd food rituals May refuse to eat in front of others	Binges (seen as eating large amounts of food in a short period of time) Followed by purging—such as vomiting, laxatives, diuretics Prefers to eat alone	Binges (seen as eating large amounts of food in a short period of time) May engage in strict/rigid dieting between binges Prefers to eat alone
Physical Symptoms and Medical Complications	Extreme weight loss Low blood pressure Heart problems Kidney problems Hair loss and/or lanugo Loss of normal muscle fat Fatigue and weakness Digestive/gastrointestinal problems May stop menstruating Decreased sexual interest Osteoporosis Sudden death	Changes in weight Ulcers Esophageal tears Gastrointestinal problems (heartburn, abdominal pain, cramps, bloating) Sore throat Russell's signs (knuckles have callous malformation) Dental problems (yellow eroded teeth) "Chipmunk" cheeks Weakness/fatigue Acute electrolyte imbalance Irregular menstrual cycle Constipation (rebound from laxatives) Poor hair texture Dehydration	Excessive weight gain High blood pressure Diabetes Joint pain Fatigue
Emotional Signs	Excessive fear of gaining weight Depression Anxiety Obsessive-compulsive behaviors Denial there may be a problem	Depression Anxiety Feelings of guilt Self-destructive behavior	Depression Feeling of guilt or self-loathing

Table 11.5 Summary Comparison Between the DSM-IV-TR and DSM-5 Diagnoses for the Feeding and Eating Disorders
The disorders of pica, rumination disorder, and avoidant/restrictive food intake disorder (formerly feeding disorder) have been moved from the DSM IV-TR chapter of "Disorders Usually First Diagnosed in Infancy, Childhood or Adolescence" to the Feeding and Eating Disorders in DSM-5
Criteria for pica and rumination disorder were changed, and diagnostic criteria can now be applied to people of any age
Feeding disorder, a diagnosis rarely used in the DSM-IV-TR chapter of "Disorders Usually First Diagnosed in Infancy, Childhood or Adolescence," was renamed Avoidant/Restrictive Food Intake Disorder and Diagnostic Criteria Expanded
Criteria for anorexia nervosa were changed by eliminating the requirement for amenorrhea
Requirements for bulimia nervosa and binge-eating disorder were changed from "at least twice weekly for 6 months" to at least once weekly for over the past 3 months
Binge-eating disorder was moved from the DSM-IV-TR Appendix of "Other Conditions That May Be a Focus of Clinical Attention" to status as a full disorder

Practitioner's Reflections

The syndromes included in the feeding and eating disorders chapter are characterized by persistent disturbances of eating or eating-related behaviors that result in changes in how food is consumed. The key features of these disorders are significant impairments in the individual's physical health, and/or psychosocial functioning. Each disorder causes a certain amount of stress for the individual, and her or his family. Some people hide their patterns of eating while others may hold unrealistic expectations for the "ideal weight," and yet still others may feel a sense of shame and disgust, thus challenging the practitioner to listen and look for "competencies" in the person's life history.

Activities

Competency 2 a

1. There are cultural differences in attitudes about ideal body weight. Identify cultures where a heavy body type is valued. Describe how you would develop a culturally responsive therapeutic relationship with a client who struggles with an eating disorder; be sure to be attentive to your own cultural beliefs and those of your client.

Competency 7 b

2. Negative stereotypes are often perpetuated in the media.
   a. Browse through a popular magazine and identify the number of advertisements that portray individuals who you consider "thin" and those with a heavier body frame. How many are portrayed as thin, and how many have more body weight?
   b. Next, identify how many are female and how many are male.
   c. Finally, identify how many are from various ethnic or cultural backgrounds.
   d. Describe how refining your understanding of negative stereotypes found in the media will influence how you will go about collecting, organizing, and interpreting client data when assessing a client with an eating disorder.

Competency 6 b

3. This activity is designed to begin to sensitize you to what it might be like to have an eating disorder and how all-consuming thoughts about food and weighing oneself can be. Keep a diary for 1 week and record everything that you eat, the time of day you ate, whether or not you were hungry, whether or not the food satisfied you, whether or not you had cravings for certain foods, and whether or not you thought about food more often than you regularly do. In addition, weigh yourself every time you eat something. How will this level of self-awareness about your own eating habits help you to eliminate the influence of your personal biases and values in working with clients who struggle with an eating disorder?

Competency 7 c and 7 b

4. Review the case of Joy Walker. (Alternatively, consider using use any of the other case stories in this chapter.) Refer to the following list of topics to answer the questions below:
   - Feelings about her appearance.
   - Things she likes to eat and what she does not like.
   - Her "ideal" appearance, and what that would look like.
   - Concerns that she may have had with her appearance in the past.
   - Current health problems (e.g., feeling weak or dizzy, heart palpitations, sore throat, hair loss, and so on).
   - Possible long-range worries about health issues.
   - Past medical problems.
   - Attempts to keep healthy, fit, and attractive (e.g., her exercise regimen and diet).

   a. Which topics do you think Joy would feel comfortable discussing with you?
   b. Which topics do you imagine would be the most difficult for her to talk about?
   c. Assume that you are the practitioner assigned to work with Joy and illustrate how you would go about developing a mutually agreed-on focus for working together.
   d. Based on what you know about Joy, how would you assess her readiness for change?

5. The majority of eating disorders are first noticed during late childhood or early adolescence. Imagine for a moment that you are a social worker working in the school system. Among the schools you are assigned to, one of them has teachers and staff eating with the students. One afternoon, you notice a student; she looks to be about 13 years old, sitting by herself in the cafeteria. Although she has been there for about 20 minutes, you notice the food on her tray has been untouched. What, if anything, should you do? Explain your answer. Next, share this activity with one (or several) of your colleagues and review the similarities and differences in responses. Next, share this information with your supervisor for her/his input.

Competency 6 b

COMPETENCY NOTES

Competency 2 a—Social workers apply and communicate understanding of the implications of diversity and difference in shaping life experiences in practice at the micro, mezzo, and macro levels (pp. 318, 335): Social workers understand how diversity and difference characterize and shape the human experience and that these features are critical to the formation of identity.

Competency 6 a—Social workers apply knowledge of human behavior and the social environment, person-in-environment, and other multidisciplinary theoretical frameworks to engage with clients (and constituencies)

(pp. 315, 327): Social workers understand theories of human behavior and the social environment and critically apply this knowledge to facilitate engagement with clients (and constituencies) including families, groups, organizations, and communities.

Competency 6 b—Social workers use empathy, personal reflection, and interpersonal skills effectively to engage clients (and constituencies) (p. 336): Social workers value the importance of human relationships.

Competency 7 b—Social workers are able to apply knowledge of human behavior and the social environment, person-in-environment, and other multidisciplinary theoretical frameworks in the analysis of assessment data (pp. 302, 306, 310, 311, 313, 317, 318, 323, 331, 335, 336): Social workers understand theories of human behavior and the social environment and critically evaluate and apply this knowledge in the assessment process.

Competency 7 c—Social workers develop mutually agreed-on intervention goals and objectives based on the assessment of strengths, needs and challenges within clients and constituencies (pp. 303, 310, 311, 336): Social workers recognize the implications of the larger practice context in the assessment process.

Competency 8 c—Social workers use interprofessional collaboration, as appropriate, to achieve beneficial practice outcomes (pp. 307, 310, 316, 317, 324, 326): Social workers value interprofessional teamwork and recognize the beneficial outcomes that require interdisciplinary, interprofessional, and interorganizational collaboration.

References

Agras, W. S. (2001). The consequences and costs of eating disorders. *Psychiatric Clinics of North America*, *24*, 371–379.

American Psychiatric Association (APA). (2000). *Diagnostic and statistical manual of mental disorders* (4th ed., text revision). Washington, DC: Author.

American Psychiatric Association (APA). (2013). *Diagnostic and statistical manual of mental disorders* (5th ed.). Arlington, VA: Author.

Anderson-Frye, E. (2009). Cross-cultural issues in body image among children and adolescents. In L. Smolak & J. K. Thompson (Eds.). *Body image, eating disorders, and obesity in youth: Assessment, prevention, and treatment* (2nd ed. pp. 113–133). Washington, DC: American Psychological Association.

Andrist, L. C. (2003). Media images, body dissatisfaction, and disordered eating in adolescent women. *American Journal of Maternal Child Nursing*, *28*, 119–123.

Blinder, B. J., & Salama, C. (2008). An update on pica: Prevalence, contributing causes, and treatment. *Psychiatric Times*, *25*(6), 66, 72–73.

Caballero, B. (2007). The global epidemic of obesity: An overview. *Epidemiologic Review*, *29*, 1–5.

Carter, J. C., Bewell, C., Blackmore, E., & Woodside, D. B. (2006). The impact of childhood sexual abuse in anorexia nervosa. *Child Abuse and Neglect*, *30*(3), 257–269.

Celio, A. A., Zabinski, M. F., & Wilfley, D. E. (2002). African-American body images. In T. F. Cash & T. Pruzinsky (Eds.), *Body image: A handbook of theory, research, and clinical practice* (pp. 234–242). New York: Guilford Press.

Chial, H. J., Camilleri, M., Williams, D. E., Litzinger, K., & Perrault, J. (2003). Rumination syndrome in children and adolescents: Diagnosis, treatment, and prognosis. *Pediatrics*, *111*(1), 158–162.

Fairburn, C. G., Cooper, Z., Shafran, R., & Wilson, G. T. (2008). Eating disorders: A transdiagnostic protocol. In D. H. Barlow (Ed.), *Clinical handbook of psychological disorders: A step-by-step treatment manual* (4th ed., pp. 578–614). New York: Guilford Press.

Fairburn, C. G., Stice, E., Cooper, Z., Doll, H. A., Norman, P. A., & O'Connor, M. E. (2003). Understanding persistence in bulimia nervosa: A 5-year naturalistic study. *Journal of Counseling and Clinical Psychology*, *71*, 103–109.

Fisher, M., Rosen, D. S., Ornstein, R. M., Mammel, K. A., Katzman, D. K., Rome, E. S., ... Walsh, T. (2014). Characteristics of avoidant/restrictive food intake disorder in children and adolescents: A "new disorder" in DSM-5. *Journal of Adolescent Health*, *55*(1), 49–52.

Flegal, K. M., Carroll, M. D., Ogden, C. L., & Curtin, L. R. (2010). Prevalence and trends in obesity among US adults, 1999–2008. *Journal of the American Medical Association*, *303*(3), 235–241.

Fox, M., Young, A., Anggiansah, R., Anggiansah, A., & Sanderson, J. (2006). A 22 year old man with persistent regurgitation and vomiting: Case outcome. *British Medical Journal*, *333*, 133–137.

Franco, D. L., Wonderlich, S. A., Little, D., & Herzog, D. B. (2004). Diagnosis and classification of eating disorders. In J. K. Thompson (Ed.), *Handbook of eating disorders and obesity* (pp. 58–80). New York: John Wiley & Sons.

Gearhardt, A. N., Yokum, S., Stice, E., Corbin, W. R., & Brownell, K. D. (2011). Neural correlates of food addiction. *Archives of General Psychiatry*, *68*(8), 808–816.

Glazer, J. L. (2008). Eating disorders among male athletes. *Current Sports Medicine Reports*, *7*, 332–337.

Goel, M. S., McCarthy, E. P., Phillips, R. S., & Wee, C. C. (2004). Obesity among U.S. immigrant subgroups by duration of residence. *Journal of the American Medical Association*, *292*, 2860–2867.

Gonzalez, A., Kohn, M. R., & Clarke, S. D. (2007). Eating disorders in adolescents. *Australian Family Physician*, *36*(8), 614–619.

Grabe, S. & Hyde, J. S. (2006). Ethnicity and body dissatisfaction among women in the United States: A meta-analysis. *Psychological Bulletin*, *132*, 622–640.

Gull, W. W. (1873). Anorexia hysterical (Apepsia hysteria). *British Medical Journal*, *2*, 527.

Henderson, K. E., & Brownell, K. D. (2004). The toxic environment and obesity: Contribution and care. In J. K. Thompson (Ed.), *Handbook of eating disorders and obesity* (pp. 339–348). New York: John Wiley & Sons.

Hersen, M., Turner, S. M., & Beidel, D. C. (2007). *Adult psychopathology and diagnosis*. Hoboken, NJ: John Wiley & Sons.

Hill, A. J. (2006). Motivation for eating behavior in adolescent girls: The body beautiful. *Proceedings of the Nutrition Society*, *65*, 376–384.

Hudson, J. I., Hiripi, E., Pope, H. G., & Kessler, R. C. (2007). The prevalence and correlates of eating disorders in the national comorbidity survey replication. *Biological Psychiatry*, *61*, 348–358.

Iacovino, J. M., Gredysa, D. M., Altman, M., & Wilfley, D. E. (2012). Psychological treatments for binge eating. *Current Psychiatry Reports*, *14*(4), 432–436.

Jacobi, C., Hayward, C., deZwan, M., Kraemer, H. C., & Agras, W. S. (2004). Coming to terms with risk factors for eating disorders: Application of risk terminology and suggestions for a general taxonomy. *Psychological Bulletin*, *130*, 19–65.

Johnson, C. D., Shynett, B., Dosch, R., & Paulson, R. (2007). An unusual case of tooth loss, abrasion, and erosion associated with culturally accepted habit. *General Dentistry*, *55*(5), 445–448.

Kearney, C. A., & Trull, T. J. (2012). *Abnormal psychology and life: A dimensional approach*. Belmont, CA: Wadsworth Cengage Learning.

Keel, P. K., Dorer, D. J., Eddy, K. T., Franko, D., Charatan, D. L., & Herzog, D. B. (2003). Predictors of mortality in eating disorders. *Archives of General Psychiatry*, *60*, 179–183.

Kilgus, M. D., Maxmen, J. S., & Ward, N. G. (2009). *Essential psychopathology and its treatment* (3rd ed.). New York: W. W. Norton.

Kreipe, R. E., & Palomkaki, A. (2012). Beyond picky eating: Avoidant/restrictive food intake disorder. *Current Psychiatry Reports*, *14*(4), 421–431.

Lasegué, C. (1873). L'anorexia hysterique. *Archives Generales de Medicine*, *1*, 385–403.

Levine, J. K., Lanningham-Foster, L. M., McCrady, S. K., Krizan, A. C., Olson, L. R., Kane, P. H., ... Clark, M. M. (2005). Interindividual variation in posture allocation: Possible role in human obesity. *Science*, *307*, 584–586.

Marazziti, D., Corsi, M., Baroni, S., Consoli, G., & Catena-Dell'Osso, M. (2012). Latest advancements in the pharmacological treatment of binge eating disorder. *European Review for Medical and Pharmacological Sciences*, *16*(15), 2012–2017.

Marcé, L. V. (1860). On a form of hypochondriacal delirium occurring consecutive to dyspepsia, and characterized by refusal of food. *Journal of Psychological Medicine and Mental Pathology*, *13*, 264–266.

Mascola, A. J., Bryson S. W., & Agras, W. S. (2010). Picky eating during childhood: A longitudinal study to age 11 years. *Eating Behavior*, *11*, 253–257.

McGee, B. J., Hewitt, P. L., Sherry, S. B., Parkin, M., & Flett, G. L. (2005). Perfectionistic self-presentation, body image, and eating disorder symptoms. *Body Image*, *2*, 29–40.

Meengs, J. S., Roe, L. S., & Rolls, B. J. (2012). Vegetable variety: An effective strategy to increase vegetable intake in adults. *Journal of the Academy of Nutrition and Dietetics*, *112*(8), 1211–1216.

MentalHealth.gov. (2015). Binge eating. Retrieved on May 29, 2015 from: http://www.mentalhealth.gov/what-to-look-for/eating-disorders/binge-eating/index.html

National Center for Health Statistics. (2005). Chart book on trends in the health of Americans. *Health, United States*. Hyattsville, MD: Public Health Service.

Nicholls, D., Christie, D., Randall, L., & Lask, B. (2001). Selective eating: Symptom, disorder or normal variant. *Clinical Child Psychology and Psychiatry*, 6(2), 257–270.

Ogden, C. L., Carroll, M. D., Curtin, L. R., Lamb, M. M., & Flegal, K. M. (2010). Prevalence of high body mass index in US children and adolescents, 2007–2008. *Journal of the American Medical Association*, *303*(3), 242–249.

Olden, K. W. (2001). Rumination. *Current Treatment Options in Gastroenterology*, *4*(4), 351–358.

Papadopoulos, V., & Mimidis, K. (2007). The rumination syndrome in adults: A review of the pathophysiology, diagnosis and treatment. *Journal of Postgraduate Medicine*, *53*(3), 203–206.

Parry-Jones, B., & Parry-Jones, W. L. (2002). History of bulimia and bulimia nervosa. In K. D. Brownell & C. G. Fairburn (Eds.), *Eating disorders and obesity: A comprehensive handbook* (2nd ed., pp. 145–150). New York: Guilford Press.

Polivy, J., & Herman, C. P. (2002). Dieting and its relation to eating disorders. In K. D. Brownell & C. G. Fairburn (Eds.), *Eating disorders and obesity: A comprehensive handbook* (2nd ed., pp. 83–86). New York, NY: Guilford Press.

Pomeroy, C. (2004). Assessment of medical status and physical factors. In J. K. Thompson (Ed.), *Handbook of eating disorders and obesity* (pp. 81–111). New York: John Wiley & Sons.

Rasquin-Weber. A., Hyman, P. E., Cucchiara, S., Fleisher, D. R., Hyams, J. S., Milla, P. J., & Staiano, A. (1999). Childhood functional gastrointestinal disorders. *Gut*, *45*(Suppl. 2), 1160–1168.

Rogers, B., Stratton, P., Victor, J., Cennedy, B., & Andres, M. (1992). Chronic regurgitation among persons with mental retardation: A need for combined medical and interdisciplinary strategies. *American Journal of Mental Retardation*, *96*(5), 522–527.

Rome, E. S., & Ammerman, S. (2003). Medical complications of eating disorders: An update. *Journal of Adolescent health*, *33*(6), 418–426.

Rose, E. A., Porcerelli, J. H., & Neale, A. V. (2000). Pica: Common but commonly missed. *The Journal of the American Board of Family Practice*, *13*(5), 353–358.

Sassaroli, S., Romero Lauro, L. J., Maria Ruggerio, G., Mauri, M. C., Vinai, P., & Frost, R. (2008). Perfectionism in depression, obsessive-compulsive disorder and eating disorders. *Behaviour Research and Therapy*, *46*, 757–765.

Schwartz, M. B., & Brownell, K. D. (2007). Actions necessary to prevent childhood obesity: Creating the climate for change. *Journal of Law, Medicine, and Ethics*, *35*, 78–79.

Stice, E. (2002). Risk and maintenance factors for eating pathology: A meta-analytic review. *Psychological Bulletin*, *128*, 825–848.

Stice, E., Ng, J., & Shaw, H. (2010). Risk factors and prodromal eating pathology. *Journal of Child Psychology and Psychiatry and Allied Disciplines*, *51*(4), 518–525.

Stice, E., Shaw, H., & Marti, C. N. (2007). A meta-analytic review of eating disorder prevention programs: Encouraging findings. *Annual Review of Clinical Psychology*, *3*, 207–231.

Sudi, K., Ottl, K., Payerl, D., Baumgard, P., Tauschmann, K., & Miller, W. (2004). Anorexia athletica. *Nutrition*, *20*, 657–661.

Sullivan, P. B. (1997). Gastrointestinal problems in the neurologically impaired child. *Baillieres Clinical Gastroenterology*, *11*(1), 529–546.

Swanson, S. A., Crow, S. J., Le Grange, D., Swendsen, J., & Merikangas, K. R. (2011). Prevalence and correlates of eating disorders in adolescents. Results from the national comorbidity survey replication adolescent supplement. *Archives of General Psychiatry*, *68*(7), 714–723.

Talley, N. J. (2011). Rumination syndrome. *Gastroenterology Hepatology*, 7(2), 117–118.

Thompson, J. K., & van den Berg, P. (2002). Measuring body image attitudes among adolescents and adults. In T. F. Cash & T. Pruzinsky (Eds.), *Body image: A handbook of theory, research, and practice* (pp. 142–154). New York: Guilford Press.

Tiggerman, M., & Slater, A. (2001). A test of objectification theory in former dancers and non-dancers. *Psychology of Women Quarterly*, *25*, 57–64.

Timimi, S., Douglas, J., & Tsiftsopolou, K. (1997). Selective eaters: A retrospective case note study. *Child Care Health Development*, *23*, 265–278.

Utter, J., Neumark-Stainzer, D., Wall, M., & Story, M. (2003). Reading magazine articles about dieting and associated weight control behaviors among adolescents. *Journal of Adolescent Health*, *32*, 78–82.

Vitiello, B., & Lederhendler, I. (2000). Research on eating disorders: Current status and future prospects. *Biological Psychiatry*, *47*, 777–786.

Wade, T. D., Bulik, C. M., Prescott, C. A., & Kendler, K. S. (2004). Sex influences on shared risk factors for bulimia nervosa and other psychiatric disorders. *Archives of General Psychiatry*, *61*, 251–256.

Wang, S. (2010, July 5). No age limit on picky eating. *Wall Street Journal*. Retrieved on April 2, 2013 from: http://online.wsj.com/article/SB1000142 4052748704699604575343130457388718.html

Westerburg, D. P., & Waitz, M. (2013). Binge-eating disorder. *Osteopathic Family Physician*, *5*(6), 230–233.

Young, S. S., Wilson, M. J., Miller, D., & Hillier, S. (2008). Toward a comprehensive approach to the collection and analysis of pica substances, with emphasis on geophagic materials. *PLoS ONE*, *3*(9), e3147.

Zipfel, S., Lowe, B., Deter, H. C., & Herzog, W. (2000). Long-term prognosis in anorexia nervosa: Lessons from a 21-year follow-up study. *Lancet*, *355*, 721–722.

CHAPTER

Elimination Disorders

INTRODUCTION

Bladder and bowel control are two important developmental tasks during the developmental stage of toddlerhood. Almost any parent can tell you stories of sitting together with their toddler in the bathroom and celebrating the joy of "going poopy or pee-pee in the potty." When the child experiences persistent problems with toileting and there is no medical reason, for example, a physical condition or the side effects of a drug, then an elimination disorder is considered. It is more common for the elimination disorders to be caused by medical conditions than psychiatric ones and the soiling is unintentional (Davidson, 2003).

The DSM elimination disorders are organized around the inappropriate elimination of urine or feces. They are first seen in childhood or adolescence, and the diagnosis is made when a child does not accomplish control over his or her bladder (enuresis) and/or bowels (encopresis) within a reasonable expected time frame or if there has been a regression (APA, 2013). Psychiatric factors may place the individual at a higher risk; for example, a child may begin wetting the bed or soiling their pants at 7 or 8 years of age after a difficult time in their life. Joinson and colleagues (2008) observed that a child's delayed development, a difficult temperament, and maternal depression or anxiety were associated with an increase in the odds of a child experiencing problems with bladder and bowel control. Absence of the expected bladder and/or bowel control should first be explored medically. When the causes are psychiatric, the soiling may also be unintentional, but not always. Table 12.1 lists the specific elimination disorders found in the DSM-5.

This chapter provides a review of the elimination disorders, beginning with enuresis.

TABLE 12.1 THE DSM-5 ELIMINATION DISORDERS
Enuresis
Encopresis
Other Specified Elimination Disorder
Unspecified Elimination Disorder

ENURESIS

Bed-wetting or nocturnal enuresis is the most common elimination disorder (APA, 2013). Enuresis can have either medical or psychiatric circumstances. From a medical perspective, enuresis has been associated with various forms of physical trauma, indicative of a seizure disorder, or may be related to malformations of the urinary system or hormonal imbalances that affect the ability to concentrate urine. Psychiatric factors, such as psychosocial stress or delayed or lax toilet training, place the child at a higher risk for developing enuresis (APA, 2013). In particular, von Gontard and colleagues (2011) noted that the effects of wetting on the child's self-esteem, quality of life, and related distress, and the rate of comorbid disorders, can also contribute to the increased risk of enuresis. Most commonly, enuresis runs in families. When the cause is related to genetics, it is not effected by counseling. Enuresis declines as the child continues to mature and he or she will most likely stop bed-wetting without intervention by adolescence.

PREVAILING PATTERN

Enuresis is a common condition among younger children in the United States, and rates vary by age with a gradual decline through childhood. For example, the disorder can be found in 5 to 10 percent of 5-year-olds, 3 to 5 percent among 10-year-olds, and approximately 1 percent among persons who are 15 years of age and older (APA, 2013). A family history of enuresis increases the likelihood of the disorder. Arnell and colleagues (1997) found a family history of bed-wetting in 50 percent of children with enuresis. Sirangam Shreeram, Jian-Ping, Kalaydian, Brthers, and Merikangas (2009) call attention to an association between attention-deficit/hyperactivity disorder and enuresis, but only 26 percent of the enuretic children they studied in a nationally representative sample had received mental health services.

DIFFERENTIAL ASSESSMENT

Enuresis involves repeated voiding of urine; for example, into the bed or clothes. This behavior can be voluntary or involuntary, though the latter is more common. This diagnosis is considered when the child is 5 years old and when the wetting occurs at least twice a week for 3 months. A mental age of at least 5 years is considered for children with developmental delays. The diagnosis is made if there are no physiological effects of a substance (such as a diuretic, antipsychotic medication, or any other medications that may bring about incontinence) or another medical condition (for instance, diabetes, a seizure disorder, or spina bifida, and so forth) that may better explain the wetting.

There are three specifiers: (1) nocturnal only, or the passage of urine during nighttime sleep, commonly referred to as bed-wetting; (2) diurnal, or passage of urine during waking hours; and (3) nocturnal and diurnal, which consists of a combination of the nocturnal and diurnal subtypes.

The course of enuresis can be described as primary or secondary. **Primary enuresis** is when a child has never been successfully trained to control urination and, by definition, begins before 5 years of age. **Secondary enuresis** refers to children who have been successfully trained or have established good bladder control for a substantial period of time and then begin wetting again in response to some sort of stressful situation. Secondary enuresis usually occurs between 5 and 8 years of age and, as we will see in the case of Ricky Crouse, it can also happen at any time.

Let's turn to the case of Ricky Crouse illustrating enuresis.

CASE The Case of Ricky Crouse

Mrs. Crouse begins her conversation with the social worker with, "It has been rough for me and Ricky this past year." She resumed, "You see, it all went downhill when I started to suspect that my husband, Ray, had a little something going on the side. First it was the late nights at work. Then he had to go into the office weekends. Finally he had these business trips. I mean Ray's never traveled for work, so it seemed a little odd. Of course he denied having a relationship, but at home he seemed so distant and preoccupied. Well, I'm no dummy. I started looking at our phone bills and you guessed it. Several late night calls to the same number. Unexplained expenses on our charge card, too. One day I got up the nerve and called the number. Somehow I was not surprised when some woman answered. Worse yet, she hung up on me when I told her who I was. So I confronted Ray. He finally confessed that he fell out of love with me. What? We've been married for 25 years but, yes, he fell in love with his 22-year-old secretary, Bambi. No joke, that's really her name."

Tears welled up in her eyes and Mrs. Crouse added, "The divorce was rough, especially on Ricky. He always looked up to his father and somehow felt that it was all his fault. I can't tell you how many times I tried to explain to him that his dad and I just drifted apart and it had nothing to do with him. Ricky just didn't believe me. His father moved into a separate bedroom and the tension in the house was so thick you could cut it with a knife. When Ray and I did talk we usually ended up in a shouting match. This went on for a year before the divorce was finalized and Ray moved out. To be honest, I think I neglected Ricky. I had so much on my mind. I've always been a stay-at-home mom and here I was job hunting and worrying how I would manage alone. I tried not to think of Ray living with his lover 'cause it would just consume me. Then I started working and Ricky was left alone in the house after school. I hate to admit it but I'm sure I put pressure on Ricky to be the man of the house. I know better but I was just so overwhelmed."

A tear rolled down Mrs. Crouse's cheek and she brushed it aside. I waited for her to collect her thoughts. Mrs. Crouse continued, "I feel like I'm starting to come out of that dark tunnel, but now I'm worried about Ricky. He has his life ahead of him and I want to do what it takes to get him back on track. He's such a handsome, bright, and sensitive boy. He used to be a straight 'A' student but now he's close to failing. He lost his interest in sports too, and doesn't seem to be as involved with his friends, either. That's why I'm here. His pediatrician suggested counseling might help.

CASE THE CASE OF RICKY CROUSE (CONTINUED)

There's nothing medical to explain his bed-wetting. Honestly, I think I could also use some help learning how to connect with Ricky again."

The social worker asked Mrs. Crouse to elaborate her concerns. She responded, "Its start was so insidious. At first I noticed a faint odor on Ricky's sheets. He's 11 years old, and active in sports so I thought nothing of it. Then I started to smell a clear odor. I thought maybe he just had an accident so I simply changed the sheets, but it kept happening. Sometimes there were big dark spots. I didn't say anything to Ricky and couldn't figure out what could be happening. I hoped he would outgrow it ... at least that's what I kept telling myself. Then I started keeping track. This had been going on for the past 6 months and would happen about 2 or 3 times a week. One thing I can tell you for sure is that I hate the color yellow and I can detect the smell of urine better than anyone else I know."

Mrs. Crouse's demeanor shifted, and the best way I could describe it was she looked defeated. She continued, "Then it was time for Ricky's visit to the doctor for his checkup for summer camp. The timing couldn't be better. So off we went. By now I was changing his sheets almost every other day. I went in to see the doctor first. Ricky didn't seem to mind. You see, I was so afraid Ricky might have some bad health problem and didn't want to break down in front of him. I told the doctor about Ricky's bed-wetting and then he saw Ricky. Afterward, I learned from the doctor that Ricky had come clean about his worries and mentioned how much he was confused about his father. On the one hand Ricky loves his dad, and on the other he's mad that he left us. Still feels it's his fault. That's where you come in." Mrs. Crouse mentioned the doctor's referral to the social worker.

"No offense," added Mrs. Crouse, "but I thought I could handle this on my own. So when we got home, I sat Ricky down and attempted to talk with him. At first he would shift from, 'Leave me alone,' to 'There's nothing wrong with me.' We were getting nowhere but I held my ground. I think what pushed me over the edge to call to you was when Ricky finally said, 'You make me talk about things I want to forget,' and added, 'When I wake up wet I feel so bad about myself. If you must know, it makes me want to cry. I'm looking forward to being dry again because then I'll be able to feel normal.' I reached over and there were a lot of hugs and tears. Ricky and I have always been close but this divorce put a wedge between us. I think we both could use your help to get back on track."

RICKY CROUSE'S DSM DIAGNOSIS IS AS FOLLOWS:
Enuresis, nocturnal only

Competency 8 c

ASSESSMENT SUMMARY By the time Ricky Crouse had been referred to the social worker, his pediatrician ruled out any medical problems that might better explain his bed-wetting. Additionally, Ricky was not taking any medications that may better explain his enuresis. In fact. He is in good health and not taking any medication. The social worker begins to organize data from Mrs. Crouse's description of what has been happening to Ricky in order to better understand his inability to control urination.

Ricky's symptom picture supports the pattern of enuresis. For example, he had been continent but then began to wet at night 2 to 3 times a week for the past 6 months. In addition, the entire family was under a great deal of stress beginning with Mr. Crouse's extramarital affair. Tension increased in the home as the couple moved toward what sounded like a difficult divorce process that lasted for about a year. Eventually, Mr. Crouse moved out in order to live with his lover and Mrs. Crouse was confronted with a difficult transition; that is, having to look for a job and managing

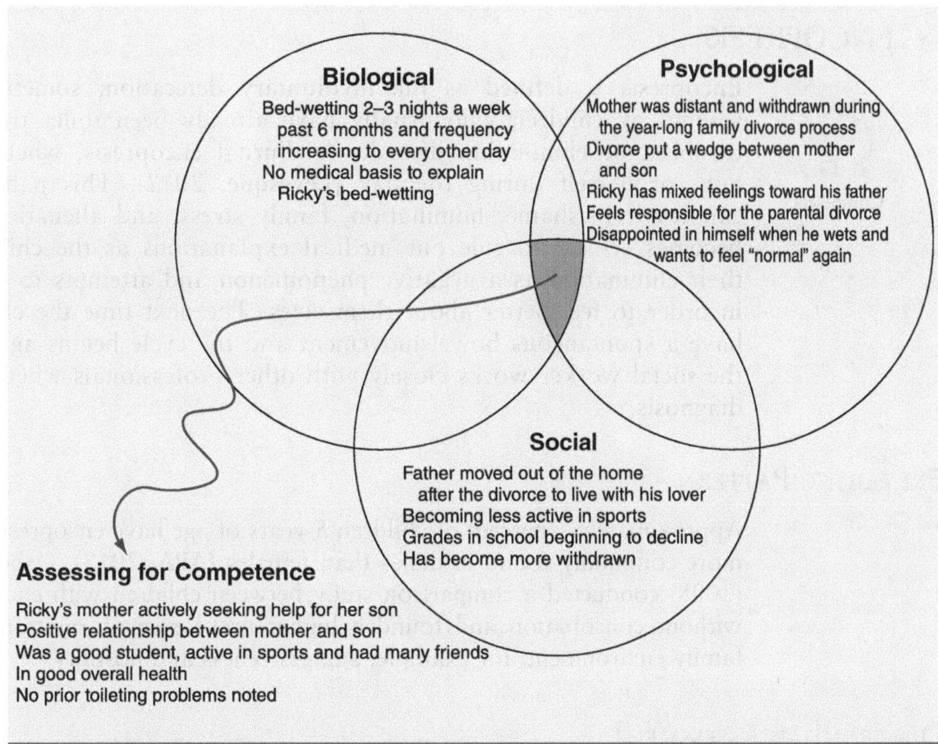

FIGURE 12.1 › ENURESIS
The interactions of the biological, psychological, and social variables in Ricky Crouse's life.

as a single mother. Mrs. Crouse showed good insight into her relationship with her son and admitted to being consumed with her own feelings and neglecting Ricky's emotional needs during this difficult family transition. Despite his mother's reassurances, Ricky felt responsible for the parents' breakup. His grades began to decline, he lost interest in sports, and was less engaged with his friends. It was around this time that the pattern of nocturnal wetting began. Ricky's self-esteem appeared to be affected and, in his own words, "When I wake up wet I feel so disappointed in myself and I want to cry." He talked about wanting to stop wetting so he could feel normal again.

Competency 7 c

Looking to the competencies in Ricky's life, his mother describes him as a "handsome, bright, and sensitive boy." While we don't know about Mr. Crouse's involvement with his son, we do know that Mrs. Crouse is extremely concerned about Ricky and sought the social worker's help to get their relationship back on track. Although the conversation after the doctor's visit between mother and son around his enuresis was difficult, they somehow managed. Tears and hugs were exchanged, suggesting a strong relationship between the two. Ricky's mother sought help for her son's bed-wetting beginning with a medical appointment for a checkup, and she followed through with the referral to the social worker. Prior to the stress of the divorce, Ricky was a good student, involved in sports, and seemed to have many friends. He is also in good general health (Figure 12.1).

We now turn to a review of encopresis.

ENCOPRESIS

Competency 8 c

Encopresis is defined as the involuntary defecation, sometimes called fecal soiling, by children who usually have already been toilet trained. The more troublesome elimination disorder is diurnal encopresis, where the child soils him- or herself during the day (Levesque, 2012). This pattern of behavior can result in shame, humiliation, family stress, and alienation from peers. It becomes critical to rule out medical explanations as the child tends to view their elimination as a negative phenomenon and attempts to retain their feces in order to feel better about themselves. The next time the child relaxes, they have a spontaneous bowel movement and the cycle begins again. Accordingly, the social worker works closely with other professionals when formulating the diagnosis.

PREVAILING PATTERN

Approximately 1 percent of children 5 years of age have encopresis. The disorder is more commonly found in males than females (APA, 2013). Lisboa and colleagues (2008) conducted a comparison study between children with encopresis and those without constipation and found a higher prevalence of emotional aspects in the family environment, for example, aggressiveness and hostility.

DIFFERENTIAL ASSESSMENT

Encopresis describes the child who is at least 4 years old and cannot control his or her bowel movements so they pass feces into inappropriate places, such as in their underwear. Control is either involuntary or intentional. At least one soiling event must occur each month for 3 months in order to consider the diagnosis. Another medical condition, or the effects of a substance such as laxatives, does not better explain the child's bowel movements.

In most situations, encopresis develops as a result of long-standing constipation, and is specified as "with constipation and overflow incontinence" that is supported by a physical exam or history. The child with constipation has fewer bowel movements than normal. The bowel movements they do have can be hard, dry, and difficult to pass. Over time, the large intestine slowly fills with stool and stretches out of shape. Consequently, liquid stool from the small intestine begins to "leak" around the more formed stool in the colon. At the outset, the leakage usually comes in small amounts that may just streak or stain the child's underwear. Understandably, most parents attribute this to the child's failure to thoroughly wipe him- or herself. As the large intestine continues to fill and stretch further, the leakage increases to the point where the child has "accidents"; that is, they pass bowel movements in their underwear. At this point the stool is not completely digested and usually is very dark and sticky, smells badly, and has to be scraped off the child's skin and clothes.

Encopresis can also be specified as "without constipation and overflow incontinence." These situations occur less commonly. The child's feces are likely to be of normal form and consistency. Soiling is intermittent and yet may be displayed in a prominent location; for example, smeared on the wall or floor. In this situation, a comorbid disorder is most likely, such as oppositional defiant disorder or conduct disorder (APA, 2013). Anal masturbation may be another contributor.

The case of Jimmy Clark illustrates encopresis.

CASE The Case of Jimmy Clark

Mrs. Clark begins, "I started to potty train my little Jimmy when he was 3 years old. He didn't seem ready. You know, not letting me know when he had to go 'poopy' let alone knowing why he had to sit on the potty. Long stretches of sitting with him in the bathroom and singing the praises of going poopy in the potty got to be a bit tiresome, so I put it off for a while. When he seemed ready, we accomplished it. I was so happy but then the holdings started. At first it was just a couple of times a month, and then it gradually got worse. Seemed like he had more important things going on ... like playing."

The social worker encouraged Mrs. Clark to continue. She said, "I hate to admit it now but back then I would get so frustrated with Jimmy. I thought his accidents were because he was lazy. He would do well for a while and then go back to square one. I don't think there are many people out there who understand what it's like to have a child who poops in his pants. This is a very lonely problem." Mrs. Clark asked the social worker, "Do you have children?" The social worker could sense Mrs. Clark's discomfort and responded, "When you ask me if I have children, I'm wondering if you are more concerned that I may not understand what you've gone through. I'll be glad to answer your question but first I'm wondering if we could talk about what worries you so." Mrs. Clark looked relieved and shared how guilty she felt about the way she had treated Jimmy for the past several months. She commented, "He was always a very active, intelligent, and hyperfocused little boy so I just thought he was not paying attention to when he needed to go." Before she found out about his diagnosis, Mrs. Clark confided that she thought Jimmy was simply lazy and acting out. She described how hard she tried to get Jimmy to "make poopy in the potty." When he didn't, she felt helpless. Then Jimmy's self-esteem and confidence would deteriorate, and especially when he had an accident.

Mrs. Clark continued, "I'm at a loss to find the words to describe how it was to see Jimmy suffer. Until I understood what was really going on, I just hammered him. He resisted going to the bathroom like he used to. He would fight it, and when he had to go I could see him break out into a sweat. Jimmy would look at me with those big blue eyes of his and say, 'Mommy, I'm trying to push it out,' but in reality I knew he was doing all he could to avoid it. Then he would try to clean himself and usually ended up making a mess of things. That's usually when I lost it."

Mrs. Clark added, "In the middle of all this the husband and I were having problems, so I buried myself in my work. Looking back, I think I neglected Jimmy when he needed me the most. At the time I wasn't worried since Jimmy got along great with his uncle, my husband's brother, so he did a lot of babysitting. Jimmy wasn't getting any better, so I started looking on the Internet and talked to a friend studying psychology. I finally realized that there could actually be a reason why my son was soiling and it wasn't because he was lazy or naughty. I decided it was time to take him to our pediatrician. My 4½-year-old son has never really been fully poop trained and he was finally diagnosed. He has encopresis but ..." Tears started rolling down Mr. Clark's cheeks.

Mrs. Clark shared that the doctor also found some "irregularities" with Jimmy's anus. "Something about the sphincter muscles," she added. It emerged that the uncle had been sexually abusing Jimmy with anal penetration. She started to cry.

As Mrs. Clark began to regain her composure, she said, "I know I have a lot of work ahead, but I feel better taking this first step." The social worker referred her to a group at the agency consisting of

CASE The Case of Jimmy Clark (Continued)

mothers with children having similar struggles, individual counseling, and individual counseling for Jimmy.

As a postscript, the social worker did answer Mrs. Clark's question about having children. The social worker shared that she did not have children and added, "Mrs. Clark, your feelings are very important to me. If for some reason, as we work together, you feel that I'm not understanding, could you please let me know?" Mrs. Clark responded that talking about her uncomfortable feelings instead of getting angry and yelling would be something new for her, but she would give it a try.

Jimmy Clark's DSM Diagnosis Is as Follows:

Encopresis with constipation and overflow incontinence

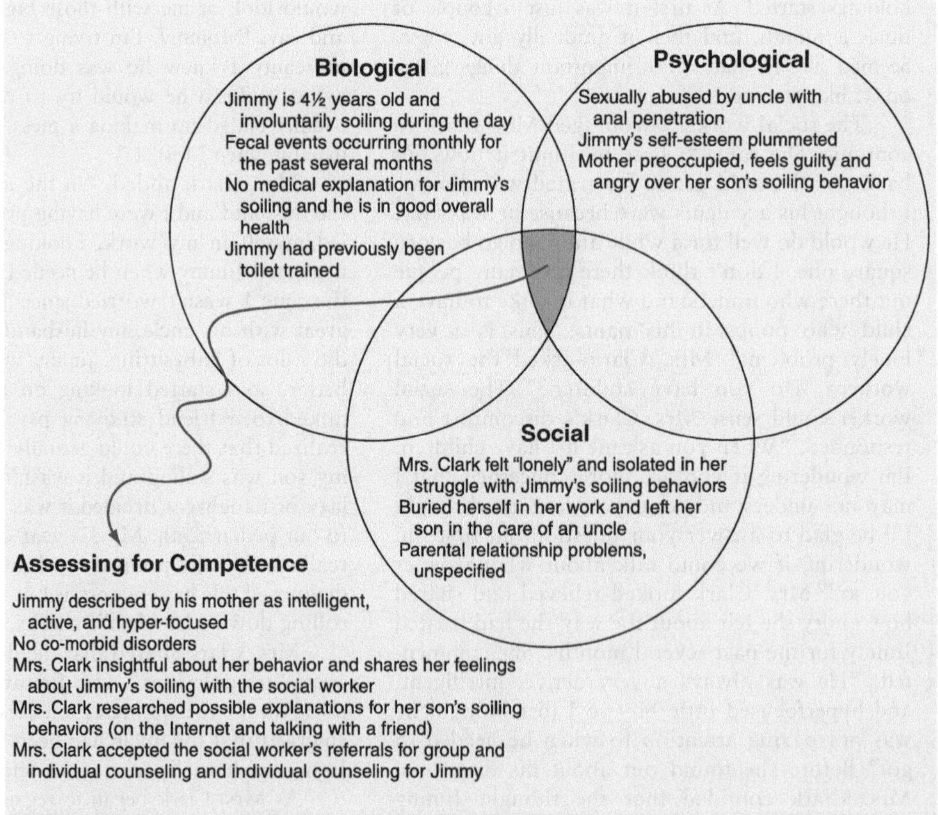

FIGURE 12.2 › ENCOPRESIS
The interactions of the biological, psychological, and social variables in Jimmy Clark's life.

Competency 7 d

Assessment Summary Jimmy had a complete medical checkup, and there was no medical condition that could better explain his encopresis. Unfortunately, a history of sexual abuse by his uncle was discovered. Mellon, Whiteside, and Friedrich (2006) report that it is not unusual to discover sexual abuse, with or without penetration, among children who are soiling.

Jimmy's symptoms support the picture of diurnal encopresis. He is now 4½ years old, involuntarily soils in his pants primarily during the day, had previously been toilet trained, and fecal elimination events were occurring monthly for the past several months (three at a minimum). Jimmy's self-esteem plummeted. Additionally, Mrs. Clark was having problems with her husband, admits to neglecting Jimmy, and leaving him in the care of his uncle who sexually abused him.

Competency 7 b

Despite the stress of Jimmy's behavior, Mrs. Clark describes her son positively; that is, she sees him as intelligent, active, and hyperfocused. There are no other behaviors in her "story" that would support another disorder, such as conduct disorder or oppositional defiant disorder. Any "mess" that Jimmy makes is the result of trying to clean himself up after soiling. Mrs. Clark is insightful about her behavior in response to Jimmy's soiling, and describes feeling angry and guilty. She is candid with the social worker and accepts referrals for group and individual counseling for herself and individual counseling for Jimmy (Figure 12.2).

OTHER RELATED DISORDERS

Two additional elimination disorders are other specified elimination disorder, and unspecified elimination disorder. The category of other specified elimination disorder is used when the individual does not meet full criteria for any of the elimination disorders. The practitioner may specify the reason, such as "low frequency enuresis" (APA, 2013, p. 359). Unspecified elimination disorder is used in situations where the individual does not meet full diagnostic criteria for an elimination disorder and the practitioner may not have sufficient information to make a diagnosis; for example, the client who is seen in the emergency room.

SUMMARY

There are two key developmental tasks that must be successfully accomplished during the stage of toddlerhood, and they are bladder and bowel control. When the child experiences persistent problems with toileting and there is no medical explanation, for instance, a bladder infection or diabetes, then an elimination disorder is considered. The symptom picture for enuresis, or the involuntary voiding of urine, more commonly called bed-wetting, was reviewed; followed by a review of encopresis, seen as repeated inappropriate passage of feces. Both disorders are most often involuntary behaviors found in childhood but can also extend into adolescence. Additionally, both disorders can occur during the day (diurnal) or at night (nocturnal).

As the DSM transitions from the DSM-IV-TR (APA, 2000) to the current edition of the manual, Table 12.2 provides a brief summary of the changes made to the diagnostic classifications.

TABLE 12.2	SUMMARY COMPARISON BETWEEN THE DSM-IV-TR AND DSM-5 DIAGNOSES FOR THE ELIMINATION DISORDERS
Both enuresis and encopresis have been moved to a new chapter called "elimination disorders"	
Overall, there have been no significant changes made to the diagnostic criteria between the former manual and the current DSM-5	

PRACTITIONER'S REFLECTIONS

Children diagnosed with an elimination disorder can often experience feelings of shame or embarrassment. If there is no medical basis for wetting or soiling, the diagnosis of enuresis and/or encopresis is considered. Diagnostic criteria include clinically significant distress or impairment in important areas of functioning such as poor self-esteem, declining grades in school or a reluctance to engage in social activities such as sleep overs to list a few. Talking about these behaviors can be difficult for parents and/or caregivers.

Competency 1 c

ACTIVITIES

Competency 2 b

1. Imagine for a moment that Ricky Crouse is your client. How would you begin to address his feelings around his parents' divorce? What questions would you bring to your clinical supervisor? As a part of relationship building, can you think of any events in your own childhood that evoked feelings of shame or embarrassment? As a parallel, address whether this level of introspection would be helpful in your work with Ricky.

Competency 1 c

2. Looking to the case of Jimmy Clark, consider the point in the interview when Mrs. Clark asks the social worker if she has any children. Discuss the social worker's response with a colleague and/or your supervisor. Would you have responded in the same way or differently? Role-play your response to a question like Mrs. Clark asked. Can you think of any other questions that a client may ask that would make you feel uncomfortable in the interview? List them and consider your potential responses.

Competency 7 a

3. Jimmy Clark's mother agreed to the social worker's referrals to group and individual counseling, and individual counseling for her son, Jimmy. She comments in the interview, "I don't think there are many people out there who understand what it's like to have a child who poops in his pants. This is a very lonely problem." Reflect on how different relational, organizational, and community systems may impact clients like Mrs. Clark.

Competency 7 b

4. The prevalence rates for enuresis and encopresis point to the reality that few individuals or their families seek out mental health services, even when there is a co-occurring disorder. Reflect on reasons why families (and their children) may not seek help. Discuss with your supervisor and/or a colleague what can be done to reach out in order to provide needed services to these populations.

Competency 2 b

5. Many families struggling with a child with an elimination disorder could be considered "high functioning"; that is, they have not had any problems that would require professional counseling and/or other supportive services. Unfortunately, when the disorder is diagnosed, it tends to dominate family life. Keeping in mind the competency-based perspective, how would you go about addressing the struggles confronting a family with a child diagnosed with an elimination disorder and simultaneously explore the strengths found in each client's story. If you do not have a client with these issues on your caseload, use the case studies in this chapter as a springboard. Also interview a colleague (or your supervisor) who has had experience in this field of practice.

Competency Notes

Competency 1 c—Social workers demonstrate professional demeanor in behavior, appearance, and oral/written/electronic communication (p. 350): Social workers understand how their personal experiences and affective reactions can influence their professional judgment and behavior and also understand emerging forms of technology and the ethical use of technology in practice.

Competency 2 b—Social workers present themselves as learners and engage clients (and constituencies) as experts in their own experiences (pp. 350, 351): Social workers appreciate the dimensions of diversity as the intersectionality of multiple factors.

Competency 7 a—Social workers collect and organize data and apply critical thinking in order to interpret information from clients and constituencies (p. 350): Social workers understand that the assessment process is ongoing and conducted with, and on behalf of, diverse individuals, families, groups, organizations, and communities.

Competency 7 b—Social workers are able to apply knowledge of human behavior and the social environment, person-in-environment, and other multidisciplinary theoretical frameworks in the analysis of assessment data (pp. 349, 350): Social workers understand theories of human behavior and the social environment and critically evaluate and apply this knowledge in the assessment process.

Competency 7 c—Social workers develop mutually agreed-on intervention goals and objectives based on the assessment of strengths, needs and challenges within clients and constituencies (p. 345): Social workers recognize the implications of the larger practice context in the assessment process.

Competency 7 d—Social workers select appropriate intervention strategies based on the assessment, research knowledge, and values and preferences of clients and communities (p. 349): Social workers understand methods of assessment with diverse clients (and constituencies) to advance practice effectiveness.

Competency 8 c—Social workers use interprofessional collaboration, as appropriate, to achieve beneficial practice outcomes (pp. 344, 346): Social workers value interprofessional teamwork and recognize the beneficial outcomes that require interdisciplinary, interprofessional, and interorganizational collaboration.

References

American Psychiatric Association (APA). (2000). *Diagnostic and statistical manual of mental disorders* (4th ed., text revision). Washington, DC: Author.

American Psychiatric Association (APA). (2013). *Diagnostic and statistical manual of mental disorders* (5th ed.). Arlington, VA: Author.

Arnell, H., Hjalmas, K., Jagervall, M., Lackgren, G., Stenberg, A., Bengtsson, B., ... Dahl, N. (1997). The genetics of primary nocturnal enuresis: Inheritance and suggestion of a second major gene on chromosome 12q. *Journal of Major Genetics*, *34*, 360–365.

Davidson, T. (2003). Elimination disorders. *Gale Encyclopedia of Mental Disorders*. Retrieved June 23, 2014 from: http://www.encyclopedia.com/doc/1G2-3405700140.html

Joinson, C., Heron, J., von Gontard, A., Butler, U., Golding, J., & Emond, A. (2008). Early childhood risk factors associated with daytime wetting and soiling in school-age children. *Journal of Pediatric Psychology*, *33*, 739–750.

Levesque, R. J. R. (2012). Enuresis and encopresis. In R. J. R. Levesque (Ed.), *Encyclopedia of adolescence* (Vol. 2, pp. 843–846). New York: Springer.

Lisboa, V. C. A., Felizola, M. C. M., Martins, L. A. N., Tahan, S., Neto, U. F., & de Morias, M. B. (2008). Aggressiveness and hostility in the family environment and chronic constipation in children. *Digestive Diseases and Sciences*, *53*(9), 2458–2463.

Mellon, M. W., Whiteside, S. P., & Friedrich, W. N. (2006). The relevance of fecal soiling as an indicator of child sexual abuse: A preliminary analysis. *Journal of Developmental and Behavioral Pediatrics*, *27*, 25–32.

Sirangam Shreeram, S., Jian-Ping, M. S., Kalaydian, A., Brthers, S., & Merikangas, K. R. (2009). Prevalence of enuresis and its association with attention-deficit/hyperactivity disorder among U.S. children: Results from a nationally representative study. *Journal of the American Academy of Child & Adolescent Psychiatry*, *48*(1), 35–41.

von Gontard, A., Baeyens, D., van Hoecke, E., Warzak, W. J., & Bachmann, C. (2011). Psychological and psychiatric issues in urinary and fecal incontinence. *The Journal of Urology*, *185*(4), 1432–1437.

CHAPTER 13

Disruptive, Impulse-Control, and Conduct Disorders

INTRODUCTION

The disruptive, impulse-control, and conduct disorders are a new chapter to the DSM-5. They include oppositional defiant disorder, the disruptive behaviors as seen in intermittent explosive disorder, conduct disorder, pyromania, and kleptomania. These disorders are distinguished by problems in emotional and behavioral self-control.

All of us have lost our temper at one time or another. What differentiates the disruptive, impulse-control, and conduct disorders is that they include very severe problems in the self-control of emotions and behaviors. While there are other disorders that may involve problems in emotional and/or behavioral regulation, the disorders in this chapter are unique in that the individual's problems are shown in behaviors that violate the rights of others (for example, aggression or destruction of property) and/or bring the person into conflict with societal norms or authority figures. Interestingly, these disorders are more common in males and emerge in childhood and adolescence. This diagnostic category also includes the more rare disorders of pyromania and kleptomania that are characterized by poor impulse control related to specific behaviors, such as fire setting or stealing.

The specific DSM-5 disorders involving problems in the self-control of emotions and are listed in Table 13.1.

Competency 6 a

Since these disorders tend to have first onset in childhood or adolescence, it is helpful for the practitioner to keep in mind that a child's behavior is affected by a number of factors such as family and home life, spiritual influences, culture, community, and economic issues, as well as inborn characteristics, such as genetic makeup (Ashford & LeCroy, 2011). The development of mental health disorders in children is influenced by the interaction of these complex psychosocial and biological features. A child diagnosed with a mental disorder is set apart from other

TABLE 13.1 THE DSM-5 DISRUPTIVE, IMPULSE-CONTROL, AND CONDUCT DISORDERS

Oppositional Defiant Disorder
Intermittent Explosive Disorder
Conduct Disorder
Pyromania
Kleptomania
Unspecified Disruptive, Impulse-Control, and Conduct Disorder

children by significant deviations from developmentally appropriate behaviors, emotions, or relationships (Webb, 2011). This underscores the comprehensive approach of the competency-based assessment model that keeps the whole child in perspective as the practitioner formulates a DSM diagnosis. Paying attention to the child's contexts and sources of strength and resilience becomes an integral part of the diagnostic process and serves to reinforce and improve adaptation.

CULTURAL PERSPECTIVES

Competency 2 a

Ethnicity and culture can also affect the behaviors parents perceive in their child as "normal" versus "abnormal" (Slade, 2004). It is important for the practitioner to recognize the importance of "difference" in shaping the child's life experiences and to be able to communicate this understanding to those who are a part of the child's life. For example, what the parent thinks about the child's behavior and their parenting efforts can play a role in the assessment process. Surprisingly, there are no generally available assessment guidelines beyond the Cultural Formulation in the DSM-5 section on "Emerging Measures and Models" (Rousseau, Measham, & Bathiche-Suidan, 2008). It falls upon the practitioner to differentiate between what may appear as illness behaviors as specified in the DSM and those inherent to specific cultural beliefs and practices. Two fundamental questions come to mind:

- Are the child's behaviors functional and adaptive or do they produce conflict?
- Do these behaviors cause distress?

Competency 2 a

Canino and Alegria (2008) point out that a child's cultural background influences every facet of the illness experience and should always be taken into account in order to fully and accurately comprehend a child's symptoms of mental illness. The competency-based assessment looks beyond dysfunctional behaviors and explores strengths and coping. To avoid prematurely labeling particular behaviors as a mental disorder within a specific culture, consider the degree to which a child's emotional and behavioral problems fall along a continuum beginning with pathology and ending with adjustment and resilience. As a rule of thumb, it is helpful for the practitioner to explore whether the child's behaviors are adaptive, or whether they produce conflict and cause suffering or distress.

From the competency-based perspective, the practitioner asks about everyday activities and relationships within the family (and the child's relationship with peers), and also looks into the attitudes and feelings that others in the child's life may have about the symptom picture. The practitioner elicits both the child's and the parents' view of the problem, expectations of help, and prior experiences with services. The competency-based approach to the assessment process also includes a review of the daily stresses associated with a child's problematic behavior and the practical problems encountered when trying to manage a troubled child. It is helpful to keep in mind that each cultural and ethnic group will differ with regard to practices and activities related to adaptation and survival.

Competency 7 b

Organized around the competency-based assessment, the following guidelines are offered to facilitate exploration of the extent to which culture affects how symptoms of the disruptive, impulse-control, and conduct disorders are shown in children:

- *Assess lifestyle behaviors, expected standards of behavior, and everyday activities relevant for cultural adaptation and survival.* Ask about everyday activities, peer relationships, and family routines in order to better understand the symptom picture within the context of the child's culture. The assessment of lifestyle and daily activities helps to determine what is considered to be pathological versus what is regarded as normal and expected in the child's environment.
- *Comprehend meanings, labels, and interpretations commonly used to describe a child's behavior or emotional problems.* Attempt to understand the child's culture, related terminology, and commonly regarded symptoms of distress or pathology. Before labeling a particular behavior as a psychiatric symptom (or disorder), identify the specific words used to label the child's problematic behaviors or emotions in order to distinguish how people in a specific culture know that the child has a problem. The recognition of symptoms and the labeling of distress as being either deviant or pathological depend on the norms of behavior accepted in the child's particular culture.

Competency 5 a

- *Evaluate the cultural context of what, on the face of it, appears as illness behaviors to determine whether they essentially support the DSM diagnostic criteria.* Consider whether the child's behavior is functional and adaptive or if it produces conflict and causes distress or suffering—both for the child and for the parents or caregivers. Find out if these behaviors and symptoms influence the child's personal identity, what he or she does, or how others perceive the child (Kleinman & Benson, 2006). Further, ask both the child and the parents (or caregivers) about what they are afraid would happen if these behaviors and symptoms had any special significance if seen as a psychiatric illness.
- *Determine whether the DSM diagnostic criteria are valid for the specific population to be assessed.* Consider if the symptoms of a particular disorder (e.g., temper tantrums) have the same meaning or relevance for certain cultures. Cauce and colleagues (2002) point out that asking parents (or a child) whether symptomatic behaviors occur more or less often than in a typical similar-aged child might be hard to answer when the parents (as well as the child) do not share the DSM's diagnostic concepts. It goes without saying that getting

accurate information would be difficult. Even so, a psychiatric illness cannot be automatically ruled out.

- *Consider the child's and the parents' (and that of significant others in the child's life) threshold of stress and how they cope with the child's behavioral problems.* Determine if the parents (or others in the child's life) are under stress themselves; if so, how does this affect their response to the child? Consider cultural influences on the types of problems that parents (or significant others) consider serious. Conversely, evaluate whether the parents have a high tolerance for certain behavioral problems while the child sees them as problematic (Roberts, Alegria, Roberts, & Chen, 2005). Also take into account the child who may have a high distress threshold and might be reluctant to talk about certain symptoms or traumatic events, especially with the practitioner.
- *Recognize how the client perceives the practitioner's social position.* Acknowledge that the assessment process can be influenced by the identity and social positioning of the practitioner and the client (Groleau, Young, & Kirmayer, 2006). For example, take into account the family's social position, religion, education, national origin, sexual orientation, immigration history, integration into the community, and intergenerational conflicts in the family, to list a few. As a first step, strive to establish an atmosphere of trust and to explain what information is or is not disclosed (confidentiality).
- *Show self-awareness.* Remember to ask yourself if you are generalizing the child's behaviors or symptoms and not paying full attention to the child's specific cultural background. Avoid the temptation to stereotype, especially when little is known about a client's specific culture or context (Hwang, 2006).

We now turn to a review of the specific disruptive, impulse-control, and conduct disorders, beginning with a disorder that is the major reason children are referred for mental health services, oppositional defiant disorder.

OPPOSITIONAL DEFIANT DISORDER

Oppositional defiant disorder (ODD) can be found in children who have a history of a succession of different caregivers or who live in families with harsh, inconsistent, neglectful child-rearing practices (Noble & Jones, 2006). It should come as no surprise that those with this disorder by and large show symptoms only at home and only with members of the family. Common features of ODD include excessive, often persistent anger, frequent temper tantrums or angry outbursts, and disregard for authority. It is the pervasiveness of the individual's symptom picture that serves as an indicator of severity.

PREVAILING PATTERN

The lifetime prevalence of ODD is estimated to be 10.2 percent of the U.S. population (Nock, Kazdin, Hiripi, & Kessler, 2007). Of those, 11.2 percent are males and 9.2 percent are females. ODD is a common child- and adolescent-onset disorder associated with substantial risk of secondary mood (45.8 percent), anxiety (62.3 percent), impulse-control (68.2 percent), and substance use (47.2 percent) disorders. Prior to adolescence, the disorder is more commonly seen in males (APA, 2013).

Differential Assessment

ODD is characterized as an ongoing pattern of disobedient, hostile, and defiant behavior toward authority figures that goes beyond the bounds of normal childhood behavior. Children and adolescents who have it may appear to be very stubborn and angry people. The essential feature of ODD is the recurrent pattern of angry and irritable mood, or vindictiveness that lasts for at least 6 months. In order to meet criteria for a diagnosis, the individual must show at least four symptoms from any of three categories: angry/irritable mood, argumentative/defiant behavior, and vindictiveness. Specific symptoms illustrative of an angry/irritable mood can include: frequent loss of temper, touchy or easily annoyed, or often angry and resentful. Argumentative/defiant symptoms can be seen as: arguing with adults or other authority figures, being noncompliant, annoying others, or blaming others for mistakes or misbehavior. Vindictiveness is taken into account when the individual has been spiteful or malicious at least twice within the past 6 months. The practitioner considers the persistence and frequency of these behaviors in order to separate them from a behavior that would normally be expected. In other words, all of these behaviors can be seen more frequently than in most children of a comparable age. In addition, the child's behaviors must cause some level of impairment in key areas of functioning such as interpersonal relationships or in school.

These behaviors can be seen on most days for at least 6 months for children under 5 years of age. For those who are 5 years of age and older, the behavior should occur at least once a week for at least 6 months. A psychotic, substance use, depressive, or bipolar disorder does not better explain the symptom picture. Looking to measures of severity, mild symptoms are considered when behavior is confined to one setting, such as at home. Moderate symptoms are reserved for when some symptoms are present in at least two settings, and severe is assigned when symptoms are seen in three or more settings.

The case of Jerry Sheppard illustrates oppositional defiant disorder.

CASE The Case of Jerry Sheppard

Mrs. Sheppard showed up for the intake interview with her 12-year-old son, Jerry. Mrs. Sheppard was seen first. She explained that she had contacted the counseling center based on the advice of her AA sponsor. The intake form noted that Mrs. Sheppard was reportedly having a lot of trouble controlling her son lately. He was constantly getting into trouble and increasingly defiant toward Mrs. Sheppard. In addition, the family was recently in turmoil over Mr. Sheppard's incarceration. Now that he was out of the house, the level of fighting between Jerry and his mother was becoming intolerable. According to Mrs. Sheppard, "Therapy might be a good way of getting things on track with Jerry." She added, "I'm in recovery and doing okay for the first time in my life so now I guess its Jerry's turn."

Mrs. Sheppard made it clear to the intake worker that if her husband, Frank, was not in jail she was sure he would have come with her to the appointment. Since her husband's incarceration, Mrs. Sheppard started working part-time to help out with the financial strain on the family that was made worse by her husband's absence. She added, "Sometimes Frank's a little hard on Jerry but I know he loves him. We don't always agree on what's right for the boy but that's all Frank knows. My husband had a hard childhood himself." Mrs. Sheppard explained that she

CASE THE CASE OF JERRY SHEPPARD (CONTINUED)

disagreed with her husband about how to discipline Jerry, and this led to inconsistent punishment. Mr. Sheppard preferred corporal punishment in contrast to Mrs. Sheppard, who tried to negotiate with her son and reward good behavior. "That's when I wasn't drinking," added Mrs. Sheppard. "You might say I just wasn't there for Jerry. Guess he just about raised himself. Now that I'm sober I want to be there for him. I have a lot of missed time to make up for. Like I said, most of the time when Jerry was growing up I was battling my addiction." She continued, "On top of that, we struggled financially, too. Frank always had a hard time keeping a job. He drank too, but not like me. Seems like we were always a paycheck away from being homeless. Whenever Frank was laid off, I had to apply for food stamps. When Frank had a job, he worked long hours. He didn't have much education so he usually found unskilled work. He had to work a couple of jobs and was not home a lot," she said. Mrs. Sheppard was insistent that her husband loved Jerry "in his own way."

Last year in the sixth grade, Jerry was suspended from school for several days each month; some of the reasons included talking back to his teacher, another time for showing a poor attitude, and yet another for throwing a temper tantrum. Finally the school principal and Jerry's teacher requested a meeting with Mr. and Mrs. Sheppard. During this meeting, Mrs. Sheppard learned that Jerry had a long-standing pattern of misbehavior in the classroom. He argued with the teacher and annoyed his classmates by teasing them every chance he could. This had been going on for most of the school year. She added that Jerry constantly argues with her when she's home but she just locks herself in her room. "It beats arguments with him that go nowhere. Besides, I'm afraid I might do the wrong thing. Jerry usually cools down and I spend a lot of time in my room. I don't know what happened. He just seems so angry all the time," said Mrs. Sheppard.

Mrs. Sheppard indicated she had no birth problems with Jerry and developmental milestones occurred within normal limits. He is in good overall health. However, Mrs. Sheppard admitted to being at a loss to understand her son's behavior. She added that she was becoming increasingly concerned about her ability to manage her son now that he was almost a teenager. At the point of the school meeting, Jerry was refusing to do most of his school work and his grades were poor. With signed consent, the social worker contacted the school, and Mrs. Sheppard's account of Jerry's behavior and poor academic performance was confirmed.

After battling an addiction to drugs for more than 10 years, Mrs. Sheppard found inspiration from a social worker who spoke at a drug and alcohol support group meeting she started attending after her discharge from rehab. "Somehow we just seemed to connect," said Mrs. Sheppard. "She sort of took me under her wing. She saw potential in me to go on and get better. That's why I came here. I'm hoping one of your social workers will be able to hit it off with my Jerry," she added. "Do you have somebody like that here?" asked Mrs. Sheppard. The social worker remembered reading the report of Jerry's intake session with another social worker on staff and said to herself, "I sure hope so." The report noted that Jerry was sullen and uncooperative. He challenged the other social worker to explain why he needed to come in and then abruptly walked out after 20 minutes.

JERRY SHEPPARD'S DSM DIAGNOSIS IS AS FOLLOWS:

Oppositional Defiant Disorder, Severe

ASSESSMENT SUMMARY As Jerry's mother describes her son's behavior in this vignette, highlighted are the key features of ODD. Jerry demonstrates an ongoing pattern of negative, defiant, argumentative, and hostile behavior. School reports indicate that Jerry argues with his teacher, annoys his classmates, loses his temper to the point of being suspended, and constantly argues with his mother at home. He is seen as defiant and angry just about all the time. When seen during the intake interview, Jerry was hostile and uncooperative. Since his behavior is apparent at home, in school, and in the social worker's office, his symptom picture is specified as severe.

Competency 7 a

Using the competency-based assessment, the social worker is able to assess Jerry's coping strategies. Hopefully they will set the stage to reinforce and improve his adaptation to life situations, circumstances, and events. Despite a history of neglectful and harsh child-rearing often found in children with ODD, there are a number of parallel strengths in Jerry's life. His mother is making a serious attempt at her own recovery and wants to be more available to raise her son. Mrs. Sheppard also reports that her husband loves Jerry "in his own way." Although Jerry's school grades and behavior are problematic, he does attend school and no learning problems are noted. Mrs. Sheppard followed through on the school referral, and her motivation is to learn how to better manage his behavior. Figure 13.1 shows the interactions of the biological, psychological, and social variables in Jerry Sheppard's life.

The diagnosis of other specified disruptive, impulse-control, and conduct disorder would be assigned if Jerry did not meet full criteria for ODD. This diagnosis

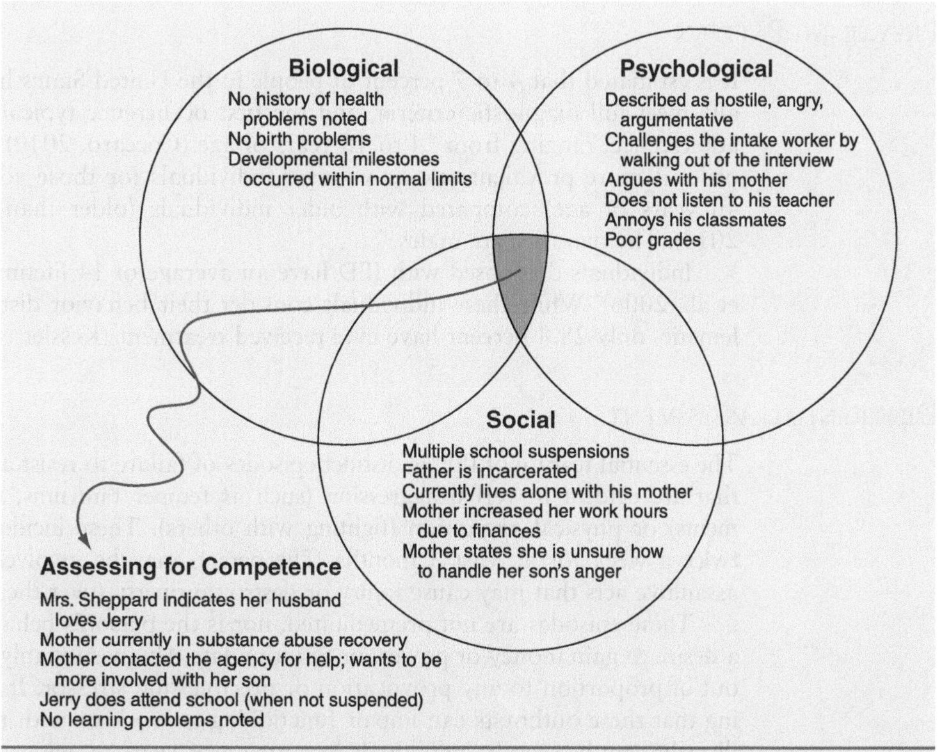

FIGURE 13.1 › Oppositional Defiant Disorder
The interactions of the biological, psychological, and social variables in Jerry Sheppard's life.

applies when the practitioner does not have enough information about the client's situation. Additionally, the diagnosis of unspecified disruptive, impulse-control, and conduct disorder is considered when diagnostic criteria are not met and the practitioner chooses not to specify the reasons. In both cases, the individual experiences significant distress or impairment.

The following discussion reviews intermittent explosive disorder.

INTERMITTENT EXPLOSIVE DISORDER

Intermittent explosive disorder (IED) can be seen in explosive outbursts wherein the person is unable to control his or (less often) her aggressive impulses. They occur rapidly and without warning, lasting for a very short time; roughly for less than half an hour. These outbursts are commonly unprovoked and usually directed toward someone close to the individual.

The individual's explosive behavior is preceded by a sense of tension or arousal followed almost immediately by a sense of relief. It is not uncommon for individuals to describe these aggressive episodes as "spells" or "attacks." Afterward, the person may describe feeling upset, remorseful, regretful, or embarrassed about his or her aggressive behavior.

PREVAILING PATTERN

It is estimated that 4 to 7 percent of people in the United States have IED and usually meet full diagnostic criteria, and the first occurrence typically occurs in early adolescence, ranging from 14 to 18 years of age (Coccaro, 2010). Further, this disorder is more prevalent among younger individuals (or those younger than 35 to 40 years of age) compared with older individuals (older than 50 years) (APA, 2013). The majority are males.

Individuals diagnosed with IED have an average of 14 lifetime attacks (Kessler et al., 2006). While these individuals consider their behavior distressing and problematic, only 28.8 percent have ever received treatment (Kessler et al., 2006).

DIFFERENTIAL ASSESSMENT

The essential feature of IED is distinct episodes of failure to resist aggressive impulses that are evident in verbal aggression (such as temper tantrums, tirades, and arguments) or physical aggression (fighting with others). These incidents happen about twice a week for at least 3 months. The person may be involved in more serious assaultive acts that may cause injury or destroy property (over the past year).

These episodes are not premeditated, nor is the person's behavior motivated by a desire to gain money or power, or to intimidate. Unquestionably, the aggression is out of proportion to any provocation or precipitating stressor. It goes without saying that these outbursts can impair functioning at work or with relationships. This disorder can be seen in individuals as young as 6 years of age.

IED can occur in the context of many other mental disorders. The practitioner should consider other syndromes that are associated with aggressive behavior or impulses; for example, antisocial personality disorder, borderline personality disorder, a psychotic disorder, a manic episode, conduct disorder, or attention-deficit/hyperactivity disorder. The practitioner also rules out the direct physiological effects of a substance such as a drug of abuse, a medication, or a general medical condition such as head trauma or Alzheimer's disease.

The case of Tommy Lusk highlights the key features of intermittent explosive disorder. Since we know little of his life history, the biological, psychological, and social features of his life are not detailed. However, his competence is evident around how he struggled with his diagnosis.

CASE The Case of Tommy Lusk

Tommy Lusk is 38 years of age, and he contacted Bayside Community Mental Health Center for "anger issues." As he settled into the social worker's office, she couldn't help but notice how tense Tommy looked. His neck muscles were stiff, and he seemed very uncomfortable. He sat upright and on the edge of the chair, fidgeted with the buttons on his shirt, and overall, looked very uneasy. Tommy looked intently at the social worker, and she felt like his dark brownish black eyes were staring right through her. She started, "My name is Susan Gray but please call me Susan. Can I call you Tommy?" He nodded affirmatively. Susan attempted small talk to ease Mr. Lusk's tension, but that only seemed to make him more uncomfortable, so she shifted directly to what prompted him to make an appointment.

Tommy began, "I've always suffered from temper tantrums and rage attacks for as long as I can remember. When I was little, what would begin as a tantrum usually ended up in a full-blown rage. I remember times when I was flipping furniture over and totally destroying my bedroom. These attacks would last anywhere from half an hour to 2 hours or more. My parents simply didn't know what to do with me. I'm adopted, you see. So they really didn't know anything about me. Anyway, they would try anything they could to hold me down so I wouldn't cause any damage to myself ... or to them."

Susan noticed that Tommy had no emotion to his voice. She thought, "It's as if he told this story so many times." He continued, "I think I was about 6 or 7 when the temper tantrums started. At first, they weren't such a big deal, but by the time I was 11, I had destroyed my bedroom so many times that my parents took everything out except for my bed and a dresser." Tommy added, "My parents finally gave up on me and I was made a ward of the court. Can't say I blame them. Next thing you know I was shuffled around from group homes to shelters to different mental institutions and back again. In some of those places I was stripped of my belt and had my shoes taken away. Seemed there was no place for me. I clearly remember when I turned 16. That was a banner year for me. I got so angry that I took out two dozen car windshields with a baseball bat. Looking back, that must have caused a coupla thousand dollars' worth of damage."

For a brief moment, Tommy looked lost in thought, but he quickly continued, "I once remember being locked in a room about 4 by 8 feet with no windows or door knob on the inside. Oh, yeah ... and they gave medication, too. Ritalin, valium, lithium ... you name it! But nothing helped the 'explosions.' Then at one of those places, I met a social worker who really seemed to care about me. She told me that I had a mental disorder and it was called, intermittent explosive disorder. Just knowing there was a name to what I was going through made all the difference in the world to me. To this day I don't think that social worker knows the difference she made in my life."

Over the years, Tommy learned all he could about his diagnosis and taught himself how to survive with it. "First thing I did was to give up cigarettes and booze. Just take each day at a time, you know? Then I discovered that I have a great sense of humor and started performing in local comedy clubs. Somehow it was easy for me to make jokes about my background. Just to see people laugh about what I went

CASE THE CASE OF TOMMY LUSK (CONTINUED)

through felt really good ... and my life was no picnic, believe me! You might say I have a lot of material to work with." He found that he had a unique ability to joke about his troubled past.

Tommy added that these stand-up performances are a great outlet for his aggression. Susan thought, "This guy has been through a lot. Seems like his life has been filled with lemons and yet he was able to make some lemonade. He's able to appreciate the absurdity of life without falling victim to it. Laughter might just be the best therapy for him." Susan noticed that Tommy seemed to exude what could best be described as a compelling presence in her office. She thought, "If Tommy looks like that on stage I'm sure he can easily hold the audience's attention." He added, "I'm writing a book about my life, too. It's called *Taming the Tiger*. Don't know if it will be a best seller, but I'm hoping that by telling my story I'll be able to motivate others who struggle like me."

Tommy continued, "That's why I came in. I'm in between gigs right now and can feel the tension building up. You see, my day job is driving a cement truck. There are so many f——king a——holes on the road. Lately I've been feeling like slamming my truck right into them."

For the past 6 months, Tommy described a pattern where he started arguing with coworkers several times a week and usually over nothing. He added, "It's weird. I don't drink anymore but that doesn't help. If one of the guys says something I don't like, the next thing you know my fist is in his face. It's like a switch or something goes off in my head. Then I feel so bad afterwards. It doesn't matter what they say, either." Needless to add, Tommy has very few friends at work.

As the interview was drawing to a close, Susan asked if this session was helpful. Tommy abruptly stood up, and headed straight for the door. He turned back and said, "Yes, you've been helpful but I won't be back for a while. Today was enough—to look too much into my past isn't good for me. You seem really nice and interested and all but.... Tell you what, I'll call you when I need to blow off steam again. Besides, an appointment here is a lot cheaper than a bar tab." Susan admitted to herself that she was taken aback by the force of Tommy's emotion and the intensity of his feelings somehow made her office feel very small. She thought to herself, "This guy is not like a lot of the clients I see here. They'll make a follow-up appointment and then they're a 'no show.' At least Tommy is honest about not coming back next week."

TOMMY LUSK'S DSM DIAGNOSIS IS AS FOLLOWS:

Intermittent Explosive Disorder

Competency 7 b

ASSESSMENT SUMMARY Tommy's aggressive outbursts first became apparent when he was about 6 years of age and escalated in early adolescence. He remembers these episodes as unprovoked. Tommy recently noticed that it really does not matter what somebody may say to him when the next thing he knows, his fist is in somebody's face. He describes it "like a switch or something goes off in my head," indicating his inability to control his aggressive behavior. The episodes seem to happen at random, and afterward he feels remorseful. When Tommy noticed these episodes had been happening several times a week, he decided to seek counseling. While his aggressive behavior seem random and unmotivated, we do know that Tommy feels his stand-up comedy performances appear to help curb his aggression. Since Tommy was "in between gigs," he decided to contact the mental health center.

Competency 7 a

While the social worker had no opportunity to get to know Tommy further, several strengths and competence can be seen in his story. Despite being made a ward of the court and living in a series of institutions, once Tommy realized his diagnosis, he was able to make positive changes in his life. He shared that he was able to stop smoking and drinking, holds a steady job, and uses stand-up comedy performances to control his aggression. His use of humor serves not to evade the situation but to minimize its intensity, and he realizes it will pass. From a neurobiological perspective, laughter reduces cortisol (a hormone released when the body experiences stress); it is soothing and stimulating. For Tommy, it works as a social lubricant that helps him to wiggle out of challenges; that is, he has a choice to get angry or to laugh at the craziness of his life. He is also writing a book about his experiences. Tommy hopes that by telling his story, he will be able to help other people.

We now turn to an overview of conduct disorder, another disorder that commonly begins in childhood and is more prevalent in males than females.

CONDUCT DISORDER

The early years of a child's life represent a sensitive period for development, especially the regulation of emotion and affect. Higher rates of conduct disorder (CD) have been observed in children of depressed mothers where a lack of emotional stability and availability have adversely influenced the emotional environment (Dawson, Frey, Panagiotides, Osterling, & Hessl, 1997). CD can be seen in children who have also experienced inconsistent child-rearing practices such as harsh discipline, a lack of supervision, maternal smoking during pregnancy, and exposure to violence (Noble & Jones, 2006).

The essential feature of conduct disorder is a consistent pattern of violating the rights of others, or violating major age-appropriate societal norms or rules (Henggeler & Sheidow, 2003). Studies have shown that those with conduct problems during childhood or adolescence are at a higher risk for other mental disorders, legal problems, and premature mortality (Kim-Cohen et al., 2003; Simonoff et al., 2004). Unfortunately, children who are diagnosed with CD report higher levels of distress and impairment in virtually all areas of living than youth with other mental disorders.

Prevailing Pattern

Estimates for the lifetime prevalence of CD in the U.S. population range from 2 percent to more than 4 percent (APA, 2013). Prevalence seems to be higher for males than for females (Maughan, Rowe, Messer, Goodman, & Meltzer, 2004). The symptoms for CD tend to be seen before age 16 and are believed to be influenced by environmental as well as genetic factors. The median age of onset is approximately 11 years of age (Nock et al., 2006).

Differential Assessment

The diagnosis of CD requires the presence of any 3 of the following 15 symptoms for at least 12 months, with at least one symptom present over the past 6 months.

These symptoms are organized around four major categories of behavior and include:

Aggression to people and animals:

- Bullying, threatening, or intimidating others.
- Starting fights.
- Using a weapon that can cause serious harm (i.e., a bat, brick, broken glass bottle, knife, or gun).
- Being physically cruel to people.
- Being physically cruel to animals.
- Stealing while confronting the person (i.e., mugging, purse snatching, extortion, armed robbery).
- Committing sexual assault.

Destruction of property:

- Setting fires with the intention of causing serious damage.
- Destroying property.

Deceitfulness or theft:

- Breaking into another's property.
- Lying.
- Stealing without confronting the person (i.e., shoplifting or forgery)

Serious violation of rules:

- Staying out at night.
- Running away from home.
- Refusing to attend school.

It may be easier to organize assessment data by remembering that these behaviors are grouped into four major categories. The practitioner specifies childhood onset when symptoms are present before 10 years of age, and adolescent onset is specified when symptoms are seen after 10 years of age. Severity may be noted as mild, moderate, or severe. Limited prosocial emotions can be specified if these features characterize the person's typical emotional functioning or pattern of relating for at least a year. When considering this specifier, it is helpful to obtain information from those who know the client, such as a teacher, family members, or coworkers, as well as what the client shares with you. Prosocial emotions and behaviors include a lack of remorse or guilt; callousness or a lack of empathy; showing no concern about his or her performance at school, at work, or in other important activities; and showing shallow or no emotions.

Someone with CD shows significant social, school, or work problems. The behaviors typically seen in boys would be fighting, stealing, vandalizing property, and breaking school rules. Girls with CD are more likely to lie, run away from home, be truant, use drugs, and become involved in prostitution. Both boys and girls can show little empathy and concern for others, callousness, lack of guilt and remorse, low self-esteem, irritability, poor frustration tolerance, recklessness, and high levels of aggression. Overall, these children (and adolescents) are also more likely than their peers to engage in early sexual behaviors, smoking, drinking, drug use, fighting, reckless acts, and gang-related activity. They are more likely to contract sexually transmitted diseases, become pregnant, or get injured from accidents or fighting.

The case of Norman Gibson illustrates the symptom picture for CD.

CASE The Case of Norman Gibson

After his most recent arrest, Norman Gibson, a 15-year-old male, was referred to the Guidance Clinic by his juvenile probation officer. Norman was scheduled to appear before a judge for his most recent charges. Since this was his second arrest in less than a year, there was a good chance that he might receive a stronger sentence. Norman's father was motivated to get help for his son, indicating, "Maybe the judge will go easier on the boy since we're in family counseling this time around."

Norman was belligerent and dismissive right from the very beginning of the interview. He sat with his leg swung over the side of the chair and announced, "Call me Namron. You see, Norman is my slave name." He went on to say that he would not answer any questions that "I don't feel like answering." The social worker's first thought was that she really didn't like this youngster but then remembered the first thing she learned in graduate school about the social worker's role. In order to be professional, she had to be nonjudgmental and offer unconditional positive regard. "Well, this is going to be tough," reflected the social worker. Gently, she asked Namron about why he thought he was here. His response was confrontational as he began, "Well just ask me all your f——kin' questions so we can get this over with and I can get out of here. I got better things to do." The social worker was surprised by Norman's response and found she was feeling a little angry. "This is really not very professional of me. If I had my druthers, I would just tell this kid off. I'd better watch my behavior," she thought.

The social worker remembered the intake report described a history of problems. Specifically, a year ago and almost to the day of the intake interview, Norman was arrested for vandalism at his local high school. He and a group of his friends were caught on the security cameras breaking windows, spray-painting graffiti on the walls, and trashing several of the classrooms. Since this was his first offense, Norman was placed on probation for 6 months. When the social worker asked about the charges, Norman just laughed. "Hell, that's only half of what I've done." He went on to describe several shoplifting sprees with his friends, missing school, and smoking marijuana. "But I only smoke on the weekends," he added with a wink in her direction. "Good grief! This kid is a sarcastic little bugger," thought the social worker. His record indicated missing school for 61 days, just about the first half of the school year.

The social worker asked Norman what had happened that brought him to the clinic. He described his recent arrest 4 months ago for torturing and killing raccoons that were eating food from the garbage bins located behind a local grocery store. For several months, Norman, along with several of his friends, started hanging out at night behind the store. They would usually drink or get high. When they noticed the raccoons, the boys would provoke the animals, but then one thing led to another. "Those raccoons were a nuisance so what do I care? I was doing that store a favor. Then some goody two-shoes animal rights a——hole comes along and reports us. I'm pretty sure I know who it was, too. It's that skinny old gray-haired bum who feeds the cats in the front of the store every day. I think he's some kind of war veteran. PTSD and all that. People who shop there even give him money to buy more cat food. What a bunch of jerks!" said Norman. "We'll take care of him," he added ominously. "Was this a threat?" wondered the social worker. She thought, "I also need to explore the extent of his drug use. I'm hoping he'll be more honest with me once we develop a relationship."

Norman was the only one who was caught abusing the raccoons, and he blamed his friends for leaving him behind. "But I'm not going to rat on my friends. It's against the code," he said. At that point, the social worker noticed that Norman wore his baseball cap backwards and had a red bandanna hanging out of his left-side back pocket. She recognized these as the markings of a local gang and wondered if Norman was a member. She made a mental note to explore this further. "He's so belligerent and confrontational right now so this might take a little time. And I've got to get my negative feelings toward this kid in check, too. I hope they don't show right now," she reflected.

The social worker asked Norman about his goals for the future. He immediately responded that he didn't think much was going to come out

CASE The Case of Norman Gibson (Continued)

of his upcoming court appearance. "The judge is such a f——king prick," he said adding that several of his friends had been in court with this judge and "all they got was community service." Norman was indifferent about school and brushed off the social worker's suggestions for work-study or part-time programs. Emphatically he stated, "Look lady. I can take care of myself. I've been doing it for most of my life. The old man is always working and never seems to have time for me. Forced me to look out for 'number one.' That would be me, in case you're wondering.... and I've been doing okay in that department." As the session drew to a close, Norman stood up and on his way out the door he abruptly turned around and stated, "Look lady, thanks for all your sweet talk but I really don't care what happens to me." The social worker was surprised when Norman went on to add that he really didn't like himself very much anymore.

Norman's father was also interviewed. The social worker had the impression that while Mr. Gibson was cooperative, he was also careful to justify his actions as a parent. "My wife left me a while back, and then 3 years ago she dumped Norman back on me. Norman has always been in good health, but the wife started saying he was too much for her to handle. Claimed he didn't get along with her latest boyfriend and their new baby. Whatever that means. Since Norman has been with me she doesn't even call, let alone remember the boy on Christmas. No wonder he has problems," added Mr. Gibson.

As a single parent, Mr. Gibson claimed that he had to work a lot and admitted his son was alone for most of the day. He seemed unaware of what Norman did and guessed that his son was either on the computer or hanging out with his friends. The social worker had the impression that their relationship was cordial, but distant. Mr. Gibson said, "The boy and I have a good relationship and I want to get help for him. Norman just needs someone to get through to him and get him back on track. Since you're the professional, I hope you know the right way to get some sense into him. You can't depend on the school. After all, nobody even let me know about all his absences until it was too late. Now he'll probably be suspended big time. Frankly, I think he was the one arrested this time around instead of the other boys because he got off so easy with the vandalism stuff. You see, we live in a small town and the school resource officer is married to the police chief. So she tells her husband about what happens at the school and next thing you know, Norman gets arrested for the supermarket episode. I think the police had it in for Norman all along. They were just waiting for the right opportunity to arrest him."

The social worker scheduled up follow-up appointments and asked for consent to contact the school counselor, the juvenile probation officer, and Norman's mother. She wanted to get a bigger picture of Norman's behavior in other contexts.

Norman Gibson's DSM Diagnosis Is as Follows:

Conduct disorder, adolescent-onset type with limited prosocial emotions, unspecified alcohol-related disorder, unspecified substance-related disorder, moderate

Assessment Summary Norman's story illustrates one of the central features of CD—a persistent pattern of behavior where the rights of others are ignored and age-appropriate societal rules are broken. Over the past year, Norman described shoplifting, missing school, and smoking marijuana. While we do not know the details of his academic performance, the social worker did ask his father for consent to contact the school counselor to further clarify Norman's status. Further information will help the practitioner to rule out other similar disorders such as oppositional defiant disorder, attention-deficit/hyperactivity disorder, a depressive disorder, intermittent explosive disorder, or an adjustment disorder.

In addition, Norman was arrested for destroying school property and more recently for torturing and killing raccoons behind a local supermarket. While his demeanor is described as belligerent, he has not physically assaulted anyone. Because this is the first known episode of cruelty to animals and there is no evidence that he has further harmed any animals, Norman's diagnosis of CD is specified as moderate.

Competency 8 c

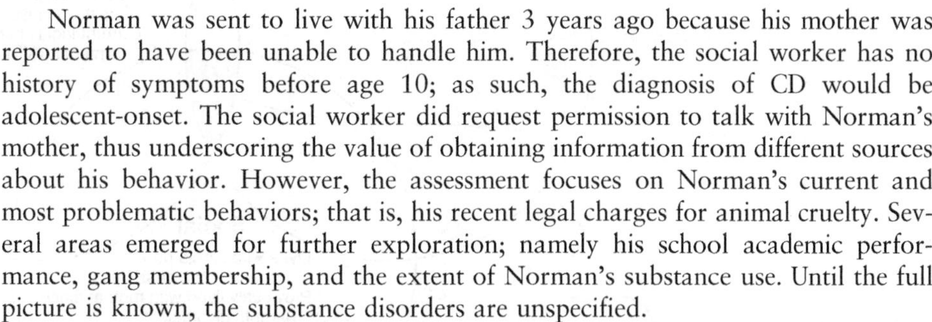

Norman was sent to live with his father 3 years ago because his mother was reported to have been unable to handle him. Therefore, the social worker has no history of symptoms before age 10; as such, the diagnosis of CD would be adolescent-onset. The social worker did request permission to talk with Norman's mother, thus underscoring the value of obtaining information from different sources about his behavior. However, the assessment focuses on Norman's current and most problematic behaviors; that is, his recent legal charges for animal cruelty. Several areas emerged for further exploration; namely his school academic performance, gang membership, and the extent of Norman's substance use. Until the full picture is known, the substance disorders are unspecified.

Competency 1 c

Norman's behavior toward the social worker was belligerent, confrontational, and challenging. Clients like this can challenge any practitioner's ability to demonstrate professional demeanor in behavior, appearance, and communication. Norman used foul language and was, at times, sarcastic. He evoked reactions of fear and hostility in the social worker. His sarcasm was evident when he gave the social worker a knowing wink as he described his substance use. Interestingly, his preferred name was "Namron," which is Norman spelled backwards. The social worker's struggle "to be professional" can be seen when she wondered if her negativity would be conspicuous and how this might affect the professional relationship.

Competency 7 a

Norman's life history of what seems to be inconsistent parenting and a lack of caregiving seems to puts him at a higher risk for CD. His father, though concerned, seemed cordial and distant. As well, his friends could best be characterized as delinquents. The practitioner is challenged to look for strengths in Norman's life story and find coping strategies to improve his adaptation to life situations, circumstances, and events. The practitioner, via the competency-based assessment, looks for strengths and resources while balancing the negatives such as Norman's erratic school attendance, legal charges, shoplifting, animal cruelty, and an overall belligerent and hostile attitude. In addition, Norman's mother is absent, and his father appears minimally involved in his son's life. However, Mr. Gibson did follow up on the probation officer's referral for counseling. While not directly stating that he wants to be involved in family counseling, Norman's father did express the hope of getting help for his son in order to improve his life. As the social worker's interview ended with Norman, he was able to admit that he did not like himself very much anymore. Hopefully this recognition of low self-esteem can set the stage for a working relationship aimed at making positive changes in his life. Figure 13.2 shows the interactions of the biological, psychological, and social variables in Norman Gibson's life.

We now turn to a review of two lesser-known disorders, pyromania and kleptomania. They are included to help the practitioner to refine the understanding of the disruptive, impulse-control, and conduct disorders. We begin with pyromania.

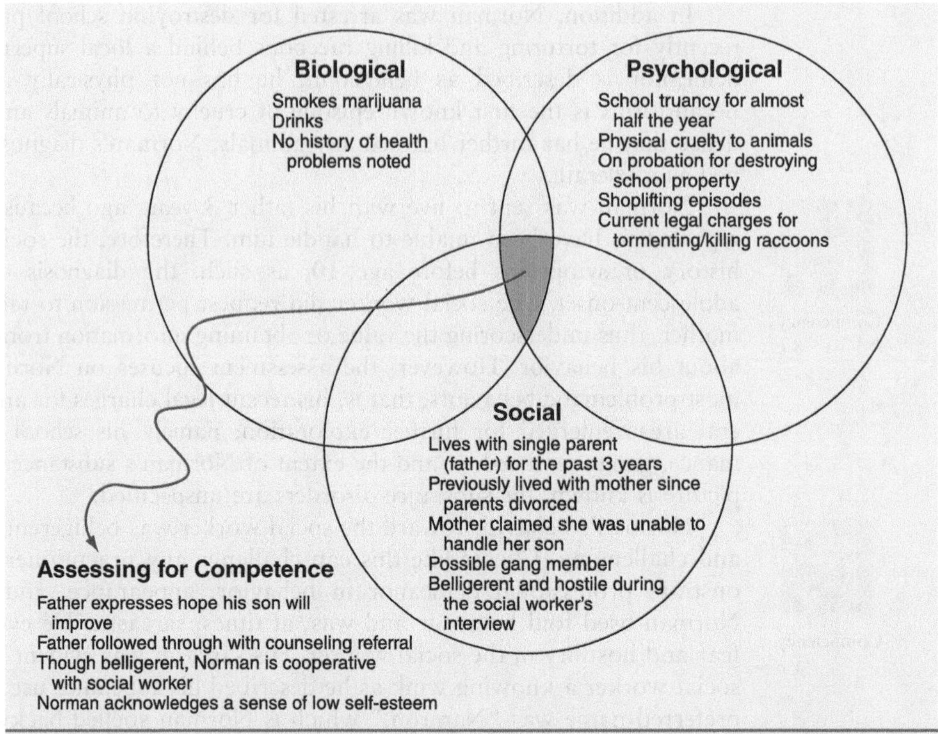

FIGURE 13.2 › CONDUCT DISORDER
The interactions of the biological, psychological, and social variables in Norman Gibson's life.

PYROMANIA AND KLEPTOMANIA: AN OVERVIEW

PYROMANIA

The essential feature of pyromania is the deliberate and purposeful setting of a fire on more than one occasion. Someone who struggles with this disorder experiences tension or emotional arousal before setting the fire. The prevalence of this disorder is unknown (APA, 2013). However, what we do know is that this is an individual who is fascinated, interested, curious about, or attracted to fire and its situational contexts. They may set off fire alarms, take pleasure in fire equipment, and show interest in how it is used. The person might even be seen spending time at the local fire department. There is a sense of relief experienced when setting fires, witnessing its effects, or participating in its aftermath. However, there seems to be no motivation for setting a fire, such as financial gain, to conceal a criminal act, or to express anger or vengeance. As well, the person is not driven to set a fire in response to delusions or hallucinations or because of impaired judgment. When considering the diagnosis, it is important for the practitioner to take into consideration reasons for setting the fire; for example, if it was set for revenge, to hide a crime, or to make a political statement. Some fires are set accidentally, such as a child playing with matches. Others may be motivated to set a fire, and then to "discover" it to save the day. As a part of the assessment process, the practitioner rules out other very similar symptom pictures seen in conduct disorder, a manic episode, or antisocial personality disorder.

An interesting example of someone with pyromania is John Leonard Orr, former captain of the Glendale California Fire Department. He was an arson investigator who eventually became a serial arsonist himself. Bestselling author Joseph Wambaugh wrote the nonfiction book *Fire Lover: A True Story,* featuring Orr, who was ultimately convicted for serial arson in 1992 and later for first-degree murder for the lives lost in the fires he set in 1998.

KLEPTOMANIA

The central feature that distinguishes kleptomania is the individual's inability to resist stealing something that has no personal use nor any monetary value. The prevalence of this disorder is very rare; however, the disorder is more prevalent in females than in males by a ratio of 3:1 (APA, 2013). The person experiences a sense of tension just before the theft and feelings of relief or gratification at the time of the theft. This syndrome is distinguished from shoplifting, which is motivated and deliberate. Some people may shoplift based on a dare, especially adolescents, or as a rite of passage.

Keep in mind that the diagnoses of other specified (and unspecified) disruptive, impulse-control, and conduct disorders provide additional diagnostic options. As an example, the former impulse-control disorder not otherwise specified (NOS) found in the DSM-IV is now categorized as the other specified and unspecified disruptive impulse-control disorders.

SUMMARY

The diagnoses listed in this chapter bring together disorders characterized by self-control. Individuals with any one of the disorders reviewed will run into problems following expected standards of behavior seen in anger, aggression, destruction of property, violating the rights of others, or conflicts with authority figures. Antisocial personality disorder is a diagnosis considered part of the disruptive, impulse-control, and conduct disorders but is fully detailed in the chapter on personality disorders.

As the DSM transitions from the DSM-IV-TR (APA, 2000) to the current edition of the manual, Table 13.2 provides a brief summary of the changes made to the diagnostic classifications in this chapter.

PRACTITIONER'S REFLECTIONS

The disorders discussed in this chapter represent a number of conditions involving self-control of emotion and behaviors. We have seen three individuals who struggle with different types of self-control: Jerry Sheppard, Tommy Lusk, and Norman Gibson. One form, found in conduct disorder, consists of behaviors that violate the rights or others or major social norms. At the extreme end of the behavioral spectrum is the individual whose behavioral outbursts are

TABLE 13.2 Summary Comparison Between the DSM-IV-TR and DSM-5 Diagnoses for the Disruptive, Impulse-Control, and Conduct Disorders
Oppositional defiant disorder and conduct disorder were moved from the DSM-IV chapter "Disorders Usually First Diagnosed in Infancy, Childhood, or Adolescence"
Intermittent explosive disorder, pyromania, and kleptomania were moved to this chapter from the DSM-IV chapter "Impulse-Control Disorders Not Otherwise Specified"
While antisocial personality disorder is listed in this chapter, it is detailed further in the chapter on "Personality Disorders"
Symptoms for oppositional defiant disorder are of three types: angry/irritable mood, argumentative/defiant behavior, and vindictiveness; the conduct disorder exclusion has been deleted; criteria were also changed with a note on frequency requirements; and specifiers are included for severity
For the most part, diagnostic criteria for conduct disorder remain unchanged from the DSM-IV but a specifier was added for individuals with limited "prosocial" emotions
Individuals over the minimum of at least 6 years of age may be diagnosed with intermittent explosive disorder without outbursts of physical aggression that are not better explained by another mental disorder, attributed to a medical condition, or the effects of a substance; criteria were added for frequency

so poorly controlled, or they show outbursts of anger that are clearly not related to any provocation or other psychosocial stressors in their life. Unfortunately, there seems to be no logical explanation for this lack of behavior and emotional control, and it is not uncommon for the practitioner to encounter family members or those close to the client who are frustrated and puzzled.

Activities

Competency 1 b

1. Children, regardless of their mental status or diagnosis, eventually grow up and mature into adulthood. Do you think persons with disruptive, impulse-control, and conduct disorders should have the opportunity to marry and have children of their own? Explain why or why not.

Competency 2 a

2. Explain why you think that many of the disorders discussed in this chapter are more commonly found in boys than in girls. How might parents (and teachers) deal differently with boys and girls?

Competency 6 a

3. Select any one of the case stories representing the disruptive behavior disorders (such as Jerry Sheppard diagnosed with oppositional defiant disorder, Tommy Lusk diagnosed with intermittent explosive disorder, or Norman Dixon diagnosed with conduct disorder) and discuss with another colleague or your supervisor what challenges you might encounter developing, managing, and maintaining the professional relationship with these clients. Keep in mind the person-in-environment and strengths perspectives as you identify these relationship challenges.

Competency Notes

Competency 1 b—Social workers use reflection and self-regulation to manage personal values and maintain professionalism in practice situations (p. 370): Social workers recognize personal values and make the distinction between personal and professional values.

Competency 1 c—Social workers demonstrate professional demeanor in behavior, appearance, and oral/written/electronic communication (p. 367): Social workers understand how their personal experiences and affective reactions can influence their professional judgment and behavior and also understand emerging forms of technology and the ethical use of technology in practice.

Competency 2 a—Social workers apply and communicate understanding of the implications of diversity and difference in shaping life experiences in practice at the micro, mezzo, and macro levels (pp. 354, 370): Social workers understand how diversity and difference characterize and shape the human experience and that these features are critical to the formation of identity.

Competency 5 a—Social workers identify social welfare and economic policies at the local, state, and federal levels impact well-being, service delivery, and access to social services (p. 355): Social workers understand that human rights and social justice, as well as social welfare and services, are mediated by policy and its implementation on several levels—local, state, and federal.

Competency 6 a—Social workers apply knowledge of human behavior and the social environment, person-in-environment, and other multidisciplinary theoretical frameworks to engage with clients (and constituencies) (pp. 353, 370): Social workers understand theories of human behavior and the social environment and critically apply this knowledge to facilitate engagement with clients (and constituencies) including families, groups, organizations, and communities.

Competency 7 a—Social workers collect and organize data and apply critical thinking in order to interpret information from clients and constituencies (pp. 359, 363, 367): Social workers understand that the assessment process is ongoing and conducted with, and on behalf of, diverse individuals, families, groups, organizations, and communities.

Competency 7 b—Social workers are able to apply knowledge of human behavior and the social environment, person-in-environment, and other multidisciplinary theoretical frameworks in the analysis of assessment data (pp. 355, 362): Social workers understand theories of human behavior and the social environment and critically evaluate and apply this knowledge in the assessment process.

Competency 8 c—Social workers use interprofessional collaboration, as appropriate, to achieve beneficial practice outcomes (p. 367): Social workers value interprofessional teamwork and recognize the beneficial outcomes that require interdisciplinary, interprofessional, and interorganizational collaboration.

References

American Psychiatric Association (APA). (2000). *Diagnostic and statistical manual of mental disorders* (4th ed., text revision). Washington, DC: Author.

American Psychiatric Association (APA). (2013). *Diagnostic and statistical manual of mental disorders* (5th ed.). Arlington, VA: Author.

Ashford, J. B., & LeCroy, C. W. (2011). *Human behavior in the social environment: A multidimensional perspective* (5th ed.). Pacific Grove, CA: Cengage Learning.

Canino, G., & Alegria, M. (2008). Psychiatric diagnosis—is it universal or relative to culture? *Journal of Child Psychology and Psychiatry, 49*(3), 237–250.

Cauce, A., Rodriguez, M., Paradise, M., Cochran, B., Shea, J., Srebink, D., & Baydar, N. (2002). Cultural and contextual influences in mental health help seeking: A focus on ethnic minority youth. *Journal of Clinical Psychology, 70*, 44–55.

Coccaro, E. F. (2010). A family history study of intermittent explosive disorder. *Journal of Psychiatric Research, 44*(5), 1101–1105.

Dawson, S., Frey, K., Panagiotides, H., Osterling, J., & Hessl, D. (1997). Infants of depressed mothers exhibit atypical frontal brain activity: A replication and extension of previous findings. *Journal of Child Psychology and Psychiatry, 38*, 179–186.

Groleau, D., Young, A., & Kirmayer, L. (2006). The McGill Illness Narrative Interview (MINI): An interview schedule to elicit meanings and modes of reasoning related to illness experience. *Transcultural Psychiatry, 43*, 671–691.

Henggeler, S. W., & Sheidow, A. J. (2003). Conduct disorder and delinquency. *Journal of Marital and Family Therapy, 29*, 505–522.

Hwang, W. (2006). The psychotherapy adaptation and modification framework. *American Psychologist, 61*, 702–715.

Kessler, R. C., Coccaro, E. F., Fava, M., Jaeger, S., Jin, R., & Walters, E. (2006). The prevalence and correlates of DSM-IV intermittent explosive disorder in the National Comorbidity Survey Replication. *Archives of General Psychiatry, 63*(6), 669–678.

Kim-Cohen, J., Caspi, A., Moffitt, T. E., Harrington, H., Milne, B. J., & Poulton, R. (2003). Prior juvenile diagnoses in adults with mental disorder: Developmental follow-back of a prospective-longitudinal cohort. *Archives of General Psychiatry, 60*(7), 709–717.

Kleinman, A., & Benson, P. (2006). Anthropology in the Clinic: The problem of cultural competency and how to fix it. *Public Library of Science Medicine, 3*, 1673–1676.

Maughan, B., Rowe, R., Messer, J., Goodman, R., & Meltzer, H. (2004). Conduct disorder and oppositional defiant disorder in a national sample: Developmental epidemiology. *Journal of Child Psychology and Psychiatry, 45*(3), 609–621.

Noble, D. N., & Jones, S. H. (2006). Mental health issues affecting urban children. In N. K. Phillips & S. L. Straussner (Eds.), *Children in the urban environment: Linking social policy and clinical practice* (2nd ed., pp. 97–121). Springfield, IL: Thomas.

Nock, M. K., Kazdin, A. E., Hiripi, E., & Kessler, R. C. (2006). Prevalence, subtypes, and correlates of DSM-IV conduct disorder in the National Comorbidity Survey Replication. *Psychological Medicine, 36*(5), 699–710.

Roberts, R., Alegria, M., Roberts, C., & Chen, I. (2005). Concordance of reports of mental health functioning by adolescents and their caregivers: A comparison of European, African and Latino Americans. *Journal of Nervous and Mental Disease, 193*, 528–534.

Rousseau, C., Measham, T., & Bathiche-Suidan, M. (2008). DSM-IV, culture and child psychiatry. *Journal of the Canadian Academy of Child and Adolescent Psychiatry, 17*(2), 69–75.

Simonoff, E., Elander, J., Holmshaw, J., Pickles, A., Murray, R., & Rutter, M. (2004). Predictors of antisocial personality: Continuities from childhood to adult life. *British Journal of Psychiatry, 184*, 118–127.

Slade, E. P. (2004). Racial/ethnic disparities in parent perception of child need for mental health care following school disciplinary events. *Mental Health Services Research, 6*, 75–92.

Webb, N. B. (2011). *Social work practice with children* (3rd ed.). New York: Guilford Press.

CHAPTER

Substance-Related and Addictive Disorders

INTRODUCTION

The spectrum of the substance use is one of our most challenging public health problems and, left untreated, places a burden on the workplace, health care system, and communities. The last available estimate from the Office of National Drug Control Policy estimates economic costs at $193 billion in 2007 (Office of National Drug Control Policy, 2014). This includes approximately $20 billion in lost productivity related to labor participation costs, involvement in treatment, incarceration, and premature death. Health care costs are estimated at $11 billion for drug treatment and medically related consequences. Criminal justice costs are at $61 billion for criminal investigations, prosecution and incarceration, and victim costs.

Most of us have used psychoactive substances (which alter mood and/or behavior) at one time or another. For instance, most of us start the day with a cup of coffee to help us wake up; or maybe we have an alcoholic drink in the evening with friends to socialize and relax. Some people admit to occasionally smoking "grass" (marijuana), snorting some "candy" (cocaine), or swallowing a little "black beauty" (amphetamine). We rationalize that it's all right as long as it does not interfere with our job or relationships with others. Most of us do not misuse drugs.

However, some people do abuse drugs or use them illegally—conservative political radio talk show host Rush Limbaugh made headlines over illicit drug use. In early 2006, Limbaugh accepted a plea bargain for charges of "doctor shopping." He agreed to submit to periodic drug testing and treatment as a part of the agreement. A few months later, Limbaugh was detained at the Palm Beach, Florida, airport for carrying unlabeled prescription drugs. They turned out to be Viagra (to treat erectile dysfunction), and did not have his name on the label in an effort to protect his privacy. Limbaugh's very public struggle with substance use raises an interesting question: Are people increasingly turning to drugs to solve their problems?

In 1992, Congress established the Substance Abuse and Mental Health Services Administration (SAMHSA) under the U.S. Department of Health and Human Services in order to collect, analyze, and disseminate public health data. Each year, the National Survey on Drug Use and Health (NSDUH) is conducted. Current trends on substance use in America from 2012, the most recent year for which NSDUH survey data have been analyzed, show that illicit drug use has been increasing (National Institute on Drug Abuse, 2014). An estimated 23.9 million individuals age 12 or older, or 9.2 percent of the American population, had used an illicit drug or medication (i.e., pain relievers, stimulants, or tranquilizers) in the past month. This is up from 8.3 percent in 2002.

We live in a culture where most people drink alcohol. Excess intake from time to time is far from unusual but the critical question is, "Who among those who use substances like drugs or alcohol is likely to become dependent on them or addicted to them?" Looking at drug habits, most people use drugs for the first time when they are teenagers. There were a slightly over 2.8 million new users of illicit drugs in 2012, and a little over half, or 52 percent, were under 18 years of age (National Institute on Drug Abuse, 2014). However, drug use is highest among those in their late teens and twenties. In 2012, 23.9 percent of individuals between 18 and 20 years of age reported using an illicit drug in the past month. Drug use is increasing among those people in their late fifties. It is speculated that these are the aging baby boomers, whose rates of illicit drug use have historically been higher than other age cohorts (National Institute on Drug Abuse, 2014). Looking to alcohol use, the National Comorbidity Survey Replication (NCS-R) found 13.2 percent of the U.S. population met lifetime criteria for alcohol abuse with an additional 5.4 percent for alcohol dependence for a total of slightly over 18 percent (Kessler, Chiu, Demler, Merikangas, & Walters, 2005). In 2012, 30.4 percent of men ages 12 and older and 16 percent of women reported **binge drinking** (five or more drinks on the same occasion) in the past month (National Institute on Drug Abuse, 2014). Additionally, almost 10 percent (9.9 percent) of men and 3.4 percent of women reported **heavy alcohol use** (binge drinking on at least 5 separate days in the past month).

The use of chemicals alters the way we feel and see things, and a person may not want to stop using them, even when they cause serious physical and social problems. All drugs taken in excess activate the brain's reward system. Each different class of drugs produces a reward sensation that is different but typically produces feelings of pleasure, often referred to as a "high." Instead of activating the reward system through adaptive behaviors, drugs of abuse directly activate the brain's reward pathways, and normal activities become neglected. A person can become addicted to legal drugs prescribed by a physician just as readily as they can to illegal drugs. Many people become addicted to things (such as alcohol, cigarettes, or smokeless tobacco) they don't even think of as drugs. Some may be surprised to learn that nicotine is rated ahead of methamphetamine and crack cocaine as the most addictive of drugs. Then, there are all the legal substances that, when used improperly, can become addictive (e.g., inhalants like nail polish, certain types of glue, or gasoline). Including the behavioral disorder of gambling, the DSM-5 responds to the evidence that gambling behaviors activate reward systems in the brain similar to those activated by drugs of abuse (Petry et al., 2013). To add to the picture, individuals with lower levels of self-control may have impairments in the brain's inhibitory mechanisms. As such, these individuals may be particularly predisposed to develop substance use disorders.

Competency 7 b

Table 14.1 lists the substance-related and addictive disorders found in the DSM-5.

In order to fully appreciate the many factors related to developing a substance-related disorder, the competency-based assessment organizes the practitioner's understanding of the interplay of theories of human behavior and the interplay

TABLE 14.1 THE DSM-5 SUBSTANCE-RELATED AND ADDICTIVE DISORDERS
Alcohol-Related Disorders *Alcohol Use Disorder* *Alcohol Intoxication* *Alcohol Withdrawal*
Caffeine-Related Disorders *Caffeine Intoxication* *Caffeine Withdrawal*
Cannabis-Related Disorders *Cannabis Use Disorder* *Cannabis Intoxication* *Cannabis Withdrawal*
Hallucinogen-Related Disorders *Phencyclidine Use Disorder* *Other Hallucinogen Use Disorder* *Phencyclidine Intoxication* *Other Hallucinogen Intoxication* *Hallucinogen Persisting Perception Disorder*
Inhalant-Related Disorders *Inhalant Use Disorder* *Inhalant Intoxication*
Opioid-Related Disorders *Opioid Use Disorder* *Opioid Intoxication* *Opioid Withdrawal*

TABLE 14.1 CONTINUED

Sedative-, Hypnotic-, or Anxiolytic-Related Disorders *Sedative, Hypnotic, or Anxiolytic Use Disorder* *Sedative, Hypnotic, or Anxiolytic Intoxication* *Sedative, Hypnotic, or Anxiolytic Withdrawal*
Stimulant-Related Disorders *Stimulant Use Disorder* *Stimulant Intoxication* *Stimulant Withdrawal*
Tobacco-Related Disorders *Tobacco Use Disorder* *Tobacco Withdrawal*
Other (or Unknown) Substance-Related Disorders *Other (or Unknown) Substance Use Disorder* *Other (or Unknown) Substance Intoxication* *Other (or Unknown) Substance Withdrawal*
Non-Substance-Related Disorders *Gambling Disorder*

with a client's social environment. For example, there is growing evidence that suggests genetic factors contribute between 50 and 60 percent of vulnerability to alcoholism (Foroud, Edenberg, & Crabbe, 2010). Although alcoholism seems to run in families, it is difficult to separate genetic factors from environmental influences (Nurnberger et al., 2004). While genetic predisposition does seem to play some role, the process is a lot more complex than originally thought (Heath et al., 2002). The substance-related disorders cannot be linked definitively to a specific gene—however, a person with a family history of substance use is at higher risk for developing a substance use disorder.

Competency 5 a

Social workers are also aware of contexts that shape practice. In particular, practitioners attend to the social factors that have been identified as contributors to the development of substance disorders. For example, drug-addicted parents spend less time monitoring their children than parents without drug problems, and this seems to be a contributing factor to early substance use in adolescents (Barnes, Hoffman, Wolfe, Farrell, & Dintcheff, 2006). Additionally, a child's prenatal development is placed at risk when the fetus has been exposed to drugs like alcohol, tobacco, or cocaine. Also consider the child born addicted to illicit substances. These infants tend to be easily agitated and aroused, experience difficulty achieving state regulation, and may be difficult to soothe (Shapiro, Shapiro, & Paret, 2001). As reviewed earlier (in Chapter 1), chronic stress has been identified as a risk to early brain development. Further, a substance-abusing parent may present a range of problems in the developing child's social context including inattention and neglect.

To some extent, all psychoactive drugs provide a pleasurable experience and the social contexts for drug taking may also encourage its use (Sadock, Sadock, & Ruiz, 2014). Looking at development over the life span, alcohol affects people differently at different life stages. For example, we do know that the brains of adolescents continue developing into young adulthood and they also tend to engage in risky behaviors, such as alcohol and drug use. Further, Windle and Zucker (2010) observe that adolescents tend to experience the effects of alcohol differently from adults; that is, they are less sensitive to the negative effects of drinking such as sleepiness but are more likely to have trouble with more complex tasks such as driving.

Similarly, neurobiological influences play a role in the substance-related disorders. The pleasurable experience in taking psychoactive substances helps to understand why some people continue to use them. The pleasure center in the brain is believed to include the dopaminergic system and its opioid-releasing neurons, which begin in the midbrain ventral tegmental area and then work their way forward through the nucleus accumbens and then on to the frontal cortex. Researchers are only beginning to understand how different drugs affect different neurotransmitter systems that converge to activate the pleasure pathway, which is primarily made up of dopamine-sensitive neurons. This pleasure response activity in the brain produces similar effects in gambling disorder (APA, 2013).

Temperament is considered as another factor in the etiology of the substance use disorder spectrum. One personality trait closely related to the substance disorders is impulsivity; generally referred to as risk-taking, lack of planning, chaotic lifestyle, desire for immediate gratification, and explosiveness (Ivanov, Schultz, London, & Newcorn, 2008). Research has found that measures of impulsivity or lower levels of self-control suggest impairments of the brain's inhibitory mechanisms can be found in people with substance use, craving, and withdrawal symptoms (APA, 2013; Moeller et al., 2001; Petry, 2001).

Competency 2 a

Diversity shapes the client's experience, and the social worker understands its importance in the client's life experiences. Gender, for example, plays a role. Women whose partners have had alcohol problems are more likely to experience victimization, injury, depressive disorders, and anxiety disorders (Dawson, Grant, Chou, & Stinson, 2007). Needless to say, these women have experienced more life stressors, and they have greater rates of substance-related and addictive disorders than women whose partners did not have alcohol problems. The risk factors for substance-related disorders among women include having a partner who drinks, a violent partner, and/or a history of childhood sexual abuse (Jaffe, 2006). So far, the leading predictor of substance use in women is a history of sexual abuse in childhood (Cormier, Dell, & Poole, 2004; Jaffe, 2006). Women also develop substance use problems in the context of their relationships. Ashley, Marsden, and Brady (2003) found that many have become involved with drugs or alcohol through their partner. Women also tend to bear the burden of family responsibilities and may turn to the use of substances as a way to cope with stress.

Sociocultural factors also play a role in influencing attitudes toward substance use. Every society has its own values, beliefs, and traditions around the use of mood-altering substances, as well as differences in their availability. The elderly, for example, present certain challenges for the practitioner. Many elderly people are at risk for developing substance problems due to their misuse of alcohol in combination with prescription medications and over-the-counter remedies (Memmott, 2003).

Globally, adults age 65 years or older will increase from 516 million in 2009 to an estimated 1.53 billion in 2050 (Wu & Blazer, 2014). It is anticipated that the number of adults who are over 50 will increasingly encounter problems with substance use. The Woodstock generational cohort, popularly known as the baby boomers, is comfortable taking medications for a wide range of problems—as a result, they are more vulnerable to abusing substances later in life. Older substance users are at risk for substance-related consequences due to substance use at earlier ages that may continue into later life, and ageing-related changes in medical conditions. For instance, the 60-something celebrity Rush Limbaugh mentioned at the beginning of the chapter was legally charged with prescription drug fraud in connection with his addiction to painkillers. He is considered representative of the new kind of patient who is now showing up in treatment centers.

Cultural attitudes and beliefs also play a role when diagnosing the substance-related and addictive disorders in the elderly. Vinton and Wambach (2005) observe that many health care providers are reluctant to bring up the issue of substance use or addiction with elderly clients because of the lack of a perceived benefit from treatment (such as rehab) or improvement in quality of life as a result of this kind of intervention. Further, who wants to entertain the thought that his or her grandmother is addicted to drugs, alcohol, and/or gambling? Moreover, the reliability of an elder self-report may be questionable. It can be difficult to determine if the physical and cognitive problems found in the elderly are due to the normal process of aging or if they are the effects of consuming a substance. Factors associated with substance use disorder in older adults include being a female, social isolation, history of a substance-use or mental health disorder, and medical exposure to prescription drugs with addictive potential (Simoni-Wastila & Yang, 2006). Substance use among older adults is a growing concern with alcohol, opioids/heroin, and cocaine the most likely substances of choice (Wu & Blazer, 2011).

Other populations are also affected by substance use. Lesbian women, gay men, and bisexual and transsexual persons (LGBT) are at increased risk for the substance-related and addictive disorders, primarily because one of the few remaining legitimate places for meeting and socializing with others remains the gay bar scene, and its association with alcohol. The LGBT community is also vulnerable to the loss of friends and acquaintances, both inside and outside their support network. In addition, many LGBT individuals do not have the full range of support commonly found in family, friends, coworkers, and neighbors—which often leaves them feeling isolated and alone, and which may contribute to turning to substances as a way of coping.

Competency 7 b

The ecological factors of poverty and limited resources also tie in to the incidence of substance use. Wright (2001) describes the effects of cultural factors and poverty influencing substance use among African Americans. In addition, poor neighborhoods have a high concentration of liquor stores, thus making access to alcohol easier.

In sum, the substance-related and addictive disorders are associated with a wide range of factors in a person's life, including, for example, genetics, individual traits or temperament, gender, family history, sociocultural attitudes, and neighborhood. The competency-based assessment provides a framework for the practitioner to evaluate and consider the complicated reasons a person misuses drugs and alcohol.

THE ESSENTIAL FEATURES OF THE SUBSTANCE-RELATED AND ADDICTIVE DISORDERS

Notice that the DSM section for substance-related now consists of substance use disorder, substance-induced disorder accompanied by the criteria for intoxication and withdrawal, substance/medication-induced mental disorders, and the (behavioral) addictive disorders (APA, 2013). For those disorders related to the use of a substance, the DSM developed criteria that can be applied to all 10 classes included in this chapter (except caffeine). Likewise, for those disorders induced by a substance, there are two categories describing the effect: intoxication or withdrawal.

The DSM-5 also refined the criteria of certain conditions. For example, less sensitive diagnostic criteria like "committing illegal acts" have been removed and a new criterion of "craving" has been added. Another modification to the substance-related disorders is that there is no longer any categorical difference between substance abuse and addiction. The earlier DSM-IV distinction between abuse and dependence (or addiction) was regarded as confusing in that it obscured the distinctions between the physical and psychological needs for a substance (O'Brien, 2011). Somehow, dependence was linked with the concept of addiction, when in reality dependence can be a normal body response to a substance. The DSM-5 work group recognized the potential for those persons who suffer from chronic pain and are taking medications as prescribed to experience tolerance and withdrawal symptoms. When that happens, they run the risk of being labeled as an "addict." Consequently, the DSM-5 makes a distinction between what is medically prescribed to manage pain and what is not. When medication is medically prescribed, the presence of tolerance and withdrawal symptoms are not counted to support the diagnosis of a substance use disorder. However, as a part of the assessment process, the practitioner needs to clearly document that these symptoms are occurring in the context of appropriate medical treatment and related prescribed medications.

The DSM-IV categories of substance abuse and dependence have been combined into a single disorder, substance use disorder. This reorganization is intended to better match the symptoms that clients experience. Accordingly, addiction is identified by a dimensional rating system from mild to severe based on severity (Shields, Howell, Potter, & Weiss, 2007). Rather than the earlier mix-and-match approach to diagnosis, nearly all substances are now diagnosed on the same overarching criteria.

Gambling disorder is a non-substance-related disorder and a new diagnosis to the DSM-5 addressing problematic gambling behaviors. Also included is a related disorder called "Internet gaming disorder" listed in the area of the manual reserved for further study, Section III. This potential disorder involves the persistent and recurrent use of the Internet to engage in games resulting in impairment that significantly impacts social and occupational functioning.

Let's begin with a review of the general criteria established for the substance use disorders.

SUBSTANCE USE DISORDER

The DSM-5 defines a substance use disorder as "a cluster of cognitive, behavioral, and physical symptoms indicating that the individual continues using the substance despite significant substance-related problems" (APA, 2013, p. 483). The diagnosis is based on a maladaptive pattern leading to clinically significant impairment or distress for at least 12 months with features that must meet 2 or more of the following 11 symptoms grouped according to impaired control, social impairment, risky use, and pharmacological criteria:

- Impaired control:
  1. Taking the substance in larger amounts and for longer than originally intended.
  2. Unsuccessful efforts at cutting down despite a persistent desire to cut down (or discontinue use).
  3. Spending time to use or obtain the substance, using the substance, or recovering from its effects; in more severe instances the person's activities revolve around the substance.
  4. Craving or a strong desire (or urge) to use a specific substance.
- Social impairment:
  5. Failure to fulfill major role obligations (i.e., work, school, or home).
  6. Recurrent substance use despite persistent or recurrent social or interpersonal problems caused by (or made worse by) the effects of the substance.
  7. Giving up or reducing other activities (i.e., social, occupational, or recreational) because or substance use.
- Risky use:
  8. Continued use in situations that are physically hazardous.
  9. Continuing use despite knowing of the problems caused (or made worse) by the substance.
- Pharmacological criteria:
  10. Tolerance as defined by:
      - Needing an increased amount of the substance in order to achieve the desired effect or
      - A significantly reduced effect when the usual amount is consumed.

  (Reminder: Does not include medications taken under medical supervision.)
  11. Withdrawal is considered for those who have maintained a heavy and prolonged use of a substance, stop using, and develop symptoms; individuals may likely consume the substance (or a closely related substance) to relieve symptoms.

  (Reminder: Does not include medications taken under medical supervision.)

Except for caffeine (which cannot be diagnosed as a substance use disorder), each of the 10 substance-related classifications (refer to Table 14.1 for a listing) follows the same general guidelines except for withdrawal. The DSM-5 considers withdrawal as a syndrome that occurs when "blood or tissue concentrations of a substance decline in an individual who had maintained prolonged heavy use of the substance" (APA, 2013, p. 484). Correspondingly, the characteristic symptoms of withdrawal vary based on the actual substance used, so the DSM-5 provides separate criteria for each of the drug classes. However, withdrawal symptoms have not been documented for selected substances. In those instances, you will find that this criterion is not included as a part of the diagnostic picture. These specific substance use disorders are:

- Phencyclidine use disorder.
- Other hallucinogen use disorder.
- Inhalant disorder.

SEVERITY, SPECIFIERS, AND RECORDING

Severity: Rather than making a distinction between abuse and dependence as was required in the earlier editions of the DSM, the practitioner assesses the severity of use. The term "dependence" is characterized by tolerance and withdrawal criteria. This shift in the approach to making the diagnosis was made in order to better reflect a person's actual experiences with substance use and is in keeping with the dimensional perspective of the DSM-5. Mild severity is the presence of two–three symptoms, moderate severity is four–five symptoms, and severe is the manifestation of six or more symptoms.

Severity can increase or decrease over time if the individual changes how much or how often he or she uses substances. Adjustments to the level of severity can be made based on the practitioner's observations, descriptions by those who know the client, the client's self-report, and/or biological testing.

Specifiers: The course of an individual's substance use is described in terms of remission, and the practitioner further considers the following specifiers: in early remission (considered after full criteria for substance use were previously met, but none of the disorder criteria have been met for at least 3 months, but for less than 12 months), in sustained remission (used after full criteria for a substance use disorder were previously met, but currently none of the criteria have been met during a 12-month period or longer), on maintenance therapy (applied if the person is taking a prescribed agonist medication—a drug that is capable of producing a response similar to the original drug—and none of the criteria for a substance use disorder have been met for that class of medication), and in a controlled environment (used if the person is in a place where access to a substance is limited). The criteria for a specific substance use disorder includes when to consider specifiers.

Recording: The process of making a diagnosis begins with noting the actual substance within the substance-related category. For example, if someone was compulsively using amphetamines to the point that it was causing significant problems in his or her life (meeting at least two diagnostic criteria within a 12-month period), then the diagnosis would be "amphetamine-type substance." The level of severity is indicated by the specific code assigned. In order to refine the diagnosis even further, the DSM adds remission specifiers that may apply. Say for example, the person is now in the early stages of recovery—still has some lingering problems (i.e., has used amphetamines within the previous 12 months), but has not used the substance for at least 3 months—the specifier would be noted as in early remission.

Later in this chapter, two case studies, one for alcohol use disorder and another representing the person's use of several classes of drugs (including alcohol and evidence of a depressive disorder), will be presented to facilitate understanding the key symptomatic features of the substance-related disorders and applying the competency-based assessment model.

We now turn to the organization of the substance-induced disorders.

SUBSTANCE-INDUCED DISORDERS

The substance-induced disorders are categorized in the DSM according to the manifested effects of the substance on the individual. They are:

SUBSTANCE INTOXICATION

Substance intoxication refers to the occurrence of a reversible substance-specific syndrome due to recent ingestion or exposure to a substance. The diagnostic criteria for intoxication are as follows: recent ingestion or use; clinically significant problematic behavioral or psychological changes (and described individually for each class of substances); and the signs or symptoms are not attributable to another medical condition and not better explained by another mental disorder, including intoxication with another substance. (Note: This category does not apply to tobacco.) The more common changes associated with intoxication involve disturbances of perception, wakefulness, attention, thinking, judgment, psychomotor behavior (or behavior involving both physical and psychological components), and interpersonal behavior. The signs are very different in the short-term or acute phase than from someone who is in the chronic stage of intoxication. For instance, somebody who moderately uses cocaine may initially be extroverted and outgoing in contrast to the social withdrawal that can develop in frequent longer-term users. In some instances, a substance may continue to effect the central nervous system even after the substance is no longer detected in the body; the person's recovery from intoxication may continue.

SUBSTANCE WITHDRAWAL

Substance withdrawal is shown as a problematic substance-specific behavior change with both physiological and cognitive elements that are due to stopping or attempting to cut down heavy and prolonged substance use. The diagnostic criteria for withdrawal are as follows: ending (or reducing) substance use that has been heavy and prolonged and development of distinctive signs and symptoms particular to the substance within a specific time frame, which causes significant distress or impairment in social, occupational, or other important areas of functioning. These signs or symptoms are not attributed to another medical condition and cannot be better explained by another mental disorder, including intoxication and withdrawal with another substance. It is not uncommon for the practitioner to find someone in withdrawal reusing the substance in order to reduce their symptoms.

When recording the diagnosis for intoxication or withdrawal, the practitioner first records the name of the specific substance. For instance, if the person is taking methamphetamine, the diagnosis is recorded as "methamphetamine intoxication" (rather than stimulant intoxication). If the substance does not fit into any of the classes, such as anabolic steroids, the practitioner codes for "other substance intoxication." If the substance taken is unknown, then the practitioner indicates the appropriate code for "other (or unknown)" substance. Further, if the clinical picture shows symptoms but full criteria are not met, then the disorder is coded in the unspecified category.

Substances have different effects on different people, and their effects will vary according to how they are used. Substances may be taken into the body in the following ways: oral ingestion (swallowing), inhalation (breathing in) or smoking, injection into the veins (shooting up), or depositing into the mucosa (moist skin) of the mouth or nose (snorting). As a part of the competency-based assessment process, it is helpful for the practitioner to be aware of the many effects of substance use. An assessment for substance use must explore the following (APA, 2013):

- Route of administration and speed of substance effects—How a substance is taken determines the effect it will have (e.g., people "snort" cocaine because the nasal mucosa absorb it more rapidly into the bloodstream than, say, swallowing it; the more rapid absorption also results in a more intense high or intoxication).
- Duration of effects—Some substances are relatively short acting (i.e., they leave the body quickly), and others linger in a person's system, dissipating very slowly. As noted earlier, the longer-acting substances tend to have a longer period of withdrawal.
- Use of multiple substances—Sometimes a person will use multiple agents to achieve a desired effect; for example, one who is dependent on cocaine may also use sedating substances such as alcohol or marijuana to counteract the cocaine-induced anxiety. In these cases, each substance should be recorded separately.
- Associated laboratory findings—Analysis of a person's blood or urine may be necessary to determine recent use of a substance. For example, it is possible for a person who chronically uses alcohol to be intoxicated without showing any overt signs of intoxication and suggests the person has considerable tolerance. If someone presents with symptoms of withdrawal but the actual substance is unknown, laboratory tests can help to identify the substance. In addition, the tests may also help differentiate withdrawal from other mental disorders.

The substance-related disorders can create problems in many aspects of people's lives as well as for their families. In most instances, the practitioner will find that those with any of the substance disorders usually seek help for a wide range of problems other than substance use—such as family conflict, depression, anxiety, financial and/or legal difficulties, and declining school or work performance, to name just a few. However, because the person rarely sees the use of substances as a problem, he or she may not "volunteer" information to the social worker about use of alcohol and/or other substances, and therefore it is helpful to be attentive to the different effects of substances.

SUBSTANCE/MEDICATION-INDUCED MENTAL DISORDERS

Some substance/medication-induced disorders can cause symptoms that are characteristic of other disorders; for instance, taking certain medications can cause delirium. When that is the case, the disorder is not diagnosed as substance-related per se, but as delirium according to the class of the neurocognitive disorders. Here, the practitioner specifies "[specific medication]-induced delirium" (and the practitioner specifies the class of substance taken). Each of the substance/medication-induced mental disorders is described in the relevant diagnostic classification in the DSM; for example, the psychotic disorders are delineated in the schizophrenia spectrum and other psychotic disorders chapter. Table 14.2 summarizes the substance/medication-induced mental disorders that are more appropriately classified in other sections of the DSM-5.

Because these disorders develop in the context of using different substances, medications, or certain toxins, a brief description is offered here. In particular, it is helpful for the practitioner to keep in mind that the substance/medication-induced disorders do share a number of features with the 10 classes of substances that produce the substance-related disorders. However, the symptoms of a mental disorder that can result from using or abusing substances is diagnosed as substance/medication induced—and the DSM-5 recognizes it can be difficult to distinguish this symptom picture.

To begin, someone with a substance/medication-induced mental disorder shows symptoms of a specific mental disorder (Table 14.2) supported by evidence (i.e., history, physical exam, or laboratory findings) of its development during (or within 1 month of) substance intoxication, withdrawal, or taking a substance (or medication) capable of producing the mental disorder. Additionally, these symptoms are not better explained by an independent mental disorder (i.e., one that is *not* substance- or medication-induced) so if the person does have another mental

TABLE 14.2 SUBSTANCE/MEDICATION-INDUCED MENTAL DISORDERS ASSOCIATED WITH THE 10 CLASSES OF SUBSTANCES
Psychotic Disorders
Bipolar Disorders
Depressive Disorders
Anxiety Disorders
Obsessive-Compulsive and Related Disorders
Sleep Disorders
Sexual Dysfunctions
Delirium
Neurocognitive Disorders

disorder, it can generally be diagnosed before the substance/medication-induced disorder (or lasts for at least a month after taking the substance). For example, someone might have bipolar disorder that has been managed with treatment (or in full remission) and a co-occurring alcohol use disorder in sustained remission. Add to this picture the reality that this same client is now experiencing amphetamine-induced auditory hallucinations and paranoia from amphetamine use over the past 3 weeks. When that happens, the client's additional diagnosis would be amphetamine-induced psychotic disorder. While delusions and hallucinations are a part of the bipolar picture (bipolar I), the practitioner's differential assessment determines that these symptoms are more directly linked to the recent amphetamine use. Thus the amphetamine-induced psychotic disorder diagnosis is added. Keep in mind that there are two disorders that continue beyond acute intoxication or withdrawal: substance-induced neurocognitive disorders and hallucinogen persisting perception disorder (commonly referred to as flashbacks).

Table 14.3 summarizes the 10 classes of drugs and their diagnostic classifications of substance use, the substance-induced disorders including intoxication and

TABLE 14.3 THE 10 CLASSES OF SUBSTANCE USE DISORDERS INDICATING SUBSTANCE USE, SUBSTANCE-INDUCED (INTOXICATION WITHDRAWAL) AND THE SUBSTANCE/MEDICATION-INDUCED DISORDERS

Substance	Use	Intoxication	Withdrawal	Other Substance/ Medication-Induced Disorders
Alcohol	✓	✓	✓	✓
Caffeine		✓	✓	✓
Cannabis	✓	✓	✓	✓
Hallucinogens				
✱ Phencyclidine	✓	✓		✓
✱ Other	✓	✓	*Note:* Hallucinogen Persisting Perception Disorder	✓
Inhalants	✓	✓		✓
Opioids	✓	✓	✓	✓
Sedatives, hypnotics, or anxiolytics	✓	✓	✓	✓
Stimulants	✓	✓	✓	✓
Tobacco	✓		✓	✓
Other or Unknown	✓	✓	✓	✓

withdrawal, and their potential to contribute to a diagnosis of the substance/medication induced disorders.

Competency 4 a

In sum, diagnosing someone with a substance-related disorder is difficult, and critical thinking plays an essential role in the diagnostic process as the social worker distinguishes, evaluates, and integrates multiple sources of information including both research-based as well as practice wisdom. The competency-based assessment helps the practitioner to look at the full spectrum of the person's experiences with a particular drug (legal and illegal), alcohol, medication, and/or toxin. Table 14.3 highlights the far-reaching consequences of the substance-related disorders in a client's life. The competency-based assessment provides a framework for the practitioner to take into account—in addition to the symptoms of the particular syndrome—the multiple personal, relational, social, medical, legal, financial, and/or occupational problems that are often at the center of the substance-related disorders.

OTHER DIAGNOSTIC CONSIDERATIONS

In some situations a person may have other mental problems in tandem with the substance-related disorders, and that individual is given a dual diagnosis. Examples appear later in this chapter. For instance, the case of Chris Oghee describes someone suspected of having an avoidant personality disorder in addition to alcohol use. However, at the time the diagnosis was made, the social worker had not been able to distinguish all of the symptoms of a comorbid disorder, so it was listed as "unspecified personality disorder." Our case of Janet Sellar highlights a co-occurring depressive disorder.

The essential feature of the substance-related disorders is the constellation of maladaptive physical, behavioral, and cognitive changes associated with the pathologic use of psychoactive substances. In essence, a person continues using a substance despite the significant problems they cause. Since all 10 classes of the substance-related disorders (except for caffeine) share the same diagnostic criteria for substance use, you will find the review of the specific substance-related disorders will have a somewhat different format from that of other chapters in the book. For example, a number of the diagnostic criteria for substance use includes symptoms of withdrawal. Since the signs of withdrawal are different for each class of substances, they are introduced as a part of the differential assessment discussion. Keep in mind that the criterion of withdrawal is not required to make the diagnosis of substance use disorder. However, withdrawal symptoms can support as a separate diagnosis, and tend to play a more prominent role in the drug history of those who stop or reduce a pattern of heavy and prolonged substance use; specifically those with higher levels of substance intake and a greater number of substance-related problems. Similarly, intoxication is a separate diagnosis in which the practitioner considers the physiological reactions to ingested substances (commonly referred to as getting "high").

We begin our review of the 10 classes of the specific substance-related disorders with the alcohol-related disorders.

ALCOHOL-RELATED DISORDERS

Alcohol is the most commonly used drug in the United States and is legal for anyone over the age of 21. Alcohol is not a product of modern decadence; it has been used throughout history, and there are reports of finding wine and mead (beer) in pottery jars at the site of a Sumerian trading post in western Iran dating back for at least 6,000 years (Hernandez-Avila & Kranzler, 2011).

Alcoholic beverages are created by capturing the ethanol produced by the action of yeast on sugars from grapes, grains, or berries that are then distilled to liquids. The alcohol in this liquid form can be absorbed into the human bloodstream rather quickly—in 5 to 10 minutes—and can stay in the body for several hours. Alcohol is carried through the blood vessels into the stomach, internal organs, liver, kidneys, and muscles or just about everywhere in the body.

PREVAILING PATTERN

Alcohol use is very common in the United States. According to the Behavioral Risk Factor Surveillance System (BRFSS) survey, more than half of the U.S. adult population drank alcohol in the past month (CDC, 2014). In addition, approximately 5 percent of the total population drank heavily while 17 percent binge drank.

In the United States, the 12-month prevalence of alcohol use disorder is estimated to be 4.6 percent among those 12 to 17 years of age and 8.5 percent among adults 18 years of age and older (APA, 2013). Looking to gender, prevalence rates are greater among adult men (reported as 12.4 percent) than among adult women (or 4.9 percent). Historically, women consume less alcohol than men, drink less frequently, and are less likely to develop alcohol-related problems. However, when women do develop problems related to drinking alcohol, those problems tend to be more severe (Paris & Bradley, 2001). For instance, women have been found to have a higher prevalence of the co-occurring problems of anxiety and depressive disorders (Williams & Cohen, 2000).

Alcohol consumption has declined among white Americans since the mid-1980s, but ethnic and minority groups continue to be disproportionately affected by alcohol-related problems. The differences in prevalence among different ethnic and racial subgroups indicate that the greatest rates reported for Hispanics (6.0 percent) followed by Native Americans and Alaska Natives (5.7 percent) relative to whites (5.0 percent), African Americans (1.8 percent), and lastly, Asian Americans and Pacific Islanders (4.5 percent) (APA, 2013). Studies show an increase of alcohol-related difficulties among Blacks and Hispanics, and they tend to experience more negative health and social consequences of drinking such as unemployment, poor education outcomes, and legal problems connected to alcohol (Boyd, Phillips, & Dorsey, 2003).

Just about everyone can describe an episode of being intoxicated to some degree. In the United States, the average age reported for intoxication is at about 15 years, with the highest prevalence being between 18 and 25 years of age (APA, 2013); for instance, 22 percent of seniors in high school and 70 percent of college students in the United States have admitted to being drunk in the past year (APA, 2013).

Approximately half (50 percent) of highly functioning individuals with an alcohol use disorder have experienced alcohol withdrawal (APA, 2013). For those who are homeless or hospitalized, rates can increase to more than 80 percent.

ALCOHOL USE DISORDER

Alcohol affects the human central nervous system and the brain. Although it is considered a depressant (a chemical agent that diminishes the function or activity of a specific part of the body), the initial effect on the user apparently is one of stimulation. A person who ingests alcoholic beverages generally experiences a sense of well-being, reduced inhibitions, and the ability or willingness to be more outgoing than he or she usually is. These effects are the result of the inhibitory centers of the brain being slowed down. Alcohol sensitizes NMDA (N-methyl-D-aspartate) receptors in the brain (important for the transmission of some aspects of pain in the central nervous system) making them more responsive to the excitatory neurotransmitter glutamate (the neurotransmitter that produces feelings of excitability), boosting brain activity. These effects are most pronounced in areas of the brain that are associated with thinking, memory, and pleasure. Low doses (one to two drinks) can lower a person's inhibitions and make him or her feel more comfortable; but for reasons not yet understood, some individuals become more aggressive than they would customarily be. With continued drinking, alcohol depresses more areas of the brain, which further impedes the ability to function properly. This increased amount of alcohol desensitizes the same brain receptors and activates the inhibitory GABA (gamma-aminobutyric acid) system. GABA's task is to calm the central nervous system and to promote sleep. Higher doses depress the central nervous system and initially produce a feeling of relaxation but then lead to "drunkenness" or intoxication characterized by poor physical coordination (staggering), memory loss, cognitive impairment (or becoming confused), slurred speech, and blurred vision. The individual's reaction time is slowed, and his or her ability to make judgments is reduced. Very high doses of alcohol can cause vomiting, coma, and even death.

DIFFERENTIAL ASSESSMENT

The DSM-5 defines alcohol use disorder as, "a cluster of behavioral and physical symptoms, which can include withdrawal, tolerance and craving" (APA, 2013, p. 492). O'Neill and Sher (2000) conducted a longitudinal study of alcohol use and found that tolerance and withdrawal symptoms reported in early adulthood were associated with a substantial risk for later alcohol use disorder. In other words, someone who struggles with alcohol at an early age engages in a number of problematic behaviors organized around use. For example, a person's social interactions and work performance may be adversely affected by alcohol use either from the aftereffects of drinking or actual intoxication while attempting to carry on with responsibilities. The consequences may also include injury or death from attempting to operate vehicles or machinery while intoxicated and/or legal difficulties because of public intoxication or drinking while driving. Unfortunately, once a

Table 14.4	Symptoms of Alcohol Withdrawal
Stopping or cutting down heavy and prolonged alcohol use	
Two (or more) of: autonomic hyperactivity; increased hand tremor; insomnia; nausea or vomiting; transient visual, tactile, or auditory hallucinations or illusions; agitation; anxiety; or/and generalized tonic-colonic (grand mal) seizures	

pattern of compulsive use develops, people who struggle with alcohol use may spend substantial periods of time obtaining and consuming alcoholic beverages.

To diagnose alcohol use, the individual must meet 2 (or more) of the 11 overall criteria for substance use within a 12-month period. After stopping (or reducing) a pattern of heavy and prolonged drinking, symptoms of withdrawal can look like: autonomic hyperactivity (such as sweating or a pulse rate greater than 100 bpm); increased hand tremor; insomnia; nausea or vomiting; transient visual, tactile, or auditory hallucinations or illusions; agitation; anxiety; and/or grand mal seizures (Table 14.4). Since they are so unpleasant, the individual may drink more. This explains that popular expression "hair of the dog," or when someone is hung over and takes another drink the very next day supposedly to feel better. Alternatively, the individual may take a closely related substance (such as benzodiazepine) to relieve or avoid withdrawal symptoms.

A review of alcohol intoxication symptoms follows.

Alcohol Intoxication

When considering alcohol intoxication, the general rule of thumb is that an average person can process about one beer or one shot of liquor each hour. Any more than that and alcohol collects in the bloodstream and intoxication ensues. While this may be true for most people, a number of factors contribute to the rate at which alcohol is metabolized; for example, gender, size, genetics, and how frequently one drinks. This makes everyone's speed of metabolizing alcohol a little different. The contents of one's stomach, overall health, and efficiency of the liver (the main organ that metabolizes alcohol) will also play a determining role in metabolism rates. Binge drinking occurs when a person drinks a large amount in a short period of time to intoxication. For men, this is five or more drinks at a time; for women, the amount is usually four or more.

The criteria for alcohol intoxication include recent drinking and significant behavioral or psychological changes—such as inappropriate sexual or aggressive behavior, mood lability, impaired judgment, and problems in social or work interactions that developed during or shortly after alcohol ingestion (APA, 2013). In addition, the person shows one or more of the following signs: slurred speech, lack of physical coordination, unsteady gait, nystagmus (rapid involuntary movements of the eyes in a side-to-side or occasionally up-and-down direction or "eye wiggles"), impairment in attention or memory, stupor, or coma. For an assessment of alcohol intoxication, these symptoms are not better explained by a general medical condition or another mental disorder.

We now turn to alcohol withdrawal.

ALCOHOL WITHDRAWAL

Those who drink heavily on a regular basis and find they cannot gradually cut down are at risk for the diagnosis of alcohol withdrawal. While the disorder is more common in adults, it can be seen in teenagers or even children who drink excessively. Having experienced previous withdrawal symptoms or needed medical detox further increases the risk for this diagnosis.

Heavy and prolonged drinking, especially on a daily basis, disrupts the brain's neurotransmitters. As noted, alcohol initially enhances the effect of GABA, which is the most abundant inhibitory neurotransmitter in the brain. However, a chronic pattern of alcohol consumption eventually suppresses GABA activity, so that the person needs more and more alcohol to produce the desired effects, commonly referred to as tolerance. Chronic drinking also suppresses the activity of glutamate. To maintain equilibrium, the glutamate system responds by functioning at a higher level than for those who are moderate or nondrinkers. When someone who is a heavy drinker suddenly stops or significantly reduces his or her alcohol consumption, the neurotransmitters previously suppressed by alcohol are no longer suppressed. As a result, they rebound resulting in brain hyper excitability. Consequently, the effects associated with alcohol withdrawal—such as anxiety, irritability, agitation, tremors, seizures, or DTs (delirium tremens, the most severe form of alcohol withdrawal manifested by an altered mental status—global confusion—and autonomic hyperactivity that can progress to cardiovascular collapse; clearly a medical emergency)—are the opposite of those associated with alcohol consumption.

Withdrawal symptoms (Table 14.4) typically emerge after the person stops or reduces a heavy and prolonged pattern of drinking and, as a consequence, blood concentrations of alcohol decline sharply. Two or more symptoms are required for a diagnosis, and they can begin as early as several hours to a few days after the person's last drink and can persist for weeks. They can range anywhere from mild anxiety and shakiness to the more severe complications seen in the DTs. However less than 10 percent of people will develop the more severe withdrawal symptoms (APA, 2013). Symptoms must cause significant distress or impairment in social, work, or other important areas of one's functioning, and they cannot be better accounted for by another mental disorder or general medical condition.

In order to test how much alcohol is in someone's system, a physician may perform a toxicology screen (referring to various tests to determine the type and approximate amount of legal and illegal drugs a person has taken, using a blood or urine sample) along with a physical exam. Physical signs a physician may look for include: hand tremors, an irregular heart rate, dehydration, and a fever. Unfortunately, the symptoms of withdrawal can be so unpleasant (such as depression, blackouts, liver disease, and other sequelae such as seizures and hallucinations) that a person may continue to drink (APA, 2013).

The following vignette describes Chris Oghee's struggle with alcohol and features the diagnosis of substance use.

CASE The Case of Chris Oghee

It is Susan's last day on the job. She has been promoted to an administrative position in her agency and will no longer be seeing clients. As she cleans out her desk in preparation for moving upstairs, she spots a small crumpled piece of paper in the bottom of a drawer. It's a note that she had written almost a year and a half ago reminding her to call back a client by the name of Chris O. "Chris Oghee," Susan says softly, as the memories of the case flood back into her mind. It feels as if she saw him just yesterday.

Chris is not someone you can easily forget. He was always on time for his appointments, and (unlike many of her court-mandated clients) Chris seemed eager to work on his problems. He was articulate and reflective as he spoke about his struggles with alcohol and the problems they caused him.

At his first visit with Susan, Chris was a 32-year-old white male who was referred to the agency for counseling by the courts. He had been convicted for driving while intoxicated—apparently his car was weaving and crossing over the center line. Fortunately, it was late at night when there was hardly any traffic on the road. However, his erratic driving was noticed by a police officer who pulled Chris over.

"Do you know why I stopped you?" The officer shined his flashlight into the car, checking for any open alcohol bottles or cans. Chris's slurred speech added to the officer's suspicions, so Chris was asked to step out of the car. The dashboard camera in the patrol car later showed that Chris stumbled getting out of his car. With his unsteady gait and smelling of alcohol, Chris did not even think to object to a roadside sobriety test. The video displayed that he had a hard time walking a straight line, let alone putting his finger on his nose. The Breathalyzer showed an illegal level of intoxication, confirming the obvious. Chris had been arrested immediately, his third for a DUI.

When he went to court, the judge sentenced Chris to a 6 month work/release program and mandated therapy during that time. Chris never had any type of counseling before.

During their first interview, Susan had taken Chris's psychosocial history, which revealed that Chris had started abusing alcohol when he was a freshman in high school. He had been drinking excessively ever since (almost 15 years at the time). Chris's father always said a real man could handle his liquor—and Chris had grown up watching his father and grandfather down a "couple of shots and a beer" together after work. To Chris, that kind of hard drinking was a sign of manhood.

After high school, Chris landed a good job in construction and married his high school sweetheart, Katie Rose. They had two children right out of the box, but after 5 years the marriage ended in divorce—partly because Katie Rose couldn't tolerate Chris's drinking. The next five years were a blur. Chris loved his kids and tried to maintain contact with them. After the divorce, Katie Rose struggled to make ends meet—so it was understandable that she would get angry with Chris when support payments were either late or skipped entirely. Katie Rose would immediately petition the court; it had almost become a routine.

In the meantime, Chris was struggling to work his construction job and go to school at the same time. He realized that he was going to need a college degree if he wanted to support a family—and he had discovered pretty early during that first semester that he couldn't continue to drink the way he had been and "do school."

Chris hadn't had anything alcoholic to drink for about 6 months when he met Diane. She was fun and crazy, and she made Chris laugh—something he felt he deserved after everything that had happened. From Chris's point of view, everything finally seemed to be coming together for him. He and Diane got along great together, and gradually he started sharing a few beers with her at the end of the day. Chris really liked Diane's parents, too, and they made him feel just like family. Diane's mom had trouble sleeping, so the doctor had prescribed some sleeping pills for her, which she usually swallowed with a cocktail (occasionally watered down with club soda). Diane's mother was usually "in the bag" by about 10 in the evening. Her father got started much earlier in the day. He believed that a beer or two was the best way to

CASE THE CASE OF CHRIS OGHEE (CONTINUED)

kick back and relax—and he usually started relaxing right after breakfast. For Chris, things were starting to feel like home.

Chris had been fairly successful at keeping his drinking under control when he and Diane were first married, but after their daughter Sylvia was born, he began to feel the pressure of being responsible for yet another child. For most of his life, Chris had felt like a failure. Even though he always loved his job in construction and had dreamed that maybe someday he could start his own company, he never really saw himself going any further in life—until college opened his eyes. With the encouragement of one of his professors, Chris discovered creative talents that he never knew he had.

Somehow, Chris eventually completed college and landed a job in a large advertising firm in New York City. Chris was quite talented, and everyone at the agency could see that he had real potential. Over time, the office staff and assistants realized that there were going to be some occasions when Chris needed them to "cover" for him—and nobody minded. Chris was a great guy. His bosses overlooked his slow starts at the beginning of the week, and, despite frequent absences (usually on a Monday after a weekend of heavy drinking), Chris had been steadily promoted. Seven years passed.

When Chris first came to see Susan, he was responsible for the national promotional campaign for a popular brand of wines, and was involved in designing the product displays you see in stores. He seemed to have a good eye for what would appeal to people. Chris consumed little alcohol during the day, but would begin drinking a shot and a beer as soon as he got home from work (much as his father and grandfather had done). Chris readily admitted to Susan that there had been several weekend episodes of binge drinking as well as occasional blackouts. She remembered very clearly what Chris said in that first interview about his drinking. "When I drink, I don't have a care in the world. Nothing really bothers me. I'm on top of the world! It's when I'm not drinking that my troubles come back, so I drink again. You know, the problems will always be there, but when I'm drinking I don't have to think about them. That's why I drink."

Chris didn't seem to mind the hangovers. His solution was to have a little "hair o' the dog that bit him" (yet another drink to chase off the headache and grogginess). He accepted the hangovers as just a part of the picture. Diane had significantly cut back on alcohol when she was pregnant, and then stopped drinking altogether shortly after Sylvia's arrival. Over the years, it had gotten so that Diane and Chris were not much company to each other. It seemed to Diane that his drinking had increased, and they were arguing more and more—usually about his drinking. Chris made a rule that he would stop drinking by midnight, but Diane would often awaken in the wee hours and hear the ice tinkling in his glass downstairs.

They really had no social life. Chris pretty much just sat in front of the TV with his drink after work and on weekends. He convinced himself that it was no big deal to Diane because she was always so absorbed with Sylvia. Diane worried about Chris's health. He started losing weight and gobbled down antacids like they were gumdrops. Chris would complain about a gnawing pain in his stomach between his breastbone and his navel. Sometimes the pain radiated to his back. After a particularly heavy bout of drinking, Chris experienced a bitter-tasting regurgitation. But he never complained, he just swallowed it back down.

Susan was packing some books into boxes as she recalled how Chris had described himself to her that first day as a "quiet guy." She smiled at the memory because, at the time, he was so sincere. "When things get really bad between me and Katie Rose—you know, my ex-wife—I just want to be by myself. I'll find some isolated place to go and just be alone. I'm a loner," he had said as if he believed it. However, he later admitted that he really enjoyed being around people. His friends from work all liked to stop off at a bar for a pick-me-up before going home. Chris's eyes literally sparkled as he recounted, "I'm usually the last guy to arrive because of my overseas phone calls and whatnot—and, I gotta say, it warms my heart to walk in the door and have everybody yell out, 'Hey, Oggie's here! Set him up, Charlie.' Charlie's been the bartender there since the place opened—way before I moved here." Chris seemed to love the idea that there was a place where he felt welcome, no questions asked. He confessed, "Drinking helps me feel more like one of the guys. Let's face it, I'm a small-town guy from New Jersey ... pretending to be a big shot in Manhattan. It's just a lot easier for me to make friends when I'm loosened up. Always has been."

By the time Chris completed the mandated counseling program, he had not had a drink for the past 3 months. However, he told Susan at their last session, "I recognize I've got a lot of work to do. My relationship with Diane isn't great ... I feel like I've neglected Sylvia ... and I know I have to find a better way of dealing with Katie Rose and the kids."

Susan had been very encouraged when Chris said he'd decided to continue their counseling sessions on a voluntary basis.

CHRIS OGHEE'S DSM DIAGNOSIS IS AS FOLLOWS:
Alcohol use disorder (and coded as severe) in early remission
Unspecified personality disorder

Competency 7 c

ASSESSMENT SUMMARY Although the focus of this case discussion revolves around Chris Oghee's struggle with alcohol, the discussion also points to his coping strategies and areas where the social worker might be able to help him improve his adaptation to life circumstances and events. When Chris was initially pulled over for erratic driving, he showed signs of alcohol intoxication. His recent ingestion of alcohol was evident by the "smell" of alcohol on his breath when the police officer approached him. Chris's speech was slurred, and when he got out of his car he was unsteady on his feet. The officer asked him to walk a straight line and then put his finger to his nose. Chris was not coordinated enough to do either, so he failed the roadside sobriety test. He was subsequently arrested for a DUI.

Chris's pattern of drinking at the time appeared to be related to significant behavioral changes in his life; a prior divorce, responsibilities for three children, a stressed relationship with his current wife, health problems, and legal charges for driving while intoxicated to name a few. However, for almost 15 years, Chris had been suffering from alcohol use. Although Chris promised himself that he would stop drinking at midnight, it was usually in the predawn hours when he actually stopped or simply blacked out. He had been able to stay away from alcohol when he met his wife Diane, but 6 months later he returned to his prior drinking habits. Subsequently they both started to argue over his drinking. Chris had been married before and divorced his first wife due to his drinking. This relationship was currently troubled. His first wife routinely pressed charges against Chris for failure to provide support payments for the two children they had together. Chris also had several outstanding legal charges due to his drinking. By the time he was mandated to attend counseling, he had three convictions for driving while intoxicated. Remarkably, Chris was doing well on the job, although his superiors overlooked his frequent absences at the beginning of the week, usually on a Monday. Chris began to lose weight, complained of abdominal pain, and experienced waterbrash (or bitter regurgitation), all symptoms of a gastric ulcer. He chewed antacids with limited relief. Despite this discomfort, he continued to drink.

As is common for those with an alcohol-related disorder, Chris reported a family history of substance use. His father and grandfather drank and conveyed the message to Chris that "real men" enjoyed a "shot and a beer" at the end of the day. Chris's drinking affected important interpersonal areas of his life. Relationships with his ex-wife and current wife were strained due to his drinking. He faced legal charges due to drinking while under the influence of alcohol. Although he wanted friends, Chris reported being a loner and described himself as shy. Drinking made him feel more confident and able to make friends, although these friends were much like him. An underlying disorder of avoidant personality disorder was considered. However, the practitioner deferred making this diagnosis until Chris experienced a period of time without alcohol in order to determine if the full symptom picture of the personality disorder would emerge with abstinence.

The diagnosis of alcohol use disorder was made since Chris exhibited the full spectrum of compulsive alcohol use, including tolerance, withdrawal, and craving. Chris was starting to drink more, and tried (unsuccessfully) to stop drinking by midnight but was really unable to stop until the predawn hours. In his words, he would take "a hair o' the dog" that bit him to ward off the aftereffects of hang-

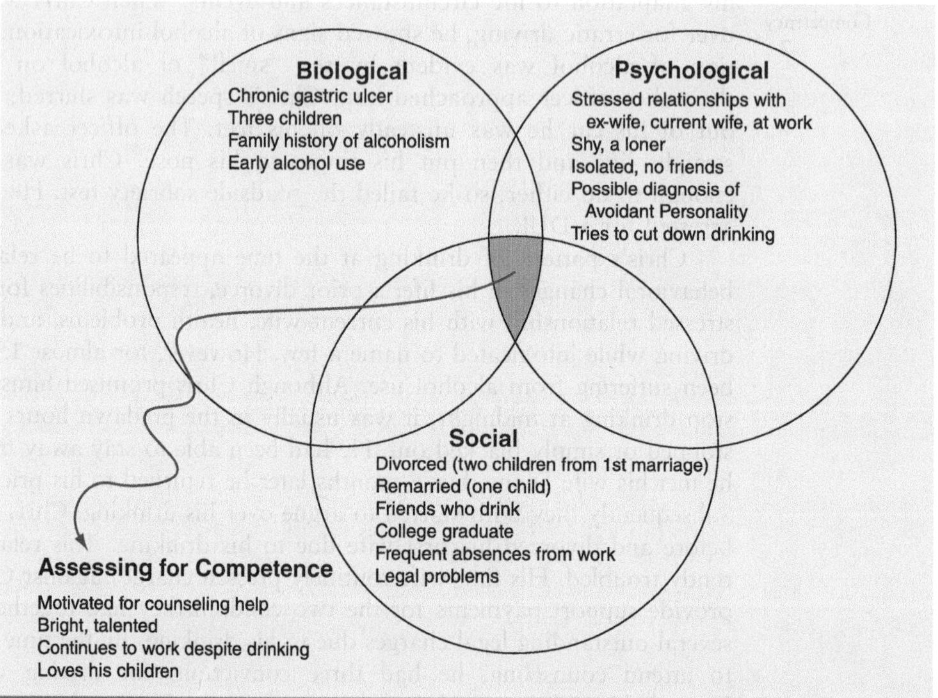

FIGURE 14.1 › ALCOHOL USE DISORDER
The interactions of the biological, psychological, and social variables in Chris Oghee's life.

overs, and his relationship with Diane was becoming increasingly stressed due to his drinking.

Despite a consistent pattern of drinking, Chris was able to work steadily and was even given the responsibility for major marketing campaigns. Although their relationship was troubled, Diane stayed with him. Chris also worked hard to remain connected to his children. When Chris completed the course of mandated counseling, he had not been drinking for at least 3 months but for less than a year. He recognized that he needed to address the other problems in his life related to his alcohol use and planned to continue seeing the social worker. At that point, the specifier, in early remission, can be applied to his diagnosis. Figure 14.1 illustrates the interactions of the biological, psychological, and social variables in Chris Oghee's life. It also identifies the areas of competency Chris possesses—the strengths that he can draw on to succeed in his battle against alcohol.

LONG-TERM EFFECTS OF ALCOHOL USE

There are two types of brain damage that can persist beyond the usual duration of intoxication and withdrawal. One is syndrome, also known as Korsakoff psychosis, which is a chronic memory disorder (and detailed in the neurocognitive disorders). Essentially a degenerative disease of the brain, Korsakoff's syndrome is characterized by abnormal eye movements, difficulties with muscle coordination, and confusion. The other is Wernicke encephalopathy (an acute brain reaction to severe lack of thiamine). Wernicke's encephalopathy was first described in 1881 and is now known to be caused by thiamine deficiency resulting from malnutrition usually brought on by chronic alcohol use. It is a medical emergency that causes life-threatening brain disruption, confusion, staggering and stumbling, a lack of coordination, and abnormal involuntary eye movements. Wernicke encephalopathy is almost always accompanied by or followed by Korsakoff's syndrome. In essence, an individual can expect to experience problems with memory and cognitive skills as a result of excessive drinking over a period of years. Long-term alcohol use can also lead to serious liver, heart, and stomach problems.

There are a number of additional issues associated with long-term alcohol use. Many people who abuse alcohol or are dependent on it fluctuate between drinking heavily, drinking socially without negative effects, and not drinking at all (or being abstinent). About 20 percent of those with severe alcohol use can have a spontaneous remission or stop drinking on their own, and will not re-experience problems with drinking (Sadock, Sadock, & Ruiz, 2014). Unfortunately, severe alcohol use is often associated with using (or abusing) other substances such as cannabis, cocaine, heroin, amphetamines, sedatives, or nicotine. This combined substance use increases the risk for suicide, accidents, or violence (Canapary, Bongar, & Cleary, 2002; Stuart et al., 2003). As a matter of fact, 40 percent of people in the United States will experience an alcohol-related accident at some time in their lives (SAMHSA, 2004). Absenteeism from work, job-related accidents, and low employee productivity, all related to alcohol use, have been well documented (National Institute on Alcohol Abuse and Alcoholism, 2005).

We now turn to the caffeine-related disorders. Notice there is no diagnosis for caffeine use.

CAFFEINE-RELATED DISORDERS

Coffee beans are indigenous to Ethiopia, and historical evidence has revealed that, in the period around 575 AD, coffee beans had become a form of currency and were consumed as food (Nawrot et al., 2003). By the fourth century, coffee beans had been introduced to Arabia, where they were called "gahwah" (a poetic term for wine). The Turkish equivalent is "kahveh," which translates to "café" in French and "kaffee" in German (Weinberg & Bealer, 2002). Coffee shops were fashionable in Europe as early as the seventeenth and eighteenth centuries. Some suggest that the Boston Tea Party of 1773 was the genesis of Americans' present-day coffee-drinking habits. Protesting against the excessive taxes on tea, the citizens of Boston boarded British ships and dumped their cargoes of tea overboard. Since that time, the United States has been considered a leader in coffee consumption. Almost a century later, in the 1880s, the first caffeinated soft drinks were created.

Caffeine is a plant alkaloid that is naturally produced in the leaves, seeds, or fruits of many plants. The primary source of caffeine is the coffee bean (or seed of the coffee plant) from which coffee is brewed. Other, less common sources of caffeine include the plants yerba mate and guarana, which are sometimes used in the preparation of teas and energy-boosting drinks. When caffeine is removed from the plant and reduced to its natural state, it forms a white powder. This powdered form of caffeine is bitter, which is probably why many beverages containing caffeine also have a lot of sugar or other sweeteners added. Caffeine can also be produced artificially.

Caffeine is considered a drug because it stimulates the central nervous system. It can be found in many beverages besides coffee and coffee-based drinks like latte. Caffeine is in many types of soda (aka pop, soda pop, soft drink), many fizzy drinks, some teas, several energy drinks, chocolate (including hot chocolate), weight-loss aids, and some over-the-counter medications such as pep pills and cold and flu remedies, for instance, Excedrin and NoDoz. Caffeine increases alertness, decreases fatigue, and improves muscle coordination. It is very similar in chemical structure to another substance in our bodies called adenosine, whose function is (among other things) to dilate blood vessels in the head. Caffeine blocks this dilation, causing a mild stimulating effect on the central nervous system. Because of this arterial dilation, caffeine is commonly found in headache and migraine medications. It also has the ability to enhance the effects of aspirin.

PREVAILING PATTERN

It is unlikely that the practitioner will encounter someone with caffeine intoxication in his or her practice. For example, Griffiths, Juliano, and Chausmer (2003) conducted a telephone survey and found that only 7 percent of current caffeine users met criteria for caffeine intoxication and experienced symptoms that interfered with their functioning at work, school, or home. Typically, a cup of coffee is around 150 milligrams of caffeine (depending on strength)—just enough to increase alertness and promote wakefulness, but not enough to result in intoxication. As such, the prevalence of caffeine intoxication is unclear. The DSM-5 notes that in the United States, approximately 7 percent of the population may experience five or more symptoms of caffeine intoxication and the impairment required to support the diagnosis (APA, 2013).

As with caffeine intoxication, the prevalence of caffeine withdrawal in the general U.S. population is unclear (APA, 2013). Headaches seem to be a common symptom and seen in 50 percent of those attempting to stop caffeine use. The symptom picture varies whether one is attempting to permanently stop caffeine use or to decrease use. A gradual reduction of caffeine intake tends to decrease the severity of withdrawal symptoms.

Caffeine Intoxication

In the United States, the average daily caffeine intake per person is about 280 milligrams—the equivalent of two mugs of coffee or three to five cans (or bottles) of soft drinks. Caffeine, the world's most common psychoactive substance, is consumed by 90 percent of adults in North America on a daily basis (Lovett, 2005; Mednick, Cai, Kanady, & Drummond, 2008). Caffeine is legal and considered generally safe; thus it could be characterized as the most commonly used and least harmful substance. It is readily available and inexpensive, and the need for it does not lead to the compulsive drug-seeking behaviors discussed in relation to other substances. It is possible to skip that cup of coffee in the morning, which contributes to the misconception that caffeine is easy to give up. However, more than 50 percent of regular caffeine users report difficulties giving up or reducing caffeine use (Meredith, Juliano, Hughes, & Griffiths, 2013). Because it is socially acceptable and so widely consumed, the negative effects of caffeine often go unrecognized.

Differential Assessment

The DSM-5 diagnostic guidelines define caffeine intoxication as the recent daily consumption of caffeine of at least more than 250 milligrams, which, typically, is the equivalent of two-and-a-half cups of brewed coffee (APA, 2013). Symptoms may develop during or shortly after caffeine use—and five or more of the following signs must be present for a diagnosis of intoxication: restlessness, nervousness, excitement, insomnia, flushed face, diuresis, gastrointestinal disturbance, muscle twitching, rambling flow of thought and speech, tachycardia (a faster than normal heart rate at rest) or cardiac arrhythmia (a disturbance of the heart rhythm), periods of inexhaustibility, or psychomotor agitation (unintentional and purposeless motions). However, intoxication may not occur for some who develop tolerance. The diagnosis of intoxication calls for significant distress or impairment in social, occupational, or other important areas in a person's life.

We now turn to the symptom picture for caffeine withdrawal.

Caffeine Withdrawal

Individuals with anxiety disorders are especially sensitive to the effects of caffeine but may not recognize the role that it plays in their anxiety symptoms. Caffeine disrupts sleep. When it is consumed just before bedtime (or continuously throughout the day), sleep onset may be delayed, total sleep time reduced, normal stages of sleep altered, and the overall quality of sleep diminished.

DIFFERENTIAL ASSESSMENT

If you missed your cup of coffee this morning and now have a headache or are having difficulty concentrating, you could be experiencing caffeine withdrawal. Juliano and Griffiths (2011) conducted a comprehensive review of the literature regarding caffeine withdrawal and identified the following symptoms: headache, fatigue, decreased energy/activity level, decreased alertness, drowsiness, decreased contentedness, depressed mood, difficulty concentrating, irritability, foggy/not clearheaded, and flu-like symptoms of nausea/vomiting and muscle pain/stiffness. According to the authors, these symptoms can be mild or severe—but about 13 percent of people who drink coffee develop symptoms so significant that they cannot do what they normally would do, such as leaving the house or performing on the job.

Caffeine is absorbed into the bloodstream very quickly but takes a relatively long time to leave our bodies. Its effects can last from 12 to about 24 hours, which explains why starting the day with a cup of coffee is a morning ritual for so many people. Typically, the onset of withdrawal symptoms occurs 12 to 24 hours after abstinence and can last from 2 to 9 days. The essential features of caffeine withdrawal emerge after someone who uses caffeine on a daily basis abruptly stops (APA, 2013). Since caffeine ingestion can be so much a part of someone's habit or daily ritual, these withdrawal symptoms are unexpected. Drinking as little as one cup of coffee can cause these symptoms.

The next category of substance-related disorders considered are the cannabis-related disorders.

CANNABIS-RELATED DISORDERS

Although cannabis can have hallucinogenic effects, it is discussed separately in the DSM because of differences in its other psychological and behavioral effects. Cannabis is the most routinely used illicit psychoactive substance in the United States. It comes from the leaves, buds, flowers, and resin from the cannabis plant (*Cannabis sativa* or *Cannabis indica*) native to Central Asia. Marijuana is the name given to these plants, which tend to grow wild (Iversen, 2000). Over the past 2 decades, an increase in the potency of seized cannabis has been found. There are more than 200 street names for marijuana, and they can vary from city to city and from neighborhood to neighborhood. Some of the most common names are weed, pot, grass, herb, Mary Jane, reefer, dagga, dope, bhang, skunk, boom, gangster, kif, chronic, and ganga (sometimes spelled ganja).

PREVAILING PATTERN

The 12-month prevalence for cannabis use disorder is about 3.4 percent among those age 12 to 17 years of age, and 1.5 percent for adults 18 years and older, making it the most widely used illicit drug in the United States (APA, 2013). There are differences in the rates of use among males and females; that is, cannabis use increases among adult males (by 2.2 percent) than among adult females (0.8 percent). When considering age, cannabis use decreases with age and the lowest use is found among those age 65 years and older (0.01 percent).

Prevalence of cannabis intoxication is difficult to determine. However, it is more than likely that most users will have at some time or another met diagnostic criteria. That said, it is highly likely that prevalence rates for cannabis use are more than likely similar to those of intoxication.

Cannabis withdrawal is a clinically significant phenomenon for those who quit use with or without treatment. Among adolescents and adults in treatment, approximately 50 to 95 percent report cannabis withdrawal (APA, 2013). Studies of withdrawal experiences conducted in the United States and Australia of non-treatment-seeking adults report a range of 40.9 percent to 80 percent (Copeland, Swift, & Rees, 2001; Swift, Hall, & Teesson, 2001).

Cannabis Use Disorder

The cannabis plants contain a number of psychoactive compounds called cannabinoids that are believed to alter mood and behavior, the most potent of which is delta-9-tetrahydrocannabinol (THC). Cannabis is usually smoked in the form of dried leaves and buds or as dried resin (hashish). When smoked as a cigarette, it is commonly called a "joint" or a "reefer"; and when made into cigars, they are called "blunts." Some users also mix marijuana into foods (e.g., brownies) or brew it as tea. Another recent device is vaporization, where the plant material is heated to release the psychoactive cannabinoids for inhalation. The THC latches onto specific receptors in the brain known to be involved in appetite regulation and the perception of pain. Precisely how this process works is not fully understood. Typically, people who use cannabis value the relaxation, increased sensory awareness, and elevated mood it provides. Typically, cannabis use disorder develops over time, although the progression is quicker in adolescents, particularly those with conduct problems. Considered a gateway drug, an individual can progress from legal drugs, such as alcohol and cigarettes, to the illicit use of cannabis. Somehow cannabis is perceived as less harmful, which, more than likely, contributes to increased use (APA, 2013).

Synthetic formulations in the form of a pill or capsule are also available and approved for medical purposes, such as for the nausea and vomiting caused by chemotherapy, or for anorexia and weight loss in individuals with AIDS. Other newly emerging synthetic forms of marijuana are available known as "fake weed" and called K2, spice, Yucatan fire, skunk, or moon rocks (National Institute on Drug Abuse, 2012a). They contain dry, shredded plant material and chemical additives that are responsible for their psychoactive (mind-altering) effects.

Mood swings are the typical reaction to marijuana. Smoked in moderate amounts, cannabis produces a vague or fuzzy feeling many people describe as mellowness and a sense of general well-being. Others might enter a dreamlike state where time seems to stand still. For some people, it can interfere with memory and increase appetite (a condition popularly referred to as "the munchies"). However, more than any other drug, marijuana can cause some very different reactions in different people. Some individuals may experience nausea, anxiety, and paranoia.

TABLE 14.5 SYMPTOMS OF CANNABIS WITHDRAWAL

Stopping a pattern of heavy and prolonged cannabis use—usually on a daily or almost daily over a period of at least a few months
Three (or more) of the following that develop within about 1 week: irritability; anger or aggression; nervousness or anxiety; sleep difficulties such as insomnia or disturbing dream; a decreased appetite or weight loss; restlessness; a depressed mood; or uncomfortable physical symptoms such as stomach pain, shakiness or tremors, sweating, fever, chills, or a headache

Iversen (2000) observes that the feeling of well-being evoked by a small dose of marijuana can change to paranoia, hallucinations, and dizziness when larger doses are taken. Coordination can be affected, which increases the risk of accidents. If eaten, the resin has a hallucinogenic effect. Those who are frequent long-term users of marijuana risk impairments of memory, concentration, motivation, self-esteem, difficulties in relationships with others, and problems at work.

DIFFERENTIAL ASSESSMENT

The diagnostic criteria for cannabis use disorder follow the same general criteria established for substance use disorders. However, the specific symptoms for withdrawal include: within approximately 1 week of withdrawal after a pattern of heavy and prolonged use (usually daily or almost daily), a person may experience three or more of the following: irritability, anger or aggression, nervousness or anxiety, sleep difficulties such as insomnia or disturbing dreams, a decreased appetite or weight loss, restlessness, a depressed mood, or uncomfortable physical symptoms such as stomach pain, shakiness or tremors, sweating, fever, chills, or a headache (Table 14.5). Because the cannabinoids are fat soluble, they stay in the bodily fluids for an extended period of time and are excreted slowly. Urine testing, especially for those who deny use, is an especially helpful method to confirm the diagnosis.

When considering cannabis use disorder, it is important for the practitioner to remember that when cannabis is used for legitimate medical reasons, it is possible for someone to experience either tolerance or withdrawal reactions. However, because these effects can naturally occur when taken as prescribed, they should not be used to support the diagnosis of a cannabis use disorder. It is the individual who compulsively uses the drug and has the associated social or occupational problems who is considered for cannabis use disorder. This is the individual who is often seen as passive; lacking in ambition; and prone to depression, suspiciousness, panic or anxiety attack, and impaired judgment.

We now turn to cannabis intoxication.

CANNABIS INTOXICATION

Cannabis intoxication is considered when problematic behavioral or psychological changes develop during (or shortly after) cannabis use. Cannabis produces euphoria (intense feelings of joy or elation) or a drug "high," which includes feelings of intoxication and detachment, relaxation, altered perception of time and distance, intensified sensory experiences, laughter, talkativeness, decreased anxiety, decreased alertness, and depression. These effects are dependent on the amount taken, expectations of the user, mode of administration (i.e., smoked, swallowed), the social environment, and the individual's personality.

The symptoms of cannabis intoxication emerge after recent use and include maladaptive behavioral or psychological changes (such as impaired coordination, euphoria, anxiety, sensation of slowed time, impaired judgment, social withdrawal) that developed during or shortly after using cannabis and two (or more) of the following: conjunctival injection (or bloodshot eyes); increased appetite; dry mouth; and tachycardia (APA, 2013). These symptoms are not due to a general medical condition and not better explained by another mental disorder. The practitioner considers the specifier of perceptual disturbances (or hallucinations).

An examination of cannabis withdrawal as a separate diagnosis follows.

Cannabis Withdrawal

Cannabis withdrawal occurs in frequent users who quit. In a study conducted by Gorelick and colleagues (2012), there seems to be no correlation between the symptoms of cannabis withdrawal and sex, race, and the type of cannabis preparation used. However, the frequency of use prior to attempts at quitting, and shorter periods of abstinence, contribute to the withdrawal diagnosis.

The diagnostic criteria for cannabis withdrawal (Table 14.5) are reserved for those who have had a pattern of heavy and prolonged use, usually on a daily basis or over a period of several months (APA, 2013).

We now turn to the hallucinogen-related disorders. Note that the signs and symptoms for withdrawal have not been established for the phencyclidines, and so this criterion does not apply to our discussion of diagnostic criteria.

HALLUCINOGEN-RELATED DISORDERS

The hallucinogens are a broad class of natural and synthetic compounds that alter a person's perception and consciousness. Included are the less potent but similarly acting compounds such as ketamine, cyclohexamine, and dizocilpine. Other hallucinogen use disorder includes the hallucinogens other than the phencyclidines. In the 1990s, the two most commonly used drugs of this class were LSD (acid), mescaline, and MDMA or ecstasy (Adam) (APA, 2013).

We begin with the phencyclidines.

THE PHENCYCLIDINES

The phencyclidines (or phencyclidine-like substances) are a class of hallucinogenic drugs that produce feelings of depersonalization and detachment from reality—qualities with great appeal to recreational drug users who value escapism. It should come as no surprise that entrepreneurial chemists have been able to manipulate the chemical structure of known drugs of abuse and produce a seemingly endless lineup of new drugs. Obviously, these "designer drugs" are not listed as controlled substances by the Drug Enforcement Administration. Their street names vary from location to location and can change over time. The phencyclidines include phencyclidine (PCP, Angel Dust, Sernylan) and ketamine (Ketalar, Ketaject), which is a derivative of cyclohexamine and phencyclidine. Ketamine is generally considered a chemical cousin to PCP. Another dissociative drug is dizocilpine (DZ, MK-801). The phencyclidines were first developed as dissociative anesthetics in the 1950s and became street drugs in the 1960s. They can be taken orally, intravenously, or smoked.

PREVAILING PATTERN

The prevalence of phencyclidine use disorder is unknown. The DSM-5 approximates that about 2.5 percent of the U.S. population reports having ever used phencyclidine with rates increasing with age; for instance from 0.3 percent of those 12 to 17 years of age, to 1.3 percent of 18- to 25-year-olds, to 2.9 percent of individuals age 26 years or older (APA, 2013). Ketamine use is assessed separately and past-year use among 12th graders seems relatively stable (at 1.6 percent to 1.7 percent over the past 3 years).

Phencyclidine intoxication reflects estimates of phencyclidine use or about 2.5 percent of the population (APA, 2013). Among 12th-grade high school students, 2.3 percent report ever having used phencyclidine with 57 percent having used over the past 12 months. Ketamine intoxication parallels ketamine use prevalence rates or 1.7 percent of 12 graders over the past year.

PHENCYCLIDINE USE DISORDER

The phencyclidines include PCP, a white crystalline powder with a distinctively bitter chemical taste. It is a popular drug for illicit chemists to experiment with, and at least 30 forms of PCP have been identified (Doweiko, 2014). The forms of PCP on the illegal market are tablets, capsules, and colored powders—and they are known by a variety of names including PCE, TCP, PCC, Angel Dust, Hog, Trang, PeaCe Pill, wack, rocket fuel, and "Eu4ia" (an amphetamine-like drug synthesized from legally purchased over-the-counter chemicals). PCP can be snorted, smoked, or eaten. When smoked, PCP is often applied to tobacco or marijuana or to a leafy herb such as mint or parsley. When mixed with marijuana, PCP is called "crystal super grass" and "killer joints."

Low doses of phencyclidine cause the user to experience dizziness, ataxia (or impairment in control of voluntary muscle coordination), nystagmus, mild hypertension, abnormal involuntary movements, slurred speech, nausea, weakness, slowed reaction times, euphoria or affective dulling, and lack of concern. Medium-sized doses of PCP produce reactions of disorganized thinking, changed body image and sensory perception, depersonalization, and feelings of unreality. At high doses, the user may experience amnesia and coma, with analgesic (decreased sensation of pain) effects sufficient for surgery. Seizures and respiratory depression can also occur at the highest doses. For individuals who also have a diagnosis of schizophrenia, their psychotic symptoms may be exacerbated. (Refer to the chapter on schizophrenia spectrum and other psychotic disorders.) Peak effects usually occur about 2 hours after oral doses

Ketamine is a surgical anesthetic, which, unlike some others, does not cause respiratory or cardiac depression. Liquid ketamine was developed in the early 1960s and was used on the battlefields in Vietnam. It has been useful in combat, natural disasters, and other situations when an emergency anesthetic is necessary (Schultz, 2007). Powdered ketamine first surfaced as a recreational drug in the 1970s and was known as Vitamin K or Super-K. It resurfaced in the 1990s with the rave scene and became known as Special K. Although ketamine can be manufactured in illicit laboratories, it is a difficult chemical process—so most of the drug found on the streets is diverted from human or veterinary supplies (Gahlinger, 2004). The drug is made by drying ketamine in a stove until it turns from a liquid into a powder.

The effects of ketamine kick in within 30 to 45 minutes, depending on the dose, and the high lasts anywhere from 30 minutes to 2 hours. Users of illicit drugs typically take a low dose and experience feelings of euphoria, visual hallucinations, a sense of unreality, depersonalization, and vivid dreams (Freese, Miotto, & Reback, 2002; Gahlinger, 2004). Some individuals report flashback experiences that occur days or even weeks after taking the drug (Gahlinger, 2004). An out-of-body experience has been described by some individuals who took high doses of ketamine. The person describes losing all sense of self and feeling a detachment of mind and body, leading to a trance-like state. In this trance, the person reports experiencing a "superior reality" filled with dazzling insights and visions. Some find this experience wonderful—others are frightened by it.

Long-term use, especially at high doses, may result in memory problems. This effect, coupled with its effectiveness at doses lower than those needed to produce anesthesia, has reportedly made ketamine popular as a date-rape drug (Gahlinger, 2004). The drug is usually inhaled through the nose (or snorted) but is sometimes sprinkled on tobacco or marijuana and smoked. Special K is frequently used in conjunction with other drugs such as ecstasy, heroin, or cocaine.

Dizocilpine was originally developed for treating traumatic brain injury and neurodegenerative diseases such as Huntington's, Alzheimer's, and amyotrophic lateral sclerosis (ALS) or Lou Gehrig's disease. The drug is an anticonvulsant. It had a promising future until neurotoxic-like effects were seen in certain regions of the brain. When this occurred, the pharmaceutical company Merck stopped further legal development of the drug. Some recreational users report unpleasant experiences such as strong aural (or auditory) hallucinations.

DIFFERENTIAL ASSESSMENT

With the exception of symptoms of withdrawal (which are not established for the phencyclidines), use is diagnosed using the general criteria for substance use. Heavy phencyclidine use is associated with craving. Phencyclidine is easy to obtain and individuals often use the drug several times a day, thus spending a significant part of their day using the substance. Increased amounts of the phencyclidines are needed to achieve intoxication or the desired effects. Some individuals may continue to use the drug despite psychological problems (e.g., anxiety, rage, aggression, or flashbacks) or medical problems (e.g., hyperthermia, hypertension, seizures). Due to a lack of insight and judgment while intoxicated, a person might also get into situations (such as fighting) that can result in legal problems. The person may neglect obligations at home, work, or school, and the person's behavior while intoxicated may contribute to arguments or risky behaviors such as driving while under the influence of the drug.

We now review the symptom picture for phencyclidine intoxication.

PHENCYCLIDINE INTOXICATION

When considering intoxication, the practitioner looks for clinically significant behavior changes (e.g., belligerence, assaultiveness, impulsiveness, unpredictability, agitation, impaired judgment, or impaired social or occupational functioning) that develop during or shortly after phencyclidine use. Within an hour of swallowing the drug (or less when smoked, snorted, or used intravenously), intoxication is seen when the user experiences two or more of the following symptoms: vertical or horizontal nystagmus; hypertension or tachycardia; numbness or diminished responsiveness to pain; ataxia; dysarthria (or slurred speech); muscle rigidity; seizures or coma; or hyperacusis (sensitivity to sound). The diagnosis of intoxication is made only if these symptoms are not associated with a general medical condition or better explained by another mental disorder. A mild level of intoxication may resolve itself after 8 to 20 hours, whereas severe intoxication may last for several days.

THE OTHER HALLUCINOGENS

The hallucinogens are a diverse group of substances that can cause hallucinations, perceptual anomalies, and other subjective changes in a person's thoughts, emotion, and consciousness. They can be classified by their subjective effects, mechanisms of action, and chemical structure and typically include the psychedelics such as LSD, mescaline, or ecstasy. Many different names for this class of drugs have been proposed over the years, but the most common designation is hallucinogens (Nichols, 2004).

PREVAILING PATTERN

Other hallucinogen use disorder is considered as one of the rarest of the substance use disorders (APA, 2013). Overall, rates are higher among males (0.2 percent) compared to females (0.1 percent). Interestingly, the rates are the opposite among the adolescent population; that is, the rates are slightly higher for females (0.6 percent) than for males (0.4 percent). The highest rates are seen in persons younger than 30 years of age, peaking in those 18 to 29 years of age (0.6 percent) and decreasing to virtually 0 percent for those 45 years of age and older.

Much like hallucinogen use disorder, prevalence rates for other hallucinogen intoxication are higher for males (2.4 percent) than in females (1.2 percent). Additionally, use is higher among younger individuals showing rates of 3.1 percent among those 12 to 17 years of age, to 7.1 percent of those age 18 to 25 years (APA, 2013). Rates decrease to 0.7 percent for those age 26 years and older.

Other Hallucinogen Use Disorder

Other hallucinogen use disorder follows the diagnostic criteria for substance use with the exception of the symptoms of withdrawal. The hallucinogens are usually taken orally although some forms can be smoked (such as DMT) or rarely sniffed or by injection (for instance, ecstasy). The amphetamine derivative MDMA (3, 4-methylenedioxy-N-methylamphetamine) is sold as ecstasy on the street; however, the street version often contains no MDMA. Ecstasy is a synthetic drug that acts both as a stimulant and a hallucinogen. Technically known as a hallucinogenic amphetamine (or an empathogen), MDMA produces feelings of energy, empathy, openness (and a desire for physical contact), teeth clenching, plus mild visual, and auditory hallucinations. Some individuals have been known to experience dangerous reactions such as jumping out of a window because they believe they can fly. A number of users describe a hangover the following day characterized by feelings of fatigue, drowsiness, and sore jaw muscles. The drug causes the brain to dump large amounts of serotonin into the synapses and raises dopamine levels. MDMA is not toxic, but it can cause death due to overheating and dehydration. It also inhibits the production of urine and can lead to a fatal buildup of fluid in the tissues.

The most widely used hallucinogens are the LSD group, including LSD (lysergic acid), LSA (d-lysergic acid amide), mescaline (found in the peyote cactus plant), DMT (dimethyltryptamine, found in ayahuasca), and psilocybin (the main active ingredient found in certain species of mushrooms; known by the street names shrooms or mushies). Ayahuasca has primarily been prepared for its folk-medicinal and religious purposes. Sections of a vine of the Virola tree found in South and Central America are ground up and boiled alone or with leaves from other plants, resulting in a brew with hallucinogenic effects.

LSD is considered the most common hallucinogen and is one of the most potent mood-changing chemicals. Made from lysergic acid, it is found in a fungus that grows on rye and other grains. Commonly referred to as "acid," LSD is sold illegally in tablet form, capsules, and occasionally as a liquid. It is odorless and colorless with a slightly bitter taste. The hallucinogenic experience is often referred to as a "trip," and adverse reactions are known as a "bad trip." After one has taken the drug, they may experience flashbacks and can be diagnosed as having hallucinogen persisting perception disorder (APA, 2013).

We now turn to hallucinogen intoxication.

Hallucinogen Intoxication

The diagnostic criteria for hallucinogen intoxication are similar to that of marijuana. The behavioral or psychological changes can be seen as marked anxiety or depression, ideas of reference (or experiencing casual events or people's remarks and believing they refer to oneself when in fact they are not), a fear of losing one's mind, paranoid ideas, or impaired judgment. The person also experiences perceptual changes such as the subjective intensification of perceptions, depersonalization, derealization, illusions, hallucinations, and synesthesias (intersensory, intersensual associations—e.g., "Can't you just hear the changing colors on the trees?"). The physical symptoms the practitioner considers during intoxication (or shortly after) are two (or more) of: pupillary dilation; tachycardia (or rapid heartbeat); sweating; palpitations; blurred vision; tremors; and lack of coordination. Tolerance develops quickly to a number of the hallucinogens, and without the symptoms of withdrawal (Pechnick & Ungerleider, 2011).

The following discussion reviews hallucinogen persisting perception or flashbacks.

HALLUCINOGEN PERSISTING PERCEPTION DISORDER

Hallucinogen persisting perception disorder is the re-experiencing of perceptual disturbances, typically visual, when the drug experience has ended. The disorder is characterized by transient perceptual experiences that are reminiscent of those generated when using hallucinogenic drugs; for example, LSD and PCP. They are commonly called flashbacks and occur days, weeks, or months after the last dose. Hallucinogen persisting perception disorder is common in heavy users and disappears with time (Halpern & Pope, 2003). This seems to be a relatively rare disorder and its cause is unknown (Drummer & Odell, 2001).

After one stops taking the hallucinogen, he or she re-experiences one or more of the perceptual symptoms that were experienced while intoxicated; for example, geometric hallucinations, false perceptions of movement in the peripheral visual fields, flashes of color, intensified colors, trails of images of moving objects, positive afterimages, halos around objects, macropsia (where objects look larger than they actually are), and micropsia (like the rearview mirror in your car where objects look smaller than they are in reality). These symptoms cause significant distress or impairment in social, occupational, or other important areas of functioning.

The majority of flashbacks consist of visual sensory distortion, but there are also somatic flashbacks that involve feelings of depersonalization and emotional flashbacks involving periods when the individual re-experiences distressing emotions felt during the active use of LSD (McDowell, 2005). Doweiko (2014) observes that seasoned LSD users seem to accept the occurrence of flashbacks much like chronic alcohol users accept a hangover as the price one pays for chemical use.

Hallucinogen persisting perception disorder is not due to a general medical condition or better accounted for by another diagnosis (e.g., delirium, major neurocognitive disorder, schizophrenia) or hypnopomic hallucinations (generally considered as natural effects of REM sleep where an individual perceives visual or aural or auditory illusions upon waking; as a result, images and sounds can be carried over into a person's conscious perception).

The inhalant-related disorders are reviewed next.

INHALANT-RELATED DISORDERS

The inhalants are a chemically diverse group of psychoactive substances found in volatile solvents that can be breathed directly into the lungs. These substances are normally found in more than 1,000 ordinary household products—the most commonly abused of which are spray paint, paint thinner, gasoline, amyl nitrate, nitrous oxide (or laughing gas), nail polish remover, felt-tipped markers, airplane glue, contact cement, dry-cleaning fluid, and spot remover. According to the National Institute on Drug Abuse (2014), the primary users of inhalants are young children and adolescents, and they are the only class of substances used by younger rather than older teens. Sadly, the inhalants are readily available, inexpensive, and easy to conceal, thus making it easier to use them (National Institute on Drug Abuse, 2012b).

Although inhalant users tend to prefer one particular substance because of its smell or taste, a variety of substances may be used to achieve the same effects or due to availability and/or cost. Most inhalants act directly on the central nervous system (CNS) to produce psychoactive or mind-altering effects. Substances are inhaled and absorbed rapidly by the capillary surface of the lungs. This method of ingestion results in a rapid peak in blood levels. The substances enter the brain at such a rapid pace that the intensity resembles the effects that can be produced by an intravenous injection of other psychoactive drugs.

Prevailing Pattern

The prevalence of inhalant use disorder in the past 12 months is about 0.4 percent of youngsters between 12 to 17 years of age in the U.S. population (APA, 2013). Of those, use is highest in the Native American population and lowest in African Americans.

Prevalence rates for inhalant intoxication are unknown, but it is assumed that most users will eventually experience intoxication (APA, 2013). As such, rates approximate those of inhalant use.

Inhalant Use Disorder

The most common form of ingestion involves sniffing the inhalant directly from an open container or "huffing" from a rag soaked in the substance and held to the face. Another method is to place an open container or a rag soaked in the substance in a bag where the vapors concentrate before being inhaled. This is called "bagging." In the 1996 movie *Citizen Ruth*, the character Ruth is seen huffing patio sealant from a paper bag. Inhalant abusers sometimes spray aerosols directly into the nose. The former *Howard Stern Show* cast member John Melendez would inhale the compressed nitrous oxide found in whipped cream cans ("whippits"). The use of inhalants can cause brain, nerve, liver, and other damage to the body. If the user is startled while high, he or she may go into cardiac arrest, an event known as Sudden Sniffing Death Syndrome.

Differential Assessment

A diagnosis of inhalant use disorder follows the same general guidelines for the substance use disorders with the exception of the withdrawal criterion. A person may continue to use an inhalant substance despite the reality that the individual is aware of the serious problems they cause. Typically, the individual misses school (or work) or is unable to meet his or her social responsibilities. They may begin to withdraw from family and/or friends. Some individuals may continue to use inhalants even in hazardous situations.

Effects of inhalants that the practitioner may come across include: behavior that resembles alcohol inebriation; stimulation and a loss of inhibition that is followed by depression; euphoria; lethargy; distortion in perceptions of time and space; headache; nausea or vomiting; slurred speech; dizziness; loss of motor coordination; sneezing; or "glue sniffer's rash" around the nose and mouth. Most inhalants produce a rapid high that looks like alcohol intoxication with initial excitation, then drowsiness, disinhibition, lightheadedness, and agitation. If sufficient amounts are inhaled, nearly all solvents and gases can produce a loss of sensation, dulling of pain responses or anesthesia, and even loss of consciousness.

Tolerance developing within several hours to a few days after use has been reported with heavy or sustained use of inhalants. There are a number of long-term health problems associated with inhalant use such as loss of hearing; brain and nervous system damage that could result in personality changes and learning disabilities; blood oxygen depletion; bone marrow damage; and heart, lungs, liver, and kidney damage (Sadock, Sadock, & Ruiz, 2014).

Following is a discussion of inhalant intoxication.

INHALANT INTOXICATION

Inhalant intoxication includes volatile hydrocarbons such as gasoline and other volatile compounds or toxic gases from glues, and paints that clear up within a few minutes to a few hours after use. Toluene, a clear liquid solvent that smells like paint thinner, is also used as an inhalant due to its intoxicating properties. Consequently, the pattern of intoxication usually occurs in brief episodes. After a recent (or unintended) and short-term high dose of inhalant substances, the physical symptoms of intoxication that develop during or shortly after use include (two or more of) the following: dizziness; nystagmus; lack of coordination; slurred speech; unsteady gait; lethargy; depressed reflexes; psychomotor retardation; tremor; generalized muscle weakness; blurred vision or diplopia (or double vision); stupor or coma; and euphoria.

Problematic psychological changes are also evident, such as belligerence, assaultiveness, apathy, or impaired judgment. A medical condition or another mental disorder (including intoxication with another substance) do not better explain this symptom picture.

We now turn to the opioid-related disorders.

OPIOID-RELATED DISORDERS

In the nineteenth century, the opioids were prescribed for a variety of medical conditions. Dr. H. H. Kane's textbook written in 1880, *The Hypodermic Injection of Morphia, Its History, Advantages, and Dangers, Based on Experience of 360 Physicians*, listed 54 diseases believed to benefit from morphine injections. They were diverse—anemia, angina pectoris, diabetes, insanity, nymphomania (or an abnormally excessive and uncontrollable sexual desire in women), tetanus, and vomiting from pregnancy. Physicians often referred to opium (or morphine) as G.O.M., or God's Own Medicine (Earle, 1880). Another commonly accepted practice during this era was to substitute opiates for alcohol. Dr. J. R. Black (1947), in a paper entitled "Advantages of Substituting the Morphia Habit for the Incurably Alcoholic," noted that it had a calming effect and led to a more healthy life for a person than one of alcohol use.

Prevailing Pattern

The DSM-5 notes that the 12-month prevalence of opioid use is approximately 0.37 percent of those age 18 years and older (APA, 2013). However, this figure may be underestimated due to the number of individuals who are incarcerated and have opioid use disorders. Rates for males (0.49 percent) are higher than for females (0.26 percent). Interestingly, female adolescents are considered more likely to develop opioid use disorders.

Opioid intoxication, and overdose in particular, can be life threatening. An overdose can occur with shooting up (intravenous) or snorting (intranasal use), illicit use of opioid medications, an accidental misuse of prescription pain medications, or an unintentional overdose induced by a physician (Fareed et al., 2011). Opioid withdrawal has been reported in 60 percent of individuals in clinical settings who have used heroin at least once in the prior 12 months (APA, 2013).

Opioid Use Disorder

Currently, the opioids are widely used as strong pain relievers. Sometimes referred to as narcotics, they are a class of drugs that depress the central nervous system. The opioids have long been used to treat acute pain, like the kind experienced by individuals post-operatively. They have also been used in palliative care to alleviate the severe, chronic, and disabling pain of terminal conditions such as cancer. When prescribed by a physician, they are considered safe and are not considered to meet criteria for opioid use disorder—but unfortunately, they have a high potential for abuse. The opioids include the naturally occurring alkaloids such as morphine, the main active ingredient of opium, derivatives of these such as heroin, and synthetic compounds such as methadone. Prescription opiates include morphine, meperidine (Demerol), methadone, codeine, and various opioid drugs for coughing and pain. They come in a variety of forms including capsules, tablets, syrups, solutions, and suppositories.

Illicit opioids include heroin, whose street names include junk, smack, horse, boy, brown sugar, H, big H, skag, and dope. Heroin can be a white or brownish powder that is usually dissolved in water and then injected. Most street preparations of heroin are diluted (or "cut") with other substances such as sugar, starch, powdered milk, or quinine. Street heroin can also be cut with strychnine or other poisons. The term *opioid* is derived from opium, the narcotic resin extracted from the unripe seedpods of the opium poppy (*Papaver somniferum*). Opium appears as dark brown chunks or as a powder and is usually smoked or eaten.

Heroin, a highly addictive substance, is commonly described as a "downer" that affects the brain's pleasure systems and interferes with its ability to perceive pain. The 2012 National Survey on Drug Use and Health estimated that about 669,000 Americans reported using heroin in the past year, a number that has been on the rise since 2007 (SAMHSA, 2013). The number of people using heroin for the first time in 2012 is 156,000, which is nearly double the number of people reported in 2006. Heroin induces feelings of euphoria, a dreamy sense of drowsiness, and a general sense of well-being. Some have described the effects of injecting the drug as a "whole body orgasm," while others may experience unpleasant effects. It can also cause nausea, constipation, sweating, itchiness, and depressed breathing and heart rate. Sharing needles or syringes puts users at risk for infections such as hepatitis and HIV. High doses of the drug itself can cause death.

Heroin can be injected into a vein (called "mainlining") or into a muscle. Years ago, just the idea of using a needle kept many potential heroin users away from the drug; however, today it can be smoked through a water pipe or a standard pipe, mixed in a marijuana "joint" or cigarette, inhaled as smoke through a straw ("chasing the dragon"), or inhaled as powder through the nose. It is a fast-acting drug, especially when injected or smoked. Heroin users quickly develop tolerance and need more and more of the drug to achieve the same high.

The opiates tend to relax the user. The person may go "on the nod" or go back and forth from feeling alert to drowsy. Physical dangers associated with the opiates depend on the specific drug used, its source, the dose, and the way it is ingested. Most of the risks for the person who uses this drug are from using too much and becoming dependent upon it. Other hazards are related to using unsterile (or dirty) needles, contaminated drugs, or combining the drug with other substances. Infections from unsterile solutions, syringes, and needles can cause illnesses such as liver disease, tetanus, HIV, and hepatitis B and C. Chronic heroin injection can cause scarred and/or collapsed veins, bacterial infections of the blood vessels and heart valves, abscesses (boils) and other soft-tissue infections, as well as liver or kidney disease and congested lungs. These lung complications (including various types of pneumonia and tuberculosis) may be as much the result of the poor health of the user as from heroin's depressing effects on respiration. The most common adverse reactions include nausea and vomiting, drowsiness, dizziness, headache, orthostatic hypotension (decreased blood pressure) when standing that may result in fainting, itch, dry mouth, miosis (decreased pupil eye size), urinary retention, and constipation (Rossi, 2005). Chronic users may experience serious constipation that leads to bowel obstruction, fecal impaction, or paralytic ileus (loss of movement in the small intestine resulting in gas and fluid buildup).

Differential Assessment

Opioid use disorder follows the general guidelines for the substance use disorders. Keep in mind that tolerance makes it necessary for the person to use ever-increasing doses of opioids in order to achieve the same effects and can be detected within 12 to 24 hours of taking the drug (Rang, Dale, Ritter, Flower, & Henderson, 2012). Regular use of an opioid induces physical dependence, which becomes apparent with the symptoms of withdrawal when regular doses are abruptly discontinued or

Table 14.6 Symptoms of Opioid Withdrawal
Stopping or reducing heavy and prolonged opioid use lasting for several weeks (or longer) or administration of an opioid antagonist after a period of use
Three (or more) of the following that emerge within minutes to several days: severe dysphoria; nausea or vomiting; muscle aches or cramps; lacrimation or rhinorrea; dilated pupils, piloerection, or sweating; diarrhea; yawning; fever; or insomnia.

the dosage is rapidly reduced. Most people with the diagnosis of opioid use disorder will have significant levels of tolerance and will experience withdrawal symptoms—with onset in a matter of minutes or up to several days after the last dose. The administration of an opioid antagonist (or a substance that tends to nullify the action of another) can also prompt withdrawal symptoms.

The symptoms of withdrawal (Table 14.6), as with other substances, are opposite to those of the drug when initially taken and include three or more of the following: severe dysphoria; nausea or vomiting; muscle aches or cramps; lacrimation (or shedding more tears than normal) or rhinorrea (runny eyes or nose); dilated pupils, piloerection (goose bumps), or sweating (the combination of chills or cold flashes with goose bumps is referred to as "cold turkey"); diarrhea; yawning; fever; or insomnia. Currently, the diagnosis of opioid use requires two substance use criteria and does not imply that a withdrawal syndrome is imminent if the opioids are discontinued.

Opioid intoxication is addressed next.

Opioid Intoxication

Opioid intoxication is considered when the person has recently used an opioid. The key elements of intoxication are clinically significant maladaptive behavior or psychological changes (such as euphoria followed by apathy, dysphoria, agitation or psychomotor retardation, impaired judgment, or impaired social or occupational functioning) that develop during or shortly after opioid use. In addition, the person's pupils constrict (or dilate due to deficient oxygen from a severe overdose) and one or more of the following signs develop: drowsiness or coma, slurred speech, and impairment in attention or memory. Again, the diagnosis of opioid intoxication requires that symptoms cannot be better explained by a general medical condition or another mental disorder.

We now address opioid withdrawal.

Opioid Withdrawal

It is helpful for the practitioner to keep in mind that opioid withdrawal develops after stopping or reducing heavy and prolonged substance use. Symptoms (detailed in Table 14.6) can also be triggered by the administration of an opioid antagonist such as naloxone or naltrexone. It goes without saying that these symptoms can cause significant distress or impaired social or occupational functioning. They are not attributed to a medical condition or better explained by another mental disorder (including intoxication or withdrawal from another substance).

Following is a review of the sedative-, hypnotic-, or anxiolytic-related disorders.

SEDATIVE-, HYPNOTIC-, OR ANXIOLYTIC-RELATED DISORDERS

The sedative-, hypnotic-, or anxiolytic-related disorders are a group of depressants that include substances that have similar but subtle differences in their outcome—the sedatives (which are calming), the hypnotics (which are sleep-inducing), and the anxiolytics (which are anxiety reducing) (Hales, Yudofsky, & Gabbard, 2010). The benzodiazepines and barbiturates are also included in this subcategory. The benzodiazepines are considered to be a safer drug than the barbiturates, which carry greater risk for abuse and dependence. They all are Schedule IV drugs under the Federal Controlled Substances Act (meaning that they are drugs with a currently accepted medical use and must be prescribed by a physician, physician assistant, or nurse practitioner). These substances are used to reduce tension, irritability, agitation, and serious anxiety, or to prevent anxiety attacks.

PREVAILING PATTERN

The most recent prevalence rates available are defined by DSM-IV for sedative, hypnotic, or anxiolytic use disorder and shows a decrease with age; for example, use is greatest among those 18 to 29 years of age (0.5 percent) and lowest among individuals who are 65 years and older (0.4 percent) (APA, 2013). Rates are slightly higher for adult males than for adult females. However, looking to the younger population, defined as those who are 12 to 17 years of age, rates for females (0.4 percent) are higher than for males (0.2 percent).

The prevalence of sedative, hypnotic, or anxiolytic intoxication found in the general U.S. population is unclear. As well, the prevalence of sedative, hypnotic, or anxiolytic withdrawal is also unclear (APA, 2013).

SEDATIVE, HYPNOTIC, OR ANXIOLYTIC USE DISORDER

The first benzodiazepine, chlordiazepoxide (Librium), was discovered in 1954 by an Austrian scientist named Dr. Leo Sternbach for the pharmaceutical company Hoffman-Laroche. He stopped his work on the drug but "rediscovered" it when an assistant was cleaning up the laboratory (Sternbach, 1972). Sternbach's further research revealed that the drug was a very effective tranquilizer. In 1963, government approval for use was given to diazepam (Valium), a simplified version of Librium, to offset anxiety symptoms. In 1965, nitrazepam (Mogadon) was introduced to treat sleep-related problems, and in 1973, flurazepam (Dalmane) was released (O'Brien, 2005). These drugs are usually prescribed for short-term relief of severe and debilitating anxiety. Although they have proven helpful in the treatment of the anxiety disorders, they do have the potential for abuse and may cause dependence or addiction when not used as medically prescribed. The benzodiazepines were at one time known as minor tranquilizers or antianxiety drugs. Physical dependence develops when these medications are used at high doses and/or for prolonged periods of time. Common withdrawal symptoms for the benzodiazepines include anxiety, insomnia, restlessness, agitation, muscle tension, and irritability. Seizures and depression may sometimes occur. People can experience unpleasant withdrawal symptoms if they abruptly stop taking these medications.

The barbiturates (Amytal, Seconal, Nembutal) were first prescribed to help people sleep and replaced alcohol and opium. They were commonly used in the 1930s and 1940s, before their addictive properties were known—and by the 1950s they had become the most abused drug in the United States. At low doses, the barbiturates relax muscles and produce a mild feeling of well-being. Larger doses can produce effects that resemble those of heavy drinking; in particular, slurred speech, problems with walking, and inability to concentrate. Extremely high doses can relax the diaphragm muscles to the point of causing death by suffocation. Barbiturate use has declined since the introduction of the benzodiazepines in the early 1960s.

The anxiolytics are generally divided into two groups: the benzodiazepines and non-benzodiazepines. This category also includes herbs, such as St. John's Wort and Kava (Kava Kava); however, there is limited evidence available for their efficacy. In Europe, the root of the valerian is a popular anxiolytic. The group of anxiolytics known as the non-benzodiazepines lack the sedation and potential for dependence associated with the benzodiazepines. Buspirone (Buspar) is a new non-benzodiazepine anxiolytic agent and described as a serotonin 1A agonist but is not included in this class of substances as it does not appear to be associated with significant misuse. Barbiturates and the sedative drug meprobamate (Miltown, Equanil, Meprin) have an anxiolytic effect but the risk of abuse and addiction is high. However, they can be valuable for the short-term treatment of insomnia.

The most common antianxiety medications (followed by their brand name) include:

- Alprazolam (Xanax)
- Chlordiazepoxide (Librium)
- Clonazepam (Klonapin, Rivotril)
- Diazepam (Valium)
- Lorazepam (Ativan)
- Oxazepam (Serax)

Commonly prescribed medications with a hypnotic or sedative effect are:

- Flurazepam (Dalmane)
- Triazolam (Halcion)

The drug midazolam (Versed, Hypnovel) is mostly used as an intravenous injection for sedation before surgery or for emergency procedures such as intubation (a procedure for inserting a tube into the mouth or nose and then advanced into the airway when a person is not breathing).

Differential Assessment

Diagnostic criteria for sedative, hypnotic, or anxiolytic use disorder follow the same general guidelines for the substance use disorders. Use of this group of drugs may

TABLE 14.7 SYMPTOMS OF SEDATIVE, HYPNOTIC, AND ANXIOLYTIC WITHDRAWAL
Stopping or reducing prolonged sedative, hypnotic, or anxiolytic use
Two or more of the following that develop within several hours to a few days: autonomic hyperactivity (such as sweating or a pulse rate greater than 100); increased hand tremor; insomnia; nausea that is sometimes accompanied by vomiting; transient visual, tactile, or auditory hallucinations or illusions; psychomotor agitation; anxiety (or panic attacks); or grand mal seizures

occur in conjunction with the use of other substances (e.g., a person might use intoxicating doses of a benzodiazepine to come down from a cocaine high).

The benzodiazepines are commonly divided into three groups: (1) short-acting compounds (for 6 hours or less), (2) intermediate compounds (lasting for 6 to 10 hours), and (3) long-acting compounds (with sedative effects that persist). However, with most of the benzodiazepines, noticeable effects usually wear off within a few hours. With frequent use, tolerance develops for many of the therapeutic effects of the benzodiazepines. Unlike tolerance to other drugs such as the opioids or stimulants, tolerance to the benzodiazepines can create an iatrogenic syndrome (or a spectrum of side effects that can be worse than the original condition). For that reason, the benzodiazepines are generally prescribed for a limited period of time (e.g., 2 to 4 weeks). Typically, tolerance to the hypnotic effects happens within days, and the anxiolytic effects usually do not last beyond a few months. Tolerance can cause a range of symptoms related to nervous system dysfunction, and they are the same as withdrawal symptoms. If a person abruptly stops taking the benzodiazepines, severe and unpleasant symptoms may occur such as convulsions, confusion, psychosis, and effects similar to delirium tremens. Therefore, it is recommended that the person who has been taking a benzodiazepine for a long period of time be weaned off the drug over a period of months.

Withdrawal symptoms for the sedative, hypnotic, and anxiolytic drugs (summarized on Table 14.7) appear when dosage is either reduced or the person stops taking the drug entirely. Within several hours to a few days after stopping (or reducing) the drugs, two (or more) of the following symptoms emerge: autonomic hyperactivity (such as sweating or a pulse rate greater than 100); increased hand tremor; insomnia; nausea that is sometimes accompanied by vomiting; transient visual, tactile, or auditory hallucinations or illusions; psychomotor agitation; anxiety (or panic attacks); or grand mal seizures. These symptoms are the opposite of the acute effects seen in the first-time user, who generally feels drowsy and uncoordinated. The specifier with perceptual disturbances may be noted when hallucinations occur.

We now turn to a review of sedative, hypnotic, or anxiolytic intoxication.

SEDATIVE, HYPNOTIC, OR ANXIOLYTIC INTOXICATION

The DSM-5 criteria for diagnosis of intoxication do not differ substantially from those for other substance use disorders, particularly alcohol intoxication (APA, 2013).

Recurrent use of sedatives, hypnotics, and anxiolytics increases their toxic effects and can involve maladaptive behavioral changes (e.g., sexual or aggressive behavior), mood changes, or impaired judgment. One (or more) of the following symptoms can be seen during or shortly after use: slurred speech, incoordination, unsteady gait, nystagmus, impairment in attention or memory, and stupor or coma. Additionally, these symptoms are not better explained by a general medical condition or another mental disorder including intoxication with another substance.

A review of the differential assessment for sedative, hypnotic, or anxiolytic withdrawal follows next.

SEDATIVE, HYPNOTIC, OR ANXIOLYTIC WITHDRAWAL

The criteria for withdrawal (Table 14.7) can cause difficulties in the person's social and work functioning. Additionally, symptoms are not better accounted for by another medical condition or another medical condition (including intoxication and withdrawal from another substance). The duration of the withdrawal syndrome is usually related to the half-life of the substance. The practitioner may specify perceptual disturbances when hallucinations are present (in the absence of delirium). Additional long-term but less intense symptoms may endure for several months (e.g., moodiness, anxiety, or problems sleeping) and could be incorrectly diagnosed as an anxiety or mood disorder.

We now turn to the stimulant-related disorders.

STIMULANT-RELATED DISORDERS

The stimulant-related disorders capture a range of problems associated with the use of a wide variety of stimulant drugs that include the amphetamines (and methamphetamines) and cocaine. The amphetamines, otherwise known as speed or pep pills, are CNS stimulants that are usually synthetically made in illegal labs. Amphetamine was first synthesized in 1887 by the Romanian chemist Lazar Edeleneau at the University of Berlin. He called this new drug phenylisopropylamine. The experimental use of amphetamines in the United States began in the 1920s and was introduced in the form of the pharmaceutical called Benzedrine. At that time, the drug was used by the military, especially the Air Force, to fight fatigue and increase alertness. Pilots used amphetamines (Dexadrine) as stimulants, calling them go-pills. After completing a mission, the pilots were given a no-go-pill (Ambien or Temazepam) to help them sleep (Caldwell, Caldwell, & Darlington, 2003). Despite what we now know of the dangers of amphetamines, 65 percent of U.S. pilots in combat during the Desert Storm campaign of 1991 admitted to having used an amphetamine compound at least once (Emonson & Vanderbeek, 1995). Although military officials suspended the program in 1992, it was later reinstated with more strict medical regulations (Bonne, 2003).

In the mid-1950s, the amphetamines were limited to prescription use, but illegal use was common. The drug became popular among truck drivers, construction workers, and factory workers whose jobs required long or irregular shift work or automatic repetitive tasks. Although it was popularized as a "redneck drug," college students who kept long hours studying also used the amphetamines in order to keep up their grades. President John F. Kennedy was rumored to have used methamphetamine during his term in office in the early 1960s (Owen, 2008). White-collar workers who tried to stay alert during long and busy days also used it. The amphetamines are a class of synthetic drugs also used (and still used) as appetite suppressors.

Amphetamines may come in the form of tablets and capsules. A recent appearance is Yaba, which in Thai means "crazy medicine." The tablets are sometimes flavored to taste like candy (grape, orange, or vanilla) and marketed to a young audience. The tablets may also be reddish-orange or green and shaped so that they fit inside the end of a drinking straw. The straws are marked with a variety of logos—WY is the most common. These drugs can also appear as powders, off-white crystals, or chunks that look like ice. The smokable methamphetamine looks like shaved glass slivers or clear rock salt that can be swallowed (bomb), sniffed or snorted (ingested through the nose), or injected. A relatively rare method of ingestion involves rubbing the drug into the gums—this is known as dabbing.

When methamphetamine is either smoked or injected, the individual experiences an intense sense of euphoria, a "rush" or a "flash" that lasts only a few minutes. The effects of smokable methamphetamine are comparable to crack cocaine in intensity—the high is reported to be too intense for the casual drug user. A practitioner known to the author shared a comment from a former client who said, "It was just like getting hit with a sledgehammer." Snorting produces effects within 3 to 5 minutes, but the high is not an intense rush. Oral ingestion produces effects within 15 to 20 minutes. The experience is variously described as speeding, tweaking (or tweaked), spinning (or spun), or up.

The amphetamines are available through a prescription by a medical doctor or from illegal sources that manufacture look-alike drugs synthetically in secret laboratories. Recipes are readily available on the Internet for anyone who wants to look, although some of the chemicals may be difficult to obtain. Crystal meth can easily be produced in small clandestine labs (even in a kitchen or bathroom) by mixing a cocktail of about 15 substances, including ammonia, paint thinner, ether, Drano, and the lithium from batteries. "Christmas tree meth" describes green methamphetamine produced using Drano crystal. "Bathtub crank" is the street term for a poor-quality methamphetamine that is literally produced in bathtubs. A "crankster" is someone who is known to manufacture (or use) methamphetamine, and "cooking" refers to the manufacturing process. This level of availability increases the risk of abuse and dependence for people of all ages.

We now shift to a review of cocaine. In the late nineteenth century, a gentleman by the name of John Stith Pemberton developed a product in response to a decision by the city of Atlanta, Georgia, to prohibit the use of alcohol. He thought his product would be seen as the "temperance drink" (Martensen, 1996, p. 1615). The product contained 60 milligrams of cocaine per 8-ounce serving and later became known around the world as Coca-Cola. During this era, it was not uncommon to use drugs that were potentially addictive, and its use did later become regulated by the Pure Food and Drug Act of 1906. Cocaine once again became fashionable in the 1970s and 1980s as a popular recreational drug and currently remains a significant part of the drug-abuse scene in the United States (Paczynski & Gold, 2011).

Results from the National Survey on Drug Use and Health (NSDUH) report that in 2008, there were an estimated 1.9 million current (past-month) cocaine users, and of those, approximately 359,000 were current crack users (National Institute on Drug Abuse, 2010).

How cocaine is produced has changed little. Cocaine comes from the leaves of the coca plant (Erythroxylon coca), a native of the eastern slopes of the Andes. The climate is well suited for the plant to grow. It is one of the most powerfully addictive drugs. Cocaine comes in two main forms. One is cocaine hydrochloride, a white crystalline powder that can be snorted into the nostrils or dissolved in water and injected. Snorting cocaine may cause erosion of the membranes inside the nose. Street names for cocaine in the powder form are coke, snow, candy, flake, blow, big C, lady, white, and snowbirds. The other form is crack cocaine hydrochloride that has been processed with ammonia or baking soda and water into a freebase cocaine, which makes it smokable. The drug's appearance is in chips, chunks, or rocks. Smoking allows the cocaine to reach the brain very quickly and results in a rapid high. Heavy use of cocaine can produce hallucinations, paranoia, aggression, insomnia, and depression.

PREVAILING PATTERN

Looking to the amphetamine-type stimulants, the estimated 12-month prevalence for use in the United States is 0.2 percent among those 12 to 17 years of age and 0.2 percent among individuals 18 years and older. Rates are similar for males and females; but among those who are younger, specifically persons 12 to 17 years of age, the rate for females (0.3 percent) is greater than for males (0.1 percent). Looking to intravenous use, the ratio of male-to-female use is 3:1 or 4:1 (APA, 2013).

Prevalence rates for cocaine use indicate that the 12-month prevalence in the United States is estimated to be about 0.2 percent among individuals age 12 to 17 years and 0.3 percent for persons age 18 years and older (APA, 2013). Rates are higher for males (0.4 percent) than for females (0.1 percent). The highest prevalence rates occur for persons 18 to 29 years of age (0.6 percent) and lowest among those age 45 to 64 years (0.1 percent).

We turn to an examination of stimulant use disorder.

STIMULANT USE DISORDER

In the United States, the amphetamines are Schedule II controlled drugs, which means that they have a currently accepted medical use that is severely restricted, but also have a high potential for abuse. The amphetamines (and methamphetamines) are stimulants that cause a release of the neurotransmitters dopamine and noradrenaline (norepinephrine) from storage vesicles in the CNS. Following is a list of just some of the amphetamines and amphetamine derivatives along with their street names:

- Amphetamine (uppers, bennies, pep pills, black beauties, white bennies)
- Methamphetamine (speed, meth, chalk)
- Methamphetamine combined with marijuana and heroin (brown)

- Methamphetamine used with Viagra (Tina)
- Smokable methamphetamine (batu, crystal, crank, glass, ice)
- Dextroamphetamine (dexies, beans)

Cocaine is a very powerful stimulator of the central nervous system. A typical dose, about 50 to 100 milligrams, rapidly induces feelings of self-confidence, exhilaration, and energy that can last for about 15 to 45 minutes before giving way to fatigue and melancholy. Crack cocaine condenses these effects into a shorter and more intense high. The drug also increases heart rate and blood pressure, sometimes causing death. Very high doses can potentially lead to cardiac arrest and respiratory failure. The principal effect of cocaine is to block the re-uptake of dopamine, serotonin, and noradrenalin into neurons leading to higher than normal levels of these neurotransmitters in the brain.

In small amounts, cocaine boosts a person's sense of self-esteem and optimism, increases mental and physical abilities, and conveys feelings of power. Extended use leads to a number of negative symptoms such as anxiety, depression, suicidal ideation, weight loss, aggressiveness, sexual dysfunction, sleeping problems, and paranoid delusions and hallucinations (Barlow & Durand, 2012). It is estimated that two-thirds or more of those individuals who are chronic cocaine abusers will develop a drug-induced psychosis that looks very much like paranoid schizophrenia, sometimes called coke paranoia (Kalayasiri et al., 2006).

Differential Assessment

Stimulant use affects all racial, ethnic, socioeconomic, age, and gender groups. Making the diagnosis seems related to societal factors, such as being arrested, suspended from school, or laid off from the job. It is not uncommon for the practitioner to find that the person who uses stimulants to also have a number of legal problems. They may also be involved in illegal activities (e.g., stealing in order to obtain the drug). The diagnosis of stimulant use disorder follows the substance use disorder general guidelines and is given to someone who has a pattern of problematic use of amphetamine, cocaine, or other stimulants (except caffeine or nicotine). However, when the individual is taking stimulant medication under medical supervision (such as medications prescribed for attention-deficit/hyperactivity disorder), the criteria for tolerance do not apply.

Tolerance to stimulants develops rapidly. As the person's body adapts to the drug, he or she needs larger doses to achieve the same effects. This means that the person uses more and more of the drug to achieve a high. After chronic use, even at low doses, a person can develop tolerance. The user feels a sense of well-being and increased energy. The effects of the amphetamines are similar to the effects of cocaine but last longer, so amphetamines are usually taken fewer times per day. As is true with cocaine use, a person may use amphetamines on a chronic or episodic basis with binges (speed runs) combined with brief periods of time where he or she may be entirely drug free.

Withdrawal symptoms (summarized on Table 14.8) are considered when the person stops or reduces use that has been heavy and prolonged. The symptom picture can be both psychological and physiological; that is, the individual has a dysphoric mood and shows two (or more) of the following within a few hours to several days: fatigue; vivid, unpleasant dreams; insomnia or hypersomnia (when

TABLE 14.8	SYMPTOMS OF STIMULANT USE WITHDRAWAL
Stopping or reducing prolonged amphetamine-type substance, cocaine, or other stimulants	
Evidence of a dysphoric mood and two (or more) of the following: fatigue; vivid, unpleasant dreams; insomnia or hypersomnia; increased appetite; and psychomotor retardation or agitation	

one sleeps for an excessively long time); increased appetite; and psychomotor retardation or agitation (APA, 2013). The person may develop craving in an effort to avoid the "down" feeling when he or she is no longer taking drugs. Restlessness, anxiety, depression, insomnia, and suicidal behavior may be seen.

We now review stimulant intoxication.

STIMULANT INTOXICATION

Intoxication is characterized by the presence of significant maladaptive changes that develop during, or shortly after, the use of amphetamine or a related substance. Intoxication usually begins with a "high" feeling followed by problematic psychological behaviors such as euphoria with enhanced energy or affective blunting, changes in sociability such as becoming extremely gregarious, hypervigilance, sensitivity to others, anxiety, tension, anger, stereotypical and repetitive behaviors, and impaired judgment. The person exhibits two (or more) of the following:

- Tachycardia (fast heart beat) or bradycardia (slow heart rate)
- Dilated pupils
- Elevated or lowered blood pressure
- Perspiration or chills
- Nausea or vomiting
- Evidence of weight loss
- Psychomotor agitation or retardation
- Muscular weakness, respiratory depression, chest pain, or cardiac arrhythmias (abnormal heart rhythm)
- Confusion, seizures, dyskinesias (impaired ability to control movement), dystonias (muscle spasms), or coma

These symptoms are not better explained by another medical condition and are not better explained by another mental disorder (including intoxication with another substance). When making the diagnosis, the practitioner specifies the specific intoxicant and considers the specifier of perceptual disturbances.

A review of stimulant withdrawal follows.

STIMULANT WITHDRAWAL

Withdrawal symptoms (summarized on Table 14.8) occur when a person abruptly stops taking amphetamines, cocaine, or other stimulants. These symptoms are generally the opposite of those seen during intoxication (e.g., the person may develop a dysphoric mood—an exaggerated feeling of depression—instead of the euphoria of intoxication). Withdrawal can be an unpleasant experience causing the person distress. He or she may experience problems in social relationships, on the job, or in other important areas of life. The symptoms are not related to a general medical condition and not better explained by another mental disorder.

The severity of these withdrawal symptoms depends on the degree of use. Crashing (marked withdrawal symptoms) often follows an episode of intense high doses (speed runs). However, there is considerable variation in people's sensitivity to the effects of the stimulants (Doweiko, 2014). Anhedonia (or the inability to experience pleasure) and drug craving may also be present as an associated feature. Bradycardia is often present and regarded as a reliable measure of stimulant withdrawal.

Associated features can include the short-term effects of a decreased appetite; increased stamina and energy; increased sexual drive/response; involuntary bodily movements; nystagmus; increased perspiration; hyperactivity; jitteriness; nausea; itchy, blotchy, or greasy skin; increased heart rate; irregular heart rate; increased blood pressure; sleep disturbance; and headaches. The short-term psychological effects may consist of alertness; a sense of euphoria; increased concentration; rapid talking; increased confidence; release of social inhibitions; feelings of cleverness, competence, and power; increased social responsiveness; and hallucinations.

A number of physical complications are associated with long-term use of amphetamines and may include tremor, restlessness, insomnia, drying of the skin and increased itchiness, and/or obsessively picking at the skin (sometimes until it bleeds); hyperreflexia (overactive reflexes such as tremors); tachypnea (rapid breathing); gastrointestinal narrowing; weight loss; and a weakened immune system. Regular amphetamine use can lead to gingivitis (inflammation of the gums), and long-term use can result in dental caries (tooth rot) (Hasan & Ciancio, 2004; Shaner, 2002). Erectile dysfunction, heart problems, stroke, and liver, kidney, and lung damage can result from prolonged use. When the drug is snorted, the person may experience a deterioration of the lining of the nostrils. The long-term psychological effects can include a mental state similar to schizophrenia, irritability, confusion, panic, and violent and aggressive behavior. More than any other drug, the amphetamines are associated with violence and antisocial behavior.

Subsequent discussion provides a review of the tobacco-related disorders.

TOBACCO-RELATED DISORDERS

Early Europeans, most notably Christopher Columbus, visiting the New World saw Native Americans smoking cigars and chewing tobacco. When the Spanish introduced tobacco to Europe in the early 1500s, it was thought to be of medicinal value and was used to treat diseases of the ear, eyes, nose, and mouth. Apparently, the treatment involved blowing smoke into all openings of the head.

Nicotine is a poisonous oily liquid that comes from the nightshade family (*Solanaceae*) of plants called *Nicotiana tabacum*. (This tobacco plant was named in honor of a French ambassador, Jean Nicot, who promoted it for its medicinal value (Rang et al., 2012). Interestingly, small amounts of nicotine are found in foods of other plants in the nightshade family (e.g., tomatoes and eggplants). Nicotine is introduced into the body in various ways: via the smoke of cigarettes, cigars, and pipe tobacco; through smokeless tobacco (for chewing); and snuff (finely ground tobacco that is "snuffed" into the nose or "dipped" and held in the cheek or lower lip). Manufacturers are increasingly prepackaging moist snuff into small paper or cloth packets to make the product more convenient. Cigarette smoking is the most popular form of nicotine ingestion—and nicotine is the substance in tobacco that causes dependence.

Social and cultural influences also contribute to who uses nicotine. The country singer Gretchen Wilson has helped to popularize smokeless tobacco through her 2005 record album *All Jacked Up*, which has a song entitled "Skoal Ring." (There is a smokeless tobacco product marketed under the brand name Skoal, and it is packaged in a round tin.) A self-declared "redneck woman," Wilson's song glamorizes the attributes of a man whose habit of carrying a can of chewing tobacco in the back pocket of his jeans produces a Skoal ring. Teens are generally resistant to antismoking messages (U.S. Department of Health and Human Services, 2012). Use of smokeless tobacco products also gets a boost from the fact that many professional baseball players chew tobacco or dip snuff—and, through the worshipful eyes of little boys just learning to love the sport, all of that "chewin' and spittin'" becomes just another one of the rituals, along with tugging on the bill of a cap or adjusting the fit of a glove.

Anyone who has ever smoked knows how hard it is to quit. Only about 4 to 7 percent of people are able to quit smoking on any given attempt without medicines or other help (American Cancer Society, 2014; Tobacco Use and Dependence Guideline Panel, 2008). Needless to add, quitting smoking requires several attempts. Mark Twain was reported to have said, "To cease smoking is the easiest thing I ever did. I ought to know, because I've done it a thousand times." About 90 percent of smokers are persistent daily users and 55 percent become dependent. A small percentage (perhaps 5 to 10 percent) are not dependent. Those who are episodic nicotine users are known as "chippers" (Doweiko, 2014).

The nicotine in tobacco smoke rides on small particles of tar. American cigarettes contain about 9 milligrams of nicotine, but much of the nicotine is burned off. As a result, a smoker gets about 1 milligram of nicotine in every cigarette. The cigarette smoke with the nicotine/tar mixture is immediately absorbed by the lungs, and within 7 seconds it reaches the smoker's brain (Gray, 2006). About 90 percent of inhaled nicotine is actually absorbed—making the cigarette a very efficient drug-delivery system. Neuro-chemical changes occur in the brain after just a few cigarettes, which suggests that a limited exposure to nicotine can initiate dependence (Mansvelder, Keath, & McGehee, 2002). Nicotine mimics the effect of acetylcholine (the neurotransmitter in the brain that appears to be involved in learning and memory), causing the release of acetylcholine and norepinephrine. The user experiences a sense of release from stress and even may experience feelings of euphoria. Additional physical effects may include increases in blood pressure and heart rate; faster respiration; constriction of arteries producing cool, pale skin; and stimulation of the central nervous system. At high doses, nicotine produces convulsions and death.

The most recent contribution to cigarette smoking is the electronic cigarette (or e-cigarette). According to the United States Patent Office, Herbert A. Gilbert obtained a patent for the device in 1963 (U.S. Patent 3200819 A, 2014). Also known as the personal vaporizer or electronic nicotine delivery system (ENDS), the electronic cigarette is essentially a battery-powered vaporizer which has a similar experience of tobacco smoking. Electronic cigarettes do not contain tobacco but do use nicotine obtained from tobacco plants (O'Connor, 2012). Most people who use the electronic cigarette have a history of smoking, but a number of young people who have never smoked cigarettes have tried the electronic cigarette at least once (Chapman & Wu, 2014). Use of these devices has increased dramatically. Sales have climbed from 50,000 in 2008 to 3.5 million in 2012 (Koch, 2012). At this point, the benefits and risks of these e-cigarettes are unknown (Harrell, Simmons, Correal, Padhya, & Brandon, 2014).

Prevailing Pattern

Cigarettes are the most commonly used tobacco product in the United States, representing over 90 percent of tobacco/nicotine use distinguished from those who use smokeless tobacco (5 percent) or pipes and cigars (less than 1 percent). Using data available from the DSM-IV criteria, the 12-month prevalence of nicotine dependence in the United States is 13 percent of adults age 18 years and older. However, since dependence criteria are a subset of tobacco use disorder, we can anticipate the actual figures of use to be greater. Rates do not differ significantly between males (14 percent) and females (12 percent). Looking to cultural differences, nicotine dependence is greater among Native American and Alaskan Natives (23 percent) than among whites (14 percent) but less so among African Americans (10 percent), Asian Americans and Pacific Islanders (6 percent), and Hispanics (6 percent) (APA, 2013).

Tobacco use is more prevalent in people with other mental disorders than in the general population. Based on a national survey in the United States, Strat, Ramoz, and Gorwood (2010) found that tobacco use was seen in almost half (or 48 percent) of adults diagnosed with alcohol use disorder. Another study by Meyer, Rumpf, and Hapke (2004) observed increased rates of mental disorders among smokers, especially those diagnosed with depressive or anxiety disorders. Smoking is also commonly seen among those with the diagnosis of schizophrenia (Leonard, Mexal, & Freedman, 2007). More than 80 percent of those diagnosed with schizophrenia smoke compared to 25 percent of the general population—meaning that people with this mental illness are twice as likely to smoke. The reasons for this are unclear, but practitioners often comment that smoking gives their clients something to do and provides a framework for organizing the day.

A review of tobacco use disorder follows.

Tobacco Use Disorder

Chronic use of tobacco leads to changes in the brain and therefore in behavior. One of the first changes is tolerance, or a decrease in the effects of nicotine. Tolerance occurs rapidly in response to some of the early unpleasant effects such as dizziness, nausea, and vomiting. Most who have smoked will remember that first cigarette as an unpleasant experience. As these effects subside and the pleasurable effects of nicotine surface, the person usually continues with his or her further use of the drug. With the development of physical dependence, further nicotine use is necessary to avoid a physiological disturbance (i.e., withdrawal). The person wants to or has tried to cut down; spends a great deal of time using tobacco (e.g., the person chain smokes); reduces important social or occupational activities because of tobacco use; and continues to use despite recurrent physical or psychological problems (e.g., continuing to smoke despite a diagnosis of high blood pressure). In addition, the person's tobacco use may create negative interactions among friends or family members.

Withdrawal is considered when the person abruptly stops using tobacco, and within 24 hours, they show four or more of the following symptoms: irritability, frustration, or anger; anxiety; difficulty concentrating; increased appetite (or weight gain); restlessness; a depressed mood; and insomnia (summarized on Table 14.9) (APA, 2013).

Since it provides an almost immediate "kick" from the neurochemical changes in the brain, nicotine is seen as highly addictive (National Institute on Drug Abuse, 2005). Nicotine is not stored in the body, so its effects last only a few minutes. It is metabolized in the body fairly quickly and disappears within a few hours—therefore, some tolerance is lost overnight when the person is sleeping. Those who smoke often comment that the first cigarette of the day is the strongest and the most satisfying. As the day continues and acute tolerance develops, the cigarettes have less of an effect. The person needs to absorb more and more nicotine to be able to experience effects.

For some people, handling the cigarette, the smell of it, and the ritual of lighting and actually smoking it are all part of the pleasant sensation. This can make withdrawal or craving worse. These rituals offer a sense of security and can contribute to a person's tendency to smoke when he or she is anxious or nervous (Doweiko, 2014). Many smokers come to associate having a cigarette with other pleasant activities such as having a cup of coffee or an alcoholic drink, or enjoying a good meal. Smoking can even be tied to having a good time with friends. For many, smoking requires taking a break from daily responsibilities. A colleague of the author would routinely take a break from meetings in order to smoke a cigarette. She returned feeling "refreshed." In other words, people may also learn to connect smoking with the temporary relief of tension, boredom, or fatigue. This is a habit that is easily reinforced. For instance, let's say smokers take an average of 10 puffs on each cigarette. If they smoke one pack a day, this amounts to 200 puffs

TABLE 14.9 SYMPTOMS OF TOBACCO WITHDRAWAL
Daily use of tobacco for at least several weeks
After stopping using (or reducing) tobacco, within 24 hours, the person shows four (or more) of the following: irritability, frustration, or anger; anxiety; difficulty concentrating; increased appetite (or weight gain); restlessness; a depressed mood; and insomnia

(or "kicks") of nicotine a day—more than 72,000 puffs a year for that pack-a-day habit.

Some of the associated features of tobacco use that the practitioner might look for are a tobacco odor, cough, very wrinkled skin, and/or the medical diagnosis of chronic obstructive pulmonary disease, shortness of breath, lung and other cancers, cardiac disease, or perinatal problems. In addition, the availability of cigarettes, the small number of legal and social consequences of tobacco use, and the sophisticated marketing and advertising methods used by tobacco companies play a role in continued tobacco use.

The Fagerstrom Test for Nicotine Dependence (FTND) is a helpful tool for practitioners to evaluate the extent of tobacco use (Heatherton, Kozlowski, Frecker, & Fagerstrom, 1991). Two of the six questions on the test account for most of the person's score and help to determine total tobacco intake and craving. Those two questions are:

How many cigarettes per day do you smoke?

How soon after you wake up do you smoke your first cigarette?

If the person reports smoking more than 30 cigarettes a day and the time after getting up before smoking the first cigarette is less than five minutes, the practitioner will more than likely come across additional symptoms supporting the severity of tobacco use. The mother of a very close friend of the author had the habit of smoking her first cigarette of the day as soon as she stepped into the shower.

We now turn to tobacco withdrawal.

TOBACCO WITHDRAWAL

Withdrawal symptoms result when a person tries to stop using nicotine. Symptoms usually begin within 2 hours of the last use of tobacco, peak within 24 hours, and then begin to decline over the next 10 days to several weeks (Sadock, Sadock, & Ruiz, 2014). For some, the discomfort associated with withdrawal and cravings continue for 6 months or longer. Withdrawal symptoms (Table 14.9) can be unpleasant for the chronic user and make it difficult to stop using tobacco. They seem to be more intense for those who smoke cigarettes or use smokeless tobacco (APA, 2013).

Although each person's experience will be different, other symptoms might include fatigue, feeling light-headed, a tingling sensation in the limbs, constipation, and increased coughing (Schmitz, Jarvik, & Schneider, 2004). Withdrawal symptoms vary and typically produce clinically significant mood changes and functional impairment.

Discussion of other (or unknown) substance-related disorders ensues.

OTHER (OR UNKNOWN) SUBSTANCE-RELATED DISORDERS

To put the finishing touches on the practitioner's understanding of the substance-related disorders, the category of other (or unknown) substance-related disorders is reviewed. Overall, this diagnostic class is reserved for those who use an intoxicating substance but do not have enough symptoms to be diagnosed within the specific diagnostic groupings of alcohol, caffeine, cannabis, hallucinogen (including phencyclidine and others), inhalant, opioid, sedative, hypnotic or anxiolytic, stimulant, or tobacco.

OTHER (OR UNKNOWN) SUBSTANCE USE DISORDER

In practice, the social worker may encounter clients who are clearly intoxicated and it is not possible to identify the substance taken. There may be other instances where a substance is so new that it has not yet been identified. Then again, it may be an "old" familiar drug but marketed under a different name. Depending on the symptom picture, the practitioner considers the diagnoses of other (or unknown) substance-related disorders use. Unfortunately, the person continues using the substance despite serious consequences.

OTHER (OR UNKNOWN) SUBSTANCE INTOXICATION

Other (or unknown) substance intoxication is considered when the practitioner encounters someone who experiences intoxication from a substance that has not been addressed in this chapter. This is a challenging diagnosis because if the drug is unknown, then its effects are unknown. The practitioner is encouraged to ask if the person has had similar experiences. In most situations, the practitioner relies on his or her clinical judgment and experience when considering this diagnosis.

OTHER (OR UNKNOWN) SUBSTANCE WITHDRAWAL

The symptom picture for other (or unknown) substance withdrawal develops during (or within a few hours to days after) the time when a person cuts down on or stops taking a substance. While it is clear that the individual has taken a substance, the challenge is to identify the specific symptoms of the withdrawal process causing significant distress or impairment when the specific drug is unknown.

UNSPECIFIED OTHER (OR UNKNOWN) SUBSTANCE-RELATED DISORDER

The practitioner considers this diagnosis when the individual shows symptoms causing significant distress or impairment but does not meet full criteria for any of the substance-related disorders. This diagnosis also applies when the person does not meet full criteria for any of the other (or unknown) substance-related disorders (i.e., other or unknown substance use, intoxication, or withdrawal).

CONCLUDING CASE REVIEW

It is not unusual for the social worker to encounter clients with a history of using multiple substances, and so we conclude the review of the substance-related and addictive disorders with the case of Janet Sellar. As she struggles to cope with her diagnosis of HIV, the multiplicative effects of her experimental use of sedatives, recreational drugs, and alcohol are highlighted. Unfortunately it is not uncommon for the practitioner to encounter clients who use recreational drugs, like ecstasy, to also have a history of using other substances like alcohol and tranquilizers as well as a co-occurring mental disorder (Wu et al., 2009). As Janet's story unfolds, we begin to see the symptom picture for an episode of major depression.

CASE The Case of Janet Sellar

On the surface, Janet Sellar's life appears to be ideal. At age 42, she is the office manager for a busy medical practice where she is held in high esteem among the entire staff, especially by the doctors and nurses. She has this uncanny ability to work with just about everyone. Her husband, Jerry, is a very successful accountant who frequently keeps long hours in the office, particularly around tax time, when weeks can pass without the couple seeing each other at all. Their combined incomes make it possible for them to live in a gated community in west Kendall, a comfortable and affluent suburb south of Miami. The couple has three sons, Scott (9), Chris (12), and Mike (15). Janet had always wanted a girl, but was afraid to take a chance with another pregnancy after Scott was born. So she and Jerry adopted a Korean girl, Stephanie, who is the light of their lives. At age 5, Steph (as she is called), is an exotically beautiful and precocious child who is extremely popular in her kindergarten class.

Behind this picture-book façade, however, all is not as it seems. This successful middle-class family has a serious problem known only to Janet and a small number of her closest friends. The Sellars' difficulties develop gradually at first, but 1 day their lives will change dramatically and forever. Things had started to fall apart when Janet was diagnosed as being HIV-positive. When their oldest son, Mike, was born, she had developed some medical problems that required several blood transfusions—one of which, it turned out, was tainted. At this point in time, her CD4 counts are such that she does not have AIDS, but naturally she worries about the day when her disease progresses to the next stage. She does receive routine medical care to monitor her status, but not from any of the physicians she works for. Janet decided she wanted to, as she says, "keep the personal from the professional." Her current medications include protease inhibitors and anti-retrovirals for the HIV.

All seemed to be progressing until a recent incident. Janet had a setback with her HIV diagnosis and was afraid that she had developed full-blown AIDS. She had always coped with her HIV diagnosis but the thought of having AIDS prompted a change. For the first time, she began to feel depressed and described symptoms of major depression on one of her regular visits to her doctor. "I feel like I've lost all my energy—and it's getting harder and harder to get up and go to work.... I've always loved my job but I just don't enjoy it anymore." Janet continued, "I feel worthless and tainted—what if I end up with AIDS?" The doctor asked if she was having any other problems, and Janet admitted that she had also started having problems falling asleep, and her appetite was spiraling out of control. She had started to gain weight. She tried to explain that she enjoys her home and is extremely proud of her children, but "lately nothing seems to give me pleasure anymore." When Janet revealed that she was plagued with thoughts of suicide, her physician immediately referred her to a psychiatrist who prescribed the antidepressant Zoloft and Ambien, a sedative for sleep.

Janet begged her physician to prescribe some kind of diet pills for her, but he was reluctant to do so because of the antidepressant medication. He finally agreed on Didrex (benzphetamine), a medication related to the amphetamines but less addictive if taken as prescribed. However, working in a doctor's office, Janet knew that she could ask one of her employing doctors "for a favor" to prescribe the same diet pills. She had been taking more than prescribed and was afraid of running out of pills. This way she had a backup source to hold her over until her medical doctor would agree to write another prescription.

As happens with most antidepressant medications, results were painfully slow in surfacing. During the time she felt depressed, Janet stopped taking her HIV medications, fatalistically stating that she had no interest in "prolonging the inevitable." Janet also stopped believing that the Zoloft would ever work for her, and she made a mental note to be sure to tell her psychiatrist at the next appointment. Jerry didn't seem to be able to cope with the entire situation because it seemed to Janet that he was staying at the office later and later.

When her friends saw what was happening, they decided to try to cheer up Janet by taking her out to some of the hot spots where dancing and "being seen" were an important part of the evening. Getting dressed up and spending the night with friends seemed to lift her spirits a little at first—but it was during one of these girl's nights out that Janet was introduced to the hallucinogenic drug, ecstasy. Her friends meant well and only intended to try and keep her spirits up. Soon, Janet started telling Jerry she was going out for "tea with the girls." That tea turned out to be cocktails—and, more often than not, ecstasy. With taking the drugs in addition to the alcohol, Janet's mood certainly changed, but not in the direction that her friends had hoped. She began to show a severe and unpredictable temper.

She often took this explosive anger out on the boys by being verbally aggressive toward them. Sometimes she would scare them by becoming physically aggressive. She would punch doors or the kitchen counter with her fist. Janet's temper seemed to flare with greater frequency and intensity when she drank. Most evenings, Janet would drink to the point where her speech was slurred, she was unsteady on her feet, and forgetful. The boys tried to stay out of her way when she was like this. They usually took Stephanie under their wing and retreated to their rooms to watch TV or play video games. Left alone, Janet found that a little "Adam" (ecstasy) would lift her spirits and give her a feeling of boundless energy. She tried not to take the whole pill because she was afraid she might grind her teeth. "How could I explain a broken tooth to Jerry?" she thought. When the effects started to wear off, it would sometimes be early in the morning, but then she had her sleeping pills to count on. After several days of drinking, ecstasy, and sedatives, Janet would be exhausted, so she depended on her diet pills to give her that needed boost of energy—and so the cycle continued.

The day that changed Janet's life started out routinely enough. The previous evening she had worked very late at the office uploading files to the new computerized record-keeping program and teaching the rest of the staff how to use it. Janet arrived home, showered, and went straight to bed. She got up around midmorning and prepared a breakfast for herself of toast slathered with lots of jelly. She also had a Bloody Mary for a pick-me-up. Stephanie was going directly from school to one of her friend's house for a sleepover, so she wasn't expected. But the boys came home at their usual time (by which point Janet had consumed about 3 ounces of alcohol).

While the boys were doing homework, Janet fixed a light dinner of fried chicken fingers for them and a salad for herself. She had another Bloody Mary and two rather large glasses of wine. Janet knew her middle son, Chris, needed a ride to baseball practice, so she decided to leave Mike home to look after Scott. Janet stashed a couple of ecstasy pills in her purse, "just in case," and left the house with Chris. Jerry was working late, as usual. If any of the boys had noticed how much Janet was drinking, no one said anything. They had learned to fear her temper. During the hour and a half of baseball practice, Janet left the ball field, went to a nearby sports lounge, and continued to drink.

By this point, Janet should not have been allowed near the wheel of her car—but there was no one around to stop her from putting the keys in the ignition. She was driving her 4-wheel drive SUV about 60 miles an hour in a 35-mile-an-hour work zone. Janet's reflexes were slowed, so it seemed to her that the road turned very suddenly and sharply to detour traffic around some heavy construction equipment. When Janet hit the brakes, it caused her SUV to veer sideways into a huge Royal Poinciana tree on the side of the road. (Fortunately, it was late in the day and no construction workers were standing there.) The car came to rest wrapped around the tree at about the midsection, between the front and back passenger side doors. Chris, who was sitting next to Janet in the front seat, was wearing his seat belt and escaped with "just" a broken right arm and scratches on his face.

Janet, who was not wearing a seat belt, did not fare as well. When the SUV hit the tree, the windshield exploded in her face and she was tossed around like a rag doll before becoming trapped in

CASE The Case of Janet Sellar (Continued)

the wreckage. The rescue team extricated Janet with the "jaws of life" and airlifted her to Jackson Hospital's Ryder Trauma Center. On admission, Janet was diagnosed with a severe cerebral contusion with significant edema, multiple fractures of her facial bones, and a severe injury to her left eye. At this point Janet's chances for survival were slim.

Miraculously, Janet's cerebral edema did not progress, and after several days she began to emerge from her coma. Jerry stayed by her side constantly until she was out of danger. Janet was extubated after 2 weeks and transferred to a nearby rehabilitation hospital where she continued to improve. Janet was finally discharged back home.

Later, Janet was charged with driving while legally intoxicated. When her SUV was searched, the ecstasy she had hidden in her purse was found. Additional charges were brought against her for felony possession of illegal drugs. As a part of her sentence, Janet was placed under house arrest to be followed by a period of probation. Counseling was also court ordered.

Jerry's punishment for Janet may be even harsher. "I want a divorce," he stated flatly after the first few weeks of shock had worn off. "How could you even dare to put our children in jeopardy? I'm so mad and I just want out of this mess." Over time, however, he seemed to soften a little. "Seeing you in the hospital, you looked so vulnerable. I remembered how much I love you. You are my wife and the mother of our children, after all." Jerry ultimately decided his ambivalence must be a sign that he should do nothing—at least for the moment.

Janet contacted a local mental health agency that specializes in treating substance disorders in order to start her court-mandated counseling. As the social worker completed Janet's psychosocial history, she was struck by the thought that drug and alcohol use are not limited to a small minority of deviants. The social worker mused, "If it can happen to someone like Janet, it can happen to anybody. But where had the opportunities been missed to intervene and avoid Janet's tragedy? Here is somebody who has access to all kinds of help. What happened?" They scheduled their next appointment, and Janet left the office. The practitioner wandered over to the window and stared out at the searing South Florida sun. "I've worked with so many clients who used multiple substances, but this situation really stands out," she thought. "Or maybe this is just another case that fell through the cracks." The social worker turned and walked back to her desk. "Everyone involved with Janet was trying to help; yet the issue of her drinking and the multiple drugs that she was taking, the prescribed and the others, was never addressed. Not by her physician or by her psychiatrist or even her husband—It's clear that Janet's friends were uneasy about her depression and upset about her refusal to comply with her HIV regimen. ... and I'm sure they feel guilty now for introducing Janet to ecstasy." The social worker shook her head slowly as she swiveled her chair idly. "And then there's Janet's husband ... he's devoted to his family, but he was away from home so much of the day and evening ... I guess he couldn't see what was happening. The poor kids just tried to cope by staying out of her way. Seems there was no one who could see the whole picture, no one suspected the extent of Janet's drug and alcohol use—or, worse yet, if they did know about it, they chose to ignore it. It took a near fatal accident for something to be done? Who is responsible?"

A light tap on the office door signaled the arrival of the social worker's next client.

Janet Sellar's DSM Diagnosis Is as Follows:
Alcohol intoxication with use disorder, severe, reason for visit
Sedative-use disorder, moderate
Stimulant use disorder, moderate

Other hallucinogen use disorder, MDMA, moderate
Major depressive disorder, single episode, moderate
Conviction in criminal proceedings without imprisonment

Competency 7 a

ASSESSMENT SUMMARY The case discussion illustrates Janet Sellar's level of intoxication by alcohol and various drugs, some prescribed (although not taken as prescribed) and some not. The case discussion also points to coping strategies that the social worker might tap into in order to improve Janet's adaption to her life situations and events. After the accident, Janet's medical diagnosis was alcohol intoxication—the legal assessment was driving under the influence and felony drug possession. The officer who searched her car and purse found her stash of ecstasy, which turned out to be a quantity that justified the charge of illegal possession. Because Janet had no prior criminal record, she was placed under house arrest followed by probation and mandated counseling.

Prior to the day of the accident, Janet's behavior showed many signs of intoxication. The clinically significant maladaptive behavioral and psychological changes resulting from ingestion of specific substances could be seen in her erratic temper, slurred speech, unsteadiness on her feet, and forgetfulness. Janet's cognitive impairment included changes in perception, wakefulness, attention deficits, and compromised judgment. Her mood instability, cognitive impairment, and belligerence caused significant stress among family members. Although Janet has been diagnosed with HIV, this medical condition does not explain her behavioral changes.

Janet had repeatedly used four groups of substances—alcohol, sedatives (Ambien), amphetamines (Didrex, a benzphetamine), and hallucinogens (ecstasy)—contributing to her diagnostic severity. Having worked in a doctor's office for many years, Janet clearly understood the dangers of mixing her medications with alcohol or other drugs and of taking more than prescribed, but unfortunately this make no difference in her intake levels.

Janet is also diagnosed with major depression, single episode, of moderate severity. Onset had been within the past few months. Due to the complications associated with her car accident, the vignette does not address the possibility of any remission. What we do know is after a setback with her HIV diagnosis, Janet felt worthless, had problems sleeping, showed a markedly diminished interest in enjoyable activities, and started gaining weight. Her suicidal ideation prompted the referral to the psychiatrist. The delay in treatment impact associated with antidepressant medications left Janet in a hellish limbo where she acted on her suicidal thoughts by stopping her medical regimen for the HIV diagnosis. Her well-meaning but misguided friends tried to "help" by introducing her to ecstasy and by enabling her heavy use of alcohol.

With this kind of pattern it is difficult to determine the extent to which Janet's alcohol and drug use added to her depression. It is not clear whether she ever received (or would have received) any benefit from Zoloft. However, this situation highlights the vulnerability of clients during the period of time it takes for any antidepressant to reach therapeutic levels. In order to fully and accurately understand

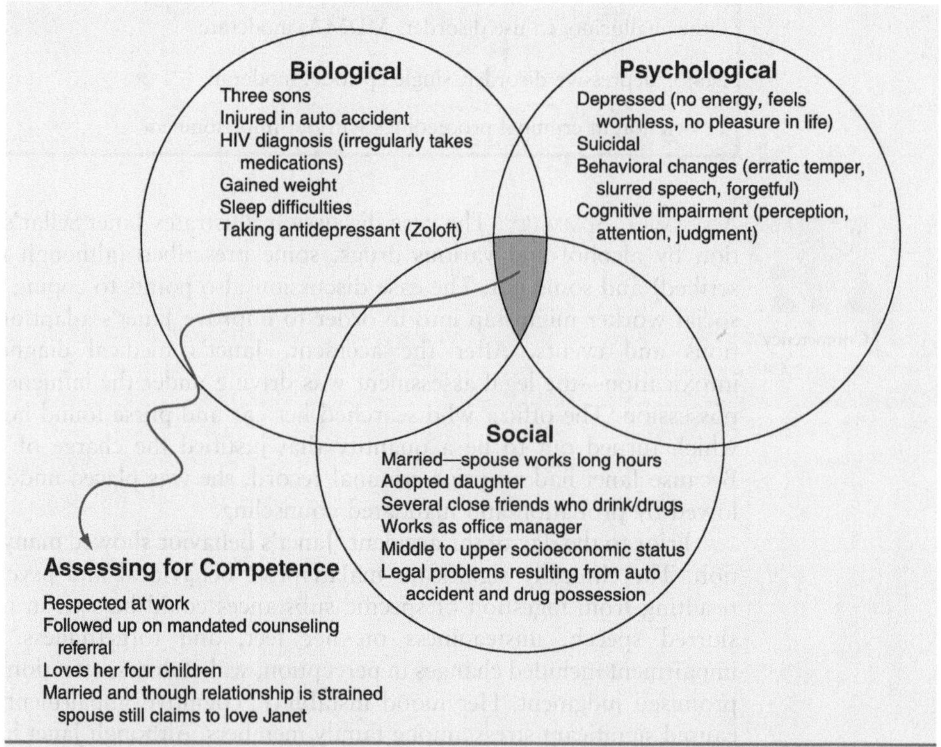

FIGURE 14.2 › THE SUBSTANCE-RELATED DISORDERS
The interactions of the biological, psychological, and social variables in Janet Sellar's life.

Janet's depression, all substances need to be withdrawn. Clearly, Janet's depression and use of multiple substances have complicated her diagnostic picture. Figure 14.2 summarizes the interactions of the biological, psychological, and social variables in Janet Sellar's life.

The following segment examines the non-substance-related disorders, specifically gambling disorder.

GAMBLING DISORDER

Gambling disorder is a non-substance-related disorder and a new addition to the DSM-5. This represents the first formal recognition of a behavioral addiction in mental health practice. Although gambling may seem of no consequence on the surface, in reality the problems they can cause are anything but. As seen in the following case story, some people who develop gambling disorder can end up in crippling debt, strained relationships, and problems on the job. It is serious consequences like these that led to the recognition of gambling as a mental health disorder (Ferentzy & Turner, 2013).

Gambling is considered to affect the brain's reward system much like the substance addictions. During brain-imaging studies, the same brain areas are activated in response to cues for either gambling or substance addictions, indicating they share the same neurocircuitry. Petry and colleagues (2013) note that gambling behaviors can become compulsive and lead to major problems in a person's life.

PREVAILING PATTERN

According to the DSM-5, the prevalence of gambling disorder over the past year has been about 0.2 percent to 0.3 percent of the U.S. general population (APA, 2013). The disorder is more prevalent for males at a rate of 0.6 percent, in contrast to females where the rate is about 0.2 percent. The rate is slightly higher for African Americans (0.9 percent) than among whites (0.4 percent), and Hispanics (0.3 percent).

DIFFERENTIAL ASSESSMENT

To meet diagnostic criteria for a gambling disorder, an individual has to have at least four of the problems listed below within the past 12 months, in conjunction with persistent and recurrent problematic gambling behavior:

- Needing to gamble with more money to get the same excitement from gambling as before.
- Feeling restless or irritable when trying to reduce or stop gambling.
- Continuing to try to reduce or stop gambling without success.
- Gambling is frequently on the person's mind, both in reliving past gambling experiences and planning future gambling events.
- Gambling when feeling depressed, guilty or anxious.
- Trying to win back gambling losses.
- Lying to cover up how much the person is gambling.
- Losing not only money, but also relationships, the job, or a significant career opportunity as a result of gambling.
- Becoming dependent on other people to give the person money to deal with financial problems that have been caused by gambling.

The practitioner considers that the person's gambling behavior is not better accounted for by a manic episode. Gambling behaviors are specified as episodic (meeting criteria at more than one point in time with symptoms subsiding between periods of gambling for at least several months), or persistent (experiencing continuous symptoms for several years). Current severity, much like the substance-related disorders, is also specified on a range from mild to severe. The practitioner also considers if the person is in early remission (no criteria have been met for at least 3 months but for less than a year) or in sustained remission (criteria have not been met for 12 months or more).

The following vignette describes Larry Dalton's struggle with gambling and illustrates the behaviors typically found in a gambling disorder. Since we know little of Larry's background, the biological, psychological, and social influences in his life are not illustrated.

CASE The Case of Larry Dalton

Larry begins, "Well, I'm on the brink of getting fired as a manager. My name is Larry and I am a compulsive gambler. It's not easy, but it has been 18 days since I've touched a slot machine. I didn't realize I was a compulsive gambler until I started getting into trouble at work. The boss claims I'm [he raises his voice to accentuate the word] 'preoccupied.' This is my dream job. All that I've been working toward for most of my adult life. In an instant, it could be gone. Hell! I'm in debt, and the wife and I aren't getting along. You might say I'm in the process of losing everything. Looking back, I guess you could say that it all started in my mid-teens."

Larry is the younger of two boys in his family. Both were involved in sports in high school and often played brotherly pickup games against each other. It was rare that these informal games against each other were played without Larry betting his allowance on the outcome. "I can remember, even to this day, that sickening feeling to lose game after game to my brother only to egg him on for just one last game. I was convinced I could win back my allowance, even double it. Never mind the fact that my brother was a better athlete than me. I just loved the action and risk of gambling my allowance although in those days I was only losing about 50 cents. Problem is, this kind of behavior continued even when I got to college. I would bet with friends on just about anything; video games, tournaments, whatever. You name it and I had a bet going. I never once considered this to be a problem. You know, the thrill of victory and all that."

After graduation from college, Larry married Becky, his high school sweetheart, and started an entry-level managerial position with a large company. Larry adds, "Paying my dues, you might say." At the time he started playing poker once a week with friends. "Looking back," Larry states, "I really took those games too seriously. I guess you might say that I was more than just a 'social gambler.' Then I started taking an occasional half day off from the job and going to the local race track. I was pretty much in control of our finances so there was little risk of Becky ever noticing any shortage of money."

Larry managed to do well on the job and was promoted to an upper-level management position that required a move—to Las Vegas, Nevada, of all places. "God, I thought I was in heaven and I don't mean it was because of the promotion," states Larry. He adds, "It was the minute I stepped off the plane and saw the slots. They had them in convenience stores, gas stations, grocery stores. Hell! They were even in the bathrooms! Slot machines were everywhere. I once heard that there's one slot machine for every 13 people in the entire state of Nevada. By the end of the year I was 100 percent addicted to the slot machines."

At first Larry played blackjack at the casinos but found the action was not fast enough for him. Then he discovered the slot machines. "There was something about trying your luck rather than being a skilled gamer that drew me in right away. They're so unpredictable and can't be controlled by anybody! You know, they're the first thing you hear once inside the casino. I love the ringing and the metal sounds as the coins hit the drop box of the slot machine. Makes me feel like I can be the next winner. Then there are those brightly colored fruits, hearts, diamonds, numerals, letters, and bells!"

Larry describes how he became totally consumed by the slot machines. "It got to the point where I couldn't concentrate at work because I was always thinking about what machines I was going to play. There are about 23 major casinos on the Strip, so I had a lot of choices. I was constantly working on a system to figure out which would be my lucky slot machine. I learned the lowest-paying slots were near the cage where you cash in your chips and by the tables. The higher payers are near the entrance. Then there's the machine's payout percentage. Once I find one with a 99 percent payout, there was no budging me. I might sit at that f——king machine for 8 hours straight. It didn't matter that I would start to get pains radiating from my neck down to my lower back from sitting there for so long. The next day I'm totally exhausted and agitated that I have to go to work."

Larry continues, "I was spending more and more money just to get the same excitement from winning at the slots. I tried to stop, but I got so restless. I needed to hear those familiar sounds of victory and the tune of the payout. Somebody once told me that slot machines are made of a special metal to give out a much noisier sound to create the illusion that money is being won by every slot machine. Personally, I think that's just sour grapes talking."

From the outside, it looked as though Larry has the perfect life. He has a great job, a loving wife, a child on the way, and a beautiful home just outside the city. However, in reality he has two second mortgages and credit card debt, all totaling about $600,000. He already tapped into his savings, and his retirement fund ... everything!

Larry adds, "Over the past 7 years I've made tons of money working only to lose it all to gambling. No one knows, and I keep it all pent up inside. I'm constantly stressed and preoccupied. Don't ask me how I did it but so far I've been away from the slots for 18 days, but I feel like I can't stop. I go to sleep thinking about how I need to try to win just one more time and then wake up thinking about playing the slots again so I can reduce my debt. This is no way to live. Becky is starting to complain that I'm 'distant' but I tell her it's just that her hormones are out of whack with the pregnancy. I can't concentrate at work because I'm constantly thinking of what machines I'm going to play."

Larry continues, "My boss is starting to notice. He told me if I mess up one more account I'm history with the company. You think that would get my attention? No! Every single waking moment somehow connects back to the slots. If somebody told me 25 years ago when I was gambling on those pickup games with my brother that when I turned 40 I'd be on the brink of losing everything, I would have told them they were crazy. I make promises to myself that I'm going to quit, but the fact of the matter is that gambling has taken over my life. I dread the day I have to tell Becky of our financial situation. I've never lied to her, but I never told her the full truth either. I am currently attending Gamblers Anonymous meetings and will attend for as long as I need to. You know, 1 day at a time. So far I've made it to 18 days without the slots. Will it ever get better?"

Larry Dalton's DSM Diagnosis Is as Follows:
Gambling disorder, persistent, moderate

Competency 6 b

Assessment Summary How many times have you been invited to share in the office pool to place a bet on the Super Bowl score or purchase a lottery ticket? Many people gamble on games and events, and most do so without experiencing problems. The case discussion highlights Larry Dalton's gambling disorder, particularly his attraction to the slot machines. Unquestionably, Larry's gambling behaviors have become compulsive, leading to major financial problems and a stressed relationship with his wife, and affecting his job performance to the point that his boss is threatening to fire him if he messes up another client account.

Gambling is frequently on Larry's mind, and he feels the need to gamble even more to get the same excitement as before. Larry is so preoccupied with playing the slot machines that his job has been compromised and his wife sees him as "distant." If Larry tries to cut down on his gambling, he feels restless and yearns for the familiar sights and sounds of the slot machines. While he has never lied to his wife, Larry has also never shared the extent of his gambling debt—well into the thousands of dollars. So far, he has been able to avoid asking others for money to relieve his debt; multiple mortgages and credit cards have carried him through. Larry is trying to stop playing the slots, but with limited success. Interestingly, Larry has a long history of gambling beginning with friendly pickup games with his older brother starting around the time he was about 15 years old. All through college he could be found gambling on just about everything and did so without experiencing any problems. After his recent promotion and job transfer to Las Vegas, Nevada, his difficulties with compulsive gambling became evident.

Competency 7 a

For reasons we do not know, Larry has made a concerted effort to cut down on his use of the slot machines and has gone 18 days without playing them—though it has been difficult. His competence is evident in seeking out the self-help provided in Gamblers Anonymous. We can anticipate there are additional strengths in Larry's life that are not evident in his story focusing on his addiction to slot machines.

Gambling disorder is comorbid with other mental disorders such as other substance use disorders, the depressive disorders, anxiety disorders, and personality disorders. Listening carefully to Larry's story, he talks about his difficulties concentrating at work and feeling restless to hear the winning sounds of the slots. While these behaviors are not sufficient to support the presence of a comorbid disorder, they are areas for further exploration.

SUMMARY

Taken together, the substance-related and addictive disorders are the most prevalent mental health issue, and more than likely practitioners can anticipate seeing someone struggling with drugs, alcohol, and/or a gambling disorder at some point in their practice. As we have seen, current trends indicate that illicit substance use is on the rise and is expected to increase. There is no clear-cut cause of substance use, though many explanations have been offered. As the case studies in this chapter illustrate, persons with substance-related and non-substance-related problems experience multiple medical, psychological, family, and social consequences.

Competency 4 a

The competency-based assessment fosters the practitioner's critical thinking by exploring the multiple dimensions of a person's life and provides an avenue to truly grasp all aspects of a client's struggle. Research, observation, and practice experience have shown that there are many determinants of substance use and the non-substance-related disorder of gambling. There are the intrapersonal or personal factors, such as genetics, temperament, or individual traits; interpersonal determinants, such as family history; and the community and environmental influences, such as cultural background and social attitudes—yet, none of this knowledge provides a clear-cut explanation or prediction for who will struggle with alcohol, drugs, and/or gambling behaviors and who will not.

The DSM-5 uses a dimensional approach to classifying the substance-related disorders and non-substance-related disorders by establishing levels of severity ranging from moderate to severe. Within the group identified as substance-induced disorders, problems are deemed to be related to either substance intoxication or substance withdrawal.

The first part of this chapter provided a review of the overall symptoms supporting the substance use disorders. The second part of the chapter was devoted to the substances themselves. The 10 classes of substances presented in the DSM were reviewed in order to provide knowledge and insight into why and how people use alcohol and drugs. Many clients who come to the attention of the social worker are not motivated to change, even if their habits are self-destructive. Clients (and their families) are usually affected on multiple levels as a consequence of the substance use (and non-substance) behaviors. Therefore, practitioners must become aware of all the various avenues of use and abuse and develop a base of knowledge that will allow them to accurately assess the nature and severity of the client's needs and resources. The last section of the chapter addressed the non-substance behavioral disorder of gambling, the only disorder considered to have enough evidence to be included as a DSM diagnosis. This overview is intended to familiarize practitioners with the behavioral disorders as they emerge in the real lives of our clients.

As the DSM transitions from the DSM-IV-TR (APA, 2000) to the current edition of the manual, Table 14.10 provides a brief summary of the changes made to the diagnostic classifications.

PRACTITIONER'S REFLECTIONS

Sooner or later the practitioner will be confronted with the substance-related and addictive disorders in his or her professional career. Despite massive efforts in the United States to eliminate recreational chemical abuse, it continues to be a major issue that results in a wide range of social, economic, and psychological problems—not just for the individual users, but for their families and communities as well. Social workers are among the "first responders" when drug- and alcohol-related problems or behavioral addictions are destroying clients' lives. Thus, it is critical that practitioners know what to look for and be able to assess clients' situations for successful intervention.

ACTIVITIES

Competency 6 a

1. Interview a friend or colleague who has given up the use of a legal substance such as alcohol, tobacco, or caffeine. Be sure to ask about what helped them to give up the particular substance (s). As you listen to these experiences, what insights can you gain that will help you to develop, manage, and maintain a therapeutic relationship with your clients who struggle with the use of substances, both legal and illegal? Address the strengths and resources that helped your friend or colleague move through his or her substance use.

Competency 6 b

2. Reflect back on the experiences of one of your clients who have struggled with using an illegal substance. What insights can you learn from their experience that will help you to develop the therapeutic relationship with your own clients from a strengths perspective found in the competency-based assessment? (If you have not worked with a client with a substance-related problem, interview a colleague with expertise in this area, and ask about what insights they can share to help inform your practice.)
3. Identify the similarities and differences between legal and illegal substance use. Be sure to include experiences with legally prescribed substances.
4. People who severely use substances often cope by denial or deceit. If you were working with someone you suspect can be diagnosed with a substance use disorder, what questions would you ask to determine if substance use is a problem and the extent of severity?

Competency 7 b

   a. After you have developed this list of questions, role-play an interview with a colleague using your questions in order to explore the suspected

Competency 7 b

abuse (or addiction). Once done, talk with your colleague about how he or she experienced these questions and what might have been "missing" in your approach. Alternatively, explore what you did well.

Competency 1 a

b. If you got stuck in the role-play interview, describe how you would use supervision or consultation to improve your skills. Develop a specific list of questions for your supervisor or consultant.

Competency 4 a

5. Find another colleague with whom to debate the following statement: "The difference among the levels of severity for a substance use disorder is really not important." (As an alternative, discuss this statement with several colleagues who have experience in the field of substance use.) Reflect on how this debate or discussion helped you to distinguish, appraise, and integrate multiple sources of knowledge to inform your perspectives on a client's use of substances.

Competency 5 c

6. People from all walks of life can be adversely affected by the use of substances. Imagine for a moment that you have been asked to develop a brochure for an agency waiting room that focuses on the prevention of substance use. Outline the key points that you would plan to cover in this preventive program. As a part of completing this "reflection," it might be helpful if you tailored this brochure to a specific agency. Alternatively, you might want to develop a brochure for the non-substance-related behavioral disorder of gambling.

Competency 7 b

Would you consider showing the prospective brochure with a client for his or her input? Explain why or why not.

Competency 2 c

7. Reflect on how people who use drugs or alcohol and/or gamble are portrayed in the popular media. Compare this image to your actual social work practice with people who use substances or have a non-substance-related disorder. If you are a professional who is not employed in the field of substance use, interview a colleague who works in this area for his or her opinion about how the media portrayal compares with their work experiences.

Competency 7 b

a. What can you conclude about how people who struggle with substance use or a non-substance-related disorder are commonly seen?
b. List at least three ways that these media images may potentially influence your own (or other professional colleagues) personal biases and values when working with diverse clients.

Competency 4 c

8. Nicotine is considered to be high on the list of the most powerfully addictive substances, which helps to explain why so many people find it difficult or impossible to stop tobacco use. Interview several people who regularly smoke, and ask them to support or refute the following statement, "Most smokers don't think of themselves as drug addicts." Based on the information they provide, what can be said about nicotine addiction?

Competency 8 c

9. Imagine that you are new to the field of working with people who struggle with the substance-related and addictive disorders. After reading this chapter, you realize that you will need to have a great deal of medically oriented information in order to be effective with your clients. Develop a plan to increase your knowledge base in this area. Be as specific as

you can (i.e., Who would you talk with? What would you read? What courses or seminars would you take? What experiences would be useful?).

Competency 5 a

10. The social worker in the vignette of Janet Sellar raises a number of questions around why Janet did not receive help for her multiple substance-related problems sooner. Review the social worker's questions in this case and attempt to answer these questions. Keep in mind that you may have to include a preventative focus in your responses.

Competency 6 b

11. Access the Competency-Based Assessment and Companion website at. Go to the case study that provides a series of reflective questions about Tim's struggles with a substance use disorder. This is a gentleman who sees alcohol use in his life as a positive, adding that nothing bothers him when he drinks. According to Tim, his problems come back when he is not drinking. Once you have identified the key criteria supporting Tim's alcohol use disorder, what challenges you can anticipate around engaging Tim to change his drinking behaviors?

COMPETENCY NOTES

Competency 1 a—Social workers make ethical decisions by applying standards of the NASW Code of Ethics and other relevant laws, regulations, and models for ethical decision-making as appropriate to context (p. 436): Social workers understand the value base of the profession and its ethical standards as well as relevant laws and regulations that may impact practice.

Competency 2 a—Social workers apply and communicate understanding of the implications of diversity and difference in shaping life experiences in practice at the micro, mezzo, and macro levels (p. 377): Social workers understand how diversity and difference characterize and shape the human experience and that these features are critical to the formation of identity.

Competency 2 c—Social workers apply self-awareness and self-regulation to manage the influence of personal biases and values in working with diverse clients (and constituencies) (p. 436): Social workers are aware of the various forms and mechanisms of oppression and discrimination and recognize the extent to which a culture's structures and values may oppress, marginalize, alienate, or create privilege and power.

Competency 4 a—Social workers use practice experience and theory to inform scientific inquiry and research (pp. 386, 434, 436): Social workers understand both quantitative and qualitative research methods and their respective roles in evaluating their practice.

Competency 4 c—Social workers use and translate research evidence to inform and improve practice, policy, and service delivery (p. 436): Social workers understand the processes for translating research findings into effective practices.

Competency 5 a—Social workers identify social welfare and economic policies at the local, state, and federal levels impact well-being, service delivery, and access to social services (pp. 376, 437): Social workers understand that human rights and social justice, as well as social welfare and services, are mediated by policy and its implementation on several levels—local, state, and federal.

Competency 5 c—Social workers apply critical thinking to analyze, formulate, and advocate for policies that advance human rights and social, economic, and environmental justice (p. 436): Social workers understand their role in policy development and implementation within their practice settings and actively engage in policy practice to effect change.

Competency 6 a—Social workers apply knowledge of human behavior and the social environment, person-in-environment, and other multidisciplinary theoretical frameworks to engage with clients (and constituencies) (pp. 433, 435): Social workers understand theories of human behavior and the social environment and critically apply this knowledge to facilitate engagement with clients (and constituencies) including families, groups, organizations, and communities.

Competency 6 b—Social workers use empathy, personal reflection, and interpersonal skills effectively to engage clients (and constituencies) (pp. 433, 435, 437): Social workers value the importance of human relationships.

Competency 7 a—Social workers collect and organize data and apply critical thinking in order to interpret information from clients and constituencies (pp. 429, 434): Social workers understand that the assessment process is ongoing and conducted with, and on behalf of, diverse individuals, families, groups, organizations, and communities.

Competency 7 b—Social workers are able to apply knowledge of human behavior and the social environment, person-in-environment, and other multidisciplinary theoretical frameworks in the analysis of assessment data (pp. 375, 378, 435, 436): Social workers understand theories of human behavior and the social environment and critically evaluate and apply this knowledge in the assessment process.

Competency 7 c—Social workers develop mutually agreed-on intervention goals and objectives based on the assessment of strengths, needs, and challenges within clients and constituencies (p. 393): Social workers recognize the implications of the larger practice context in the assessment process.

Competency 8 c—Social workers use interprofessional collaboration, as appropriate, to achieve beneficial practice outcomes (p. 436): Social workers value interprofessional teamwork and recognize the beneficial outcomes that require interdisciplinary, interprofessional, and interorganizational collaboration.

REFERENCES

American Cancer Society. (2014). Guide to quitting smoking. Retrieved on November 20, 2014 from: http://www.cancer.org/Healthy/StayAwayfromTobacco/GuidetoQuittingSmoking/guide-to-quitting-smoking-success-rates

American Psychiatric Association (APA). (2000). *Diagnostic and statistical manual of mental disorders* (4th ed., text revision). Washington, DC: Author.

American Psychiatric Association (APA). (2013). *Diagnostic and statistical manual of mental disorders* (5th ed.). Arlington, VA: Author.

Ashley, O., Marsden, M. E., & Brady, T. (2003). Effectiveness of substance abuse treatment programming for women: A review. *American Journal of Drug and Alcohol Abuse*, *29*, 19–54.

Barlow, D. H., & Durand, V. M. (2012). *Abnormal psychology: An integrative approach* (6th ed.). Belmont, CA: Wadsworth Cengage Learning.

Barnes, G. M., Hoffman, J. J., Wolfe, J. W., Farrell, M. P., & Dintcheff, B. A. (2006). Effects of parental monitoring and peer deviance on substance use and delinquency. *Journal of Marriage and the Family*, *68*, 1084–1104.

Black, J. R. (1947). Advantages of substituting the morphia habit for the incurably alcoholic. *Cincinnati Lancet-Clinic* in A. R. Lindesmith, *Opiate addiction* (p. 183). Evanston, IL: Principia Press.

Bonne, J. (January 9, 2003). "Go pills": A war on drugs? Air Force use of amphetamines raises questions. Retrieved on November 20, 2014 from: http://www.msnbc.msn.com/id/3071789/

Boyd, M. R., Phillips, K., & Dorsey, C. J. (2003). Alcohol and other drug disorders, comorbidity, and violence: Comparison of rural African-American and Caucasian women. *Archives of Psychiatric Nursing*, *17*, 249–258.

Caldwell, J. A., Caldwell, J. L., & Darlington, K. K. (2003). Utility of dextroamphetamine for attenuating the impact of sleep deprivation in pilots. *Aviation, Space, and Environmental Medicine*, *74*(11), 1125–1134.

Canapary, D., Bongar, B., & Cleary, K. M. (2002). Assessing risk for completed suicide in patients with alcohol dependence: Clinicians' views of critical factors. *Professional Psychology: Research and Practice*, *33*(5), 464–469.

Centers for Disease Control and Prevention (CDC). (2014). Alcohol and public health. Retrieved on November 1, 2014 from: http://www.cdc.gov/alcohol/data-stats.htm

Chapman, C., & Wu, L-T. (2014). E-cigarette prevalence and correlates of use among adolescents versus adults: A review and comparison. *Journal of Psychiatric Research*, *54*, 43–54.

Copeland, J., Swift. W., & Rees, V. (2001). Clinical profile of participants in a brief prevention program for cannabis use disorder. *Journal of Substance Use and Treatment*, *20*(1), 45–52.

Cormier, R. A., Dell, C. A., & Poole, N. (2004). Women and substance abuse problems. *BioMed Central Women's Health*, *4*(Suppl. 1), S1–S8.

Dawson, D. A., Grant, B. F., Chou, S. P., & Stinson, F. S. (2007). The impact of partner alcohol problems on women's physical and mental health. *Journal of Studies on Alcohol and Drugs*, *68*(1), 66–75.

Doweiko, H. E. (2014). *Concepts of chemical dependency* (9th ed.). Belmont, CA: Brooks/Cole Cengage Learning.

Drummer, O. H., & Odell, M. (2001). *The forensic pharmacology of drugs of abuse*. New York: Oxford University Press.

Earle, C. W. (1880). The opium habit: A statistical and clinical lecture. *Chicago Medical Review*, *2*, 442–446.

Emonson, D. L., & Vanderbeek, R. D. (1995). The use of amphetamines in the U.S. Air Force tactical operations during Desert Storm. *Aviation, Space, and Environmental Medicine*, *66*(3), 260–263.

Fareed, A., Stout, S., Caseralla, J., Vayalapalli, S., Cox, J., & Drexler, K. (2011). Illicit opioid intoxication: Diagnosis and treatment. *Substance Abuse: Research and Treatment*, *5*, 17–25.

Ferentzy, P., & Turner, N. E. (2013). *A history of problem gambling: Temperance, substance abuse, medicine, and metaphors*. New York: Springer.

Foroud, T., Edenberg, H. J., & Crabbe, J. C. (2010). Genetic research: Who is at risk for alcoholism? *Alcohol Research and Health*, *33*(1 & 2), 64–75.

Freese, T. E., Miotto, K., & Reback, C. J. (2002). The effects and consequences of selected club drugs. *Journal of Substance Abuse Treatment*, *23*(2), 151–156.

Gahlinger, P. M. (2004). Club drugs: MDMA., gamma-hydroxybutyrate (GHB), rohypnol, and ketamine. *American Family Physician*, *69*, 2919–2927.

Gorelick, D. A., Levin, K. H., Coperisno, M. L., Heishman, S. J., Liu, F., Boggs, D. L., & Kelly, D. L. (2012). Diagnostic criteria for cannabis withdrawal syndrome. *Drug and Alcohol Dependence*, *123*, 141–147.

Gray, S. W. (with Zide, M. R.). (2006). *Psychopathology: A competency-based treatment model for social workers*. Pacific Grove, CA: Brooks/Cole Thomson Learning.

Griffiths, R. R., Juliano, L. M., & Chausmer, A. L. (2003). Caffeine pharmacology and clinical effects. In A. W. Graham, T. K. Schultz, M. F. Mayo-Smith, R. K. Ries, & B. B. Wilford (Eds.), *Principles of addiction medicine* (3rd ed., pp. 193–224). Chevy Chase, MD: American Society of Addiction.

Hales, R. E., Yudofsky, S. C., & Gabbard, G. O. (Eds.), (2010). *Essentials of clinical psychiatry* (3rd ed.). Washington, DC: American Psychiatric Publishing.

Halpern, J. J., & Pope, H. G. (2003). Hallucinogen persisting perception disorder: What do we know after 50 years? *Drug and Alcohol Dependence*, *69*, 109–119.

Harrell, P. T., Simmons, V. N., Correal, J. B., Padhya, V. A., & Brandon, T. H. (2014). Electronic nicotine delivery systems ("e-cigarettes"): Review of safety and smoking cessation efficacy. *Otolarnygology—Head Neck Surgery*, *151*(3), 381–393.

Hasan, A. A., & Ciancio, S. (2004). Relationship between amphetamine ingestion and gingival enlargement. *Pediatric Dentistry*, *26*(5), 396–400.

Heath, A. C., Todorov, A. A., Nelson, E. C., Madden, P. A., Bucholz, K. K., & Martin, N. G. (2002). Gene environment interaction effects on behavioral variation and risk of complex disorders: The example of alcoholism and other psychiatric disorders. *Twin Research*, *5*(1), 30–37.

Heatherton, T. F., Kozlowski, L. T., Frecker, R. C., & Fagerstrom, K. O. (1991). The Fagerstrom test for nicotine dependence: A revision of the Fagerstrom tolerance questionnaire. *British Journal of Addiction*, *86*, 1119–1127.

Hernandez-Avila, C. A., & Kranzler, H. R. (2011). Alcohol use disorders. In J. H. Lowinson, P. Ruiz, R. B. Millman, & J. G. Langrod (Eds.), *Substance abuse: A comprehensive textbook* (5th ed., pp. 138–160). Philadelphia: Lippincott Williams & Wilkins.

Ivanov, I., Schultz, K. P., London, E. D., & Newcorn, J. H. (2008). Inhibitory control deficits in childhood and risk for substance use disorders: A review. *American Journal of Drug and Alcohol Abuse*, *34*, 239–258.

Iversen, L. L. (2000). *The science of marijuana*. New York: Oxford University Press.

Jaffe, E. (2006). Women and substance abuse. *Observer*, *19*(4). Retrieved on October 1, 2014 from: http://www.psychologicalscience.org/index.php/publications/observer/2006/april-06/women-and-substance-abuse.html

Juliano, L. M., & Griffiths, R. R. (2011). Caffeine. In J. J. Lowinson, P. Ruiz, R. B. Millman, & J. G. Langrod (Eds.), *Substance abuse: A comprehensive textbook* (5th ed., pp. 335–353). Philadelphia: Lippincott Williams & Wilkins.

Kalayasiri, R., Kranzler, H. R., Weiss, R., Brady, K., Gueorguirva, R., Panhuysen, C., & Malison, R. T. (2006). Risk factors for cocaine-induced paranoia in cocaine-dependent sibling pairs. *Drug and Alcohol Dependence*, *84*, 77–84.

Kane, H. H. (1880). *The hypodermic injection of morphia. Its history, advantages, and dangers. Based on experience of 360 physicians.* New York: Chas L. Bermingham and Company.

Kessler, R. C., Chiu, W. T., Demler, O., Merikangas, K. R., & Walters, E. E. (2005). Prevalence, severity, and comorbidity of 12-month DSM-IV disorders in the National Comorbidity Survey Replication. *Archives of General Psychiatry*, *62*, 617–627.

Koch, W. (2012). E-cigarettes: No smoke but fiery debate over safety. *USA Today News*. Retrieved on November 20, 2014 from: http://usatoday30.usatoday.com/news/health/story/2012–08-18/electronic-cigarettes-smokeless-vaping-risks/57121894/1

Leonard, S., Mexal, S., & Freedman, R. (2007). Smoking, genetics, and schizophrenia: Evidence for self-medication. *Journal of Dual Diagnosis*, *3*(3–4), 43–59.

Lovett, R. (2005). Coffee: The demon drink? *New Scientist*, *24*, 2518–2522.

Mansvelder, H. D., Keath, J. R., & McGehee, D. S. (2002). Synaptic mechanisms underlie nicotine-induced excitability of brain/reward areas. *Neuron*, *33*, 905–919.

Martensen, R. L. (1996). From papal endorsement to southern vice. *Journal of the American Medical Association*, *216*, 1615.

McDowell, D. (2005). Marijuana, hallucinogens, and club drugs. In R. J. Frances, S. I. Miller, & A. H. Mack (Eds.), *Clinical textbook of addictive disorders* (3rd ed., pp. 157–183). New York: Guilford Press.

Mednick, S. C., Cai, D. J., Kanady, J., & Drummond, S. P. A. (2008). Comparing benefits of caffeine, naps and placebo on verbal, motor and perceptual memory. *Behavioural Brain Research*, *193*(1), 79–86.

Memmott, J. L. (2003). Social work practice with the elderly substance abuser. *Journal of Social Work Practice in the Addictions*, *3*(2), 85–103.

Meredith, S. E., Juliano, L. M., Hughes, J. R., & Griffiths, R. R. (2013). Caffeine use disorder: A comprehensive review and research agenda. *Journal of Caffeine Research*, *3*(3), 114–130.

Meyer, J. U., Rumpf, H. J., & Hapke, U. (2004). Smoking, nicotine dependence, and psychiatric comorbidity—a population-based study including smoking cessation after three years. *Drug and Alcohol Dependence*, *76*(3), 287–295.

Moeller, F. G., Dougherty, D. M., Barratt, E. S., Schmitz, J. M., Swann, A. C., & Grabowski, J. (2001). The impact of impulsivity on cocaine use and retention in treatment. *Journal of Substance Abuse Treatment*, *21*, 193–198.

National Institute on Alcohol Abuse and Alcoholism. (2005, July). Brief interventions. *Alcohol Alert*, *66*, 1–8.

National Institute on Drug Abuse. (2005, March). Cigarettes and other nicotine products. *NIDA Info Facts*. NIF-010 National Institutes of Health—U.S. Department of Health and Human Services.

National Institute on Drug Abuse. (2010, September). What is the scope of cocaine use in the United States? Retrieved on November 30, 2014 from: http://www.drugabuse.gov/publications/research-reports/cocaine/what-scope-cocaine-use-in-united-states

National Institute on Drug Abuse. (2012a, December). Drug facts: Spice ("synthetic marijuana"). Retrieved on November 1, 2014 from: http://www.drugabuse.gov/publications/drugfacts/spice-synthetic-marijuana

National Institute on Drug Abuse. (2012b, December). Inhalants. Retrieved on November 1, 2014 from: http://www.drugabuse.gov/drugs-abuse/inhalants

National Institute on Drug Abuse. (2014). *Drug facts: Nationwide trends*. National Institute on Drug Abuse (NIDA): U.S. Department of Health and Human Services. Retrieved on October 1, 2014 from: http://www.drugabuse.gov/publications/drugfacts/nationwide-trends

Nawrot, P., Jordan, S., Eastwood, J., Rothstein, J., Hugenholtz, A., & Feeley, M. (2003). Effects of caffeine on human health. *Food Additives and Contaminants*, *20*(1), 1–30.

Nichols, D. (2004). Hallucinogens. *Pharmacology and Therapeutics*, *101*(2), 131–181.

Nurnberger, J. I., Jr., Wiegand, R., Bucholtz, K., O'Connor, S., Myer, E. T., Reich, T., ... Porjesc, B. (2004). A family study of alcohol dependence: Coaggregation of multiple disorders in relatives of alcohol dependent probands. *Archives of General Psychiatry*, *61*, 1246–1256.

O'Brien, C. P. (2005). Benzodiazepine use, abuse, and dependence. *Journal of Clinical Psychiatry, 66* (Suppl. 2), 28–33.

O'Brien, C. P. (2011). Addiction and dependence in DSM-V. *Addiction, 106*, 866–867.

O'Connor, R. J. (2012). Non-cigarette tobacco products: What have we learnt and where are we headed? *Tobacco Control, 21*(2), 181–190.

O'Neill, S. E., & Sher, K. J. (2000). Physiological alcohol dependence symptoms in early adulthood: A longitudinal perspective. *Experimental and Clinical Psychopharmacology, 8*(4), 493–508.

Office of National Drug Control Policy. (2014). *How illicit drug use affects business and the economy*. Washington, DC: Executive Office of the President. Retrieved on October 1, 2014 from: http://www.whitehouse.gov/ondcp/ondcp-fact-sheets/how-illicit-drug-use-affects-business-and-the-economy/

Owen, D. (2008). *In sickness and in power: Illnesses in heads of government during the last 100 years*. Westport, CT: Praeger.

Paczynski, R., & Gold, M. S. (2011). Cocaine and crack. In J. H. Lowinson, P. Ruiz, R. B. Millman, & J. G. Langrod (Eds.), *Substance abuse: A comprehensive textbook* (5th ed., pp. 191–213). Philadelphia: Lippincott Williams & Wilkins.

Paris, R., & Bradley, C. L. (2001). The challenge of adversity: Three narratives of alcohol dependence, recovery, and adult development. *Qualitative Health Research, 11*(5), 647–667.

Pechnick, R. N., & Ungerleider, J. T. (2011). Hallucinogens. In J. H. Lowinson, P. Ruiz, R. B. Millman, & J. G. Langrod (Eds.), *Substance abuse: A comprehensive textbook* (5th ed., pp. 267–276). New York: Lippincott Williams & Wilkins.

Petry, N. M. (2001). Substance abuse, pathological gambling, and impulsivity. *Drug and Alcohol Dependence, 63*, 29–38.

Petry, N. M., Blanco, C., Auriacomb, M., Borges, G., Bucholz, K., Crowley, T. J., ... O'Brien, C. (2013). An overview of and rationale for changes proposed for pathological gambling in DSM-5. *Journal of Gambling Studies, 30*(2), 493–502.

Rang, H. P., Dale, M. M., Ritter, J. M., Flower, R., & Henderson, G. (2012). *Rang and Dale's Pharmacology* (7th ed.). Edinburgh: Churchill Livingstone.

Rossi, S. (Ed.) (2005). *Australian medicines handbook 2005*. Adelaide: Australian Medicines Handbook.

Sadock, B. J., Sadock, V. A., & Ruiz, P. (2014). *Kaplan and Sadock's synopsis of psychiatry: Behavioral sciences/clinical psychiatry* (11th ed.). Philadelphia: Wolters Kluwer.

Schmitz, J. M., Jarvick, M. E., & Schneider, N. G. (2004). Nicotine. In J. H. Lowinson, P. Ruiz, R. B. Millman, & J. G. Langrod (Eds.), *Substance abuse: A comprehensive textbook* (4th ed., pp. 276–293). New York: Lippincott Williams & Wilkins.

Schultz, C. H. (2007). Earthquakes. In D. E. Hogan and J. L. Burstein (Eds.), *Disaster medicine* (2nd ed., pp. 185–193). New York: Lippincott Williams & Wilkins.

Shaner, J. W. (2002). Caries associated with methamphetamine abuse. *Journal of the Michigan Dental Association, 84*(9), 42–47.

Shapiro, V., Shapiro, J., & Paret, I. (2001). *Complex adoption and assisted reproductive technology: A developmental approach to clinical practice*. New York: Guilford Press.

Shields, A. L., Howell, R. T., Potter, J. S., & Weiss, R. D. (2007). The Michigan Alcoholism Screening Test and its shortened form: A meta-analytic inquiry into score reliability. *Substance Use and Misuse, 42*, 1783–1800.

Simoni-Wastila, L., & Yang, H. K. (2006). Psychoactive drug abuse in older adults. *American Journal of Geriatric Pharmacotherapy, 4*(4), 380–394.

Sternbach, L. H. (1972). The discovery of Librium. *Agents Actions, 2*, 193–196.

Strat, Y. L., Ramoz, N., & Gorwood, P. (2010). In alcohol-dependent drinkers, what does the presence of nicotine dependence tell us about psychiatric and addictive disorders comorbidity? *Alcohol and Alcoholism, 45*(2), 167–172.

Stuart, G. L., Ramsey, S. E., Moore, T. M., Kahler, C. W., Farrell, L. E., Recupero, P. R., & Brown, R. A. (2003). Reductions in marital violence following treatment for alcohol dependence. *Journal of Interpersonal Violence, 18*(10), 1113–1131.

Substance Abuse and Mental Health Services Administration (SAMHSA). (2004). *Results from the 2003 National Survey on Drug Use and Health: National finding*. (NSDUH Series H-25, DHHS Publication No. SMA 04–3964). Rockville, MD: Office of Applied Studies.

Substance Abuse and Mental Health Services Administration (SAMHSA). (2013). *Results from the 2012 National Survey on Drug Use and Health:*

Summary of national findings. Rockville, MD: Author.

Swift, W., Hall, W., & Teesson, M. (2001). Cannabis use and dependence among Australian adults: Results from the National Survey of Mental Health and Wellbeing. *Addiction, 96*(5), 737–748.

Tobacco Use and Dependence Guideline Panel. (2008). Treating tobacco use and dependence: 2008 update. Rockville, MD: U.S. Department of Health and Human Services. Available at: http://www.ncbi.nlm.nih.gov/books/NBK63952/

U.S. Department of Health and Human Services. (2012). *Preventing tobacco use among youth and young adults: A report of the Surgeon General.* Atlanta, GA: National Center for Disease Control and Prevention, National Center for Chronic Disease Prevention and Health Promotion, Office of Smoking and Health. Retrieved on June 1, 2015 from: http://www.surgeongeneral.gov/library/reports/preventing-youth-tobacco-use/exec-summary.pdf

U.S. Patent 3200819 A. (2014) Smokeless non-tobacco cigarette. Retrieved on November 30, 2014 from: http://www.google.com/patents/US3200819

Vinton, L., & Wambach, K. (2005). Alcohol and drug use among elderly people. In C. A. McNeese & D. DiNitto (Eds.), *Chemical dependency: A systems approach* (pp. 484–502). Boston: Pearson.

Weinberg, B. A., & Bealer, B. K. (2002). *The world of caffeine: The science and culture of the world's most popular drug*. New York: Routledge.

Williams, R., & Cohen, J. (2000). Substance use and misuse in psychiatric wards. *Psychiatric Bulletin, 24*, 43–46.

Windle, M., & Zucker, R. A. (2010). Reducing underage and young adult drinking: How to address critical drinking problems during this developmental period. *Alcohol Research and Health, 33*(1 & 2), 29–44.

Wright, E. M. (2001). Substance abuse in African American communities. In S. A. Ashenberg Strausser (Ed.), *Ethnocultural factors in substance abuse treatment* (pp. 31–51). New York: Guilford Press.

Wu, L-T., & Blazer, D. G. (2011). Illicit and non-medical drug use among older adults: A review. *Journal of Aging and Health, 23*(3), 481–504.

Wu, L-T., & Blazer, D. G. (2014). Substance use disorders and psychiatric comorbidity in mid and later life: A review. *International Journal of Epidemiology, 43*(2), 304–317.

Wu, L-T., Parrott, A. C., Ringwalt, C. L., Patkar, A. A., Manelli, P., & Blazer, D. G. (2009). The high prevalence of substance use disorders among recent MDMA users compared with other drug users: Implications for intervention. *Addictive Behaviors, 34*(8), 654–661.

CHAPTER

The Neurocognitive Disorders

INTRODUCTION

It is well known that people today are living longer, and it is not uncommon to find 80-, 90-, and 100-year-olds living active and productive lives. I can remember my 95-year-old aunt, the indomitable bargain hunter, looking forward to her 100th birthday so that she could get a free hearing aid from her audiologist. So how old is old? What does the concept of chronological age really mean? When is someone no longer considered productive or valuable? Beliefs about aging are maintained by language. Expressions often reserved for older people can be found in metaphors such as the "autumn years" or the "twilight of one's life." Popular characterizations that are less favorable can be seen in terms like "old codger," "curmudgeon," "doddering," or "senile." People today seem more impressed with looking young, staying healthy, and maintaining their productivity. This is often characterized as the search for the proverbial Fountain of Youth. We can find an array of lotions, creams, and surgeries all aimed at reversing the aging process. Instead of seeing aging as a normal part of the life cycle, aging is seen as something to be cured.

As people age, they continue to develop—and they experience many changes both individually and in their relationships. Their rich personal histories and experiences are a part of their "life story." During the latter part of the aging process, adults will typically retire from the workforce and may face the loss of support for their role identity. Friends and/or family have either died or moved away, prompting the loss of family relationships and friendships. As health declines, the older person is confronted with the gradual erosion of functioning. Being able to do things that one once did at a younger age becomes a source of pride. Some cultures view the elderly as productive members throughout their entire lives and treat them as treasured jewels. Others regard our elders as inconvenient burdens or nuisances.

The DSM-5 introduces the chapter on the neurocognitive disorders that was previously entitled "Delirium, Dementia, and Amnestic and Other Cognitive Disorders" in the DSM–IV (APA, 2000). This shift was made to accentuate the "neurocognitive" aspects of these disorders in order to highlight the cognitive functions associated with particular areas of the brain and represent a decline from previous levels of functioning. Only disorders whose core features are cognitive are included, and they are characterized by the syndromes of delirium as well as by major or mild neurocognitive disorders and their etiological subtypes—all of which are caused by either a general medical condition, substance use (both prescribed and illicit, and including alcohol), or a combination of these factors. Amnestic disorder became major or mild neurocognitive disorder. This chapter will review the classes of these disorders.

Delirium is characterized as a temporary condition that often follows a short and fluctuating course. People affected with delirium cannot think or reason clearly and consequently lose contact with the world around them. It includes prominent disturbances in alertness, meaning that the individual is confused and disoriented. Those suffering from delirium generally do not know what day it is or where they are. They might be able to focus on one thing, but this focus only lasts a few moments. Additionally, individuals with delirium cannot relate their present situation to anything they experienced in the past—in other words, their thinking is disconnected. One of the ways to recognize the presence of delirium is the person's tendency toward restlessness, agitated behavior, and constant moving around without purpose (specified as hyperactive). Alternatively, the person may suddenly withdraw from interacting with the outside world. They are sluggish and lethargic (specified as hypoactive). Regardless of the presentation, these behaviors are recognized by others as unusual for that person. Delirium can occur at any age, and under many different circumstances. Its effects are almost always time-limited. Once seen as a temporary condition, research is now finding that the effects of delirium can be longer-lasting and especially for older persons admitted to the hospital and in the intensive care unit (Cole, Ciampi, Belzile, & Zhong, 2009; Iwashyna, Ely, Smith, & Langa, 2010; Wilson et al., 2012).

The neurocognitive disorders (NCDs) represent a deficit in the person's cognitive functioning and they, too, are acquired rather than developmental. That is, the NCDs are those diagnoses where a person's impaired cognition has not been present since birth or very early in life but represent a decline from a previous level of functioning. These disorders are advancing, progressive, and degenerative conditions marked by a gradual deterioration of a broad range of cognitive abilities. Dementia has been incorporated under major neurocognitive disorder in the DSM-5. Typically, dementia refers to degenerative disorders in the elderly, but the DSM-5 expands the neurocognitive category to disorders seen in younger people; for example, HIV and traumatic brain injury. During the process of DSM-5 development, there was pressure to retire the designation "dementia" because of the stigma evoked by the term (Siberski, 2012). The literal Latin translation of dementia means being "without mind," but that is inaccurate. Many patients diagnosed with "dementia" maintain their faculties and awareness, and, in essence, have not lost their minds. However, dementia can be seen in the DSM-5 subtypes where the term is standard. Because of the term's long medical history and many practitioners being accustomed to the term, it was retained to ensure continuity (APA, 2013).

The U.S. population is graying rapidly. The "very old" is the fastest group, and the incidence of the neurocognitive disorders increases for those who are older than 85 (Sadock, Sadock, & Ruiz, 2014). Nearly half will have Alzheimer's disease, and it is expected that the number may quadruple by the year 2050 (Brookmeyer, Johnson, Ziegler-Graham, & Arrighi, 2007).

The neurocognitive disorders are characterized by prominent memory disturbances and central nervous system (CNS) damage, and are likely to have a protracted course. Unlike those with delirium, people are not disoriented or confused in the early stages. However, over time individuals experience a global deterioration in their intellectual, emotional, and cognitive abilities. They experience a great deal of difficulty performing tasks that require them to remember or learn things or to use information they once knew. The individual finds it increasingly difficult to maintain and sustain attention. A gradual decline in the normal richness of their thought process takes place.

Competency 7 b

The competency-based assessment is especially suited to working with people suffering from the NCDs and their families because of the integration of biological, psychological, social, environmental, and economic concerns. This integration emphasizes the unique features of each individual and his or her multiple interactions with their environment. In terms of financial cost, the NCDs (particularly major neurocognitive disorder) are extremely expensive disorders because so many people need formal services, such as nursing home care, to maintain their quality of life. This chapter will focus on the etiological subtype of Alzheimer's disease to underscore the importance of looking at its medical underpinnings.

Table 15.1 lists the neurocognitive disorders listed in the DSM-5.

Table 15.1 The DSM-5 Neurocognitive Disorders

Delirium
- Substance Intoxication/Withdrawal
- Medication-Induced
- Delirium Due to Another Medical Condition

Major or Mild Neurocognitive Disorder
- Alzheimer's Disease
- Frontotemporal Lobar Degeneration
- Lewy Body Disease
- Vascular Disease
- Traumatic Brain Injury
- Substance/Medication Induced
- HIV Infection
- Prion Disease
- Parkinson's Disease
- Huntington's Disease
- Another Medical Condition
- Multiple Etiologies
- Unspecified

We begin with a review of delirium, followed by the syndromes of mild neurocognitive disorder, major neurocognitive disorder, and their etiological subtypes.

DELIRIUM

Delirium is one of the first mental disorders to be documented in history (Berrios, 1981). People with these symptoms are described in writings more than 2,500 years old. Over time, delirium has been known by many different names, including acute confusional state, toxic psychosis, acute brain syndrome, and metabolic encephalopathy. Although the brain may be directly involved (as in the case of a seizure disorder), the actual cause of delirium is usually a process initiated outside the CNS. Delirium is known to have many causative factors, including fevers, drug allergies, chemotherapy, anesthesia, and/or the effects of drug use or an overdose of drugs. The person's impairment crosses multiple health conditions and the delirium process can include effects from hypo- or hyperactive endocrine dysfunction (thyroid disease); infections (meningitis); liver disease (hepatic encephalopathy); renal disease (uremic encephalopathy); vitamin deficiency diseases (thiamine, folic acid, nicotine acid); drug withdrawal or toxicity (anti-cholinergic agents, antipsychotic drugs, and others); poisons (carbon monoxide); and the effects of postoperative states (anesthesia). The individual may quickly switch between hyperactive and hypoactive states. The hyperactive state, often associated with medication side effects and drug withdrawal, is more commonly seen by the practitioner where the client is very active, agitated, refuses to cooperate, and exhibits mood shifts. Some may show a mixed level of activity seen as a normal level of activity but the individual's attention and awareness are disturbed.

These multiple factors highlight the interplay between cognitive functioning and biological influences and underscore the importance of making the competency-based assessment. Of particular importance to the practitioner is a thorough exploration of biological factors. For example, the practitioner considers delirium when someone has high fevers, is taking certain medications, or undergoing a surgical procedure. Because delirium can be brought on by the improper use of medications, this diagnosis can be difficult to make in older people because they are likely to be taking prescription medications more than any other age group (Cole, 2004). Most of the medical conditions are potentially treatable; therefore, delirium can often be reversed in a relatively short period of time. Delirium should be thought of as a syndrome and not a disease.

PREVAILING PATTERN

Delirium most commonly affects those who are frail and infirm. It is estimated to be found in as many as 10 to 30 percent of older adults admitted to acute care facilities, such as hospital emergency rooms (APA, 2013; Fearing & Inouye, 2009). The presence of delirium varies depending on the characteristics of the individual, the setting of care, and sensitivity to detection (Jones & Pisani, 2012). When the person is admitted to the hospital, for example, the prevalence of delirium ranges from 14 to 24 percent, and the incidence of delirium occurring during a hospitalization ranges from 6 to 56 percent of general hospital populations (APA, 2013). Delirium can be found in 15 to 53 percent of older individuals postoperatively, in 70 to 87 percent of those in intensive care, up to 60 percent of those in nursing homes or post-acute care settings, and up to 83 percent of people at the end of life (APA, 2013).

Differential Assessment

Competency 8 c

The characteristic features of delirium underscore the importance of consulting with medical professionals, as needed, to confirm the diagnosis. The disorder is characterized by impaired awareness and attention during the course of several hours or several days (Newman & Slater, 2012). Perhaps because of its transient nature (i.e., it can occur and then resolve itself quickly), delirium has been difficult to study. Estimates are lacking of the actual number of people affected. However, Sadock, Sadock, and Ruiz (2014) suggest that delirium is a common disorder and most prevalent in those who undergo general surgical procedures, cancer patients, and people with acquired immune deficiency syndrome (AIDS). While many medical conditions have been linked to the onset of delirium, it can also be caused by intoxication from drugs, toxins, and poisons; withdrawal from drugs; infections; head injuries; and various other types of trauma to the brain. Delirium often signals the presence of a medical situation or a medical emergency that is causing brain dysfunction; thus, it behooves the practitioner to intervene as soon as possible. The pattern of delirium is typically short term, and it is this feature that helps to distinguish it from the other NCDs. Delirium tends to develop quickly, and its course can vary over the day. Symptoms of delirium tend to worsen during early evening hours or at night (known as sundowning), seen as the result of fatigue or a disturbance in the brain's biological clock (Lemay & Landreville, 2010). This sundowner syndrome can also be seen when the person is in an unfamiliar and unstructured environment.

The competency-based assessment pays particular attention to the person's mental status, including clouding of consciousness (the inability to focus, sustain, or shift attention). Individuals appear confused, bewildered, or alarmed—and they may have difficulty responding to reassurance or in following directions. Impaired cognition often includes a marked disturbance of recent memory, and the individual may be unable to provide meaningful psychosocial history. The person may be disoriented to time and place; speech may have a rambling or incoherent quality; and he or she may have trouble finding words, or identifying commonly recognized objects or people. This underscores the importance of interviewing family members or friends who are familiar with the individual in order to establish a baseline of cognitive functioning.

Perceptual disturbances may also be present and may include illusions and visual hallucinations. Often, actual perceptions are misinterpreted, and ordinary noises or objects can be perceived as dangerous, threatening, and disturbing. Persecutory delusions based on sensory misperceptions are fairly common. However, once the causative factor is eliminated, the individual gradually returns to his or her prior (or premorbid) level of functioning. Delirium has a short and fluctuating course in contrast to the gradual cognitive decline that characterizes the other

NCDs. Etiology should be specified according to: substance intoxication or withdrawal, medication-induced, due to another condition, or due to multiple etiologies.

Associated features include the following:

- Symptom length—This can be seen as acute (lasting a few hours or days) or persistent (lasting weeks or months).
- Activity level—The person may appear hyperactive, hypoactive (i.e., sluggish and lethargic), or show a mixed level of activity; for the person who shows minimal responses or is hard to engage, the behavior should be considered as severe inattention (APA, 2013).
- Emotional disturbances—Periods of anxiety, fear, depression, irritability (the individual striking out), belligerence (attempting to flee), or euphoria (resulting in being injured; for example, falling out of a bed) can also occur.

The following case vignette provides an example of delirium.

CASE THE CASE OF SALVADOR CULLOTTO

Adeline Cullotto brought her husband Salvador to Memorial General Hospital's emergency room. She entered the reception area pleading, "Please, please can someone help my husband? He's talking out of his head, and I don't know where else to go!" The social worker on duty attempted to calm down Mrs. Cullotto, and she asked, "Can you tell me what's been happening to your husband?"

Mrs. Cullotto responded, "Well, Sal doesn't know his name, he doesn't know who I am, and he's talking out of his head. He seems very confused. On top of all that, he has not slept a wink all night. I'm really so worried about him. He's terribly frail right now. Do you think he's becoming senile?" The social worker said that she needed more information and asked Mrs. Cullotto, "What has been happening recently or differently that might explain your husband's current behavior?"

Mrs. Cullotto replied, "Well, Sal does have some anemia—you know, low blood counts." After a moment of thought, she replied, "Oh you mean like Sal having chemotherapy treatments for his chronic lymphocytic leukemia? Now that you mention it, Sal's doctor changed his treatment several days ago, but Sal never had any problems before with medication changes. You know, come to think of it, Sal is really out of it. While we were driving over here, he whispered to me, 'The doctor is taking blood out of one arm and putting it right back into my other arm.' Sal made me promise to tell the proper authorities—whoever that is—he says to me not to let them charge us double."

The social worker asked Mrs. Cullotto to explain further. Shaking her head, Mrs. Cullotto continued, "Sal insists that the doctor is selling his blood back. He takes blood from one arm and then puts it right back into the other arm. He doesn't want to let him get away with that." She sighed, "I've never seen Sal like this before. That's really a screwy idea, and I don't know what's gotten into him. He absolutely loves Dr. Canner. He's been taking care of Sal for years. Sal has never been in remission for his CLL but when his white blood cell count reached 100,000, Dr. Canner decided it was time to do something." Mrs. Cullotto shared that she and Sal had been married for 55 years, both are retired (she was a hairdresser, and he was a factory worker). They have one son who lives nearby.

When the emergency room social worker turned to Mr. Cullotto, she asked a series of questions about his memory and orientation. "Sir, what is your name? Do you know where you are right now? Do you know what today's date is? How old are you? What is your wife's name? Do you know what you ate for breakfast this morning? How are you feeling?" The social worker wrote in his progress notes, "Mr. Cullotto appears unable to focus, sustain, or shift his attention enough to answer the questions posed to him. His attention wanders, and he is distracted by room sounds around him. He is unable to follow instructions, complete a thought, or reply fully to questions posed to him. His speech has a rambling quality and is difficult to follow."

The emergency room social worker reassured Mrs. Cullotto and promised to speak with Mr. Cullotto's doctor. Mr. Cullotto was subsequently hospitalized. When the social worker followed up with the Cullottos after admission, she learned that Mr. Cullotto's chemotherapy protocol had indeed been changed. Reading his hospital chart, she noticed that Mr. Cullotto was taking dexamethasone as a part of his treatment. His delirium was a severe but rare side effect. The social worker thought, "Geez, something new to learn every day. That's one of the reasons why I really love working in a hospital."

Two days after admission, Mr. Cullotto's symptoms began to lessen, and he was discharged three days later. Upon discharge, Mrs. Cullotto was overheard commenting to her husband, "Sal, it's just so wonderful to see you back to your usual self. You really weren't you, and I was so scared that you were starting to get Alzheimer's. Let's go home and order a pizza! And then we'll rent that Avatar movie you've been wanting to see ... and I want you around for the sequel, too."

SALVADOR CULLOTTO'S DSM DIAGNOSIS IS AS FOLLOWS:
Dexamethasone-induced delirium, acute, hyperactive
Chronic Lymphocytic Leukemia

Competency 7 a

ASSESSMENT SUMMARY The practitioner collects, organizes, and interprets a range of client data in order to assess for delirium. The vignette is intended to illustrate the presenting symptoms, and thus the interactions of the biological, psychological, and social elements in Sal Cullotto's life are not illustrated. The key assessment issue for delirium is the recognition of causative factors. A case in point is when the social worker asked Mrs. Cullotto about the strength of her husband's belief that his blood was being sold back to him. The features of Mr. Cullotto's delirium—features in contrast to those of the neurocognitive disorders—were that they had an acute beginning, a relatively brief duration, and the minute-to-minute shifting of his mental status. Barlow and Durand (2014) point to the increasing concern by medical professionals about the occurrence of delirium, especially in view of the increased number of people who are living longer. Jacobi and colleagues (2002) recommend that the assessment for delirium be included as one of the "vital signs" (along with heartbeat, breathing rate, temperature, and blood pressure) that physicians should routinely check into when seeing older adults. Unfortunately, the diagnosis of delirium is all too often missed in medical settings, especially for those who are quiet and subdued as opposed to those who are agitated and confused (Eisenbach et al., 2010).

The NCDs can be distinguished from delirium by the absence of confusion, but the two conditions may occur concurrently. Assessment for delirium should distinguish it from other mental disorders that present with similar features (e.g., confusion, disorientation, and perceptual disturbances); for instance, brief psychotic disorder, schizophrenia, schizophreniform disorder, and other psychotic disorders as well as bipolar and depressive disorders with psychotic features.

Intoxication or withdrawal from many drugs of abuse can also cause these symptoms, but the assessment of substance-induced delirium should not be made unless the symptoms exceed those that would be expected during typical intoxication or withdrawal. When schizophrenia is present, the individual's hallucinations and apparent confusion can resemble a delirium, but the individual does not have the disorientation, memory loss, and (daily) sleep disturbance seen in delirium. Those with generalized anxiety disorder may present with agitation, but without disorientation, confusion, and memory loss. Those with malingering and factitious disorder do not have another medical condition (or substance) that is related to the cognitive disturbance seen in delirium.

The various types of delirium listed in the DSM-5 (APA, 2013) are those that are substance-induced (intoxication or withdrawal and including complications from prescribed medication), medication-induced, due to another medical condition, and have multiple etiologies. This chapter focuses on medication-induced delirium as it is commonly seen by the practitioner, especially those who work in a hospital or other medically related settings. The DSM also offers the diagnoses of Other Specified Delirium (where not all the required criteria are met for the diagnosis of delirium) and Unspecified Delirium (where not all the required criteria are met for the diagnosis of delirium including presentations where there is insufficient information to make the diagnosis).

If the delirium is caused by a medication, the practitioner should note the name of the medication when coding the delirium. In Sal's case, he is reacting to his dexamethasone medication. His medical condition, chronic lymphocytic leukemia, is also listed. As another example, if a client has delirium due to congestive heart failure, it would first be noted as Delirium Due to Congestive Heart Failure and then the medical condition listed separately as Congestive Heart Failure.

Competency 7 a

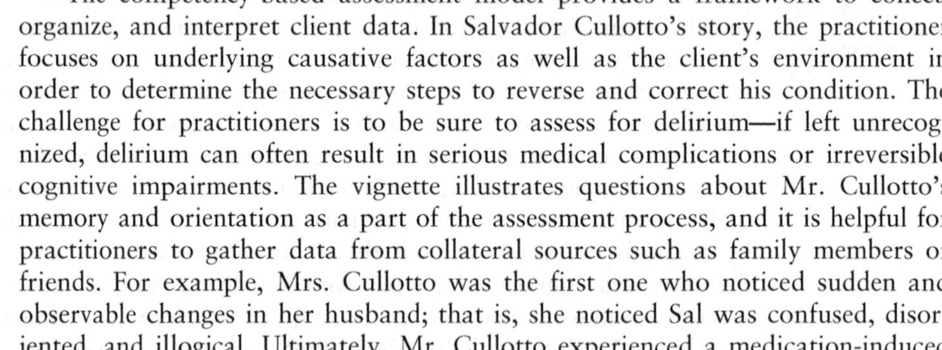

The competency-based assessment model provides a framework to collect, organize, and interpret client data. In Salvador Cullotto's story, the practitioner focuses on underlying causative factors as well as the client's environment in order to determine the necessary steps to reverse and correct his condition. The challenge for practitioners is to be sure to assess for delirium—if left unrecognized, delirium can often result in serious medical complications or irreversible cognitive impairments. The vignette illustrates questions about Mr. Cullotto's memory and orientation as a part of the assessment process, and it is helpful for practitioners to gather data from collateral sources such as family members or friends. For example, Mrs. Cullotto was the first one who noticed sudden and observable changes in her husband; that is, she noticed Sal was confused, disoriented, and illogical. Ultimately, Mr. Cullotto experienced a medication-induced delirium in reaction to his chemotherapy treatment. Once his treatment was adjusted, Sal returned to his prior level of functioning.

Let's now turn to a review the neurocognitive disorders.

THE NEUROCOGNITIVE DISORDERS

Including the neurocognitive disorders (NCDs) in the DSM-5 acknowledges the emerging literature that recognizes the neuropathology underlying these disorders emerges well before the onset of clinical symptoms (Blazer, 2013). Unlike any of the other disorders included in the DSM-5, the pathology and often the etiology of neurocognitive disorders can often be determined. The cognitive decline from a previous level of performance that characterizes the NCDs is not just the person's sense of the loss of his or her cognitive abilities, but also that it can be noticed by others. Additionally, this decline can be tested by standardized cognitive assessments.

The DSM-5 elaborates the criteria for the neurocognitive disorders based on key cognitive domains and includes a table listing each domain, symptoms or observations of impairments that can be seen in a person's everyday experiences, and examples of assessments (APA, 2003, pp. 593–595). These neurocognitive domains are summarized in Table 15.2, including examples of (major and mild) impairments that can be seen in practice.

TABLE 15.2 COGNITIVE DOMAINS, SPECIFIC FUNCTIONS, AND EXAMPLES OF MAJOR AND MILD IMPAIRMENTS

Cognitive Domains	Specific Functions	Examples of Major and Mild Impairments
Complex attention—The ability to sustain focus.	This includes sustained attention or the person's ability to pay attention over time; Allocating and dividing attention; Selective attention or the ability to resist distraction; and Processing speed or the ability to capture information, process it, and respond.	Major: The person experiences increased difficulty in environments with multiple stimuli (television, radio, conversation); is easily distracted by competing events in the environment; and input must be restricted and simplified. Mild: Normal tasks can take longer than before for the person; others begin to find errors in routine tasks; work needs more double-checking than before; thinking is easier for the person when he or she is not competing with other things like listening to the radio, watching television, or conversation.
Executive function—The ability to think abstractly and to plan initiate, sequence, monitor, and stop complex behavior, allows a person to access information, think about solutions, and to implement these solutions.	This includes the ability to plan; Make decisions; Working memory or the ability to hold information for a brief period of time and to manipulate it; Responding to feedback; Being able to benefit from feedback and correcting errors; Overriding habits/inhibition (for instance this might be the person who looks away from the direction indicated by an arrow); and Mental flexibility or being able to shift between thinking about two different concepts.	Major: The individual abandons complex projects; needs to focus on one task at a time; depends on others to plan significant activities of daily living or even to make decisions. Mild: The individual increases his or her efforts necessary to complete the multiple phases of projects; experiences difficulty returning to a task that has been interrupted, for instance by a phone call or a visitor; may complain about the extra effort needed to organize, plan, and make decisions; may avoid large gatherings finding them to be more taxing or less enjoyable due to the increased effort required to follow shifting conversations.

TABLE 15.2 COGNITIVE DOMAINS, SPECIFIC FUNCTIONS, AND EXAMPLES OF MAJOR AND MILD IMPAIRMENTS (CONTINUED)

Cognitive Domains	Specific Functions	Examples of Major and Mild Impairments
Learning and memory—The process in which information is encoded, stored, and retrieved.	This addresses immediate memory; Recent memory (including the ability to freely recall, cued recall, and recognition memory); and Very long-term memory. Note: Sometimes immediate memory is considered under the working memory seen as part of the person's executive functions.	Major: The person may now repeat him- or herself in conversations; cannot keep track of a short list of items when going out shopping or planning the day; requires numerous reminders to attend to a task at hand. Mild: The person shows difficulty recalling events; relies more and more on making lists or checking on a calendar; needs occasional reminders (or re-reading) to keep track of the different characters in a movie (or in a book); occasionally may repeat him- or herself over a few weeks to the same person; loses track of bills that have already been paid.
Language—In particular, expressive language, or one's ability to communicate with others using language or how one expresses his or her wants and needs; and receptive language, which is the understanding of language "input" or the understanding of both words and gestures.	This comprises naming; Word finding (such as proficiency in identifying objects or pictures); Fluency (such as being able to name as many things as possible in a specific category); Grammar; and Syntax or the rules of grammar that dictate how words are combined into phrases, sentences, and paragraphs.	Major: The individual has significant difficulties with expressive (or receptive) language; often uses general terms such as, "You know what I mean," and prefers general pronouns instead of names to disguise language problems; with very severe impairment, the individual may not remember the names of family and closer friends; shows errors in language or in using peculiar words; errors in grammar become evident; and in spontaneity of output; uses stereotypic speech; ecolalia (both immediate or the voluntary repetition of words or phrases just spoken by others). Mild: The individual has noticeable difficultly finding words; may substitute general terms for the specifics; may avoid using the particular names of acquaintances; shows grammatical errors involving the subtle omission or incorrect use of prepositions, auxiliary verbs, and the like.

Table 15.2 Cognitive Domains, Specific Functions, and Examples of Major and Mild Impairments (continued)

Cognitive Domains	Specific Functions	Examples of Major and Mild Impairments
Perceptual-motor—The ability to receive, interpret, and respond successfully to sensory information; more specifically, perception means to know or to interpret information, and motor refers to output or responsive movement.	This includes visual perception or the set of skills used to gather visual information from the environment and integrating them with other senses; Visuoconstructional, or the abilities that involve the coordination of fine motor skills with visuospatial abilities, usually in the reproduction of geometric figures (for instance, those who have difficulties with visuoconstruction and spatial abilities often struggle with daily tasks); Perceptual-motor, which is any skill involving the interaction and integration of perceptual processes and voluntary physical movement (such as the ability to insert pegs into a slotted board); Praxis, which refers to the act of engaging, applying, exercising, realizing, or practicing ideas; and Gnosis or perceptual awareness and recognition.	Major: The individual experiences significant difficulties with activities that were previously familiar to them (such as how to use cooking utensils despite having been a good cook, or driving despite having a drivers' license for many years), or navigating in familiar environments; becomes confused more often at dusk, especially when the early evening shadows and lowering levels of light can change perceptions. Mild: The person may need to rely more on maps for travel to familiar places or other directions; uses notes and follows others to get to a new location; may become "lost" or turned around when not concentrating; less precise in parking abilities; or shows greater effort for spatial tasks such as sewing, knitting, carpentry, or putting something together from picture directions.
Social Cognition—Focuses on how people process, store, and apply information about others and social situations.	This consists of recognition of emotions; and Theory of mind, or the ability to consider another person's mental state, thoughts, desires, etc.	Major: The individual's behavior is clearly out of the "acceptable" social range; he or she is insensitive to social standards of modesty in dress, or in conversations around political, religious, or sexual topics; focuses excessively on a topic despite disinterest or direct feedback from others; displays behavioral intent without regard for safety; typically shows little insight around these changes. Mild: There are subtle changes in the person's behavior or attitude often characterized as changes in personality—that is, the person is less able to read social cues or the facial expressions of others, shows decreased empathy, becomes increasingly extraverted (or introverted), displays decreased inhibition, episodic apathy, or restlessness.

The neurocognitive disorders generally develop much later in life and do not occur exclusively in the context of delirium. While the schizophrenia spectrum and other psychotic disorders or the bipolar disorders can have an effect on cognitive and memory functions, they are not included in the NCD classification because the person's loss of cognitive function is not the main (or causal) symptom.

Competency 8 c

Except for delirium, the first step in the assessment process is to differentiate among a person's normal neurocognitive function—mild neurocognitive disorder (or mild NCD), which provides the option of classifying less disabling symptoms; or major neurocognitive disorder (major NCD or dementia). To begin, clients with symptoms of cognitive impairments should be referred to a physician for a complete medical and neurological assessment. Practitioners who are in settings where their clients are primarily diagnosed with an NCD usually work very closely with other professionals in the medical community around assessment and related treatment planning.

Differential Assessment

Having taken a look at the cognitive domains for the NCDs and examples of what they can look like in practice, we now turn to a review of the disorders by comparing the symptom picture for major NCD and mild NCD distinguished in Table 15.3.

The primary feature of both disorders is an acquired cognitive decline in one or more cognitive domains (i.e., attention, executive functions, learning and memory, language, perception, and social cognition). This decline is not just a sense of loss of one's cognitive abilities, but can also be observed by others. This decline causes significant interference in a person's everyday independence in major NCD and less so in mild NCD. Although distinguishing mild from major impairment may, in some instances, rely on the practitioner's judgment, the DSM-5 does make an objective distinction. Specifically, mild NCD requires a "modest" cognitive decline to the extent that it does not interfere with the person's independence in everyday activities; for instance, taking medications as prescribed or paying bills on time. In contrast, the cognitive decline in major NCD meets criteria when there is "significant" impairment that is evident or reported by those who know the individual and interferes with independence to the extent that assistance is required. The distinction between mild and major NCD relies heavily on observable behavior but can also be tested by a cognitive assessment, such as a neuropsychological test battery.

The second step in the assessment process is to consider the cause and assign an etiological subtype. When previously diagnosing dementia (now considered major NCD), practitioners could use a number of different criteria sets in order to designate whether the disorder was of the Alzheimer's type, vascular dementia, or substance-induced dementia. According to the DSM-5 (APA, 2013), vascular NCD and NCD due to Alzheimer's disease have remained, and new separate criteria are now presented to further refine the diagnoses. They include: due to frontotemporal NCD, Lewy body disease, traumatic brain injury,

TABLE 15.3 THE SYMPTOM PICTURE FOR THE MAJOR AND MILD NEUROCOGNITIVE DISORDERS

Major Neurocognitive Disorder	Mild Neurocognitive Disorder
The person shows evidence of *significant* cognitive decline from a previous level of performance in one (or more) domains such as complex attention, executive function, or those mental processes that help connect past experiences with present actions such as the learning, memory, language, perceptual-motor, or social cognition domains as evidenced by: • A *significant* decline in cognitive function (as considered by the individual, or one who knows the individual such as a relative, the practitioner, or close friend). • *Significant* impairment in cognitive performance (and preferably documented by standardized testing).	Evidence of a *modest* decline from a previous level of performance in one (or more) domains such as complex attention, executive function, learning, memory, language, perceptual-motor, or social cognition evidenced by: • A *modest* decline in cognitive function (as considered by the individual, or one who knows the individual such as a relative, the practitioner, or close friend). • *Modest* impairment in cognitive performance (and preferably documented by standardized testing).
Cognitive deficits interfere with the person's independence in everyday activities.	Cognitive deficits *do not* interfere with the person's independence in everyday activities.
Cognitive deficits do not (exclusively) occur in the context of delirium.	Cognitive deficits do not (exclusively) occur in the context of delirium.
Cognitive deficits are not better explained by another mental disorder.	Cognitive deficits are not better explained by another mental disorder.
Presence or absence of behavioral disturbance is considered; if present, specify the disturbance such as psychotic symptoms, mood disturbance, agitation, apathy. Also consider current severity ranging from mild, moderate to severe.	Presence or absence of behavioral disturbance is considered; if present, specify the disturbance such as psychotic symptoms, mood disturbance, agitation, apathy.

substance/medication use, HIV infection, Prion disease, Parkinson's disease, and Huntington's disease. Another medical condition, multiple etiologies, and unspecified NCD are also considered as diagnoses. Each subgroup can be further divided into mild or major degrees of cognitive impairment on the basis of cognitive decline, especially around the ability to perform functions of daily living independently.

The DSM makes a distinction between a probable and a possible diagnosis. Only when there is tangible data known about the diagnosis is the diagnosis indicated as "probable" (and the additional medical condition is listed). The practitioner uses the term "possible" when he or she is the first to recognize the disorder but does not have evidence to support the medical diagnosis. In this instance, the additional medical condition is not listed.

Let's review a few additional distinctions between the mild and major neurocognitive disorders.

MILD NEUROCOGNITIVE DISORDER (MILD NCD)

Mild NCD was previously the diagnosis of cognitive disorder not otherwise specified in the DSM-IV (APA, 2000). The DSM-5 diagnosis goes beyond the symptoms normally associated with aging. While this is a new diagnosis in the DSM, it is believed that it will help to bridge the gap by highlighting those with a modest level of decline most commonly seen, for example, in individuals with the early stages of Alzheimer's disease, HIV, and traumatic brain injury. Mild NCD describes a level of decline to the extent where the person is seen as engaging in compensatory strategies and making the associated accommodations in order to be able to remain independent in contrast to the more debilitating decline seen in major NCD. However, to be diagnosed with mild NCD, there must be changes that impact cognitive functioning. It may be related to learning and memory, or it could be related to subtle changes in an individual's personality.

MAJOR NEUROCOGNITIVE DISORDER

The new category of major NCD is very similar to the earlier DSM diagnosis of dementia and pulls together a set of disorders from the DSM-IV (2000), specifically dementia and amnestic disorder. Similar to mild NCD, the specific etiological subtypes need to be identified when making the diagnosis. However, major NCD looks to a consideration of severity. Mild severity considers a person's difficulties with the activities of daily living (ADLs), such as the ability to manage money or doing housework. Moderate severity looks to the person's difficulties with ADLs such as being able to eat without help or dressing. Severity is specified when the person is fully dependent.

PREVAILING PATTERN

The prevalence rates of NCD vary according to the person's age and etiological subtype but overall, the disorder primarily affects the older population. The prevalence rates for dementia, which is consistent with major NCD, are approximately 1 to 2 percent at 65 years of age and reaches to as high as 30 percent by age 85 (APA, 2013). Prevalence rates are less clear for mild NCD as the person's impairment in cognitive functioning must he high enough to seek care. As such, prevalence among older individuals is fairly variable, ranging from 2 to 10 percent for those 65 years of age and increases to a range of 5 to 25 percent by age 85 (APA, 2013).

For individuals with a subtype that occurs across the life span, prevalence rates are more likely to be available. This chapter will focus on the Alzheimer's type of NCD. Alzheimer's disease is the most common disorder, with the percentage among those with the dementias ranging from about 60 percent to over 90 percent. Among the U.S. population, approximately 7 percent of those diagnosed with Alzheimer's disease are between ages 65 and 74 years, 53 percent are between ages 75 and 84 years, and 40 percent are 85 years and older (APA, 2013).

Our case illustration will highlight major NCD due to probable Alzheimer's disease to underscore the importance of looking at the medical underpinnings. The practitioner will more commonly encounter this subtype in practice. The second most common NCD the practitioner can expect to see is due to vascular disease.

NEUROCOGNITIVE DISORDER DUE TO ALZHEIMER'S DISEASE

When German psychiatrist Alois Alzheimer first described this disease in 1906, it was considered to be relatively rare. Perhaps this was because life expectancy at the turn of the century was 47 years as opposed to the current figure of 77 years. Of those with an NCD, half are found to have Alzheimer's-type, which translates to more than 5 million Americans (Alzheimer's Association, 2010). In some forms, people who are in their 40s or 50s can be affected. However Alzheimer's disease usually appears in individuals who are in their 60s and 70s. The disease is more prevalent among women and can be found in all ethnic groups, with slightly lower rates seen among American Indians (Craig & Murphy, 2009; Weiner, Hynan, Beckly, Koepsell, & Kukull, 2007).

There is no foolproof way to diagnose Alzheimer's disease (AD), other than perhaps after death at autopsy, but medical science has made several critical discoveries about how the disease affects and destroys the brain. For instance a project called the Alzheimer's Disease Neuroimaging Initiative (ADNI) uses sophisticated brain scans along with new chemical tracers to help clinicians identify the disease before the significant declines in cognitive abilities become evident (Weiner et al., 2010).

The amyloid cascade hypothesis provides a biological explanation of Alzheimer's disease. While many questions are still unanswered, researchers believe this theory best explains the cause of Alzheimer's disease (Reitz, 2012). Similar to the way cholesterol builds up on the walls of blood vessels and restricts blood supply, deposits of amyloid proteins are believed to cause cell death associated with Alzheimer's (Hales, Yudofsky, & Gabbard, 2010). During the late 1980s, scientists isolated and identified a molecule called amyloid precursor protein (APP), which is a normal protein produced by healthy neurons. The human body produces at least three enzymes—dubbed alpha, beta, and gamma secretase—that eventually cleave APP into shorter forms. The exact purpose of these enzymes is not yet known, and their specific function remains to be demonstrated conclusively (Nunan & Small, 2000). What is clear is that these secretase inhibitors can build up in the fluid surrounding neurons to form plaques. At one time, the medical community believed that individuals with Alzheimer's disease produced too many of the enzymes known as A-beta, but that has not proved to be the case; in fact, people with Alzheimer's disease produce A-beta at the same rate as healthy people.

Researchers reexamined the issue and found it was not the process of buildup in the fluid surrounding the neurons, but a matter of how these fluids are disposed. In a healthy person, A-beta usually dissolves after it drifts away from the cell—but scientists now find that sometimes A-beta folds into insoluble forms called fibrils, which stick together and form plaques. We all produce some plaques as we go through the aging process. However, problems begin when these plaques trigger an inflammatory response in the brain, generating toxic agents called free radicals, which fight off infections. The free radicals kill off indiscriminately both the fibrils and healthy neurons. Much of the current work in Alzheimer's research involves looking at how a host of agents (such as enzymes, vitamins, heredity, environmental factors, the use of anti-inflammatory drugs, and hormones) play a role in the onset of this disease. Treatment is aimed at preventing the destruction of healthy neurons while stalling the production of A-beta enzymes.

Recent research regarding brain functioning suggests that several important mental functions are localized in specific areas of the brain and that injury to these areas can result in certain types of cognitive impairment. Our understanding of the brain has greatly improved. We know the brain is divided into many different components, but in order to do its job it must function as a well-integrated system. Clearly, Alzheimer's disease disrupts that functioning. The essential feature of the resulting neurocognitive disorder is deterioration of memory, awareness, thought, and perception—which affects how a person remembers and understands language and how they learn. When that happens, the person loses interest in others and becomes more socially isolated. As the disease progresses, a person can become agitated or confused, depressed, anxious, or even combative. The overall impact on a person's life is tremendous.

Differential Assessment

The practitioner considers a neurocognitive disorder when the cognitive decline has been present for at least several months and has been shown not to be a manifestation of a fluctuating course of delirium (discussed earlier). A condition such as Alzheimer's disease often causes degeneration across many areas of the brain, producing a mosaic of cognitive problems (Albert et al., 2011). Age-related cognitive decline is an important consideration when making a competency-based assessment, in part because many diseases that cause brain deterioration more than likely affect the elderly.

The following must be present for a diagnosis of major or mild NCD due to Alzheimer's disease (APA, 2013):

- There is an insidious onset and gradual progression of cognitive impairment.
    - For Major NCD, two or more cognitive domains are impaired (unlike the other NCDs) and impaired ADLs.
    - For Mild NCD, one or more cognitive domains are impaired and ADLs are intact.
- The disorder is not better explained by cerebrovascular disease, another neurodegenerative or cerebrovascular disease, or another neurological or systemic disease, or to a condition likely contributing to a person's cognitive decline.
- Also consider:
    - Probable neurocognitive disorder due to Alzheimer's disease where there is:
        - Evidence of AD genetic mutation or
        - All three of the following: (a) impairment of memory and in one other cognitive domain; (b) progressive, gradual decline; and (c) no other possible etiology—otherwise, consider a "possible" diagnosis.
    - Possible neurocognitive disorder due to Alzheimer's disease is diagnosed if there is no evidence of Alzheimer's gene but all three factors exist; that is, decline in memory and learning; progressive, gradual decline; and no evidence of other etiologies.

As discussed above, major NCD due to Alzheimer's disease is the reduction or impairment of intellect, emotion, and behavioral functioning severe enough to be detrimental in social, occupational, and other important areas in life. It is almost as if the person has lost his or her "road map of life." Initially, the individual experiences difficulty with short-term memory and, to a lesser degree, long-term memory. For example, when short-term memory problems do occur, people forget where they left their purse or wallet, forget to turn off the stove (sometimes with food still cooking), or forget to lock the doors before going to bed. At the outset, these problems experienced with long-term memory are considered less severe; for example, the individual gets "lost" and cannot remember where he or she lives or how to get home.

Family members or others who are close to a person with Alzheimer's may talk about personality changes that can become apparent in a number of ways, such as a lack of appropriate grooming in someone who has generally been fastidious about his or her appearance. The individual might begin to wear clothing inside out (or no clothing at all), display a major decline in personal hygiene including bowel and urinary incontinence, cease oral care or shaving, and overall be unable to care for him- or herself. It is generally this loss of "good judgment" and lapse of previously "normal" behavior that prompts family members to seek help. In the author's clinical practice, a family member described her mother as someone who, at one time, "could vie for the regalness of being the Queen of England. She always had such impeccable table manners and social graces. Now mother eats butter with her fingers, and throws the bread on the floor or tries to stuff peas up her nose." It is often this heartbreak of seeing loved ones unable to sustain their former standard of behavior that is so difficult for the family to endure. Family members often describe the heartbreak of losing their loved one while having to live with the progressive decay of his or her appropriate judgment. In some cases, a person once described as easygoing and friendly may become extremely rigid, anxious, hostile, or aggressive.

Social work practitioners often encounter families struggling with caring for their loved one at home. Having to make the difficult decision to institutionalize a beloved family member with an NCD due to Alzheimer's disease usually occurs when there is an excessive amount of nighttime activity, a history of falls and injuries, immobility or difficulty in walking, incontinence, and a situation of being cared for by a female, usually a relative who is not physically able to handle someone with limited capacities. Other difficulties caretakers are faced with can include depression, emotional distress, financial worries, loss of work, and family conflict.

Undoubtedly, we can expect NCD due to Alzheimer's disease to increase in older adults as a result of the increase of "baby boomers" entering the ranks of the elderly. Making a competency-based assessment is vitally important for both clients and their families in helping to understand the personality changes that will occur. Even though only one person in a relationship is likely to have NCD due to Alzheimer's disease at any given time, the disease really has two or more victims—the affected individual's partner, the caretaker, and the family.

During the early stage of Alzheimer's, a person's cognitive deterioration is slow but becomes more rapid during the middle and late stages (Sperling et al., 2011).

Practitioners must be able to recognize the various warning signs of Alzheimer's and they are summarized as follows:

The Early Stage

- Memory loss (recent) and other cognitive impairments begin to affect the individual's performance
- Loss of initiative
- Mood or personality changes (e.g., avoiding family or friends)
- Confusion about current circumstances (e.g., being at home)
- Difficulty performing usual chores
- The person is able to compensate and continues to function independently

The Middle Stage

- Increasing problems recognizing family and/or friends
- Escalating memory loss and confusion
- Increase in making repetitive statements
- Occasional muscle jerking or twitching
- Difficulty in reading, writing, or understanding numbers
- Problems thinking logically
- Difficulty finding "the right words"
- Needs close supervision (e.g., may wander away from home)
- Becomes suspicious, irritable, or restless
- Difficulty with bathing and/or self-care
- Changes become more marked and disabling, and the person becomes more dependent on caregivers for daily activities

The Late Stage

- Difficulty swallowing/feeding self and maintaining weight
- Does not recognize their family members or lifelong friends
- Does not distinguish familiar everyday objects (e.g., how to use a fork or spoon)
- Becomes incontinent (unable to control bladder and/or bowels)
- Unable to care for self
- Difficulty communicating (e.g., cannot speak or respond to others)
- Complete personality deterioration, physical problems are dominant, and the person is totally dependent on others for even the most basic activities.

The pathophysiological process of AD is thought to begin several years before the actual diagnosis is made (Albert et al., 2011). As AD progresses, the person's memory loss gets worse, and the changes in other cognitive domains are evident. Now it takes longer to complete normal daily tasks. People are often diagnosed in the early stage. In this stage, damage occurs in areas of the brain that control language, reasoning, sensory processing, and conscious thought. By the late stage, plaques and tangles have spread throughout the brain, and brain tissue has shrunk significantly. In the late stage, individuals are not able to communicate and are completely dependent on others for care. At the very end, the person may be in bed for most or all of the time as their body begins to shut down (National Institute on Aging, 2014).

The following vignette illustrates NCD due to Alzheimer's disease.

CASE THE CASE OF SARAH JEAN PFOHL

"Mr. Pfohl, why don't you follow me and I'll show you our nursing home facility," said the social worker.

"You know, I'm still not so sure about putting Sarah Jean in here," Mr. Pfohl responded. "Actually, I'm really sick about it. This June we'll be married 55 years. You know a lot of people can't say that these days." Mr. Pfohl followed the social worker down a hallway. "Sarah Jean and I promised each other if ever the other one should ever 'get so bad' as to need a nursing home—well, we just wouldn't do it. We promised we'd do everything in our power to stay at home together, but—" Mr. Pfohl started to cry. "Things are just so terrible right now ... I hired a very nice woman who took wonderful care of my wife 6 days a week. She'd cook meals, bathe Sarah Jean—she provided 24-hour care—but then one of her own relatives got sick, and she ... I just can't take care of Sarah Jean by myself. I can't even lift her in or out of the bathtub." He stopped walking and braced himself on the handrail. Looking at the floor, he continued in a softer voice. "But the worst part was changing her diapers. I mean, how much can a person deal with? I can't stand to see the one person I love most in this world reduced to being ... a baby. It's just too much ... just too much. She's not the Sarah Jean I knew. She doesn't recognize our children, the grandchildren, her only great-grandchild—sometimes she doesn't even know ME!"

The social worker found a quiet corner in the home's formal parlor away from the activity of the residents and staff. She invited Mr. Pfohl to sit down and asked him to talk about what made him decide to visit the nursing home.

Mr. Pfohl related, "We had it pretty good for many years. Sure, we had rough times, but mostly times were good for us. We were just two young kids when we married in 1929. Neither one of us finished high school, but not many people did in those days. I left school, got a job—and a Model-T Ford—in that order," he chuckled, as his eyes brightened. "Sarah Jean was the only girl in her family, and the third of four children. She was like a mother to the other kids. Their parents died with the swine flu epidemic in 1918—Sarah Jean was still a baby herself, but she was determined that she and her brothers wouldn't be separated—and by golly they weren't! Once she made up her mind, everybody better watch out."

The social worker listened attentively, and encouraged Mr. Pfohl to go on.

"We've been married almost 56 years, and for the most part it's been a good marriage. We have two wonderful children. They both live nearby. Our daughter is divorced, but she's doing okay. She has three grown children of her own—and just last summer finished her master's degree in teaching. On top of that, she's a world-class musician." Mr. Pfohl beamed. "We've always been proud of her accomplishments."

The social worker asked about the Pfohl's other children.

"Our son is a doctor who married his high school sweetheart. At first, we didn't approve of their relationship, but as time went on we could see they really were meant for each other. Now they've got three children and are also doing very well. You know, since Sarah Jean's been having problems, the daughter-in-law has been very helpful bringing food over and whatnot. But how much can we expect her to take care of us? Our grandchildren are wonderful, too—but everybody's got their own lives to live. Me? I don't need much anyway."

The issue of the Pfohls' financial situation had not been mentioned, so the social worker inquired.

"I forgot to mention that Sarah Jean got a real estate broker's license after the kids were grown and out of the house. I won't lie, I wasn't too thrilled with her working outside of the home. You know, in those days ... but she was stubborn about this. She said she was tired of cleaning the house, and she only wanted to sell real estate for pin money. Ha!" Mr. Pfohl laughed. "She did a pretty good job, too. In a few years, Sarah Jean had three or four other people working for her. She'd buy fixer-uppers, do whatever was needed to make them nice, then she'd sell them for a nice tidy profit. Her commissions always went back into buying other houses. I tell you, she had some nose for business. We're lucky we don't have any financial worries, but that's because of Sarah Jean—it sure isn't because of what I earned in my seat

CASE THE CASE OF SARAH JEAN PFOHL (CONTINUED)

cover business. She's the brains in our family." He lowered his head, and his voice followed. "That's why her being this way is so hard for me."

After a few moments, Mr. Pfohl said softly, "These were supposed to be our golden years. We used to have lots of friends, and we went out a couple of times a week. I guess I really don't blame anybody, it's just. ..."

Sensing a need to explore other areas, the social worker gently shifted the conversation to the kinds of things that told Mr. Pfohl something was happening with his wife—something that was different from her usual behavior.

"I guess I knew things weren't going right when Sarah Jean forgot where she left her purse, or when she left the stove on. Five or six years ago, I didn't think too much of it, but then it got worse. A couple of times she almost burned the house down! After that, I wouldn't let her cook anymore." He removed his glasses and wiped his hand across his eyes. "She'd forget who she was talking to on the telephone, or else didn't remember how to get home when she went out on errands. Two times the police picked her up for driving crazy. I had to promise them I wouldn't let her drive anymore. Sometimes I think I was wrong for trying to let her continue to be normal. She's used to going out to show houses and all that—and even after she realized she couldn't do that anymore, sometimes I'd just give her the car keys and hope for the best. I just didn't want to face the truth that she was changing. She isn't the Sarah Jean I knew—I've lost my best friend."

The social worker waited a moment for Mr. Pfohl to gather himself, then asked him to describe his wife's behavior in a little more detail.

"Sometimes she's as placid as a lamb, and other times she gets so agitated that she physically lashes out at others trying to help bathe or take care of her. A couple of times she accused me of stealing her money. A few times she got so riled up that I'd give her a little change purse filled with dollar bills. Just being able to touch or feel the money seemed to calm her down. Now, if she tells me I took her money, I show her the change purse and she quiets right down again." Mr. Pfohl's eyes again filled with tears, and he again took his glasses off, this time to clean them with a well-worn wrinkled handkerchief.

"We used to go to the all the spring training baseball games; we knew all the players—especially the rookies. We'd do all the typical things, you know, eat hot dogs, drink soda pop, sing along with 'Take Me Out to the Ball Game.' My Sarah Jean sure loved going to those games. Sometimes we'd take a glove with us to try to catch pop flies. One time we actually caught a ball and gave it to our youngest grandson, Kenny." Mr. Pfohl paused and said to the social worker, "I feel like I'm about to talk your ears off. I guess I've needed someone to talk to. Am I taking up too much of your time? Do you have someone else you need to see?"

The social worker reassured Mr. Pfohl that she really wanted to hear about what had been happening to him and his wife, and added, "I have as much time as you need. You're my only priority right now."

He seemed appreciative and continued, "Sarah Jean keeps me up at night. Several times she started to open the front door and wander away. I have to watch her real close. I used to let her dress herself, but she'd get things on backwards. Now sometimes she'll just sit naked until I dress her. Until recently, she was able to walk around our condo, but she fell a couple of times—then 3 months ago she broke her arm. Let me tell you, it was no picnic taking care of her with a full arm cast. More times than not, I use a wheelchair to get her around just because she's so unsteady on her feet. It just seems easier than letting her walk. I got one of those gizmos that fits on the back of my car so it makes using a wheelchair easier. But nothing is really easy."

Mr. Pfohl sat quietly, struggling to keep his composure. He was visibly upset, and the social worker reassured him that what he is experiencing is very normal.

"Yeah, that's what everyone says. What I'm feeling is very normal, but it doesn't help when I have to break my promise and put Sarah Jean in a nursing home because I'm too weak to take care of her. I used to think of myself as a rock, a strong man—but not anymore." He looked defeated. "I guess that's the real problem of getting old. You start having health problems, financial problems, and problems with things you used to be able to do easy. I haven't had a good night's sleep in months. Sarah Jean is really restless, especially at night, and she keeps me up half the night. That's when I knew I had to hire someone to help me take care of her. Now I'm in a real bind because I don't want to put her in a nursing home, but I don't seem to have much choice. Thankfully, money's not an issue. We have good insurance. I feel like I've betrayed her somehow, but if I don't get some relief this thing is going to kill us both. I've always heard people say that getting old with the one you love is what it's all about. Well, if you ask me, getting old is really just an awful experience—especially when you have to do it without your best friend. I don't want the kids to have to go through this when they're old like me." Mr. Pfohl turns to the social worker and asks, "Is there some kind of test we can do to see if Sarah Jean's behavior runs in the family? I know you can't be sure about the future but it helps to prepare—especially for the nightmare like I'm going through!"

As a post script, the social worker did have the opportunity to talk with the physician who had been treating Sarah Jean (with the appropriate consents to obtain information) and learned that there were no medical problems that could better explain her behavior.

SARAH JEAN PFOHL'S DSM DIAGNOSIS IS AS FOLLOWS:
Alzheimer's disease
Moderate major neurocognitive disorder due to probable Alzheimer's disease with behavioral disturbance

ASSESSMENT SUMMARY When assessing NCD due to Alzheimer's disease, the practitioner rules out potential medical and neurological explanations. In the usual course of events, the nursing home social worker is among the last professionals to be consulted—and, as happened in the vignette, despite Sarah Jean's fall and broken arm, her complete medical and neurological evaluations were not mentioned on her admission to the nursing home, thus preventing the social worker from access to detailed information that may shed light on Sarah Jean's behavior. However, in this case, the social worker did have the opportunity to speak with her client's physician.

There are several ways to code NCD due to Alzheimer's disease, depending on the evidence of causative factors; such as genetic testing, a family history coupled with autopsy confirmation, or a genetic test in an affected family member. The differentiation between "probable" and "possible" is particularly important in that Alzheimer's disease is coded separately when there is evidence for major NCD due to Alzheimer's disease. The additional code for Alzheimer's disease is not listed for possible NCD due to Alzheimer's disease and behavioral disturbances cannot be coded, but the practitioner is encouraged to go ahead and indicate its presence. In our case study, Sarah Jean shows a typical symptom picture for major NCD due to Alzheimer's disease; and her physician noted evidence of a symptom picture is without extended plateaus—nor does she show evidence of mixed etiology. Sarah Jean's story shows memory decline, and with a gradual progressive decline in cognition along with no other medical problems that can better explain her behavior. Therefore, she can be diagnosed as NCD due to probable Alzheimer's disease (APA, 2013). The medical condition of Alzheimer's disease is also listed.

An assessment of NCD due to Alzheimer's disease, at least in an overall sense, is usually not difficult to make—except in the very early stages. Because effects of delirium present with features similar to the NCDs (disorientation and memory loss), NCD due to Alzheimer's disease cannot be assessed until after the delirium clears.

Figure 15.1 shows the interactions of the biological, psychological, and social variables in Sarah Jean Pfohl's life.

Competency 7 b

In looking at Sarah Jean's past and present history, the practitioner can gain greater insight into her strengths and vulnerabilities. Looking at her current functioning, specific attention focuses on understanding variables in biological, psychological (including cognitive), and social systems. The competency-based assessment notes that Sarah Jean has a very strong support system in her husband, Harry, and in her children who live nearby. Mr. Pfohl is currently in a crisis himself as he looks to a future without his "best friend." However, he is very resilient in that he is able to talk openly with the social worker about his feelings and seeks outside assistance.

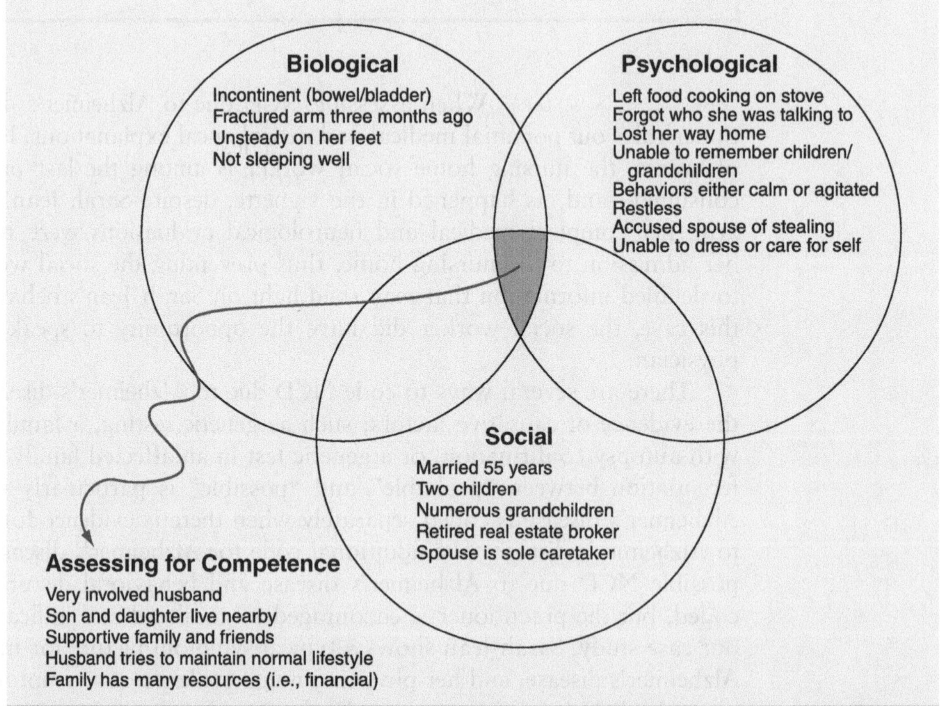

FIGURE 15.1 › MAJOR NEUROCOGNITIVE DISORDER DUE TO PROBABLE ALZHEIMER'S DISEASE WITH BEHAVIORAL DISTURBANCE
The interactions of the biological, psychological, and social variables in Sarah Jean Pfohl's life.

Competency 2 b

While Mrs. Pfohl is the "identified client," in actuality Mr. Pfohl becomes an added focus of the social worker's assessment. Undoubtedly, the social worker in this vignette had other clients to see. Yet when Mr. Pfohl asked if he was taking up too much of the social worker's time, her response was to reassure him that she wanted to hear more about what was happening to his wife and to him. In this way, the social worker engages Mr. Pfohl as the key informant regarding the entire situation. Several key competencies include Mr. Pfohl's role as the sole caretaker, a strong desire to keep his family together, and his intention to maintain a normal lifestyle.

We now turn our attention to a review of the second most commonly occurring etiological subtype of NCD, vascular disease.

VASCULAR DISEASE

After AD, the second most common neurocognitive disorder subtype the social worker may encounter in practice is vascular neurocognitive disorder or vascular disease. Sometimes referred to as multi-infarct dementia, vascular disease defines a decline in thinking skills caused by conditions that block or reduce blood flow to the brain depriving brain cells of vital oxygen and nutrients. Vascular neurocognitive disorder is a heterogeneous group of cognitive disorders associated with cerebrovascular damage, and symptoms can vary depending on the specific brain areas where blood flow is reduced (Fratiglioni et al., 2000). Sudden changes in thinking and perception after a stroke may include: confusion, disorientation, trouble speaking or understanding speech, or vision loss. Symptoms may be the most obvious soon after a major stroke.

Vascular disease is caused by at least one stroke and possibly is the result of a series of strokes. Risk factors include diabetes, hypertension (high blood pressure), heart disease, and medical disorders that lead to cerebral emboli. A neurological assessment often reveals a history of strokes and/or transient ischemic episodes (or when blood flow to part of the brain is blocked or reduced, frequently referred to as a mini-stroke) and signs of cerebral infarct (a type of stroke resulting from blockage in the blood vessels supplying blood to the brain).

The differential diagnosis for vascular neurocognitive disorder is that the person's condition worsens in a series of small debilitating steps (as these strokes occur), or when there is prominent evidence for a decline in complex attention (including processing speed) and executive functions (like planning, organizing, sequencing, or abstracting) in contrast to the more gradual deterioration of function seen in NCD due to Alzheimer's disease. Additionally, there is evidence of cerebrovascular disease from a person's history, physical exam, and/or neuroimaging to account for these deficits.

We now shift to a review of the additional subtypes of the neurocognitive disorders.

NEUROCOGNITIVE DISORDERS OTHER THAN ALZHEIMER'S AND VASCULAR DISEASE

FRONTOTEMPORAL NEUROCOGNITIVE DISORDER

Frontotemporal lobar degeneration (FTD), or frontotemporal neurocognitive disorder, is commonly diagnosed in adults under the age of 65 and is the fourth most common neurocognitive disorder in industrialized nations (Johnson et al., 2005). FTD symptoms typically appear about a decade earlier than AD, making age of onset a distinctive diagnostic feature. Although there is significant variability in the course and progression of FTD, survival rates vary from between 2 and 8 years post onset (Neary, Snowden, & Mann, 2005).

Frontotemporal neurocognitive disorder is characterized by progressive changes in personality and social conduct, and associated with degeneration of the prefrontal and anterior temporal cortex of the brain (APA, 2013). Behavioral changes are the presenting feature and dominate the clinical picture throughout the course of the disorder. They can include a loss of interest in socializing, self-care, and personal responsibilities, or the person may show varying degrees of apathy or disinhibition. Qualitative changes in language and cognitive impairments in executive function can also occur. For many years, FTD was known as Pick's disease.

Neurocognitive Disorder with Lewy Bodies

Neurocognitive disorder with Lewy bodies is a relatively new classification with about half the frequency of AD (Rahkonen et al., 2003). Age of onset is similar to AD; that is, with a mean of 68 years of age and a range of 50 to 85 years (Jellinger, Wenning, & Seppi, 2007). The individual experiences an insidious onset and gradual progression resulting in unrelenting dementia until death (McKeith, 2006). Lewy bodies is considered when the person meets criteria for a NCD (major or mild) as well as a combination of core diagnostic features (such as fluctuating cognition with pronounced variations in attention and alertness, recurrent visual hallucinations, and movement disorder or spontaneous features of Parkinsonism) and suggestive features (rapid eye movement sleep disorder, which can appear years before the onset of dementia, and severe reactions to neuroleptics or tranquilizers used to treat psychotic conditions). The disease is evident in supportive features such as repeated falls and syncope (fainting), transient and unexplained loss of consciousness, autonomic dysfunction, hallucinations, visuospatial abnormalities (like depth perception, object orientation, directional sense, and illusions) and other psychiatric disturbances such as delusions, aggression, and depression. In the late stages, global cognitive deficits lead to a person's complete functional dependence.

Neurocognitive Disorder due to Traumatic Brain Injury

Neurocognitive disorder due to traumatic brain injury is characterized by impact to the head (or other means of rapid movement) or displacement of the brain within the skull. It is among the earliest illnesses in human history and is currently a major source of morbidity and mortality. It is estimated that 2 percent of the U.S. population lives with long-term disabilities due to a prior traumatic brain injury (TBI) (Shively, Scher, Perl, & Diaz-Arrastia, 2012). Someone who has experienced a TBI in early to midlife is at an increased risk of a neurocognitive disorder in late life, in the range of 2- to 4-fold, compared with the general population (Fleminger, Oliver, Lovestone, Rabe-Hesketh, & Goria, 2003). Certain professions at a greater risk for concussive injuries have drawn attention to TBI, such as professional boxers and, more recently, football, soccer, and ice hockey players (McKee et al., 2009; McKee et al., 2010).

SUBSTANCE/MEDICATION-INDUCED NEUROCOGNITIVE DISORDER

Substance/medication-induced neurocognitive disorder, previously substance-induced persisting dementia, is characterized by neurocognitive impairments that persist beyond the usual duration of intoxication and acute withdrawal. Usually, a person's mental skills will improve considerably within a few days of discontinuing alcohol or drug use and improve as he or she moves through the detox process. Sometimes it can take months for functioning to return to normal. On other situations, problems can be persistent and normal functioning does not fully return. Therefore, it becomes important for the practitioner to make sure that the person's cognitive deficits were not present before the use of the substances or medications thought to be responsible for the impairment. The disorder is specifically coded for alcohol or the specific substance causing the neurocognitive symptoms.

Alcohol is particularly associated with major neurocognitive disorder and associated with Korsakoff syndrome (a chronic memory disorder caused by severe deficiency of thiamine or vitamin B1) that is most commonly caused by alcohol misuse. Korsakoff syndrome is often, but not always, preceded by an episode of Wernicke encephalopathy (an acute brain reaction to severe lack of thiamine). Wernicke encephalopathy is a medical emergency that causes life-threatening brain disruption, confusion, staggering and stumbling, a lack of coordination, and abnormal involuntary eye movements.

Those with Korsakoff syndrome may confabulate (or make up information they cannot remember). They are not lying per se and may actually believe their made-up explanations. The syndrome causes problems learning new information, an inability to remember recent events, and long-term memory gaps. One may find striking memory problems while other thinking and social skills are relatively unaffected. For example, you may encounter a client who can carry on a coherent conversation, but a few minutes later they are unable to remember that this conversation ever happened or that they even talked with you.

NEUROCOGNITIVE DISORDER DUE TO HIV INFECTION

HIV (human immunodeficiency virus) disease is caused by infection with human immunodeficiency virus type-1 (HIV-1) that is acquired through exposure to the bodily fluids of an infected person through injection drug use, unprotected sexual contact, or exposure, such as to a contaminated blood supply or a needle-puncture injury to medical personnel (APA, 2013). HIV enters the central nervous system soon after initial infection and is responsible for a range of neuropsychiatric complications.

Neurocognitive disorder due to HIV infection shows a more marked acquired impairment in cognitive functioning in people with HIV/AIDS (or acquired immune deficiency, the advanced form of HIV infection). The disorder produces a highly variable clinical course and a spectrum of signs and symptoms ranging from subtle cognitive and motor impairments to profound dementia. Common clinical features for those in the late stage include seizures, incontinence, and severe confusion (Antinori et al., 2007). The person typically presents with milder symptoms at the outset and, in the current era of highly active antiretroviral therapy, the condition may often go undiagnosed (Valcour, Sithinamsuwan, Letendre, & Ances, 2011). In mild NCD, the individual shows at least a mild interference in daily functioning; for example, inefficiency in work, homemaking, or social functioning. In major NCD, slowing may be prominent. However, since HIV can affect any part of the brain, the individual may show other patterns of cognitive dysfunction.

PRION DISEASE

Prion disease, or transmissible spongiform encephalopathies (TSEs), is essentially a family of rare progressive neurodegenerative disorders that can affect both humans and animals. The causative agents of the TSEs are believed to be prions (which refer to abnormal, pathogenic agents that are transmissible and are able to induce abnormal folding of specific normal cellular proteins called prion proteins that are found most abundantly in the brain).

One of the identified prion diseases is Creutzfeldt-Jakob disease (CJD), a rare illness marked by rapid mental deterioration, usually within a few months, and is always fatal leading to death usually within 1 year of onset. Initial signs and symptoms typically include: personality changes, anxiety, depression, memory loss, impaired thinking, blurred vision, insomnia, difficulty speaking, difficulty swallowing, and sudden jerky movements. As the disease progresses, the person's mental symptoms worsen. Classic CJD is not related to "mad cow" disease (bovine spongiform encephalopathy or BSE) that affects animals. However, there is another prion disease that is related to mad cow disease, called variant CJD. Those with the more rare variant CJD experience psychiatric symptoms that may be more prominent in the beginning with delayed neurological signs—seen as the loss of the ability to think, reason, and remember—developing later in the course of the illness. The person may also experience painful dyesthesiasis (a neurological condition characterized by a distortion of the sense of touch, which causes all touch to feel unpleasant). The variant form affects individuals at a younger age than the classic CJD and appears to have a slightly longer duration of 12 to 14 months (Belay & Schonberger, 2002).

NEUROCOGNITIVE DISORDER DUE TO PARKINSON'S DISEASE

Neurocognitive disorder due to Parkinson's disease (PD) is a slow and progressive neurological condition characterized by tremors, rigidity, involuntary and rhythmic movements of extremities, motor restlessness, and posturing instability. Symptoms typically begin to appear between 50 and 60 years of age with the mean onset of 60 years (Rao, Hofmann, & Shakil, 2006). The slow development of symptoms often causes them to go unnoticed at the outset by family, friends, and even the person who has the disease. Symptoms can vary from one person to another and change as the disease progresses.

As many as 70 to 80 percent of individuals with PD convert to neurocognitive disorder due to Parkinson's disease. In most instances, this occurs within the first 10 years after onset and, again, is subtle in nature (Emre et al., 2007). Neurocognitive disorder due to Parkinson's includes impairment in at least two of the following four cognitive domains: attention, executive functioning, visuospatial processing, and verbal free recall. For the diagnosis of probable NCD, the person must show at least one behavioral symptom; for example apathy, depression, hallucinations, delusions, or excessive daytime sleepiness (Emre et al., 2007).

NEUROCOGNITIVE DISORDER DUE TO HUNTINGTON'S DISEASE

Neurocognitive disorder due to Huntington's disease is inherited through a single dominant gene. It is a progressive and degenerative disease that includes difficulties in cognition, emotion, and movement. Symptoms generally begin between 30 and 50 years of age, and death usually occurs within 10 to 20 years of its onset. The individual exhibits involuntary tremors and twitching of the head, torso, and extremities, a lurching gait, and explosive speech. Huntington's is usually associated with excessive levels of dopamine, deficient GABA (or gamma-aminobutyric acid, which functions as the major inhibitory neurotransmitter in the brain), and atrophy in the caudate nucleus and frontal-temporal lobes of the brain.

ADDITIONAL NEUROCOGNITIVE DISEASES

Looking to the other neurocognitive disorder subtypes, when an individual has more than one subtype (excluding substances), he or she may be diagnosed with major or mild NCD due to multiple etiologies. The diagnosis of NCD due to another medical condition is considered when there is evidence of a medical condition; for example, primary or secondary brain tumors, hypothyroidism, systemic lupus, or renal failure, to name a few. The practitioner considers unspecified NCD when there is some degree of impairment but the individual does not meet full criteria for any of the NCDs.

SUMMARY

Delirium can be recognized by its acute onset and its brief duration. The neurocognitive disorders are a more insidious and progressively deteriorating process. NCD due to Alzheimer's type, for example, has been called "the longest good-bye" because its features can last 10 or more years. The person is present in the lives of loved ones but his or her memory and distinctive personality gradually fades away over time. The DSM-5 introduces diagnostic criteria for the neurocognitive disorders that was previously designated "Delirium, Dementia, and Amnestic and Other Cognitive Disorders" in the DSM-IV (APA, 2000). Amnestic disorder became major or mild neurocognitive disorder. Delirium and the NCDs are two of the most frequently undetected disorders in the clinical setting. While delirium can occur at any age, NCD is generally associated with those over 55. However, the inclusion of etiological subtypes such as traumatic brain injury or HIV expands the disorder to include a younger population. Table 15.4 summarizes the differential features between delirium and the neurocognitive disorders.

As the DSM transitions from the DSM-IV-TR (APA, 2000) to the current edition of the manual, Table 15.5 provides a brief summary of the changes made to the neurocognitive disorders diagnostic classifications.

TABLE 15.4 THE DIFFERENTIAL FEATURES BETWEEN DELIRIUM AND THE NEUROCOGNITIVE DISORDERS

Characteristics	Delirium	Neurocognitive Disorders
Onset	Sudden/acute Occurs at any age	Insidious Generally occurs after 55 years of age
Duration	Fluctuates, lasting hours to a few days	Long term; months to years (the "longest good-bye")
Prevailing Pattern	Temporary reversible condition while "causative factors exist"—consequence of an underlying medical condition, substance intoxication, use of medication or toxin exposure—or a combination; examples: drug allergies, chemotherapy, anesthesia, substance use	Permanent, irreversible condition Etiology can potentially be determined
Attention	Lacks direction, distractibility, fluctuates during the day	Relatively unaffected (in the mild stages)
Speech	Incoherent	Progressive, noticeable difficulties with expressive (and receptive) language
Personality Changes	No long-standing change	Person eventually becomes a "shell" of former self
Environment	Difficulties generally do not arise due to short-term nature of syndrome	Difficulties interfere with independence in everyday activities (in major stages) Interpersonal difficulties—examples include: caregiver stress, financial worries
Common Features	Memory loss Confusion Decreased alertness and orientation Problems with mood and behavior	Memory loss Confusion Decreased alertness and orientation Problems with mood and behavior

TABLE 15.5 SUMMARY COMPARISON BETWEEN THE DSM-IV-TR AND DSM-5 DIAGNOSES FOR THE NEUROCOGNITIVE DISORDERS

Dementia and amnestic disorder became major or mild neurocognitive disorder
DSM-5 has a new listing of cognitive domains
New separate diagnostic criteria are presented for major or mild neurocognitive disorder due to various conditions (or etiological sub types) such as Alzheimer's disease; frontotemporal lobar degeneration; Lewy body disease; vascular disease; traumatic brain injury; substance/medication induced; HIV infection; Prion disease; Parkinson's disease; Huntington's disease; another medical condition; multiple etiologies; and unspecified
Substance/medication-induced neurocognitive disorder and unspecified neurocognitive disorder are new diagnoses included in the DSM-5

Practitioner's Reflections

One of the key challenges the practitioner faces is knowing how to differentiate between delirium and the neurocognitive disorders, both major and mild. The competency-based assessment underscores the importance of exploring biological, psychological, and social influences.

Activities

Competency 1 b

1. As you think about the professional relationship with clients, describe the challenges to a social worker's professional demeanor in behavior and communication when interviewing a client with a diagnosis of delirium, or someone like Mr. Sal Cullotto.

Competency 2 b

2. Diversity plays a role in working with others. Early research suggests that certain populations, such the Amish or Native Americans, were less likely to be affected with neurocognitive disorder due to Alzheimer's (Pericak-Vance et al., 1996; Weiner et al., 2007). However, these differences may have actually been related to differences in those who seek assistance which can be considered unacceptable in some cultural groups. Identify how you would go about engaging someone from another culture to teach you specific perspectives around on seeking help for delirium and the neurocognitive disorders, major or mild.

Competency 8 c

3. Practitioners often are called upon to consult with other medical professionals. Imagine for a moment that you are referring one of your clients that you suspect is showing symptoms of a neurocognitive disorder to a physician to confirm the diagnosis. How would you present your case?

Competency 7 b

4. Reflect for a moment that your client presents with a delirium-like picture and you are interviewing a family member or someone close to your client (like a good friend or next-door neighbor). What kinds of questions would you ask to determine the presence of the disorder? Would you also interview the client? Explain why or why not.

Competency 5 a

5. List all of the problems, obstacles, and challenges that you anticipate that Sarah Jean Pfohl and her family (i.e., her husband, their children) might encounter with Sarah Jean's diagnosis of Alzheimer's disease. Based on your practice experience, can you add to this list?

Competency 7 a

6. Access the Competency-Based Assessment and companion website at http://www.thomsonedu.com/social_work/gray, where the case of "Mike" is highlighted. He is struggling with memory loss after being involved in an accident. Although his work has been affected, notice that he has a number of supports in his life to help him cope with his memory problems. Identify the specific coping strategies that Mike is using to improve his adaptation to living with his memory loss.

Competency Notes

Competency 1 b—Social workers use reflection and self-regulation to manage personal values and maintain professionalism in practice situations (p. 471): Social workers recognize personal values and the distinction between personal and professional values.

Competency 2 b—Social workers present themselves as learners and engage clients (and constituencies) as experts in their own experiences (pp. 465, 471): Social workers appreciate the dimensions of diversity as the intersectionality of multiple factors.

Competency 5 a—Social workers identify social welfare and economic policies at the local, state, and federal levels impact well-being, service delivery, and access to social services (p. 471): Social workers understand that human rights and social justice, as well as social welfare and services, are mediated by policy and its implementation on several levels—local, state, and federal.

Competency 7 a—Social workers collect and organize data and apply critical thinking in order to interpret information from clients and constituencies (pp. 449, 450, 471): Social workers understand that the assessment process is ongoing and conducted with, and on behalf of, diverse individuals, families, groups, organizations, and communities.

Competency 7 b—Social workers are able to apply knowledge of human behavior and the social environment, person-in-environment, and other multidisciplinary theoretical frameworks in the analysis of assessment data (pp. 445, 464, 471): Social workers understand theories of human behavior and the social environment and critically evaluate and apply this knowledge in the assessment process.

Competency 8 c—Social workers use interprofessional collaboration, as appropriate, to achieve beneficial practice outcomes (pp. 447, 454, 471): Social workers value interprofessional teamwork and recognize the beneficial outcomes that require interdisciplinary, interprofessional, and interorganizational collaboration.

References

Albert, M. S., DeKosky, S. T., Dickson, D., Dubois, B., Feldman, H. H., Fox, N. C., ... Phelps, C. H. (2011). The diagnosis of mild cognitive impairment due to Alzheimer's disease: Recommendations from the National Institute on Aging-Alzheimer's Association workgroups on diagnostic guidelines for Alzheimer's disease. *Alzheimer's and Dementia*, 7, 270–279.

Alzheimer's Association. (2010). Alzheimer's disease facts and figures. *Alzheimer's and Dementia* (Vol. 6). Chicago: Author.

American Psychiatric Association (APA). (2000). *Diagnostic and statistical manual of mental disorders* (4th ed., text revision). Washington, DC: Author.

American Psychiatric Association (APA). (2013). *Diagnostic and statistical manual of mental disorders* (5th ed.). Arlington, VA: Author.

Antinori, A., Arendt, G., Becker, J. T., Brew, B. J., Byrd, D. A., Cherner, M., ... Wojna, V. E. (2007). Updated research nosology for HIV-associated neurocognitive disorders. *Neurology, 69*, 1789–1799.

Barlow, D. H., & Durand, V. M. (2014). *Abnormal psychology: An integrative approach* (7th ed.). Stamford, CT: Wadsworth Cengage.

Belay, E., & Schonberger, L. (2002). Variant Creutzfeldt-Jakob disease and bovine spongiform encephalopathy. *Clinics in Laboratory Medicine*, *22*, 849–862.

Berrios, G. E. (1981). Delirium and confusion in the 19th century: A conceptual history. *British Journal of Psychiatry*, *139*(5), 439–449.

Blazer, D. (2013). Neurocognitive disorders in DSM-5. *American Journal of Psychiatry*, *170*(6), 585–587.

Brookmeyer, R., Johnson, E., Ziegler-Graham, K., & Arrighi, M. H. (2007). Forecasting the global burden of Alzheimer's disease. *Alzheimer's and Dementia*, *3*(3):186–191.

Cole, M. G. (2004). Delirium in elderly patients. *American Journal of Geriatric Psychiatry*, *12*, 7–21.

Cole, M. G., Ciampi, A., Belzile, E., & Zhong, K. (2009). Persistent delirium in older hospital patients: A systematic review of frequency and prognosis. *Age and Aging*, *38*(1), 19–26.

Craig, M. C., & Murphy, D. G. M. (2009). Alzheimer's disease in women. *Best Practice and Research Clinical Obstetrics and Gynecology*, *23*(1), 53–61.

Eisenbach, W. J., Hough, C. L., Crane, P. K., Haneuse, S. J., Carson, S. S., Curtis, J. R., & Larson, E. B. (2010). Association between acute care and critical illness hospitalization and cognitive function in older adults. *Journal of the American Medical Association*, *303*(8), 763–770.

Emre, M., Arsland, D., Brown, R., Burn, D. J., Duyckaerts, C., Mizuno, Y., ... DuBois, B. (2007). Clinical diagnostic criteria for dementia associated with Parkinson's disease. *Movement Disorders*, *22*(12), 1689–1707.

Fearing, M. A., & Inouye, S. K. (2009). Delirium. In D. G. Blazer & D. C. Steffens (Eds.), *The American Psychiatric Publishing textbook of geriatric psychiatry* (4th ed., pp. 229–242). Arlington, VA: American Psychiatric Publishing.

Fleminger, S., Oliver, D. L., Lovestone, S., Rabe-Hesketh, S., & Goria, A. (2003). Head injury as a risk factor for Alzheimer's disease: The evidence 10 years on, a partial replication. *Journal of Neurology, Neurosurgery, and Psychiatry*, *74*(7), 857–862.

Fratiglioni, L., Launer, I. J., Andersen, K., Breteler, M. M., Copeland, J. R., Dartigues, J. F., ... Hofman, A. (2000). Incidence of dementia and major subtypes in Europe: A collaborative study of population-based cohorts. Neurologic Diseases in the Elderly Research Group. *Neurology*, *54*(11, Suppl. 5), S10–S15.

Hales, R. E., Yudofsky, S. C., & Gabbard, G. O. (Eds.). (2010). *Essentials of psychiatry* (3rd ed.). Washington, DC: American Psychiatric Press.

Iwashyna, T. J., Ely, E. W., Smith, D. M., & Langa, D. M. (2010). Long-term cognitive impairment and functional disability among survivors of severe sepsis. *Journal of the American Medical Association*, *304*(16), 1787–1794.

Jacobi, J., Fraser, G. L., Coursin, D. B., Riker, R. R., Fontaine, D., Wittbrodt, E. T., ... Lumb, P. D. (2002). Clinical Practice Guidelines for the sustained use of sedatives and analgesics in the critically ill adult. *Critical Care Medicine*, *30*(1), 119–141.

Jellinger, K. A., Wenning, G. K., & Seppi, K. (2007). Predictors of survival in dementia with Lewy bodies and Parkinsonian dementia. *American Journal of Neurodegenerative Disease*, *4*(6), 428–430.

Johnson, J. K., Diehl, J., Mendez, M. F., Neuhaus, J., Shapira, J. S., Forman, M., ... Miller, B. L. (2005). Frontotemporal lobar degeneration: Demographic characteristics of 353 patients. *Archives of Neurology*, *62*(6), 925–930.

Jones, S. F., & Pisani, M. A. (2012). ICU delirium: An update. *Current Opinion in Critical Care*, *18*(2), 146–151.

Lemay, M., & Landreville, P. (2010). Verbal agitation in dementia: The role of discomfort. *American Journal of Alzheimer's Disease and Other Dementias*, *25*(3), 193–201.

McKee, A. C., Cantu, R. C., Nowinski, C. J., Hedley-White, E. T., Gavett, B. E., Budson, A. E., ... Stern, R. A. (2009). Chronic traumatic encephalopathy in athletes: Progressive tauopathy after repetitive head injury. *Journal of Neuropathology and Experimental Neurology*, *68*(7), 709–735.

McKee, A. C., Gavett, B. E., Stern, R. A., Nowinski, C. J., Cantu, R. C., Kowall, N. W., ... Budson, A. E., (2010). TDP-43 proteinopathy and motor neuron disease in chronic traumatic encephalopathy. *Journal of Neuropathology and Experimental Neurology*, *69*(9), 918–929.

McKeith, I. G. (2006). Consensus guidelines for the clinical and pathologic diagnosis of dementia with Lewy bodies (DLB): Report of the Consortium on DLB International Workshop. *Journal of Alzheimer's Disease and Associated Disorders*, *9*(3 Suppl.), 417–423.

National Institute on Aging. (2014). *Alzheimer's disease fact sheet.* Washington, DC: National Institutes of Health. Retrieved on August 30, 2014 from: http://www.nia.nih.gov/alzheimers/publication/alzheimers-fact-sheet

Neary, D., Snowden, J. S., & Mann, D. (2005). Frontotemporal lobar degeneration: A consensus on clinical diagnostic criteria. *Neurology*, *51*(6), 1546–1554.

Newman, J. K., & Slater, C. T. (Eds.). (2012). *Delirium: Causes, diagnosis and treatment.* Hauppauge, NY: Nova Science Publishers.

Nunan, J., & Small, D. H. (2000, October 13). Regulation of APP cleavage by alpha-, beta-, and gamma-secretases. *Federation of European Biochemical Sciences Letters*, *483*(1), 6–10.

Pericak-Vance, M. A., Johnson, C. C., Rimmler, J. B., Saunders, A. M., Robinson, L. C., D'Hondt, E. G., ... Haines, J. I. (1996). Alzheimer's disease and apolipoprotein E-4 allele in an Amish population. *Annals of Neurology*, *39*, 700–704.

Rahkonen, T., Eloniemi-Sulkava, U., Rissanen, S., Vatanen, A., Viramo, P., & Sulkava, R. (2003). Dementia with Lewy bodies according to the consensus criteria in the general population aged 75 years of older. *Journal of Neurology, Neurosurgery, and Psychiatry*, *74*(6), 720–724.

Rao, S. S., Hofmann, L. A., & Shakil, A. (2006). Parkinson's disease: Diagnosis and treatment. *American Family Physician*, *74*(12), 2046–2054.

Reitz, C. (2012). Alzheimer's disease and the amyloid cascade hypothesis: A critical review. *International Journal of Alzheimer's Disease.* Retrieved on August 30, 2014 from: http://ncbi.nlm.nih.gov/pmc/articles/pmc3313573/

Sadock, B. J., Sadock, V. A., & Ruiz, P. (2014). *Kaplan and Sadock's comprehensive textbook of psychiatry: Behavioral sciences/clinical psychiatry* (11th ed.). Philadelphia: Lippincott Williams and Wilkins.

Shively, S., Scher, A. I., Perl, D. P., & Diaz-Arrastia, R. (2012) Dementia resulting from traumatic brain injury. *Archives of Neurology*, *69*(10), 1245–1251.

Siberski, J. (2012). Dementia and DSM-5: Changes, cost, and confusion. *Aging Well*, *5* (6), 12. Retrieved on August 29, 2014 from: http://www.todaysgeriatricmedicine.com/archive/110612p12.shtml

Sperling, R. A., Aisen, P. S., Beckett, L. A., Bennett, D. A., Craft, S., Fagan, A. M., ... Phelps, C. H. (2011). Toward defining the preclinical stages of Alzheimer's disease: Recommendations from the National Institute on Aging-Alzheimer's Association workgroups on diagnostic guidelines for Alzheimer's disease. *Alzheimer's and Dementia*, *7*(3), 280–292.

Valcour, V., Sithinamsuwan, P., Letendre, S., & Ances, B. (2011). Pathogenesis of HIV in the central nervous system. *Current HIV/AIDS Reports*, *8*(1), 54–61.

Weiner, M. F., Hynan, L. S., Beckly, D., Koepsell, T. D., & Kukull, W. A. (2007). Comparison of Alzheimer's disease in American Indians, whites, and African Americans. *Alzheimer's and Dementia*, *3*(3), 211–216.

Weiner, M. F., Aisen, P. S., Jack, C. R., Jagust, W. J., Trojanowski, J. Q., Shaw, L., ... Schmidt, M. (2010). The Alzheimer's Disease Neuroimaging Initiative: Progress report and future plans. *Alzheimer's and Dementia*, *6*(3), 202–211, e207.

Wilson, R. S., Hebert, L. E., Scherr, P. A., Dong, X., Leurgens, S. E., & Evans, D. A. (2012). Cognitive decline after hospitalization in a community population of older persons. *Neurology*, *78*(13), 950–956.

CHAPTER

The Personality Disorders

INTRODUCTION

Hippocrates was an ancient Greek physician who is traditionally considered the father of Western medicine. Among his many contributions, he suggested that disease, mainly brain disease or head trauma, was responsible for mental problems. He believed that most were due to an imbalance in four essential fluids, or "humors," that circulated throughout the body. These humors, "blood, black bile, yellow bile, and lymph," were somehow responsible for characterizing an individual's worldview. In his work *Hippocratic Corus* (Maher & Maher, 1985), Hippocrates advanced the idea that the psychological disorders could be treated like any other disease. Indeed, Hippocrates described several mental disorders that are familiar to contemporary practitioners, including mania, melancholia, and paranoia.

Two thousand years later, DSM-I described 27 "personality disorders" and organized them into five specific headings: (1) personality pattern disturbance, (2) personality trait disturbance, (3) sociopathic personality disturbance, (4) special symptom reactions, and (5) transient situational personality disorders (APA, 1952). When DSM-II made its appearance, the subheadings were subsequently eliminated and the number of personality disorders was reduced from 27 to 12 categories (APA, 1968). The professional community did not endorse these as positive changes, because they were considered too limited. The next round of diagnostic revisions began in 1974, leading to the publication of the DSM-III in 1980 (APA, 1980). For the first time, the personality disorders were separated from the other clinical syndromes. This separation ensured the personality disorder designation would not be overlooked. DSM-III-R (APA, 1987) described 11 personality disorders and subdivided them into three "clusters," with each cluster representing disorders related by their symptomology. (The clusters and their corresponding disorders are discussed in detail later in this chapter.)

Although there are many schools of thought, Freudian psychodynamic theory has historically influenced the way practitioners conceptualize personality and pathology. (An in-depth discussion of psychoanalytic theory is beyond the scope of this book; however, for a thorough review, the reader is directed to Goldstein, Miehls, and Ringel [2009] and Teyber and McClure [2010].) Briefly, adult personality is viewed as the accumulation of early childhood experiences. Individuals generally learn to solve their own emotional problems during various stages of childhood development. These characteristic ways of interacting help determine adult personality traits. Freud has been credited for noticing that the emotional problems of childhood are resolved by the development of defense mechanisms aimed at decreasing anxiety. Defenses were conceptualized as unconscious processes originating within the ego, or the executive function of the individual's personality structure.

The term *personality* implies the manner in which a person interacts with his or her environment and other people. A personality disorder characterizes those individuals who usually respond poorly to changes, exhibit deficiencies in their capacity to form relationships, and have interpersonal problems in a variety of arenas, such as employment or school. Problems occur when traits, or those features that make up a personality, remain inflexible, thus impairing individuals' ability to interact within their social environment and with others.

Each person has a unique and individualized repertoire of defense mechanisms geared to maintain balance between the individual's internal drives and the external world. This repertoire is seen as personality; that is, a set of characteristics defining the behaviors, thoughts, and emotions of each individual. These characteristics become so ingrained that they usually dictate the person's worldview, lifestyle, and life choices. An individual's personality can be defined as those emotional and behavioral traits that characterize day-to-day living under normative conditions; an individual's personality is relatively predictable (Sadock, Sadock, & Ruiz, 2014).

A personality disorder is seen as a variant of character traits going far beyond the normative range found in most people. When these traits are extremely inflexible and maladaptive and cause significant functional impairment or subjective distress, they constitute a personality disorder. Individuals characterized by a personality disorder exhibit deeply ingrained, inflexible, rigid, problematic, and maladaptive patterns of relating to others and in perceiving themselves. Although this interactional style generally creates no distress for the individual, it may adversely affect others; that is, the person's behavior is considered ego-syntonic (where one's behaviors, values, or feelings are seen as acceptable and consistent with the person's personality and beliefs). This might present a major problem for the practitioner, especially when trying to foster the therapeutic relationship and develop collaborative efforts aimed at change. As a part of the assessment process, the social worker needs to take into account the influence of culture, ethnicity and/or social background; that is, someone's culture of origin may influence their habits, customs, or religious and political values.

The DSM-5 defines a personality disorder as "an enduring pattern of inner experience and behavior that deviates markedly from the expectations of the individual's culture, is pervasive and inflexible, and has an onset in adolescence or early adulthood, is stable over time, and leads to distress or impairment" (APA, 2013, p. 645). The competency-based assessment expands this definition by considering the influence of the full range of biological, psychological, sociocultural, and environmental factors that affect the individual's life.

Table 16.1 lists the personality disorders listed in the DSM-5.

TABLE 16.1 THE DSM-5 PERSONALITY DISORDERS

Cluster A Personality Disorders
- Paranoid Personality Disorder
- Schizoid Personality Disorder
- Schizotypal Personality Disorder

Cluster B Personality Disorders
- Antisocial Personality Disorder
- Borderline Personality Disorder
- Histrionic Personality Disorder
- Narcissistic Personality Disorder

Cluster C Personality Disorders
- Avoidant Personality Disorder
- Dependent Personality Disorder
- Obsessive-Compulsive Personality Disorder

Other Personality Disorders
- Personality Disorder Due to Another Medical Condition
- Other-Specified Personality Disorder
- Unspecified Personality Disorder

We all have notions about personality: Jorge, for instance, can be described as gregarious, Brett as fun-loving, and Richard as quiet and introspective. In fact, personality goes beyond the way people think or conduct themselves. Each of us has probably behaved at times in ways that can be characterized as gregarious, fun-loving, and quiet and introspective—but behavior is seen as being part of an individual's personality only if it cuts across many situations and events.

The DSM-5 notes 10 distinct personality disorders and they are grouped into three clusters—A, B, and C—with the following designations:

Cluster A: Odd and eccentric—Includes individuals who have paranoid, schizoid, and schizotypal personality disorders.

Cluster B: Emotional, dramatic, or erratic—Includes individuals with antisocial, histrionic, borderline, and narcissistic personality disorders.

Cluster C: Anxious, fearful—Includes individuals with avoidant, dependent, and obsessive-compulsive personality disorders.

There are two additional categories the practitioner may consider to further refine the personality disorders diagnosis. The first category, personality change due to another medical condition, is considered when a person's personality disturbance is due to the effects of a medical condition. It might be something like a frontal lobe lesion, such as an abnormality in the front part of the brain that might be caused by a tumor. When the criteria for any of the 10 specific personality disorders are not met, the practitioner may also consider the diagnosis of other specified personality disorder. In this case, if the practitioner chooses not to specify why criteria are not met for any of the 10 personality disorders, then the diagnosis of unspecified personality disorder may be assigned (APA, 2013, pp. 645–646).

The DSM-5 approach to the personality disorders remains essentially the same as in the DSM-IV-TR; that is, each of the disorders are seen as distinct clinical syndromes. Table 16.2 shows each cluster along with the major characteristics of each personality disorder.

TABLE 16.2 OVERVIEW OF THE PERSONALITY DISORDERS

Cluster A: Odd and eccentric		
Paranoid	*Schizoid*	*Schizotypal*
Suspicious and distrustful of other's motives as malevolent • Others seek to harm them • Preoccupied with unjust doubts about loyalty • Reluctant to confide in others • Reads hidden meanings • Bears grudges • Counterattacks or reacts angrily • Recurrent suspicion about fidelity of partner	*Socially restricted* • No desire for close friendships • Chooses solitary activities • No interest in sex • Takes little pleasure in activities • Lacks friends • Indifferent to praise or criticism • Cold, detached, or flat affect	*Perceptual disturbances; interpersonal deficits* • Ideas of reference • Odd beliefs • Unusual perceptions • Odd thinking and speech • Suspicious or paranoid ideation • Behavior appears odd, eccentric • Inappropriate affect

Cluster B: Emotional, dramatic, or erratic			
Antisocial	*Borderline*	*Histrionic*	*Narcissistic*
Violent, blatant disregard for others; behavior occurring since age 15; must be 18 before diagnosed • Failure to conform to social norms • Dishonest for own profit and purposes • Irritability and/or aggressiveness • Impulsivity • Reckless disregard for self or others • Irresponsible • Lack of remorse	*Unstable relationships; poor self-image; marked impulsivity* • Frantic efforts to avoid being abandoned • Unstable chaotic relationships • Impulsive spending, sex, substance abuse • Suicidal • Feeling "empty" • Inappropriate, intense, or difficulty controlling anger • History of mutilating	*Excessive emotionality; attention seeking* • Uncomfortable when not center of attention • Provocative behavior • Uses physical attraction to draw attention to self • Self-dramatization • Rapidly changes shifting emotions • Highly suggestible	*Requires excessive admiration* • Grandiose • Fantasizes about unlimited success, power • Striking sense of entitlement • Lacks empathy • Believes self "special" and others ordinary • Interpersonal relationships exploited; others manipulated • Envious of others and thinks others jealous of them • Arrogant

Table 16.2 Overview of the Personality Disorders (continued)

Cluster C: Anxious, fearful		
Avoidant	*Obsessive-Compulsive*	*Dependent*
Inhibited; feels inadequate	*Order; perfection; inflexible*	*Needs to be taken care of; clinging behavior*
• Avoids meaningful relationships with others • Unwilling to get involved unless "guaranteed" they will be liked • Shows restraint because they fear shame or ridicule • Preoccupied with criticism or rejection • Feels inadequate • Views self as inept, inferior • Reluctant to take risks, might be embarrassed	• Preoccupied with rules, regulations • Perfection interferes with completion of tasks • Overly conscientious • Hoards objects • Rigid and stubborn • Reluctant to delegate tasks	• Difficulty making everyday decisions • Desires others to assume responsibility for them • Lacks initiative • Excessive lengths to obtain support from others • Feels uncomfortable or helpless • Preoccupied with fears of being left alone

The DSM-5 (APA, 2013) acknowledges that "the clustering system, although useful in some research and educational situations, has serious limitations and has not been consistently validated" (p. 646). Nonetheless, this method of organization is a helpful framework for the competency-based assessment, which looks at the influence of the wide range of factors affecting client behavior and attempts to identify the impact of those factors on the client's biopsychosocial world. The personality disorders are seen as long-term, stable patterns of unusual and inflexible personality characteristics leading to pervasive impairment or interpersonal distress throughout a person's life. The pattern of impairment is evident in two (or more) of the following areas:

Cognition—Ways of perceiving and interpreting oneself, other people, and events.

Affectivity—The range, intensity, and appropriateness of emotional response(s).

Interpersonal functioning—The instability of and inability to maintain relationships; poor self-image or self-esteem.

Impulse control—The ability to withhold inappropriate verbal or motor responses while completing a task; individuals who act or speak without anticipating the repercussions of their behavior or without learning from undesirable consequences of their previous behavior that it is appropriate to delay an action are seen as having poor impulse control.

Most individuals are able to adapt their behavior to a variety of different situations. For example, someone who is considered talkative is able to be quiet during an important speech or a religious service. Individuals with a personality disorder, however, exhibit personality traits so out of proportion or inflexible that they often cause problems for themselves and those around them. These difficulties continue over an extended period of time (Kearney & Trull, 2012). It is possible that earlier in the individual's life, these traits were effective in coping with conditions in his or her family of origin.

To identify the presence of a personality disorder, the individual exhibits the following characteristics:

- Almost always inflexible across a wide range interpersonal and intrapersonal situations.
- This enduring pattern leads to significant distress or impairment in social, occupational, or other important areas of interpersonal functioning.
- The behavioral pattern is stable and of long duration, and its onset can usually be traced back to at least adolescence or early adulthood.
- Behavior is not better explained by another mental disorder.
- Behavior is not due to the direct physiological effects of a substance (e.g., a drug of abuse) or a general medical condition (APA, 2013).

The 10 personality disorders described in this chapter are certainly not the "final word," but they do arise from historical traditions of dividing the domain of personality disorders. These categories can cause assessment dilemmas when an individual's behavior pattern comes very close to what is considered "normal" behavior versus "abnormal" behavior. Identifying the boundary between one specific personality disorder and another also poses a challenge. The main point for the practitioner to recognize is that these personality disorders are considered no more than behavioral prototypes with indistinct boundaries.

Competency 7 b

The competency-based assessment underscores the uniqueness of each individual. In addition, when the influence of biopsychosocial factors is considered, an individual's life story is clearly far more complex than any listing of behavior patterns. The DSM should not be used as a "recipe" for understanding behavior. However, an awareness of the DSM guidelines for differential assessment will help practitioners approach the competency-based assessment process in a systematic way. The competency-based framework is intended to enhance, not to replace, the central role of the social worker's clinical judgment, empirical evidence to formulate a clinical diagnosis, and the wisdom of accumulated practice experience. Merging the DSM format with the competency-based assessment model helps practitioners fully explore a client's life history and the impact of biological, psychological, and social variables. This approach to the assessment helps the practitioner to better understand clients and their environment. For example, the dramatic personality disorders (Cluster B) are found to be highly comorbid with the kind of social problems social workers encounter in practice such as unemployment, poverty, violent death, incarceration, recidivism such as parole violations, and significant relationship instability (Fountoulakis, Lecht, & Kaprinis, 2008).

In what follows, descriptions of the 10 personality disorders noted in the DSM-5 will be provided. While these descriptions tap into the basic features of each personality disorder, it is important to understand that these are only abbreviated characterizations. In practice, the social worker attends to the whole person and his or her unique life history.

We now turn to a review of the Cluster A personality disorders beginning with paranoid personality disorder. Keep in mind that everyone can show some of the following personality traits from time to time, but what distinguishes the personality disorders as a diagnosable disorder is that these personality traits are inflexible and cause significant impairment and problems in interpersonal relationships.

CLUSTER A: ODD AND ECCENTRIC PERSONALITY DISORDERS

Individuals with the Cluster A personality disorders generally appear odd and eccentric. These disorders are often associated with schizophrenia. In particular, someone diagnosed with schizotypal personality disorder shows cognitive or perceptual distortions and eccentricities of behavior and is often described as having a pattern of acute discomfort in close relationships. An individual with paranoid personality disorder can be paranoid in contrast to somebody diagnosed with schizoid personality disorder, where they might have difficulty being understood by others since they have an odd or eccentric manner of speaking and lack close relationships. Unlike those with schizophrenia, people diagnosed with a Cluster A disorder tend to have a greater grasp on reality. However, these disorders do have a higher risk to occur among first-degree relatives with a diagnosis of either schizophrenia or a Cluster A personality disorder (Nolen-Hoeksema, 2014).

We begin with a more detailed review of paranoid personality disorder.

PARANOID PERSONALITY DISORDER

In paranoid personality disorder, the individual's behavior is characterized by pervasive, groundless suspiciousness and an inherent distrust of others. This person is often described as hostile, irritable, or angry, and he or she refuses to take responsibility for his or her own actions and feelings. As the name suggests, these individuals generally interpret innocent remarks as insults or threats. They often believe their personal character and reputation are being attacked when, in fact, these perceived injuries are wholly unintended. Because of the fear of exploitation, individuals with this disorder generally do not confide in or trust others.

PREVAILING PATTERN

It is estimated that as many as 1 in 10 adults in the United States may have a diagnosable personality disorder (Lenzenweger, Lane, Loranger, & Kessler, 2007), and the overall prevalence ranges from 2.3 to 4.4 percent of the U.S. population (APA, 2013). This disorder appears to be more commonly diagnosed in men than in women and does not seem to have a familial pattern (APA, 2013). Individuals with a personality disorder rarely seek help on their own, but rather are referred to treatment by others in their social environment such as a spouse or an employer.

DIFFERENTIAL ASSESSMENT

The central characteristics of paranoid personality include a pervasive pattern of distrust and suspicion seen by (four or more of) the following:

- *Suspicion*—Although the individual has no real basis or evidence of another's malfeasance, they tend to be preoccupied assuming others are somehow betraying or being unfaithful to them.

- *Unjustified doubts*—The individual is preoccupied with doubts about the loyalty or trustworthiness of friends or others in their life. They assume others are out to exploit, harm, or deceive them even if there is no evidence that others are plotting against them. The individual may lash out at any time and without reason. They are amazed when a friend shows loyalty. If the person gets into trouble, they expect others to attack or ignore them.
- *Problems with intimacy*—The individual has difficulty confiding in others, and is generally distrusting and afraid the information will be used against him or her. They may refuse to answer personal questions stating, "It's nobody's business."
- *Hidden meanings*—The person perceives demeaning or threatening intent into benign remarks or events. For instance, a casual humorous remark by a coworker is seen as a serious character attack.
- *Holding grudges*—These individuals do not forgive insults, slights, or injuries. They are predisposed to blame others for their problems, and often have a history of being litigious.
- *Paranoia*—The prominent characteristics are permanent and unshakeable suspiciousness and persecutory delusions in a person who is otherwise clear thinking. A minor slight will raise major hostility, and these hostile feelings will last for a long time. These individuals are quick to react in anger or to counterattack. They have a tendency to be chronically tense, and constantly mobilize themselves against perceived threats from others in their social environment. This worldview generally begins by early adulthood.
- *Recurrent suspicions*—The person has a strong tendency to have doubts or misgivings, without justification, about others. He or she constantly questions the fidelity of their spouse or significant other and may spend time gathering "evidence" to support their suspicions. Constant questioning or challenges as to the whereabouts, actions, intentions, and fidelity of the spouse or partner dominate the relationship. The individual is supersensitive to issues regarding rank, class, and power and resents those who have things he or she does not.

Individuals with paranoid personality disorder are prone to see insult where none exists and quick to take offense when none was intended (Sadock, Sadock, & Ruiz, 2014). They are convinced that most people cannot be trusted. Their personality can be described as chronically sarcastic, argumentative, angry, irritable, and querulous—in short, they have a "chip on their shoulder." It is not unusual for the individual to bear a grudge for an excessively long time, and he or she pursues "insults" with a righteous, moralistic tenacity. Relationships with neighbors or coworkers can be described as tense. For example, the individual characterized with a paranoid personality views a barking dog as the neighbor's deliberate attempt to annoy him or her. There exists a profound negativistic, bitter, and cynical attitude, which often pervades the person's perception of life. These individuals are cold and humorless, extremely self-protective of their own interests, jealous, controlling, and possessive in whatever relationships they secure. The practitioner should not be surprised to see such individuals fascinated with weapons, survivalist organizations, or extremist political groups.

The following vignette about Ben Rogers illustrates the characteristics of someone with a paranoid personality disorder.

CASE The Case of Ben Rogers

Ben Rogers is a 77-year-old retired pharmacist, and is being seen by the social worker at a senior citizens center for an evaluation of health care needs for himself and his 75-year-old bedridden wife, Franne. Mr. Rogers states that he is a relatively healthy individual, except for "a little" angina and high blood pressure. He has been the sole caretaker for his wife and was recently urged by their only child, Myra Schwartz, to seek help because his wife's condition is deteriorating. Ben's responsibilities around caring for Franne have become a tremendous physical drain on him. Getting help for her dad was not easy for Myra. She explains, "I just put Dad in the car, drove up to the senior center, and told him I wasn't going to budge until he got out and went inside. I told him he didn't have to have a smile on his face—he just had to go in the door of the center and ask for some help. I felt so guilty," Myra confides, "but I was desperate. This was one of the most awful things I've had to do—but I knew it was the only thing that would work with Dad."

Because Myra was the catalyst in getting her father involved with the senior citizens center, the social worker set some time aside to talk with her and get an idea of what is happening in the Rogers' home. Myra begins by telling the social worker that her parents have been married for 55 years. Her father, who retired about 15 years ago to care for her mother full time, used to have a moderately successful business as a pharmacist. Myra confides that her parents' relationship has always been somewhat rough. She shares, "My mother was the only person my father ever showed any tender feelings for." Myra also reveals that, except for her mother, "My father never trusted anyone—his attitude has always been that people can't be trusted. He's convinced that everybody is always out to get you. ... He refuses offers of help from anybody in the family, even from our friends because he thinks they just want a chance to 'get something on him' that they can use against him later."

Myra shakes her head slowly, and with a wry smile offers, "My father probably has earned a place in the *Guinness Book of World Records* for holding a grudge longer than anyone else on earth. He has never, ever, forgiven an insult." When asked if her father exhibited evidence of mood swings or psychosis, she responds, "No, he's not crazy or anything like that, he's just nasty."

According to Myra, Ben Rogers's personality issues have been fairly stable. "Oh, Dad's always acted this way—as long as I can remember, anyway. ... You know, now that I'm an adult and I look back on my relationship with him, I don't really know him very well at all. You might say that he's hard to have a relationship with." Myra is quiet for a moment and then continues. "Don't get me wrong, I love my father, but it's like I always have to walk on eggshells whenever I try to talk with him. I mean, he questions my every motive."

Ben Rogers's DSM Diagnosis Is as Follows:

Paranoid personality disorder

Competency 7 c

Assessment Summary Exploring the interaction of the biopsychosocial factors in Ben Rogers's life makes it appear that his wife's deteriorating health condition has intensified his paranoid beliefs. His wife Franne continues to decline physically, and Ben's ability to care for her becomes increasingly demanding and emotionally draining. Circumstances are conspiring; that is, they seem to force Ben, a man who usually refuses help, to reach out to others and to depend on them for assistance. As his daughter Myra points out, "Dad has a long history of not trusting people." He is suspicious of everyone and is known to hold a grudge for a long time. Even at the day care center he expects other people will take advantage of him, and sometimes he reads hidden meanings into others' innocent remarks.

Competency 7 c

The competency-based assessment focuses on strengths and positives in the client's situation. Ben Rogers has had a moderately successful career as a pharmacist, an occupation in which it was necessary for him to interact with others—and, despite evidence of interpersonal difficulties, he has continued a 55-year marriage. His daughter acknowledges that her father has always demonstrated tender feelings for his wife.

Ben has been in relatively good health in the past, but the physical demands of being the sole caretaker for his wife are beginning to take their toll on his own health status; he is currently taking medication for hypertension and angina. Though one might suspect it is difficult, Ben has been attending the senior citizens center once or twice a week after being urged by his daughter to seek help.

From the information available in this case presentation, Ben has come to the practitioner's attention because of interpersonal family issues, and he has not sought help on his own. This pattern of access to services is in keeping with people who experience intense interpersonal conflicts. Further, Ben lacks the insight to understand that his behavior creates relational difficulties with others; personality traits that produce such behavior are considered ego-syntonic. It is important for the practitioner to be attentive to the features of paranoid personality disorder, as this characteristic way of relating will also play a role in the helping relationship. Figure 16.1 illustrates the interactions of the biological, psychological, and social variables in Ben Rogers's life.

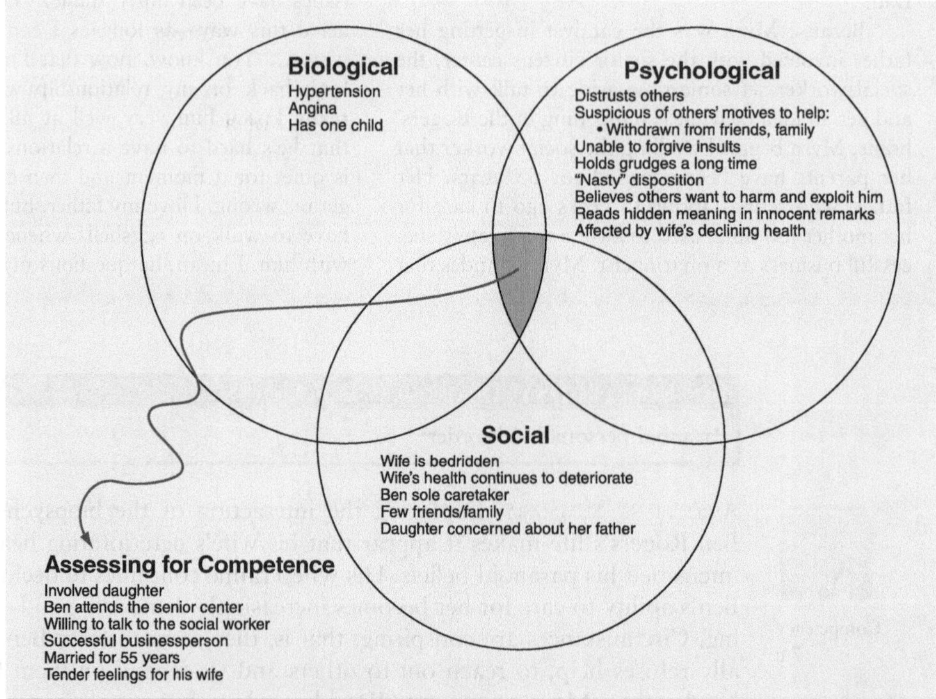

FIGURE 16.1 › PARANOID PERSONALITY DISORDER
The interactions of the biological, psychological, and social variables in Ben Rogers's life.

Competency 6 a

A number of other mental disorders with psychotic features and characterized by persistent psychotic symptoms (such as delusions and hallucinations) can be distinguished from the paranoid personality disorder (e.g., delusional disorder-persecutory subtype, schizophrenia, bipolar disorder, or depressive disorder). For instance, individuals with paranoid personality disorder display constant hypervigilance (where the person is obsessively concerned, defended, or watchful) or pervasive mistrust, which are not seen in the delusional disorder.

However, paranoid personality disorder may co-occur with these other mental disorders with psychotic symptoms. Using schizophrenia as an example, the practitioner may see the symptoms of chronic delusions or hallucinations and detect a greater degree of incoherence and illogical speech symptomatic of schizophrenia along with the symptom picture of paranoid personality disorder. When the additional (and co-occurring) diagnosis of schizophrenia is assessed along with paranoid personality disorder, the personality disorder must have been present before the onset of the psychotic symptoms and continue when the psychotic symptoms are in remission. Let's consider that the person has schizophrenia that was preceded by the paranoid personality disorder to review how to assign the diagnoses. In this instance, the practitioner records the paranoid personality disorder and the diagnosis of schizophrenia but now includes the term "premorbid" in parentheses for the diagnosis of paranoid personality disorder. In our example, the diagnosis would look like, "paranoid personality disorder (premorbid)."

It should be noted that the schizoid and schizotypal personality disorders (discussed in the following sections) share similarities with the co-occurrence of mental disorders with psychotic symptoms and the diagnoses are recorded in the same fashion; that is, the additional diagnosis of a personality disorder is given when it has been present before the psychotic symptoms and continues when the psychotic symptoms are in remission. Since the personality disorder came first, then it is subsequently coded with the term "premorbid" included in parentheses along with the co-occurring mental disorder.

There are a number of other personality disorders that share features with the paranoid personality disorder. They are the schizotypal, schizoid, borderline, histrionic, and avoidant personality disorders. Those with schizotypal traits are set apart by symptoms of magical thinking, unusual perceptual experiences, and odd thinking and speech. Those with schizoid personality disorder, while seen as strange, eccentric, cold, and aloof, usually do not have the paranoid ideation seen in paranoid personality disorder. Individuals with borderline and histrionic personality disorders are not associated with the pervasive suspiciousness seen in the paranoid personality. Those with a paranoid personality disorder desperately want relationships with others, whereas for someone with borderline personality disorder (characterized as chaotic, fractured, and difficult), relationships are extremely problematic. Individuals with avoidant personality disorder are afraid of being embarrassed or seen as inadequate in interpersonal relationships rather than suspecting the malicious intent of others as seen in paranoid personality disorder.

We now turn to a review of schizoid personality disorder.

SCHIZOID PERSONALITY DISORDER

Persons with schizoid personality disorder display a lifelong pattern of social withdrawal; that is, they tend to be introverted and remain isolated from others by choice. Often, their lifestyles are described as bland and solitary (Nirestean, Lukacs, Cimpan, & Taran, 2012), with very little human interaction. Eccentric, lonely, and ill at ease in the company of others—these are the typical ways of describing their behaviors. However, the individual with schizoid personality disorder does not exhibit the disordered thinking so apparent in those with schizophrenia, bipolar disorder, depressive disorder with psychotic features, or autism spectrum disorder. Gathering information about the individual's childhood may reveal a history of having been a loner, or of being sensitive to the teasing of other children during early school years.

PREVAILING PATTERN

Schizoid personality disorder is the least commonly diagnosed disorder in practice (APA, 2013), and knowledge about this disorder remains incomplete. However, over the past several decades research has pointed to the role of biological influences in combination with poor family socialization and early learning or relationship problems (Wolff, 2000). Onset typically occurs during early childhood years, and prevalence is estimated at 4.9 percent based on a probability subsample from the National Comorbidity Survey Replication data in the United States (Lenzenweger et al., 2007).

DIFFERENTIAL ASSESSMENT

Do you know someone you consider a loner? Someone who would rather stay home to watch television than accept an invitation to join a party? Magnify this preference for isolation many times over, and you begin to grasp the impact on someone with a schizoid personality disorder. These individuals give the impression of being reserved, indifferent, or detached from everyday events. They lead quiet, distant, reclusive, and unsociable lives with remarkably little need or desire for emotional ties to others (Sadock, Sadock, & Ruiz, 2014). The person is characterized as eccentric, isolated, detached, or lonely. These are individuals who may daydream excessively and/or become attached to animals. They usually do not marry or even form long-lasting romantic relationships. Sadly, beneath the surface of their indifference, there often exists a deep loneliness and a desire for close relationships.

The outstanding characteristics of schizoid personality disorder include at least four (or more) of the following:

- *No penchant for social relationships*—Although some individuals with this disorder may form stable relationships with family members (or others), they lack the ability to *sustain* close relationships in general.
- *Preference for solitary activities*—Typically, the individual retains low-level jobs requiring limited interpersonal contact (e.g., they might be employed as a night security worker, janitor, or computer technician). Interestingly, they often succeed at solitary jobs others might find difficult to endure.

- *Little or no sex drive*—These individuals rarely date or marry; men are more likely to remain single than women (perhaps due to problems in initiating courtship).
- *Takes pleasure in few, if any, activities*—The individual usually has less pleasure or sensory, bodily, or interpersonal experiences; for example, enjoying an evening sunset walking on the beach.
- *Lacks close friends other than first-degree relatives*—This is the individual who has few close friends or confidants.
- *Acts indifferently to praise (or criticism) of others*—The person does not seem to be bothered by what others think of them, and seems indifferent to the approval (or criticism) of others.
- *Limited range of emotions*—These individuals have a confined range of emotions in social settings, and are often described as cold and detached. The person appears indifferent to both compliments and/or criticisms, and takes little or no pleasure in life. His or her discomfort with relationships is noteworthy.

The following case discussion of Tyrone White, a young man brought to a mental health clinic by a concerned relative, illustrates what the life of someone with schizoid personality disorder might look like.

CASE THE CASE OF TYRONE WHITE

His cousin, Sabrina, referred Tyrone White to the XYZ Mental Health Clinic. With concern in her voice, she said, "Tyrone is such a lonely boy and needs someone to talk to about his troubles."

As I entered the waiting room, the first thing I noticed about Tyrone was that he seemed oblivious to those around him. His face was hidden in a movie star magazine. I went over to greet him and invite him into my office. When Tyrone entered my office, it was quite apparent to me that he did not regard the appointment as much of an event. His physical appearance said the same thing; his shorts were torn, his T-shirt tattered, and he was barefoot. My initial impression was that he was dressed for washing his car instead of going to an office appointment.

When he sat down, Tyrone continued to leaf through his magazine. I waited for about a minute for him to say something, but he did not even seem to notice that I was sitting there. As our interview began, he continued looking at his magazine.

"Hello, I'm Jeanne O'Laughlin, one of the social workers here. I understand your name is Tyrone. Is that what other people call you?"

He nodded his head in agreement.

"Most people call me Jeanne, and if you'd like, you can too. May I call you Tyrone?"

He nodded affirmatively.

"How are you doing?" I asked.

"Fine," he replied.

"Do you know why you are here today?" I asked.

"Nuh huh," he replied. (I waited again.)

"Well, what I know about why you are here is that your cousin Sabrina is worried about you and thought you might need someone to talk to. What do you think?"

"I'da know," he replied (still reading his magazine).

I asked (trying again), "Did Sabrina tell you why she was so worried about you?"

"Nuh huh," he replied.

Most of my interview with Tyrone followed this same pattern, so I will try to summarize what transpired. If I asked Tyrone a direct question, he answered but did not elaborate or volunteer additional data. He sat quietly (reading his magazine) throughout the interview, and I noticed no evidence of abnormal or eccentric behavior. When asked, he was appropriately oriented to time, place, and date,

CASE **THE CASE OF TYRONE WHITE (CONTINUED)**

and he denied any drug or alcohol use. I asked if he had ever heard any voices (that other people did not hear) or saw things (that other people did not see). His usual reply was, "Nuh huh."

Tyrone is African American, and somehow through our convoluted conversation I was able to learn that he is 27 years old and the youngest of eight children. He revealed that his father died 10 years ago from some kind of surgical complications. He volunteered no other details. His mother recently remarried, and, he added, "I don't see my family very often." He lives alone in a small apartment in the same neighborhood as his cousin, Sabrina. He supports himself as a movie projectionist. Tyrone did not finish high school, and he has held this job for the past 7 years. He has gotten several raises over the years, and was even asked to become a manager, but Tyrone replied that he does not want to "attend all those meetings with all those people." He went on, "Besides, once you're in the union, nobody can push you into something you don't want. I like that!" He stated, "I like my job a lot because I can look at movie stars all day, and nobody bothers me." He considers himself to be an "average guy" and doesn't really want friends or family around because, as he states, "I like my own good company." Tyrone does not have a history of dating nor has he been sexually active.

After the session, Jeanne O'Laughlin spoke to his cousin, Sabrina. She commented that Tyrone has always been "a loner," even when he was a child. Tyrone corroborated this, saying, "I was a street kid." He never spent much time with his family and does not remember very much time spent doing family things. Tyrone stated that the neighborhood kids "picked on me because I was so small," but he insists, "I never cared." In school, his progress was noted as "nothing special."

When asked, "What makes you happy?" he replied, "I just like being left alone." When the session was over, Tyrone stood up, carefully turned down the corner of the page he had been reading, tucked the magazine under his arm, and walked out of my office without a backward glance, never to return.

TYRONE WHITE'S DSM DIAGNOSIS IS AS FOLLOWS:
Schizoid personality disorder

Competency 2 b

ASSESSMENT SUMMARY Tyrone relates to the practitioner in a stilted but passively cooperative manner. Although he responds to the interviewer, he provides little information beyond superficial data. Tyrone seems more comfortable answering questions than initiating conversation. He appears to be poorly prepared for his session, reflected in his casual, almost shabby attire and also in his insistence that he is unaware of his cousin Sabrina's concerns about him. Tyrone appears to be oriented to his surroundings (time, place, and date) and denies hearing voices and seeing things that others do not.

Tyrone's affect during the interview, while seeming appropriate on the surface, has an underlying detached quality. Tyrone shows a greater interest in reading a magazine than in talking to the social worker. He denies having any problems, giving the impression that he would not seek counseling on his own.

Tyrone is in good health and denies alcohol or drug use. Family interactions are limited; his father died 10 years ago, and his mother recently remarried—and he gave the impression she plays no part in Tyrone's current life. Tyrone's social context is constricted, and he has few environmental resources (that is, he lives alone and professes he does not want friends or family around). His choice of job further limits any opportunity for developing social contacts.

Tyrone's biopsychosocial history reveals a pattern of being a loner from early childhood. Additionally, he was singled out for ridicule because of his small size while growing up. Although he is the youngest of eight children, very little is known about Tyrone's older siblings. His academic performance was not exceptional, and he did not complete high school. Being left alone seems to be a source of pleasure for Tyrone; he is single, does not date, lives by himself, and works alone. Tyrone does not seem interested in job promotions, primarily because the additional responsibilities would require more interaction with others.

Tyrone White tends to turn inward, and he moves away from interpersonal connections with the outside world. This inner-directed reality does not exhibit the disordered pattern of thinking commonly associated with those who have schizophrenia. As demonstrated in the interview, he has a constricted emotional range—in essence, Tyrone is a man who is unsociable, distant, indifferent, and reclusive. Based on the way he approaches interpersonal relationships, a practitioner can expect him to relate more like an observer rather than an active participant in the therapeutic relationship.

Competency 6 a

The medical model might accentuate the negatives in looking at Tyrone's behavior. The competency-based assessment pays attention to the associations between behaviors and the various positive external factors while looking for strengths and resources. (Refer to Figure 16.2 for the interactions of the biological, psychological, and social variables in Tyrone White's life.) Tyrone has worked steadily for the past 7 years; he is self-sufficient; he pays his own rent; he receives routine raises; and he has been offered opportunities for job advancement. Although Tyrone is socially isolated, his cousin Sabrina seems concerned enough to bring him to the clinic for help, and somehow she got his cooperation in coming.

As with the paranoid personality disorder, those with schizoid personality disorder share other mental disorders with psychotic symptoms. Both the disorder with psychotic symptoms and the schizoid personality disorder diagnosis is assigned in the same manner as reviewed in the earlier discussion of paranoid personality disorder.

The similarities between individuals with the schizoid personality disorder and those with schizotypal, paranoid, avoidant, and obsessive-compulsive personality disorders underscore the importance of a careful assessment. Schizoid personality disorder can be distinguished from schizotypal personality disorder by the lack of cognitive and perceptual distortions. Those with the paranoid personality are more socially connected than someone with schizoid personality disorder, and show a greater tendency to project their feelings onto others. Individuals with avoidant personality disorder are also characterized by isolation, but they show a strong desire to participate in activities; something that is absent in those with the schizoid personality disorder. Also absent are the oddities of perception, thought, behavior, and communication seen in schizotypal personality disorder (which is more similar to schizophrenia). Individuals with obsessive-compulsive personality disorder can present with a sense of detachment, but it comes from their devotion to work and

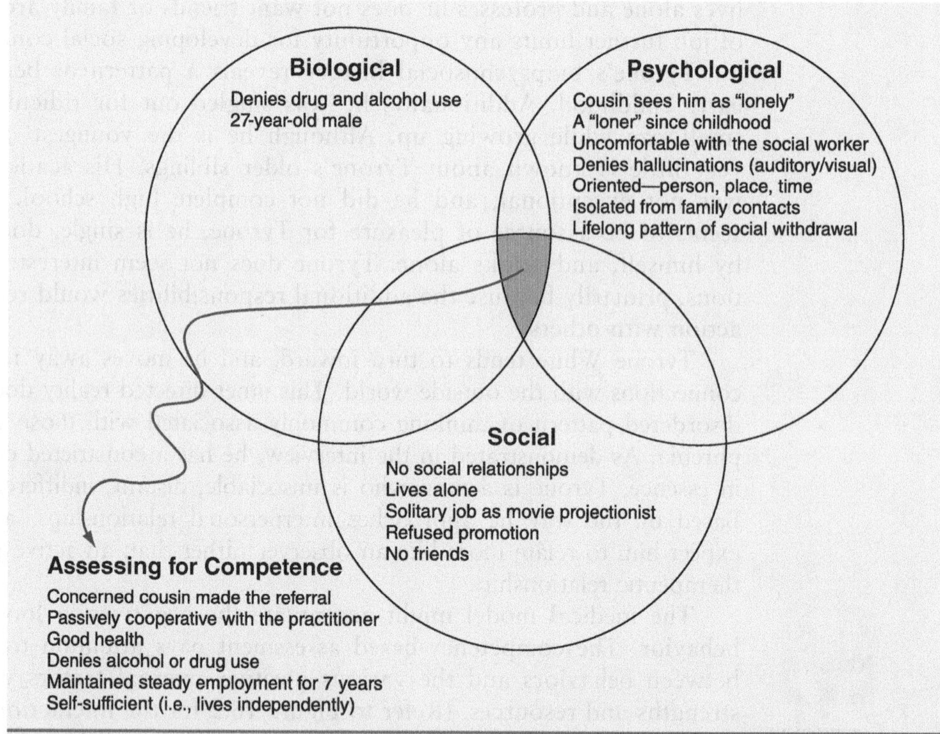

FIGURE 16.2 › SCHIZOID PERSONALITY DISORDER
The interactions of the biological, psychological, and social variables in Tyrone White's life.

discomfort with emotions. In addition, they also have an underlying capacity for intimacy, unlike the person with schizoid personality disorder.

We now review schizotypal personality disorder.

SCHIZOTYPAL PERSONALITY DISORDER

Individuals with schizotypal personality disorder exhibit strikingly odd or strange mannerisms in addition to having a very active fantasy life. This may include magical thinking (an irrational belief that one has powers that defy laws of nature and physics and thus can cause or prevent events), illusions (perceptual disturbances in which things appear differently from what they actually are in reality), derealization (loss of one's sense of reality in the external world), and ideas of reference (in which everything everyone else does somehow relates back to them). Interpersonally, these individuals are described as loners, much like Tyrone White, who was described in the previous vignette and diagnosed with a schizoid personality disorder. However, the person's solitary pursuits and social isolation may stem from strained social anxiety that does not diminish with familiarity.

PREVAILING PATTERN

Competency 7 b

Schizotypal personality disorder occurs in approximately 4.6 percent of the U.S. general population (APA, 2013). However, the disorder is less frequently seen in clinical populations and shows a higher level of prevalence (3.9 percent) in the general population. It is helpful for the practitioner to thoroughly explore the client's family history for evidence of schizophrenia, because of the greater incidence of schizotypal personality disorder found among first-degree biological relatives of people with schizophrenia.

DIFFERENTIAL ASSESSMENT

Delineation of schizotypal personality disorder in the DSM evolved from attempts to clarify the boundary between schizophrenia and borderline personality disorder. Schizotypal personality disorder is associated with schizophrenia in a number of important ways. Individuals with schizotypal personality disorder experience subtle distortions of their environment similar to those experienced by individuals with schizophrenia; but the latter have the fully developed syndrome that includes hallucinations or delusions and loss of contact with reality. Under stress, individuals with schizotypal personality disorder may decompensate and display psychotic symptoms, but these lapses are usually of brief duration. Schizotypal personality disorder can be distinguished from schizophrenia by the absence of psychosis (but, if psychotic symptoms are present, they are brief and fragmentary). In severe instances, anhedonia (or an inability to experience pleasure) and severe depression may also be present.

The notion that there is a relationship between schizotypal personality disorder and schizophrenia arises in part from how people with these two disorders behave. For example, symptoms such as ideas of reference, illusions, and paranoid thinking are similar, yet those with schizotypal personality disorder have somewhat better interpersonal skills and are more connected to their social environment (Barlow & Durand, 2014). Ongoing research into these two disorders seems to support a genetic component in each disorder. Several theorists suggest that individuals with a diagnosis of schizotypal personality can be influenced by their environment (Anglina, Cohenab, & Chena, 2008; Berenbaum, Valera, & Kerns, 2003; Hoeksema, 2014). However, there is also support for the biological theories of schizotypal personality disorder (Voglmaier et al., 2000).

The diagnostic picture for individuals with schizotypal personality disorder requires five (or more) of the following behaviors:

- *Ideas of reference*—Where the person experiences innocuous events or mere coincidences and believes they have a strong personal significant meaning for them.
- *Odd beliefs*—Magical thinking that influences behavior and is inconsistent with cultural norms seen in superstitiousness or a belief in clairvoyance, telepathy, or a "sixth sense" that goes well beyond the norms of their subculture (for instance, the person may feel they have "special powers" to be able to sense events before they happen or to read others' thoughts).

- *Unusual perceptual experiences*—A feeling of having special powers (for instance, sensing that another person is present or hearing a voice whispering his or her name).
- *Odd thinking or speech*—Where the person's speech may include unusual or idiosyncratic phrasing and construction in that a conversation is characterized by vagueness, digressions, excessive abstractions, limited vocabulary, or an unusual pattern of words (for example, the person may state he was not "talkable" at work).
- *Suspiciousness or paranoid ideation*—The person may be suspicious and paranoid (for instance, the person may believe coworkers are undermining their reputation at work).
- *Inappropriate or constricted affect*—The person is unable to negotiate a full range of affect with others or may interact in an inappropriate, stiff, or constricted manner.
- *Behavior or appearance that is odd, eccentric, or peculiar*—The individual may show unusual mannerisms, be a little sloppy in their appearance, or be dressed in a way that does not quite "fit together" (for example, they can be generally described as being unkempt, and they also show unusual mannerisms such as avoiding eye contact).
- *Lack of friends or close confidants other than relatives*—The person has few or no close friends and may seem uncomfortable relating to others, even though they may express unhappiness about a lack of relationships; in addition, the individual's behavior can suggest a decreased desire for intimate contacts (for instance, they are rarely able to form intimate relationships).
- *Anxiety in social situations*—These individuals are anxious in social situations, and especially those involving unfamiliar people; they may keep to themselves because they feel they are "different" and do not fit in (for example, it is usually impossible for them to sustain employment that requires extended social contact).

From an early age, the major characteristics of schizotypal personality disorder can be seen in individuals who are unable to have long-lasting interpersonal relationships, which leave them severely isolated and reduce their capacity for ever maintaining connections with others. They often feel anxious with strangers and cannot banter or make small talk. They exhibit distortions in their thinking, eccentric perceptions, and magical thinking, which unfortunately make them appear unusual or odd to others. Often, these individuals manifest unusual perceptual experiences, such as feeling as if another person is in the room when they are in fact alone. Their behavior is influenced by associated odd beliefs or by magical thinking inconsistent with cultural norms, including superstitions and belief in telepathy. Frequently, they believe they have special powers of thought and insight. Schizotypal personality disorder typically begins in early adulthood and is seen in a variety of contexts.

Tyrone White, as described in the earlier vignette, is distant from others and pictured as a loner. Unlike those individuals with schizophrenia, Tyrone has not lost total contact with reality. Ben Rogers, who we earlier saw as someone with a paranoid personality disorder, is characterized as hostile and suspicious. The following case, describing the social worker's encounter with Juan Enrique Martinez, highlights the different presentation of these behaviors as seen in the diagnosis of schizotypal personality disorder.

CASE The Case of Juan Enrique Martinez

Juan Enrique Martinez, a 35-year-old single (never married) Mexican American man, has been urged to attend our community mental health center's activities program by his mother. Mrs. Martinez seems somewhat older than her stated age of 58 and looks really tired. She sounds worried as she tells the social worker that her son "just needs a little help making friends."

When the social worker asks for more details, Mrs. Martinez adds that Juan has had a lifelong pattern of social isolation. She can't remember a time when her son had some "real" friends—he usually spends hours "doing nothing."

Mrs. Martinez says it all started when Juan was about 13, and he lost interest "in just about everything." During that time, she took him to her parish priest, who assured her, "Juan will grow out of it; it's just a stage he's going through."

"Well, he never grew out of it," Mrs. Martinez adds ruefully. "He hasn't been able to keep a bunch of jobs, including his last one as a postal worker." Apparently, Juan did not show up for work on multiple occasions and could not deal with the close public contact. She stated, "I'm worried that Juan will lose his room in the boarding house because he has no way to pay the rent now ... and he was picked up by the Metro Dade police. They charged him with disorderly conduct and said he was drinking. I know my son and he is not a drinker."

Mrs. Martinez confides that Juan's appearance is becoming "more strange." When asked to explain what she means, she says, "He's been getting a lot of tattoos, and now he's talking about wanting to get some body piercing done." She frowns, looks momentarily distracted, and then asks for the social worker's opinion about the health risks associated with body piercing. Mrs. Martinez quickly apologized for shifting the focus of the discussion, admitting how hard it is for her to talk about her son's odd behavior. Her main concern, the real reason she wanted Juan to come to the mental health center, was because "he is acting really weird." By that she concedes that she can live with all his tattoos, but she's concerned that Juan now believes he can sense forces around him. "He is so sure these forces exist and that they are somehow against him," Mrs. Martinez relates. She also indicates that Juan is highly suspicious about other people. "These suspicious thoughts are what caused Juan's problems in his last job—but he also does not get along with people he has known for years."

Mrs. Martinez sighs heavily and goes on to say that it is harder and harder for her to communicate with her son. She adds, "I worry that he will turn out to be just like my brother, Lorenzo, who was sent away to a mental hospital when he was 17. Everybody thought he was crazy. He used to hear voices and see things that no one else did. I remember during one visit that the doctor wanted me to convince Lorenzo to take his medicine. I asked the doctor what this medicine was for and the doctor looked at me so surprised. He told me, 'I thought you knew! Lorenzo is schizophrenic.' I don't want that to happen to my little Juan." Mrs. Martinez begins to cry.

When the social worker meets with Juan, he is distant and conveys a high level of distrust. He describes in intricate detail his somewhat uneventful everyday life. He tells the social worker that he really doesn't like people and he does not want to join any group here at the center where he will have to "talk to people." Juan then stands up, and with an almost forced air of bravado, walks out of the office saying, "If my mother wants to talk, she can join your group."

Juan Enrique Martinez's Diagnosis Is as Follows:

Schizotypal personality disorder

Competency 7 b

Assessment Summary Juan's interpersonal pattern of relating shows that he is unable to form relationships or respond to others in a meaningful way. His sense of "forces" around him, suspiciousness, and paranoia keep him socially isolated. The practitioner's conversation with Juan is difficult because of his peculiar communication style; for instance, he goes into intricate detail about his day, which in reality was uneventful. Although his communication (and his appearance) can be characterized as "odd" and his perception of his social environment is subtly distorted, Juan does not show evidence of hallucinations or delusions characteristic of those with schizophrenia. Mrs. Martinez mentions that Juan was picked up for disorderly conduct by the police, who indicated that he was drinking. She insists that her son is not a drinker. Unfortunately, the social worker was not able to explore this further with Juan, but hopefully if he can become engaged with the community mental health center's activities, this could be further clarified. What is clear are his mother's concerns, and they seem to have increased over time. Unfortunately (but not surprisingly), Juan is indifferent to his mother's worries.

Despite a close community, Juan is withdrawn from his social environment, and his recent job loss has further increased his isolation. In this case illustration, his isolation can be traced back to early adolescence, a time when peer influence is important—and yet, it was during this period that Juan began to lose interest "in just about everything," according to his mother. She characterizes him now as a socially isolated young man. Participation in the community mental health center's activities group might decrease Juan's social isolation, but his abrupt departure from the interview suggests this may be a frightening prospect for him. Mrs. Martinez points out that Juan tends to wander around doing nothing, and although Juan's behaviors and appearance might be unusual, they are not provocative.

Competency 7 c

The involvement of "significant others" is important. As in Juan's situation, this is what led him to the mental health center. Juan's mother has been a mediating influence in his social environment as seen in the biological, psychological, and social influences in his life (refer to Figure 16.3). For example, she is the person in his social environment who brings him to the center for help with socialization or to make friends. Though reluctant, Juan did come into the agency, and perhaps with time he would feel more comfortable participating in activities there.

Oddities in behavior, thinking, perception, and communication (in addition to a strong family history of schizophrenia) distinguish those individuals with schizotypal personality disorders from the general population as well as from those with other personality disorders. However, making distinctions among a number of personality disorders can be challenging as there are several that share features with schizotypal personality disorder, such as paranoid, schizoid, avoidant, narcissistic, and borderline personality disorders. For instance, both paranoid and schizoid personality disorders are characterized by social detachment and restricted affect that can look very much like the symptoms of schizotypal personality disorder, but the latter is distinguished by cognitive (or perceptual) distortions and marked eccentricity or oddness. Limited close relationships characterize both the schizoid and avoidant symptom picture, but the lack of a desire for relationships and persistent detachment differentiates schizotypal personality disorder. In addition, individuals with narcissistic personality disorder, much like Juan, experience intense discomfort in interpersonal relationships and an impaired ability to form close relationships. However, in contrast to Juan, who is extremely

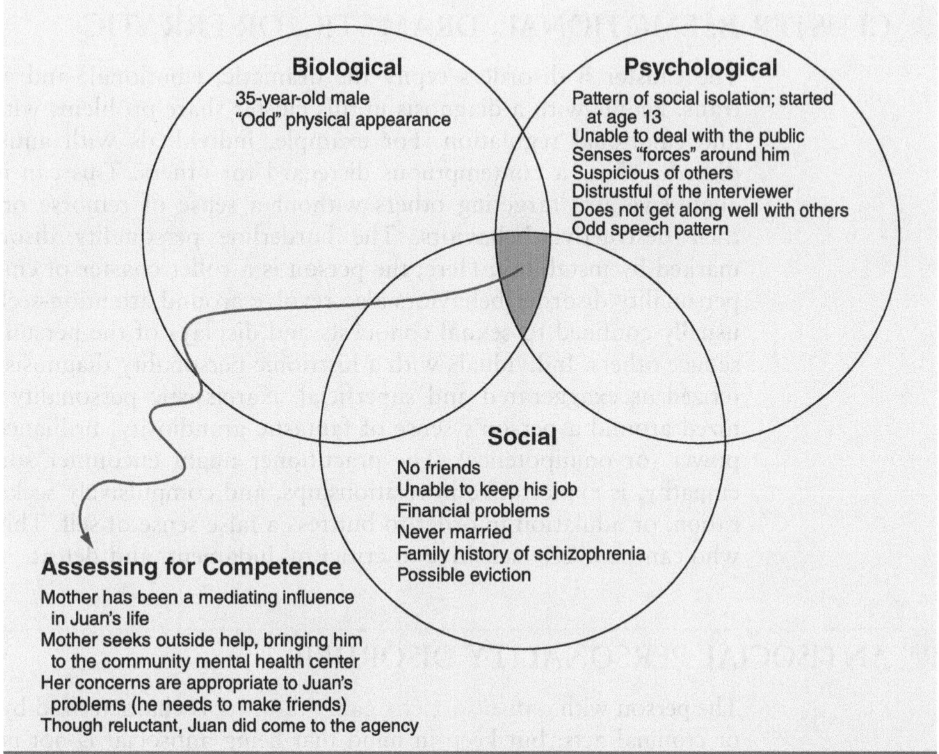

FIGURE 16.3 › Schizotypal Personality Disorder
The interactions of the biological, psychological, and social variables in Juan Enrique Martinez's life.

uncomfortable if he has to "talk to people," those with narcissistic personality disorder are primarily afraid of having their imperfections or flaws revealed. Psychotic-like symptoms are shared between borderline and schizotypal personality disorders. However, for the borderline personality disorder picture, these symptoms are more transient and more closely related to the person's intense anger or anxiety in response to stress. In contrast, the psychotic-like symptoms seen in the schizotypal personality disorder are more enduring and less likely to be associated with affect. There is a high rate of co-occurrence between borderline and schizotypal personality disorders, so making the differential diagnosis is not an easy process for the practitioner (APA, 2013).

Moreover, the qualities of social isolation, oddness, solitary behavior or the lack of friends, and speech difficulties characteristic of schizotypal personality disorder add to the difficulties of differentiating this disorder from the communication disorders and children with the neurodevelopmental disorder of autism spectrum disorder, where they, too, can be seen as "odd."

Those with schizotypal personality disorder share other mental disorders with psychotic symptoms, and the diagnosis is assigned in the same manner as reviewed in the earlier discussion of paranoid personality disorder.

CLUSTER B: EMOTIONAL, DRAMATIC, OR ERRATIC

The Cluster B disorders typify the dramatic, emotional, and erratic personality traits. People with a diagnosis in this cluster share problems with impulse control and emotional regulation. For example, individuals with antisocial personality disorder show a contemptuous disregard for others. This can involve violent or aggressive acts targeting others without a sense of remorse or guilt for any of their destructive behaviors. The borderline personality disorder diagnosis is marked by instability. Here, the person is a roller coaster of emotions. Histrionic personality disorder behaviors also revolve around attention-seeking, but they are usually confined to sexual conquests and displays of the person's irresistibility to seduce others. Individuals with a histrionic personality diagnosis are often characterized as exaggerated and superficial. Narcissistic personality disorder is organized around a person's sense of fantastic grandiosity, brilliance, perfection, and power (or omnipotence). The practitioner might encounter someone who lacks empathy, is exploitative in relationships, and compulsively seeks attention, admiration, or adulation in order to buttress a false sense of self. This is the individual who can be overly sensitive to criticism, judgment, and defeat.

ANTISOCIAL PERSONALITY DISORDER

The person with antisocial personality disorder is characterized by continual asocial or criminal acts; but keep in mind that being antisocial is not necessarily synonymous with criminality. While these individuals tend to have a long and involved history of illegal activities, they are also engaged in lying, theft, substance abuse, and rejection of social norms, and can show a lack of remorse for any hurtful actions directed toward others. These behaviors initially surface in childhood and intensify during adolescence. It is important to note the developmental nature of antisocial behavior in that many adults with antisocial personality disorder had the diagnosis of a conduct disorder as children (Salekin, 2006).

Because antisocial personality disorder results in a variety of problems with law enforcement, the legal system, and within families, it has been the subject of more clinical interest and research than any other personality disorder. Unfortunately, the studies have revealed that the future is pessimistic for those with antisocial personality disorder (Meloy, 2007).

PREVAILING PATTERN

The scenario for antisocial personality disorder is variable at best. Using criteria from previous DSMs, the 12-month prevalence rates are between 0.2 and 3.3 percent (APA, 2013). The disorder is more prevalent among men, and these individuals are also considered to be an increased risk for substance abuse, alcoholism, vagrancy, suicide, criminal activity, repeated incarceration, and death by violence (Fazel & Danesh, 2002; Moeller & Dougherty, 2001). Their antisocial disposition, tendencies, and attitudes are usually chronic and lifelong; however, this pattern can shift over time in some individuals. As they reach age 30 and beyond, many of them burn out, and gradually the frequency of their antisocial acts decreases. Often the antisocial behaviors are replaced with somatic behaviors (e.g., hypochondriasis). This is a serious disorder, and overall the long-term outcome is generally considered to be poor, regardless of the person's gender (Colman et al., 2009). It is considered as the diagnosis of last resort. Over 20 years ago, Stoudemire (1994) observed, "In the psychiatric setting, antisocial personality disorder is viewed as one of the most difficult personalities to treat" (p. 187).

DIFFERENTIAL ASSESSMENT

The essential features of this disorder include a pervasive pattern of disregard for and violation of the rights of others, usually beginning in earnest after the age of 15, with evidence of conduct disorder before age 15 (APA, 2013). As youngsters, they often acquire a reputation for being the neighborhood bully toward younger children and for being cruel toward animals. Overall, these are individuals who behave in ways that most of us would find unacceptable, such as stealing from friends and family or being deceitful, irresponsible, and impulsive (DeBrito & Hodgkins, 2009). As youngsters, these individuals appear out of control, and most efforts to discipline them have little or no lasting effect. Nothing seems to have an impact on them or be able to touch them. They remain unmoved by any kindness shown, steal and destroy property for the pleasure of it, and habitually lie even when telling the truth is just as convenient.

Competency 7 b

Although many of these individuals have a childhood marked by incorrigibility, school problems, and/or running away from home, there are a number of complex biological, psychological, and cultural factors that combine in intricate ways for someone to develop antisocial personality disorder (Gelhorn, Sakai, Price, & Crowley, 2007). This highlights the competency-based assessment and draws attention to the social worker's ability to critique and apply knowledge of human development in order to better understand the person and his or her environment. Antisocial personality disorder is more common among first-degree biological relatives, and adoption studies indicate genetic and environmental factors associated with its development. Therefore it is important for practitioners to reserve this assessment for individuals who are over the age of 18 and who have a history of conduct disorder before the age of 15 (APA, 2013; Meloy, 2007).

The major characteristics of antisocial personality disorder include three or more of the following that have been going on since the age of 15 years:

- *Defiance of or failure to conform to social norms*—They do not feel they should obey societal norms or laws, favoring instead making their own rules. They are most often concerned with their own needs, wants, and desires, and do not allow anyone or anything to get in the way of getting what they want.
- *Deceitful, or the absence of consistent truthfulness*—For these individuals, being truthful is also considered a matter of convenience; if a lie proves more useful, then that is what will be used. These individuals have no qualms about using different aliases, changing occupations, and moving from location to location—especially if they are trying to elude the law. They are excellent at running confidence schemes for their own profit, pleasure, or power.

- *Impulsive*—The individual fails to plan ahead, and decisions are made on the spur of the moment and without considering the consequences. It is not uncommon to find a history of sudden job changes, residences, or relationships.
- *Irritable and aggressive*—Reckless, violent, and cruel behavior is common among those with antisocial personality disorder. They are irritable when dealing with authority but seem comfortable using aggression against others. Frequently they are involved in physical assaults and confrontations; for example, there is a high incidence of reported domestic violence and child abuse.
- *Reckless disregard for the safety of self or others*—These are the individuals who will speed, drive while intoxicated, or be involved in multiple accidents, showing little or no concern for the safety of themselves or others. They may engage in high-risk sexual behaviors or fail to care for a child in a way that puts that child in danger.
- *Irresponsible*—Those with antisocial personality disorder tend to be consistently and extremely irresponsible as seen in problems fulfilling commitments such as those to family and employers, and they may have difficulty meeting financial obligations. Their marriages tend to be troubled, violent, and short-lived. Being faithful in a relationship, whether there is a marriage or not, is a matter of convenience, and children are often viewed as being a burden.
- *Lack of remorse or empathy*—These individuals have no feelings or remorse for those they harm. They rationalize reasons for hurting or taking advantage of others (e.g., "They should have known better than to trust me"), and often blame their victim for making them act in a harmful manner because they consider themselves smart enough to "get away with it."

For someone with antisocial personality disorder, a veneer of charm and a smooth and ingratiating seductiveness may mask the interest in exclusively meeting that person's own needs. These are people who often present themselves as fascinating, disarming, and beguiling; they are the ultimate con artists. At the same time, they are undependable, impetuous, and dishonest. They do things that others find particularly offensive (e.g., stealing from family members or friends). Very early on, Dr. Robert Hare (1993) conducted extensive studies of those with psychopathic personalities and he eloquently describes these individuals in his book *Without Conscience: The Disturbing World of the Psychopaths Among Us:*

> [They are] Social predators who charm, manipulate, and ruthlessly plow their way through life, leaving a broad trail of broken hearts, shattered expectations, and empty wallets. Completely lacking in conscience and in feelings for others, they selfishly take what they want and do as they please, violating social norms and expectations without the slightest sense of guilt or regret. (p. xi)

These individuals are often described as having a long history of being rebellious problem children, and during their adolescent years continue a pattern of activities harmful to, and violating the rights of, others (APA, 2013). Many come to the practitioner's attention through a court system mandate. They generally recount extensive histories filled with arrests for fraud, theft, embezzlement, alcohol (DUIs) and drug use, physical violence, and disregard for alimony and/or child support payments. Although most tend to have poor employment records, many individuals do display a high degree of success in the business or corporate world. It is a mistake to assume that individuals with an antisocial personality disorder live in poor neighborhoods, ride motorcycles, wear torn T-shirts, or any other stereotypical description—they can be anyone.

The following vignette describes some of the behaviors considered typical of antisocial personality disorder.

CASE: THE CASE OF LUKE ROSSEY

"I want to divorce my brother Luke," said Sara Rossey, weeping. "Isn't there anything I can do? Legal aid? The court system?" The social worker prompted her to continue.

Sara took a deep breath, and went on, "Luke is 23 and works as a cable installer—at least that's what he's doing this week. He's had at least 20 different jobs, but he can't keep any of them. It's not that he's stupid or anything. In fact, when he was in school they tested his IQ, and it was somewhere up in the 160s! Anyway, what he did last week was the last straw for me and my family, no matter how smart he is."

"What happened?" asked the practitioner.

Sara continued, "He was caught threatening an elderly woman at knifepoint at a neighborhood ATM!"

"Tell me a bit more about Luke," the social worker said as she leaned forward.

"Oh, God, I don't even know where to start, 'cause it seems like he's always been in trouble one way or another," Sara began again. "Well, when he was little, all the other kids used to pick on him because he was smaller than them. I guess he got fed up, and 1 day he killed a couple of their dogs and drowned a kitten. They left him alone after that—mostly, I think, because their parents told them to stay away from Luke." She stared at a spot on the rug as if she were transported back in time. "Now that I think about it, I guess that's when he first started to be mean ... I mean *really* mean. He would pick out some little kid and beat him up real bad for no reason. ... and that's before all the attention about bullies. Luke was suspended lots of times from school, and even when he wasn't suspended he sometimes just didn't go. I remember there were weeks at a time when he missed school. I don't think the school really cared, because when he was there he would steal from classmates, threaten teachers, and damage school property."

She continued, "My poor mother really had her hands full with him. In her heart, I think she had a hard time believing Luke could be so mean. Our dad died when Luke was 6—Dad was an alcoholic and I think maybe he used some drugs, too. So Mom raised the two of us by herself. She just couldn't control Luke. He joined a gang when he was about 13, and right after that he was sent to juvenile hall for assault and battery of a police officer ... who was just doing his job breaking up a fight Luke was in the middle of. I think it was some kind of gang initiation rite. Luke got some shrink who told the judge that Luke was a victim of conduct disorder or something like that. They just slapped his wrists, and sent him to some country-club youth ranch where he got time off for good behavior. I don't know how he fooled them, but as soon as he got out, he went right back to his old ways and his gang buddies."

"He started boozing it up nonstop and using every drug he could get his hands on. I learned a whole new language. Have you ever heard of 'shrooms'? Anyway," Sara continued, "When Luke was 16, they sent him to the state youth program for 9 months. That didn't do him any good, either. As soon as he was back home, he got busted for selling drugs to an undercover cop. They sent him up again, and after he was released they made him go to some kind of drug rehab program. Some rehabilitation!" Sara exclaimed, disgusted. "That's where I think he learned more ways of messing up. He would relapse and then was just sent away again. Eventually, Mom didn't want him to live at home anymore. She felt like a prisoner in her own home. Mom had to put a lock on every door—if she didn't Luke would steal everything that wasn't nailed down and sell it for money to buy drugs

CASE The Case of Luke Rossey (Continued)

or booze. Luke even hocked Mom's wedding ring——for 10 lousy bucks. And it was an heirloom worth a couple of thousand dollars. He got just enough for Dad's pocket watch to buy a bottle of booze. He doesn't care about anyone but himself. That's why I want to divorce him."

The social worker responded, "It sounds as if things have been pretty rough for you and your mom."

"That's not even the half of it," she sighed, and then continued. "When Luke was 19, he joined the Army, and Mom and I thought maybe he'd finally get straightened out. Three months later he was court-martialed and thrown out on his ear. He beat up a captain who caught him selling drugs in the barracks. Luke came home after that. He wasn't home more than 2 weeks when his old girlfriend sued him for support of her baby. She had named him as the father, but Luke wouldn't even bother to go for genetic testing. He just denied the baby was his. When I tried to talk to him about the situation, Luke told me, 'Alyssa is a stupid bitch who wants me to support someone else's brat.' Can you believe that? I think he probably used to beat her up, too."

Sara took a deep breath, exhaled slowly, and picked up again, "Luke lives alone now and he drinks basically every night of the week except Sundays. He says taking a day off helps him to keep from having to drink more to feel the effects. His drink of choice is vodka, and he cuts it with a little Diet Coke. Claims he has trouble falling asleep without a little booze in his system. You would think he would have a guilty conscience for all he's done and that would be the reason to keep him up but, no, not Luke. And what with all those DUIs he doesn't even have a driver's license. He depends on his current girlfriend for transportation. Luke has had so many girlfriends I don't even bother to learn their names anymore. And how does he deal with his anger, you might ask?"

Without waiting for an answer, Sara said, "Cocaine is his lifeline. Says the cocaine keeps him focused and directed. If you can believe this, Luke insists that it boosts his self-esteem. He always manages to have enough on hand for a little snort. If you look at Luke, he's in great shape. Works out regularly. I think he learned that from all those rehab programs he was in. The bottom line is that he's dependent on alcohol and cocaine. I've tried talking to him but it's like trying to reason with a 12-year-old adolescent who thinks everything is a funny joke."

When the social worker asked if Sara had ever seen any evidence of psychotic behavior, she replied, "No, he's only a mean son-of-a-...."

Luke Rossey's Diagnosis Is as Follows:
Antisocial personality disorder
Alcohol use disorder, moderate
Cannabis use disorder, moderate
Cocaine use disorder, moderate

Competency 7 c

Assessment Summary The roots of Luke's problems are recognized in his early childhood behavior, which included hurting animals, truancy from school, and stealing things from his parents with no remorse. As Luke's sister talked about her brother when they were growing up, she presented a history of his rebellious, problematic childhood and adolescence. The social worker listens to the client's life story and pays attention to the possibility for those co-occurring diagnoses commonly associated with antisocial personality disorder; for example, Sarah talks about

Luke stealing money to buy drugs or "booze," which can indicate a co-occurring substance disorder (APA, 2013).

Other comorbid diagnoses sharing common features with antisocial personality disorder are the borderline, narcissistic, histrionic, and paranoid personality disorders. However, if the person meets full criteria for one or more of the personality disorders, in addition to antisocial personality disorder, then the practitioner lists all that can be diagnosed. Luke's story indicates a pattern of substance use, particularly alcohol, cannabis, and cocaine, and each diagnosis has been listed. It should be noted that his substance use and antisocial behavior both began in childhood and continued into his adult years. Severity is based on the number of diagnostic criteria, and we see evidence of moderate use (the presence of four to five symptoms) in his story.

Competency 1 a

People with antisocial personality disorder may run into other social problems—and in this case, we find that Luke has a history of legal charges. The practitioner is cautioned to consider all aspects of a client's life before making a diagnosis. If someone does have a criminal record, no matter how long, this does not of itself serve as a qualification for a diagnosis of antisocial personality disorder. The DSM makes a distinction between individuals diagnosed with adult antisocial behavior and those with antisocial personality disorder—that is, the former manifest activities of a career criminal, but these activities do not pervade all aspects of their lives; those with antisocial personality disorder exhibit pervasive egocentricity, selfishness, reckless exploitation, lack of remorse, and failure to conform to social norms.

Competency 1 b

Clearly, it would be easy to dislike Luke, and working with someone like him underscores the importance of the social worker's professional use of self with clients. He would be a very difficult client, and his behaviors are quite complex. More than likely he does not have a great deal of insight into his problems. In addition, Luke is not motivated to come in, and he has not indicated that he thinks there is a problem with his behavior. As far as he is concerned, everyone else is the problem. There is the remote possibility that Luke might come in for counseling at the demand of others, such as an employer, the court system, or a spouse. However, it is very unlikely that he will seek out intervention on his own behalf or follow through with appropriate treatment. If Luke were to seek help, the competency-based assessment would be invaluable because it relies on observation and systematic exploration rather than on unsupported personal reactions by the practitioner. This objectivity would be essential to drawing any conclusions about how the client's behavior is being influenced in all areas of his life. Figure 16.4 shows the interactions of the biological, psychological, and social variables in Luke Rossey's life.

BORDERLINE PERSONALITY DISORDER

Borderline personality disorder is one of the most common personality disorders (Beck, Freeman, & Davis, 2007). An unstable mood, extremely poor relationships with others, and low self-image alternating between extremes of idealization and devaluation (commonly referred to as "splitting") characterize the person with a

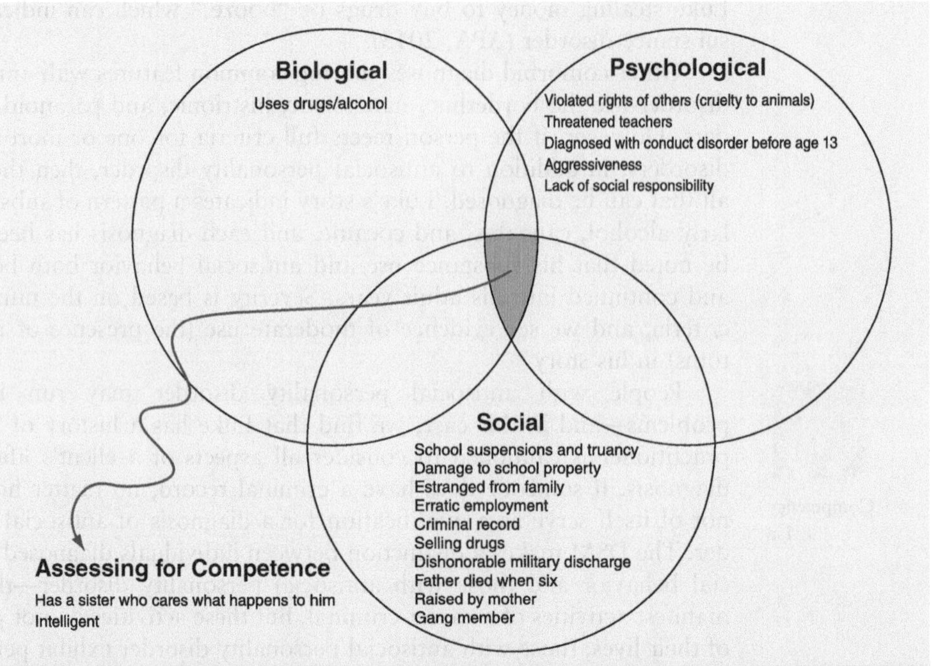

FIGURE 16.4 › ANTISOCIAL PERSONALITY DISORDER
The interactions of the biological, psychological, and social variables in Luke Rossey's life.

borderline personality disorder. These individuals are considered very intense, often going from strong feelings of anger to depression in a very short period of time. Some will engage in self-injurious behaviors, such as cutting themselves to reduce tension.

The person frequently complains of an empty feeling, and he or she is sometimes characterized as chronically bored. They might have difficulty with their own identity. One of the core features of this disorder is dysfunction in the area of emotion; that is, these individuals often engage in behaviors that are suicidal, self-mutilative, or both, cutting, burning, or punching themselves (Neacsiu & Linehan, 2014). The term *borderline personality disorder* was not widely researched until it appeared in the DSM-III in 1980, and since then it has been used too frequently, and inaccurately, to describe any observed form of personality disorder. Before this disorder was added to the DSM-III, borderline individuals often were diagnosed with schizophrenia, latent type. The term was also subjected to a wide range of definitions and continues to be one of the most controversial personality disorder diagnoses.

Although the disorder has been well described in the professional literature, there is still no consensus concerning its etiology or even the meaning of its most notable features (Distel, Trull, & Boomsma, 2009). There is a confusing hodgepodge of hypotheses suggesting that the borderline individual is trying to conceal his or her rage directed toward the mother figure; is manifesting depression over loss of his or her mother; or spending his or her life energy ambivalently pursuing, seeking, and rejecting relationships resembling the original mother–child bond. Others suggest that this disorder results from a lack of "fit" between the mother and her infant. What we do know is borderline personality disorder tends to be almost 5 times more common among first-degree biological relatives of those with the disorder (APA, 2013).

PREVAILING PATTERN

Assessing for a borderline personality disorder can usually be made by early adulthood when the individual has exhibited a pervasive pattern of unstable interpersonal relationships; undergone frantic efforts to avoid real or imagined abandonment; alternated between extremes of idealization and devaluation; experienced identity disturbance; engaged in recurrent suicidal behavior, gestures, or threats; complained of chronic feelings of emptiness; exhibited inappropriate and intense anger or difficulty coping; and exhibited impulsiveness in at least two areas, such as spending money, sexual encounters, and/or substance abuse (APA, 2013). The behaviors that make up this disorder are fairly stable and do not change very much over time. Although this is considered a chronic disorder, most individuals experience a lessening of symptoms as they reach their middle years (Zanarini, Frankenburg, Hennen, Reich, & Silk, 2006).

Approximately 1.6 percent to as high as 5.9 percent of the general population may qualify for the designation of borderline personality disorder (APA, 2013). It is one of the most common personality disorders seen in clinical practice settings and applies to a far greater proportion of clients who seek out mental health care than of those who are not seen in the mental health arena. Molly Layton's (1995) earlier characterization still holds true when she states:

> In the minds of many therapists, the borderline diagnosis has come to be a code word for trouble. The diagnosis signals a kind of impossible case—long, grueling work with the client often challenging the therapist's equanimity over and over, withdrawing in a sulk or attacking in a rage, creating melodramatic scenes, threatening suicide, demanding more and more of the therapist's love and time, while the shaken therapist feels used, abused and manipulated, thinking he or she is often making no difference at all. (p. 36)

DIFFERENTIAL ASSESSMENT

There is agreement that this disorder is characterized by a history of ambivalence, very unstable and intense relationships and moods, erratic and often self-destructive behaviors, feelings of boredom, poor self-esteem, poor impulse control, and a fear of abandonment (Cowen, Harrison, & Burns, 2012). Individuals may also have short-lived psychotic episodes (noted as micro psychotic episodes) when under severe stress, rather than a psychotic break. These symptoms are almost always transient and fleeting. The main feature of borderline personality disorder consists of a pervasive pattern of instability in interpersonal relationships, self-image, affects, and marked impulsivity. For diagnosis, five of the following must be present:

- *Frantic efforts to avoid abandonment*—Even the perception of an impending separation or rejection can lead to profound changes in the person's self-mage, affect, thoughts, and behavior.
- *Poor interpersonal relationships*—The person exhibits a pattern of unstable and intense relationships; for instance, they may idolize someone they just met, demand a lot of time together, and share a great deal of intimate information very early on only to quickly shift to devaluing them. Their primary fear (real or imagined) is of being abandoned and left alone. He or she will make heroic efforts searching for companionship yet at the same time struggle against being engulfed in a relationship.
- *Identity disturbance or unstable self-image*—The person shows sudden and dramatic shifts in his or her self-image; for instance, the person's life has been marked by uncertainty in major life issues (e.g., occupation, education, values, and relationships with others).
- *Marked impulsivity*—These individuals show impulsivity in at least two areas that are self-damaging (e.g., gambling, spending money, binge eating, abusing substances, engaging in unsafe sex, or driving recklessly); this does not include suicidal or self-mutilating behavior as this is addressed as a separate symptomatic behavior.
- *Recurrent suicidal behavior, gestures, or threats, or self-mutilating behavior*—For these individuals, self-mutilative acts (such as cutting or burning), and suicide threats and attempts are common.
- *Affective instability*—These individuals are capable of marked reactivity of mood (e.g., intense episodic dysphoria, irritability, or anxiety that usually lasts for a few hours or, rarely, for a few days); the person's dysphoria is often interrupted by periods of anger, panic, or despair, and the individual is rarely comforted by a sense of well-being.
- *Chronic feelings of emptiness*—These individuals may be troubled by a chronic feeling of emptiness.
- *Inappropriate, intense anger*—The person may have difficulty controlling his or her anger (e.g., frequent temper displays, constant anger, recurrent physical fights); this anger can be seen as extreme sarcasm, bitterness, or verbal outbursts and is often provoked when the individual believes that a lover or caregiver is neglectful, withholding, uncaring, or deserting them.
- *Transient stress-related paranoid ideation or severe dissociative symptoms*—During periods of extreme stress, the individual may experience paranoid ideation or dissociative symptoms (e.g., depersonalization) but they are of short duration, usually lasting minutes or hours, and often in response to a real or imagined abandonment.

The following case portrays a young woman whose behaviors are consistent with those commonly seen in borderline personality disorder.

CASE The Case of Suzie Hutchfield

When Suzie Hutchfield called the community mental health center, she asked for an appointment by saying, "I need someone to help me." An appointment was made for later that week.

"You know it's really hard to make something of yourself when your own father tells you that you're never gonna make much of yourself," Suzie told me. "Do you know what he told me when I was 14 years old? I had just run away from home, 'cause he always smacked me around. When the police brought me home, my dad told me that I'd better learn to be good making money on my back because that's all I'll ever be good for."

She continued, "He was such a dumb shit. You know men have always been jerks, starting with him. He was no Prince Charming. He used to beat me and my younger brother up real good, and then he'd go plant his fat butt in front of the television set and drink his booze. Oh, and he had a girlfriend too, but I bet my mother didn't care."

Suzie is currently employed as a waitress in a delicatessen. However, she admits that she has had a series of jobs, none of which lasted very long. She adds, "I've been married three times, and once I married the same man twice. Did I confuse you? Did you understand what I said?" I nodded my head, indicating that I understood. "Anyway, I can't seem to get it right, even though I'm 42 years old. You know, I'm a single mom—I've got two girls—and even at home I can't get things right. My oldest daughter, Candy, she's 16 and a real piece of work. She should be making As, but skips school a lot. One of these fine days some goody-two-shoe social worker is gonna haul me to jail because that kid's always truant." Suzie went on, "Now my little girl, Heather, she's the best. She's 11 years old, cute as a button, and a better kid you never saw." She added, "Don't that beat all? I got one good kid and one bad one."

"What did you ask? Oh yeah, I remember now. My boyfriend. Well, Bob just moved in with us, but I'm not so happy about it already. I think he's been cheating on me, but he tells me he's not. Twice last week I followed him after he left for his motorcycle repair shop. Anyway, he drove right over to his ex-girlfriend's house, and stayed there for 2 hours! When he came home, I confronted him, and he told me some cock-and-bull story that she needed some 'house maintenance' done. Some maintenance! I've been through this with him before, many, many times. I throw him out, and then he swears this is the last time, but it never is, and I still take him back." She said, "You know there's nothing I hate more than being alone, and if it means taking that bum back, well at least I know what I have, ya know? It's not that I need him. I've had lots of men in my life. I always have a man waiting in the wings. You never know what can happen. I really just don't want to ever be alone."

Suzie leaned toward me and continued in a softer voice, "Can you keep a secret?" I nodded in the affirmative. "I met this orderly last week when I was in the hospital, you know for the cutting and the cocaine."

It should be pointed out that Suzie has been hospitalized several times for suicide attempts by cutting her wrists.

"Anyway, I think he loves me," she confided, "but he's not exactly a rocket scientist, if you know what I mean. We found a broom closet when I was in the hospital and made out a coupla times. We even made a date for after I got out."

"You know, sometimes I just feel empty, so I'll do something really exciting for fun. My old social worker said I do these crazy things for attention. She's so stupid! Not like you—you seem to be real smart and I bet you can help me. What do you think?"

"I once spent $2,000 at Payless Shoes. They're still waiting for me to pay." Suzie explained that she bought all different sizes in men's, children's, and women's shoes. The store manager told her that they had a no-return policy and stamped her receipt to that effect. Despite this, Suzie still tried to return the shoes because she was worried that her credit card was charged over the limit. In fact, as a result of this incident, her credit card was canceled. Suzie also admits to using alcohol and drugs, "But I'm not a drug addict or nothing like that. I just wanna have a good time. You know, snort a little coke, drink a little wine, have a good time—I don't hurt anybody."

CASE — THE CASE OF SUZIE HUTCHFIELD (CONTINUED)

The social worker asked Suzie about her substance use. Suzie responded, "Please don't report me or anything like that but keeping this appointment was so hard that I just had a coupla glasses of wine about 5 hours ago ... just to build my confidence. Like I said, there's a lot of dysfunction in my family and I knew you would ask me about it. It's all so embarrassing. I drink just to forget about it. For years, this is how my life has become. Each day I promise myself not to have a drink or if I did, I would only have one ... just one ... or maybe two just so I could go and do what 'normal' people do. You know, make dinner, check on the girls' homework, and go to bed. Sounds easy, doesn't it? How boring! That's where I'm different. I have to drink for life to be exciting. It lifts me up, takes away my insecurities, and gives me courage and hope. So that first sip of my favorite sav blanc gives me instant relief. I can feel it send waves of calm throughout my entire body."

The social worker was surprised by Suzie's candor. It was as if Suzie had bottled up these feelings for a very long time and nobody had ever cared enough to ask her about how she was doing. Without skipping a beat, Suzie continued, "Then I found cocaine. You might say it's my soul mate. On day one I loved the feeling I got from it and started using it on a regular basis for the last 5 or 6 years. I didn't think it was a problem, let alone an addiction. It was just a social habit. Just trying to chase the buzz, you know? Of course I tried to quit and failed. Found I couldn't go a day without it. So to distract myself I turned to body piercing. Did my ears and got a nipple ring. The one I put in my belly button got infected, so I had it taken out and switched to tattoos. Finally, I started to feel like I was strong and in control of my life. Well, that's not really how I felt so the tats didn't work either. That's where you come in."

SUZIE HUTCHFIELD'S DIAGNOSIS IS AS FOLLOWS:
Borderline personality disorder
Alcohol use disorder, moderate
Cocaine use disorder, moderate

Competency 7 a

ASSESSMENT SUMMARY Suzie's interpersonal relationships have always been unstable, chaotic, and intense. She has a very poor self-image, a fear of being abandoned by others, and a tendency to engage in self-destructive behavior. Confronted with evidence that her boyfriend is cheating on her, she still tries to maintain this flawed relationship by meeting someone else when she was hospitalized for a suicide attempt. Suzie exhibits mood reactivity (a depressed mood that can brighten readily at a positive turn of events) related to her poor impulse control (demonstrated by spending $2,000 on useless shoes), multiple suicide attempts, and alcohol and drug use. While Suzie admits to using alcohol and drugs, she denies the chronic extent of use. Figure 16.5 summarizes the major interactions of the biological, psychological, and social factors particular to Suzie's life.

Competency 6 a

The borderline personality is characterized by gross impairment in behavior, cognitive and emotional styles, and interpersonal relationships. Historically, people with borderline personality disorder have been stereotyped as being very difficult, demanding, impatient, and prone to acting out. You might have encountered a practitioner who has avoided working with someone like Suzie, and they may have even characterized their client by his or her diagnosis rather than those factors

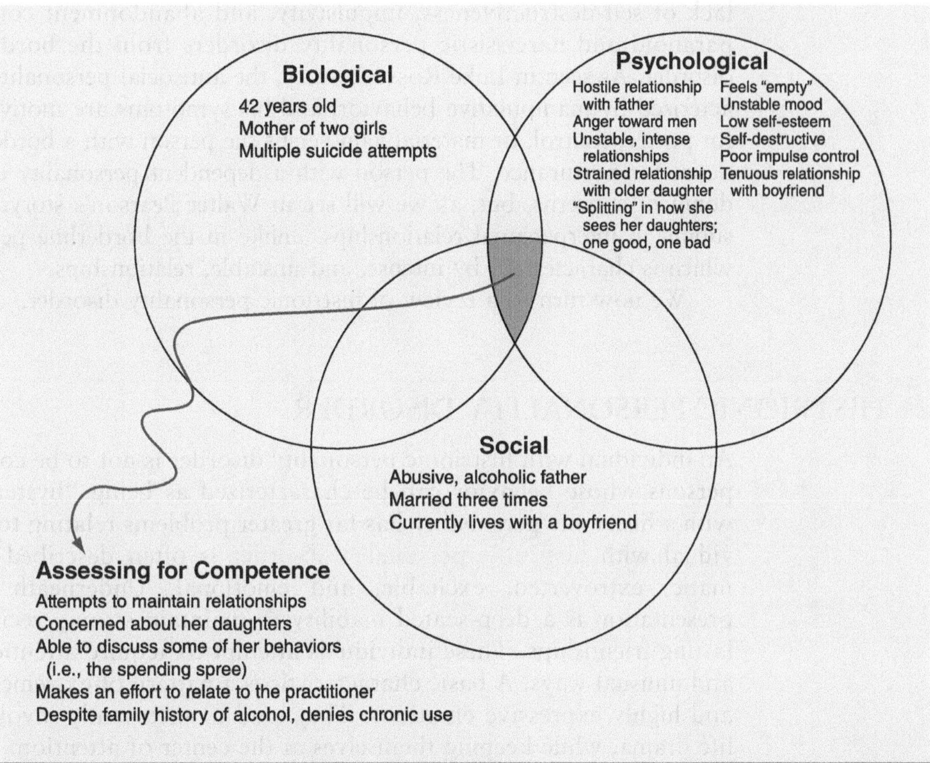

FIGURE 16.5 › Borderline Personality Disorder
The interactions of the biological, psychological, and social variables in Suzie Hutchfield's life.

that make this person unique. The competency-based assessment is concerned with individual differences and is sensitive to the factors that influence someone like Suzie in her social environment. For instance, Suzie does convey to the practitioner some sense of wanting to make changes in her life.

Competency 7 b

Clinical attention should be drawn to the possible coexistence of a mood, substance abuse, or eating disorder (Grant et al., 2008; Zanarini, Reichman, Frankenburg, Reich, & Fitzmaurice, 2010), and Suzie's story reflects a history of alcohol and substance use, specifically cocaine. Borderline personality disorder also shares features with other personality disorders highlighting the importance of a differential assessment.

The individual with histrionic personality disorder also shows extreme emotions but does not exhibit chronic feelings of emptiness or loneliness, self-destructive behaviors, or intensively impaired relationships seen in those with a borderline personality disorder. Differentiation between schizotypal personality disorder and the borderline personality disorder considers differences between prolonged episodes of paranoid ideas or illusions; that is, in borderline personality disorder, the symptoms are more transient, interpersonally reactive, and responsive to external structuring. A relatively stable self-image and relative lack of self-destructiveness, impulsivity, and abandonment concerns distinguish paranoid and narcissistic personality disorders from the borderline personality disorder. As seen in Luke Rossey's story, the antisocial personality disorder is characterized by manipulative behavior, and his symptoms are motivated by the desire for power, control, or material gain versus the person with a borderline personality's desire for nurturance. The person with a dependent personality disorder has abandonment concerns, but, as we will see in Walter Pearson's story, they appease and submit in interpersonal relationships, unlike in the borderline personality disorder, which is characterized by intense, and unstable, relationships.

We now turn to a review of histrionic personality disorder.

HISTRIONIC PERSONALITY DISORDER

An individual with histrionic personality disorder is not to be confused with those persons whose behavior can be characterized as being "hysterical"; the person with a histrionic personality has far greater problems relating to others. The individual with histrionic personality disorder is often described as colorful, dramatic, extroverted, excitable, and emotional. Underneath this flamboyant presentation is a deep-seated inability to maintain strong, reciprocal, and long-lasting friendships. These individuals attempt to acquire attention in inexplicable and unusual ways. A basic characteristic is a pattern of extreme attention seeking and highly expressive emotions. They tend to incessantly involve others in their life drama, while keeping themselves at the center of attention. Others frequently describe these individuals as superficial, disingenuous, and unconvincing. Although all of these characteristics are (mercifully) not found in everyone with histrionic personality disorder, they do serve as a means for assembling an initial basis for making an assessment.

PREVAILING PATTERN

The prevalence of histrionic disorder is 1.84 percent of the general U.S. population (APA, 2013). This is a lifelong pattern of behavior, although symptoms generally tend to be modulated by the aging process. It remains unclear whether these individuals just tend to burn out due to the amount of energy required to maintain their character throughout the years (Barlow & Durand, 2014). What we do know is that the personality disorders originate in childhood and do continue into the adult years, drawing the attention of others. When researchers have been able to follow a person's progress over the years, problems associated with the disorder continue (Ferguson, 2010). These are the individuals who may get into trouble with the law, abuse substances, and act promiscuously.

DIFFERENTIAL ASSESSMENT

Those with histrionic disorder have a long-standing pattern of excessive emotionality and attention seeking, which seeps into most areas of their lives. They are often described as being provocative and sexually seductive. They are always overly concerned with their physical attractiveness. These features are characteristic of the American culture's stereotypical female and may lead to overdiagnosis of histrionic disorder among women (Barlow & Durand, 2014). Consider histrionic disorder only if the person's emotional expression is excessive within her cultural group and causes distress or impairment. The need for approval can be so excessive at times that they will call attention to themselves through their speech, dress, behavior, and extreme emotions. Of those with histrionic personality disorder, the women tend to dress and act seductively, whereas the men act tough or "macho." Relationships (in both genders) are inclined to be stormy and short-lived, as the person becomes easily bored with others; conversely, others may become fed up with their behavior and leave. These individuals rarely maintain stable, enduring, and meaningful relationships. They are often described as shallow, lacking in substance, and incapable of having reciprocal meaningful relationships with others.

To inform the diagnosis, the major features of histrionic personality disorder are indicated by five of the following:

- *Grandiose sense of self-importance*—These individuals can be found to overestimate their abilities and inflate their accomplishments; for instance, they appear to others as boastful and pretentious.
- *Preoccupied with fantasies of unlimited success, power, brilliance, beauty, or ideal love*—These individuals can be found comparing themselves to famous people or think that they are long overdue for admiration and privilege. Relationships with others are apt to be superficial and lack genuine feelings or concern.
- *Show rapidly shifting and shallow expression of emotions*—These individuals often have rapid shifts of emotion that may seem artificial to others.
- *Concerns with "presentation" or physical appearance*—The individual with a histrionic personality disorder may change his or her "presentation" depending upon the circumstances as they attempt to engage whoever is present and to draw attention to themselves. These individuals dress in extravagant, lavish, and provocative styles, and women use makeup, hairstyles, and clothes to attract further attention.
- *Speech that is excessively impressionistic and lacks detail*—The person expresses his or her opinion with a dramatic flair that lacks substance, and he or she is usually vague and diffuse.
- *Self-dramatization, theatric, and exaggerated expression of emotion*—These individuals often have rapid shifts of emotion that may seem artificial to others. They are also quite manipulative, using strong emotional outbursts to get their own way, embarrassing friends and acquaintances (e.g., hugging a casual acquaintance with excessive ardor, sobbing uncontrollably on a minor sentimental event, or having a temper tantrum).
- *Easily influenced and susceptible*—These individuals are very impressionable, become enthusiastic about the latest fads, and base their convictions on very little evidence.
- *Considers relationships more intimate than they are*—It is not uncommon for the person with histrionic personality disorder to refer to friends or colleagues as "a dear friend" or to interact with a professional that they just met by their first name.

Making the distinction between histrionic and borderline personality disorders is admittedly difficult. Both disorders may be assessed for the same individual, but the two should be noted separately. Histrionic traits do occur in a number of other personality disorders, and the overlap has caused some to question whether the histrionic personality disorder should be reclassified (Bakkevig & Karterud, 2010). However, there are certain specific differential points that help clarify making a correct assessment:

- Individuals with a narcissistic personality may be quite self-aggrandizing, constantly searching for praise, and needing to be the center of attention—but they usually lack the intense emotion seen in those diagnosed with histrionic personality disorder.
- Individuals with borderline personality may be characterized as flamboyant and self-destructive; however, they have an enduring sense of emptiness and loneliness. In contrast, individuals with histrionic personality disorder are seen as shallow and lacking substance.
- Those with antisocial personality disorder tend to be highly impulsive, as are individuals with histrionic personality disorder; however individuals with histrionic personality disorder become dependent on or deeply attached to others, unlike the person with antisocial personality disorder.

The following case illustrates many of the features of someone with histrionic personality disorder.

CASE THE CASE OF TAMIKA BROWN

During a routine physical examination, Tamika Brown, a 43-year-old African American single parent, suddenly started crying and blurted out to her doctor that she was thinking about committing suicide. She said she had been playing with a razor and making marks on her arms. Tamika stated that she used to do this when she was a teenager to get her mother's attention. The physician immediately made an emergency referral to a nearby county mental health center.

The social worker at the center noted Ms. Brown's appearance as soon as she walked in. She was almost 6 feet tall and had what could be considered a naturally graceful style, but the most striking thing was Ms. Brown's unusual hair. It was braided but had what looked like "spikes" accentuating her forehead and was partially shaved in the back. Her clothes could be characterized as "dramatic"; everything was black, accented with animal prints, and extremely tight fitting. She wore about a dozen gold bracelets on each arm and a large, heavy gold chain around her neck. Her large hoop earrings, also in a gold color, further accented her hair style. The first three or four buttons of Ms. Brown's shirt were left unbuttoned revealing her bra (also black) and showing extensive cleavage. Her overall appearance could best be described as "distracting." The social worker asked why she had been referred for an evaluation.

Ms. Brown laughed and said, "I know something about psychotherapy and I'm hoping to find a special therapist who understands me and will really help me. I promise to be your most interesting patient. You know, [chuckling] been there, done that?"

During the interview, Ms. Brown described a tortured childhood that included an abusive alcoholic father, an absent mother, and being picked on by other children for being a "fat butt." When she became an adolescent, she lost weight and began a dedicated workout regimen. Boys began to be attracted to her, but she completely ignored them. Instead, she continued to exercise and study hard in school so she could "get out" of the neighborhood and as far away as possible from her family.

Tamika confided that she wants to be a model. In her early 20s, she had breast implants, lip augmentation, and surgical tightening of the buttock muscles to further accentuate her figure. Although she is currently working, the nature of her job is somewhat vague and mysterious. She happened to bring along her portfolio and offered to show it to the social worker. Tamika's professional photo book included several seductive poses in bikini bathing suits, lingerie, and seminude shots. As she put her portfolio away, she explained that she belongs to a gym where some very famous movie and television stars are also members. She stated, "It's just a matter of time until I get discovered. My body is way better than some of those cows," she sneered. "I can't believe they still haven't asked me to work out with them. Well, I know it's because they are jealous. They can't compete with me."

Tamika makes Herculean efforts to be seen around the hot spots in town. She dines in only the trendiest South Beach restaurants, always arriving in a super-deluxe stretch limousine. She makes a dramatic entrance because she loves to wear the most revealing clothes she can find. "If ya got, flaunt it!" she says as she bobbles her head and grins. The South Beach location is important to her, because that's the area known for attracting celebrities. Tamika went on to say that she routinely sends photographs of herself doing the town "big time" to several of the local newspapers.

When asked about the other people in her life, Tamika recounted multiple relationships that were short-lived and unsatisfying to her. She concluded, "I don't have a boyfriend right now. I dumped the last one, Geoffrey Halesander, 'cause he was so shallow—and besides, he didn't meet any of my needs. I like to be taken out and pampered, but all he wanted to do was sit around the house and watch television. How boring!"

The social worker remembered that the primary objective for this intake session was to assess suicidal ideation. Up to this point, Ms. Brown did not address the issue when asked about purpose of the referral. Instead, the conversation was dominated by Ms. Brown's interests and needs.

TAMIKA BROWN'S DIAGNOSIS IS AS FOLLOWS:
Histrionic personality disorder

Competency 7 a

ASSESSMENT SUMMARY People with histrionic personality disorder are differentiated from the other personality disorders by their attention-seeking behaviors. Tamika Brown reflects this characteristic way of relating to her social environment by being overly dramatic in her emotional displays, her attempts to be the center of attention, and her inability to be ignored. She is self-centered and appears unable to develop any degree of intimacy. Tamika has no insight about what went wrong with Geoffrey Halesander, her former boyfriend. In actuality, her ability to connect in a meaningful way had always been short-lived. There is a manipulative quality to Tamika's relationships. Individuals with antisocial personality disorder are also manipulative, but their motivation is to gain profit, power, or some other material gain. As a consequence of her very strong need to be the center of attention, Tamika has few enduring friendships in contrast to someone with dependent personality disorder, who is excessively dependent on others for praise and guidance. Those with borderline personality share Tamika's attention-seeking behaviors are set apart by their self-destructiveness, angry disruptions in close relationships, and chronic feeling of emptiness and identity disturbance.

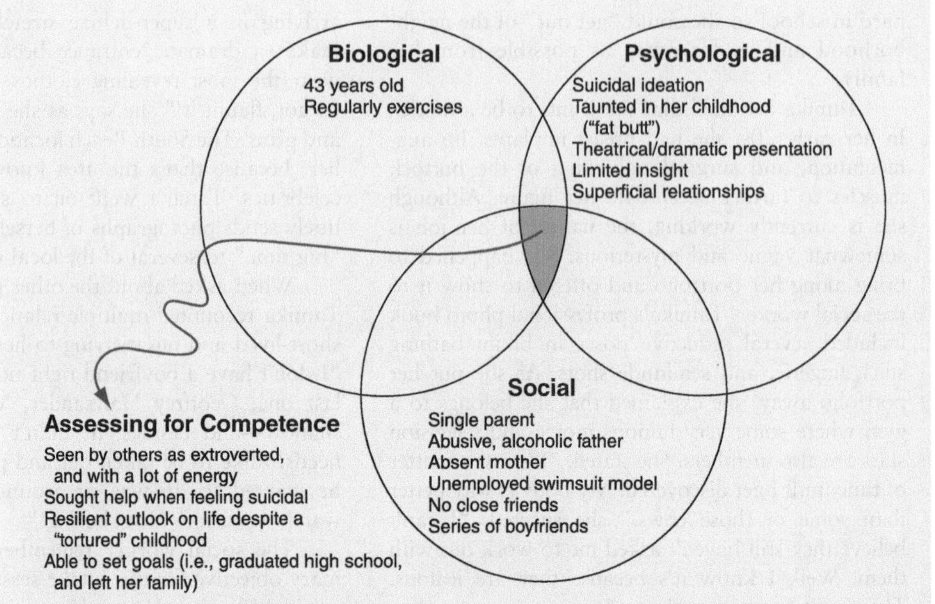

FIGURE 16.6 › HISTRIONIC PERSONALITY DISORDER
The interactions of the biological, psychological, and social variables in Tamika Brown's life.

Tamika initially presented herself to the practitioner as an engaging, yet highly emotional woman. Upon closer examination, it became apparent that those emotions were shallow, and she lacks the ability to sustain meaningful relationships. When the practitioner began the interview, Tamika connected readily and seemed eager to please with her responses. However, she was not in touch with her real feelings and was very vague about the details of her suicide attempt. While it can be difficult for some clients to address suicidal ideation, Tamika Brown's focus on herself in the interview is striking.

Competency 1 b

Using the competency-based model enables the practitioner to work collaboratively with Tamika in order to mobilize her strengths and coping abilities, locate resources, and begin to explore opportunities within her environment that may help pave the way for this client to achieve success (Refer to Figure 16.6). Despite a miserable childhood with an abusive, alcoholic father, she maintains a resilient outlook on life and has set some realistic future goals for herself. Tamika reports that she does not abuse drugs or alcohol.

We next discuss narcissistic personality disorder to complete the review of the Cluster B personality disorders.

NARCISSISTIC PERSONALITY DISORDER

Narcissistic disorder is not recognized around the world and may be a reflection of our modern Western culture that displays a number of criteria reflective of the narcissistic personality disorder; in particular, it is seen as a society that is self-centered, materialistic, and less centered on familial or interpersonal bonds (Foster, Campbell, & Twenge, 2003). A heightened sense of self-importance and unrealistic inflated self-worth, often disguising an underlying fragile sense of self, characterize the individual with narcissistic personality disorder. As the name implies, individuals with this personality disorder tend to be self-absorbed, self-important, and grandiose. They see themselves as unique and special, deserving of extraordinary treatment. Their sense of entitlement is striking. Others in their social environment might describe them as arrogant and boastful.

Prevailing Pattern

This personality disorder is somewhat uncommon; it occurs in less than 1 percent of the general population (Trull, Jahng, Tomko, Wood, & Sher, 2010). Based on DSM-IV definitions, prevalence ranges from zero to 6.2 percent in community samples (APA, 2013). Though rarely seen in practice, this is the kind of client who will be easily remembered because of the individual's flair for being the center of attention.

Information about this disorder's etiology is also somewhat limited, but it does appear more frequently in males than in females (Lynam & Widiger, 2007). The disorder has a tendency to be chronic and difficult to treat because the individual must consistently struggle with looking at the impact of their behavior or its interplay with their life experiences. The person is prone to bouts of depression, handles the aging process poorly, and is more vulnerable to midlife crises.

Differential Assessment

Most of us know people who think very highly of themselves, perhaps even a little beyond their actual abilities. However, individuals with narcissistic personality disorder take this tendency to the extreme. They exhibit an exaggerated sense of self-importance and a tremendous preoccupation with gaining attention from others. They have a lifelong pattern of needing admiration and truly believe they are unique and special. The person considers their accomplishments to be far greater than they are in reality. The major characteristics of this disorder include five or more of the following:

- *Grandiose sense of self-importance*—These individuals exaggerate their achievements and talents. Not only do they feel superior to others, but they also believe they are unique and special. They are convinced they are entitled to "special handling" simply because of who they are. Although the person may envy others, their belief is that others envy them even more. Accomplishments, physical attributes, and talents are often self-exaggerated and not equal to actual achievements. They easily criticize others but have a very difficult time receiving criticism.
- *Preoccupied with fantasies of success*—The person is engrossed with his or her ideal of unlimited power, brilliance, beauty, or ideal love.
- *Belief in being special and unique*—The individual believes he or she can only be understood by, or should associate with, other "special" people; for instance, they are likely to insist they need to be seen by the "best" doctor,

lawyer, hairdresser, and the like and devalue the credentials of those who disappoint them. It is through these associations that the individual's own self-esteem is enhanced.

- *Constant desire or need for admiration*—The person can be very charming but invariably use this "charm" to seek out adulation, admiration, and compliments from others. They think about long-overdue admiration and will compare themselves with famous or privileged people. This is the person who is constantly looking for compliments and has unreasonable expectations for favorable treatment or for others to comply with their demands/needs.
- *Sense of entitlement*—These individuals expect to be catered to and are puzzled (or angry) when this does not happen; for instance, they do not believe they need to wait in line, and they feel that, because their priorities are so important, others should cater to them.
- *Interpersonally exploitative*—As ultrasensitive as they are about their own feelings, these individuals take advantage of others to achieve their own ends, and thus relationships tend to be exploitative; for instance, this person expects to be given whatever they want or need, no matter what may be important to others.
- *Lacks empathy*—The individual has difficulty recognizing the feelings or experiences of others and assumes the focus is solely on them and their welfare. Because they are so focused on themselves, they often are incapable of empathizing with others or are oblivious to the hurt their remarks may inflict (e.g., they may talk about their own good health in front of someone who is sick, or boast about being engaged in "the best" relationship in front of a former partner). Relationships tend to wear very thin over time. As ultrasensitive as they are about their own feelings, they have poor insight regarding the emotional needs of others, often feigning empathy when none exists.
- *Envious of others or believes that others are envious of them*—The person may resent the successes of others, believing that they are more deserving of these achievements. Alternatively, the individual may devalue the contributions of others.
- *Shows arrogant, haughty behaviors/attitudes*—This person can be characterized as arrogant and haughty, showing snobbish, disdainful, or patronizing attitudes; for instance, they may loudly complain about a clumsy waiter's "stupidity" or be very condescending toward a professional who provides a service.

Essential features include "a pervasive pattern of grandiosity (in fantasy or behavior), need for admiration, and lack of empathy, beginning by early adulthood and present in a variety of contexts" (APA, 2013, p. 669). They tend to have a very rich "inner life," entertaining fantasies of masterminding their next venture, which will of course bring them fame and fortune. Interpersonal exploitation is very common among people with narcissistic personality disorder. Although this feature is not part of the DSM criteria, underneath this individual's grandiosity and excessive need for admiration is a very vulnerable person with a fragile sense of self-esteem.

The following case illustrates the major features of someone with a narcissistic personality disorder.

CASE The Case of Lawrence Shull

"Hello, is this Dr. Susan Gray?" a voice on the telephone asked.

"Why, yes," I replied. "Can I help you?"

"Well, you don't know me, but my name is Lawrence Shull, and I've just moved to South Florida from New York."

"So how did you come across my name, Mr. Shull?" I asked.

"Well, first I called the Dade County Mental Health Association, then I checked with the National Association of Social Workers, then I went to *Who's Who of Social Work Digest*, and, finally, I asked several local leaders 'Who is the best social worker in town?' That's how I got your name."

"That's very flattering, Mr. Shull," I replied. "What can I do for you?"

"Well, I want to make an appointment," he responded. I remember thinking that Mr. Shull made this sound like he was doing me a great favor.

Our session took place 3 days later. Mr. Shull presented himself as a very refined-looking gentleman. He was extremely well groomed, and what I would consider a very fashionable dresser. Although it was a typically warm tropical day, he wore a light-brown suit, matching tie, and expensive-looking dress shoes. He confessed to me that he is 55 years old but added, with a wink, "I had a little surgical help from the 'top doc' in Manhattan. Everybody says I look 10 years younger." He is 6 feet tall, 200 pounds, and looks as if he works out and takes extremely good care of himself. His nails are buffed and manicured, and he had not a hair out of place. Although he had said he is new to the South Florida area, he sported a bronzed, suntanned appearance. He looked as if he spent a lot of time at the beach.

After our initial greeting and when we were settled, I asked, "What brings you here, Mr. Shull?"

He responded saying, "Please call me Lawrence, and by the way, may I call you Susan?" (I nodded yes.) "Well Susan, dear, it's quite a long and involved story, but the bottom line is: I'm quite miffed at having to relocate because of my job. You see, I'm an underwriter for a very well-known national tire chain. The problems all started when one of the managers there got jealous of my productivity level. You see, I sold lots of tires, shock absorbers, and brakes ... actually, I sold more than all the other service techs put together." He was silent for a moment, and I prompted him to continue. Odd, I thought. He describes himself as an underwriter but he sounds more like a salesman.

"The store manager is such a jerk! No, he's more than a jerk! He's a nitwit. He doesn't know how to run a business. I've been on the job for 3 months, and I already know more than he does. I can't believe he disapproved of my selling style. Me! I was the best they ever had. He told me that I was unfair to the rest of the guys because I made deals for prices the store wouldn't support and that customers had problems with my enthusiasm for selling." Mr. Shull's face was becoming flushed. He continued, "Can you believe that! I was too enthusiastic?" (He shook his head slowly.) "They are just envious of my success. So it was suggested I relocate to South Florida. I took a big salary hit, and was demoted to, get this, [chuckling] an assistant service technician." He paused and then added, "You know Susan, they'll be sorry when I end up being the CEO and owning the damn company. They can't stop me!"

Farther along in our discussion, Mr. Shull abruptly stated that he broke up with his girlfriend of 6 months.

"She was very dependent on me, and I don't need that extra baggage to carry around. I need someone who is my intellectual equal, someone who complements me," he stated. "I'm still looking for the right woman. So far, nobody's been able to meet my needs." Mr. Shull stopped talking for a moment, smiled at me, and continued, "You know Susan, I just realized all I've been talking about is me, me, me, and me. Why don't you tell me what you think about me and my problems? Do you think you can see me five times a week?"

When our session was over, I scheduled another appointment for Mr. Shull for the following week.

LAWRENCE SHULL'S DIAGNOSIS IS AS FOLLOWS:
Narcissistic personality disorder

Competency 7 a

ASSESSMENT SUMMARY Narcissistic personality disorder often coexists with antisocial, histrionic, and borderline personality disorders, thus complicating the assessment. Lawrence Shull exhibits less anxiety and his life is less chaotic than someone with borderline personality characteristics. His presentation of the symptoms of narcissistic personality disorder is also unlike those with antisocial personality disorder. People with an antisocial personality disorder behave somewhat differently; that is, in addition to being arrogant, they almost always exploit others for financial power or material gain, tend toward impulsive behavior and alcohol or other substance abuse, and tend to have frequent problems with law enforcement. For Lawrence Shull, financial gain is not considered a key issue. Instead, he is forced to relocate and take a cut in pay, which he mentions only in passing, but continues to nurse the idea of being the company's next CEO. His sense of personal glory and entitlement is the central focus of his life. People who have a histrionic personality disorder are also seen as self-absorbed and eager to be the center of attention, but they are usually more willing to connect with others. This contrasts with Lawrence Shull, who apparently without a backward glance, abruptly ended a 6-month relationship with his girlfriend. Another complication in the differential assessment of histrionic versus narcissistic personality disorder is that those with histrionic personality disorders show qualities of exhibitionism and interpersonal manipulativeness very similar to those associated with narcissistic personalities. Suspiciousness and social withdrawal distinguish the nature of the relationship for those with schizotypal or paranoid personality disorder from someone with histrionic personality disorder.

Those with an obsessive-compulsive personality disorder also complicate the assessment process for narcissistic disorder. In both types of clients, the practitioner sees evidence of an air of superiority and marked condescension toward others, masking very vulnerable, fragile individuals underneath. The difference between the two lies in the methods used to express contempt or hostility. The person with a narcissistic personality disorder does not settle for smugness and a superior attitude, but rather gravitates toward malicious (passive-aggressive) counterattacks in response to any criticism (real or perceived) that is directed toward him or her (Miller, Campbell, & Pilkonis, 2007). Lawrence Shull, for instance, undercut the prices of his coworkers at the tire company in order to succeed, and then he perceived his boss as being envious of his success. Those with obsessive-compulsive personality disorder tend to be self-critical.

Competency 1 b

Understanding all of the various aspects of Lawrence Shull's functioning helps to provide a more complete clinical picture and to identify his areas of competency (see Figure 16.7). Within this framework, the difficulties that he brings to the interview are related to how he approaches problem solving—however, he is articulate in describing his "problems" and seeks out the social worker on his own. He also seems to have resilience (the ability to "bounce back" from adversity) despite his job demotion (Gitterman, 2014).

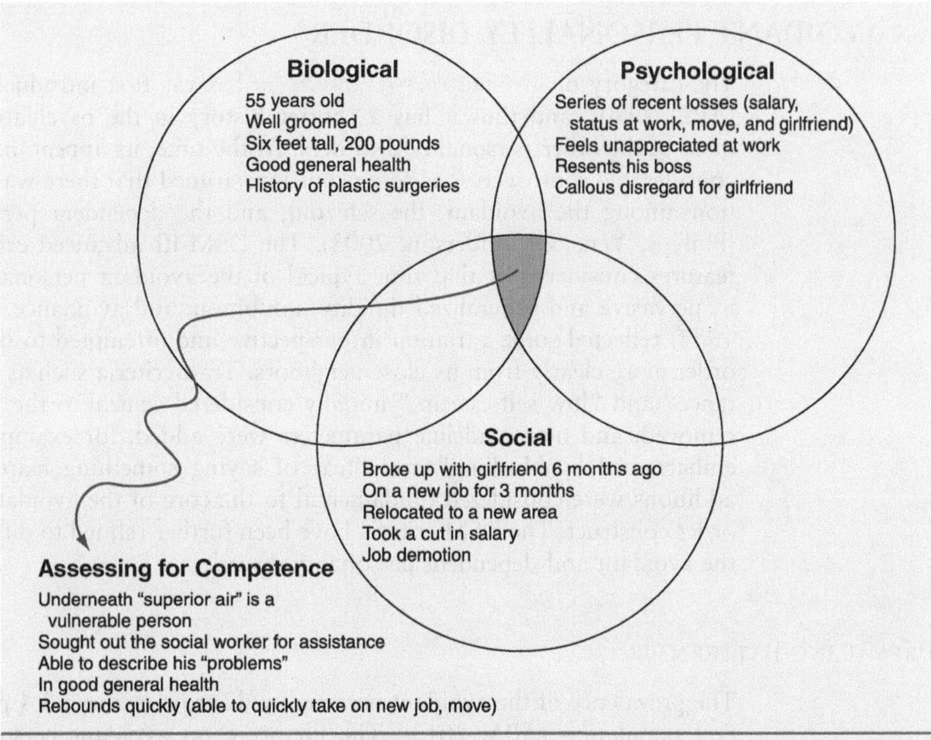

FIGURE 16.7 › NARCISSISTIC PERSONALITY DISORDER
The interactions of the biological, psychological, and social variables in Lawrence Shull's life.

CLUSTER C: ANXIOUS, FEARFUL

Cluster C is called the anxious, fearful cluster. It includes the avoidant, dependent, and obsessive-compulsive personality disorders. The disorders in this cluster all share a high level of anxiety. For instance, people with the avoidant personality disorder are intensely afraid that others will ridicule, reject, or criticize them. This leads to avoiding both social situations and interactions with others. By contrast, the core feature of dependent personality disorder is a strong need to be taken care of by others. This need to be taken care of, and the associated fear of losing the support of others, often leads to "clingy" behavior, most often seen in submission to the desires of others and frequently at their own expense. Individuals with obsessive-compulsive personality disorder are preoccupied with rules, regulations, and orderliness. This preoccupation with perfectionism and control is at the expense of flexibility, openness, and efficiency. These are the people who are great makers of lists and schedules, and who are often devoted to work to the extent that they often neglect social relationships.

AVOIDANT PERSONALITY DISORDER

The category of avoidant personality disorder was first introduced in the DSM-III (APA, 1980), and thus it has a shorter history in the psychiatric literature than most of the other personality disorders. At the time, its appearance was marked by considerable controversy, as some clinicians argued that there was too little distinction among the avoidant, the schizoid, and the dependent personality disorders (Phillips, Yen, & Gunderson, 2003). The DSM-III advanced criteria emphasizing features considered at that time typical of the avoidant personality disorder: that is, pervasive and generalized timidity, inhibition, and avoidance. DSM-III-R (APA, 1987) reflected some variation in perspective and attempted to demarcate this disorder more clearly from its close neighbors. Trait criteria such as "desire for acceptance" and "low self-esteem," initially considered central to the formulation, were removed; and new guideline parameters were added, for example, "fear of being embarrassed by blushing" and "fear of saying something inappropriate." These additions were considered fundamental to the core of the avoidant personality disorder construct. The DSM criteria have been further refined to differentiate between the avoidant and dependent personality disorders.

PREVAILING PATTERN

The prevalence of the avoidant personality disorder is about 2.4 percent of the general population (APA, 2013). The literature on avoidant personality disorder is sparse, but there is some evidence that the disorder seems to occur equally in males and females.

DIFFERENTIAL ASSESSMENT

You will find these individuals to be inhibited and overly cautious. They fear that new situations will throw them a curve for which they are not prepared. Many are able to function as long as they stay protected in a "closed" or safe environment. People diagnosed with this disorder are often confused with individuals described as "being shy." As the name suggests, people with avoidant personality disorder are highly sensitive to the opinions of others and therefore avoid most social relationships (Barlow & Durand, 2014). Because of their heightened sensitivity toward criticism and censure by others, they have a propensity to be self-effacing and eager to please. These qualities often lead to marked social detachment. Additional features include feelings of low self-esteem; being standoffish or introverted; fear of closeness to and rejection by others; social awkwardness; and a chronic fear of being embarrassed. These characteristics persist throughout adulthood, affecting nearly all aspects of daily life.

Individuals with this disorder have a chronic, lifelong pattern of social withdrawal grounded in the anticipation of being rejected. They would like to have a relationship with others; however, the person is extremely sensitive to any form of criticism, making it nearly impossible for them to develop any relationships unless there is a strong guarantee of uncritical acceptance. Some individuals with avoidant personality disorder do marry and have families; being surrounded by familiar relationships and life circumstances that do not demand spontaneity is helpful. In the workplace, these individuals will often accept subordinate jobs, thus removing themselves from the realm of having increased responsibilities and increased contact.

The main characteristics of avoidant personality disorder are a pervasive pattern of social inhibition; constant feelings of inadequacy and ineptitude, especially in social situations; and hypersensitivity to negative evaluation beginning in early adulthood. The features of the disorder are indicated by four (or more) of the following:

- *Avoids occupational activities involving significant interpersonal contact*—Individuals may ardently avoid situations at work that involve interpersonal contact out of a fear of criticism, disapproval, or rejection; for instance, they may decline a job promotion because of a fear that the new responsibilities may result in criticism from former coworkers.
- *Unwilling to get involved with others unless they can be certain they will be liked*—The person assumes that others will be critical and disapprove of them. They may well avoid making new friends unless they are somehow reassured that they will be liked and accepted. Repeated and generous offers of support and nurturance can set the stage to make it possible for the person to join in group activities. However, these individuals are almost always detached from others, afraid of being embarrassed, criticized, or ridiculed (so they withdraw from social situations whenever possible). This disengagement sets up a vicious cycle wherein the individual appears aloof and distant to others who mirror similar restraint toward him or her.
- *Shows restraint within intimate relationships*—It is possible for the person to establish close relationships when assured of uncritical acceptance but here, too, it is still difficult. They may remain inhibited and overly cautious for fear of being ridiculed or shamed. The individual longs for affection and social acceptance and is quite distressed by its absence.
- *Preoccupied with being criticized or rejected*—The person is so preoccupied with criticism or rejection that if someone even slightly disapproves, then he or she will be extremely hurt. Driven by a fear of being exposed, ridiculed, or shamed, the individual tends to be "invisible" in order to avoid attention. They believe that no matter what they say, it will be "wrong," so they may say nothing at all; for instance, these people find it hard to talk about themselves, or they keep their intimate feelings to themselves.
- *Inhibited in new interpersonal situations*—The individual views him- or herself as socially undesirable and feels inadequate, which inhibits participation in new situations. Although these individuals want to be involved with others, low self-esteem and fear of rejection keep them from becoming involved.
- *Consider themselves as socially inept, personally unappealing, or inferior to others*—Doubts about personal competence and personal appeal become evident in settings involving interactions with strangers.
- *Reluctant to take personal risks or to engage in any new activities*—These people tend to exaggerate the potential dangers of ordinary situations and restrict

their lifestyle because it is more predictable and safe. They worry about embarrassing themselves and consequently do not try anything new or different; for instance, this is the person who cancels a job interview because he or she is afraid of embarrassment by not dressing appropriately.

The following vignette portrays a young woman diagnosed with avoidant personality disorder.

CASE THE CASE OF MABEL HUMPHRIES

Mabel, a 33-year-old single woman, has been referred to the Employee Assistance Program by her supervisor. The major complaint centers on Mabel's unwillingness to change her working hours from nights to days; currently, she works the 11 p.m. to 7 a.m. shift in the hospital morgue.

As the social worker assigned to interview Mabel, I can report that my first impression of her was that she likes being alone. She expressed herself in the following way:

"Listen, it don't take much to keep me satisfied. As long as everybody stays outta my way, we'll get along just fine. I don't know what my supervisor told you, or what her problem is, but I don't want to work days. I like the peace and quiet of working the graveyard shift. That way I do my job and nobody's in my face. I guess I'm set in my ways. You see what I'm saying? I don't tell nobody my business and keep to myself. Always have, always will."

I took a wild guess and asked, "Mabel, do you try to avoid the type of work that requires a lot of contact with people?"

"Well, it's true I don't care to be around a lot of people," she answered, "but mostly it's because they might not like me, you know."

I thought this was a pretty brave admission on Mabel's part. So, I decided to go with some more relationship-oriented questions like:

Have you ever turned down a promotion because you were worried other people would be critical of you?

Do you worry about being rejected?

Do you find yourself having trouble carrying on a conversation with someone you just met?

Do you often feel inadequate in work or social situations?

Do you usually feel like you are not as interesting or as much fun as other people are?

Having answered yes to all of my questions, Mabel tried to explain. She said, "I was raised by a deadbeat alcoholic mother who never cared about anybody, including me. My mother always had trouble with people, especially men. Somewhere along the way, I remember somebody said she had borderline something-or-other. If that means One Tough Bitch, then that'd be about right."

Mabel didn't seem at all sentimental as she recounted this. She was just saying what was. After a moment, she continued, "She used to beat the hell out of me and tell me I was no good. Didn't take long for her to convince me—I mean a mother wouldn't lie, would she?" At that point, Mabel's eyes suddenly filled, so I asked if she would like a drink of water or a tissue. "No, don't waste anything on me, I'm fine," she replied.

I asked Mabel if she had any friends. She tried to laugh, but was struggling now to keep her composure. "Nobody wants to be friends with a loser," she replied. "It's not like I haven't tried. But, let's face it, I don't have a lot to offer other people. Like I said before, I'm pretty much of a loner. I don't like to go out and stuff like that, so I guess that's one reason I don't make any friends. The way I figure it, they won't like me, so why bother? And besides, what would I talk about? I don't do anything except wheel dead people around in the morgue." Mabel smiled a little and said, "Hey, I do have lots of friends, but they're all dead." Before Mabel left at the end of our session, she added, "I sure hope you can get my supervisor off my back so I can get back to work."

MABEL HUMPHRIES'S DIAGNOSIS IS AS FOLLOWS:
Avoidant personality disorder

Competency 7 a

ASSESSMENT SUMMARY Mabel desires social interaction with others and is distressed by its absence, but goes to great lengths to try to hide that—she describes herself as a loner, but she also struggles with wanting to have some interpersonal relationships. People with schizoid personality disorder spend most of their time alone and isolated. The discrete difference is that Mabel is unhappy with her lack of social interaction, whereas Tyrone White (described earlier to illustrate schizoid personality disorder) prefers having no social contacts with others.

Competency 6 a

The competency-based assessment serves as a guide to the types of information to obtain. Figure 16.8 shows the interactions of the biological, psychological, and social variables in Mabel's life. It is important for the practitioner to be knowledgeable about the many factors related to a client's presenting issues. In this way, Mabel's problems can be better understood, and the "diagnostic label" has the potential to provide additional insight into what is a complicated symptom picture. On the surface, it may appear that Mabel has problems getting along with her boss, but a thorough assessment reveals her underlying reasons for wanting to stay on the night shift. At the same time, the practitioner comes to appreciate the strengths in Mabel's personality and life situation. For

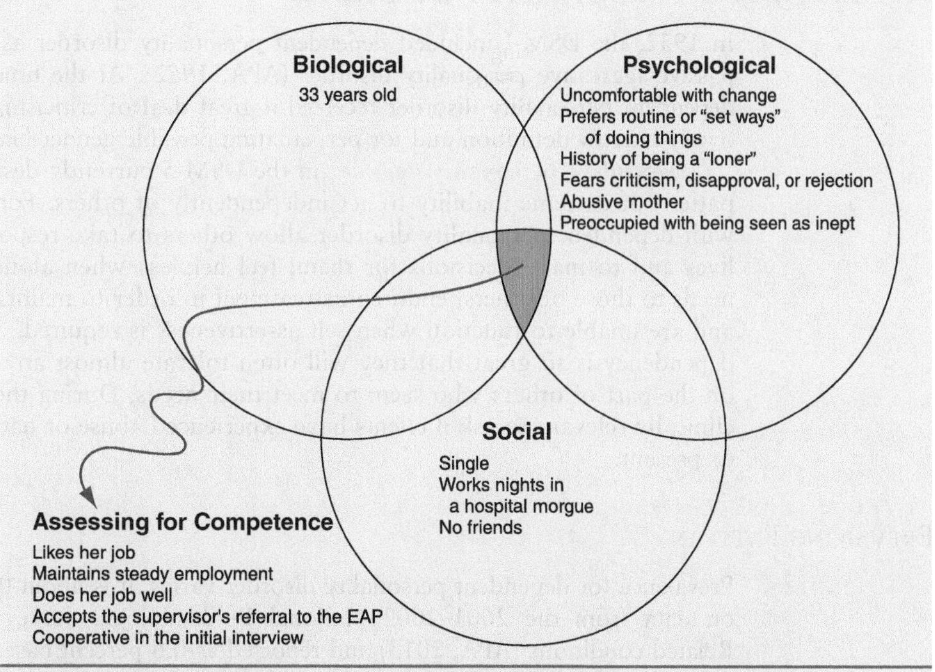

FIGURE 16.8 › AVOIDANT PERSONALITY DISORDER
The interactions of the biological, psychological, and social variables in Mabel Humphries's life.

instance, fearful as she is of criticism, she is willing to discuss "what's wrong" with the practitioner.

Competency 7 b

Avoidant personality disorder shares features with schizoid, schizotypal, and paranoid personality disorders, but perhaps the more difficult differential assessment exists between avoidant and dependent personality types. Mabel, who is avoidant, approaches interpersonal relationships with reluctance, motivated by her fear of saying something foolish and looking inept. By contrast, Walter Pearson (introduced in the upcoming vignette illustrating dependent personality disorder), is socially isolated because of a clinging, submissive relationship with his mother. Those with schizoid and schizotypal personality disorders share traits of social isolation. This differs from avoidant personality disorder in that the person wants to have relationships with others. A reluctance to confide in others is shared by both avoidant and paranoid personality disorders. The avoidant is distinguished from paranoid traits by the person's fear of being embarrassed in contrast to the paranoid fear of others' malicious intent.

Many of the features of the anxiety disorder social phobia overlap with avoidant personality disorder, particularly avoidance. The two disorders often co-occur. However, one dissimilarity can be found in the relational context. The individual with social phobia has problems around specific social situations (such as a speaking engagement) versus the tendency toward avoidance in personal relationships seen in avoidant personality disorder.

DEPENDENT PERSONALITY DISORDER

In 1952, the DSM-I included dependent personality disorder as a subtype of the passive-aggressive personality disorder (APA, 1952). At the time, the category of dependent personality disorder received a great deal of criticism for presenting an overly narrow definition and for perpetuating possible gender bias toward women.

Dependent personality disorder in the DSM-5 currently describes a pervasive pattern of extreme inability to act independently of others. For example, people with dependent personality disorder allow others to take responsibility for their lives and to make decisions for them; feel helpless when alone; subjugate their needs to those of others; endure mistreatment in order to maintain a relationship; and are unable to function when self-assertiveness is required. These individuals' dependency is so great that they will often tolerate almost any kind of behavior on the part of others who seem to meet their needs. During the assessment, it is clinically relevant to ask if clients have experienced abuse or battering, either past or present.

PREVAILING PATTERN

Prevalence for dependent personality disorder varies. It is about 0.49 percent based on data from the 2001–2002 National Epidemiologic Survey on Alcohol and Related conditions (APA, 2013) and reported as 0.6 percent based on a probability subsample from Part II of the National Comorbidity Survey Replication (APA, 2013). In clinical settings, the dependent personality disorder is more commonly diagnosed in women than in men.

However, little is known about the overall course of this disorder. What we do know is that individuals tend to exhibit impaired occupational functioning and show little or no ability to act independently and without close supervision. Social relationships are apt to be limited to those they "depend" on—as a consequence, the individual may endure mental or physical abuse as long as he or she remains unassertive and passive.

Differential Assessment

Individuals with a dependent personality disorder go to great lengths to avoid undertaking or assuming positions of responsibility or leadership. Instead, they prefer to perform tasks under someone else's direction. It is important to discern that these individuals have a problem that is more than just being indecisive. The disorder is more than being unable to choose between a tuna salad and the hamburger for lunch. What is so striking is the individual's inability to expedite decision making without exorbitant amounts of advice and reassurance. They want others to make decisions for them in all areas of their lives, including, for example, their occupation, where to live, how to dress, or even how to act. They cling tenaciously to others and make excessive sacrifices to win the slightest sign of appreciation. At first blush, this dependency might seem like a compliment to the person being depended upon; however, the excessive demands for reassurance eventually become so bothersome and irritating that most people are driven away. The tendency to be dependent on people is pervasive—which, not surprisingly, makes the mental health system, the agency, and the practitioner prime targets for dependence.

Dependent behavior begins by early adulthood and is present in a variety of contexts. To summarize, the major characteristics of someone with dependent personality disorder is the excessive need to be taken care of, leading to submissive and clinging behaviors and a fear of separation as indicated by five (or more) of the following (APA, 2013):

- *Difficulty making everyday decisions*—The individual seeks out an excessive amount of advice and reassurance from others; for instance, he or she will need help deciding on what may look like minor decisions, such as what color shirt to wear to work, or whether to bring an umbrella or not.
- *Need for others to assume responsibility for most major areas of his or her life*—Typically, the person depends on others such as a parent or spouse to make decisions in almost every aspect of their life, such as where they should live, what to eat, the kind of job they should have, or even who should be their friends. As a parallel, adolescents with dependent personality disorder will let his or her parent(s) decide on major aspects of their lives such as who should be their friends, what to wear, how to spend free time, or what school or college to attend. In essence, the need for others to make life decisions goes well beyond age-appropriate (and situation-appropriate) requests for help from others.
- *Difficulty expressing disagreement*—Coming from a fear of losing support or approval, the individual will agree with almost anything (even if he or she feels it is wrong) rather than risk losing the help of those they look to for guidance.

- *Difficulty initiating projects or doing things independently*—Coming from a lack of confidence in judgment or abilities (rather than a lack of motivation or energy), the individual will wait for others to start things and are convinced that they are incapable, thus presenting themselves as inept or needing constant assistance.
- *Goes to extreme lengths to obtain nurturance and support*—The individual is consistently willing to submit to what others want, even if the demands placed on them are unreasonable; this may include extraordinary self-sacrifice or tolerating verbal, physical, or sexual abuse. This is the person who is filled with feelings of self-doubt, passivity, pessimism, and helplessness and is uncomfortable when alone.
- *Feels uncomfortable (or helpless) when alone*—Because the individual is so afraid of being unable to care for him- or herself, they can be seen tagging along with others just to avoid being alone even if they are not interested in what's happening. It is not uncommon for this individual to live with someone who is controlling, domineering, overprotective, and infantilizing.
- *When a close relationship has ended, seeks another relationship for support*—Coming from the belief that the individual cannot function alone, he or she may urgently seek another close relationship.
- *Preoccupied with fears of being left alone to care for him- or herself*—The person considers him- or herself as totally dependent on others for advice to the extent that they have excessive and unrealistic fears about being abandoned, even when there is no basis to support these fears.

This symptom picture is illustrated in the following vignette about Walter Pearson.

CASE THE CASE OF WALTER PEARSON

Walter Pearson has been referred to the employee assistance program (EAP) for an evaluation. His boss at the bank where he works complains, "Walter requires too much direction and guidance, and he's always wasting his coworkers' time trying to get some reassurance about what he's doing. It really interferes with his job responsibilities."

Walter is a 38-year-old African American single male. He is an only child and was raised by his single-parent mother. "My momma has always spoiled me rotten," he relates proudly. At Walter's request, Mrs. Pearson has come along to his interview. She jokingly tells the social worker, "As a baby, Walter just hated when I had to drop him off at the day-care center. Oooo wee, could that little feller cry! He had problems when he started elementary school, too—I guess he just wanted his momma!"

Walter interjects, "Momma, do you remember when they sent me home from sleep-away camp? I cried so much and was so homesick, they put me on the first train that was coming in this direction." Walter and his mother chuckle at the memory. Then Walter continues, "As a youngster all the kids in the neighborhood made fun of me and called me Momma's Boy, but I didn't care. I guess because it was true."

He finished high school and was accepted to a small liberal arts college, where he earned his degree. Immediately after graduation, he came home because, as he says, "Momma needed me to help her with the business." At this point, Walter looks at his mother expectantly. The social worker has the impression that he's looking for his mother's approval. Almost imperceptibly, Mrs. Pearson smiled and nodded approvingly in Walter's direction. Walter currently lives at home with his mother. Although he tried renting an apartment of his own nearby, he commented, "I didn't like the location, and it wasn't safe—so I moved home after about 3 months."

Walter has done some dating, but hasn't found anyone special, or anyone that his mother particularly liked. He said, "Momma is very picky—she won't like anyone I date, I know that. I used to see a really nice girl, named Debbie McPhrew, but Momma complained about how talkative Debbie is." He smiles at his mother and continues, "After a while, I started to think she was right. Debbie did talk a blue streak. I know I'm an adult, but Momma does have my best interests at heart. Anyhow, my judgment hasn't always been the greatest. I've made lots of mistakes in my life."

Mrs. Pearson sat quietly by his side with a reserved but noticeable smile on her face. Periodically, she would nod in agreement as if to reinforce Walter's comments about how much he needed her. He went on to say, "When Momma helps me make decisions, things just seem to work out better."

Walter has worked as a bank teller for the past 5 years. "Momma knew the manager, so you could say she helped me get the job." Walter recently turned down a promotion, because his mother thought it would be too much responsibility for him. "I was worried that I couldn't do a good job, and that I'd make lots of mistakes. It's better that I stay in my present position," Walter concluded.

Walter Pearson's Diagnosis Is as Follows:
Dependent personality disorder

Competency 7 b

Assessment Summary Figure 16.9 illustrates the interactions of the biological, psychological, and social variables in Walter's life. His story is an example of someone with a dependent personality disorder wherein we see a middle-aged man who continues to be bound in one way or another to someone else; in this situation, it is his mother. The vignette suggests that Walter lacks the initiative to make decisions or assert himself. His dependency needs are so great that he accepts most suggestions his mother offers—even if they are not in his best interest. He accepts this advice without question in order to avoid being rejected or criticized. In fact, he has become convinced that his judgment is not "the greatest" except when his mother intercedes on his behalf.

Mrs. Pearson appears to love her son and want the best for him, but on closer examination, she seems to want to keep her son close to home. She discouraged any attempts Walter may have made in developing other relationships, such as with a girlfriend. On some level, it appears that Walter fears being separated from his mother and left to shift for himself. He maintains a submissive, clinging role in order not to be abandoned. He looks to his mother for approval. His dependence on others has now surfaced as a problem at work, so much of a problem that his supervisor has referred him to the EAP office for help. Interestingly, Walter's mother accompanies him to the appointment.

The differential assessment is a complicated process since features of dependence are found in the other personality disorders that can be confused with dependent personality disorder as well as in other disorders where dependency is an outcome of the condition, such as somatic symptom disorder and agoraphobia.

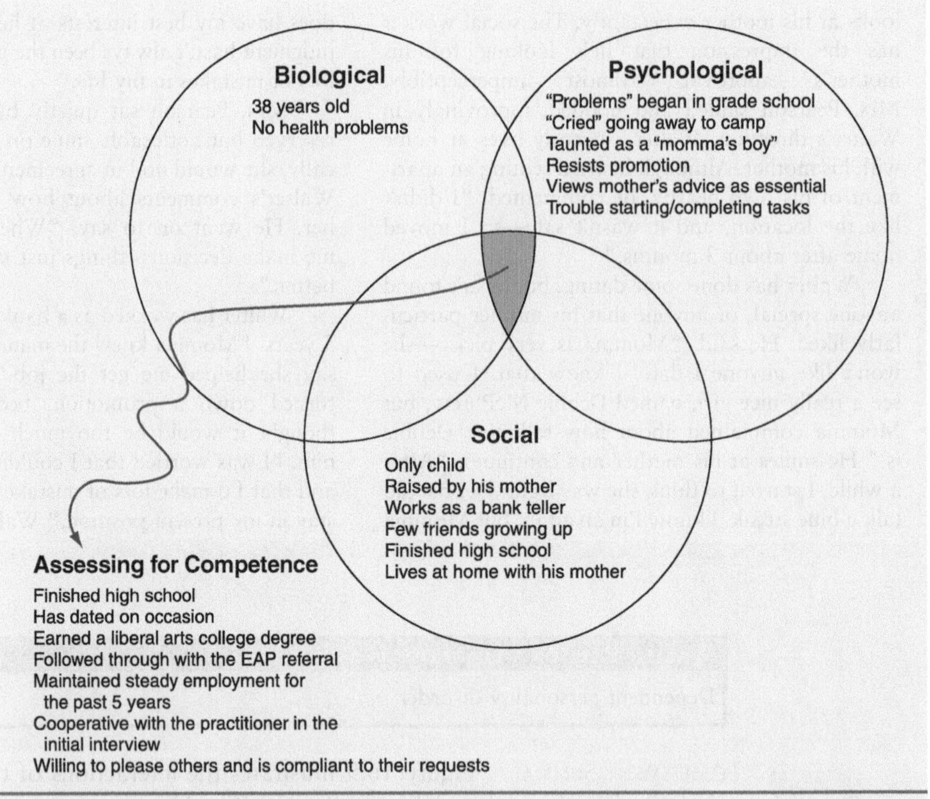

FIGURE 16.9 › DEPENDENT PERSONALITY DISORDER
The interactions of the biological, psychological, and social variables in Walter Pearson's life.

Dependence plays a role in histrionic and borderline personality disorders; however, the individual with the dependent personality disorder usually has a long-standing relationship with one main person on whom they are dependent versus a series of persons seen in the histrionic and borderline personality disorders. Those with avoidant personality disorder are afraid of being humiliated, but the dependent personality disorder is distinguished by what is evident in Walter Pearson's story; that is, his predominately submissive, reactive, and clinging behaviors.

Competency 5 a

An important social work value relates to appreciating human worth and respecting human dignity. The profession is committed to helping those who are oppressed and disempowered. In Walter's situation, his "oppression" is not related to any of the various forms of discrimination but arises from his dependence on his mother for her approval and advice—and that oppression is just as debilitating as any other would be. A competency-based assessment examines Walter's present functioning in relationship to past events, while considering biopsychosocial factors as well as environmental systems. This thorough examination adds clarity to the way Walter relates to his world. By focusing on his strengths rather than deficits, the practitioner has the opportunity to build on his eagerness to please others and foster a new relationship built on mutual respect and collaboration around problem solving.

We now turn to the last of the disorders included in Cluster C, the obsessive-compulsive personality disorder.

OBSESSIVE-COMPULSIVE PERSONALITY DISORDER

Individuals with obsessive-compulsive personality disorder do not have obsessions or compulsions in the same sense that they do in obsessive-compulsive disorder (OCD); rather, the energy of the person's entire personality is channeled into "perfectionism." These individuals are rigid, orderly, inflexible, and emotionally constricted. They often have difficulties making decisions and appear excessively moralistic. Additionally, they are frequently characterized as headstrong and preoccupied with doing things the right way. These traits can be seen in gifted children whose quest for perfection can be debilitating. As a caution against misdiagnosis, Webb and colleagues (2005) suggest a full understanding of the behavior characteristics of these youngsters.

Prevailing Pattern

The prevalence of obsessive-compulsive personality disorder is one of the most commonly found personality disorders in the general population, with estimated occurrence ranging from 2.1 to 7.9 percent. These individuals are more apt to seek intervention on their own than are people with other personality disorders. As we will see in the following case story of Geoffrey Hales, they often have stable relationships and marriages (especially if the spouse is passive) but usually have few close friends, and their lives tend to be constricted and joyless. Routines are rigidly adhered to and their occupational lives are usually formal.

Differential Assessment

This disorder is often confused with OCD, but OCD is distinguished by thinking obsessions and performing compulsions. Individuals with obsessive-compulsive personality disorder tend to become lost in details and are completely immobilized by indecision. Projects are ultimately left uncompleted. They feel more comfortable exercising control over other people and greatly resist attempts at being controlled. Individuals with this disorder appear to be supersaturated with upholding the highest level of scruples and are inflexible regarding moral and ethical matters. Consequently, they are often described as cold, insensitive, single-minded, stubbornly rigid, frugal, parsimonious, and miserly to the point of being unwilling to part with any material possessions. Although obsessive-compulsive personality disorder tends to be chronic, there is some suggestion that cognitive-behavioral therapy appears to be effective for helping people to manage their symptoms (Svartberg, Styles, & Seltzer, 2004).

With obsessive-compulsive disorder, the practitioner encounters individuals who spend a great deal of time performing ritualized behaviors such as checking, counting, or washing. In contrast, the major characteristics of obsessive-compulsive personality disorder include four (or more) of the following:

- *Preoccupied with details, rules, lists, order, organization, or schedules*—These individuals can be characterized as "careful" and extremely attentive to detail, repeatedly checking for mistakes. He or she may overanalyze things, which has the effect of distancing and detaching them. The alternative, emotional spontaneity, is too threatening to tolerate.
- *Perfectionism*—Inflexible ethical standards characterize these individuals that they believe everyone should follow. He or she does not delegate work to others because they fear things will not be done to their own exacting standards. To all outward appearances, they seem to stride through life with meticulous, regimental thoroughness.
- *Excessively devoted to work and productivity*—The person's leisure activities and friendships are adversely affected as the person tends to devote more time to work and productivity.
- *Overconscientious, scrupulous, and inflexible about matters of morality ethics, or values*—The individual tends to follow rigid moral principles (and insist others comply, as well), and are inflexible and self-critical about their own mistakes; these qualities are not better accounted for by the person's culture or religious identification.
- *Difficulty discarding worthless objects*—The individual is known to accumulate seemingly useless or worn-out possessions. They are often described as "pack rats" and stingy.
- *Difficulty delegating tasks or to work with others*—The person can be stubborn or unreasonable insisting things be done "their way."
- *Miserly or stingy toward self and/or others*—These individuals may live far below what they can legitimately afford, believing expenses must be controlled in order to save for a "rainy day."
- *Shows rigidity or stubbornness*—This is the person who is concerned with having done the "correct" way and has trouble accepting the ideas of others. Plans are meticulous, and the person is unwilling to make any changes; compromise is not considered and he or she argues that it is because of "the principle of the thing."

The following vignette illustrates the most salient features of obsessive-compulsive personality disorder.

CASE — The Case of Geoffrey Hales

Geoffrey Hales is 45 years old, married, and has two children: a boy who is 11, and a girl who is 9. He is employed as an electrical engineer for a nationally known company. Geoffrey and his wife Irene have come in (at Irene's insistence) because of marital problems. Here is a synopsis of their initial interview.

After greetings and introductions, when everyone is seated, Irene turns to the social worker and blurts out, "My husband is driving me crazy! No, I take that back—he's driven me crazy already! You gotta help him."

I ask them both to tell me about what has brought them to my office. They exchange a quick glance, and Irene goes ahead. "Where do I start? He's never home, he's always working, we haven't been on a vacation in the 15 years we've been married. He's overworked, and he never seems to sleep. He always brings work home with him and stays up until 3 a.m. most mornings working on the computer. Forget about dinner. He sits there with his phone talking or texting. " She took a breath, and then continued, "Everything has to be just letter perfect—but it rarely is, because he's constantly changing his reports for work so nothing is ever finished. He can't even keep a secretary for more than 3 months—they can't stand his perfectionism either. He doesn't have time for the kids or for me. We never go out because he's too involved with his work. I mean, how many times can he rewrite a report? His current secretary calls him 'Mr. Four-Rs.' It stands for rules, rigidity, regulation, and regimen. Boy! She sure pegged Geoffrey!"

Geoffrey finally spoke up. "Irene, you know other people just don't do things the way I want them done."

I asked if other difficulties were affecting their relationship. Irene replied, "The house looks like we're ready to move out. He's got boxes scattered all around the place, and no one is allowed to touch anything. He says he is saving important information that he's going to use, but he never does. I jokingly call him a 'pack rat,' but it's not funny anymore. He can't throw anything away. We've got newspapers dating back 10 years sitting in a corner of the living room! What's he going to do with all that junk?"

Geoffrey shrugged and answered, "I guess I am a collector, but I think of it as 'waste not, want not.' Actually, I think it's Irene who has the problem, not me. Why don't we talk about how disorganized she is around the house? She doesn't even know how to balance a checkbook."

Geoffrey went on to say that he runs his life by meticulous planning and making lists. As he describes the processes he uses in minute detail, I notice that he is totally absorbed, as if he must make sure that I see the rightness of his approach. "I know that other people think that I'm a perfectionist but that's the only way you get things done in this world."

Irene retorted, "You might see yourself that way, but everyone else sees you as indecisive, preoccupied with details, and a procrastinator who never gets the job done." She went on to say, "One of the reasons I insisted you come for help is that I've put up with your behavior for 15 years, and now it's time to stop. I'm tired of your 'it's my way or the highway' attitude."

Geoffrey looked somewhat chastened, and he replied tentatively, "I guess I am inflexible sometimes, and I know I turn people off—but it's only because I want things done right. I can't stand it when people bend the rules and try to cut corners."

Irene turned to me and asked, "Do you think there is any hope for our marriage?"

GEOFFREY HALES'S DIAGNOSIS IS AS FOLLOWS:
Obsessive-compulsive personality disorder

Competency 7 b

ASSESSMENT SUMMARY Figure 16.10 provides a summary of the major biological, psychological, and social features of Geoffrey Hales's life. Although his wife is quite unhappy and dissatisfied with his behaviors, Geoffrey is unaware of the extent of her discontent and continues to defend his need for orderliness and perfectionism. He is always working, and when he finishes a project, he then feels the need to rework the details. As a matter of fact, getting the job done "correctly" seems to irritate his coworkers, as indicated by his secretary's comments. Aside from an already troubled marriage, he seems to have no friends or interests outside of his job. In addition, Geoffrey Hales's preoccupation at getting things done properly comes at the expense of spending time with his family—never mind a family vacation.

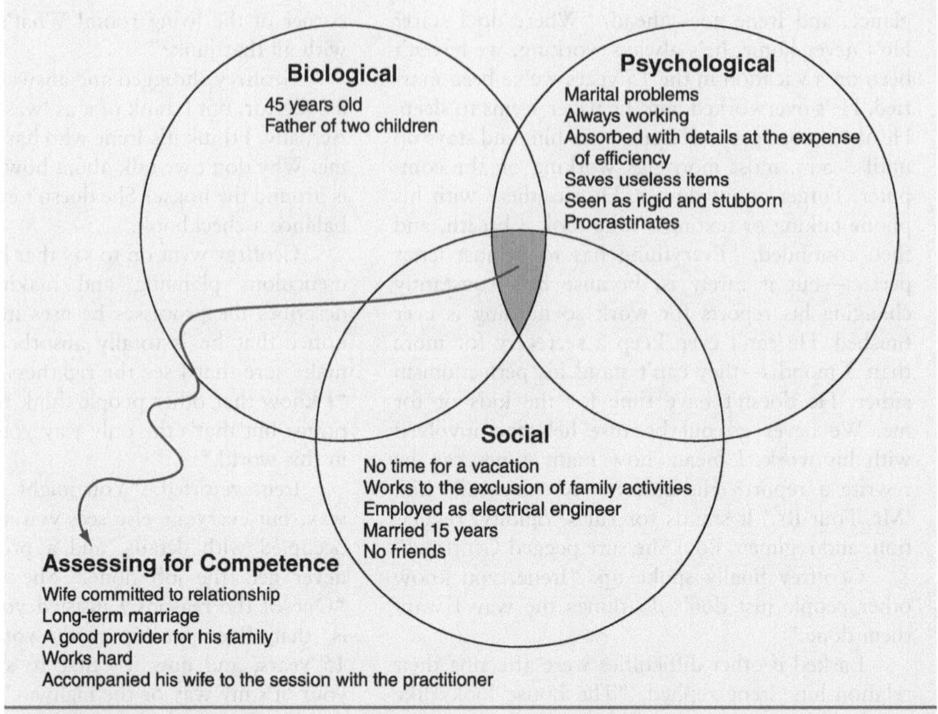

FIGURE 16.10 › OBSESSIVE-COMPULSIVE PERSONALITY DISORDER
The interactions of the biological, psychological, and social variables in Geoffrey Hales's life.

Competency 1 b

Geoffrey's demeanor changed when he described the minutiae of his daily routine to the social worker—he became quite preoccupied. This kind of observation by the practitioner can prove to be very helpful and highlights the significance of the professional relationship in the helping process. When relating to the practitioner, clients tend to replicate the preoccupations that dominate their lives. It is important to recognize this parallel process, as it can provide clinical insight into the characteristic patterns that these individuals follow in relating to their social world. It is not surprising that Irene is seeking out counseling—people with personality disorders are often unaware of the impact their behavior has on others.

Competency 7 b

Clients do not exist in a vacuum. There is more to Geoffrey than his life story and a description of symptoms. The competency-based assessment helps to individualize Geoffrey while exploring the full range of factors affecting his life. He is very committed to his family, married for 15 years (despite his wife's concerns about his behavior), has two children who are not seen as problems, and is being a good provider. Since personality disorder features are ego-syntonic, Geoffrey has been genuinely unaware of the distress his behavior creates for his family.

When making the assessment for obsessive-compulsive personality disorder, other disorders that should be ruled out include narcissistic, antisocial, and schizoid personality disorders and obsessive-compulsive disorder (OCD). Individuals with a narcissistic personality disorder, albeit concerned with perfection and correctness, are focused on seeking adulation versus maintaining these behaviors out of a preoccupation with orderliness, and perfectionism. Antisocial personalities tend to lack generosity but can be seen to indulge themselves, in contrast to the person with obsessive-compulsive personality disorder, wherein the person adopts what could be characterized as a miserly spending style. Schizoid traits can be seen in formality and social detachment, whereas these features come from a place of discomfort with emotions and excessive devotion to work seen in the obsessive-compulsive personality symptom picture. Individuals with obsessive-compulsive disorder have true obsessions and compulsions that are not found in persons with obsessive-compulsive personality disorder. However, that is not to say that the person might not eventually develop OCD. While Geoffrey Hales tends to keep boxes and newspapers around to the extent that his wife calls him a "pack rat," it is not to the extreme that would warrant consideration of the diagnosis of a hoarding disorder.

THE PROPOSED ALTERNATIVE DSM-5 MODEL FOR DIAGNOSING THE PERSONALITY DISORDERS

The DSM-5 made several refinements to the personality diagnoses. Included in Section III of the manual, "Emerging Measures and Models," is another approach to diagnosing the personality disorders, and the DSM-5 work group looks to future clinical evaluation and research on the alternative model. Described as a hybrid dimensional-categorical model, this approach to diagnosing personality disorders seeks to keep the most familiar and useful aspects of the categorical system which practitioners are more accustomed to using. Within this framework, the general diagnostic criteria for personality disorder requires:

- An assessment of self and personality functioning (or how the individual typically experiences him- or herself as well as others) as well as interpersonal functioning.
- The presence of one or more pathological personality traits.
- These traits are consistent across social situations and stable over time.

Alternative explanations for impairments are also explored; for example, another mental disorder, use of a substance or another medical condition, or the person's developmental stage or sociocultural environment.

In keeping with the categorical model used for diagnosing personality disorders, the alternative hybrid approach proposes the following personality disorders of:

- Antisocial,
- Avoidant,
- Borderline,
- Narcissistic,
- Obsessive-compulsive, and
- Schizotypal personality disorders.

The alternative DSM-5 model characterizes these specific personality disorders by impairments in personality functioning and pathological personality traits.

Next, the alternative model describes the diagnosis of personality disorder-trait specified (PD-TS), which identifies pathological trait profiles. This diagnosis is intended to replace the former DSM-IV diagnosis of personality disorder not otherwise specified. The proposed PD-TS diagnosis applies to those individuals who meet general criteria for a personality disorder but do not have any one of the six specified disorders. PD-TS does not conform to a named personality disorder, for example, schizoid or paranoid personality disorder. Instead, the diagnostic criteria address impairment in personality functioning and by what are seen as personality trait domains. Supporting the practitioner's assessment of personality functioning and pathological personality traits (Hopwood et al., 2011), the DSM-5 presents a Level of Personality Functioning Scale (beginning on page 775 of the DSM-5) and definitions of trait domains (starting on page 779 of the manual).

The American Psychiatric Association is offering a number of "emerging measures." One measure that facilitates the evaluation of an individual's personality traits is the Personality Inventory for DSM-5 (PID-5) (Krueger, Derringer, Markon, Watson, & Skodol, 2012). This instrument is a 220-item, self-rated personality trait assessment scale for adults 18 years of age or older (and can be obtained from: http://www.psych.org/practice/dsm/dsm5/online-assessment-measures). There is also a measure for children. This instrument can also be administered to someone who knows the individual, such as a spouse. However, if using the scale is not possible due to time constraints, the practitioner can ascertain a general portrait of the individual's personality traits by reviewing the "Definitions of DSM-5 Personality Disorder Trait Domains and Facets" (APA, 2013, pp. 779–781).

Shaped around the widely used five-factor model of personality (Digman, 1990), the proposed trait domain system for diagnosing PD-TS disorder consists of a series of five personality "trait domains." The domains include: negative affectivity, detachment, antagonism, disinhibition, and psychoticism. Variations in the descriptions of these specific trait domains are intended to distinguish the personalities of each individual client. Using the "Definitions of DSM-5 Personality Disorder Trait Domains and Facets," for example, you may encounter two people who are both characterized by pathological traits of detachment, as seen in the features (or facets) of withdrawal, anhedonia, and suspiciousness. However only one of the two individuals may also show psychoticism as seen by the specific feature of eccentricity. The specific trait domains (that is, detachment and psychoticism) are seen as the specifiers for PD-TS. Table 16.3 shows what these trait differences might look like for each person; in our example, let's call them Al and Billy. In this way, the proposed diagnosis of PD-TS and relevant specifiers are intended to help the practitioner to better focus treatment efforts that target the pertinent areas of each client's personality.

As shown is this example, both Al and Billy have traits of detachment, but there are overall differences in their personalities. Al can be characterized as withdrawn, the kind of person who does not seem to enjoy anything and is suspicious of others. Further, you might say that Al looks a little funny—he has a weird haircut and wears what could best be characterized as mismatched clothes—and he is unpredictable. You never know what Al might say. Billy may also be withdrawn, unhappy, and suspicious of others, but since he does not have the pathological trait of psychoticism, he looks more "normal." The key difference between these two people is that Billy's interpersonal relationships, while stressed, are somewhat

TABLE 16.3 AN EXAMPLE OF USING THE DEFINITIONS OF DSM-5 PERSONALITY DISORDER TRAIT DOMAINS AND FACETS

Individual Features	*Negative Affectivity*	*Detachment*	*Antagonism*	*Disinhibition*	*Psychoticism*
Al		*Withdrawal* preference for being alone over being with others; reticence in social situations; avoidance of social contacts and activity; lack of initiation of social contact *Anhedonia* lack of enjoyment from, engagement in, or energy for life's experiences; deficits in the capacity to feel pleasure and take interest in things *Suspiciousness* expectations of—and sensitivity to—signs of interpersonal ill-intent or harm; doubts about loyalty and fidelity of others; feelings of being mistreated, used, and/or persecuted by others			*Eccentricity* odd, unusual, or bizarre behavior, appearance, and/or speech; having strange and unpredictable thoughts; saying unusual or inappropriate things
Billy		*Withdrawal* preference for being alone over being with others; reticence in social situations; avoidance of social contacts and activity; lack of initiation of social contact *Anhedonia* lack of enjoyment from, engagement in, or energy for life's experiences; deficits in the capacity to feel pleasure and take interest in things *Suspiciousness* expectations of—and sensitivity to—signs of interpersonal ill-intent or harm; doubts about loyalty and fidelity of others; feelings of being mistreated, used, and/or persecuted by others			

"easier" for him. Using this approach to the PD-TS diagnosis, the practitioner has the opportunity to individualize the personalities of each client by differentiating their expression of different personality traits through the use of trait domain specifiers. As a parallel, treatment planning can also be particularized for each client.

SUMMARY

Individuals with a personality disorder relate to others and to their social environment in rigid and inflexible ways. As they attempt to cope with stress or respond to problems in their usual ways, matters only become worse. Unfortunately, the individual is largely unaware of the difficulties these behavioral patterns may pose and fails to recognize the connection to their personality. As a result, they generally do not seek out counseling on their own. If they do come to the practitioner's attention, it is usually through a referral or coercion by others in their social environment.

The ego-syntonic nature of their behavior makes change difficult, and they are largely unmotivated to give up this characteristic disposition. The individual's behavior frequently elicits the kind of response from others that reinforces his or her maladaptive traits. It is helpful for the practitioner to be aware of those distinctive ways that individuals with a personality disorder relate, because this process will more than likely emerge in the counseling relationship. The case vignettes in this chapter demonstrate that individuals with a personality disorder are very different from one another—not just in terms of their symptoms, but in the various strengths they have developed to cope with their life situations.

As a final note, it is helpful for the practitioner to keep in mind that a person's personality may change as a consequence of another medical condition; for example, temporal lobe epilepsy. When that happens, the diagnosis should include the name of the other medical condition and be coded separately. Then the diagnosis of personality disorder due to another medical condition is assigned and specifiers describing the affective change are assigned; that is, labile, disinhibited, aggressive, apathetic, paranoid, other combined or unspecified types.

Figure 16.11 provides an overview summarizing the major features of personality disorders.

As the DSM transitions from the DSM-IV-TR (APA, 2000) to the current edition of the manual, Table 16.4 provides a brief summary of the changes made to the personality disorders diagnostic classifications.

PRACTITIONER'S REFLECTIONS

Perhaps the greatest challenge the social worker faces when trying to assess for personality disorders is to distinguish among those features that may be helpful and those that may get in the way of how a person copes and adapts to life's problems. The following activities are designed to encourage further reflections about the diagnostic categories of personality disorders.

ACTIVITIES

Competency 1 c

1. People with a personality disorder generally do not come to the practitioner without some kind of external catalyst. Problem-solving behaviors, though troublesome to others, are ego-syntonic, and the person's motivation for change, especially those behaviors that define his or her distinct "personality," is often limited. Looking back on the cases discussed in this chapter, select one and imagine for a moment that the client in the vignette is coming to your agency or office for the first time. Role-play with a colleague or your supervisor how you would conduct yourself in the interview and consider the following:
   a. How would you start the initial interview?
   b. What strengths can you identify?

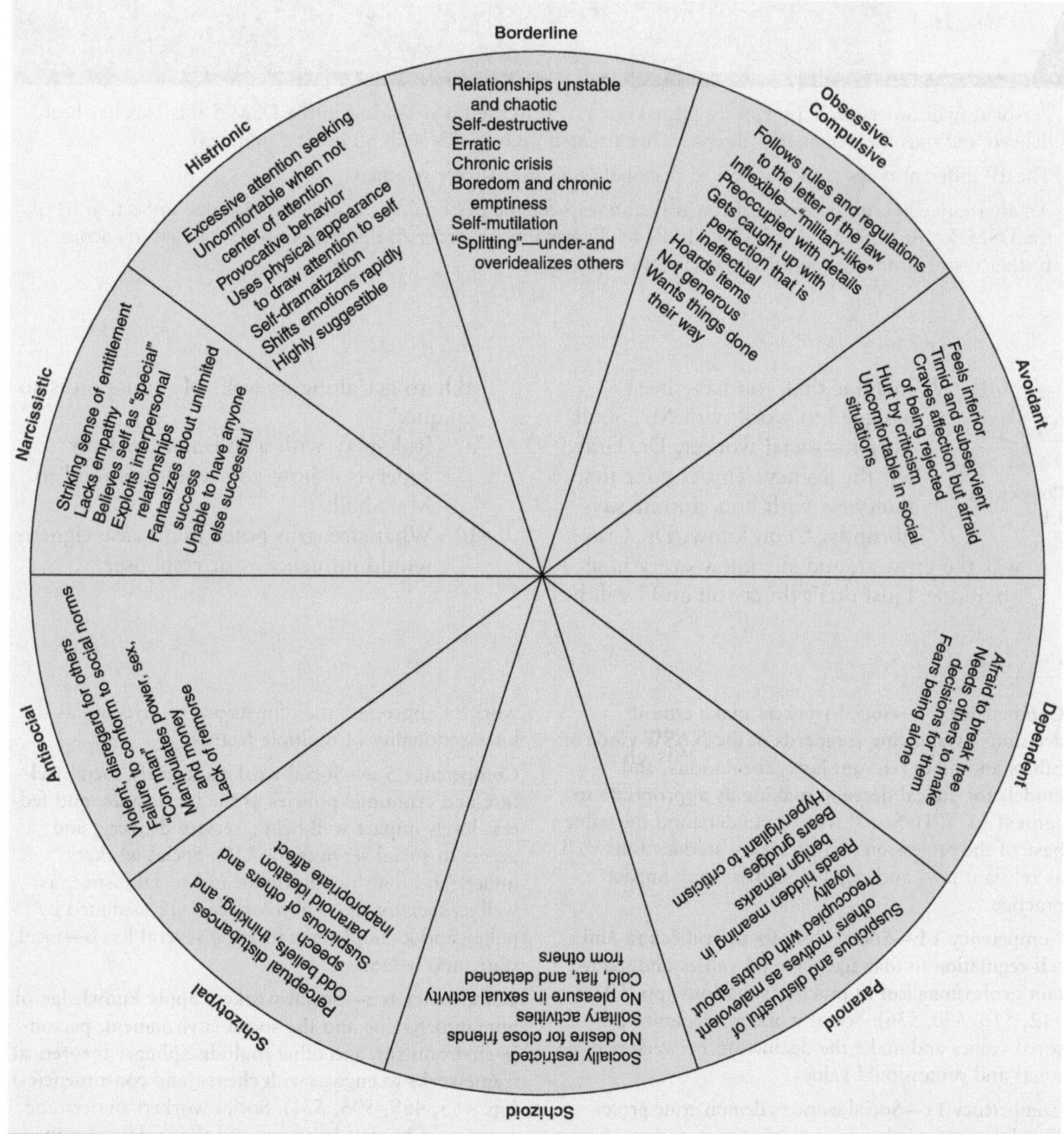

FIGURE 16.11 ❯ MAJOR CHARACTERISTICS OF EACH PERSONALITY ORGANIZED BY CLUSTER

c. What might potentially get in the way of developing a therapeutic relationship with this client (and their family)?

d. What is going on in this client's life that may be helpful in forming a therapeutic relationship?

TABLE 16.4 SUMMARY COMPARISON BETWEEN THE DSM-IV-TR AND DSM-5 DIAGNOSES FOR THE PERSONALITY DISORDERS

Personality disorders were previously placed on Axis II in the DSM-IV, but in the DSM-5 this axis has been deleted and thus the personality disorders are situated on one axis with all other diagnoses
The 10 different types (and clusters) of personality disorders were retained
An alternative hybrid dimensional-categorical model for the personality disorders is included in Section III of the DSM-5, "An Alternative DSM-5 Model for Personality Disorders"; this insertion is intended to encourage further research on this modified classification system

Competency 1 b

2. Imagine that you have been assigned to work with Mr. Shull after his social worker, Dr. Gray, left the agency. This is your first interview with him, and he says abruptly, "You know, Dr. Gray was the greatest, and she knew everything about me. I just don't think you and I will be able to get along as well. My situation is so unique."
   a. Role-play with a colleague or your supervisor how you would respond to Mr. Shull.
   b. What strengths noted in his case vignette would influence your response?

COMPETENCY NOTES

Competency 1 a—Social workers make ethical decisions by applying standards of the NASW Code of Ethics and other relevant laws, regulations, and models for ethical decision-making as appropriate to context (p. 501): Social workers understand the value base of the profession and its ethical standards as well as relevant laws and regulations that may impact practice.

Competency 1 b—Social workers use reflection and self-regulation to manage personal values and maintain professionalism in practice situations (pp. 501, 512, 516, 530, 536): Social workers recognize personal values and make the distinction between personal and professional values.

Competency 1 c—Social workers demonstrate professional demeanor in behavior, appearance, and oral/written/electronic communication (p. 534): Social workers understand how their personal experiences and affective reactions can influence their professional judgment and behavior and also understand emerging forms of technology and the ethical use of technology in practice.

Competency 2 b—Social workers present themselves as learners and engage clients (and constituencies) as experts in their own experiences (p. 488): Social workers appreciate the dimensions of diversity as the intersectionality of multiple factors.

Competency 5 a—Social workers identify social welfare and economic policies at the local, state, and federal levels impact well-being, service delivery, and access to social services (p. 526): Social workers understand that human rights and social justice, as well as social welfare and services, are mediated by policy and its implementation on several levels—local, state, and federal.

Competency 6 a—Social workers apply knowledge of human behavior and the social environment, person-in-environment, and other multidisciplinary theoretical frameworks to engage with clients (and constituencies) (pp. 485, 489, 506, 521): Social workers understand theories of human behavior and the social environment and critically apply this knowledge to facilitate engagement with clients (and constituencies) including families, groups, organizations, and communities.

Competency 7 a—Social workers collect and organize data and apply critical thinking in order to interpret information from clients and constituencies (pp. 506, 511, 516, 521): Social workers understand that the assessment process is ongoing and conducted with, and on behalf of, diverse individuals, families, groups, organizations, and communities.

Competency 7 b—Social workers are able to apply knowledge of human behavior and the social environment, person-in-environment, and other multidisciplinary theoretical frameworks in the analysis of assessment data (pp. 480, 491, 493, 497, 507, 522, 525, 529, 530): Social workers understand theories of human behavior and the social environment and critically evaluate and apply this knowledge in the assessment process.

Competency 7 c—Social workers develop mutually agreed-on intervention goals and objectives based on the assessment of strengths, needs and challenges within clients and constituencies (pp. 483, 484, 494, 500): Social workers recognize the implications of the larger practice context in the assessment process.

REFERENCES

American Psychiatric Association (APA). (1952). *Diagnostic and statistical manual of mental disorders*. Washington, DC: Author.

American Psychiatric Association (APA). (1968). *Diagnostic and statistical manual of mental disorders* (2nd ed.). Washington, DC: Author.

American Psychiatric Association (APA). (1980). *Diagnostic and statistical manual of mental disorders* (3rd ed.). Washington, DC: Author.

American Psychiatric Association (APA). (1987). *Diagnostic and statistical manual of mental disorders* (3rd ed., revised). Washington, DC: Author.

American Psychiatric Association (APA). (1994). *Diagnostic and statistical manual of mental disorders* (4th ed.). Washington, DC: Author.

American Psychiatric Association (APA). (2000). *Diagnostic and statistical manual of mental disorders* (4th ed., text revision). Washington, DC: Author.

American Psychiatric Association (APA). (2013). *Diagnostic and statistical manual of mental disorders* (5th ed.). Arlington, VA: Author.

Anglina, D. M., Cohenab, P. R., & Chena, H. (2008). Duration of early maternal separation and prediction of schizotypal symptoms from early adolescence to midlife. *Schizophrenia Research, 103*(1), 143–150.

Bakkevig, J. F., & Karterud, S. (2010). Is the Diagnostic and Statistical Manual of Mental Disorders, fourth edition, histrionic disorder category a valid construct? *Comprehensive Psychiatry, 51*(5), 462–470.

Barlow, D. H., & Durand, V. M. (2014). *Abnormal psychology: An integrative approach* (7th ed.). Stamford, CT: Wadsworth Cengage.

Beck, A. T., Freeman, A., & Davis, D. P. (2007). Cognitive therapy of personality disorders. New York: Guilford Press.

Berenbaum, H., Valera, E. M., & Kerns, J. G. (2003). Psychological trauma and schizotypal symptoms. *Schizophrenia Bulletin, 29*(1), 143–152.

Colman, L., Murray, J., Abbott, R., Maughan, B., Kuh, D., Croudace, T., ... Jones, P. B. (2009). Outcomes of conduct problems in adolescence: 40 year follow-up of national cohort. *British Medical Journal, 338*, a2981.

Cowen, P., Harrison, P., & Burns, T. (2012). *Shorter Oxford textbook of psychiatry* (6th ed.). Oxford: Oxford University Press.

DeBrito, S. A., & Hodgkins, S. (2009). Antisocial personality disorder. In M. McMurran & R. C. Howard (Eds.), *Personality, personality disorder and violence: An evidence based approach* (pp. 133–154). New York: John Wiley & Sons.

Digman, J. M. (1990). Personality structure: Emergence of the five-factor model. *Annual Review of Psychology, 41*, 417–440.

Distel, M. A., Trull, T. J., & Boomsma, D. I. (2009). Genetic epidemiology of borderline personality disorder. In M. H. Jackson & L. F. Westbrook (Eds.), *Borderline personality disorder: New research* (pp. 1–31). Hauppage, NY: Nova Science Publishers.

Fazel, S., & Danesh, J. (2002). Serious mental disorder in 23,000 prisoners: A systematic review of 62 surveys. *The Lancet, 359*(9306), 545–550.

Ferguson, C. (2010). Genetic contributions to antisocial personality and behavior: A meta-analytic review from an evolutionary perspective. *The Journal of Social Psychology, 150*(2), 160–180.

Foster, J. D., Campbell, W. K., & Twenge, J. M. (2003). Individual differences in narcissism: Inflated self-views across the lifespan and around the world. *Journal of Research in Personality, 37*, 469–486.

Fountoulakis, K. N., Lecht, S., & Kaprinis, G. S. (2008). Personality disorders and violence. *Current Opinion in Psychiatry*, *21*, 84–92.

Gelhorn, H. L., Sakai, J. T., Price, R. M., & Crowley, T. J. (2007). DSM-IV conduct disorder criteria as predictors of antisocial personality disorder. *Comprehensive Psychiatry*, *48*, 529–538.

Gitterman, A. (Ed.). (2014). *Handbook of social work practice with vulnerable and resilient populations* (3rd ed.). New York: Columbia University Press.

Goldstein, E. G., Miehls, D., & Ringel, S. (2009). *Advanced clinical social work practice: Relational principles and techniques*. New York: Columbia University Press.

Grant, B., Choi, S., Goldstein, R., Huang, B., Stinson, F., Saha, T., ... Pickering, R. P. (2008). Prevalence, correlates, disability, and comorbidity of DSM-IV borderline personality disorder: Results from the Wave 2 National Epidemiologic Survey on Alcohol and Related Conditions. *The Journal of Clinical Psychiatry*, *69*(4), 533.

Hare, R. D. (1993). *Without conscience: The disturbing world of the psychopaths among us*. New York: Pocket Books.

Hoeksema, S. N. (2014). *(Ab)normal Psychology*. New York: McGraw-Hill.

Kearney, C. A., & Trull, T. J. (2012). *Abnormal psychology and life: A dimensional approach*. Belmont, CA: Wadsworth Cengage Learning.

Hopwood, C. J., Malone, J. C., Ansell, E. B., Sanislow, C. A., Grilo, C. M., Pinto, A., ... Morey, L. C. (2011). Personality assessment in the DSM-5: Empirical support for rating severity, style, and traits. *Journal of Personality Disorders*, *25*, 305–320.

Krueger, R. F., Derringer, J., Markon, K. E., Watson, E., & Skodol, A. E. (2012). Initial construction of a maladaptive personality trait model and inventory for DSM-5. *Psychological Medicine*, *42*(9), 1879–1890.

Layton, M. (1995). Emerging from the shadows. *Family Therapy Networker*, May–June, 35–41.

Lenzenweger, M., Lane, M., Loranger, A., & Kessler, R. (2007). DSM-IV personality disorders in the National Comorbidity Survey Replication. *Biological Psychiatry* *62*(6), 553–564.

Lynam, D. R., & Widiger, T. A. (2007). Using a general model of personality to understand sex differences in the personality disorders. *Journal of Personality Disorders*, *21*, 583–602.

Maher, B. A., & Maher, W. B. (1985). Psychopathology: I From ancient times to the eighteenth century. In G. A. Kimble & K. Schlesinger (Eds.), *Topics in the history of psychology* (pp. 251–294). Hillsdale, NJ: Erlbaum.

Meloy, J. R. (2007). Antisocial personality. In G. O. Gabbard (Ed.), *Treatments of psychiatric disorders* (4th ed., pp. 775–790). Arlington, VA: American Psychiatric Press.

Miller, J. D., Campbell, W. K., & Pilkonis, P. A. (2007). Narcissistic personality disorder: Relations with distress and functional impairment. *Comprehensive Psychiatry*, *48*, 170–177.

Moeller, F. G., & Dougherty, D. M. (2001). Antisocial personality disorder, alcohol, and aggression. *Alcohol Research and Health*, *25*(1), 1–10.

Neacsiu, A., & Linehan, M. (2014). Borderline personality disorder. In D. H. Barlow (Ed.), *Clinical handbook of psychological disorders* (5th ed., pp. 365–461). New York: Guilford Press.

Nirestean, A., Lukacs, E., Cimpan, D., & Taran, L. (2012). Schizoid personality disorder—the peculiarities of their interpersonal relationships and existential roles. *Personality and Mental Health*, *6*(1), 69–74.

Nolen-Hoeksema, S. (2014). *Abnormal Psychology* (6th ed.). New York: McGraw-Hill.

Phillips, K. A., Yen, S., & Gunderson, J. G. (2003). Personality disorders. In R. E. Hales & S. C. Yudofsky (Eds.), *Textbook of clinical psychiatry* (4th ed., pp. 804–832). Washington, DC: American Psychiatric Press.

Sadock, B. J., Sadock, V. A., & Ruiz, P. (2014). *Kaplan and Sadock's comprehensive textbook of psychiatry: Behavioral sciences/clinical psychiatry* (11th ed.). Philadelphia: Lippincott Williams and Wilkins.

Salekin, R. T. (2006). Psychopathy in children and adolescents: Key issues in conceptualization and assessment. In C. J. Patrick (Ed.), *Handbook of psychopathy* (pp. 389–414). New York: Guilford Press.

Stoudemire, A. (Ed.). (1994). *Clinical psychiatry for medical students* (2nd ed.). Philadelphia: J. B. Lippincott.

Svartberg, M., Styles, T. C., & Seltzer, M. H. (2004). Randomized, controlled trial of the effectiveness of short-term dynamic psychotherapy and cognitive therapy for cluster C personality disorders. *American Journal of Psychiatry*, *161*, 810–817.

Teyber, E., & McClure, F. (2010). *Interpersonal process in psychotherapy: An integrative model* (6th ed.). Belmont, CA: Brooks/Cole Cengage.

Trull, T. J., Jahng, S., Tomko, R. L., Wood, P. K., & Sher, K. J. (2010). Revised NESARC personality disorder diagnoses: Gender, prevalence, and comorbidity with substance dependence disorders. *Journal of Personality Disorders*, *24*, 412–426.

Voglmaier, M. M., Seidman, L. J., Niznikiewicz, M. A., Dickey, C. C., Shenton, M. E., & McCarley, R. W. (2000). Verbal and nonverbal neuropsychological test performance in subjects with schizotypal personality disorder. *American Journal of Psychiatry*, *157*, 787–793.

Webb, J. T., Amend, E. R., Webb, N. E., Goerss, J., Beljan, P., & Olenchak, F. R. (2005). *Misdiagnosis and dual diagnoses of gifted children and adults: ADHD, bipolar, OCD, Asperger's, depression and other diagnoses*. Scottsdale, AZ; Great Potential Press.

Wolff, S. (2000). Schizoid personality in childhood and Asperger syndrome. In A. Kline, F. R. Volkmar, & S. S. Sparrow (Eds.), *Asperger syndrome* (pp. 278–305). New York: Guilford Press.

Zanarini, M. C., Frankenburg, F. R., Hennen, J., Reich, D. B., & Silk, K. R. (2006). Prediction of the 10 year course of borderline personality disorder. *American Journal of Psychiatry*, *163*, 827–832.

Zanarini, M. C., Reichman, C. A., Frankenburg, F. R., Reich, D. B., & Fitzmaurice, G. (2010). The course of eating disorders in patients with borderline personality disorder: A 10-year follow-up study. *International Journal of Eating Disorders*, *43*(3), 226–232.

APPENDIX

ASSESSING FOR COMPETENCY IN PSYCHOPATHOLOGY

The following questions are designed to test your competency in psychopathology. Some items require you to apply what you know to a case study involving a hypothetical client. Other questions ask you to remember information about the various diagnostic categories. The section heading indicates the chapter where the answer can be found. You may want to answer these questions before reading the book in order to test your understanding of psychopathology. On the other hand, you might try to answer the questions after reading the book and then review those chapters where you had the most incorrect answers. All in all, I hope this "quiz" will better prepare you for knowing about psychopathology. Good luck with the questions!

CHAPTER ONE–AN INTRODUCTION TO THE COMPETENCY-BASED ASSESSMENT MODEL

1. The DSM, or *Diagnostic and Statistical Manual,* is considered the:
   a. Classification system for general medical disorders
   b. Psychological evaluation measurement
   c. Handbook to the treatment of mental illness
   d. Standard reference used to diagnose all mental disorders
2. Competency-based practice emphasizes:
   a. The importance of identifying client competencies
   b. A review of historical information in a client's life
   c. A focus on the effects of deficits
   d. Exploring biological factors in a client's life
3. Interprofessional collaboration refers to when professionals from different disciplines:
   a. Work cooperatively to understand their respective Code of Ethics
   b. Work together to formulate a more accurate diagnosis
   c. Attend interdisciplinary workshops and conferences focusing on mental health topics
   d. Define what is unique about their professional perspective

4. Subtypes are subgroupings within a particular diagnosis and they are indicated by:
   a. Neurotransmitters
   b. Axon terminals
   c. Specifiers
   d. Endorphins
5. Section II of the DSM-5 includes all of the following features except:
   a. A delineation of the categorical diagnoses including other conditions that may be a focus of clinical attention
   b. An organization around the life span, and developmental progression
   c. A listing of assessment measures including self-assessment tools and a cultural formulation for understanding the cultural context
   d. A total of 20 chapters that describe specific disorder categories

CHAPTER TWO–NEURODEVELOPMENTAL DISORDERS

6. Paul's behavior is typified by uncontrollable squeals, odd grunting sounds, and sniffing. His diagnosis is:
   a. Persistent (chronic) motor or vocal tic disorder
   b. Provisional tic disorder
   c. Tourette's disorder
   d. Unspecified tic disorder
7. Children with this disorder may have problems with symptoms of inattention, hyperactivity, and impulsivity. This disorder is:
   a. Attention-deficit/hyperactivity disorder, combined presentation
   b. Attention-deficit/hyperactivity disorder, predominantly inattentive presentation
   c. Attention-deficit/hyperactivity disorder, predominantly hyperactive/impulsive presentation
   d. Unspecified attention-deficit/hyperactivity disorder
8. The essential feature of children with ________ disorder is impaired skills requiring motor coordination; for instance, it's hard for a child to use scissors, ride a bike, and/or participate in sports or team activities in school.
   a. Stereotypic movement disorder
   b. Tic disorder
   c. Provisional tic disorder
   d. Developmental coordination disorder
9. ________ describes those who have problems with pronunciation and articulation to the extent that they interfere with being understood or prevent verbal communication.
   a. Language disorder
   b. Speech sound disorder
   c. Childhood-onset fluency disorder (stuttering)
   d. Social (pragmatic) communication disorder

10. _________ is a disorder that appears before adulthood characterized by an individual's significantly impaired cognitive functioning, and deficits in adaptive behaviors.
    a. Global developmental delay
    b. Intellectual disability (Intellectual developmental disorder)
    c. Unspecified intellectual disability (Intellectual developmental disorder)
    d. Other specified intellectual disability disorder

CHAPTER THREE–SCHIZOPHRENIA SPECTRUM AND OTHER PSYCHOTIC DISORDERS

11. Mrs. Stacy Hill contacted the XYZ Mental Health Center because she is concerned about her 24-year-old daughter, Violet, who lives at home and is displaying several symptoms that seem to be cause for concern. Violet's symptoms include persecutory delusions, auditory hallucinations, incoherence, and loosening of associations. According to Mrs. Hill, her daughter was just fine until 3 months ago when this "strange behavior suddenly developed." There is some family history of schizophrenia. What would your diagnosis be?
    a. Schizophrenia
    b. Schizophreniform disorder
    c. Schizoid personality disorder
    d. Brief psychotic disorder
12. Sarah, age 23, gave birth to her first child 3 days ago. Her initial complaints consisted of insomnia, restlessness, and emotional lability that progressed to confusion, irritability, delusions, and thoughts of wanting to harm her baby. What is the most correct diagnosis?
    a. Brief psychotic disorder, postpartum onset
    b. Autoscopic psychosis
    c. Cotard's syndrome
    d. Induced delusional disorder
13. Mario Walters believes that he has developed a major plan that would end all hunger, homelessness, and crime in the world. In addition, he believes the President of the United States, the Queen of England, and various important heads of state support his plan. This is an example of:
    a. Persecutory type delusions
    b. Tangential thought
    c. Grandiose type delusions
    d. Neologism
14. Delusional disorder is characterized by:
    a. At least 1 month of delusions but no other psychotic symptoms
    b. Symptomatic presentation of schizophrenia lasting more than 1 day and remits by 1 month
    c. Delusions lasting for at least 6 months and includes at least 1 month of active-phase symptoms
    d. A mood episode and active-phase symptoms of schizophrenia

15. The erotomanic type specifier of delusional disorder applies when:
    a. The central theme of the delusion is the conviction of having some great but unrecognized talent or insight, or having made some important discovery
    b. The central theme of the individual's delusion is that his or her spouse or lover is unfaithful
    c. The central theme of the delusion is that another person is in love with the individual
    d. The central theme of the delusion involves bodily functions or sensations

CHAPTER FOUR–BIPOLAR AND RELATED DISORDERS

16. Which of the following list of symptoms is the first sign of the beginning of a manic episode?
    a. Racing thoughts
    b. Hallucinations
    c. Hypergraphia
    d. A change in sleeping patterns
17. Which of the following symptoms is not apparent in a manic episode?
    a. The person is more talkative than usual or evidences pressured speech
    b. Distractibility—attention too easily drawn to irrelevant stimuli
    c. Excessive sleeping
    d. Excessive involvement in pleasurable activities
18. One specifier of bipolar disorder is characterized by four or more episodes a year with mania and depression following each other. Which type is this?
    a. Seasonal affective disorder
    b. Double depression
    c. Rapid cycling
    d. Cyclothymia
19. Euphoria, boundless optimism, inflated self-esteem, and grandiosity are characteristic symptoms of:
    a. Bipolar disorder, manic type
    b. Schizophrenia, catatonic type
    c. Delusional disorder
    d. No mental disorder is present

CHAPTER FIVE–DEPRESSIVE DISORDERS

20. _________ was formerly known as depressive neurosis and was considered less severe than major depressive disorder. This disorder is more common in women than in men and is chronic. Its onset is insidious and occurs more often in persons with a history of long-term stress or sudden loss. This disorder often coexists with other psychiatric disorders (e.g., substance abuse, personality disorders, and obsessive-compulsive disorder). This diagnosis requires

the presence of at least two of the following symptoms: poor appetite, overeating, sleep problems, fatigue, and/or low self-esteem. What is this disorder?
   a. Panic disorder
   b. Persistent depressive disorder (dysthymic disorder)
   c. Schizoaffective disorder
   d. Posttraumatic stress disorder
21. Which of the following would not be present during a major depressive disorder episode?
   a. Changes in sleep and/or appetite habits
   b. Anxiety
   c. Anhedonia
   d. Grandiosity
22. Maria Gonzalez was agitated and screaming when her family brought her to the emergency room of a local hospital. The previous week, Maria had learned that her former husband had remarried in their home country, the Dominican Republic. Since then, she has become increasingly agitated, has developed insomnia, and is unable to eat—and by the time she arrived at the emergency room, she alternated between being mute and mumbling unintelligibly in both Spanish and English. She was admitted to the psychiatric unit and was given a small dose of an antipsychotic medication with no response. The social worker reported that Ms. Gonzalez had outbursts of bizarre behavior, had ideas of reference, complained of headaches, and felt "out of control." In addition, she cried, pulled her hair, rocked back and forth, and could not be consoled. Over a period of 3 days, Maria's family assured her that she and her children would be well cared for, and the psychotic-like symptoms resolved, at which time she was released from the hospital. Ms. Gonzalez's diagnosis would be:
   a. Ataque de nervios, a culture-bound syndrome
   b. Hysterical conversion disorder
   c. Panic disorder without agoraphobia
   d. Bipolar II disorder
23. Mary Kathryn Mc Kinney seems to have the perfect life—a husband who is devoted to her, two beautiful children, and a job she loves. "I work as a substitute teacher at a school near my home," said Mary Kathryn. There is nothing in her life she would change, but there is something that she has kept hidden; something she was ashamed of that happens every month. Mary Kathryn continued, "I just want those that are the closest to me to vanish. I don't want my husband to come home and I don't want the kids to come home either. I get so sad ... and for no reason. Then I cry at the drop of a hat. My moods can change in an instant. During this time she feels bloated and her breasts are tender. She adds, "This can start the week just before my period, and then within a few days of my period things begin to get better." These symptoms then stop altogether a couple of days after her period has stopped—about a week later, on average. Her most likely diagnosis is:
   a. Premenstrual dysphoric disorder
   b. Premenstrual dysphoric disorder provisional
   c. Persistent depressive disorder (dysthymia)
   d. No mental disorder present

24. For this disorder, a depressed mood is present most of the day and nearly every day as indicated either by the person's report of symptoms of feeling sad, empty, hopeless, or seen by others such as tearfulness. It is:
    a. Persistent depressive (dysthymia) disorder
    b. Disruptive mood dysregulation disorder
    c. Major depressive disorder
    d. Bipolar disorder

CHAPTER SIX–ANXIETY DISORDERS

25. Six-year-old Christina has been telling her brothers about her field trip to the zoo with her Girl Scout Brownies troop. She was fascinated with the petting zoo and what she fed the goats that day. This behavior would come as a surprise to her teachers in school who never heard her talk. Christina's diagnosis would be:
    a. Childhood disintegrative disorder
    b. Selective mutism
    c. Tourette's disorder
    d. Disruptive behavior NOS
26. The basic symptoms of panic attack include all of the following except:
    a. Situationally predisposed
    b. Culture-specific
    c. Physical
    d. Cognitive
27. A panic attack may be characterized by all of the following except:
    a. An abrupt experience of intense fear or discomfort
    b. Heart palpitations
    c. Sweating
    d. Elevated mood
28. David is extremely afraid of snakes. He makes every effort to never be in the presence of them or even to look at pictures of snakes. His phobia is considered:
    a. Social anxiety disorder
    b. A complex phobia
    c. Agoraphobia
    d. A specific phobia
29. The essential feature of ________ is a marked, or intense, fear or anxiety triggered by the real (or anticipated) exposure to a wide range of situations.
    a. Social anxiety disorder
    b. Generalized anxiety disorder
    c. Agoraphobia
    d. Panic disorder
30. ________ disorder is characterized by excessive anxiety and worry (apprehensive expectation) about a number of events or activities.
    a. Panic attack disorder
    b. Generalized anxiety disorder
    c. Social anxiety disorder
    d. Anxiety disorder due to another medical condition

CHAPTER SEVEN–OBSESSIVE-COMPULSIVE AND RELATED DISORDERS

31. Hope Udall is a shy, anxious-looking 29-year-old homemaker who was hospitalized after an overdose of Valium washed down with some vodka. While in the hospital, Hope met with the social worker in a darkened room and insisted on wearing a scarf that covered her hair, eyes, and nose. When the social worker asked what had happened to bring Hope in, she replied, "I have no friends, and my husband just left me. It's just so hard to talk about. I don't know if I can, it's too embarrassing." After some discussion, she revealed that the overdose was because of her nose, which she described as "grotesque and deformed." She related to the social worker that her nose has "huge pock marks and ugly bumps." The social worker did not note any such appearance and, in fact, saw a lovely young woman of normal appearance. According to the DSM-IV criteria, what would Hope's diagnosis be?
    a. Narcissistic personality disorder
    b. Body dysmorphic disorder
    c. Histrionic personality disorder
    d. Generalized anxiety disorder
32. The obsessions seen in obsessive-compulsive disorder are characterized by all of the following except:
    a. Recurrent and persistent thoughts, urges, or images
    b. Intrusive and unwanted thoughts, urges, or images
    c. Behaviors or mental acts aimed at preventing or reducing anxiety or distress
    d. Seen as time consuming causing significant distress or impairment
33. Sherry Meads has difficulty discarding or parting with things. Just the thought of giving something away or throwing it out causes her great distress. Her apartment is so filled with useless items ranging from books and newspapers to napkins from take-out meals, to list a few, that she has to carve out paths just to get from one room to another. Forget about using the bathtub, because it is filled with boxes of receipts that she is convinced she needs to save, "just in case." She doesn't cook anymore because the sink and table are also filled with clutter. Sherry's likely diagnosis would be:
    a. Obsessive-compulsive disorder
    b. Social anxiety disorder
    c. Hoarding
    d. Specific phobia
34. The central feature of _________ disorder is picking at one's skin. The most common sites are on the face, arms, and hands. It is:
    a. Trichotillomania
    b. Obsessive-compulsive
    c. Body dysmorphic
    d. Excoriation
35. People with this disorder recurrently pull out their own hair—it can be from any part of the body where hair grows. The disorder is called:
    a. Pyromania
    b. Trichotillomania

c. Hypomania
d. Complex mania

36. Kevin is an 18-year-old recent high school graduate with a problem that's starting to get in the way of his socializing with his friends. For Kevin, the simple act of looking in a mirror is sheer torture. It all started about a year and a half ago when a friend made a casual comment about his appearance. "I've never been the same since," commented Kevin. He has been obsessed with the size of his chest. Brian adds, "It's just not right. It doesn't fit the rest of my body. It's kinda sunken in, and makes my stomach stick out. I look sickly." Kevin's diagnosis is:
    a. Body dysmorphic disorder
    b. Trichotillomania
    c. Excoriation
    d. Complex mania
37. Other specified (and unspecified) obsessive-compulsive and related disorder is used when the person does not meet full criteria for one of the obsessive-compulsive and related disorders and the practitioner may indicate reasons for using this diagnosis such as jikoshu-kyofu, which means:
    a. An intense anxiety that the penis will recede into the body
    b. Intense fear of having a deformity
    c. An intense fear of having a foul body odor
    d. An intense fear of having a body defect

CHAPTER EIGHT–TRAUMA- AND STRESSOR-RELATED DISORDERS

38. One of the central characteristics of children with _________ disorder is that they have experienced inadequate caregiving environments and show a distinct pattern of being inhibited and withdrawn.
    a. Disinhibited social engagement disorder
    b. Reactive attachment disorder
    c. Acute stress disorder
    d. Posttraumatic stress disorder
39. One of the symptoms of children with this disorder is the failure to seek and respond to comfort when distressed.
    a. Disinhibited social engagement disorder
    b. Reactive attachment disorder
    c. Acute stress disorder
    d. Posttraumatic stress disorder
40. Individuals with this disorder may have problems subsequent to exposure to actual or threatened death, serious injury, or sexual violence. The disorder is called:
    a. Obsessive-compulsive disorder
    b. Reactive attachment disorder
    c. Adjustment disorder
    d. Posttraumatic stress disorder

41. Someone with this disorder may show problems related to a single event or multiple stressors, but for diagnostic purposes, the person's distress is out of proportion to the severity or intensity of the stressor(s). This disorder is called:
    a. Conduct disorder
    b. Disinhibited social engagement disorder
    c. Adjustment disorder
    d. Posttraumatic stress disorder
42. Posttraumatic stress disorder may arise after any of the following events except:
    a. A traumatic wartime experience
    b. An earthquake, flood, or hurricane
    c. Sudden death of a loved one
    d. An allergic medication reaction
43. Immediately after experiencing a tornado, Louise Ann's symptoms emerged almost immediately—her hands started shaking uncontrollably, and she had difficulty grasping the enormity of the event. Fortunately, these symptoms stopped after 3 weeks. Her disorder is called:
    a. Adjustment disorder
    b. Acute stress disorder
    c. Posttraumatic stress disorder
    d. Reactive attachment disorder

CHAPTER NINE–DISSOCIATIVE DISORDERS

44. Nathan Roberts's complaints include: "My perception of my environment often feels distorted or strange. Like, sometimes I have a sudden overwhelming sense of being detached from my own body. During some of these episodes, I can't understand people when they talk to me. The best way I can describe it is that I feel like a robot—or like I'm really outside of my body." Mr. Roberts says that he has been experiencing these episodes since he was a teenager and that they are often accompanied by feelings of anxiety, panic, or depression. What is your beginning assessment?
    a. Dissociative amnesia with dissociative fugue
    b. Depersonalization/derealization disorder
    c. Dissociative amnesia
    d. Dissociative identity disorder
45. Ling Wong is a 34-year-old woman who recently survived the sinking of a ferryboat on the Mississippi River. She claims she has no memory of the events surrounding this disaster, including how she got ashore. Her physical examination was unremarkable, and her cognitive ability is intact. She is very distraught about the unknown fate of her husband, who was also aboard the ferry. She can remember everything but the event. Which of the following is Ling Wong's diagnosis?
    a. Amnesia due to transient cerebral anoxia
    b. Dissociative amnesia
    c. Dissociative fugue
    d. Derealization disorder

46. Which of the following factors contributes to the difficulty in assessing dissociative identity disorder?
    a. These individuals are difficult to hypnotize because it is impossible to gain access to each of the separate "alters"
    b. Some of the presenting symptoms may appear similar to symptoms of schizophrenia
    c. Few individuals report gaps in memory
    d. The different personalities are usually in conflict with each other
47. Which of the following is true of dissociative identity disorder?
    a. The separate identities are always fully developed
    b. There are rarely more than two separate identities
    c. It was previously known as multiple personality disorder (MPD)
    d. Each of the identities is completely aware of the others
48. In almost all cases of dissociative identity disorder, an apparent cause is found in the client's history, which includes:
    a. An overactive imagination
    b. Lack of social support
    c. Severe physical and/or sexual abuse during childhood
    d. Familial predisposition

CHAPTER TEN–SOMATIC SYMPTOM AND RELATED DISORDERS

49. The following symptoms are all necessary for a DSM-5 diagnosis of illness anxiety disorder except:
    a. Preoccupation with the fear of acquiring a serious or life-threatening disease
    b. Preoccupation with suing one's doctor for not finding a serious or life-threatening disease
    c. A misperception of one's own bodily symptoms
    d. Significant distress in one's everyday functioning
50. Kenny Marks, a third-year medical student, returned to the student health services for the fifth time with complaints of diarrhea. After a thorough medical workup that included a barium enema and various other procedures, Kenny was told that there was no organic disease present. Despite this reassurance from several doctors, Kenny continued to test his stool for blood, and remained convinced that the doctors missed making the correct diagnosis. Kenny is exhibiting:
    a. Factitious disorder
    b. Illness anxiety disorder
    c. Psychological factors affecting other medical conditions
    d. Conversion disorder
51. Malingering disorder differs from factitious disorder in the following way:
    a. "Clanging" is more prominent in the factitious disorder than in malingering
    b. In malingering, there is an identifiable external gain

c. There is evidence of displacement of anxiety left over from the oral stage
d. Malingering is similar to factitious disorder but with fewer symptoms

52. Josette Saint-Jean, aged 27, recently experienced an episode of blindness following a physical assault that occurred while she was walking home from work. Upon physical examination in a local emergency room, her eyes were found to exhibit normal dilation when exposed to light. Josette related that her blindness developed spontaneously when the police officers at the scene asked her to come down to the station and go through mug shots. What is Josette's diagnosis?
    a. Dissociative disorder
    b. Panic disorder
    c. Somatic symptom disorder
    d. Conversion disorder
53. _________ is characterized by the voluntary production of signs, symptoms, or disease for no other apparent goal than to be cast in the role of being "sick." What is this disorder called?
    a. Conversion disorder
    b. Somatic symptom disorder
    c. Illness anxiety disorder
    d. Factitious disorder imposed on self
54. Which of the following disorders was originally known as Briquet's syndrome?
    a. Dissociative identity disorder
    b. Somatic symptom disorder
    c. Factitious disorder
    d. Illness anxiety disorder
55. The essential feature of this disorder is an individual's intentional production of an illness; that is, grossly exaggerating physical and/or psychological symptoms motivated by external incentives such as obtaining financial compensation through litigation or disability status or to avoid military duty. This criterion meets which diagnosis?
    a. Malingering disorder
    b. Neuropsychiatric organizational disorder
    c. Body dysmorphic disorder
    d. Somatothymic disorder
56. Marion Moon is anxious and worried about not being able to lose weight. This is especially important since her doctor strongly advised her that this would be better for her diabetes. She has tried several kinds of diets but to no avail. Each time Marion diets she ends up gaining more weight and this only makes her more anxious. She's desperate and decided to adjust her insulin "just a little." Marion has the signs of:
    a. Somatic symptom disorder
    b. Illness anxiety disorder
    c. Psychological factors affecting other medical conditions
    d. Panic disorder

CHAPTER ELEVEN–EATING AND FEEDING DISORDERS

57. Which of the following is a feature found in both bulimia nervosa and anorexia nervosa?
    a. Excessive concern with body weight
    b. Excessive fear of being fat
    c. Bingeing
    d. Weight loss
58. Which of the following is considered the most severe medical complication associated with bulimia?
    a. Dental erosion
    b. Irregular heartbeat
    c. Electrolyte imbalance
    d. Hypertension
59. Which of the following is not considered an eating disorder by the DSM-IV?
    a. Binge-eating disorder (BED)
    b. Obesity
    c. Anorexia nervosa
    d. Bulimia nervosa
60. Twarla Jones is just less than 5 feet tall and weighs 80 pounds. She has always been involved in her school's cheerleading, swim team, and gymnastics. When she turned 16 several months ago, she became extremely fearful about gaining weight. Twarla initially began to limit her food and caloric intake. In addition, she began exercising excessively in order to prevent herself from gaining weight. Twarla calls herself "a blimp." However, her parents, teachers, and friends all reassure her that she is quite thin. Twarla's diagnosis is probably:
    a. Bulimia nervosa, purging type
    b. Anorexia nervosa, restricting type
    c. Eating disorder, not otherwise specified
    d. Bulimia nervosa, nonpurging type
61. ________ refers to self-induced vomiting or laxative misuse to influence body weight.
    a. Purging
    b. Excessive exercise
    c. Restricting
    d. Binge eating
62. Each of the following medical complications, except ________, is associated with anorexia nervosa.
    a. Dry yellowish skin
    b. High blood pressure
    c. Bradycardia (slow heartbeat)
    d. Electrolyte imbalance

CHAPTER TWELVE–ELIMINATION DISORDERS

63. Enuresis is an elimination disorder characterized by:
    a. Sporadic voiding of urine into the bed or clothes
    b. Repeated voiding of urine into the bed or clothes

c. Occasional voiding of urine during waking hours
d. Rarely occurring voiding of urine during nighttime sleep

64. There are two types of enuresis described. They are:
a. Primary and secondary
b. Tertiary and adjuvant
c. Principal and subordinate
d. Retrograde and reversing

65. Which of the following statements is true?
a. Very few children with enuresis are evaluated for a comorbid disorder
b. Developmental delays are rarely present in children with enuresis
c. Most children with enuresis have a comorbid mental disorder
d. Most children with enuresis do not have a comorbid disorder

66. Encopresis is an elimination disorder characterized by:
a. Sporadic passage of feces into inappropriate places
b. Repeated passage of feces into inappropriate places
c. Occasional passage of feces during waking hours into inappropriate places
d. Rarely occurring passage of feces during nighttime sleep into inappropriate places

67. Other specified elimination disorder applies to presentations in which symptoms characteristic of an elimination disorder do not meet full criteria. This allows the practitioner to communicate:
a. The presence of unusual symptoms
b. Low frequency of symptom occurrence
c. The specific reason that the client does not meet criteria
d. Low-grade medical complications

CHAPTER THIRTEEN–DISRUPTIVE, IMPULSE-CONTROL, AND CONDUCT DISORDERS

68. One of the symptoms shown in individuals with this disorder is the consistent violation of others. This disorder is called:
a. Oppositional defiant disorder
b. Conduct disorder
c. Rett's disorder
d. Childhood disintegrative disorder

69. Doug is sitting in a neighborhood bar and having a conversation with another man sitting next to him. At one point, Doug feels insulted by something the guy said. Instead of finding out whether the remark was intended as an insult or answering the supposed insult verbally, Doug jumps up and impulsively punches him in the face. Afterwards, Doug feels genuinely sorry for his actions, upset, and embarrassed by his impulsive and aggressive behavior. Doug's likely diagnosis is:
a. Conduct disorder
b. Antisocial personality disorder

c. Intermittent explosive disorder
d. Dysthymia

70. This disorder is distinguished by the individual's inability to resist stealing something that has neither personal use nor any monetary value. This disorder is:
a. Pyromania
b. Kleptomania
c. Hypomania
d. Hypopnea

71. Individuals who will run into problems following expected standards of behavior seen in anger, aggression, destruction of property, violating the rights of others, or conflicts with authority figures are characterized by all of the following disorders except:
a. Oppositional defiant disorder
b. Conduct disorder
c. Conversion disorder
d. Intermittent explosive disorder

72. Jack Martin is the former captain of the Glendale, California, Fire Department. He was an arson investigator who eventually became a serial arsonist himself. He was later convicted for first-degree murder for the lives lost in the fires he set. Jack's diagnosis is:
a. Dysphoria
b. Dysthymia
c. Kleptomania
d. Pyromania

CHAPTER FOURTEEN–SUBSTANCE-RELATED AND ADDICTIVE DISORDERS

73. Which one of the following is not recognized in the DSM-5 as an alcohol-related disorder?
a. Alcohol use
b. Alcohol dependence
c. Alcohol intoxication
d. Alcohol withdrawal

74. Which one of the following non-substance-related addictive disorders is included in the DSM-5?
a. Internet addiction
b. Computer dependence
c. Gambling
d. Compulsive shopping

75. The diagnosis of substance _________ is given when a person uses a drug without a legitimate medical need to do so.
a. Intoxication
b. Withdrawal
c. Use
d. Dependence

76. When assessing for the substance-related disorders, it is helpful to explore:
    a. Route of administration
    b. Duration of effects
    c. Use of multiple substances
    d. All of the above
77. The following drugs are prescribed for short-term relief of severe, debilitating anxiety and may be abused when not used as directed:
    a. Benzodiazepines
    b. Barbiturates
    c. Opioids
    d. Sedatives
78. These drugs, also known as speed or pep pills, are central nervous system stimulants that are usually synthetically make in illegal labs.
    a. Cocaine
    b. Amphetamines
    c. Opioids
    d. Hallucinogens
79. Hallucinogen persisting perception disorder is commonly referred to as:
    a. A "bad trip"
    b. Snorting
    c. Flashbacks
    d. A hangover
80. The diagnostic criteria for hallucinogen use disorder follows the same guidelines as for other substance-related disorders with one exception. Which of the following does not support hallucinogen use disorder?
    a. Withdrawal
    b. Tolerance
    c. Desire or efforts to cut down or stop use
    d. Use in situations in which it is physically hazardous
81. All of the ten classes of substances listed in the DSM-5 follow guidelines for a substance use disorder with the exception of one. Of the following, which substance or class of substances is not associated with a substance use disorder?
    a. Inhalants
    b. Stimulants
    c. Caffeine
    d. Tobacco
82. ________ are a chemically diverse group of psychoactive substances that includes a variety of substances found in common household products.
    a. Hallucinogens
    b. Inhalants
    c. Phencyclidines
    d. Green hornets
83. The substance use disorders include the following criteria except:
    a. Dependence and abuse
    b. Intoxication and withdrawal
    c. Polysubstance dependence
    d. None of the above

CHAPTER FIFTEEN–NEUROCOGNITIVE DISORDERS

84. Dr. Johnson, a physician, referred his 73-year-old patient, Abner Smith, to you for a consultation. Mr. Smith has been having difficulty remembering and concentrating for the last 3 years. He came to the interview with his son, Jake. Abner Smith admitted to feeling depressed and anxious. His wife of 48 years died several years ago, and since that time he has lived alone in their house. Jake Smith added that his father seems to have changed over time; that is, his father leaves food cooking on the stove unattended; was found wandering around the neighborhood as if he was lost; and forgets the names of family members. These symptoms support the diagnosis of:
    a. Neurocognitive disorder due to Alzheimer's disease
    b. Delirium
    c. Paranoid personality disorder
    d. Schizophrenia, paranoid type
85. Kenny Grayson accepted a new job in another town several hundred miles away, and he is worried about leaving his 72-year-old father behind. Kenny's father lives alone, is very confused, and is bowel and bladder incontinent. In addition, the senior Grayson suffered a mild stroke several years ago, which left a number of areas in his brain damaged. He is now showing signs of neurological impairment. What is the most likely DSM-IV diagnosis for Kenny's father?
    a. Neurocognitive disorder due to another medical condition
    b. Neurocognitive disorder due to Alzheimer's disease
    c. Dissociative fugue
    d. Vascular neurocognitive disorder
86. The clinical picture of neurocognitive disorder due to Alzheimer's disease, includes all of the following symptoms, except:
    a. Sudden onset
    b. Individual gets lost in familiar places
    c. Night restlessness and difficulty falling asleep
    d. Short-term memory loss
87. The majority of people who experience an episode of delirium:
    a. Tend to progress rapidly to dementia without recovery
    b. Usually recover within several days or weeks after the causative factor is eliminated
    c. Do not recover unless treated with a carbamazepine protocol
    d. Should have psychosocial rehabilitation to support social and functioning skills that the individual may have lost in the earlier phase of the episode
88. Edna Trybus states that her mother, Hilda Walker, 75 years old, has become increasingly irritable and reclusive over the last 4 or 5 years. Mrs. Walker accuses her children of plotting to steal her house and her life savings. Mrs. Walker has been unable to care for herself; for example, she cannot cook her own meals, dress herself, or clean her home. Mrs. Walker is often confused in that she cannot remember her home address, her phone number, or her

children's names. What DSM-5 diagnosis best describes Mrs. Walker's signs and symptoms?
a. Agoraphobia, without panic disorder
b. Delirium
c. Frontotemporal neurocognitive disorder
d. Neurocognitive disorder due to Alzheimer's disease

89. The DSM-5 distinguishes between mild neurocognitive disorder and major neurocognitive disorder based on:
a. Whether or not the person is concerned about a decline in cognitive function
b. Whether or not the cognitive impairment is sufficient to interfere with independent completion of the activities of daily living
c. The presence of impairment on cognitive testing
d. Co-occurrence with delirium

CHAPTER SIXTEEN–PERSONALITY DISORDERS

90. Perry Max lives his life following a very strict schedule every day. Perry must have everything perfect, in its place, and organized. He is devoted to his job as a plant manager, and he insists on following all rules and regulations without deviation. Perry has not taken a vacation in 10 years. Although he loves his job, Perry has tremendous difficulty completing projects and getting his reports done in a timely fashion. Which of the following best characterizes his personality type?
a. Paranoid
b. Obsessive-compulsive
c. Dependent
d. Avoidant

91. Jamie is a 19-year-old young man who was mandated to therapy by the court and assigned to you for an intake appointment. Reviewing the background materials, you notice that the client has exhibited significant signs of conduct disturbance since the age of 14. He has a history of lying, stealing, and selling drugs—he physically attacked his mother on several occasions. He shows no remorse and is indifferent to others' suffering. In session, the client seems surly and irritable. He blames others for his problems with the law. The best diagnosis for this client is:
a. Cluster A personality disorder
b. Antisocial personality disorder
c. Oppositional defiant disorder
d. Borderline personality disorder

92. Nancy has recently been assigned to you because her prior worker left the agency. You note from the psychosocial history in her file that she has a tendency to sexualize all relationships and displayed irrational emotional outbreaks to her previous worker; more specifically, on one day she "loved" her worker and on the next day "hated" her. Nancy likes to be the center of

attention. She also shows a tendency toward suggestibility, dramatization, and chaotic behavior. Her diagnosis would be:
a. Schizoid personality disorder
b. Histrionic personality disorder
c. Borderline personality disorder
d. Narcissistic personality disorder

93. According to his family, Barry, 28 years of age, has always been shy. He did not do well in grade school and dropped out of high school before graduating. He is described as being isolated, having no friends, and showing no interest in dating or sexual activity. Despite adequate intelligence, Barry has never been able to keep a job. He lives at home with his father—he is so unmotivated and so isolated that he has never bothered to obtain a driver's license. He plays computer games all day. Beyond Barry's reclusive nature and emotional aloofness, he has no desire to change and refuses to go for counseling. What is Barry's diagnosis?
a. Avoidant personality disorder
b. Borderline personality disorder
c. Schizoid personality disorder
d. Dependent personality disorder

94. According to the DSM-5, the ten personality disorders are divided into _________ clusters that are based on certain descriptive characteristics.
a. 1
b. 2
c. 3
d. 4

95. Cluster _________ personality disorders are characterized by odd and eccentric behaviors.
a. A
b. B
c. C
d. D

96. A pervasive distrust and suspiciousness of others characterize _________ personality disorder, such that the motives of others are interpreted as malevolent, and hidden meanings are read into benign remarks.
a. Paranoid
b. Schizoid
c. Dependent
d. Histrionic

97. Which of the following personality disorders is most closely related to schizophrenia?
a. Borderline
b. Antisocial
c. Schizotypal
d. Schizoid

98. Which of the following personality disorders is best characterized by feelings of inadequacy, extreme sensitivity to negative remarks, and social inhibition?
    a. Avoidant
    b. Schizoid
    c. Dependent
    d. Borderline
99. Cluster C personality disorders are characterized by ________ behaviors.
    a. Aggressive and hostile
    b. Dramatic, emotional, and erratic
    c. Odd and eccentric
    d. Anxious and fearful
100. Cluster B personality disorders include all of the following except ________.
    a. Antisocial
    b. Borderline
    c. Histrionic
    d. Paranoid

ANSWER KEY

1. (d) Standard reference used to diagnose all mental disorders
2. (a) The importance of identifying client competencies
3. (b) Work together to formulate a more accurate diagnosis
4. (c) Specifiers
5. (c) A listing of assessment measures including self-assessment tools and a cultural formulation for understanding the cultural context
6. (c) Tourette's disorder
7. (a) Attention-deficit/hyperactivity disorder, combined presentation
8. (d) Developmental coordination disorder
9. (b) Speech sound disorder
10. (b) Intellectual disability (Intellectual developmental disorder)
11. (b) Schizophreniform disorder
12. (a) Brief psychotic disorder postpartum onset
13. (c) Grandiose type delusions
14. (a) At least 1 month of delusions but no other psychotic symptoms
15. (c) The central theme of the delusion is that another person is in love with the individual
16. (a) Racing thoughts
17. (d) Excessive involvement in pleasurable activities
18. (a) Seasonal affective disorder
19. (a) Bipolar disorder, manic type
20. (b) Persistent depressive disorder (dysthymia)
21. (d) Grandiosity
22. (a) Ataque de nervios, a culture-bound syndrome
23. (b) Premenstrual dysphoric disorder provisional

24. (c) Major depressive disorder
25. (b) Selective mutism
26. (a) Situationally predisposed
27. (d) Elevated mood
28. (d) A specific phobia
29. (c) Agoraphobia
30. (b) Generalized anxiety disorder
31. (b) Body dysmorphic disorder
32. (c) Behaviors or mental acts aimed at preventing or reducing anxiety or distress
33. (c) Hoarding
34. (d) Excoriation
35. (b) Trichotillomania
36. (a) Body dysmorphic disorder
37. (c) An intense fear of having a foul body odor
38. (b) Reactive attachment disorder
39. (b) Reactive attachment disorder
40. (d) Posttraumatic stress disorder
41. (c) Adjustment disorder
42. (d) An allergic medication reaction
43. (b) Acute stress disorder
44. (b) Depersonalization/derealization disorder
45. (b) Dissociative amnesia
46. (b) Some of the presenting symptoms may appear similar to symptoms of schizophrenia
47. (c) It was previously known as multiple personality disorder (MPD)
48. (c) Severe physical and/or sexual abuse during childhood
49. (b) Preoccupation with suing one's doctor for not finding a serious or life-threatening disease
50. (b) Illness anxiety disorder
51. (b) In malingering, there is an identifiable external gain
52. (d) Conversion disorder
53. (d) Factitious disorder imposed on self
54. (b) Somatic symptom disorder
55. (a) Malingering disorder
56. (c) Psychological factors affecting other medical conditions
57. (b) Excessive fear of being fat
58. (c) Electrolyte imbalance
59. (b) Obesity
60. (b) Anorexia nervosa, restricting type
61. (a) Purging
62. (b) High blood pressure
63. (b) Repeated voiding of urine into the bed or clothes
64. (a) Primary and secondary
65. (d) Most children with enuresis do not have a comorbid disorder
66. (b) Repeated passage of feces into inappropriate places
67. (c) The specific reason that the client does not meet diagnostic criteria

68. (a) Oppositional defiant disorder
69. (c) Intermittent explosive disorder
70. (b) Kleptomania
71. (c) Conversion disorder
72. (d) Pyromania
73. (b) Alcohol dependence
74. (c) Gambling
75. (c) Use
76. (d) All of the above
77. (a) Benzodiazepines
78. (b) Amphetamines
79. (c) Flashbacks
80. (a) Withdrawal
81. (c) Caffeine
82. (b) Inhalants
83. (c) Polysubstance dependence
84. (a) Neurocognitive disorder due to Alzheimer's disease
85. (d) Vascular neurocognitive disorder
86. (a) Sudden onset
87. (b) Usually recover within several days or weeks after the causative factor is eliminated
88. (d) Neurocognitive disorder due to Alzheimer's disease
89. (b) Whether or not the cognitive impairment is sufficient to interfere with independent completion of the activities of daily living
90. (b) Obsessive-compulsive
91. (b) Antisocial personality disorder
92. (c) Borderline personality disorder
93. (c) Schizoid personality disorder
94. (c) 3
95. (a) Cluster A
96. (a) Paranoid
97. (c) Schizotypal
98. (a) Avoidant
99. (d) Anxious and fearful
100. (d) Paranoid

Glossary

Acetylcholine a neurotransmitter found in the hippocampus, an area of the brain responsible for forming new memories

Adrenal cortex produces hormones to initiate or control stress reactions

Agonist medication a drug that is capable of producing a response similar to the original drug

Affective liability refers to mood swings

Agoraphobia a disorder characterized by a marked or intense fear or anxiety triggered by the real or anticipated exposure to a wide range of situations; for example, using public transportation, being in open spaces or in enclosed spaces, standing in line, or being outside of the home alone

Alcohol intoxication known as drunkenness or inebriation; is the physiological state induced by induced by the ingestion of ethyl alcohol

Alcohol use disorder a diagnosis where the individual engages in problem drinking

Alter refers to the shorthand term for a different identity or personality seen in the dissociative disorders

Alogia seen in those diagnosed with schizophrenia, is a negative symptom involving a speech disturbance in which there is a lack of fluency and productivity of thought and speech or poverty in its content

Alzheimer's disease a condition such as often causes degeneration across many areas of the brain, producing a mosaic of cognitive problems

Amok a trance syndrome, common in Southeast Asia, characterized by a sudden outburst of unrestrained violent and aggressive behavior, usually of a homicidal nature, preceded by a period of anxious brooding and followed by exhaustion

Amygdala the part of the brain located near the hippocampus and involved in fear responses and memory of that fear

Anhedonia an inability to experience pleasure or recall previously pleasurable experiences and can be a negative symptom of schizophrenia

Animal Phobia an excessive or unreasonable fear of animals

Anorexia nervosa, binge eating/purging type the individual regularly engages (minimally for at least the past 3 months) in weight control behaviors such as self-induced vomiting and/or misuse of laxatives, enemas, or diuretics.

Anorexia nervosa, restricting type the individual severely limits caloric intake (for at least the past 3 months), but does not regularly engage in binge eating or purging behavior

Anosognosia seen as a lack of awareness of (or poor insight) into a disorder

Antisocial personality disorder a personality disorder characterized by continual asocial or criminal acts

Anxiety a mood state wherein the person anticipates future danger or misfortune with apprehension

Anxiety disorders a category of disorders that share features of excessive fear and anxiety and related disturbances

Anxious distress specifier a specifier applicable to the bipolar disorders that is intended to identify individuals who have symptoms of anxiety that are not part of the bipolar diagnostic criteria

Aphonia inability to create sounds or speak

Asociality refers to the person's lack of interest in social interactions and is a negative symptom for schizophrenia

Ataques de nervios a commonly noted response to acute stress in Latin American and Hispanic cultures where features include uncontrollable crying, screaming, shouting, seizure-like behaviors, and a failure to remember the episode afterward

Ataxia impairment in control of voluntary muscle coordination

Attention-deficit/hyperactivity disorder (ADHD) a neurodevelopmental disorder that affects the areas of social skills, behavior, and communication; key behaviors are inattention or a lack of focus, executive functioning difficulties, impulsivity, and hyperactivity beyond what can be expected of a person's normal developmental age

Atypical features specifier applicable only to bipolar I disorder, this specifier applies when the person's mood brightens during his or her most recent major depressive episode

Auditory hallucinations a hallucination consisting of the person hearing voices and is considered the most common feature of schizophrenia

Autism spectrum disorder (ASD) sometimes just referred to as "autism"; is a neurodevelopmental disorder characterized by social deficits and communication difficulties, stereotyped or repetitive behaviors and interests, and, in some instances, cognitive delays; this DSM-5 disorder includes the previous DSM-IV-TR diagnoses of autism, Asperger's syndrome, pervasive developmental disorders not otherwise specified (PDD-NOS), childhood disintegrative disorder, and Retts syndrome

Avoidant personality disorder the main characteristics of this personality disorder are a pervasive pattern of social inhibition; constant feelings of inadequacy and ineptitude, especially in social situations; and hypersensitivity to negative evaluation beginning in early adulthood

Avoidant/restrictive food intake disorder (ARFID) is an eating disorder that prevents the consumption of certain foods

Avolition a loss of goal-directed behavior seen in those diagnosed with schizophrenia

Axon this is attached to the soma, and its function is to carry messages out to other cells

Bezoar a hard, indigestible mass trapped in the gastrointestinal system, usually the stomach, causing a bowel obstruction or an intestinal obstruction

Binge ingesting a much larger amount of food than most people would eat under similar circumstances in a limited period of time

Binge drinking consuming 5 or more drinks on the same occasion

Binge eating an episode in which the individual eats "out of control" and is unable to resist the temptation to consume certain foods

Binge eating disorder or BED, is characterized by recurrent binge eating, but without subsequent purging episodes that are part of the bulimic picture

Biopsychosocial framework validates the potential importance of biogenetic, psychological, social, and environmental factors in understanding human behavior and is an element supporting the competency-based assessment

Bipolar disorder a disorder characterized by the presence of mania or hypomania

Bipolar I a bipolar disorder that refers to severe manic episodes accompanied by one or more periods of major depressive episodes which can have psychotic features

Bipolar II a specific bipolar disorder that refers to a pattern of symptoms ranging from hypomanic (or manic) episodes accompanied by one or more periods of depression, but with a major distinction in the degree of severity; typically, this disorder does not lead to psychotic behavior or require hospitalization

Bloating abdominal distension seen in the eating and feeding disorders caused by the amount of food eaten

Blood-injection-injury phobia individuals with this type of phobia fear needles and invasive medical procedures

Body dysmorphic disorder (BDD) a diagnosis that characterizes the person's preoccupation about some imagined defect in their body

Body mass index (BMI) a measure of one's weight calculated in kilograms in relationship to height calculated in meters

Borderline personality disorder one of the most common personality disorders where the person shows an unstable mood, extremely poor relationships with others, and low self-image alternating between extremes of idealization and devaluation (commonly referred to as "splitting")

Bradycardia slow heartbeat

Brain stem the part of the brain located at the top of the spinal cord

Brief psychotic disorder also known as brief reactive psychosis; is a disorder that seems to be triggered by major stress or a traumatic event characterized by its sudden onset and relatively short duration wherein the individual returns full return to functioning

Caffeine intoxication the recent daily consumption of caffeine of at least more than 250 milligrams, which typically is the equivalent of two and a half cups of brewed coffee

Cannabinoids the term used to describe a number of psychoactive compounds found in cannabis plants

Cardiac arrhythmia an irregular heartbeat

Cataplexy a sudden and transient episode of paralysis (with no loss of consciousness) and affecting nearly all voluntary muscles

Catatonia specifier applies when the person shows catatonic behaviors during most of the bipolar episode of mania or depression; it also can be seen in neurodevelopmental, psychotic, depressive disorders, which refer to a series of psychomotor features that may involve decreased motor activity, decreased engagement during an interview, or excessive and peculiar motor activity

Catatonic behavior seen as the person's decreased ability to react to his or her environment; manifests itself in several ways such as not actively relating to one's environment, showing odd mannerisms, repetitive movements, agitation or grimacing to list a few

Catatonic excitement a form of catatonic behavior where the person shows purposeless and excessive motor activity without an obvious cause

Central nervous system a biological system that consists of the brain and spinal cord; receives, processes, interprets, and stores information; and then sends messages to the muscles, glands, and organs

Cerebellum about the size of a small fist, this is the part of the brain involved in cognitive and emotional learning along with contributing to a sense of balance and coordination of muscle movements

Cerebral cortex the largest part of the brain; can best be described as a cauliflower-like structure that is covered by several thin layers of densely packed cells

Cerebral infarct a type of stroke resulting from blockage in the blood vessels supplying blood to the brain

Cerebrovascular accident (CVA) the sudden death of some brain cells due to a lack of oxygen when blood flow to the brain is impaired by a blocked vein or artery; commonly referred to as a stroke

Childhood onset fluency disorder (stuttering) a neurodevelopmental communication disorder subcategory reserved for frequent, persistent, and marked instances of stuttering that causes problems for the individual such as anxiety about speaking, limited effective communication, or changes in social participation or job performance (or any combination)

Cingulate cortex resembles a collar surrounding the frontal part (or anterior section) of the corpus callosum and plays an important role in emotional and cognitive processing

Clanging seen in those with the diagnosis of schizophrenia and characterizes speech where someone uses rhyme or puns

Clouding of consciousness the inability to focus, sustain, or shift attention

Communication disorder a cluster of neurodevelopmental disorders that affects how a person speaks and communicates to the extent that it interferes with school, work, or even relationships; namely, language disorder, speech sound disorder, childhood onset fluency disorder (stuttering), social (pragmatic) communication disorder, and unspecified communication disorder

Competency-based assessment an approach to the assessment process that provides a conceptual framework using bio-psycho-social-spiritual theories and the DSM classification systems

Competency-based practice this approach to practice emphasizes the importance of identifying client competencies, and it focuses on assets instead of deficits

Complex motor tics last longer (seconds) than simple motor tics and can include a combination of simple tics such as simultaneous head turning and shoulder shrugging

Conduct disorder (CD) the essential feature of this disorder is a consistent pattern of violating the rights of others, or major age-appropriate societal norms or rules are violated

Confabulate or when a person makes up information he or she cannot remember

Conjunctival injection referred to as bloodshot eyes

Conversion disorder a type of somatic symptom disorder where the affected individual experiences a loss or change in physical functioning that suggests the presence of a physical disorder but cannot be explained on the basis of any known physiologic mechanism

Coprolalia seen in tic disorders and involves uttering socially unacceptable words including obscenities, racial slurs, and the like

Copropraxia a complex motor tic behavior characterized by making an obscene gesture

Cortisol a hormone released when the body experiences stress

Creutzfeldt-Jakob disease (CJD) one of the more common prion diseases; is a rare illness marked by rapid mental deterioration, usually within a few months, and is always fatal, leading to death usually within one year of onset; initial signs and symptoms typically include personality changes, anxiety, depression, memory loss, impaired thinking, blurred vision, insomnia, difficulty speaking, difficulty swallowing, and sudden jerky movements

Cyberchondria a mutation of hypochondria; refers to easy access to medical and diagnostic information via the Internet

Cyclothymic disorder a disorder within the classification of the bipolar and related disorders that refers to a chronic or cyclic mood disturbance that has many of the same features found in major depressive episodes

Defense mechanisms processes geared to maintain balance between the individual's internal drives and the external world

Delirium a neurocognitive disorder characterized as a temporary condition that often follows a short and fluctuating course

Delusional disorder a disorder characterized by the person's persistent belief about something that is contrary to reality

Delusions refer to the false and fixed beliefs based on incorrect deductions or misrepresentations in a person's reality

Delusions of control the delusional belief where the person believes his or her body is being affected by some outside force

Dendrites the parts of the neuron that receive messages from other cells

Dental caries this term refers to tooth rot

Dependent personality disorder a personality disorder that describes a person's pervasive pattern of extreme inability to act independently of others

Depersonalization/derealization disorder a disorder where the person will experience themselves or their surroundings as strange or unreal in some way

Depressant a chemical agent that diminishes the function or activity of a specific part of the body

Derailment interruptions to thought and jumping from one thought to another disconnected thought or loose associations

Derealization the loss of one's sense of reality in the external world

Developmental coordination disorder also known as dyspraxia or clumsy child syndrome; is a neurodevelopmental disorder subcategory of the motor disorders characterized by impaired skills requiring motor coordination; for instance, it's hard for a child to use scissors, ride a bike, and/or participate in sports or team activities in school

Diminished emotional expression seen in those diagnosed with schizophrenia; characterized as a reduced expression of emotions seen in the person's face, eye contact or intonation of speech

Diplopia this term refers to double vision

Disinhibited social engagement disorder core diagnostic features of this disorder can be seen in the child's behavior, described as an inappropriate approach to unfamiliar adults, a lack of wariness of strangers, and a willingness to wander off with strangers

Disruptive, impulse-control, and conduct disorders this classification of disorders is a new chapter to the DSM-5; specific disorders include oppositional defiant disorder, the disruptive behaviors as seen in intermittent explosive disorder, conduct disorder, pyromania, and kleptomania

Disruptive mood dysregulation disorder (DMDD) a relatively new diagnosis to the DSM; is included to capture children with frequent temper tantrums and irritability and to prevent the overdiagnosis of other closely related disorders such as bipolar disorder or oppositional defiant disorder

Dissociative amnesia disorder formerly known as psychogenic amnesia, this is a completely reversible amnesia that is associated with some form of emotional, traumatic, or psychological stress

Dissociative disorders a disorder wherein people forget who they are, where they are, and what they have been doing—in extreme cases of dissociation, people may acquire one or more distinct identities

Dissociative fugue a specifier for dissociative amnesia, wherein the person experiences unexpected travel away from their home or work, suffer an inability to recall their past, assume a new identity, and cannot remember important personal details about their past

Dissociative identity disorder formerly known as multiple personality disorder (MPD); is considered the most severe of all the dissociative disorders because the most common and fundamental alteration includes the presence of more than one discrete identity

Disorganized behavior involves physical actions that do not appear to be goal directed—for example, taking off one's clothes in public, assuming or maintaining unusual postures, pacing excitedly, or moving fingers or extremities in idiosyncratic and repetitive ways

Disorganized speech a form of speech commonly seen in the diagnosis of schizophrenia that is not governed by logic; sometimes it is exhibited in rhymes or puns, and at other times it may take the form of mimicking speech patterns of those around the person

Diuresis the removal of excess fluid from the body through increased urine output

Dizygotic twin refers to fraternal twins

Dopamine a neurotransmitter found in the brain that can have differing effects, depending on its exact location; for instance, if too little dopamine is released in certain areas of the brain, the result is Parkinson's disease, and if too much is released in other areas, the result is a cluster of symptoms that may be a part of schizophrenia

Dyesthesiasis a neurological condition characterized by a distortion of the sense of touch, which causes all touch to feel unpleasant

Dysarthria refers to slurred speech

Dyscalculia an alternative term used to refer to a pattern of difficulties characterized by problems processing numerical information, learning arithmetic facts, and performing accurate or fluent calculations

Dyskinesias impaired ability to control movement

Dyslexia an alternative term used to refer to a pattern of learning difficulties characterized by problems with accurate or fluent word recognition, poor decoding, and poor spelling difficulties

Dysphonia refers to difficulty in speaking, usually evidenced by hoarseness

Dysphoria a state of feeling unhappy or unwell

Dystonias refers to muscle spasms

Dystonic movements refers to tremors

Echolalia seen when the individual is repeating the last heard word or phrase of another and then he or she may copy the tone, words, or fragments of overheard conversations

Echopraxia a tic-like imitation of another's physical gestures and movements similar to a pantomime

Ecological perspective an aspect of the competency-based assessment that serves to draw attention to the client's multiple interactions with his or her environment; within this framework, "goodness of fit" between individuals and their surroundings is a]achieved through mutual interaction, negotiation, and compromise

Ego according to Freudian psychoanalytic theory, this is seen as the executive function of the individual's personality structure

Ego-dystonic where one's behaviors, values, or feelings are seen as incompatible with the person's view of him- or herself

Ego-syntonic where one's behaviors, values, or feelings are seen as acceptable and consistent with the person's personality and beliefs

Electroconvulsive therapy (ECT) a treatment procedure where an electric shock is administered directly through the brain for a very brief period of time (less than a second), producing a seizure and a series of brief convulsions; a treatment used for major depressive disorder

Elimination disorders organized around the inappropriate elimination of urine or feces, these are first seen in childhood or adolescence, and the diagnosis is made when a child does not accomplish control over their bladder (enuresis) and/or bowels (encopresis) within a reasonable expected time frame, or if there has been a regression; nocturnal refers to passage only during nighttime sleep, and diurnal refers to passage during waking hours

Encopresis an elimination disorder where the child repeatedly passes feces into inappropriate places such as clothing or the floor (either involuntary or intentional)

Endorphins one set of neuropeptides that influences pain-controlling chemicals in the body

Enteral feeding refers to tube feeding

Enuresis an elimination disorder characterized by repeated voiding of urine into bed or clothes (either involuntary or intentional)

Erotomanic delusional disorder this type of delusional disorder characterizes the individual who believes that someone else, often someone important or famous, is in love with him or her

Erotomanic delusions the erroneous delusional belief that someone is in love with the person

Erythrophobia a term that refers to blushing

Euphoria or euphoric intense feelings of joy or elation or a drug "high"

Euthymic refers to a normal non-depressed, reasonably positive mood

Excoriation (skin-picking) disorder a disorder characterized by recurrent skin-picking, most commonly on the arms, face, and hands, resulting in skin lesions.

Externalizing disorders a group of disorders that are characterized by symptoms of prominent antisocial behaviors, disruptive conduct, substance use, and impulsive behaviors

Factitious disorder this disorder applies to the person who displays physical and psychological symptoms that are intentionally produced and are completely under the person's voluntary control (as with malingering), but there is no obvious reason for voluntarily producing the symptoms except, possibly, to take on the sick role and receive increased attention

Falling out also known as blacking out; is characterized by the individual collapsing, sometimes without warning, in a trance

Flat affect a form of affect seen in those diagnosed with schizophrenia that is exhibited by gazing with "vacant eyes" and can be seen in someone who is seemingly unaffected by what is going on around him or her and displays little change in facial expressions

Free-floating anxiety the kind of anxiety experienced but not attached to any specific situation

Frontotemporal neurocognitive disorder a neurocognitive disorder characterized by progressive changes in personality and social conduct, and associated with degeneration of the prefrontal and anterior temporal cortex of the brain

Frozen watchfulness a behavior where the individual is sitting and staring as if frozen

Gaba-aminobutyric acid the major neurotransmitter producing inhibition in the brain

Gambling disorder a non-substance-related disorder addressing problematic gambling behaviors newly added to the DSM-5

Gastroesophageal reflux disease (GERD) a condition in which the stomach contents, food or liquid, leak backwards from the stomach into the esophagus or the tube from the mouth to the stomach

Gastroparesis clinically similar to rumination disorder, this is a condition in which the stomach cannot empty food properly

Generalized anxiety disorder a disorder characterized by excessive anxiety and worry (seen as apprehensive expectation) about a number of events or activities

Gingivitis refers to the inflammation of the gums

Global developmental delay a neurodevelopmental disorder diagnosis used for individuals who are 5 years of age or younger and fail to meet expected developmental milestones in several areas of intellectual functioning; it is reserved for the child who is not able to undergo a systematic assessment of intellectual functioning or is unable to participate in standardized testing

Globus refers to having a lump in the throat

Glutamate the neurotransmitter that produces feelings of excitability

Grandiose delusional disorder the person with this type of delusional disorder has an overinflated sense of worth, or having some great but unrecognized talent or insight, or has made an important discovery

Grandiose delusions the delusional belief that one is special, famous, or important

Grazing an individual eats small amounts of food almost continuously throughout the day

Grisi siknis also known as Pibloktoq, but found among the Miskito Indians of Central America

Hallucinations this term characterizes experiences of sensory events in the absence of environmental stimulation

Hallucinogen persisting perception disorder commonly referred to as flashbacks

Heavy alcohol use binge drinking on at least 5 separate days in the past month

Hippocampus located toward the middle temporal lobe on each side of the brain; is instrumental in forming long-term permanent memories that are then stored elsewhere in the brain

Histrionic personality disorder a personality disorder that characterizes someone who is often described as colorful, dramatic, extroverted, excitable, and emotional

Hoarding disorder a disorder that characterizes the individual's persistent difficulties in discarding or parting with possessions regardless of their actual value because of a perceived need to save them or sentimental attachment.

Hyperacusis refers to sensitivity to sound

Hyperreflexia refers to overactive reflexes such as tremors

Hypersomnia a term that characterizes when one sleeps for an excessively long time

Hypervigilance seen when the person is obsessively concerned, defended, or watchful

Hypnopomic hallucinations generally considered as natural effects of REM sleep where an individual perceives visual or aural or auditory illusions upon waking; as a result, images and sounds can be carried over into a person's conscious perception

Hypokalemic alkalosis a condition caused by the kidneys' reaction to an extreme lack or loss of potassium, which may be caused by some diuretic medications

Hypomania a less severe form of mania seen in bipolar disorders

Hypomanic episode seen in the bipolar II disorder where many of the features found in mania may be present, but overall the mood disturbance is less severe

Hypotension refers to chronically low blood pressure

Hypothalamus this part of the brain sits just below and in front of the thalamus and regulates body temperature, thirst, hunger, sleeping and waking, sexual activity, and the aggression we feel

Iatrogenic syndrome a spectrum of side effects that can be worse than the original condition

Ideas of reference seen where the person experiences innocuous events or mere coincidences and believes they have a strong personal significant meaning for that person, in which everything everyone else does somehow relates back to him or her

Iich'aa also referred to as amok, but found among the Navajo.

Illness anxiety disorder this disorder is characterized by the person who has physical complaints that are without a clear cause.

Illusions refers to perceptual disturbances in which things appear differently from what they actually are in reality

Indisposition also referred to as falling out but occurs in Haitians

Individuals with Disabilities Education Act (IDEA) the U.S. federal statute that guides how early intervention and special education services are provided to infants, toddlers, children, and youth with disabilities

Inhalants a chemically diverse group of psychoactive substances found in volatile solvents that can be breathed directly into the lungs

Insomnia refers to when an individual cannot sleep

Intellectual disability (intellectual developmental disorder) formerly called mental retardation; is a neurodevelopmental disorder that appears before adulthood, characterized by an individual's significantly impaired cognitive functioning and deficits in adaptive behaviors; the individual shows significantly sub-average general intellectual functioning, existing concurrently with deficits in adaptive behavior and manifested during the developmental period, that adversely affects educational performance

Intermittent explosive disorder (IED) the behaviors supporting this diagnosis can be seen in explosive outbursts wherein the person is unable to control his (or, less often, her) aggressive impulses.

Internalizing disorders a group of disorders characterized by high levels of negative activity and represented by prominent symptoms of anxiety, depressive, and somatic symptoms

International Classification of Diseases also commonly referred to as the ICD; refers to a coding system used to classify morbidity data from inpatient and outpatient records, physician offices, and most National Center for Health Statistics (NCHS) surveys

Interoceptive avoidance a type of avoidance where the person removes him- or herself from situations or activities that might evoke the physiological arousal that resembles the beginnings of a panic attack

Interprofessional collaboration the term reserved for when the social worker may consult with other professional disciplines to confirm a diagnosis or to monitor a client's medication

Intubation refers to a procedure for inserting a tube into the mouth or nose and then advancing it into the airway when a person is not breathing

Ipecac a solution that induces vomiting

Jealous type of delusional disorder someone with this type of delusional disorder believes that his or her spouse or sexual partner is unfaithful

Kleptomania the central feature that distinguishes this disorder is the individual's inability to resist stealing something that has no personal use or any monetary value

Korsakoff syndrome a chronic memory disorder caused by severe deficiency of thiamine or vitamin B1) is most commonly caused by alcohol misuse

La belle indifference refers to showing inappropriate indifference in the face of seemingly tragic and overwhelming medical events

Lability the state where the person emotionally moves from the peaks of elation to the depths of despair

Lacrimation refers to the shedding of more tears than normal

Language disorder a neurodevelopmental communication disorder characterized by difficulties in learning and using language that involve the processing of linguistic information due to deficits in comprehension or production; specifically, the person has problems with vocabulary, grammar, and putting sentences together

Lanugo refers to "peach fuzz" or baby fine hair found on the trunk, face, and extremities

Latah primarily thought of as a Malay-Indonesian syndrome, is a set of trance-like symptoms that occur in response to startling stimuli

Leaden paralysis refers to a heavy or leaden feeling in the arms or legs

Limbic system the part of the brain involved in emotions, motivation, memory, and learning

Loose associations interruptions to thought and jumping from one thought to another disconnected thought or derailment

Macropsia where objects look larger than they actually are

Magical thinking an irrational belief that one has powers that defy laws of nature and physics and thus can cause or prevent events

Major depressive disorder those with this disorder usually report experiencing a dampening or lowering of mood lasting for more than a day or two; people with this disorder do not bounce back, and their "down feeling" consumes their entire lives to the extent that nothing is interesting or fun anymore

Mal de pelea refers to a form of amok but found in Puerto Rico

Mania seen in the bipolar disorders and defined as a distinct period during which the predominant mood is either elevated, expansive, or irritable, and there is increased activity or energy

Mambo a female voodoo priest in Haitian culture

MAO inhibitors a class of antidepressant medications that work by blocking the enzyme MAO that breaks down neurotransmitters—like norepinephrine and serotonin

Melancholic features specifier this specifier applies to bipolar I disorder and features a nearly complete loss of pleasure in all or almost all activities or a lack of a response to pleasurable stimuli

Micropsia where objects look smaller than they are in reality, much like the rear view mirror in your car

Miosis a term that refers to decreased pupil eye size

Mitosis cell division upon fertilization of the female's egg

Mixed features specifier this specifier replaces the earlier DSM bipolar I diagnosis of "mixed episode" and now applies to both bipolar disorders applied when symptoms of the opposite pole are present (i.e., symptoms of depression in mania/hypomania or, alternatively, the person shows symptoms of mania/hypomania in a depressive episode)

Mixed reuptake inhibitors a class of newer antidepressant medications that work by blocking reuptake of norepinephrine (which affects the neurons that are involved in increased heart rate, the slowing of intestinal activity associated with stress, and the neurons involved in learning, memory, dreaming, waking from sleep, and emotion)

Mixed type of delusional disorder people with this type of delusional disorder do not seem to have one predominant delusional theme

Monohy-pochondriacal paranoia a delusional disorder, somatic type, where the individual harbors delusional beliefs in which one particular part of their bodies play a part; for example, a person might think his or her eyes are grossly deformed or distorted, and the person emotionally moves from the peaks of elation to the depths of despair (referred to as lability)

Monozygotic twin refers to an identical twin

Mood lability a condition where the person emotionally moves from the peaks of elation to the depths of despair

Mood reactivity a depressed mood that can brighten readily at a positive turn of events

Motor disorders a new DSM-5 subcategory of the neurodevelopmental disorders that includes developmental coordination disorder, stereotypic movement disorder, and the tic disorders including Tourette syndrome

Movements of the articulation the ability to coordinate the jaw, tongue, and lips

Munchausen by proxy a variant of the factitious disorder, typically occurring within the context of a relationship between the parent and child; the diagnosis is assigned to the perpetrator, not the victim, and occurs when the parent or caregiver deliberately falsifies the child's (or another adult's or pet's) medical history and subjects the child to unnecessary medical procedures (including unnecessary surgeries) and unneeded hospitalizations

Muscle dysmorphia a diagnostic specifier for body dysmorphic disorder where people are more uniquely focused on muscle defects and body building

Mutism a form of catatonic behavior where the person shows a lack of verbal response

Myelin sheath wraps around the axon and serves to increase the speed at which nerve impulses are transmitted from one nerve cell to another

Narcissistic personality disorder a personality disorder where the person tends to be self-absorbed,self-important, and grandiose; they see themselves as unique and special, deserving of extraordinary treatment

Natural environment phobia describes fears of situations or events occurring in nature; common examples include a fear of heights, storms, or water

Negativism refers to a form of catatonic behavior that describes the person's resistance to instructions

Neologism when the person may create his or her own words

Nervous system the assembly of neurons; considered the most complex system in the body

Neurobiology a subdiscipline of both biology and neuroscience that studies the physiological, genetic, and developmental aspects of behavior

Neurocognitive disorder due to Alzheimer's disease the reduction or impairment of intellect, emotion, and behavioral functioning severe enough to be detrimental in social, occupational, and other important areas in life

Neurocognitive disorder due to HIV infection a neurocognitive disorder producing a highly variable clinical course and a spectrum of signs and symptoms ranging from subtle cognitive and motor impairments to profound dementia

Neurocognitive disorder due to Huntington's disease a neurocognitive disorder that is inherited through a single dominant gene; is a progressive and degenerative disease that includes difficulties in cognition, emotion, and movement

Neurocognitive disorder due to Parkinson's disease a slow and progressive neurological condition characterized by tremors, rigidity, involuntary and rhythmic movements of extremities, motor restlessness, and posturing instability

Neurocognitive disorder due to traumatic brain injury is characterized by impact to the head (or other means of rapid movement) or displacement of the brain within the skull

Neurocognitive disorders a class of disorders that represent a deficit in the person's cognitive functioning

Neurocognitive disorder with Lewy bodies a neurocognitive disorder consisting of symptoms of a combination of core diagnostic features (such as fluctuating cognition with pronounced variations in attention and alertness, recurrent visual hallucinations, and movement disorder or spontaneous features of Parkinsonism) and suggestive features (rapid eye movement sleep disorder, which can appear years before the onset of dementia and severe reactions to neuroleptics)

Neurodevelopmental disorders a cluster of disorders characterized by abnormalities in brain development affecting emotion, learning ability, self-control, and memory with a typically early onset that unfolds as a person grows

Neuroleptics refers to the type of tranquilizers used to treat psychotic conditions

Neurons the basic building blocks of the nervous system

Neuropeptides a group of substances that can serve as neurotransmitters or hormones, or influence the action of other neurotransmitters

Neurotransmitters chemical substances (such as epinephrine or dopamine) that transmit nerve impulses across synapses to either inhibit or excite a target cell

Nihilism or nihilistic term used to characterize a viewpoint that traditional values or beliefs are unfounded and that existence is senseless or useless

Nihilistic delusions the delusional conviction that a major catastrophe will happen

Nicotine a poisonous, oily liquid that comes from the nightshade family of plants called *Nicotiana tabacum*

Nymphomania refers to an abnormally excessive and uncontrollable sexual desire in women

Nystagmus rapid involuntary movements of the eyes in a side-to-side or occasionally up-and-down direction or "eye wiggles"

Obesity excess body fat resulting from the long-term excess of energy intake relative to energy expenditure

Obsessive-compulsive disorder a disorder that has two components—obsession (which involves thinking, doubts, and ideas) and compulsion (which involves doing, acting out, and performing)—and is characterized by obsessive, distressing, intrusive thoughts and the related compulsive actions that attempt to neutralize them

Obsessive-compulsive personality disorder often confused with obsessive-compulsive disorder, this personality disorder is characterized by a pervasive pattern of preoccupation with orderliness, perfectionism, and mental and interpersonal control, at the expense of flexibility, openness, and efficiency

Oocyte the female's immature egg or immature ovum, which divides 23 times before the time of birth

Oppositional defiant disorder (ODD) common features of this disorder include excessive, often persistent anger, frequent temper tantrums or angry outbursts, and disregard for authority

Other Specified (and Unspecified) Obsessive-Compulsive and Related Disorder this diagnosis is used in situations in which the symptoms do not meet all of the criteria of an obsessive-compulsive or related disorder and the clinician does not have sufficient information to make a more specific diagnosis

Palilalia refers to a complex vocal tics characterized by repeating one's own sounds or words

Panic disorder a disorder characterized by recurrent and unexpected panic attacks that last for a very short time, usually within minutes, accompanied by intense fear or discomfort

Paranoid personality disorder a personality disorder where the individual's behavior is characterized by pervasive, groundless suspiciousness and an inherent distrust of others

Paresthesias a term describing numbness or tingling

Paruresis refers to "bashful bladder"

Pathognomonic term used for indicative of a disease

Peripartum onset applicable to the bipolar disorders, this specifier is considered when the current or most recent episode of mania, hypomania, or major depression occurs during pregnancy or the 4 weeks following delivery

Peripheral nervous system allows the brain and spinal cord to communicate with the sensory systems of the eyes, ears, skin, and mouth, and allows the brain and spinal cord to control the muscles and glands of the body

Peristalsis a wave-like movement that propels food particles through the digestive tract

Persecutory delusional disorder this type of delusional disorder applies when the person believes that he or she (or someone close to them) is being mistreated, or that someone is spying on them or planning to harm them

Persecutory delusions refers to a delusional belief that others intend harm

Perseveration when someone may continuously repeat the same words or sentence; seen in the diagnosis of schizophrenia

Persistent depressive disorder also referred to as dysthymia; is characterized by a depressed mood that occurs for most of the day, for more days than not, for at least 2 years and 1 year for children and adolescents

Personality refers to those emotional and behavioral traits that characterize day-to-day living under normative conditions

Personality disorder an enduring pattern of inner experience and behavior that deviates markedly from the expectations of the individual's culture, is pervasive and inflexible, has an onset in adolescence or early adulthood, is stable over time, and leads to distress or impairment

Phii Pob refers to a common type of spirit possession

Phobia a term that describes an extreme and irrational fear of simple things or social situations

Phonological knowledge knowledge of speech sounds that enables an individual to produce speech

Pibloktoq sometimes called arctic hysteria; is a Polar Eskimo trance syndrome seen as an abrupt dissociative episode accompanied by extreme excitement of up to 30 minutes' duration and frequently followed by convulsive seizures and coma lasting up to 12 hours

Pica a disorder characterized by a person's appetite for substances that are largely nonnutritive

Piloerection refers to goose bumps

Pituitary gland the master gland that controls or influences all of the other endocrine glands that release a variety of hormones

Positron emission tomography or PET refers to brain imaging studies

Posttraumatic stress disorder this disorder is marked by close exposure to trauma; combat experiences and sexual assault are the most common traumas

Posturing a form of catatonic strange behavior where postures can be held for very long periods of time, making the person look like a figure in a wax museum

Primary enuresis is when a child has never been successfully trained to control urination and, by definition, begins before 5 years of age

Primiparious women a term used to describe women who have given birth only once

Prion disease a disease characterized by a group of transmissible spongiform encephalopathies (TSEs), which are essentially a family of rare progressive neurodegenerative disorders that can affect both humans and animals

Prions refer to abnormal, pathogenic agents that are transmissible and are able to induce abnormal folding of specific normal cellular proteins, called prion proteins, that are found most abundantly in the brain

Prodromal phase refers to the period before the features of schizophrenia become very apparent; during this time, the person's level of functioning deteriorates

Prosody term used to refer to the intonation of one's speech

Pseudocyesis refers to a false pregnancy

Psychological factors affecting other medical conditions this diagnosis is considered when the individual has a symptom (or actual medical condition) as well as significant psychological or behavioral factors that adversely affect the medical condition

Psychomotor agitation refers to a person's unintentional and purposeless motions

Psychomotor behavior behavior involving both physical and psychological components

Psychosis a term often used interchangeably with schizophrenia; refers to a group of incapacitating disorders traditionally defined as the loss of reality testing and the impairment of mental functioning manifested by delusions (or irrational beliefs) and/or hallucinations (or sensory experiences in the absence of external events) as well as confusion, impaired memory, and the inability to function within the interpersonal domain

Psychotic features specifier this specifier applies when a person may experience delusions or hallucinations at any point in a bipolar episode, but if psychotic features are present, they may be *mood-congruent psychotic features* (seen as themes of suspiciousness or paranoia along with the typical delusions and hallucinations—grandiosity, invulnerability, and so forth—seen in manic episodes) or *mood-incongruent psychotic features* (or the content of the person's delusions and hallucinations is inconsistent or a mixture of mood-congruent and mood-incongruentthemes).

Purging any activity aimed at ameliorating the perceived negative effects of a binge on body shape and weight

Pyloric stenosis refers to a problem with a baby's stomach that causes forceful vomiting; this happens when the baby's narrowed (stenosed) pylorus, which connects the stomach and the small intestine, swells and thickens, keeping food from moving into the intestine

Pyromania the essential feature of this disorder is the deliberate and purposeful setting of a fire on more than one occasion

Rapid cycling specifier this specifier is indicated for the bipolar disorders when the individual experiences at least 4 mood episodes (in any combination) within a 1-year period; in other words, the person may experience a major depressive episode and then switch to the opposite polarity of mania or hypomania, or the person may experience a full remission between episodes

Reactive attachment disorder a childhood disorder that results from inadequate caregiving environments in early childhood and encompasses a distinct pattern of a child who is emotionally withdrawn and inhibited

Referential delusions refers to the delusional belief that certain gestures, comments, environmental cues, and the like are directed to the person

Rhinorrea the term used for runny eyes or nose

Rumination disorder is a disorder that involves the repetitive regurgitation of undigested food (or rumination) from the stomach back up into the mouth

Russell's signs the by-products of repeated and constant friction of fingers being scraped back and forth across incisor teeth to induce vomiting, as seen in bulimia nervosa

Schedule II controlled drugs drugs that have a currently accepted medical use that is severely restricted, but also have a high potential for abuse

Schedule IV drugs under the Federal Controlled Substances Act, these are drugs with a currently accepted medical use and must be prescribed by a physician, physician assistant, or nurse practitioner

Schizoid personality disorder a personality disorder where the person displays a lifelong pattern of social withdrawal; that is, they tend to be introverted and remain isolated from others by choice; often, their lifestyles are described as bland and solitary

Schizotypal personality disorder a personality disorder where the person exhibits strikingly odd or strange mannerisms in addition to having a very active fantasy life

Seasonal pattern this specifier, is applicable to the bipolar disorders, and involves a regular seasonal pattern (within a 2-year period) for those who tend to experience at least one type of mood episode (i.e., mania, hypomania, or depression)

Secondary enuresis refers to children who have been successfully trained or have established good bladder control for a substantial period of time and then begin wetting again in response to some sort of stressful situation

Selective mutism a disorder characterized by consistent failure to speak in specific social situations in which there is an expectation for speaking, such as at school, despite speaking in other situations

Selective-serotonin reuptake inhibitors (SSRIs) refer to the class of drugs considered the first-line choice of treatment for depression; they work by selectively inhibiting or blocking the presynaptic reuptake of serotonin (the neurotransmitter that can have either an excitatory or inhibitory effect associated with sleep, mood, anxiety, and appetite) in the brain

Separation anxiety disorder a disorder characterized by excessive fear or anxiety concerning separation from home or attachment figures

Serotonin a neurotransmitter originating in the lower part of the brain that can have either an excitatory or inhibitory effect; it is associated with sleep, mood, anxiety, and appetite

Shin-byung a Korean syndrome that involves initial feelings of anxiousness, somatic complaints (such as weakness, dizziness, fear, anorexia, insomnia, or gastrointestinal problems) followed by dissociation and possession by ancestral spirits

Simple motor tics refers to body movements that are of short duration (i.e., milliseconds) and include eye blinking, shoulder shrugging and extension of the extremities, and simple vocal tics include throat clearing, sniffing, and grunting

Situational phobia people with this type of phobia have difficulty using public transportation (e.g., buses, trains, and airplanes), or being in enclosed places such as elevators

Social anxiety disorder also known as social phobia; refers to a condition in which a person fears performing publicly lest he or she be revealed as inept, foolish, or inadequate, thereby suffering disgrace, humiliation, or embarrassment

Social (pragmatic) communication disorder a neurodevelopmental communication disorder describing difficulties in social use of verbal (and nonverbal) communication, which affects social participation, relationships, academic achievement, or job performance (or any combination)

Soma a term that refers to the part of the neuron that contains the nucleus, which keeps the entire cell alive and functioning

Somatic term used to refer to physical symptoms

Somatic delusional disorder a type of delusional disorder that involves bodily functions or sensations, and the person believes that he or she has a physical defect or medical problem

Somatic delusions a delusional preoccupation with one's health

Somatic symptom disorder this disorder emphasizes the individual's experiences of distressing somatic symptoms plus abnormal thoughts, feelings, and behaviors in response to these symptoms rather than the absence of a medical explanation for these somatic symptoms

Somatosensory amplification refers to the person's tendency to experience their own bodily sensations as being unusually intense, aversive, and distressing

Specific learning disorder a neurodevelopmental disorder describing difficulties learning and using academic skills; affects a child's ability to acquire and apply reading, writing, and/or math skills

Specific phobia a disorder that describes any persistent, unreasonable, and irrational fear of a specific object (dogs or cats) or situation (flying, heights, animals, receiving an injection, or seeing blood) that causes intense distress

Speech sound disorder a neurodevelopmental communication disorder describing those who have problems with pronunciation and articulation to the extent that they interfere with being understood or prevent verbal communication

Stereotypic movement disorder a neurodevelopmental motor disorder characterized by repetitive, nonfunctional motor behaviors (for example, hand waving or head banging) that markedly interferes with normal activities or can result in bodily injury

Stereotypy a type of movement described as seemingly purposeless repetitive movements such as folding a piece of paper along the same creases until it disintegrates

Strengths perspective an aspect of the competency-bases assessment that serves to draw attention to the attributes, capacities, experiences, and resources in a person's life that contribute to a positive and satisfying life and effective social functioning

St. John's wort a natural herbal extract, also referred to as hypericum, taken for depression

Stupor a form of catatonic behavior where the person shows a lack of motor responses

Substance/medication-induced neurocognitive disorder previously known as substance-induced persisting dementia; is characterized by neurocognitive impairments that persist beyond the usual duration of intoxication and acute withdrawal from a substance or medication

Substance/medication-induced disorders these disorders are potentially severe and usually temporary and apply as the result of substance use, abuse, intoxication, or withdrawal rather than an underlying mental illness—symptoms are characteristic of other disorders; for instance, taking certain medications can cause hallucinations

Substance-induced disorders disorders categorized in the DSM-5 according to the manifested effects of the substance on the individual

Substance intoxication refers to the occurrence of a reversible substance-specific syndrome due to recent ingestion or exposure to a substance

Substance use disorder a disorder that describes a cluster of cognitive, behavioral, and physical symptoms indicating that the individual continues using the substance despite significant substance-related problems

Substance withdrawal shown as a problematic substance-specific behavior change with both physiological and cognitive elements that are due to stopping or attempting to cut down heavy and prolonged substance use

Suicidal ideation refers to thoughts about killing oneself

Sundowning when symptoms of delirium tend to worsen during early evening hours or at night; seen as the result of fatigue or a disturbance in the brain's biological clock

Synapses placed at the end of the axon (called the axon terminal), these specialized structures are located where neurotransmitter chemicals are released to communicate with target neurons

Synaptic cleft a very small space where the axon terminal of one neuron almost touches the dendrite or cell body of another neuron

Synaptic vesicles tiny sacs in the axon terminal that open and release a few thousand molecules of a chemical substance called a neurotransmitter

Syncope refers to fainting

Synesthesias refers to intersensory, intersensual associations—e.g., "Can't you just hear the changing colors on the trees?"

Systems theory an aspect of the competency-based assessment, this theory serves to organize the practitioner's understanding of human development aimed at appreciating the complex interactions between the individual and all aspects of that individual's biopsychosocial life

Tachycardia refers to a faster-than-normal heart rate at rest

Tachypnea a term referring to rapid breathing

Tactile hallucinations hallucinations that include sensations similar to electrical tingling or burning sensations and that are considered the least common in the diagnosis of schizophrenia

Tangentiality term used for a form of disorganized speech that describes the person's failure to answer specific questions or when a person is going off on a tangent

Thalamus a somewhat round structure located in the center of the brain that acts as a relay station for incoming information from the sensory organs to the cerebral cortex.

Thought insertion seen in those with schizophrenia, this is the belief that thoughts have been put into the person's mind

Thought withdrawal seen in those with schizophrenia, this is the belief that the person's thoughts have been removed from them by some kind of outside force

Tic disorders a subcategory of the neurodevelopmental motor disorders, distinguished by the presence of motor and/or vocal tics and organized around the categories of Tourette's disorder (also known as Gilles de la Tourette syndrome), persistent (chronic) motor or vocal tic disorder, provisional tic disorder, and other specified and unspecified tic disorders

Toxicology screen refers to the various tests used to determine the type and approximate amount of legal and illegal drugs a person has taken—using a blood or urine sample

Transient ischemic episodes when blood flow to part of the brain is blocked or reduced, frequently referred to as a mini-stroke

Trichotillomania (hair-pulling) disorder a disorder that involves the recurrent pulling out (or twisting) of one's own hair, resulting in hair loss

Tricyclic antidepressants a class of antidepressant medications that seem to block the reuptake of certain neurotransmitters, allowing them to collect in the synapse and, desensitize or down-regulate the transmission of that particular transmitter—at least initially

Unspecified communication disorder a neurodevelopmental communication disorder reserved for those who have symptoms of a communication disorder but who do not meet all criteria and whose symptoms cause distress or impairment

Unspecified type delusional disorder this type of delusional disorder applies when the individual's dominant delusional belief cannot be clearly determined or cannot be described in the specific types of delusional disorders

Vascular disease (VaD) sometimes referred to as multi-infarct dementia, VaD defines a decline in thinking skills caused by conditions that block or reduce blood flow to the brain depriving brain cells of vital oxygen and nutrients

Vascular neurocognitive disorder refers to a heterogeneous group of cognitive disorders associated with cerebrovascular damage; symptoms can vary depending on the specific brain areas where blood flow is reduced

Vegetative features refers to the presence of physical changes seen in the depressive disorders

Waxy flexibility a term used in catatonia wherein someone else may try to manipulate or move the individual's limbs, but once moved, the limbs can then remain fixed for hours or days

Wernicke encephalopathy an acute brain reaction to severe lack of thiamine; is a medical emergency that causes life-threatening brain disruption, confusion, staggering and stumbling, a lack of coordination, and abnormal involuntary eye movements

World Health Organization commonly abbreviated as WHO; the entity that is responsible for coordination of all official disease classifications

Zar refers to the experience of spirits possessing an individual; is found in Ethiopia, Somalia, Egypt, Sudan, Iran, and other North African and Middle Eastern societies

Name Index

Subject Index

Note: Figures are indicated by f and tables by t following the page reference.